Monetary Dynamics and Socio-Economic Development in Emerging Economies

Cláudio Canguende-Valentim
Instituto Superior Politécnico Jean Piaget de Benguela, Angola

Mara Madaleno
GOVCOPP, DEGEIT, Portugal & University of Aveiro, Portugal

Samuel Carlos Victorino
Universidade Jean Piaget de Angola, Angola

João Jungo
GOVCOPP, University of Aveiro, Portugal

IGI Global
Scientific Publishing
Publishing Tomorrow's Research Today

Vice President of Editorial	Melissa Wagner
Director of Acquisitions	Mikaela Felty
Director of Book Development	Jocelynn Hessler
Production Manager	Mike Brehm
Cover Design	Jose Rosado

Published in the United States of America by
IGI Global Scientific Publishing
701 East Chocolate Avenue
Hershey, PA, 17033, USA
Tel: 717-533-8845
Fax: 717-533-7115
Website: https://www.igi-global.com E-mail: cust@igi-global.com

Library of Congress Cataloging-in-Publication Data

LCCN: 2025005802 (CIP Data Pending)
ISBN13: 9798369397657
Isbn13Softcover: 9798369397664
EISBN13: 9798369397671

British Cataloguing in Publication Data
A Cataloguing in Publication record for this book is available from the British Library.

Table of Contents

Detailed Table of Contents

The purpose of the study is to provide a holistic approach in exploring monetary policy concepts in developing economies. The study uses a systematic review by identifying and evaluating peer-reviewed journals in monetary policy issues that is published within the period, 2009-2020, from different contexts. The study targets at directing future research efforts to critical areas that require immediate attention. With several gaps in theoretical, methodologies and empirical evidence, the paper signals promising lines of inquiry for both theoretical and empirical research. It is therefore important for researchers and policy makers to provide an extensive research that addresses these concerns.

This chapter discusses the pivotal role of monetary policy in enabling sustainable development with a focus on Sustainable Development Goal 8 (SDG 8). We explore the potential implications of traditional monetary policy tools like interest rate cushions, quantitative easing for economic growth, and inequality and environmental impacts. This chapter suggests a paradigm shift to a more sustainable monetary policy. It involves embedding sustainability into day-to-day operations by enabling the dual push of green finance through focused lending schemes and green bonds, developing climate-aware risk management, and pushing social responsibility investment.This chapter highlights a growing call for central banks to proactively work together to use monetary policy to help build a just and sustainable future.

Planning can be considered as the result of socio-economic development efforts and advanced socialization for a country. This judgment is also very valid for Turkey, which is the only Afro-Eurasian country in the world, a candidate for the European Union, a G-20 economy and one of the emerging economies. The subject and purpose of this study is to examine the monetary, interest and exchange rate policies in Turkey on the basis of primary development plans. Five-yearly development plans covering all main and sub-sectors have been prepared in Turkey since 1963, but after the famous IMF stability decisions dated January 24, 1980, which ensured the transformation to liberal-global capitalism in macroeconomics, other development plans remained at a formal or symbolic level. Here, the monetary and development targets achieved and the handicaps encountered in the first 20-year "planned development" period, which included 4 development plans prepared between 1963-1983, are analyzed.

This chapter examines the potential of Central Bank Digital Currencies (CBDCs) to enhance financial inclusion and economic growth in emerging economies. Unlike decentralized cryptocurrencies, CBDCs are government-backed digital currencies that offer secure and regulated alternatives to traditional money. The chapter explores how CBDCs can improve access to financial services, reduce transaction costs, and promote financial stability, particularly in countries with limited banking infrastructure. It also discusses the challenges and risks associated with CBDCs, such as financial stability concerns and the displacement of commercial banks. Through case studies from China and India, the chapter highlights how well-designed CBDCs can act as a catalyst for inclusive economic development, while emphasising the need for robust regulatory frameworks for successful implementation.

The digital economy is expanding quickly, particularly in emerging nations. This paper aims to explain the digital economy—its meaning, estimation, government initiatives, and challenges. After analyzing the various definitions proposed by credible organizations and researchers across different reports, the paper selects the most appropriate definition for the estimation. Also, it ranks different nations in terms of digital advancement in their economies. Further, the paper gives an insight into the government's steps to increase digital penetration in India and its future plans.

The integration of Artificial Intelligence (AI) and the IoThas led to significant advancements in the banking and finance sector, providing personalized, efficient, and data-driven services. However, these AI-IoT enabled systems also introduce complex security and privacy challenges that need to be addressed to protect sensitive financial data and maintain customer trust. This paper surveys the key security and privacy issues in AI-IoT enabled banking, including data breaches, cyber-attacks, unauthorized access, and data misuse. We examine current methodologies for securing AI-IoT systems, such as encryption, blockchain, alongside AI-driven threat detection and response techniques.The survey explores regulatory considerations and compliance requirements that shape security protocols in financial services. By identifying gaps in existing security measures and highlighting advanced privacy-preserving technologies, this study aims to provide a comprehensive understanding of the challenges and future directions in securing AI-IoT applications within banking and finance.

The interplay between exchange rates, trade, and economic policies shapes the way nations engage with each other economically. Understanding exchange rates, their fluctuations, and how they influence trade flows is crucial for governments, businesses, and individuals involved in international trade. This overview will explore the concept of exchange rates, stability and growth. On the other hand, political instability or economic uncertainty can lead to depreciation, as investors seek safer assets in other countries.Government interventions, particularly in the form of monetary and fiscal policies, can also affect exchange rates. Conversely, a currency appreciation can worsen a trade deficit by making exports more expensive and imports cheaper. moreover, exchange rate movements can affect the timing of trade flows. For instance, if a country expects its currency to appreciate in the future, it may delay its purchases of foreign goods to take advantage of lower prices later.

International trade facilitates efficient resource allocation and economic growth but is highly sensitive to external factors such as Exchange Rate Fluctuations (ERV). ERV represents frequent and unpredictable changes in currency values that can increase transaction costs, reduce competitiveness in export markets, and discourage cross-border investments. This research investigates the relationship between ERV and International Trade in Emerging economies. The gravity model of trade model is used to analyze panel data collected from 20 emerging market countries over 2000-2022 to examine the effect of ERV on export and import flows. The results indicate a significant negative impact of exchange rate volatility on exports and imports, with exports being more sensitive to volatility. Macroeconomic stability and financial development are found to moderate the adverse effects of volatility on trade flows. These findings have important implications for policymakers in emerging economies seeking to promote international trade and mitigate the risks associated with exchange rate fluctuations.

In this paper, we analyze the connectedness between the Tunisian growth rate and its key macroeconomic drivers, namely Foreign Direct Investment, inflation, and exchange rate. The purpose is to evaluate how economic growth responds to shocks induced by a variety of economic indicators using the Time- Varying Parameter Vector autoregressive (TVP-VAR). The findings indicate that the 90s and 2000s reform policies were critical in restructuring the dynamics of Tunisia's macroeconomic network. In particular, the network visualization analysis shows that the behavior of the Tunisian growth rate in the past years has changed from being a net shock receiver to net shock transmitter. Interestingly, there has been a declining shock transmission between the Tunisian growth rate and the Foreign Direct Investment, showing that over time the economy was diversified, while policy response mechanisms have strengthened. Such findings, therefore, provide insights from the perspective of an investor as well as policymakers who strive to understand the dynamics of the Tunisian economy.

This study examines how economic impact analysis is conducted through the Input-Output Model. The paper discusses the structure of Input-Output tables in detail, examines the mathematical dimension of the model based on matrices, and discusses how multipliers are determined. Unlike other studies, after examining how all these variables are calculated, how the economic impact analysis is conducted is explained with examples from the Canadian economy. In other words, the mathematical and economic dimensions of the model are examined together, the Input-Output analysis is compared with other analyses, and a detailed contribution to the literature is made.

Preface

Monetary dynamics serve as a cornerstone in guiding the socio-economic evolution of emerging economies. Encompassing key elements such as inflation management, interest rate strategies, currency stabilization, and central bank interventions, these factors directly shape patterns of investment, consumption, and income distribution. As nations pursue sustainable and inclusive growth, the relationship between monetary policy and development outcomes grows increasingly intricate, demanding a delicate equilibrium between economic expansion and financial resilience. Grasping this interplay is crucial for crafting policies that foster advancement while minimizing inequality and guarding against systemic vulnerabilities.

Monetary Dynamics and Socio-Economic Development in Emerging Economies delves into the pivotal challenges faced by emerging nations as they strive for monetary stability and sustained economic growth. It highlights both the obstacles and the transformative opportunities that define this journey, examining how evolving monetary trends intersect with development goals amid a rapidly shifting global landscape.

Through a multidisciplinary lens, the book explores critical topics such as digital innovation, international trade, and strategic monetary policy, offering rich insights into the mechanisms shaping contemporary economies. This volume serves as an essential resource for a wide spectrum of readers—including business leaders, economists, policymakers, computer scientists, academics, and researchers—seeking to understand and influence the future of economic development in emerging contexts.

The many academic areas covered in this publication include Accounting and Finance, Artificial Intelligence, Digital Technology, Economics and Economic Theory, Exchange Rates, International Trade, Internet of Things, Monetary Policy, Security and Privacy, Socio-Economic Development, Sustainable Development, and Trade Dynamics.

Emerging economies today find themselves at a pivotal crossroads, where monetary policy, digital transformation, and socio-economic imperatives converge in unprecedented ways. This volume seeks to illuminate the complex interplay between financial mechanisms and development trajectories across diverse geographies.

From traditional monetary instruments to cutting-edge digital currencies, and from exchange rate volatility to housing crises and trust in financial institutions, each chapter unravels a different thread in this intricate tapestry. The studies span regions such as Turkey, India, Tunisia, and Canada, offering empirical insights and policy reflections tailored for scholars, policymakers, and practitioners aiming to understand the nuances of economic transformation. At its heart, this book is a dialogue between evidence and possibility—a commitment to framing the challenges and opportunities that will shape the emerging economic order.

Deep diving into each chapter contribution, we have:

CHAPTER OVERVIEW

Chapter 1: Monetary Policy in Developing Economies - A Review

This study adopts a comprehensive approach to examining monetary policy frameworks within developing economies. Through a systematic review of peer-reviewed literature published between 2009 and 2020, it analyzes diverse perspectives and contexts surrounding key monetary policy challenges. The primary aim is to guide future research by highlighting critical areas in need of urgent attention. Notable gaps in theoretical foundations, methodological approaches, and empirical evidence underscore the need for deeper exploration. As such, the study calls on scholars and policymakers to advance robust research initiatives that address these pressing concerns and enrich the discourse on monetary dynamics and development.

Chapter 2: Monetary Policy, Growth and Sustainable Development

This chapter examines the essential role of monetary policy in advancing sustainable development, with a particular emphasis on Sustainable Development Goal 8 (SDG 8). It analyzes the broader socio-economic and environmental implications of conventional monetary instruments, including interest rate buffers and quantitative easing, highlighting their impact on economic growth, inequality, and ecological outcomes. Recognizing the limitations of traditional approaches, the chapter advocates for a paradigm shift toward a more sustainability-oriented monetary framework. It proposes integrating green finance into routine policy operations through targeted lending programs, the issuance of green bonds, and the adoption of climate-sensitive risk management practices. By promoting socially responsible investment strategies, the chapter underscores an emerging consensus: central banks must play a proactive role in shaping a just, resilient, and sustainable future through their monetary policy agendas.

Chapter 3: Monetary, Interest and Exchange Rate Policies in Turkey: An Analysis for the Planned Development Period of 1963-1983

Planning represents both the outcome and driving force of socio-economic development and societal advancement. This perspective holds particular relevance for Turkey, an Afro-Eurasian nation uniquely positioned as a European Union candidate, a G-20 economy, and a prominent emerging market. This study explores Turkey's monetary, interest rate, and exchange rate policies through the lens of its primary development plans. Since 1963, Turkey has implemented comprehensive five-year plans covering major sectors. However, following the landmark IMF stabilization measures of January 24, 1980—which marked a decisive shift toward liberal global capitalism—these plans gradually became more symbolic than operational. Focusing on the initial 20-year "planned development" era, spanning four key plans from 1963 to 1983, this analysis assesses both the monetary policy goals that were achieved and the challenges that emerged during this transformative period.

Chapter 4: Central Bank Digital Currencies (CBDC) as Catalysts for Financial Inclusion and Economic Expansion in Emerging Asian Economies

This chapter explores the transformative potential of Central Bank Digital Currencies (CBDCs) in fostering financial inclusion and driving economic growth within emerging economies. Unlike decentralized cryptocurrencies, CBDCs are state-issued digital currencies, offering secure, regulated alternatives to conventional cash and payment systems. Focusing on their impact in settings with limited banking infrastructure, the chapter investigates how CBDCs can expand access to financial services, lower transaction costs, and strengthen financial stability. It also addresses key implementation challenges, including risks to financial stability and the potential displacement of commercial banking functions. Drawing from case studies in China and India, the chapter illustrates how well-structured CBDC frameworks can serve as catalysts for inclusive development. It concludes by underscoring the importance of comprehensive regulatory systems to ensure safe, equitable, and scalable deployment.

Chapter 5: Global Digital Economy and Initiatives of Government of India

The digital economy is experiencing rapid expansion, particularly across emerging nations where technological transformation is accelerating development. This paper seeks to clarify the concept of the digital economy by examining its definition, measurement methodologies, government-led initiatives, and prevailing challenges. Drawing from a range of authoritative sources and academic literature, it identifies the most suitable definition to guide digital economy estimation. The paper also presents a comparative assessment of countries based on their level of digital integration. Special attention is given to India's strategic efforts to deepen digital inclusion, outlining current initiatives and future policy directions aimed at enhancing nationwide digital connectivity.

Chapter 6: Security and Privacy in AI: IoT Enabled Banking and Finance Services

The convergence of Artificial Intelligence (AI) and the Internet of Things (IoT) has ushered in transformative advancements across the banking and financial services landscape, enabling highly personalized, efficient, and data-centric solutions. Yet, these AI-IoT integrated systems also present a host of intricate security and privacy challenges that must be proactively addressed to safeguard sensitive financial data and preserve user trust. This paper offers a comprehensive review of the primary security and privacy risks associated with AI-IoT-enabled banking systems, including data breaches, cyberattacks, unauthorized access, and misuse of financial information. It evaluates prevailing security methodologies such as encryption protocols, blockchain technologies, and AI-powered threat detection and response strategies. Additionally, the study examines evolving regulatory frameworks and compliance obligations that shape cybersecurity standards within financial institutions. By identifying persistent vulnerabilities and exploring cutting-edge privacy-preserving innovations, the paper provides critical insights into the current state and future directions of securing AI-IoT applications in the banking sector.

Chapter 7: Exchange Rates and Trade Dynamics

The dynamic relationship between exchange rates, international trade, and economic policy plays a central role in shaping how nations interact within the global economy. Understanding the mechanisms behind exchange rate fluctuations and their impact on trade flows is essential for governments, enterprises, and individuals participating in cross-border commerce. This overview delves into the concept of exchange rate stability and its influence on economic growth. Political instability and economic uncertainty often trigger currency depreciation, as investors reallocate assets toward more stable markets. Likewise, government interventions—through monetary and fiscal policy—can alter exchange rate trajectories. While currency appreciation may strengthen purchasing power, it can also widen trade deficits by rendering exports less competitive and imports more affordable. Exchange rate expectations further influence the timing of trade activity. For example, if market participants anticipate future currency appreciation, they may postpone foreign purchases in hopes of securing more favorable prices later. These strategic decisions underscore the critical role of exchange rate dynamics in shaping international trade behavior and macroeconomic outcomes.

Chapter 8: The Influence of Exchange Rate Volatility on International Trade in Emerging Economies

International trade plays a vital role in promoting efficient resource allocation and driving economic growth. However, it remains highly susceptible to external shocks, particularly Exchange Rate Fluctuations (ERV). ERV refers to frequent and unpredictable changes in currency valuations, which can elevate transaction costs, erode export competitiveness, and deter cross-border investment activities. This study examines the relationship between ERV and international trade within emerging economies, utilizing the gravity model of trade to analyze panel data from 20 emerging market countries spanning 2000 to 2022. The analysis reveals that exchange rate volatility exerts a significant negative influence on both exports and imports, with exports exhibiting heightened sensitivity to fluctuations. Furthermore, the findings suggest that macroeconomic stability and financial sector development serve as buffers, mitigating the adverse impacts of ERV on trade flows. These insights carry meaningful policy implications for emerging economies aiming to bolster international trade while navigating the risks associated with currency volatility.

Chapter 9: Unraveling Dynamic Shock Transmission Between Tunisian Economic Growth and Key Economic Indicators

This paper investigates the dynamic relationship between Tunisia's economic growth rate and its primary macroeconomic indicators—namely, foreign direct investment (FDI), inflation, and exchange rate movements. Utilizing the Time-Varying Parameter Vector Autoregressive (TVP-VAR) model, the study assesses how growth responds to shocks originating from these key variables. Findings reveal that reform initiatives during the 1990s and 2000s played a pivotal role in reshaping the interconnectedness of Tunisia's macroeconomic system. Notably, network visualization analysis indicates a structural shift in the Tunisian growth rate's role, from predominantly absorbing shocks to actively transmitting them. Over time, a noticeable decline in shock transmission between growth and FDI suggests increased economic diversification and enhanced policy responsiveness. These insights carry significant implications for both investors and policymakers seeking a deeper understanding of Tunisia's evolving economic landscape and its resilience in the face of external shocks.

Chapter 10: Economic Impact Assessment through Input-Output Modeling: The Case of Canada

This study explores the application of the Input-Output Model in conducting economic impact analysis, offering a comprehensive examination of both its structural and mathematical foundations. It delves into the composition of Input-Output tables, analyzes the matrix-based framework of the model, and explains the derivation and significance of multipliers. Distinguishing itself from previous studies, this chapter not only clarifies the methodological processes behind variable calculations but also illustrates their practical use through case examples drawn from the Canadian economy. By integrating both mathematical rigor and economic interpretation, the study positions Input-Output analysis within a broader analytical context, comparing its utility to alternative approaches and providing a substantive contribution to the literature on economic modeling.

Chapter 11: RBI's Decision of Moratorium and Trust of Middleclass Depositors in India: An Analytical Study

The Reserve Bank of India (RBI) occasionally imposes temporary moratoriums on specific banking institutions following the identification of irregularities within their operations. Such actions require prior approval from the Government of India and are aimed at containing systemic disruptions while safeguarding depositor interests. This research paper investigates the impact of RBI-imposed moratoriums on the trust levels of middle-class depositors within the Indian banking context. Data was collected through a self-designed questionnaire administered to customers in the Delhi region, with 474 valid responses analyzed using statistical techniques. The findings indicate a significant erosion of trust among middle-class depositors, who are increasingly reluctant to retain accounts with banks subject to moratoriums, highlighting long-term reputational consequences for affected institutions.

Chapter 12: Navigating the Housing Crisis in Turkey: Monetary Policy, Fiscal Tools, and Structural Challenges

Housing occupies a pivotal space at the nexus of social necessity and economic influence, serving not only as a basic human requirement for shelter but also as a powerful engine of economic activity and wealth generation globally. In Turkey, however, persistent increases in housing prices, combined with monetary policy uncertainty, supply-side constraints, and surging demand, have rendered the housing sector a significant source of macroeconomic volatility. This study provides a descriptive analysis of the primary trends shaping Turkey's housing market, with a particular focus on the influence of monetary policy. It further investigates structural determinants—including housing supply, fiscal strategies, demographic shifts, external capital inflows, and social dynamics—that collectively define market conditions. The findings demonstrate that housing prices in Turkey are highly responsive to monetary policy interventions and that addressing the crisis requires multidimensional strategies. Accordingly, the study advocates for integrated policy solutions that incorporate not just economic levers but also social and spatial dimensions, offering sustainable recommendations aimed at stabilizing and strengthening the Turkish housing market.

Chapter 13: An Empirical Analysis of Borsa Istanbul: Some Answers to the Questions on Investors' Minds

Investors frequently face uncertainty when evaluating which financial instruments deliver superior returns. Sharpe ratio assessments reveal that, for risk-averse investors in Türkiye, the Borsa Istanbul 100 (BIST-100) index ranks as the second-best investment option after gold. Notably, among various alternatives, the BIST-100 demonstrates the highest probability of outperforming the risk-free rate. From an international portfolio diversification perspective, empirical evidence suggests a declining correlation between Türkiye and global markets heading into the 2020s. Analysis of exchange rate trends and stock market performance indicates that the depreciation of the Turkish lira (TL) has played a significant role in driving down stock prices. Although the Turkish stock market's contribution to economic growth is somewhat indirect, it remains positive, supporting long-term economic expansion. Findings further show a general alignment between stock returns and inflation; however, this relationship is not linear in Türkiye's case. As a result, Borsa Istanbul typically offers returns that fall short of fully offsetting inflation.

There are some policy implications to be derived from the book's chapters. First, strengthening monetary policy frameworks by implementing inflation-targeting regimes supported by transparent communication from central banks, enhancing monetary transmission mechanisms by promoting financial sector depth and accessibility, and encouraging the use of data-driven tools for forecasting and managing monetary dynamics in volatile environments. Second, promoting financial inclusion. This may be done by supporting digital payment systems and fintech innovations as entry points for underserved populations, developing regulatory sandboxes that allow safe experimentation with digital financial products, or expanding mobile and microfinance infrastructure, especially in rural and low-income communities. Third, through currency stabilization and exchange rate policies, while designing flexible exchange rate regimes paired with strategic foreign exchange reserves management, fostering regional currency cooperation or swap lines to buffer external shocks, with correct monitoring and mitigation of speculative capital flows through targeted macroprudential policies. Fourth, by integrating the Sustainable Development Goals. This can be achieved by aligning monetary and fiscal policies with green financing incentives (e.g., green bonds, ESG frameworks), introducing monetary tools that reward climate-resilient investments and penalize unsustainable practices, and facilitating public-private partnerships to fund infrastructure that balances growth and sustainability. Finally, building institutional trust by prioritizing policy credibility and transparency, especially in times of crisis (e.g., moratoriums, bailouts), enabling strong legal frameworks that protect depositor rights and investor interests, and cultivating financial literacy to deepen trust and participation among citizens. However, these implications aren't one-size-fits-all, but they offer direction for tailoring responsive, resilient, and inclusive monetary strategies in fast-changing global and local contexts.

Therefore, the main message to be derived from here is "Harnessing Monetary Dynamics for Inclusive Socio-Economic Development in Emerging Economies". Emerging economies are navigating complex fiscal landscapes marked by rapid digitalization, demographic shifts, and global market volatility. Monetary policies play a critical role in stabilizing economies, fostering financial inclusion, and aligning national development goals with global sustainability frameworks. The objectives are simply to:

a) To strengthen monetary policy effectiveness and responsiveness.

b) To promote inclusive economic growth through financial innovation.
c) To build institutional resilience and public trust in financial systems.

For its effectiveness, we should modernize the Monetary Policy Frameworks, ensure Digital Transformation, Financial Access, and safeguard Exchange Rate Stability and Trade Support. At the same time, Linking Growth with Sustainability, and Building Financial Trust and Institutional Credibility. From these, it should be expected an enhanced macroeconomic stability and reduced volatility, a broader financial inclusion across income and geographic divides, a stronger trust and participation in formal economic institutions, and sustainable growth pathways aligned with global development benchmarks.

Acknowledgment

We would like to thank all the contributors to this book. First, the authors of the book chapters, without whose effort and commitment, none of this would be possible. Moreover, we thank the reviewers who dedicated their time to improving the chapter's quality and ensuring a timely release of the book. The editors would like to thank all those who have directly or indirectly contributed to this achievement, personally and professionally. Finally, we would like to thank the conditions provided by all host institutions that offer the necessary conditions for research to be developed, either in the form of book chapters, scientific articles, or even policy briefs, which is the only route available for scientific progress. This work was also supported by UID/04058 - Research Unit on Governance, Competitiveness and Public Policies (GOVCOPP), financed by national funds through FCT - Foundation for Science and Technology.

Chapter 1
Monetary Policy in Developing Economies: A Review

Daniel Ofori-Sasu
https://orcid.org/0000-0001-8012-2478
Business School, University of Ghana, Ghana

Joshua Yindenaba Abor
Business School, University of Ghana, Ghana

Elikplimi Komla Agbloyor
Business School, University of Ghana, Ghana

ABSTRACT

The purpose of the study is to provide a holistic approach in exploring monetary policy concepts in developing economies. The study uses a systematic review by identifying and evaluating peer-reviewed journals in monetary policy issues that is published within the period, 2009-2020, from different contexts. The study targets at directing future research efforts to critical areas that require immediate attention. With several gaps in theoretical, methodologies and empirical evidence, the paper signals promising lines of inquiry for both theoretical and empirical research. It is therefore important for researchers and policy makers to provide an extensive research that addresses these concerns.

1. INTRODUCTION

Recently, the quest to stabilize developing economies has raised concerns about different mechanisms employed in proper reaction to monetary policy – making

DOI: 10.4018/979-8-3693-9765-7.ch001

monetary policy a crucial macroeconomic and financial regulation framework (Akan, 2024; Nguyen *et al.*, 2022; Schmeling *et al.*, 2022; Bussière *et al.*, 2021). Monetary policy is the actions undertaken by a nation's central bank to control money supply and achieve sustainable economic growth. The goal of finding potential macroeconomic indicators that predicts monetary policy shocks has awakened many scholars. Theoretically and empirically, the important role of monetary policy in understanding macroeconomic fluctuations has been well documented (see Nguyen, Dridi, Unsal & Williams, 2015; Srithilat and Sun, 2017; Waknis, 2014). Studies from literature recognises monetary policy as a dominant force in achieving financial stability (BIS, 2018; Goldberg *et al*, 2020) and the role of monetary policy in propelling financial and economic development worldwide (Hiroshi & Yuan, 2018; Effiong, Esu & Chuku, 2017; Ikhide & Uanguta, 2010; Al-Jasser & Banafe, 2008; Mohanty & Turner, 2006). Again some studies have been shown on the transmission of monetary policy in stabilizing the financial sector (Kashyap & Stein, 2000; Albertazzi *et al*, 2020) and interesting evidence has been provided in relation to banks' behaviour and their roles in response to monetary policy transmission (Ahumada & Fuentes, 2004; Alfaro, Franken, Garcia & Jara, 2003; Hulsewig, Mayer & Wollmershauser, 2009; Afanasyeva & Guntner, 2020). Despite monetary policy attracting the attention by many scholars and practitioners in recent times, evidence shows that studies on the drivers of monetary policy and banks' behaviour and channels in response to monetary policy in developing economies context continue to lag in finance literature (Waknis, 2016).

This review stems from the recent focus on monetary policy and its impact on the real economy and banking sector, both from an academic perspective and from a professional perspective. Most economists appreciate that monetary policy significantly propels the real economy through credit channels, at least if not in the long run (Bernanke & Gertler, 1995). Although some studies have led to the role of monetary policy in financial sector development, academic research on conceptual, theoretical, methodological, and empirical understanding of monetary policy, its determinants as well as its impact on the financial sector and real economy appear relatively little in the face of increasing changes in the global economy. To this end, there is a call for further research to explore current issues of monetary policy in development economies to address relevant gaps in the literature and create clear pathways for future studies in this area (Waknis, 2016; Jawadi, Malick & Souza, 2017).

From the literature, in particular, monetary policy issues indicate that the choice of monetary policy strategy, according to Walsh (2004), is a complex framework that defines the macroeconomic goals and targets that central banks use to achieve their stated goals. For instance, Lubis, Alexiou, and Nellis (2019) provide a review of monetary policy and macro-prudential in achieving the financial stability goal of the central bank. They investigate the channels through which macro-prudential and monetary policies interact to withstand financial and economic shocks. Stone and Bhundia (2004) identified five types of monetary policy strategies. These include three strategies with a single target, a strategy with multiple targets (Patra and Kapur, 2012), and a non-explicit nominal strategy (Cuaresma and Gnan, 2008). Alternatively, one type of monetary strategy can be adopted by one country at a time. The clear objective of the monetary policy strategy includes monetary targeting, inflation targeting, and exchange rate targeting (Roger, 2009). Marjan (2013) argues that central banks can make a wise decision that allows them to choose from a variety of monetary policy strategies and that countries can change from one type of monetary strategy to another.

The banking sector is critical to the transmission of monetary policy to the real economy. For instance, loose monetary policy reflects low policy rates which may induce banks' to lower their lending standards and grant more and riskier loans (Gertler *et al*, 2012). Despite a vast literature developed in recent times on the channels through which monetary policy operates, this renewed interest in monetary policy needs to be viewed within the context of current issues that stress on the impact of monetary policy on the financial system and real economy.

Ho and Yeh (2010) called for studies looking at the effect of monetary policy changes on macroeconomic shocks and transfers (Issahaku, Harvey & Abor, 2016), as well as monetary policy volatility responses to capital flows (Rey, 2013). Prior to this call, monetary policy research focused primarily on advanced economies (Kashyap and Stein, 2000; Ashcraft, 2006; Matousek, 2009) and on Africa (Ground & Ludi, 2006); and more recently in developed countries, particularly in the US economy (Tong, 2017; Igan *et al*, 2017; Lawal *et al* (2018). A new classification review of monetary systems by Stone and Bhundia (2004) presented in the International Monetary Fund (IMF) conference, revealed issues related to monetary policy, with few published papers on monetary policy in developing countries. Contrary, advent literature on it appears vague, inconsistent, and scattered in both developed and developing countries. The purpose of this study is to determine the current issues and research evidence on monetary policy in developing countries – providing key directions for further conceptual, contextual, methodological, and empirical studies. Also, it highlights reviews on determinants of monetary policy and the impact of monetary policy on the financial sector and real economy. The study intends to contribute significantly to the literature space by presenting a systematic review approach close to the work of Boateng and Duncombe, (2009)

This paper attempts to address questions by reviewing and assessing the state of knowledge regarding monetary policy issues in developing economies.

The specific objectives of this paper are:

i. To provide a literature review of issues on monetary policy in developing countries in developing market economies.
ii. To categorize and evaluate conceptual and theoretical approaches for understanding issues underpinning the role of monetary policy in the economy as well as its determinants from developing economies.
iii. To categorise and analyse the methodologies employed in several related studies and evaluate the empirical findings revealed by those studies.
iv. To identify and map key research gaps and trends in line with geographical distribution, concepts, methodologies, issues addressed with evidence presented as well future research directions in the area under research.

The next section presents the methodology for the reviews, literature discussion, methodological and empirical gaps and implications for theory and practice.

2. METHODOLOGICAL REVIEW

The paper intends to use a systematic review to provide projections of relevant information for future research (Keranen *et al*, 2012). Tranfield *et al* (2003) describe the systematic review approach as allowing the researcher to capture broader literature coverage with high transparency, reproducibility, and methodological rigor (Petticrew & Roberts, 2006). This approach has been categorized in this section as: (1) the scope of the review and (2) the search approach.

2.1 Scope of the review

A wide range of articles from business journals, particularly finance and economics, were the basis for the study's systematic review. However, the scope of the review was limited to monetary policy studies with specific focus on factors driving monetary policies from different context and economic settings. Further, studies on monetary policy, as a standalone indicator are not included because they are out of the scope of this research and it is broad in scope. Moreover, the study is limited to years of publication as well as journal recognition. In this regard, the study reviews articles published over 10 year period (2009-2020). This take into account a structural break in dataset as a result of the global financial crisis 2007/2008. The scope of the study was also limited to articles published in academic journals (David & Han, 2004) and articles from conference proceedings whose acceptable level of quality is based on a rigorous peer review of the English language. Thus, excluding articles published outside the English language, as well as essays and thesis in the study area. A total of ninety-nine (99) articles were used for the study. However, some of the articles were outside the scope of the reviewed articles categorized within the last 10 years publications.

2.2 Search approach

The search approach employed for the literature was through a review strategy, particularly "subject pearl growing" technique (Dolan *et al.*, 2005). In this approach, the researcher locates useful information related to the subject under study – by using an electronic databases with keyword descriptors (Ramer, 2005). The researcher, first, identifies some key subjects, information on appropriate topics and empirical research articles in the study and then proceeds to conduct the search. In the search process, diverse range of possible published journal articles were found within several online journal databases: Google Scholar, Wiley, Elsevier, SAGE, Emerald, JSTOR, Sci. Hub search, Routledge (Taylor and Francis Group), Oxford University Press, Springer, Thomson Reuters, World scientific publishing and EBSCOhost. The researcher searched and selected the articles based on year of publication, authors in the subject area, volume and issue number. Over 90 percent of the articles were in the field of academia whiles few of the articles in practitioner-oriented journals were considered. Some of the keywords and phrases used in the subject search are: "Monetary policy", "Monetary policy in developing economies", "Monetary policy and its determinants in developed countries", "Monetary policy and macroeconomic factors in developing economies", Monetary policy channels and transmissions", as well as "the impact of monetary policy on bank behaviour and financial sector". These keywords were used to cover a broad or general areas rather than specific areas since monetary policy is a macroeconomic variable for individual country or economic level, but not specific industries or sectors within an economy.

Out of over 200 search results from the databases, the researcher identified, after careful observation that the abstracts of some articles are overlapping because of the phrases used for the search. The researcher selected the relevant articles and eliminated the ones that overlapped. Although the study used 99 articles for this exercise (as shown in reference list), some were outside the year specification scope. Moreover, abstracts without full texts were omitted, leaving a total of 80 articles. Subsequently, out of the 80 articles, 70 relevant articles were used as a basis for the review (see Appendix I). A worklist of sixty (70) related articles has been created for this review. Table 1 shows the summary of the sources of the experimental literature and the year of publication.

Table 1. Summary of Literature Sources and Year of Publication

	2009	2010	2011	2012	2013	2014	2015	2016	2017	2018	2019	2020	2021	2022	2023	2024	Total
"Peer Reviewed Journal Articles"																	
1. Japan and the World Economy	**1**																**1**
2. Journal of International Money and Finance							1		1					**2**			**4**
3. The Quarterly Review of Economics and Finance									1								**1**
4. Applied Economics Letters									1	2							**3**
5. Research in International Business and Finance									2	1							**3**
6. Journal of Development Economics						1											**1**
7. Environmental Science and Policy										1							**1**
8. Economic Systems								1									**1**

continued on following page

Table 1. Continued

	2009	2010	2011	2012	2013	2014	2015	2016	2017	2018	2019	2020	2021	2022	2023	2024	Total
9. Review of Development Finance						2	1	1									**4**
10. Physica A 506										1							**1**
11. Journal of Economic Integration		1															**1**
12. Journal of Policy Modelling							1		2	1							**4**
13. Economic Modelling	1				1	2	2	1		1							**8**
14. Journal of Banking & Finance								1									**1**
15. Economics Letters								1									**1**
16. International Journal of Forecasting				1													**1**
17. Journal of Development Economics						1					**1**						**2**
18. Pacific-Basin Finance Journal						1											**1**

continued on following page

Table 1. Continued

	2009	2010	2011	2012	2013	2014	2015	2016	2017	2018	2019	2020	2021	2022	2023	2024	Total
19. Journal of African Development								1									**1**
20. Future Business Journal										1							**1**
21. Macroeconomics and Finance in Emerging Market Economies				1													**1**
22. Qualitative Research in Financial Markets,			1	1				1									**3**
23. Borsa _ Istanbul Review							1										**1**
24. Journal of Economics and Behavioral Studies								1									**1**
25. International Review of Economics and Finance							1										**1**
26. China Economics			1														**1**

continued on following page

Table 1. Continued

	2009	2010	2011	2012	2013	2014	2015	2016	2017	2018	2019	2020	2021	2022	2023	2024	Total
27. Journal of Asian Economics				1													**1**
28. Journal of Monetary Economics												**1**					**1**
29. Emerging Markets Finance and Trade												**1**					**1**
30. International Journal of Monetary Economics and Finance								1		1	**1**	**1**					**4**
31. Journal of Financial Economics														**1**			**1**
32. Econometrica														**1**			**1**
33. The Journal of Economic Asymmetries																**1**	**1**
34. Journal of Asian Economics																**1**	**1**
35. Review of International Economics													**1**				**1**

continued on following page

Table 1. Continued

	2009	2010	2011	2012	2013	2014	2015	2016	2017	2018	2019	2020	2021	2022	2023	2024	Total
36. Cogent Business & Management														**1**			**1**
37. Energy Policy																**1**	**1**
38. The Journal of Finance														**1**			**1**
Non-Peer-Reviewed Journal Articles																	
39. IMF working paper	1																**1**
40. The Chinese University of Hong Kong								1									**1**
41. Goethe University Frankfurt Am Main Working Paper Series				1													**1**
42. City University Working Paper			1														**1**
43. Federal Reserve Board									1								**1**
44. Book Review										1							**1**
Total	**3**	**1**	**3**	**5**	**1**	**7**	**7**	**10**	**8**	**10**	**2**	**3**	**1**	**6**		**3**	**70**

3. DESCRIPTION OF LITERATURE

In the systematic approach, the researcher identified sixty-four (64) peer-reviewed journals and six (6) non-peer-reviewed articles, ranging from 2009 to 2024 on monetary policy issues in developed and developing countries (see Appendix II). There have been earlier publications on the subject area, but the review considered journal articles with 14-year period and years after the 2008/2009 financial crises. The subject, "Monetary policy", has gained much concern in literature. Over the past years (within the years of review), a number of theoretical and empirical literature has been documented around issues on monetary policy and dynamics in macroeconomic variables. The literature posits that fluctuations in output and inflation (Rafiq & Mallick, 2008; Waal & Eyden, 2012; Nguyen, Dridi, Unsal & Williams, 2015); household consumption (Owusu-Sekyere, 2017); house prices (Simo-Kengne, Balcilar, Gupta, Reid, Ayeet, 2013); credit and investment (Ndikumana, 2016); exchange rates (López-Villavicencio & Mignon, 2017); industrial sector performance (Kutu & Ngalawa, 2017); exchange rate volatility, currency substitution (Yinusa & Akinlo, 2008); market integration (Caporin, Pelizzon and Plazzi, 2017); and financial systems (Ncube, 1999); economic and industrial sector performance (Balolgun, 2007; Kutu & Ngalawa, 2016); risk taking and spillovers (Powel, 2014) – all have a direct and reverse influence on monetary policy instruments.

From the review, special attention was given to *Economic Modelling,* followed by *Journal of International Money and Finance*, *Review of Development Finance* and *Journal of Policy Modelling*, with significant increase in publications from 2011 to 2024. Moreover, three key journals (*Economic Modelling, Journal of Policy Modelling, International Journal of Monetary Economics and Finance* and *Review of Development Finance*) within the 14 years made significant contributions to the growth of publications on monetary policy issues. There has been an increasing trend in journal publications of the subject matter under investigation and evidence of the growing scope started from 2010 to 2012, it then declined in 2013 and increased again from 2014 to 2016, but decreased in 2017 (8 articles) with the same number of articles recorded in the first quarter in 2018. The period 2019-2021 and 2024 are in their development stages. However, 2010, 2013, and 2019 recorded the least within the growing trend while the year, 2020 recorded 2 publications that matched the search criteria.

In terms of the authors for the reviewed articles, it appears that there exists a relatively low-frequency rate of single-authored articles identified (i.e., 15 single authors), twenty-three (23) reviewed articles were mainly two authors and the majority (27) were more than two authors. The studies (reviewed articles) focus on macroeconomic indicators in various economic contexts. it came mainly from the field of finance and economics. Overall, the reviewed articles on the subject matter had certain macroeconomic indicators interacting with monetary policy.

4. FINDINGS AND GAPS FOR THE REVIEW

A systematic classification for the articles were developed and articles were categorized as follows:

1. Theoretical review and conceptual framework
2. Themes under monetary policy
3. methodologies
4. Geographic representation of research
5. Future research direction

The study discuss in detail, each of the five segments listed above. It spells out the issues addressed and the questions raised in the articles reviewed – pointing to future research considerations.

4.1 Brief Theoretical Review

One significant element required to drive macroeconomic policy is monetary policy (Seleteng, 2016). The goal of monetary policy, which has been widely accepted by economists, is to maintain price stability. It is broadly classified as either expansionary or contractionary. It consists of the management of money supply and interest rates, aimed at controlling inflation, consumption, growth and liquidity. The tools used to achieve monetary policy are open market operations, direct lending to banks, bank reserve requirements, unconventional emergency lending programs, and managing market expectations subject to central bank's credibility. Expansionary monetary policy is when central bank uses its tools to stimulate the economy. In this case, increases in money supply, lowers interest rates, and increases demand. This boosts economic growth, lowers the value of currency and thereby decreases the exchange rates. On the other hand, contractionary monetary policy is when a central bank uses its monetary tools to fight inflation. In this case, economic growth slows down. The banks will raise interest rates to make lending more expensive, thus, reducing the amount of money and credit that banks lend. This lowers the money supply by making loans, credit cards and mortgages more expensive. Thus, monetary policy is of great importance, regarding stabilizing real exchange rate and inflation.

4.2 Monetary policy concepts

In mapping the review, the current studies were identified based on the concept of the monetary policy transmission mechanism. From the literature, the concepts of monetary policy were captured into two areas of development, namely: financial sector transmission channels, macroeconomic interaction with monetary policy and impacts on banking behaviour and financial system.

4.2.1 Theoretical Underpinnings

The study used theories to explain these two concepts. The discussions are entails below.

4.2.1.1 Financial Sector Transmission of Monetary Policy

The fast-growing financial system has a direct impact on central banks' monetary policy. According to Kashyap and Stein (2000), monetary policy operates effectively through financial systems and any development that has the potential to influence the structure of the financial system will also have an impact on the transmission mechanism. In addition, credit channel theory demonstrates that a higher level of financial friction is associated with a stronger mechanism for the transmission of monetary policy, and the theory supports the effect of monetary policy on bank lending behavior (Kashyap and Stein, 2000). In the bank lending channel, a high interest rate indicates a close relationship between bank lending rates and the policy rate (money market rate). It can be said that these articles are the bulk of the studies focusing on the banking industry in various economies. They include the work of Hazra (2017) that captures the relationship between alternative payment methods and whether each is linked to costs and benefits. The results show that the trade-off between alternative means of payment can be critical to the transmission of monetary policy when costs are associated with both methods of payment. A study by Gunji and Yuan (2018) examined the relationship between monetary policy effectiveness and business diversification between banks and companies using data at the bank level in 11 Asian countries from 1995 to 2008. Gunji, Miura, and Yuan (2009) show that there is a theoretical contradiction between the effects of monetary policy shocks to economies with different competitive banking sectors. The study examines the impact of the level of bank competition on the monetary policy of 22 countries in the United States, Europe and Asia-Oceania, including developing countries. A recent study by Matusk and Solomon (2018) examines the bank lending channel (BLC) in Nigeria between 2002 and 2008 of 23 consolidated banks. They indicated that loan increases were more sensitive to changes in the bank's size and capitalization. Consequently, the monetary policy of the central bank restructuring activities improved the central bank's influence in Nigeria.

In a 2014 paper by Mishra, Montiel, Pedroni and Spilembergo (2014), the study examined the transmission of monetary shocks to lending rates in a large sample (132) of developed, emerging and low-income countries during the period 1978-2013. Matemilola Bany-Ariffin, and Muhtar (2015) analyzed the effect of monetary policy on bank lending rates in South Africa and found that commercial banks in South Africa adjust their lending rates down or by lowering interest rates. Jeon Wu (2014) examines the role of foreign banks in transmission of monetary policy, an evidence from Asia during the 2008-2009 crisis. They noted that the increased penetration of foreign banks has weakened the effectiveness of the monetary policy transmission mechanism in emerging Asian economies. In addition, most of these studies raise concerns about the impact of monetary policy changes on the banking sector. Although monetary policy plays an important role in both growth and development economies, the approaches used in each case is different. This presents lack of understanding of the concept of monetary policy as a transmission mechanism in the financial sector. Other limitation found in the review is linked to data scope, measurement inconsistencies and time lags. As a result, a robust measurement of variables, well defined data scope, particularly an extended year periods and recent data must be given priority for monetary policy research.

There are some key areas of concern raised from the literature, which are:

Research questions

RQ1. "How do banks respond to host country monetary policy differently depending on the extent to which their parent banks are affected by the global financial crisis of 2008–9? "

RQ2. "How does parent banks' reliance on the wholesale funding market impact their subsidiaries abroad to host monetary policy? "

RQ3. "Are the roles of foreign banks in the monetary policy transmission affected by the different modes of entry to the host banking markets in different markets? "

RQ4. "What is the median response of the lending rate to a country-specific monetary shock? "

RQ5. "What factors determine the response of the lending rate to monetary policy shocks? "

4.2.1.2 Macroeconomic and Banking Behaviour Interactions with Monetary Policy Concept

Extant research on this concepts discusses the role of monetary policy in influencing macroeconomic indicators like exchange rate, inflation, stock returns, financial stability, financial development, remittances, and capital flows. From the articles reviewed - focusing on this idea, Issahaku, Harvey and Abor, (2016) investigate on whether growth financing poses an additional risk to monetary policy. Qin, Ge and Lu (2018) examined the effectiveness of monetary policy in China and Kenya (Were *et al*, 2014) and in small open economies (Primus, 2018). López-Villavicencio and Mignon (2017) examined exchange rate fluctuations in emerging countries and examined whether the inflation environment, monetary policy and central bank behavior mattered. Ma and Lin (2016) analyzed economic growth and effectiveness of monetary policy while Tong (2017) observed that US monetary policy has a significant impact on global financial stability. Kabundi, Schaling and Some (2015) examined monetary policy and heterogeneous inflation prospects in South Africa. Suhaibua, Harvey and Amidu (2017) investigated the effect of monetary policy on stock market performance from twelve (12) African countries. Recent studies of monetary policy in developing countries document a weak bank lending channel (Abuka *et al*, 2019) while output effects of monetary policy in emerging and developing countries has been evidenced in empirical studies (Nguyen, 2020). Again Afanasyeva and Guntner (2020) provide evidence on bank market power and the risk channel of monetary policy. The results from all the studies in this category reinforce the various proposals from different context in developing economies.

However, some notable areas that demand in-depth investigation are pointed out below.

Research questions

RQ6. What are the factors that influence monetary policy in developing economies?
RQ7. How effective are these factors in enhancing monetary policy in developing economies?
RQ8. How does monetary policy affect financial system and stability in developing economies?
RQ9. What are the challenges confronting monetary policy behaviour in developing economies?

4.2.2 Methodological Issues in Monetary Policy Research

This section highlights the different methods underlining the reviewed articles from the literature. Although, some studies have been proven to be conceptual (Tarullo, 2017) empirical and case study (Filho *et al*, 2018) in nature, the study draws both the qualitative and quantitative methods from the review. Drawing from the review, the quantitative research method was predominant whiles the qualitative method was less conducted in the literature. However, the application or use of the models adopted in the quantitative method was not consistent across the studies. For instance, whiles recent works by Issahaku, Harvey and Abor (2016), Gunji and Yuan (2018), Matousek and Solomon (2018) used the panel model approach, Aleem, and Lahiani (2014), Matemilola Bany-Ariffin, and Muhtar (2015), Primus (2018) employed the time series approach.

Primarily, data for the studies have been on macro-level data from the World Development Indicator, World Bank and Bank Scope. At the macro-level, data have been from monthly data sample, quarterly data sample and yearly with historical sample data. Regarding macro-level, several studies have evaluated macroeconomic variables interaction with monetary policy and the sample data have been analysed on specific countries (Qin, Ge & Lu, 2018; Tong, 2017) and in developed economies (Aleem & Lahiani, 2014; Rubio and Schuh, 2017) and developing economies (Suhaibua, Harvey & Amidu, 2017).

The researcher noted that the level of analyses continues to reveal the importance of monetary policy, not only at country level, but also across different countries in the international markets. In developing economies in Africa, the scope of data, methodology, models, and country selection criteria used in the analysis vary from one study to another. The analysis of all the reviews is based on macro level data analyses. Table 2 presents a "mapping of some key research concepts and methodological approaches underlying these studies. "From the table, it is obvious that there exist gaps in the qualitative, descriptive, and mixed research methods in relation to the two basic concepts of monetary policy research.

Table 2. Mapping of monetary policy issues/concepts and methodological approaches

	Qualitative	Quantitative	Mixed	Descriptive
Effectiveness of Monetary Policy and its Determinants	16,46	3,42,49,50,59,64, 61, 62, 66	39	4, 18, 32, 38
Monetary policy impact on Bank Behaviour, Lending, Channels and transmission mechanism of Monetary Policy	33, 10, 28, 43	7, 8, 12, 13,15, 21,29,30,31, 35, 52, 53, 54, 55, 57, 63, 68, 70		40
Impacts of monetary policy on output (real economy) and other factors		51,60, 65, 69		
Monetary Policy interaction with macroeconomic variables.	6, 41	1, 2, 5, 9, 11, 14, 17, 19, 20, 22, 23, 24,25,26,27,36, 37,44,45,47,48,58, 67		34

4.2.3 Geographic Representations

This section shows the topographical distribution of recent articles conducted in monetary policy studies.

Within almost all developed countries, monetary authorities like the Federal Reserve System in US, the Bank of England, the European Central Bank, Bank of Japan and the People's Bank of China exist to execute monetary policy and are frequently independent of the executive. In relation to financial system, these governmental institutions, called the central banks, are responsible for supervising the smooth operation of financial systems of an economy. Open market operation, a monetary policy tool, entails the control of quantity of money in circulation through the sales and purchases of various financial assets or financial instruments (IEA-Ghana, 2012). In the short term, open market operation aims to achieve a short term interest target or specific exchange rate target relative to some foreign currency or reserves like gold. For instance, in the US, Federal Reserve targets the federal funds rate (lending rate); which indicates the rate at which member banks may lend to one another. From the extant works that have been revealed so far, the majority of the works have been done in developed countries, particularly in Asia (Akan, 2024; Schmeling *et al.*, 2022; Gunji & Yuan, 2018; Ma, 2016; Jeon & Wu, 2014; Aleem & Lahiani, 2014); empirical works in U.S. or Latin America (Aleem, & Lahiani, 2014; Hammoudeh, Nguyen & Sousa, 2015; Igan *et al*, 2017; Tong, 2017; Balcilar *et al*, 2017), developing countries (Nguyen *et al.*, 2022; Issahaku, Harvey & Abor, 2016), emerging markets (Zehri *et al.*, 2024; Wong & Chong, 2016; Hove at al, 2015) and Africa (Ouedraogo & Sourouema, 2018; Filho *et al*, 2018; Harvey & Cushing, 2015; Mullineux & Murinde, 2014). The less represented regions are the Europe, Middle East, and Australia. Within these regions that have been represented, differences occur with respect to analysis, methodologies, models and number of times article have been published in a year. For instance, from the context of Africa and concentrated on countries such as South Africa (Naraidoo & Paya, 2012; Matemilola Bany-Ariffin, & Muhtar, 2015; Kabundi, Schaling & Some, 2015) with less presented in specific countries like Nigeria (Matousek & Solomon, 2018; Lawal *et al* 2018), Kenya (Were *et al* 2014), Ghana (Quartey & Afful-Mensah, 2014) and emerging economies in Africa (Suhaibua, Harvey & Amidu, 2017).

A critical look has focused less on the distribution of publications, case studies, and quality in monetary policy across all economies and within empirical works, and there are relatively rare evidence from emerging or developing and less developed market contexts.

4.2.4 Conceptual focus

The study presents a significant dispersal of conceptual approaches used in the study of monetary policy in a variety of theoretical perspectives are presented as follows:

Theoretical approaches are studies that define theories and test these theories.

Framework-based approaches are studies that follow a specific framework of analysis and this framework can be derived from theoretical work.

Model-based approaches are studies that apply multiple models and do not refer to a cognitive group.

Conceptual approaches are studies that follow specific concepts but are not based on theoretical foundations.

Category-based approaches are studies or researches that adopt a specific set of factors for conducting analysis.

The revised articles were assigned according to geographical distribution and theoretical approaches on studies relating to monetary policy. This is presented below.

Table 3. Mapping of geographical contexts and conceptual approaches

	"Theory-based approaches"	**Framework-based approaches**	**"Model-based approaches"**	**"Concept-based approaches"**	**"Category-based approaches"**	**TOTAL**
U.S, Latin America	46, 48, 55, 63		31, 25, 47, 1, 15, 9, 12, 62, 69, 70	17, 41,43, 61		**18**
Asia and Middle East	32	4, 56	7, 8, 26, 21,13,27,39, 53, 57, 59, 66, 68			**15**
Europe/Euro Area	54, 64		3			**3**

continued on following page

Table 3. Continued

	"Theory-based approaches"	Framework-based approaches	"Model-based approaches"	"Concept-based approaches"	"Category-based approaches"	TOTAL
Africa	40, 44	2	36, 30, 11, 38, 49, 5, 34, 29, 22, 45, 24, 23, 33,35,52,58,60	6		**21**
Across Different Regions	37, 65	14,19	20, 42; 50, 16, 18, 51, 67	10, 28		**13**
TOTAL	**11**	**5**	**47**	**7**	**0**	**70**

From the reviewed articles, little or no studies on monetary policy have been conducted with focus on theory-based approaches (11), framework-based approaches (5), and concept-based approaches (7); however, none was recorded for category-based approaches. Thus, evidence from the literature indicates that studies on monetary policy take the form of model-based approaches (47). Studies in the European market economies were the least recorded with the majority done in Europe and Africa. Most of the search also focussed on the African region to establish gaps in the work done within this region.

5. DISCUSSIONS AND RESEARCH IMPLICATIONS

In economic research literature (Kim, 2000; Gali and Monacelli, 2005), the main concern is an investigation into what has been the main impact of monetary policy on the economy of several markets (Akan, 2024; Effiong, Esu and Chuku, 2017; Al-Jasser and Banafe, 2008; Mohanty and Turner, 2006). Previous studies focus on developed economies (Srithilat and Sun, 2017), and studies of monetary policy devoted to methodological issues (Saiti, 2016). However, monetary policy from developing countries in Africa is scanty. In developing economies, previous studies focused on bank lending channels and there has been extensive research on the banking lending channels in developed economies (Matousek, 2009). However, the transmission of monetary policy lending patterns or behaviour of the banking sector in Africa – has not been studied extensively. In addition, how monetary policy influences the impact of financial development (Krause & Rioja, 2006) on GDP growth volatility – is yet to gain attention in developing economies in Africa.

The study refers to the Current Systematic Review - to conduct a literature review on monetary policy in various market contexts. The literature review captures accumulated scientific data and finds gaps in the literature, coupled with some research questions. The study maps the review to future research by identifying trends and issues in extant literature focused on monetary policy issues.

The study found that there is a call for advancement of theories, concept approaches and qualitative methods in monetary policy research. SubsequentlySome of the concerns expressed by previous scholars seem to have been handled, whereas others are yet to be given future consideration. Empirical studies on the interactions of the various macroeconomic indicators with monetary policy have not been extensively been studied from the African context. The study observed lack of cross-sectional research, focusing more on single countries, dominance of quantitative studies and model-based approaches. Thus, a significant gap in the study of monetary policy exists, particularly in Africa. Most of the studies did not focus on less-developed countries and this could be attributed to lack of data. Moreover potential determinants of monetary policy are not yet revealed and explored in different context as well as longitudinal research approaches. Institutional quality and country-level characteristics can be moderated to know the true effect of these determinants on monetary policy.

Some key main methodological concerns are the lack of mixed methods and qualitative methods in studies. In contrast to this there is a significant use of quantitative methods, which tend to dominate these areas of study. Moreover, there is the lack of case studies, practitioner research approaches and the literature review fails to provide a meta-analysis on monetary policy for different economies. It is therefore important for researchers, scholars in academia and practitioners, policy makers and organizations to provide an extensive research that addresses these concerns.

6. CONCLUSIONS AND LIMITATIONS

The study highlights reviews on current issues, theories, methodologies and research approaches used in monetary policy research. It attempts to address questions raised in existing literature on the subject of monetary policy and it does this by reviewing and assessing the state of knowledge regarding monetary policy issues in developing economies. By comprehensively, providing literature review on issues of monetary policy in developing countries; categorising and evaluating conceptual and theoretical approaches for understanding issues underpinning the role of monetary policy in the economy as well as its determinants from developing market economies perspective; analysing the methodologies employed in several related studies and evaluate the empirical findings revealed by those studies; identifying and mapping key research gaps and trends in line with geographical distribution, concepts, methodologies, issues addressed with evidence presented as well future research directions in the area under research. The study used a systematic review to ensure a provision for relevant insights for future research. An evidence from mapping the results give an opportunity for the future direction of research in the study of the concept of monetary policy and in the understanding of the theoretical and experimental foundations.

In summary, the researchers conclude some of the gaps in the issues by presenting a series of questions and projecting current concerns about further studies to be conducted in an effort to develop a comprehensive empirical approach to monetary policy. However, the authors prudently acknowledge that this research has some limitations. First, it presents a general overview of evidence existing in the literature, without carefully and explicitly checking specific studies, journals or online databases. In addition, the study was limited to published articles for both peer reviewers and non-peer reviewers who could access and publish in English. In this light, the articles reviewed may not represent the total coverage of the publications in the study area. Although the concerns and questions raised in the study may not be comprehensive, the researcher hopes that the concerns and questions serve as a pointer to further studies. This also signals prospects for novel research ideas and investigations.

REFERENCES

Akan, T. (2024). The impact of monetary policy on climate change through the mediation of sectoral renewable energy consumption. *Energy Policy*, *192*, 114244. DOI: 10.1016/j.enpol.2024.114244

Al-Jasser, M., & Banafe, A. (2008). Monetary policy transmission mechanism in Saudi Arabia. In *BIS Papers No. 35*. Bank for International Settlements.

Albertazzi, U., Fringuellotti, F., & Ongena, S. (2020). Monetary policy and bank stability: The analytical toolbox reviewed. *ECB Working Paper Series No. 2377*. European Central Bank. https://doi.org/DOI: 10.2866/13576

Aleem, A., & Lahiani, A. (2014). Monetary policy credibility and exchange rate pass-through: Some evidence from emerging countries. *Economic Modelling*, *43*, 21–29. DOI: 10.1016/j.econmod.2014.06.020

Allegret, J. P., & Benkhodja, M. T. (2015). External shocks and monetary policy in an oil exporting economy (Algeria). *Journal of Policy Modeling*, *37*(4), 652–667. DOI: 10.1016/j.jpolmod.2015.03.017

Ashcraft, A. B. (2006). New evidence on the lending channel. *Journal of Money, Credit and Banking*, *38*(3), 751–775. DOI: 10.1353/mcb.2006.0037

Balcilar, M., Demirer, R., Gupta, R., & van Eyden, R. (2017). The impact of US policy uncertainty on the monetary effectiveness in the Euro area. *Journal of Policy Modeling*, *39*(6), 1052–1064. DOI: 10.1016/j.jpolmod.2017.09.002

Bianchi, J., & Bigio, S. (2022). Banks, liquidity management, and monetary policy. *Econometrica*, *90*(1), 391–454. DOI: 10.3982/ECTA16599

Bussière, M., Cao, J., de Haan, J., Hills, R., Lloyd, S., Meunier, B., Pedrono, J., Reinhardt, D., Sinha, S., Sowerbutts, R., & Styrin, K. (2021). The interaction between macroprudential policy and monetary policy: Overview. *Review of International Economics*, *29*(1), 1–19. DOI: 10.1111/roie.12505

Caporin, M., Pelizzon, L., & Plazzi, A. (2017). Does monetary policy impact market integration? Evidence from developed and emerging markets. *Journal of International Money and Finance*, *70*, 147–168. DOI: 10.1016/j.jimonfin.2016.08.004

Cham, T. (2016). Does monetary integration lead to an increase in FDI flows? An empirical investigation from the West African Monetary Zone (WAMZ). *Borsa Istanbul Review*, *16*(1), 9–20. DOI: 10.1016/j.bir.2016.01.002

Chebbi, T., & Derbali, A. (2019). US monetary policy surprises transmission to European stock markets. *International Journal of Monetary Economics and Finance*, *12*(1), 3–14. DOI: 10.1504/IJMEF.2019.098633

Cortés, G. S., Gao, G. P., Silva, F. B., & Song, Z. (2022). Unconventional monetary policy and disaster risk: Evidence from the subprime and COVID–19 crises. *Journal of International Money and Finance*, *122*, 102543. DOI: 10.1016/j.jimonfin.2021.102543 PMID: 34949899

Cuaresma, J. C., & Gnan, E. (2008). Four monetary policy strategies in comparison: How to deal with financial instability? *Monetary Policy & The Economy*, (Q1/08), 65–102. https://ideas.repec.org/p/onb/oenbfs/y2008iq1b3.html

David, R. J., & Han, S. K. (2004). A systematic assessment of the empirical support for transaction cost economics. *Strategic Management Journal*, *25*(1), 39–58. DOI: 10.1002/smj.359

Dolan, P., Shaw, R., Tsuchiya, A., & Williams, A. (2005). QALY maximization and people's preferences: A methodological review of the literature. *Health Economics*, *14*(2), 197–208. DOI: 10.1002/hec.924 PMID: 15386656

Duncombe, R., & Boateng, R. (2009). Mobile phones and financial services in developing countries: A review of concepts, methods, issues, evidence and future research directions. *Development Informatics Working Paper No. 37*. Centre for Development Informatics, University of Manchester. https://diodeweb.files.wordpress .com/2010/09/di_wp37.pdf

Filho, W. L., Balogun, A. L., Ayal, D. Y., Bethurem, E. M., Murambadoro, M., Mambo, J., Taddese, H., Tefera, G. W., Nagy, G. J., Fudjumdjum, H., & Mugabe, P. (2018). Strengthening climate change adaptation capacity in Africa: Case studies from six major African cities and policy implications. *Environmental Science & Policy*, *86*, 29–37. DOI: 10.1016/j.envsci.2018.05.004

Gali, J., & Monacelli, T. (2005). Monetary policy and exchange rate volatility in a small open economy. *The Review of Economic Studies*, *72*(3), 707–734. DOI: 10.1111/j.1467-937X.2005.00349.x

Ground, M., & Ludi, K. L. (2006). Investigating the bank-lending channel in South Africa: A VAR approach. *Working Paper 2006-4*, Department of Economics, University of Pretoria. https://ideas.repec.org/p/pre/wpaper/200604.html

Gunji, H., Miura, K., & Yuan, Y. (2009). Bank competition and monetary policy. *Japan and the World Economy*, *21*(2), 105–115. DOI: 10.1016/j.japwor.2007.11.001

Gunji, H., & Yuan, Y. (2018). Bank diversification and monetary policy. *Applied Economics Letters*, *25*(15), 1087–1090. DOI: 10.1080/13504851.2017.1397845

Hammoudeh, S., Nguyen, D. K., & Sousa, R. M. (2015). US monetary policy and sectoral commodity prices. *Journal of International Money and Finance*, *57*, 61–85. DOI: 10.1016/j.jimonfin.2015.06.003

Hanim, T. F., Abdul Rahman, R., & Omar, N. (2011). Empirical evidence on the risk management tools practised in Islamic and conventional banks. *Qualitative Research in Financial Markets*, *3*(2), 86–104. DOI: 10.1108/17554171111155339

Harvey, S. K., & Cushing, M. J. (2015). Is West African Monetary Zone (WAMZ) a common currency area? *Review of Development Finance*, *5*(1), 53–63. DOI: 10.1016/j.rdf.2015.05.001

Hassen, G., & Hamdi, K. (2020). The impact of monetary policy on overall and sectoral economic growth: Evidence from Tunisian Central Bank in crisis periods. *International Journal of Monetary Economics and Finance*, *13*(5), 471–484. DOI: 10.1504/IJMEF.2020.110558

Hazra, D. (2017). Monetary policy and alternative means of payment. *The Quarterly Review of Economics and Finance*, *65*, 378–387. DOI: 10.1016/j.qref.2016.11.002

Ho, T., & Yeh, K. (2010). Measuring monetary policy in a small open economy with managed exchange rates: The case of Taiwan. *Southern Economic Journal*, *76*(3), 811–826. DOI: 10.4284/sej.2010.76.3.811

Hove, S., Mama, A. T., & Tchana, F. T. (2015). Monetary policy and commodity terms of trade shocks in emerging market economies. *Economic Modelling*, *49*, 53–71. DOI: 10.1016/j.econmod.2015.03.012

Igan, D., Kabundi, A., De Simone, F. N., & Tamirisa, N. (2017). Monetary policy and balance sheets. *Journal of Policy Modeling*, *39*(1), 169–184. DOI: 10.1016/j.jpolmod.2016.09.003

Ikhide, S., & Uanguta, E. (2010). Impact of South Africa's monetary policy on the LNS economies. *Journal of Economic Integration*, *25*(2), 324–352. DOI: 10.11130/jei.2010.25.2.324

International Monetary Fund (IMF). (2015). Monetary policy and financial stability. *IMF Policy Paper*. https://www.imf.org/en/Publications/Policy-Papers/Issues/2016/12/31/Monetary-Policy-and-Financial-Stability-PP5059

Issahaku, H., Harvey, S. K., & Abor, J. Y. (2016). Does development finance pose an additional risk to monetary policy? *Review of Development Finance*, *6*(2), 91–104. DOI: 10.1016/j.rdf.2016.06.001

Issing, O., & Wieland, V. (2012). Monetary theory and monetary policy: Reflections on the development over the last 150 years. *Institute for Monetary and Financial Stability, Goethe University Frankfurt*. Working Paper No. 67. https://www.imfs-frankfurt.de/de/forschung/imfs-working-papers.html

Jawadi, F., Mallick, S. K., & Sousa, R. M. (2017). US monetary policy and global financial stability. *Research in International Business and Finance*, *39*, 466–485. DOI: 10.1016/j.ribaf.2016.09.001

Jeon, B. N., & Wu, J. (2014). The role of foreign banks in monetary policy transmission: Evidence from Asia during the crisis of 2008–2009. *Pacific-Basin Finance Journal*, *29*, 96–120. DOI: 10.1016/j.pacfin.2014.03.005

Kabundi, A., Schaling, E., & Some, M. (2015). Monetary policy and heterogeneous inflation expectations in South Africa. *Economic Modelling*, *45*, 109–117. DOI: 10.1016/j.econmod.2014.11.002

Kang, K. H., & Do, K. (2024). Korea's neutral interest rate: Estimates, determinants, and monetary policy stance. *Journal of Asian Economics*, *92*, 101732. DOI: 10.1016/j.asieco.2024.101732

Kashyap, A. K., & Stein, J. C. (2000). What do a million observations on banks say about the transmission of monetary policy? *The American Economic Review*, *90*(3), 407–428. DOI: 10.1257/aer.90.3.407

Keränen, J., Piirainen, K. A., & Salmanen, R. T. (2012). Systematic review on B2B branding: Research issues and avenues for future research. *Journal of Product and Brand Management*, *21*(6), 404–417. DOI: 10.1108/10610421211264892

Kim, J. (2000). Constructing and estimating a realistic optimizing model of monetary policy. *Journal of Monetary Economics*, *45*(2), 329–359. DOI: 10.1016/S0304-3932(99)00054-9

Krause, S., & Rioja, F. (2006). Financial development and monetary policy efficiency. *Working Paper*, Department of Economics, Georgia State University.

Kutu, A. A., & Ngalawa, H. (2016). Monetary policy shocks and industrial sector performance in South Africa. *Journal of Economics and Behavioral Studies*, *8*(3), 26–40. DOI: 10.22610/jebs.v8i3(J).1286

Lawal, A. I., Somoye, R. O., Babajide, A. A., & Nwanjia, T. I. (2018). The effect of fiscal and monetary policies interaction on stock market performance: Evidence from Nigeria. *Future Business Journal*, *4*(1), 16–33. DOI: 10.1016/j.fbj.2017.11.004

López-Villavicencio, A., & Mignon, V. (2017). Exchange rate pass-through in emerging countries: Do the inflation environment, monetary policy regime, and central bank behavior matter? *Journal of International Money and Finance*, *79*, 20–38. DOI: 10.1016/j.jimonfin.2017.09.004

Ma, Y. (2016). Nonlinear monetary policy and macroeconomic stabilization in emerging market economies: Evidence from China. *Economic Systems*, *40*(4), 461–480. DOI: 10.1016/j.ecosys.2015.12.003

Ma, Y., & Lin, X. (2016). Financial development and the effectiveness of monetary policy. *Journal of Banking & Finance*, *68*, 1–11. DOI: 10.1016/j.jbankfin.2016.03.002

Masood, O., & Ashraf, M. (2012). Bank-specific and macroeconomic profitability determinants of Islamic banks: The case of different countries. *Qualitative Research in Financial Markets*, *4*(2/3), 255–268. DOI: 10.1108/17554171211252565

Matemilola, B. T., Bany-Ariffin, A. N., & Muhtar, F. E. (2015). The impact of monetary policy on bank lending rate in South Africa. *Borsa Istanbul Review*, *15*(1), 53–59. DOI: 10.1016/j.bir.2014.09.003

Mishra, P., Montiel, P., Pedroni, P., & Spilimbergo, A. (2014). Monetary policy and bank lending rates in low-income countries: Heterogeneous panel estimates. *Journal of Development Economics*, *111*, 117–131. DOI: 10.1016/j.jdeveco.2014.08.005

Mohanty, M. S., & Turner, P. (2006). Monetary policy transmission in emerging market economies: What is new? *BIS Papers No. 35*. Bank for International Settlements. https://www.bis.org/publ/bppdf/bispap35.htm

Morgan, S. (2011). *Dynamic differentiated RRR adjustment to become the primary monetary policy tool.* Morgan Stanley Research Asia/Pacific.

Mullineux, A. W., & Murinde, V. (2014). Financial sector policies for enterprise development in Africa. *Review of Development Finance*, *4*(2), 66–72. DOI: 10.1016/j.rdf.2014.05.001

Naraidoo, R., & Paya, I. (2012). Forecasting monetary policy rules in South Africa. *International Journal of Forecasting*, *28*(2), 446–455. DOI: 10.1016/j.ijforecast.2011.04.006

Ncube, M. (1999). Financial systems and monetary policy in Africa (*Working Paper No.* 20, Graduate School of Business Administration, University of the Witwatersrand). https://wiredspace.wits.ac.za/handle/10539/19804

Ndikumana, L. (2016). Implications of monetary policy for credit and investment in Sub-Saharan African countries. *Journal of African Development*, *18*(2), 1–18. DOI: 10.5325/jafrideve.18.2.0001

Nguyen, A. D. M., Dridi, J., Unsal, F. D., & Williams, O. H. (2015). On the drivers of inflation in Sub-Saharan Africa (*IMF Working Paper No.* WP/15/189). International Monetary Fund, African Department. https://doi.org/DOI: 10.5089/9781513519240.001

Nguyen, H. H., Nguyen, T. P., & Tran, A. N. T. (2022). Impacts of monetary policy transmission on bank performance and risk in the Vietnamese market: Does the COVID-19 pandemic matter? *Cogent Business & Management*, *9*(1), 2094591. Advance online publication. DOI: 10.1080/23311975.2022.2094591

Ouedraogo, R., & Sourouema, W. S. (2018). Fiscal policy pro-cyclicality in Sub-Saharan African countries: The role of export concentration. *Economic Modelling*, *71*, 1–11. DOI: 10.1016/j.econmod.2018.05.017

Owusu-Sekyere, E. (2017). The impact of monetary policy on household consumption in South Africa: Evidence from vector autoregressive techniques. *Suid-Afrikaanse Tydskrif vir Ekonomiese en Bestuurswetenskappe*, *20*(1), 1–12. DOI: 10.4102/sajems.v20i1.1660

Patra, M. D., & Kapur, M. (2012). A monetary policy model for India. *Macroeconomics and Finance in Emerging Market Economies*, *5*(1), 16–39. DOI: 10.1080/17520843.2011.576453

Petticrew, M., & Roberts, H. (2006). *Systematic reviews in the social sciences*. Blackwell. DOI: 10.1002/9780470754887

Picault, M., Pinter, J., & Renault, T. (2022). Media sentiment on monetary policy: Determinants and relevance for inflation expectations. *Journal of International Money and Finance*, *124*, 102626. Advance online publication. DOI: 10.1016/j.jimonfin.2022.102626

Powel, J. H. (2014, June). Monetary policy accommodation, risk-taking, and spillovers. *Global Research Forum on International Macroeconomics and Finance*, Federal Reserve Bank of New York.

Primus, K. (2018). The effectiveness of monetary policy in small open economies. *Journal of Policy Modeling*, *31*(1), 1–31. DOI: 10.1016/j.jpolmod.2018.03.001

Qin, J., Ge, J., & Lu, X. (2018). The effectiveness of monetary policy in China: New evidence from long-range cross-correlation analysis and the components of multifractality. *Physica A, 506*, 1026–1037. DOI: 10.1016/j.physa.2018.04.068

Quartey, P., & Afful-Mensah, G. (2014). Financial and monetary policies in Ghana: A review of recent trends. *Review of Development Finance*, *4*(2), 115–125. DOI: 10.1016/j.rdf.2014.07.001

Rafiq, M. S., & Mallick, S. K. (2008). The effects of monetary policy on output in EMU-3: A sign restriction approach. *Journal of Macroeconomics*, *30*(4), 1756–1791. DOI: 10.1016/j.jmacro.2007.12.003

Ramer, S. L. (2005). Site action pearl-growing methods and librarianship history and theory. *Journal of the Medical Library Association: JMLA*, *93*(3), 397–403. DOI: 10.3163/1536-5050.93.3.397 PMID: 16059431

Rey, H. (2013, August). Dilemma not trilemma: The global financial cycle and monetary policy independence. *Symposium on "Reassessing the Fed's Roles"*, Jackson Hole. Federal Reserve Bank of Kansas City.

Rubio, M., & Schuh, S. (2017). Monetary policy and the role of inventory investment. *Applied Economics Letters*, *24*(21), 1605–1612. DOI: 10.1080/13504851.2017.1363855

Saiti, B. Y. B. (2016). The effects of monetary policy on the Islamic financial services industry. *Qualitative Research in Financial Markets*, *8*(3), 218–228. DOI: 10.1108/QRFM-02-2016-0006

Schmeling, M., Schrimpf, A., & Steffensen, S. A. (2022). Monetary policy expectation errors. *Journal of Financial Economics*, *146*(3), 841–858. DOI: 10.1016/j.jfineco.2022.09.005

Simo-Kengne, B. D., Balcilar, M., Gupta, R., Reid, M., & Aye, G. C. (2013). Is the relationship between monetary policy and house prices asymmetric across bull and bear markets in South Africa? Evidence from a Markov-switching vector autoregressive model. *Economic Modelling*, *32*, 161–171. DOI: 10.1016/j.econmod.2013.02.006

Srithilat, K., & Sun, G. (2017). The impact of monetary policy on economic development: Evidence from Lao PDR. *[Conference paper]*.

Stone, M. R., & Bhundia, A. J. (2004). A new taxonomy of monetary regimes (*IMF Working Paper No. 04/191*). International Monetary Fund. https://doi.org/DOI: 10.5089/9781451866390.001

Suhaibu, I., Harvey, S. K., & Amidu, M. (2017). The impact of monetary policy on stock market performance: Evidence from twelve African countries. *Research in International Business and Finance, 42*, 1372–1382. DOI: 10.1016/j.ribaf.2017.07.075

Tarullo, D. K. (2017, February 10). Monetary policy without a working theory of inflation [Speech]. Federal Reserve Board. https://www.federalreserve.gov/newsevents/speech/tarullo20170210a.htm

Tong, E. (2017). US monetary policy and global financial stability. *Research in International Business and Finance, 39*, 466–485. DOI: 10.1016/j.ribaf.2016.09.001

Tranfield, D., Denyer, D., & Smart, P. (2003). Towards a methodology for developing evidence-informed management knowledge by means of systematic analysis. *British Journal of Management, 14*(3), 207–222. DOI: 10.1111/1467-8551.00375

Waal, A., & van Eyden, R. (2012, October). Monetary policy and inflation in South Africa: A VECM augmented with foreign variables (*ERSA Working Paper No. 316*). Economic Research Southern Africa.

Waknis, P. (2014). A Leviathan central bank: Modeling seignorage in a money search model. *Economics Letters, 125*(3), 386–391. DOI: 10.1016/j.econlet.2014.10.027

Waknis, P. (2016). Competitive supply of money in a new monetarist model. *Economics Letters*, •••, 1–25. DOI: 10.1016/j.econlet.2016.02.008

Walsh, C. E. (2004). Implications of a changing economic structure for the strategy of monetary policy (*Working Paper 03/18*). University of California, Santa Cruz, Center for International Economics.

Wang, Y., Whited, T. M., Wu, Y., & Xiao, K. (2022). Bank market power and monetary policy transmission: Evidence from a structural estimation. *The Journal of Finance, 77*(4), 2093–2141. DOI: 10.1111/jofi.13159

Were, M., Nyamongo, W., Kamau, A. W., Sichei, A. W., & Wambua, J. (2014). Assessing the effectiveness of monetary policy in Kenya: Evidence from a macroeconomic model. *Economic Modelling, 37*, 193–201. DOI: 10.1016/j.econmod.2013.11.004

Wong, K. M., & Chong, T. T. L. (2016). Does monetary policy matter for trade? *Department of Economics, The Chinese University of Hong Kong*. (Unpublished manuscript).

Yinusa, D. O., & Akinlo, A. E. (2008). *Exchange rate volatility and the extent of currency substitution in Nigeria (MPRA Paper No. 16257)*. University Library of Munich.

Zehri, C., Madjd-Sadjadi, Z., & Ammar, L. S. I. (2024). Asymmetric impacts of US monetary policy on emerging markets: Contagion and macroeconomic determinants. *Journal of Economic Asymmetries*, *29*, e00354. Advance online publication. DOI: 10.1016/j.jeca.2024.e00354

APPENDIX I

Table 4. Numbered Papers Cited in Table 2 and Table 3

No.	Author(s)
1.	Aleem, A, & Lahiani, A. (2014).
2.	Allegret, J.P. & Benkhodja. M.T (2015).
3.	Balcilar, M., Demirerd, R., Guptab, R. & vanEydenb, R. (2017).
4.	Balfoussia, H., Brissimis, S.N. & Manthos D. Delis, M.D. (2011).
5.	Cham, T. (2016).
6.	Filho, W.L., Balogun, A.L, Ayal, D.Y., Bethurem, E.M., Murambadoro, M., Mambo, J., Taddese, H., Tefera, G.W., Nagy, GJ., Fudjumdjum, H. & Mugabe, P. (2018).
7.	Gunji, H. & Yuan, Y. (2018).
8.	Gunji, H., Miura, K., & Yuan, Y (2009).
9.	Hammoudeh S. Nguyen, D.K & Sousa, R.M. (2015).
10.	Hanim T.F., Abdul Rahman, R. and Omar, N. (2011),
11.	Harvey, S.K, & Cushing, M.J (2015).
12.	Hazra, D (2017)
13.	Hiroshi G. & Yuan Y. (2018)
14.	Hove, S., Mama, A.T. & Tchana, F.T. (2015).
15.	Igan, D. Kabundib, A., De Simonec, F.N., & Tamirisa, N. (2017).
16.	Ikhide, S. & Uanguta, E. (2010).
17.	IMF (2015),
18.	Issahaku, H., Harvey, S.K. & Abor, JY. (2016).
19.	Issing, O. & Wieland, V. (2012).
20.	Jawadi, F., Mallick, S.K. & Sousa, R.M. (2016).
21.	Jeon, B.N & Wu, J. (2014).
22.	Kabundi, A., Schaling E., Some, M. (2015).
23.	Kutu, A.A, & Ngalawa, H. (2016).
24.	Lawal, A.I., Somoyeb, R.O. Babajidec, A.A. & Nwanjia. T.I. (2018).
25.	López-Villavicencio, A & Mignon, V. (2017)
26.	Ma, Y & Lin, X. (2016).
27.	Ma, Y. (2016),
28.	Masood, O. and Ashraf, M. (2012),
29.	Matemilola, B.T., Bany-Ariffin, A.N. & Muhtar, F.E. (2015).
30.	Matouseka, R. & Solomon, H. (2018).

continued on following page

Table 4. Continued

No.	Author(s)
31.	Mishra, P., Montiel, P., Pedroni, P. and Spilimbergo, A. (2014).
32.	Morgan S. (2011),
33.	Mullineux, A.W, & Murinde, V. (2014)
34.	Naraidoo, R. & Paya, I. (2012).
35.	Ndikumana L. (2016)
36.	Ouedraogo, R., and Sourouema, W.S (2018).
37.	Patra, M. D. and M. Kapur (2012).
38.	Primus, K. (2018).
39.	Qin, J., Ge, J. & Lu, X. (2018)
40.	Quartey, P., & Afful-Mensah, G. (2014).
41.	Roger, S. (2009),
42.	Rubio, M and Schuh, S. (2017).
43.	Saiti, B.Y.B. (2016),"
44.	Simo-Kengne, B.D., Balcilar, M., Gupta, R., Reid, M. & Aye, G.C (2013).
45.	Suhaibu, I. Harvey, S.K & Amidu, M. (2017).
46.	Tarullo, D.K. (2017).
47.	Tong, E. (2017).
48.	Waknis, P. (2016)
49.	Were, M., Nyamongo, W., Kamau, AW., Sichei, A.W. & Wambua, J. (2014).
50.	Wong, K.M & Chong, T.T.L. (2016)
51.	Nguyen, T.M.L (2020)
52.	Abuka, C. Alinda, R.K, Minoiu, C & Peydro, J.L., and Presbitero, A. (2019).
53.	Zulkhibri, M, (2012)
54.	Hulsewig, Mayer and Wollmershauser (2009)
55.	Afanasyeva and Guntner, (2020)
56.	Waknis P. (2018)
57.	Attasuda, L. (2018)
58.	Umar, M., Dahalan, J & Aziz, MIA (2016)
59.	Chebbi, T & Derbali, A. (2019)
60.	Hassen, G. & Hamdi, K. (2020)
61.	Schmeling, M., Schrimpf, A., & Steffensen, S. A. (2022).
62.	Cortes, G. S., Gao, G. P., Silva, F. B., & Song, Z. (2022).
63.	Bianchi, J., & Bigio, S. (2022).
64.	Picault, M., Pinter, J., & Renault, T. (2022).

continued on following page

Table 4. Continued

No.	Author(s)
65.	Zehri, C., Madjd-Sadjadi, Z., & Ammar, L. S. I. (2024).
66.	Kang, K. H., & Do, K. (2024).
67.	Bussière, M., Cao, J., de Haan, J., Hills, R., Lloyd, S., Meunier, B., ... & Styrin, K. (2021).
68.	Nguyen, H. H., Nguyen, T. P., & Tram Tran, A. N. (2022).
69.	Akan, T. (2024).
70.	Wang, Y., Whited, T. M., Wu, Y., & Xiao, K. (2022)

APPENDIX II

Table 5. Mapping of issues, methods of analysis and contextual approach

Authors	Research Issues (Topic)	Method of Analysis	Level of Analysis (Macro/Meso/Micro)	Timing: Cross-sectional, time series/panel	Context
Nguyen (2020)	Output effects of monetary policy in emerging and developing countries: Evidence from a Meta-Analysis	Meta Regression Analysis, VAR	Macro	32 emerging and developing countries, 4001-2014	World
Abuka *et al*, (2019).	Monetary Policy and bank lending in developing countries: Loan applications, rates and real effects	Maximum Likelihood Estimation	Micro and Macro	Developing country	Africa
Ouedraogo & Sourouema, (2018)	Fiscal policy pro-cyclicality in Sub-Saharan African countries: The role of export concentration	GMM	Macro	40 countries over the period 1995–2015,	Sub-Saharan Africa
Gunji & Yuan (2018)	Bank diversification and monetary policy	Random Effect, GMM	Macro	11 Asian countries from 1995 to 2008	Asia
Matousek & Solomon, (2018)	Bank lending channel and monetary policy in Nigeria	GMM	Macro	23 banks in Nigeria between 2002 and 2008	Nigeria
Mishra *et al* (2014)	Monetary policy and bank lending rates in low-income countries: Heterogeneous panel estimates	structural panel VAR	Macro	Dataset at a quarterly frequency. Our estimation sample covers a total of 132 countries over the period 1978–2013, which includes 16 advanced, 25 emerging, and 91 LICs	large sample of advanced, emerging, and low-income countries.
Filho *et al* (2018)	Strengthening climate change adaptation capacity in Africa- case studies from six major African cities and policy implications	Qualitative, case study approach	Macro	Qualitative	African cities: (Douala, Lagos City, Dar-es-Salaam, Accra, Addis Ababa and Mombasa

continued on following page

Table 5. Continued

Authors	Research Issues (Topic)	Method of Analysis	Level of Analysis (Macro/Meso/Micro)	Timing: Cross-sectional, time series/panel	Context
Harvey & Cushing (2015)	Is West African Monetary Zone (WAMZ) a common currency area?	SVAR model	Macro	10 countries from the West African monetary zone	West Africa
Issahaku, Harvey, & Abor (2016)	Does development finance pose an additional risk to monetary policy?	panel vector autoregressive (PVAR) model	Macro	106 developing countries from1970 to 2013,	developing countries
Qin, Ge & Lu (2018)	The effectiveness of the monetary policy in China: New evidence from long-range cross-correlation analysis and the components of multifractality	qualitative and quantitative basis,	Macro	2,503 daily closing prices over the period from October 8, 2006, to September 30, 2016. Chinese Renminbi (RMB) and the Shanghai Interbank Offered Rate (Shibor) markets	China
Primus (2018)	The effectiveness of monetary policy in small open economies	Vector Autoregressive model	Macro	Barbados, Jamaica and Trinidad and Tobago	
Were *et al*, (2014)	Assessing the effectiveness of monetary policy in Kenya: Evidence froma macroeconomic model		Macro	Emerging country	Kenya
López-Villavicencio & Mignon, (2017)	Exchange rate pass-through in emerging countries: Do the inflation environment, monetary policy regime and central bank behavior matter?	GMM	Macro	sample of 14 emerging countries over the 1994Q1-2015Q3 period	Brazil, Colombia, Czech Republic, Hungary, Indonesia, South Korea, Mexico, Philippines, Poland, Romania, Slovak Republic, South Africa, Thailand and Turkey

continued on following page

Table 5. Continued

Authors	Research Issues (Topic)	Method of Analysis	Level of Analysis (Macro/Meso/Micro)	Timing: Cross-sectional, time series/panel	Context
Cham (2016)	Does monetary integration lead to an increase in FDI flows? An empirical investigation from the West African Monetary Zone (WAMZ)	Ordinary Least Squares (OLS) and fully-modified OLS (FMOLS).	Macro	West African Monetary Zone (WAMZ) using annual time series for the period 1980e2013	
Mullineux & Murinde (2014)	Financial sector policies for enterprise development in Africa	Qualitative	Macro		African countries
Quartey, & Afful-Mensah, (2014)	Financial and monetary policies in Ghana: A review of recent trends	Descriptive: Trend analysis	Macro	12 companies over 1997–2012 in Ghana.	Ghana
Ma & Lin (2016)	Financial development and the effectiveness of monetary policy	panel data models (PVAR)	Macro	panel data of 41 economies over 2005Q1 to 2011Q4	
Tong (2017)	US monetary policy and global financial stability	Panel VAR	Macro	panel of 257 banks across 26 countries	US
Jawadi, Mallick & Sousa (2016)	Fiscal and monetary policies in the BRICS: A panel VAR approach	Panel Vector Auto-Regressive (PVAR) model	Macro	data for the BRICS (Brazil, Russia, India, China and South Africa). quarterly frequency over the period 1990:1–2013:2,	Brazil, Russia, India, China and South Africa (BRICS
Naraidoo, & Paya (2012)	Forecasting monetary policy rules in South Africa	Forecasting model	Macro	1986-2004 The number of out-of-sample observations used above (132) is complemented with sizes of 180 (insample: 1986–1993); 108 (in-sample: 1986–2000); and 48 (in-sample: 1986–2004) observations	South Africa
Rubio & Schuh, (2017)	Monetary policy and the role of inventory investment	dynamic stochastic general equilibrium (DSGE) model	Macro		Developed country

continued on following page

Table 5. Continued

Authors	Research Issues (Topic)	Method of Analysis	Level of Analysis (Macro/Meso/Micro)	Timing: Cross-sectional, time series/panel	Context
Aleem, & Lahiani, 2014	Monetary policy credibility and exchange rate pass-through: Some evidence from emerging countries	semistructural vector autoregressive model	Macro	Monthly data (1994-2009)	Latin American countries and East Asian countries
Igan *et al*, 2017	Monetary policy and balance sheets	Factor-Augmented Vector Autoregression (FAVAR)model	Macro	From 1990Q1 to 2008Q2 at quarterly frequency.	US
Matemilola Bany-Ariffin, & Muhtar, (2015)	The impact of monetary policy on bank lending rate in South Africa	MTAR, VECM	Macro	South African, monthly data from January 1978 to December 2012	South Africa
Kabundi, Schaling & Some (2015)	Monetary policy and heterogeneous inflation expectations in South Africa	Autoregressive model (AR-model)	Macro	quarterly survey observed from 2000Q1 to 2013Q1	South Africa
Wong & Chong, (2016)	Does monetary policy matter for trade?	Fixed Effect, OLS	Macro	4,078 observation	Emerging markets
Ma & Yin (2016)	Nonlinear monetary policy and macroeconomic stabilization in emerging market economies: Evidence from China	New Keynesian DSGE model, nonlinear Taylor rule	Macro	Chinese economy over the period 1998–2013.	China
Jeon & Wu (2014)	The role of foreign banks in monetary policy transmission: Evidence from Asia during the crisis of 2008–9	System GMM	Macro	emerging Asian economies during the period from 2000 to 2009,	Asia
Hammoudeh, Nguyen & Sousa, (2015)	US monetary policy and sectoral commodity prices	Structural VAR (SVAR) model	Macro	US data period from 1957:1 to 2008:3	US
Suhaibua, Harvey, & Amidu (2017)	The impact of monetary policy on stock market performance: Evidence from twelve (12) African countries	system of panel VAR	Macro	12 African countries, data from 1979:2013	Ghana, South Africa, Namibia, Nigeria, Morocco, Mauritius; Kenya, Egypt, Botswana, Ivory coast, Zambia and Zimbabwe.

continued on following page

Table 5. Continued

Authors	Research Issues (Topic)	Method of Analysis	Level of Analysis (Macro/Meso/Micro)	Timing: Cross-sectional, time series/panel	Context
Allegret & Benkhodja, (2015)	External shocks and monetary policy in an oil exporting economy (Algeria)	a New Keynesian Dynamic Stochastic General Equilibrium (DSGE) model	Macro	over the period 1990–2010 for Algerian economy	Algeria
Hove at al (2015)	Monetary policy and commodity terms of trade shocks in emerging market economies	New Keynesian Dynamic Stochastic General Equilibrium (DSGE) model	Macro		Emerging Market Economies (EMEs)
Balcilar *et al*, (2017)	The impact of US policy uncertainty on the monetary effectiveness in the Euro area	structural Interacted Vector Autoregressive (IVAR) model	Macro	US in the Euro area over the period 1999:01–2015:3, we	US and Euro area
Lawal *et al* (2018)	The effect of fiscal and monetary policies interaction on stock market performance: Evidence from Nigeria	EGARCH models	Macro	Data from January 1985 to December 2015 on the Nigerian economy.	Nigeria
Zulkhibri (2012)	Policy rate pss-through and the adjustment of retail interest rates: Empirical evidence from Malaysian financial institutions	Symmetric Error Correction Model	Macro	Data over the 1983-2005 period	Malaysia
Schmeling *et al.* (2022)	Monetary policy expectation errors.	Structural Models-Predicting Expectation Errors and Excess Returns	Macro	Data over the 1990-2021 period	US
Cortes *et al.* (2022)	Unconventional monetary policy and disaster risk: Evidence from the subprime and COVID–19 crises.	Impulse response and systems of autoregressive and error correction models	Macro	Data over the 1996-2021 period	US and global economies
Bianchi & Bigio (2022)	Banks, liquidity management, and monetary policy. .	OLS and Volatility models	Macro	Data over the 2000-2015 period	US
Picault *et al.*, (2022)	Media sentiment on monetary policy: Determinants and relevance for inflation expectations.	Review	Macro	25,000 newspaper articles published between 2006 and 2017.	Europe

continued on following page

Table 5. Continued

Authors	Research Issues (Topic)	Method of Analysis	Level of Analysis (Macro/Meso/Micro)	Timing: Cross-sectional, time series/panel	Context
Zehri *et al.* (2024)	Asymmetric impacts of US monetary policy on emerging markets: Contagion and macroeconomic determinants.	OLS, GMM, Panel VAR-GMM	Macro	Data over the 2000-2020 period	EMEs
Kang & Do (2024	Korea's neutral interest rate: Estimates, determinants, and monetary policy stance. .	Impulse response	Macro	Data over the 2003-2023 period	Korea
Bussière *et al*, (2021)	The interaction between macroprudential policy and monetary policy: Overview.	a structural macroeconomic VAR	Macro	Extending the Gertler and Karadi (2015) specification to 2018	Advanced Economies and EMEs
Nguyen *et al* (2022)	Impacts of monetary policy transmission on bank performance and risk in the Vietnamese market: Does the Covid-19 pandemic matter?.	S-GMM	Macro	between the first quarter of 2017 and the fourth quarter of 2020	Vietnam
Akan (2024)	The impact of monetary policy on climate change through the mediation of sectoral renewable energy consumption	Descriptives, bootstrapped structural equation modeling (SEM)	Macro	from 1973M2–2023M5	US
Wang *et al* (2022)	Bank market power and monetary policy transmission: Evidence from a structural estimation.	VAR models	Macro	The sample period is 1994 to 2017.	US

Chapter 2
Monetary Policy, Growth, and Sustainable Development

Sakshi
https://orcid.org/0009-0007-8467-8079
Lovely Professional University, India

Shivani Dhand
https://orcid.org/0000-0002-4809-1365
Lovely Professional University, India

ABSTRACT

This chapter discusses the pivotal role of monetary policy in enabling sustainable development with a focus on Sustainable Development Goal 8 (SDG 8). We explore the potential implications of traditional monetary policy tools like interest rate cushions, quantitative easing for economic growth, and inequality and environmental impacts. This chapter suggests a paradigm shift to a more sustainable monetary policy. It involves embedding sustainability into day-to-day operations by enabling the dual push of green finance through focused lending schemes and green bonds, developing climate-aware risk management, and pushing social responsibility investment.This chapter highlights a growing call for central banks to proactively work together to use monetary policy to help build a just and sustainable future.

DOI: 10.4018/979-8-3693-9765-7.ch002

INTRODUCTION

Modern monetary policy, as we know it, evolved starting in the early 20th century, with central banks actively engaging in managing economic fluctuations. Decisive figures like Keynes brought the power of monetary interventions to the forefront, using them to treat the malady of unemployment and the stagnation of demand brought on by recessionary conditions. Monetary policy definition later widened to include price stability, financial stability, and economic growth (Bernanke, 2020). However, in the 21st century – the era of globalization, technological advancement, and the climate crisis – these traditional growth models have proved inadequate and must be re-evaluated." These models prioritize short-term over long-term financial, social, and environmental outcomes to the planet's detriment (Bocken & Short, 2021; Dikau & Volz, 2021). The publication of the Sustainable Development Goals (SDGs) Goals by the United Nations as the 2030 agenda for well-being on the planet in 2015 then served as a comprehensive framework (Nunes et al., 2016). More specifically, SDG 8 promotes Sustained, inclusive, sustainable economic growth, full and productive employment, and decent work. It highlights the importance of economic policies that promote growth and tackle development's environmental and social aspects. As the passage reveals, central banks are uniquely positioned to engage with this agenda, given their status as a key orientation point for various macro-financial variables, including those related to investment, consumption, and employment (Zehri et al., 2024). Central banks can support sustainable practices, create incentives for green investments, and reduce the adverse effects of economic inequality (Dikau & Volz, 2021) by influencing financial conditions. Accommodative monetary policies boost economic activities through job creation. It is still important, however, that these policies are not made at the price of environmental devastation or social equity. This required a paradigm shift in monetary policymaking and its decision-making towards sustainability (Faruq & Huq, 2024).

Role of Monetary Policy

Monetary policy is how a country's central bank or monetary authority manages the money supply to achieve specific goals (Bernanke, 2019). The focus is on interest rates, accessibility of credit, and other monetary instruments to drive economic activity and ensure financial stability. This has become a significant aspect of macroeconomic management that governments and central banks rely on to affect significant economic variables, including inflation, unemployment, and economic growth (Muhammad, 2023). If used correctly, monetary policy can promote stability, encourage economic vitality, and act as a steadying force in achieving sustainable development goals (Muzayyanah et al., 2023). Monetary policy pauperization: The role of monetary policy is crucial for the haters of boom-bust cycles when it comes to challenges like financial instability, economic inequality, and external economic shocks.

Objectives of Monetary Policy

The key objectives of monetary policy include:

- **Price Stability**: The primary objective of monetary policy is to keep price stability. Stable prices maintain the currency's purchasing power, moderate uncertainty, and create confidence among consumers and investors. When inflation is high, real income and savings erode, and when it is deflationary, it acts to dissuade spending and investment, with the potential risk of economic stagnation (Blanchard & Brancaccio, 2019).
- **Full Employment**: Monetary policy aims to reach full employment by establishing conditions encouraging productive economic activity. Low unemployment rates are important for improving living standards, cutting down on poverty, and helping create social stability. This connects well with Sustainable Development Goal 8 (SDG 8), which focuses on decent work and inclusive economic growth.
- **Economic Growth**: Maintaining economic growth is one of monetary policy's primary goals. Monetary policy helps boost living standards and strengthen the economy by encouraging investments, advancing technology, and improving productivity (Ufoeze et al., 2018).
- **Financial Stability**: Central banks work to guarantee the financial system's stability to avoid disturbances that can affect the whole economy (Padoa-Schioppa, 2003). Financial crises like the 2008 worldwide financial crisis highlight the crucial need to preserve the stability of institutions and financial markets (Otker-Robe & Podpiera, 2013).

Instruments of Monetary Policy

Central banks use various tools to control liquidity, guide economic behavior, and fulfill their missions. These tools are classified as conventional tools and unconventional tools.

- **Interest Rates**: Modifying the benchmark interest rates is the most potent monetary policy tool. Interest rates affect how much it costs to borrow money, how much people invest, and how much they spend. For example, lower interest rates lower the cost of borrowing, spurring investment and consumption, whereas higher rates can help curb inflation by limiting demand that exceeds supply (Taylor, 1999).

- **Open Market Operations (OMO)**: Open market operations are when central banks buy or sell government securities in financial markets to control liquidity. Central bank purchases of securities infuse liquidity into the economy, encouraging lending and investment. On the other hand, sales of securities effectively shrink the money supply and affect moderating inflationary pressures (Schwartz, 2003).
- **Reserve Requirements**: These are the minimum reserves that a commercial bank must have with the central bank. This means credit becomes more or less available when central banks tinker with these requirements. Insurance on reserve requirements expands the money supply and increases economic activity, whereas increasing them restricts credit conditions to tackle inflation (Blanchard & Brancaccio, 2019).
- **Quantitative Easing (QE)**: Quantitative easing is an unconventional monetary policy instrument used during economic crises when traditional measures, like interest rate adjustments, are insufficient. Traditionally, central banks have resorted to open market purchases of long-term financial instruments such as government bonds as an effective measure for using liquidity to lower interest rates and thus stimulate lending and investment. The last time QE was extensively used during the COVID-19 pandemic-related financial crisis, during which it was applied to stabilize financial markets and recover from the crisis by easing monetary conditions (Bernanke, 2020).

Adapting them toward changing economies achieves a delicate balance between growth and the stabilization of the markets. Such tools are also essential for fighting many ills of the times-from inequality to environmental degradation to economic volatility.

Monetary Policy and Economic Growth

Monetary policy is an important mechanism central banks can use to influence macroeconomic conditions such as economic growth. Through monetary instruments like interest rates, open-market operations, and reserve requirements, policymakers can stimulate demand, promote investment, and create a favorable environment for long-term growth. This section then presents the channels of monetary policy, including ways and reasons why it can promote economic growth. However, there are limitations-"sustainable development goals" is one of them.

Figure 1. Monetary policy affects the economy's growth

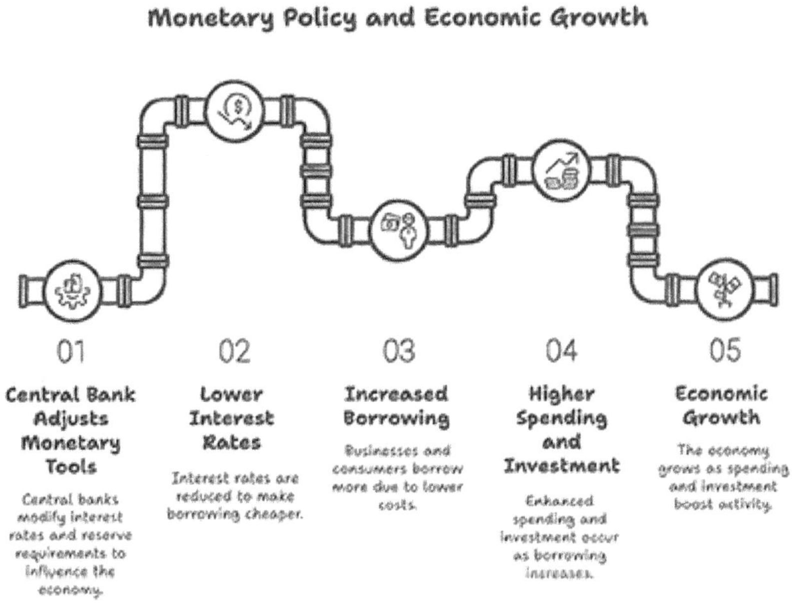

Figure 1 shows how monetary policy affects the economy's growth. The central bank determines the monetary tools, such as interest rates, reserve requirements, and open market operations. The adjustments should target the economy, inflation control, and financial stability. By lowering interest rates, the central bank gains by lowering the cost of borrowing, making loans cheaper for businesses and consumers. Borrowing encourages consumption, investment, or business expansion when credit becomes more straightforward with the increase in borrowing, spending, and investment increase. Businesses invest in new projects, equipment, and technologies, while consumers invest more in goods and services. This leads to increased demand across sectors of the economy. Demand stimulates output, job creation, and economic activity. These economies grow and produce a fuller effect of all such events: more significant employment levels, higher income per capita, and overall living standards. This process stimulates economic growth but requires careful long-term sustainability consideration since rapid growth sometimes harms the environment, causes income imbalances, and causes financial deterioration.

Stimulating Growth through Monetary Policy

When monetary policy aims to create the right conditions in financial markets, it can effectively stimulate economic growth. Central banks create an environment for borrowing by cutting interest rates or pursuing expansionary policies to incentivize businesses and consumers to spend and invest. The actions in the context of SDG 8 aim to promote inclusive and sustainable economic growth, employment, and decent work for all (Isibor et al., 2023).

- **Investment**: Lower interest rates reduce the cost of borrowing for companies. This makes it easier for firms to purchase new projects, hire new workers, and engage in R&D. The boost in productivity and job creation multiplies the economy. There is empirical evidence that lower borrowing costs increase private-sector levels of investment, especially in capital-intensive industries (Evemy et al., 2024).
- **Consumption**: Lower interest rates mean cheaper consumer loans, encouraging spending on products and services. Increased consumer spending boosts aggregate demand, which, in turn, increases production and drives economic growth. During economic decline, central banks tend to lower interest rates to promote confidence and consumer spending (Kallianiotis, 2017).
- **Export Competitiveness**: Another way monetary policy supports growth is through exchange rates. Lower interest rates (and therefore more debt) usually mean worsening the currency value, making exports cheaper and more competitive on world markets. Excellent export activity promotes economic growth and will also contribute to alleviating trade disequilibria, which is a primary objective of many developing economies (Taylor, 1999).

These channels play a role in stimulating economic growth, smoothing over fluctuations in the short run, and creating opportunities in the long run. However, this does not help with sustainability.

Limitations of Monetary Policy

While effective in the short run for stimulating economic growth, monetary policy is limited by broader sustainability objectives. However, inclusive and environmentally sustainable growth challenges reinforce the need for complementarity and a holistic approach to economic policymaking.

- **Inequality**: Lowering interest rates or more extraordinary quantitative easing tends to enrich asset holders more than the rest of the population. For example, rising asset prices, driven by low interest rates, raise the wealth of people who own real estate, stock, or other financial assets, while lower-income groups might not benefit much. This widening gap defeats the purpose of inclusive growth and goes against the equitable development principles highlighted under SDG 8 (Meurs et al., 2019).
- **Environmental Considerations**: The traditional monetary policy tool maximizes economic output without explicitly considering environmental sustainability. For example, low interest rates could unintentionally promote investments in resource-intensive industries that degrade the environment (e.g., fossil fuels or agriculture driving deforestation). Consequently, traditional modes of monetary policy could be at odds with international initiatives to mitigate climate change and restore ecological symmetries (Boneva et al., 2022).
- **Long-Term Sustainability**: Monetary policy can effectively address short-term economic challenges but may not resolve structural issues that prevent long-term sustainable growth. For example, if it takes much monetary easing to stimulate demand but the economy is already heavily reliant on it, it will only generate unsustainable debt levels, speculative bubbles, misallocating resources, etc. Temporary economic growth spurts might forestall the painful reforms in labor markets, education, and infrastructure needed to sustain development (Dinh et al., 2024).

Sustainable Development and Monetary Policy

Sustainable development is the balance between prosperity, equity, and ecological integrity. Central banks, founded on the need for economic stability and growth, are increasingly aware of their contribution to sustainability. Overview of Sustainable Development and Development-Related Goals—This section provides an overview of sustainable development, bonds, how monetary policy can be adjusted to facilitate sustainable development objectives, and best practices from key institutions. The starting point of sustainable development is that it is a multidimensional concept where current and future generations should have the opportunity to meet their own needs. It comprises three interconnected pillars: economic, environmental, and social sustainability.

- **Economic Growth**: Inclusive and sustainable economic growth is one of the major principles of sustainable development (Gupta & Vegelin, 2016). This includes making economic opportunities available to all sections of society and narrowing wealth and income disparities. Inclusive growth also emphasizes the creation of decent work, as highlighted in SDG 8, as well as building resiliency against economic shocks.

- **Environmental Protection**: Sustainability needs to preserve natural resources and use them to limit environmental degradation. That includes reducing greenhouse gas emissions, promoting the use of renewable energy, and applying principles of the circular economy to keep the long-term ecological balance (Stern, 2006).
- **Social Inclusion**: One of the nominations for social sustainability is equity, inclusivity, and justice, which guarantee that all these benefits of economic growth will be counted equally in all communities. It is related to gender equality, access to education and health care, and protection of disadvantaged populations (Batool & Bhatti, 2020).

Monetary policy, while reflecting the traditional macroeconomic dimensions, can provide an effective leaver for boosting aspects of sustainability.

Integrating Sustainability into Monetary Policy

Central banks must create creative tactics that handle social and environmental issues with economic priorities to match monetary policy with sustainable growth. The following strategies show how a financial policy could propel long-term development:

- **Green Financing**: Central banks may promote investments in sustainable projects, including renewable energy, green infrastructure, and energy-efficient technologies. Green bonds have become popular in the financial market to raise funds through issuing bonds for environmentally sustainable projects. Thus, to make green ends-cum-means equilibrating operations in which central banks can include such bonds in their asset portfolios for employment generation and economic development, the purchase of these types of bonds could be included as part of central bank asset portfolios (Campiglio, 2016).
- **Climate Risk Assessment**: Monetary policies must abide by climate-related risks as global warming turns to a systemic risk at every level; disappointment within these lines, and so much has to be incorporated into this (D'Orazio and Popoyan, 2023). Climate risks could vary from extreme weather events to resource scarcity; it could cause disruptions in economic activity and undermine financial institutions. They also intend to require the financial institution to disclose the exposure to that climate risk and encourage the alignment of institutional portfolios to sustainability goals (Carney, 2015).

- **Socially Responsible Investment**: the monetary policy may facilitate achieving social accomplishments through investments in affordable housing, healthcare, and education ownership. Such investments will foster social equity and promote better living conditions among underserved communities (Capelle-Blancard et al., 2021). Central banks can offer preferential financing, for instance, to projects that create jobs in low-income neighborhoods or enhance access to vital services.

Integration of such strategies under reference to monetary policy might, as such, provide a sustainable economy to which SDG 8, among others, would theoretically correspond.

Case Studies

This dynamism in incorporating sustainability into monetary policies and regulatory frameworks shapes central banks and other monetary institutions worldwide.

- **European Central Bank (ECB)**: The ECB considers climate change a systematic risk regarding financial stability. They explored how environmental criteria may have been incorporated into its asset purchasing programs. Moreover, it has extended its holdings of green bonds funded by projects to net carbon emissions and renewable energy (Bevilacqua, 2022). It sets and promotes suitable employment and environmental sustainability activities, which are the hallmark of SDG 8 for sustainable economic growth.
- **Bank of England**: The Bank of England has developed techniques for measuring climate-related financial risks. The law mandates that financial services firms declare their exposure to climate risks and stress-test their businesses in different climate scenarios. Furthermore, the Bank is in favor of green financing as it invests in projects that are both environmentally friendly and socially responsible. These promote the financial system's stability and create conditions for purposeful, inclusive, and environmentally sustainable growth.
- **Reserve Bank of India (RBI)**: The RBI has promoted financial inclusion, a crucial element of social sustainability. Its projects include promoting digital payment systems and microfinance institutions, enabling rural and marginalized populations to access financial services. The RBI also stressed that green financing in India underlined that banks must finance renewable energy projects and practice sustainable lending (Vishwakarma et al., 2024).

Challenges and Considerations

Monetary policy's role in fostering sustainability is fraught with challenges and trade-offs that policymakers must address. This section explores the inherent tensions between economic growth and sustainability and the complexities of navigating a global economic context.

Trade-offs Between Growth and Sustainability

Creating balanced economic growth with environmental and social sustainability is a critical challenge. These trade-offs often occur because ecosystem services diffuse objective economic gains, and long-term system services are not always aligned.

- **Short-term Gains vs. Long-term Sustainability**: Policies enacted to achieve that accelerate this, for example, low-interest rates or encouraging significant industrial investments, prefer immediate financial gain over sustainability. For example, the onset of rampant industrialization can also cause soil degradation and depletion of natural resources, and there we are, involving high greenhouse gases. Likewise, focusing on near-term performance to the detriment of investments in green technologies (in tech) or sustainable infrastructure will result in future challenges, including climate-related risks, resource scarcity, etc. (Stern, 2006)
- **Political and Social Pressures**: Policymakers face intense pressure from their communities to produce premature results, especially during election cycles or economic downturns. Unfortunately, under such circumstances, the best opportunity is to deliver an increase in short-term employment or GDP growth to the detriment of sustainable development. Industries that provide immediate employment opportunities at the cost of long-term environmental, e.g., coal mining, become a severe constraint to achieving long-term sustainability. They are also particularly relevant for Goal 8, which focuses on the decency of work and economic growth.
- **Economic Inequality**: Monetary policies that emphasize aggregate economic focus inadvertently exacerbate disparities. For example, quantitative easing and low-interest rate policies favor wealthier classes, mainly those who own financial assets, without necessarily translating into benefits to lower-income groups. This emerging gulf weakens the social inclusion section of sustainable development and calls for more equitable approaches to monetary policy (Kohler, 2015).

Global Context

In the contemporary world of interlinked global economies, the reach of any monetary policy extends beyond borders. This requires policymakers to consider global phenomena affecting domestic economies and sustainability endeavors.

- **Capital Flows**: Capital flows present significant challenges to central banks, especially in developing nations. For instance, expansionary monetary policies in developed countries like the United States can cause hot money to fly out of emerging economies and destabilize the countries' financial systems. Conversely, capital inflows may trigger asset price bubbles, heighten volatility, and make domestic monetary policy less effective. These dynamics address the careful management of capital flows toward sustainable development ends (Eichengreen & Bordo, 2002).
- **Cooperation and Coordination**: International cooperation is also needed to solve global problems, as climate change and financial instability require this. For this purpose, the central banks and monetary authorities for such policies should be able to engage with development goals that are aligned towards sustainability. For example, initiatives like the Network for Greening the Financial System (NGFS) develop a holistic approach to integrating climate-related risks into financial decision-making. Hence, coordination of sustainability-oriented monetary policies could enhance their impact, especially in increasing resilience against global shocks.
- **Technology and Innovation**: The world's shift to digital technologies and green innovations brings challenges and opportunities to monetary policy. Rapid technological changes, innovations in digital currencies, and blockchain technology compel policymakers to rethink old assumptions about financial systems. Innovations may assist the inclusion of finance and transparency while providing challenges to traditional mechanisms of monetary policy. In addition, to foster investments in green technologies, central banks must develop new frameworks that do not stymie innovation while maintaining stability (Campiglio et al., 2018).

Monetary policy has a unique potential to further sustainability goals but poses challenges and trade-offs that must be thoughtfully negotiated. In navigating these complex global economic considerations, policymakers face the challenge of nurturing short- and long-lasting sustainability. Overcoming these challenges will need creative solutions, global cooperation, and a dedication to harmonizing monetary policy with the ideals of sustainable development.

CONCLUSION

Monetary policy is one of the pillars of modern economic governance, and its crucial aspects are economic growth and sustainable development. Central banks somehow hold the key to affecting major economic parameters such as inflation, employment, and financial stability using finely tuned tools from the interest-rate-changing arsenal, open market operations, and reserve requirements. However, due to the changing global economic landscape with globalization and environmental and social challenges threatening the very framework of nature, monetary policy can be rethought to reflect better sustainable development goals. This chapter has analyzed the complex interrelations among monetary policy, growth, and sustainability. It illustrated that through investment, consumption, and export competitiveness, monetary policy can enhance growth, which is vital to realizing Sustainable Development Goal 8 on inclusive and sustainable economic growth, full and productive employment, and decent work. The downsides of traditional monetary policy tools in amplifying income inequality and detachment from environmental problems have made a wider lens an imperative. Sustainability concerning monetary policy could imply appraising novel strategies ranging from green financing to climate risk assessments and social governance of capital. In this connection, the European Central Bank and the Bank of England have demonstrated that such integration could be realized toward resilient and inclusive economies. These instances further illustrate the proof of concept for central banks as usable enablers of sustainable development as they internalize environmental-social considerations into their policy framework. Unfortunately, this transition carries its own set of challenges. Policymakers are confronted with quite a difficult task; short-term recovery against long-term sustainability must be weighed into the equation, together with considerations regarding global economic linkages and the trade-offs brought about by political, social, and economic pressure in the system. Therefore, achieving these objectives will entail concerted international efforts, demanding multiple stakeholder engagements and the establishment of comprehensive forward-looking monetary policy frameworks. The world is facing unprecedented challenges driven by climate change, social inequality, and economic volatility, and thus, there is a need for a radical change in the perspective of monetary policy. Central banks and governments must take on a broader remit that treats sustainability as a core aim so that economic advances today are not made at the expense of future generations. Strategic innovations, interdisciplinary collaboration, and commitment to long-term resilience will allow monetary policy to become a key driver of establishing a more just, sustainable, and prosperous global economy. This chapter finishes with the assertion that monetary policy can change society; however, this can only happen by integrating sustainable development goal criteria into its working framework. Nevertheless, financial outcomes for all vested interests in their present form may only require a significant paradigm shift in how policymakers consider growth and prosperity and to ensure that this paradigm foregrounds positive agendas in environmental conservation and community welfare.

REFERENCES

Batool, Z., & Bhatti, A. A. (2020). Macroeconomic policies and social inclusion in the developing world. [LASSIJ]. *Liberal Arts and Social Sciences International Journal, 4*(2), 114–129. DOI: 10.47264/idea.lassij/4.2.10

Bernanke, B. S. (2019). Monetary policy in a new era.

Bernanke, B. S. (2020). The new tools of monetary policy. *The American Economic Review, 110*(4), 943–983. DOI: 10.1257/aer.110.4.943

Bevilacqua, E. (2022). European cooperative banks and sustainability. In *Contemporary Trends in European Cooperative Banking: Sustainability, Governance, Digital Transformation, and Health Crisis Response* (pp. 165–192). Springer International Publishing. DOI: 10.1007/978-3-030-98194-5_8

Blanchard, O., & Brancaccio, E. (2019). Crisis and revolution in economic theory and policy: A debate. *Review of Political Economy, 31*(2), 271–287. DOI: 10.1080/09538259.2019.1644730

Bocken, N. M., & Short, S. W. (2021). Unsustainable business models–Recognising and resolving institutionalized social and environmental harm. *Journal of Cleaner Production, 312*, 127828. DOI: 10.1016/j.jclepro.2021.127828

Boneva, L., Ferrucci, G., & Mongelli, F. P. (2022). Climate change and central banks: What role for monetary policy? *Climate Policy, 22*(6), 770–787. DOI: 10.1080/14693062.2022.2070119

Campiglio, E. (2016). Beyond carbon pricing: The role of banking and monetary policy in financing the transition to a low-carbon economy. *Ecological Economics, 121*, 220–230. DOI: 10.1016/j.ecolecon.2015.03.020

Campiglio, E., Dafermos, Y., Monnin, P., Ryan-Collins, J., Schotten, G., & Tanaka, M. (2018). Climate change challenges for central banks and financial regulators. *Nature Climate Change, 8*(6), 462–468. DOI: 10.1038/s41558-018-0175-0

Capelle-Blancard, G., Desroziers, A., & Zerbib, O. D. (2021). Socially responsible investing strategies under pressure: Evidence from Covid-19. *Journal of Portfolio Management, 47*(9), 178–197. DOI: 10.3905/jpm.2021.1.288

Carney, M. (2015). Breaking the tragedy of the horizon–climate change and financial stability. *Speech given at Lloyd's of London, 29*, 220-230.

D'Orazio, P., & Popoyan, L. (2023). Do monetary policy mandates and financial stability governance structures matter for the adoption of climate-related financial policies? *Inter Economics*, *173*, 284–295. DOI: 10.1016/j.inteco.2023.01.004

Dikau, S., & Volz, U. (2021). Central bank mandates, sustainability objectives and the promotion of green finance. *Ecological Economics*, *184*, 107022. DOI: 10.1016/j.ecolecon.2021.107022

Dinh, L. Q., Oanh, T. T. K., & Ha, N. T. H. (2024). Financial stability and sustainable development: Perspectives from fiscal and monetary policy. *International Journal of Finance & Economics*.

Eichengreen, B., & Bordo, M. D. (2002). Crises now and then: What lessons from the last era of financial globalization.

Evemy, J., Berry, C., & Yates, E. (2024). Low interest rates, low productivity, low growth? A multi-sector case study of UK-based firms' funding and investment strategies in the context of loose monetary policy. *New Political Economy*, *29*(2), 240–259. DOI: 10.1080/13563467.2023.2240237

Faruq, A. T. M., & Huq, M. T. (2024). The Role of Central Banks in Advancing Sustainable Finance. arXiv preprint arXiv:2411.13576.

Gupta, J., & Vegelin, C. (2016). Sustainable development goals and inclusive development. *International Environmental Agreement: Politics, Law and Economics*, *16*(3), 433–448. DOI: 10.1007/s10784-016-9323-z

Isibor, A., Omankhanlen, A., Ehikioya, B., Osuma, G., Oladipo, A., Bunmi-Alo, A., & Ajalaadebowale, K. (2023). Achieving Sustainable Economic Growth in Sub-Saharan African Countries Using the Tool of Monetary Policy Effectiveness. *Journal of Central Banking Theory and Practice*, *12*(3), 111–132. DOI: 10.2478/jcbtp-2023-0027

Kallianiotis, J. N. (2017). Central Banks, Monetary Policy, and their Efficiency. *Chapter in Monetary Policy: Perspectives, Strategies and Challenges, Harriet Ward (editor), New York: Nova Science Publishers.*

Kohler, P. (2015). Redistributive policies for sustainable development: looking at the role of assets and equity.

Meurs, M., Seidelmann, L., & Koutsoumpa, M. (2019). How healthy is a 'healthy economy'? Incompatibility between current pathways towards SDG3 and SDG8. *Globalization and Health*, *15*(1), 83. DOI: 10.1186/s12992-019-0532-4 PMID: 31791366

Muhammad, A. A. (2023). Examining the Relationship among Unemployment, Inflation, and Economic Growth. *Journal of Business and Economic Options*, *6*(2), 23–31.

Muzayyanah, M., Triyana, E., & Aura, K. A. N. (2023). Evaluating the impact of fiscal and monetary policies on Indonesia's macroeconomic stability and growth (2015-2019). [JIEMB]. *Journal of Islamic Economics Management and Business*, *5*(2), 203–226. DOI: 10.21580/jiemb.2023.5.2.21672

Nunes, A. R., Lee, K., & O'Riordan, T. (2016). The importance of an integrating framework for achieving the Sustainable Development Goals: The example of health and well-being. *BMJ Global Health*, *1*(3), e000068. DOI: 10.1136/bmjgh-2016-000068 PMID: 28588955

Otker-Robe, I., & Podpiera, A. M. (2013). The social impact of financial crises: Evidence from the global financial crisis. *World Bank Policy Research Working Paper*, , 6703. DOI: 10.1596/1813-9450-6703

Padoa-Schioppa, T. (2003). Central banks and financial stability: exploring the land in between. The transformation of the European financial system, 25, 269-310.

Schwartz, A. J. (2003). Asset price inflation and monetary policy. *Atlantic Economic Journal*, *31*(1), 1–14. DOI: 10.1007/BF02298459

Stern, N. (2006). Stern Review: The economics of climate change.

Taylor, J. B. (1999). The robustness and efficiency of monetary policy rules as guidelines for interest rate set by the European Central Bank. *Journal of Monetary Economics*, *43*(3), 655–679. DOI: 10.1016/S0304-3932(99)00008-2

Ufoeze, L. O., Odimgbe, S. O., Ezeabalisi, V. N., & Alajekwu, U. B. (2018). Effect of monetary policy on economic growth in Nigeria: An empirical investigation. *Annals of Spiru Haret University. Economic Series*, *9*(1), 123–140.

Vishwakarma, D., Sonkar, S., Keshari, S. K., & Jaiswal, A. K. (2024). Achieving Sustainable Development Goals Through Microfinance: An Incremental Steps Towards Growth. [EEL]. *European Economic Letters*, *14*(1), 2022–2031.

Zehri, C., El Amin, B. M., Inaam, Z., & Sekrafi, H. (2024). Exploring the nexus of decent work, financial inclusion, and economic growth: A study aligned with SDG 8. *Sustainable Futures : An Applied Journal of Technology, Environment and Society*, *7*, 100213. DOI: 10.1016/j.sftr.2024.100213

Chapter 3
Monetary, Interest, and Exchange Rate Policies in Turkey:
An Analysis for the Planned Development Period of 1963–1983

İrfan Kalaycı
İnönü University, Turkey

ABSTRACT

Planning can be considered as the result of socio-economic development efforts and advanced socialization for a country. This judgment is also very valid for Turkey, which is the only Afro-Eurasian country in the world, a candidate for the European Union, a G-20 economy and one of the emerging economies. The subject and purpose of this study is to examine the monetary, interest and exchange rate policies in Turkey on the basis of primary development plans. Five-yearly development plans covering all main and sub-sectors have been prepared in Turkey since 1963, but after the famous IMF stability decisions dated January 24, 1980, which ensured the transformation to liberal-global capitalism in macroeconomics, other development plans remained at a formal or symbolic level. Here, the monetary and development targets achieved and the handicaps encountered in the first 20-year "planned development" period, which included 4 development plans prepared between 1963-1983, are analyzed.

DOI: 10.4018/979-8-3693-9765-7.ch003

INTRODUCTION

The subject and purpose of this study is to examine the interaction of monetary, interest and exchange rate policies with national development in the period from the 1960s, when all sectors in Turkey began to be planned according to the mixed economy model, to January 24, 1980, when this model began to be replaced by liberalism and liberal economic stability decisions were taken in line with the International Monetary Fund (IMF). The years 1963, the beginning of the first five-year development plan discussed here, and 1983, the end of the fourth development plan of the same nature, draw the chronological boundary of this study. Therefore, later periods and national and international liberal economic developments, their effects on Turkey's development process and macroeconomic indicators are excluded from the scope. Turkey was a typical underdeveloped economy in the 1960s-1970s. It began to integrate with the liberal Western bloc by implementing the outward-oriented growth and financial liberalization model within the context of the famous free market "January 24 Economic Decisions" and was included in the category of developing countries by this bloc, which was its economic ally. At that time, neither the ideology of planning had yet fallen into disfavor nor was the popular term emerging markets, which would erase the traces of central planning, in circulation.

The idea of "planning", one of the key words of this study, can be considered as the result of both a country or society's desire and effort for socio-economic development and an advanced level of socialization. Asking *"Are planning and development Siamese twins?"*, Küçük (1985: 34-36) opened an interesting discussion in the context of economic order, and argued that the basic dynamics of development are imbalances in the economy and that when a socialist order is established in today's advanced capitalist countries, the development problem will disappear, but planning will necessarily continue in order to maintain fair distribution together with the advanced production that has been achieved.

Although its philosophy and political essence are different, it consists of three technical components as goals, tools and the economic structure that acts as a bridge between the two. As Kılıçbay (1990: 78-79) stated, there are many types of plans and/or planning according to their duration, size, centrality, monetary measures, and ability to change the established order. These are mostly identified with five-year development plans (DPs) in Turkey, and are also mentioned together with the mixed economic model. According to Samuelson's definition, a *mixed economy* is a system in which the public and private sectors coexist, the free market and political decisions and preferences work together, personal freedoms and social responsibilities are intertwined, individual welfare and social welfare are reconciled and harmonized, and it is difficult to implement it in a measurable mold within this framework (Kılıçbay, 1990: 608).

As a result of the 1961 Constitution of the Republic of Turkey linking socio-economic development to macro plans, the State Planning Organization (SPO, DPT) was established (subordinate to the Prime Minister) and five-year DPs were prepared and implemented starting in 1963. Turkey switched to central planning in the context of a mixed economic order. During the central planning period that began after the ten-year rule of the Democrat Party (1950-1960), the objective and instrument variables within the scope of monetary policy were changed and developed in accordance with the conjuncture. In this new period, an interactive relationship began between the Central Bank of the Republic of Turkey (CBRT, TCMB), which was responsible for monetary policy, and the government, which implemented fiscal policy.

DPs in Turkey arose from macroeconomic needs. At the end of the 1950s, the country had entered an environment of external payment difficulties and hyperinflation. In order to get out of the crisis and ensure stability, it was necessary to leave the use of capital either to price indicators and free market conditions or to DPs and development programs. The second method was adopted due to the existing internal and external conditions (Kepenek, 2014: 138).

While three five-year DPs were implemented during the 1963-1980 period, which is the chronological subject of this analysis, the 4th Plan was prepared one year later in 1979 due to the government and parliament being virtually deadlocked due to intense terrorist incidents in 1978. The famous *"structural transformation and stability decisions in the economy"* dated January 24, 1980 coincided with the 4th Plan. The "January 24 Decisions", which increased the number of institutions and rules of the free market economy and expanded the scope of liberal policies, did not prevent DPs from being made after 1980, which witnessed the *"September 12"* military coup, but they were based on a planning approach focused on privatization and deregulation, which limited the public sector and expanded the private sector. Monetary, interest and exchange rate policies were also shaped according to this changing planning approach.

While the term of the 10th DP (2014-2018), which is completely different from the traditional (status quo) planning that symbolizes the subjective conditions of the 1960s and 70s, ended on the date of the transition to the Presidential government system, the 11st DP (2018-2023), which was prepared based on high geoeconomic targets and neoliberal policies, ended on the 100th anniversary of the foundation of the Republic.

In the periods when DPs that guide monetary policy implementations are implemented, the heads of government (prime minister) who make the plans and the CBRT governors responsible for monetary policies have a special importance. Eighteen governments (between the 27th and 44th) were able to fit into the first four plan periods due to political instability (Table 1).

Table 1. Prime Ministers and Central Bank Governors in the Planned Development Periods in Turkey

	1st DP (1963-67)	*2nd DP (1968-72)*	*3rd DP (1973-77)*	*4th DP (1979-83)*
Governments of the Republic of Turkey; Prime Ministers (Terms of office, political parties)	-27th Goverment; İ. İnönü (1962-63; CHP) -28th Goverment; İ. İnönü 1963-65; CHP) -29th Goverment; S. H. Ürgüplü (1965; AP); -30th Goverment; S. Demirel (1965-69; AP)	-31st Goverment; S. Demirel (1969-1970; AP) -32nd Goverment; S. Demirel (1970-71; AP) -33rd Goverment; N. Erim (1971; Milli Birlik) -34th Goverment; N. Erim (1971-72; MB) -35th Goverment; F. Melen (1972-73; Temporary)	-36th Goverment; N.T Talu (1973-74; Temporary) -37th Goverment; B. Ecevit; (1974, CHP) -38th Goverment; S. Irmak (1974-75; Temporary) -39th Goverment; S. Demirel (1975-77, AP) -40th Goverment; B. Ecevit (1977, CHP) -41st Goverment; S. Demirel (1977-78, AP)	--42nd Goverment; B. Ecevit (1978-79, CHP) -43th Goverment; S. Demirel (1979-80, AP) -44th Goverment; B. Ulusu (1980-83, Provisional Military Government)
Governors of the CBRT (Terms of Office)	-İ. M. Mostar (1960-62) -Z. Kayla (1963-66)	-M. N. Talu (1967-1971)	-M. Güpgüpoğlu (1972-75) -C. T. Sadıklar (1976-78)	-İ. H. Aydınoğlu (1979-81) -O. Şıklar (1981-84)
Abbreviations	CHP: Cumhuriyet Halk Partisi (Republican People's Party); AP: Adalet Partisi (Justice Party) MBK: Milli Birlik (National Unity) CBRT: The Central Bank of the Republic of Turkey			

As seen in Table 1, the 1st DP has worn out four governments and two CBRT governors. A similar situation is also valid in other DP periods where different governments changed hands for one or two years due to political instability. It is understood that governments generally do not act with much political preference in changing CBRT governers who are seen to have completed their terms of office.

In these periods, a sensitive central bank independence of a legal nature and above-party level is noteworthy in Turkey.

MONETARY AND EXCHANGE RATE POLICIES IN THE 1st, 2nd, 3rd and 4th FIVE-YEARLY DEVELOPMENT PLANS (DPs): SIMILARITIES AND DIFFERENCES

During the planned development period, monetary and exchange rate policies were implemented in accordance with the mixed economy system that brought together the public sector (state intervention) and the private sector (free market). The common aspect of these policies is to ensure monetary and price stability by pumping the liquidity required by the markets as a component of national development. The four development plans (DPs) prepared in the twenty-year period covering the years 1963-83 were imperative for the public sector and guiding for the private sector in accordance with the planning philosophy and technique, while they exhibited some differences depending on the domestic and foreign economic conjunctural changes.

The First Five-Yearly Development Plan (1st DP) Covering the Years 1963-1967

The 1st DP is the first 15-year long-term perspective plan, which was described by the Prime Minister of the period, İsmet İnönü, as the main goal of "rapid and balanced development in accordance with social justice within democracy" (Cumhuriyet 11/11/1962, quoted by Sezen, 1999: 187). In the context of monetary and credit policies, the 1st DP's goals regarding the Turkish economy can be listed as follows (DPT-SPO, 1963: 501-4):

> a- The realization of private sector investments will be based on auto financing and savings to be obtained from the capital market, while on the other hand, it will be fed by financing from commercial and other banks and credit institutions. Public economic enterprises (SEEs) will benefit from special funds to be established for investment and business loans that they will desperately need.
> b- It is normal and necessary for there to be an expansion in circulation and therefore in the credit volume in parallel with the increase in production and national income, but in a way that will not lead to inflation.
> c- Efforts will be made to bring the interest rates to be set for various loans closer to the economic interest. This goal will be achieved by easing and eventually removing the price increases currently on interest as the economy develops during the plan period. ("The economic interest" mentioned here

is an original term used in the development plan of the period. Although it reminds us of today's policy interest, its equivalent may be nominal interest.)
d- In addition to long-term loans that meet the investment credit needs of enterprises, especially through the Turkish Industrial Development Bank and the Ziraat Bank, one-year medium-term loans and loans that meet the revolving fund needs of sectors such as industry, agriculture and tourism will be allocated. A "State Investment Bank" will be established for the financing needs of SEEs. A consortium will be established with the participation of banks to meet the medium-term credit needs of the private sector.

The following developments were recorded regarding targeted money and credits during the 1st DP period (DPT-SPO, 1968: 33-5):

a- In the 1st DP, monetary policy was implemented in a way that would prevent the development of inflationary/deflationary tendencies that prevented the full use and effective distribution of resources, and care was taken to ensure that the rate of increase in the circulation volume was in line with the increase in production and national income. In the first four years of the 1st DP, the money supply increased by an average of 15.9% per year, rising from 10.9 billion Turkish Lira (TL) in 1962 to 19.7 billion TL in 1966. In the same period, the annual average increase in the circulation volume was 12.1%, the increase in the volume of registered money (bank money) was 13.1%, and the increase in demand savings deposits was 20.2%. While the gross national product (GNP) increased by an average of 6.5% annually, the general price level increased by an average of 4.2% annually.
b- In the years known as the implementation result of the 1st DP, the bank credit volume increased by an average of 19.5% annually and increased from 11.2 billion TL in 1962 to 19.1 billion TL in 1965. Despite this, the credit measures envisaged for the purpose of private enterprises were insufficient and the necessary organization could not be made.

The Second Five-Yearly Development Plan (2nd DP) Covering the Years 1968-1972

The 2nd DP includes new targets that develop the 1st Plan and various measures that can be taken (DPT-SCO, 1968: 111-20):

a- The deflationary tendencies that developed in the first months of 1964 have made it necessary to use monetary policy tools. These measures generally include increasing the resources of banks whose resources have decreased due to the increase in the public's "liquidity preference" (Keynesian money demand).

b- In calculating the emission increase in line with the expected developments in money demand, it has been assumed that the tendency to hold bank money instead of cash money, which increased in 1965 and 1966 and accelerated the development in money supply, will continue.

c- A significant portion of the resources created by the emission increase in the past period (more than 90%) has been used by the public sector. In the Second Plan period, it was envisaged that the Central Bank (CBRT) resources would be used to meet short-term Treasury needs in the event of normal development of the public sector.

d- As one of the measures, coordination regarding monetary policies will be provided by the Money-Credit Board to be established between the SPO, the Ministry of Finance and the CBRT. The relations of the TCMB with the Treasury and the banking system will be organized in accordance with the modern economic understanding.

e- Another measure, instead of short-term advances to the Treasury, in order to increase the efficiency and flexibility in practice by improving open market transactions, the method of increasing the emission by selling short-term bonds to banks and, when necessary, by purchasing these bonds from banks by the TCMB will be preferred and this method will be developed.

f- In addition, in order to increase the banking system and resources, policies that will mobilize idle savings, increase the attractiveness of deposits and develop the check payment system will be emphasized. The conditions for banks to obtain long-term funds by issuing bonds will be facilitated. Interest and discount rates will be used as a tool to ensure the distribution of loans in accordance with the Plan targets.

The Third Five-Yearly Development Plan (3rd DP) Covering the Years 1973-1977

The 3rd DP was prepared in 1972 with a 22-year long-term perspective, taking into account Turkey's accession process to the "European Common Market", which is the intermediate integration phase of the current European Union, and emphasized that the monetary-credit policy should be consistent with the fiscal policy. This Plan aimed to provide the financing needed by the economy with an application that would not disrupt price stability, create pressure on the balance of payments and encourage inefficient activity, and to make the following arrangements necessary for the supervision and effective operation of the monetary-credit system (DPT-SPO, 1975: 875-etc.):

a- In order to increase the possibility of directing bank loans to priority sectors and regions in accordance with the Development Plan and annual programs, the rediscount relations of the CBRT with commercial banks will be developed.
b- In order to reduce the credit price and, when necessary, open subsidy application based on interest difference refund will be implemented. In order to prevent the distribution of savings deposits, regulations will be made in the application regarding the taxation of deposit interests.
c- In meeting the medium and long-term credit needs of the industry, short-term credits of commercial banks are insufficient and the chance of success of industrial initiatives based on the own resources of capitalist-entrepreneurial individuals and family groups will decrease.
d- Foreign currency and TL resources of active industrial investment and credit banks will be increased. A "Development Bank" will be established to operate in the fields of crediting the industry and meeting the medium-term credit needs of industrial investments, especially in regions with priority in development.
e- It is important to provide credit to export-oriented agricultural and livestock projects. In addition to loans for the tradesmen sector, loans primarily for social housing construction and to meet demand will also be provided through the Turkish Real Estate Credit Bank.

The Fourth Five-Yearly Development Plan (4th DP) Covering the Years 1979-1983

While the 4th DP covers the last year of the traditional planned period (1979), it coincides with the period when the liberal stability decisions of January 24, 1980, namely the economic policies, began and continued. Accordingly (DPT-SPO, 1979: 261-etc.):

a- It will be ensured that the resources of the CBRT will be used less in meeting the financial deficits of the public sector and it will be essential to provide this sector with more economically sound financial resources.
b- It will be used as a flexible and effective tool in the context of the general interest policy, in a way that provides a compromise between the objectives of directing savings to an organized financial order, encouraging investment in areas required by development, and avoiding price increases.
c- All kinds of deposit and bond interests and the interest rates applied by institutions that make installment sales will be differentiated in a way that will provide a flow of resources compatible with the principles envisaged by the Plan. Instruments such as interest and rediscount differentiations, interest difference refunds, deposit reserve requirement ratio differentiations that al-

low selective application in lending will be used in harmony and effectively, taking into account the risk and profitability of the fields of activity and the bottlenecks encountered in financing.

d- In the agricultural sector, the principle will be to partially adopt a financing structure based on the sector's own resources, as the price support policy, which is currently carried out mainly with the resources of the Central Bank of Turkey and the Ziraat Bank. In this model, if the world price develops above the income growth trend, the difference will be transferred to a fund, and if the prices develop below this trend, the method of making payments to the producer from the fund will be applied. In this way, the producer will be prevented from suffering losses due to fluctuations in world prices of products subject to foreign trade and will provide stability to his income.

e- The Turkish People's Bank will follow a credit policy that supports the initiatives that develop the production activities of tradesmen and craftsmen and facilitates them to change their profession and art branch when economic and technological change requires it. The State Industrial and Worker Investment Bank (SIWIB) will be used as a tool to eliminate imbalances between regions and income groups by expanding the industry through multi-partner companies at the domestic level and also to evaluate the savings of citizens working abroad domestically.

f- An "Export Bank" with the status of a state-economic enterprise (SEE) will be established, the capital of which will be provided by the Treasury, other public specialized and commercial banks and the Turkish Industrial Development Bank, and which will primarily perform tasks such as detailed and continuous evaluation of export markets, determination of domestically marketable goods and services, provision of communication between producers and foreign buyers, provision of short and medium-term foreign exchange and TL credits to exporters, financing of exporters on a project basis and export insurance.

Comparison of Planned Development Periods or Development Plans (DPs)

It should be noted that the first two plans are of 'critical' importance in the planned development period. Because planning represents a new period that started after the Democrat Party governments that managed the economy with liberal discourses but statist practices, and indirectly claims to increase the benefits and reduce the burdens of the mixed economy.

The monetary policies such as money supply and monetary base followed in the 1st and 2nd DP periods were determined by public authorities, not independently of development policies. While banknote emission was influenced by credit increases in the 1st DP period, it was more influenced by net gold and foreign exchange increases in the 2nd DP period. In the 1960-68 period, the public finance sector received the highest share in the distribution of credits and advances of the TCMB with 36%, agricultural policy institutions with 30% and the private sector with 27%, while the lowest share was received by SEEs with 6%. The Money Lending Transactions Law was amended and with a new decree, the highest interest rate was first determined as 12%, and the loan interests applied to agricultural enterprises were kept at a lower level than other enterprises. After 1960, term deposit interests varied between 2.5% and 6.5% (Parasız, 2003: 183-187).

The budget deficits that increased during the 2nd DP period were financed by the TCMB resources, the money supply increased by 16% in 1969 and the inflation rate started to increase. With the stability package of August 4, 1958, the value of the TL was reduced from 9 TL against the US Dollar ($) to 15 TL on August 10, 1970 through an official devaluation of 67%. On the same date, the bank loan interest rate was increased to 11.5% and the term deposit interest rate was increased to 9% with the expectation that it would shrink the money volume. A stand-by loan of $90 million was received from the IMF within the scope of the stability program based on orthodoxy monetary and fiscal policies, where interest and exchange rates were nominal anchors against inflation and current deficit (Parasız, 2003: 220-230).

The reorganization of the duties and authorities of the TCMB, which is responsible for monetary policies, was mentioned in the first two development plans and programs and became official in January 1970. Even the banknotes currently in use in Turkey still state "Issued according to the law numbered 1211 and 14 January 1970". The quantitative and selective objectives, tools, transactions and bodies of the TCMB in the field of money and credit have been brought into line with the development plans in order to meet the needs of the growing Turkish economy.

The monetary policies of the 3rd and 4th DP periods, which exhibited an inflationary structure like the first two plans identified with a stable structure in the economy, did not develop on a very different line in essence compared to the previous liberal Democrat Party period. Due to the acceleration of the conjuncture and industrialization, a loose monetary strategy was resorted to and this strategy was not inflationary at first, but the economy, which encountered external cost inflation, soon came to the brink of crisis. The crisis deepened when the basic monetary indicators, namely interest rates and exchange rates, were not adjusted freely upwards and could not have a braking effect due to rising inflation (Güneş, 1998: 187).

In the planned period, a fixed exchange rate regime was adopted, which worked with rare but large-scale changes in exchange rates. If a mobile fixed exchange rate regime was adopted after the implementation of the liberal 24 January Stability Decisions in 1980 in order to eliminate some of the drawbacks of the fixed exchange rate regime that contradicted the mixed economy, one reason for this was the increase in fluctuations in cross rates, and the other reason was to determine the exchange rates parallel to inflation in order to prevent the large current deficits experienced in the past (Akat, 2004: 57). In fact, the CBRT applied a de facto "devaluation as much as inflation" rule against the crisis conjunctures experienced in the 1990s.

A method that directly determined the exchange rate could not be found in the planned period, but exchange rates could be used as a tool for development. Within this framework, by keeping the value of the TL extremely high (by decreasing the exchange rates), the price of imported goods was artificially cheapened at the expense of damaging the foreign trade balance, but import substitution was encouraged in industry. As a result of the intervention in exchange rates, exports increased by 30% and imports by 11% during the 1st DP period, when exchange rates were kept constant; in the 2nd DP period, foreign trade was left to the influence of exchange rates as desired by the IMF; in the 3rd DP period, as imports increased twice as much as exports, the foreign trade deficit increased to a record level of 265%. The economy entered the 4th DP period (1979, the first year of the plan) with a foreign trade deficit of approximately $2.8 billion (i.e. almost ten times the equivalent of the year the first plan was implemented) (Oksay, 2001:123-6).

Turkey, which became a member of the IMF in 1947 and entered into its first stand-by arrangement with the IMF in 1961, when planning had not yet begun, adopted an adjustable fixed exchange rate regime based on the gold-foreign exchange standard until July 1971, during the 3rd DP period within the scope of the Bretton Woods (BW) system. In addition, the banking sector, where the first reaction to monetary, interest and exchange rate policies was given, also experienced a change in this process (Parasız, 2011: 23-5; Kazgan, Ateş, et al., 1999: 261): While large private banks were established between 1944-1967, the banking sector witnessed major public interventions between 1961-1980. The accelerating conjuncture "from stone-built public banks to glass-fronted private banks" would reach its peak in the 1980s.

The BW system referred to here is the name given to a series of decisions taken at the international monetary and financial conference held in the town of Bretton Woods (New Hampshire) in the USA in 1944. The most important of these decisions can be summarized as follows: i) The simultaneous establishment of two liberal-capitalist twin financial institutions, the IMF and the World Bank. ii) The tying of other countries' currencies to the US dollar, the US dollar to gold, and therefore all members' currencies to gold. iii) Permission to obtain permission from the IMF for devaluations or revaluations above 10%. iv) The US Federal Reserve selling gold at a fixed rate to foreign central banks that would supply the US dollar. As a result, the BW system collapsed in 1973, the year of the oil crisis, when some of the member countries left their national currencies floating.

One of the common features of the first four development plans (DP) implemented before 1980 is that they took the growth of the Turkish economy at a certain positive rate (as it happened between 6-7%) as the basic variable as an indirect aim of monetary policy and based economic growth on the import substitution industrialization strategy (Öztürk and Aslanoğlu, 1998: 2008). Economic growth was followed by monetary growth. As seen in Table 2, in the years when the development plans were implemented, the money in circulation, the loans given by the CBRT and banks and the deposits they collected constantly increased and the ratio of these indicators to the GNP always had positive values in the fluctuating movement. For example, while the amount of money in circulation increased from approximately 7.5 billion TL in 1965, when the 1st DP was in force, to 217.5 billion TL at the end of 1980, when the 4th DP was still in force, the ratio of this amount to GNP decreased from 9.9% to 6.3% in the same years.

Table 2. Course of monetary indicators in the years of development plans (1965-1980)

Indicator/ Year	*1965*	*1969*	*1970*	*1975*	*1979*	*1980*
Currency in Circulation*	7 571	11 264	14 235	32 309	143 676	217 501
Currency in Circulation / GNP**	9.9	9.0	9.6	7.7	8.4	6.3
CBRT Credits*	4 665	12 920	14 565	66 198	382 138	655 183
CBRT Credits / GNP**	6.1	10.3	10.5	12.4	17.4	25.0
Bank Deposits*	14 785	30 759	36 246	144 847	446 188	789 515
Bank Deposits / GNP**	19.3	24.6	24.5	27.0	20.3	17.8
Bank Credits*	16 242	33 714	37 543	140 311	594 453	966 457
Bank Credits / GNP**	21.2	27.0	25.4	26.2	27.0	21.8

Notes: (*) As of the end of the year; million TL. (**) As a proportional percentage.
Source: Pakdemirli, 1991: 167-168.

REASONS AND RESULTS OF THE APPLICATION OF MULTIPLE EXCHANGE RATE

A multiple exchange rate regime is when the government/central bank determines different exchange rates for current transactions consisting of different goods and services in an economy. For example, by applying a high exchange rate, the import of some goods is reduced or prevented and/or their export is encouraged.

The transition to a multiple exchange rate regime in Turkey was a process. It was devalued on August 4, 1958 to "$1 = 9 TL". Similarly, with the Decision No. 18 on "Protection of the Value of the Turkish Currency" (PVTC) dated August 10,

1970, a new exchange rate was set and determined as "$1 = 15 TL". The purpose of this devaluation was stated to be to reduce import demand and increase the competitiveness of export goods in foreign markets. The introduction of a new application in the exchange rate regime in 1974 was the main reason for frequent devaluations. According to the method prepared by the IMF, it was stated that there should be a maximum of 2% difference between any two buying or two selling rates in the exchange rates between the currencies of countries' own currencies and those of other members. The exchange rates were adjusted 3 times in 1976, 2 times in 1977, 3 times in 1978, 3 times in 1979, 16 times in 1980 when the January 24 Decisions were announced, and many times in the following years. In Turkey, the exchange rate regime was changed on January 24, 1980, a crawling parity regime was introduced, and the value of $1 was increased to 70 TL. As of May 1, 1981, a single exchange rate was implemented, and exchange rates began to be announced daily by the CBRT. According to developments in international markets and money markets, the exchange rates were changed 164 times in 1981, 245 times in 1982, and 246 times in 1983. In other words, the exchange rates were determined anew every business day (Arat, 2003: 37-38).

Between January 24, 1980 and May 1, 1981, which coincided with the 4th DP period, small devaluations were made in exchange rates, not exceeding 5%, in other words, the external value of the TL was regularly reduced (exchange rates were increased) and an effective exchange rate policy was implemented to increase exports. As of May 1, 1981, the TCMB was authorized to determine and announce the parity between the TL and foreign currencies daily, thus closing the difference between the official and market rates and the strategy of reaching a "realistic balance rate" in the long term was started. The foreign exchange regime was also liberalized with the Decision No. 28 on the PVTC, which came into force on December 29, 1983. Within the scope of simplifying the foreign exchange legislation, the main exchange rate application determined by the Central Bank (1984) was terminated and the exchange rates started to be determined by the banks (1985). However, due to the significant disruptions in the banking system, this policy was also abolished (Parasız 2004 and İşgüden-Akyüz 1990, cited in Hepaktan, Çınar and Dündar, 2011: 64).

Flexible anchors, which were on the agenda from the 1970s to the second half of the 1990s, were thought to be a very effective policy element against high and chronic inflation, to reduce uncertainty by reducing exchange rate risk, and to be superior in terms of international investments and external borrowing. In contrast, it has been argued that flexible anchors are not resistant to external shocks, cause a current account deficit, create uncertainty due to reliability problems, and do not reduce hyperinflation much due to the stickiness of inflation. Turkey, which implemented a controlled and multiple exchange rate policy until the decisions of January 24, 1980, decided to switch to a "more realistic and flexible exchange rate regime" within the framework of the decisions it made on this date. Within this scope, the TL was devalued by approximately 50% against foreign currencies and multiple exchange rate practices were abolished except for chemical fertilizer imports. In addition, importers of raw materials and intermediate goods were also included in the foreign exchange allocation application granted to exporters (İnan, 2002: 2-3).

Meanwhile, when the studies on the exchange rate regimes implemented in Turkey before 1980 are examined, it is seen that in addition to the fixed exchange rate regimes based on currencies such as the British pound (1930-1931, 1936-1939), the French franc (1931-1936), the US dollar (1960-1961, 1970-1971), exchange rate regimes such as crawling bands (1971-1976) and managed floating (1953-1960) were implemented (as cited in Yalçıner, Çetinkaya and Çevik, 2017: 268).

REASONS AND RESULTS OF NEGATIVE INTEREST POLICIES

Negative interest was first defined by the German economist S. Gessel in the late 19th century as "a tax paid for holding money". Keynes similarly described it as a tax on carrying or holding money. It is seen that the nominal interest rate is applied negatively in the USA and some European economies, especially when a financial crisis occurs or in return for safekeeping of money. (For details, see Köse, Atik and Yılmaz, 2015: 322-3).

In Keynesian terms, interest, which is the price of giving up money or the opportunity cost of money, is normally applied at a positive rate in debt transactions. In an inflationary conjuncture, the real interest rate must be positive, otherwise neither the lenders will be able to protect the real purchasing power of their money nor will it be easier to combat consumer inflation. In theoretical terms, there are a number of reasons or purposes that require negative interest rate decisions for countries, ceteris paribus, such as increasing the income of the real sector by making savers spend in a way that will stimulate the economy, providing banks with a source of cheap credit, preparing the ground for an increase in exports by decreasing the value of the domestic currency and facilitating the flow of foreign exchange from abroad to inland.

Negative interest is the determination of the interest rate applied by the central bank to the current accounts of commercial banks as a monetary policy tool below the country's inflation rate. Negative interest rate practices, which have the message of "I will not give interest for the money you deposit to me, I will receive money on top. Instead of depositing this money to me, give me a loan", aim to break the increasing inflationary expectations caused by demand, reduce the downward pressures on exchange rates and finally regain dynamism in economic growth (Dünya Gazetesi, 2016; Ergin-Ünal and Yetiz, 2017: 69, 72; Eroğlu and Erdoğmuş, 2017:

85). However, since the negative interest rate policy leads decision-making units to prefer to keep the cash in their own safes instead of depositing it in the bank in order not to be burdened with interest costs and has the handicap of starting currency wars between countries, it does not have the chance to be implemented for a long time.

In Turkey, before 1980, deposit and loan interest rates were under the control of the public, nominal interest rates were kept at low levels in order to encourage investments on the one hand and to reduce the public's borrowing cost on the other, and real interest rates generally remained negative with the rise in inflation. For this reason, deposit interest rates were always below inflation. The most significant feature of this period was that the CBRT imposed interventionist restrictions on interest rates within the framework of general economic policy. Therefore, the function of banks was limited to only keeping money, money transfers and collecting checks and promissory notes. This situation pushed banks to a strategy of spreading to a wide base with multiple branches, banks entered into a race to expand their branch networks as much as possible and implemented attractive methods such as lotteries and promotions in order to provide resources (Takım and İslamoğlu, 2012: 182-3).

In the 1970s, which coincided with the 2nd DP period, banks and other financial intermediary institutions were reluctant to finance new investments due to negative real interest rates, and preferred to finance affiliates and physical assets they wanted to purchase as a precaution against asset decreases due to inflationary conjuncture. In accordance with development plans, it was desired to develop some sectors with various interest and credit privileges. Since the efficiency of credits would be increased by interest rate differentiation, unlike previous periods, importance was given to minimizing the difference between credit and deposit interest rates (Parasız, 2003: 256-7).

Before the oil crisis in 1973, the developments that increased and decreased emission depending on gold and foreign exchange reserves followed their normal course. In order to curb the inflationary effect of the increase in emission, deposit reserves (up to 30%) and rediscount rates (1%) were increased. The rate of increase in banknotes decreased in 1975. The CBRT's credits increased by 81% in 1977 and 27.5% in 1978, reaching 242 billion TL. In 1973, the nominal value of deposit interests was 9%, and due to high inflation, their real value fell to -17%, and in 1979, the nominal 20% deposit interests exceeded -27%. Throughout the development plans, it was aimed to bring deposit interest rates closer to the equilibrium interest rates and to collect savings in financial intermediary institutions, but an interest regime suitable for this goal could not be established (Parasız, 2003: 248-257).

ECONOMIC EFFECTS OF THE 1973-74 OIL CRISIS

The oil crisis (October 1973) occurred while the 3rd DP was being implemented in Turkey. This crisis was an oil embargo launched by the Organization of Arab Petroleum Exporting Countries (OAPEC) against Western states that supported the Israeli army in the Arab-Israeli War that broke out in the same year and threw the Middle East into a chaotic process. As a result of the embargo, oil prices increased approximately fourfold in the short term, oil revenues changed direction and began to flow towards Middle Eastern countries, production costs increased in Western economies dependent on Arab oil, consumers' purchasing power decreased due to the escalation of inflation caused by oil, and world economies in general entered a “stagflation” (i.e. stagnation within inflation) conjuncture (Öztürk and Saygın, 2017: 1 and 6). In addition, the 1973 oil crisis affected energy security in many ways, for example, from the definition of the concept of energy supply security to the increased importance given to energy independence, from the adoption of new energy policies by developed countries and their turning to alternative energy providers, sources and routes to the establishment of institutions such as the International Energy Agency and the adoption of policies based on joint struggle and the adoption of saving measures (Yılmaz and Kalkan, 2017: 186). Finally, as Yergin (2023) reminds us, the 1973 crisis, which turned into an embargo for the West, shook the global energy market, reset geopolitics, reorganized the global economy, and ushered in the modern energy era.

The 1973 oil crisis also disrupted Turkey's periodic development plan. Due to this regional energy crisis and the accompanying wrong and inconsistent monetary and fiscal policies, the Turkish economy experienced production declines (i.e. recession) and the paths leading to hyperinflation were shortened. The increasing inflation phenomenon was fed by factors such as the increase in imported input prices and oil prices, the direct and indirect costs in the economy caused by the Aegean Problem and the Cyprus Peace Operation, the reduction of foreign aid, the foreign exchange bottleneck, and the support for oil consumption in the country in contrast to the oil savings in the West. The increase in the price of crude oil by four times at the end of 1973 and five times in 1974 (from $2.5 to $11.6) shook the balances in the world economy and tripled the foreign trade deficit of oil importer Turkey. When the foreign trade deficit was $2.3 billion and the budget deficit was $303 million, almost all export revenues were not enough to pay the high oil bills and Turkish workers returned to the country, foreign borrowing became inevitable. The solution to the financing problem of the public sector due to political concerns of high oil prices was left to the CBRT. In addition, while oil companies and organizations all over the world entered into intensive drilling investments due to the great oil crisis, Turkey implemented the “Petroleum Reform Law” numbered 1702, which indicated that oil exploration should be carried out by the state instead of foreign capital (Öztürk and Saygın, 2017: 6; Eğilmez and Kumcu, 2004: 256; Parasız, Ekren and Eroğlu, 2016: 419).

Later, despite the planning, fluctuations in the value of the TL and market prices began, and statist economic policies centered on fiscal policy that required market interventions and, to some extent, heterodox policies that meant restrictions and control on rent, interest and similar incomes along with prices were followed (Eğilmez and Kumcu. 2004: 257).

DEVALUATIONS PERIOD 1977-1980: REASONS AND RESULTS OF FREQUENT DEVALUATIONS

Turkey's monetary economic history is a history of devaluations. Devaluation, which means reducing the value of national currency in terms of foreign currencies, is applied in economies with a fixed exchange rate regime. Devaluation, which is applied to close the balance of external payments, is expected to increase foreign exchange earnings and reduce foreign exchange expenditures.

After each devaluation, Turkey's goods and services have become cheaper for foreigners at the rate of the devaluation, and thus export and tourism revenues have increased, while foreign goods and services have become more expensive and import and tourism expenditures have decreased, thus partially reducing the current account deficit. Devaluation, which definitely reduces foreign expenditures, has always had a relative effect on the Turkish economy in terms of increasing foreign exchange earnings. Theoretically, if foreigners' demand for domestic (Turkey's) goods and services is not elastic enough (>1), that is, if exports do not increase proportionally more than the devaluation, or if domestic production in the country is insufficient to meet this demand even if foreign demand for export goods increases, export earnings will not increase after devaluation or will be less than before (Aren, 1991:

Meanwhile, sometimes, in order to neutralize the devaluation, other countries may have to enter into a "devaluation competition" and make new devaluations in order to protect or not lose foreign markets. In this case, the expected positive effect of devaluation will not be realized. Instead of developing countries with a current account surplus, which is the opposite of devaluation, and achieving a current account balance by revaluation, they wait for the countries they do foreign trade with to devalue. Because when one country devalues, the other country will be considered to have made a revaluation (Aren, 1991: 108).

As seen in planned development periods, the Turkish economy has experienced a vicious cycle of devaluation-inflation. A negative effect of devaluation, in contrast to its positive effects, is that while imports are fixed, the domestic supply of goods and services is narrowed or made scarce due to the increase in exports, and these goods and services become more expensive after a while -while aggregated supply (AS) is fixed and aggregated demand (AD) is increasing- and this leads to inflation. When imports are increased while exports are fixed in order to combat inflation, the current account balance, if any, will turn into a deficit and if there is a deficit, it will deepen. A high interest rate policy has been followed to break the inflationary effect of devaluation. On the one hand, high interest rates have reduced investment demand since they have increased (reduced) investment costs (profits), and on the other hand, they have increased the savings that can be spent. Thus, while AS is fixed, this interest policy has narrowed the high AD, which is a source of inflation, consisting of private sector consumption expenditures and investment expenditures. In order for the mechanism to work well, interest rates should be above inflation (real interest rate positive).

Devaluation has been a policy that has toppled governments in Turkey and similar developing countries. The devaluations made by the Menderes government in 1958 and by the Demirel and Ecevit governments in the 1970s as a solution to their high current account deficits and debts led to their withdrawal from government or their defeat in elections. It has been observed that devaluations, which cannot be made without the knowledge of the IMF, were sometimes attempted in Turkey despite the IMF and its reaction (Doğan, 1986: 34).

The IMF, whose main duty is to close the deficits in the member country's account of payments, applies a financial model when providing short-term loans: This model includes two targets and two projections. The target is to provide low inflation ( ) and a sustainable balance of payments, while the projection is the change in the real growth rate (g) and the money velocity rate (V). According to the known inflation formula, " $= \Delta M / M - g + \Delta V / V$": The increase in the money supply (M or Ms) minus g plus V are the variables that determine the inflation target. "$\Delta M / M = + g - \Delta V / V$" is applied to reach the target inflation. For this, it is necessary to estimate the increase in M, g and V (Yaşar, 2005: 78).

Turkey operated Convertible Deposit Accounts (CDC) against the foreign exchange bottleneck during the coalition governments called the Nationalist Front between 1975-78. They were first implemented between 1967-73 to attract the foreign exchange savings of workers in Germany to the country in order to close the foreign trade balance, and these accounts, which affected the exchange rate system, created a significant credit volume. In essence, CDC, which is a foreign exchange flow from foreign economies to the Turkish economy, mainly consisting of German Marks and Swiss Francs, is an account opened in a bank in the name of a certain person in Turkey by Turkish/foreign real/legal persons residing in Turkey or abroad, to collect foreign exchange that they do not have to bring to Turkey. CDC accounts collected by banks were transferred to theCBRT, and exchange rate differences and interest income were reflected in favor of the account holder with the Treasury guarantee. CDCs, which are observed to constitute a significant portion of foreign exchange reserves, disrupted the fight against inflation and put the country into a different debt trap. The credits sent by international financial institutions through the CDC were used in trade, not investments. In addition, by reducing the dependency of banks on the CBRT, it rendered monetary policy dysfunctional. The CDC entry was frozen by the government of the period in 1978 due to the interest burden it brought to the banking sector, the exchange rate difference burden it brought to the treasury, the excessive profit it provided to those who used it as a credit and cross-rate application, and the fact that it became a source of inflation (Doğan, 1986: 128-132). During the 4th DP period, monetary policies were tried to be implemented without the CDC and, if possible, without devaluation.

DISCUSSION

Since the late 1970s, many developing countries, including Turkey, have been forced to adopt neoliberal policies through agreements made with the World Bank and the IMF under the name of structural adjustment or stabilization programs. As Alagöz (2012) points out, neoliberal policies and harsh debt-credit conditions have devastated the socio-economic structures of fragile countries such as Turkey. A severe crisis balance sheet emerged in Türkiye in the form of high unemployment, poverty, and the shrinking of the public sector.

The 1970s are important because they encompass the chain of events that led to the collapse of the Bretton Woods system (BWS) (1944-1970), which included the establishment of the IMF and the World Bank. The BWS was an adjustable fixed exchange rate system in which each country pegged its currency to a peg currency (the US dollar) and the value of the peg currency was pegged to gold. The fact that all currencies were indexed to the dollar created great tension in financial markets and made it difficult to convert the dollar, whose reliability had decreased due to reasons such as inflation and large external deficits in the US, into gold. As a result, the US stopped indexing the dollar to gold in 1971; when gold got out of control at high market prices, the BWS collapsed (Garber, 1991; Jin, Liu and Li, 2018; Pinder 2023). When the oil shocks came after this collapse, monetary, interest and exchange rate policies began to change in all world economies, including Turkey, and the wheels of neoliberalism began to form. In the 1980s, central banks immediately switched to a more daring floating exchange rate system.

The BWS system collapsed, but its main institutions, the IMF and the World Bank, continued to survive. Emerging markets like Turkey were left dependent on IMF standby loans to cover short-term foreign exchange deficits and World Bank loans to finance long-term regional and sectoral development (Şenses, 1991; Lavy & Rapoport, 1992; WB, 1976 and 1980). In the 1970s and 1980s, Turkey, which was in debt and in a conjuncture of chronic high inflation, had one leg of its five-year development plans left to the initiative of these remaining institutions of the BWS. While the devaluation decisions of the central bank, as expected by the government, provided temporary relief to the balance of payments through cheap exports and the inflow of workers' remittances, they were also paving the way for imported and cost-driven inflations by increasing the costs of inputs such as imported oil. And Turkey was unable to plan its national development on the slippery ground of monetary and foreign exchange policies, and it fell on that slippery ground every time and was looking for ways to get back on its feet. One of those ways was the neoliberal economic decisions of January 24, 1980. However, it was seen that these decisions brought about a political economy crisis full of class inequalities, heavy unemployment, brutal inflation and high cost of living instead of stability due to the military coup of September 12, 1980.

GENERAL CONCLUSION

The planned development period covering the years 1960-1980 (and four development plans) does not represent a period in which the economic order in Turkey was radically changed, but a period in which socio-economic development processes supported by monetary policies were tied to plans. The planning understanding and approach of this period, as far as can be observed, was neither the rigid-hard central planning of the Soviet style nor the liberal-market planning of the Western style. This was a pragmatic approach specific to the social structure of the country and in line with the mixed economy order that was actually maintained. The main reason for wanting to carry out development with plans was to effectively supply and distribute national resources, including money and credit, according to social needs. It can be said that these plans partially met the expectations of the people and the goals of the governments during the periods they were implemented and to the extent that domestic/external conjunctural developments (terrorism, oil shocks, etc.) allowed.

Since the twenty-year planned development period examined here for Turkey coincides with a person's childhood and early youth, it should be considered normal for there to be errors and deficiencies in the plans – in the content preparation phases of technocrats and in the implementation phases of bureaucrats – and for them to develop over time and be implemented as they are. Although the latest plans are more advanced versions of the previous plans – depending on the development of the CBRT responsible for monetary policies and the banking sector that reflects those policies firsthand, and the change in political preferences of governments due to concerns about gaining the most votes – this fact does not change. The liberal economic policies declared and implemented in Turkey on January 24, 1980 ended the traditional planned development period and initiated a new planned development period in which the mixed economy evolved into liberalism. Thus, the scope of monetary policy was expanded with new regulations that increased the activities and functionality of the central bank and financial institutions, encouraged the private sector with public loans, encouraged privatizations, and supported foreign exchange trading and all kinds of financial liberalization.

REFERENCES

Akat, A.S. (2004). Dalgalı Kur ve Para Politikası: Bir Parasal Kural Önerisi. iç. *Gülten Kazgan'a Armağan: Türkiye Ekonomisi.* İstanbul: İstanbul Bilgi Üniversitesi Yayınları, ss.57-80.

Alagöz, R. (2012). The Impacts Of Neo-Lıberal Polıcıes On Turkey In 2000-2001. City University of New York (CUNY) *CUNY Academic Works.* https://academicworks.cuny.edu/cc_etds_theses/133

Arat, K. (2003). Türkiye'de Optimum Döviz Kuru Rejimi Seçimi ve Döviz Kurlarından Fiyatlara Geçiş Etkisinin İncelenmesi. Uzmanlık Yeterlilik Tezi. Ankara: TCMB Dış İlişkiler Genel Müdürlüğü.

Aren, S. (1991). *100 Soruda Para ve Para Politikası.* 4.b., İstanbul: Gerçek Yayınevi.

Doğan, Y. (1986). *IMF Kıskacında Türkiye 1946-1980. 2.b.* Tekin Yayınevi.

DPT. (1968). *İkinci Beş Yıllık Kalkınma Planı 1968 – 1972.* Ankara. http://www.sbb.gov.tr/ Lists/Kalknma%20Planlar/Attachments/8/plan2.pdf

DPT. (1973). *Üçüncü Beş Yıllık Kalkınma Planı 1973 – 1977.* Ankara. http://www.sbb.gov.tr/ Lists/Kalknma%20Planlar/Attachments/7/plan3.pdf

DPT. (1979). *Dördüncü Beş Yıllık Kalkınma Planı 1979 – 1983.* Ankara. http://www.sbb.gov.tr/ Lists/Kalknma%20Planlar/Attachments/6/plan4.pdf

DPT-SPO (Devlet Planlama Teşkilatı). (1963). *Birinci Beş Yıllık Kalkınma Planı 1963 – 1967.* Ankara. http://www.sbb.gov.tr/ Lists/Kalknma%20Planlar/Attachments/9/plan1.pdf

Dünya Gazetesi (2016). Negatif faiz nedir, neden uygulanır? https://www.dunya.com/ finans/haberler/negatif-faiz-nedir-neden-uygulanir-haberi-307723

Eğilmez, M., & Kumcu, E. (2004).Ekonomi Politikası: Teori ve Türkiye Uygulaması. 22.b., İstanbul: Remzi Kitabevi.

Ergin Ünal, A. & Yetiz, F. (2017). Parasal Genişlemeye Alternatif Arayışları: Negatif Faiz. *PEK-Politik Ekonomik Kuram,* c.1, S.2, ss.66-78.

Eroğlu, İ. & Erdoğmuş, M. (2017). Merkez Bankalarının Krizle Mücadele Çabaları: Negatif Faiz Politikası Tercihi ve İktisadi Yansımaları. *Namık Kemal Üniversitesi Sosyal Bilimler Metinleri Dergisi,* İCOMEP'17 Özel sayı, ss.82-97.

Garber, P. M. Garber (1991). The Collapse of the Bretton Woods Fixed Exchange Rate System. NBER Chapters, in: *A Retrospective on the Bretton Woods System: Lessons for International Monetary Reform*, pp. 461-494, National Bureau of Economic Research, Inc. https://www.nber.org/system/files/chapters/c6876/c6876.pdf

Güneş, H. (1998). Dünden Bugüne Para Politikaları. iç. *75 Yılda Paranın Serüveni.* M. Sönmez (Ed.), İstanbul: Tarih Vakfı Yayınları, ss.187-194.

Hepaktan, E., Çınar, S. & Dündar, Ö. (2011). Türkiye'de Uygulanan Döviz Kuru Sistemlerinin Dış Ticaret İle İlişkisi. *Akademik Araştırmalar ve Çalışmalar Dergisi,* c.3, S.5, Kasım, ss.62-82.

İnan, E. A. (2002). *Kur Rejimi Tercihi ve Türkiye.* TBB-Türkiye Bankalar Birliği.

Jin, Y., Liu, D., & Li, Y. (2018). Factors That Have Led to the Collapse of the Bretton Woods System. *American Journal of Industrial and Business Management, 8*(10), 2133–2142. DOI: 10.4236/ajibm.2018.810141

Kazgan, H., & Ateş, T. vd. (1999). *Osmanlı'dan Günümüze Türk Finans Tarihi.* c.2, İstanbul: Creative Yayıncılık.

Kepenek, Y. (2014). Türkiye Ekonomisi. 28.b., İstanbul: Remzi Kitabevi.

Kılıçbay, A. (1990). *İktisadi Planlama.* İ.Ü. İktisat Fakültesi Yayını.

Köse, Y., Atik, M. & Yılmaz, B. (2015). Türkiye İçin Negatif Faiz Oranının Uygulanabilirliği ve Analitik Olarak İncelenmesi. *Finansal Araştırmalar ve Çalışmalar Dergisi,* c.7, S.13, Temmuz, ss.321-339.

Küçük, Y. (1985), Planlı Kalkınma ve Türkiye, 4.b., İstanbul: Tekin Yayınevi.

Lavy, V., & Rapoport, H. (1992). External Debt and Structural Adjustment: Recent Experience in Turkey. *Middle Eastern Studies, 28*(2), 313–332. https://www.jstor.org/stable/4283495. DOI: 10.1080/00263209208700903

Oksay, S. (2001). *Döviz Kuru ve Ödemeler Bilançosu Politikaları: Türkiye (1923-2000).* Beta Yayınevi.

Öztürk, A., & Aslanoğlu, M. (1998). *Ekonomik Planlama.* Ekin Kitabevi.

Öztürk, S. & Saygın, S. (2017). 1973 Petrol Krizinin Ekonomiye Etkileri ve Stagflasyon Olgusu. *BJSS-Balkan Sosyal Bilimler Dergisi,* c. 6, S. 12, ss. 1-12.

Pakdemirli, E. (1991). *Ekonomimizin 1923'ten 1990'a Sayısal Görünümü.* Milliyet Yayınları.

Parasız, İ. (2003). *Türkiye Ekonomisi.* Ezgi Kitabevi.

Parasız, İ. (2011). *Türkiye'de ve Dünyada Bankacılık*. Ezgi Kitabevi.

Parasız, İ., Ekren, N., & Eroğlu, İ. (2016). Para Politikası ve Türkiye Uygulaması. 7.b., Bursa: Ezgi Kitabevi.

Pinder, R. (2023). Was the Bretton Woods system bound to fail? *Knowles Review of Economic History*, *2*(1), 36–45.

Şenses, F. (1991). Turkey's Stabilizatıon and Structural Adjustment Program in Retrospect and Prospect. *The Developing Economies*, *29*(3), 210–234. DOI: 10.1111/j.1746-1049.1991.tb00208.x

Sezen, S. (1999). Devletçilikten Özelleştirmeye Türkiye'de Planlama. Ankara: TODAİE Yayını (No 293).

Takım, A. & İslamoğlu, M. (2012). Serbest Piyasa Ekonomisine Geçiş Sürecinde Türkiye'de Uygulanan Para Politikaları İle İlgili Tartışmalar. *Afyon Kocatepe Üniversitesi İİBF Dergisi,* c.XIV, S.1, ss.179-189.

WB. (1976). *Turkey - Country economic memorandum.* Washington, D.C.: World Bank Group. http://documents.worldbank.org/curated/en/509561468172148573

WB. (1980). *Turkey - Postscript special economic report.* Washington, D.C.: World Bank Group. http://documents.worldbank.org/curated/en/621131468121489159

Yalçıner, K. & Çetinkaya, M. – Çevik, Y. E. (2017). Türkiye'nin 'De Facto' Döviz Kuru Rejiminin Belirlenmesi. *Selçuk Üniversitesi Sosyal Bilimler Enstitüsü Dergisi*, S.37, ss.265-272.

Yaşar, S. (2005). *Global Ekonomide Makro Ekonomi Yönetimi*. Beta Yayınevi.

Yergin, D. (2023). The 1973 Oil Crisis: Three Crises in One—and the Lessons for Today. Testimonies & Speeches by Daniel Yergin, Columbia-SIPA, October 16. https://www.energypolicy.columbia.edu/ publications/the-1973-oil-crisis-three-crises-in-one-and-the-lessons-for-today/

Yılmaz, S. & Kalkan, D. K. (2017). Enerji Güvenliği Kavramı: 1973 Petrol Krizi Işığında Bir Tartışma. *ANKASAM Uluslararası Kriz ve Siyaset Araştırmaları Dergisi,* 1 (3), ss.169-199.

Chapter 4

Central Bank Digital Currencies (CBDC) as Catalysts for Financial Inclusion and Economic Expansion in Emerging Asian Economies

Akarshi Chopra
https://orcid.org/0009-0007-6388-2361
Christ University, India

Pankaj Dhaundiyal
https://orcid.org/0000-0002-4815-1647
Christ University, India

Abhinav Kataria
https://orcid.org/0009-0009-6362-0569
Christ University, India

ABSTRACT

This chapter examines the potential of Central Bank Digital Currencies (CBDCs) to enhance financial inclusion and economic growth in emerging economies. Unlike decentralized cryptocurrencies, CBDCs are government-backed digital currencies that offer secure and regulated alternatives to traditional money. The chapter explores how CBDCs can improve access to financial services, reduce transaction costs, and promote financial stability, particularly in countries with limited banking

DOI: 10.4018/979-8-3693-9765-7.ch004

infrastructure. It also discusses the challenges and risks associated with CBDCs, such as financial stability concerns and the displacement of commercial banks. Through case studies from China and India, the chapter highlights how well-designed CBDCs can act as a catalyst for inclusive economic development, while emphasising the need for robust regulatory frameworks for successful implementation.

1. INTRODUCTION

In recent years, Central Bank Digital Currencies (CBDCs) have emerged as a pivotal innovation in the global financial system. With the potential to redefine how money is used and circulated, CBDCs have garnered significant attention, particularly from central banks seeking to modernize monetary frameworks while addressing issues of financial inclusion and stability. Unlike cryptocurrencies, which operate independently of central authorities, CBDCs are government-issued digital currencies that are fully regulated and controlled by central banks. This distinction makes them an attractive option for policymakers who aim to harness the benefits of digital currencies while mitigating the risks associated with decentralized cryptocurrencies. Despite the growing interest in CBDCs, there remain significant gaps in the literature regarding their specific impact on financial inclusion and stability (Philippon, 2016; Kim & Kwon, 2019). Current research tends to highlight the opportunities that CBDCs provide without fully addressing the potential risks or outlining clear channels through which CBDCs influence financial inclusion and financial stability.

The purpose of this chapter is to examine the role of CBDCs in promoting financial inclusion and stability, with a particular focus on emerging economies. CBDCs have become a central point of discussion among central banks, especially in light of their potential to offer secure, efficient, and inclusive financial systems. The onset of the COVID-19 pandemic further underscored the importance of digital financial systems, as physical banking operations became more limited. CBDCs present a unique opportunity to address the limitations of traditional financial systems, particularly in underserved regions where access to banking services is constrained. By analyzing the potential of CBDCs, this chapter aims to clarify their role in transforming global financial systems and explore how they can foster financial inclusion while maintaining financial stability (Tronnier, 2020; Ozili, 2018).

CBDCs offer several advantages over traditional financial mechanisms. First, they provide an alternative to physical cash, which can be costly to produce and manage. By issuing digital currencies, central banks can reduce the costs associated with printing and distributing money. Moreover, CBDCs can streamline cross-border transactions, reducing the friction and time associated with international payments. This feature is particularly important in the global economy, where trade and investment flows depend on the efficient movement of capital across borders. Beyond cost and efficiency gains, CBDCs hold immense potential for increasing financial inclusion. In countries where financial infrastructure is limited, CBDCs could serve as a gateway for the unbanked population to access formal financial services (Tronnier, 2020).

Financial inclusion has long been a challenge, especially in developing economies where vast portions of the population remain excluded from the traditional banking system. This exclusion prevents individuals from participating fully in the economy, limiting their ability to save, invest, or engage in financial transactions. CBDCs can address this issue by providing a digital platform that allows individuals to access banking services without needing to rely on physical bank branches or costly intermediaries. By lowering the barriers to entry into the financial system, CBDCs can empower underserved populations and promote greater financial inclusion (Ozili, 2018).

Despite their potential benefits, CBDCs also raise concerns regarding financial stability. The introduction of a digital currency by a central bank could disrupt the traditional banking system by altering the dynamics of how money is distributed and managed. Commercial banks, which currently play a central role in the provision of credit and liquidity, could see their functions change if CBDCs are widely adopted. For instance, if individuals and businesses choose to hold their funds in CBDC accounts directly with the central bank, commercial banks could face a reduction in deposits, which might affect their ability to provide loans and manage liquidity (Kim et al., 2018). This shift could lead to unintended consequences, such as a destabilization of the banking sector if not managed properly. Additionally, central banks would need to develop new mechanisms to ensure that CBDCs do not exacerbate existing financial risks or introduce new ones. The regulatory framework surrounding CBDCs will play a crucial role in determining their impact on financial stability. Central banks must balance the benefits of CBDCs with the potential risks they pose to the banking system and broader financial markets. This includes developing policies that mitigate the risk of bank runs, ensure the security of digital currency systems, and prevent cyberattacks that could threaten the stability of the financial system (Carbó-Valverde & Sánchez, 2013). As central banks continue to explore the feasibility of CBDCs, they must also consider how these innovations will integrate with existing financial infrastructure and how they will affect the regulatory landscape.

This chapter aims to contribute to the existing literature by providing a comprehensive analysis of how CBDCs can promote financial inclusion and financial stability in emerging economies. By focusing solely on CBDCs, this chapter seeks to offer a clearer understanding of the opportunities and challenges presented by this particular digital financial innovation. It highlights the importance of thoughtful regulation and careful implementation to ensure that CBDCs can serve as a tool for enhancing financial inclusion without compromising the stability of the financial system. As CBDCs continue to gain traction among central banks worldwide, their role in shaping the future of financial systems, particularly in emerging economies, will be of paramount importance.

2. BACKGROUND

The advent of Central Bank Digital Currencies (CBDCs) has become a hub of controversy for policy-makers and academics, principally with respect to financial inclusion. Financial inclusion, which clients and underserved populations have been defined as having access to basic financial services at a reasonable cost, is still an important goal for governments. There are regions in the world where a traditional banking system does not exist, and CBDCs, as government- endorsed electronic currencies do have the ability to advance financial inclusion in such areas.

Many authors from the vast majority of literature point out that CBDCs have a positive impact on financial inclusion and address the problem of unbanked people with this form of digital currency. As stated by Ozili (2022b) Also adopt responsibility in conclusively performing certain functions, where for example, CBDCs would enhance financial inclusion by enabling only a few basic features or transactions that require no financial institution. Harnessing the proposition related to identifying ID systems is also useful in accessing formal financial services by the unbanked population. As stated previously about simplicity of supporting documents required, CBDCs have the required effect in including the vulnerable communities into the economy as transactions become more straightforward.

Scholars have looked into some of the particular design features of CBDCs which have potential to enhance financial inclusion. For instance, Beck (2020) points out that new delivery channels, products and technologies like mobile money and crowdfunding platforms can increase the access to financial services. He goes on to state that due to such innovations, which are also built into the frameworks of the CBDC, it is possible for more people to be "banked". This is particularly the case for developing economies which mobile money platforms have proven to be effective for widening the scope of financial inclusion. With the use of mobile wallets and other digital systems, the CBDCs could use such advantages and further build on them by decreasing the reliance on traditional banking systems (Beck, 2020).

The other factor in the ability of the CBDCs to foster financial inclusion has to do with the way existing systems will be interlinked with the current financial system. Schindler (2017) draws attention to the fact that CBDCS as out of many financial innovations are not ordinary technologies. Nonetheless, their use for these types of emerging financial products and types of financial services has received increased focus as they offer potential for disrupting the economies.

Although CBDCs show some potential avenues in augmenting the financial inclusion of the people, there are new risks that will come with CBDCS. The very contour of the banking industry could be upset with the introduction of CBDC. Ward and Rochemont (2019) flag a very real possibility of deposit substitution risks, where customers transfer their traditional deposits to CBDC wallets. Such an evolution might cause an outflow of deposits in commercial banks and will affect their capacity to lend and to maintain liquidity which does threaten the stability in the financial sector. Likewise, Kumhof and Noone (2018) concede with this perspective asserting that great CBDCs adoption might breed bank disintermediation as some duties vested with commercial banks could be handed to central banks. Some would argue that this may improve the delivery of banking services to the masses, however it presents liquidity risk issues together with funding issues of established banks which may have adverse implications on financial inclusion in the long run.

Another important consideration in the literature is the regulatory framework surrounding CBDCs. Lumpkin (2010) points out that financial innovation, while beneficial in some contexts, can also lead to financial crises if not properly regulated. To ensure that CBDCs promote financial inclusion without destabilizing the financial system, regulators must find a balance between allowing innovation to thrive and maintaining the safety and soundness of the financial ecosystem. Proper regulation of CBDCs, coupled with clear frameworks for their implementation, can ensure that the benefits of financial inclusion are realized without exacerbating financial risks.

A growing body of research also explores how CBDCs can complement existing financial inclusion efforts, particularly in addressing challenges in underbanked and unbanked communities. Ozili (2021a) highlights a bidirectional relationship between financial inclusion and financial innovation, suggesting that the introduction of innovative financial products can significantly close gaps in financial access. Kabir (2022) supports this claim, demonstrating that financial innovation, such as CBDCs, has the potential to bring unbanked populations into the formal financial sector. This is particularly significant in developing economies, where financial infrastructure is often lacking, and traditional banking services are inaccessible to large segments of the population. Moreover, the literature underscores the role of CBDCs in fostering long-term societal transformation. Salampasis and Mention (2018) argue that Fintech innovations, including CBDCs, have the potential to close the gap between unbanked, underbanked, and banked populations. These innovations, when properly designed, can have profound societal impacts, enabling individuals and small businesses to participate more fully in the economy. The decentralized nature of some digital financial systems, while potentially risky, also presents opportunities for broadening financial inclusion and reducing the reliance on traditional financial intermediaries (Ozili, 2022e).

In summary, the literature presents a compelling case for the potential of CBDCs to promote financial inclusion, especially in underserved regions. By reducing the barriers to accessing financial services and providing digital alternatives to traditional banking systems, CBDCs could play a crucial role in bringing unbanked populations into the formal financial sector. However, the design and implementation of CBDCs must be carefully managed to avoid unintended disruptions to financial stability, and appropriate regulatory frameworks must be put in place to mitigate these risks. As CBDCs continue to evolve, their role in promoting financial inclusion will depend largely on how effectively they are integrated into the broader financial ecosystem and how well they are regulated to ensure the safety and soundness of the financial system.

3. CENTRAL BANK DIGITAL CURRENCIES AND FINANCIAL INCLUSIONS

Central Bank Digital Currencies (CBDCs) have significant potential to advance financial inclusion, especially in emerging economies where a large portion of the population remains unbanked. By providing a direct digital financial service, CBDCs can bypass traditional financial intermediaries, thus reducing access barriers for underserved communities (Ozili, 2022b). Financial inclusion is a key objective for policymakers worldwide, as it allows individuals to participate in the formal financial system, gain access to savings and credit, and reduce their dependence on informal financial networks that often charge high fees and carry substantial risks. In this context, CBDCs represent a transformative tool, offering secure, government-backed digital currency that can reach unbanked populations without the prerequisites of conventional banking structures.

One major challenge to financial inclusion is the requirement for a traditional bank account, which necessitates extensive documentation, credit history, and sometimes substantial fees. For the unbanked population, particularly in low-income or remote areas, these requirements can be a formidable barrier. CBDCs, however, could operate independently of conventional bank accounts, allowing users to transact via digital wallets managed by central banks or authorized financial agents. This method significantly reduces entry requirements, enabling unbanked adults to hold and use digital currency with only a digital identification (ID), which can be relatively easy to obtain and free from cumbersome documentation requirements (Ozili, 2022b).

This unique digital ID serves as a gateway to financial inclusion, allowing users to access the CBDC system and perform transactions directly without a formal bank account. A CBDC designed with this approach can integrate with national digital ID systems, such as India's Aadhaar program, creating a streamlined and accessible entry point for financial services. Such IDs ensure that unbanked adults can securely access financial services without the need for multiple proofs of identity, which are often inaccessible for rural and marginalized populations. Thus, a digital ID combined with a CBDC wallet provides a direct, inclusive channel to participate in the financial system (Ozili, 2022b).

The structure of CBDC delivery also plays a crucial role in enhancing financial inclusion. As illustrated, CBDCs can be delivered in two ways: directly from the central bank to individuals or through financial institutions. Direct delivery to unbanked adults, represented by thick lines in Figure 1, bypasses the need for financial intermediaries. This approach reduces transaction costs and allows for easier access to funds, which is particularly valuable in underserved regions where banks are either scarce or charge high fees for account maintenance and transactions (Ward & Rochemont, 2019). For unbanked populations, this direct delivery model could offer a lifeline, enabling seamless transfers, payments, and access to essential financial services.

Alternatively, a CBDC can also be distributed to financial institutions, which can then transfer it to users, including unbanked adults, via existing banking apps or digital platforms, as shown by the dotted lines in Figure 1. This model leverages existing financial infrastructure and technology, which can be advantageous in more developed regions with higher digital penetration. However, this method may not have the same impact on financial inclusion as direct CBDC delivery, as it relies on intermediaries who might impose access restrictions or fees. Additionally, using intermediaries introduces the possibility of financial exclusion for those who cannot meet specific account or documentation requirements (Kumhof & Noone, 2018).

Another essential design consideration for a CBDC promoting financial inclusion is simplicity. Many unbanked individuals lack familiarity with complex financial products, so the CBDC interface must be user-friendly, intuitive, and accessible. Ideally, CBDC platforms should support only basic, essential functions such as storing funds, making payments, and receiving transfers without requiring users to understand advanced financial concepts. Additionally, multilingual support and accessibility features can enhance usability for populations with limited literacy or technological skills. Financial literacy programs could complement the CBDC rollout, educating users on its functionality and benefits, thereby empowering them to use digital financial services more confidently (Beck, 2020).

The development of CBDCs in countries like China and India has shown that digital currency can indeed reach unbanked populations. China's Digital Yuan, for instance, has been tested with simplified user interfaces and government-backed incentives, making it more appealing for unbanked individuals. The Reserve Bank of India's Digital Rupee pilot similarly underscores the value of integrating CBDCs with digital ID systems, which can simplify the onboarding process and provide secure access to financial services for rural and low-income communities (Kabir, 2022). These case studies reveal that when designed with financial inclusion in mind, CBDCs can successfully bridge the gap between traditional financial systems and underserved communities.

Cybersecurity and fraud protection are also vital in promoting trust and stability within CBDC systems. As digital currency transactions often take place on mobile platforms, they are vulnerable to cyber threats, which could disproportionately affect unbanked users who may lack digital literacy. A well-designed CBDC must prioritize security measures, including secure encryption protocols, two-factor authentication, and fraud detection mechanisms, to ensure that users feel confident in adopting digital currency (Carbó-Valverde & Sánchez, 2013). When users are assured of the safety of their funds, they are more likely to adopt digital financial services and integrate them into their daily lives.

4. CENTRAL BANK DIGITAL CURRENCIES AND FINANCIAL STABILITY

Central Bank Digital Currencies (CBDCs) are gaining global interest for their potential to enhance monetary policy effectiveness and strengthen financial stability. At their core, CBDCs serve as digital representations of fiat currency issued by central banks, and they have the potential to transform how individuals and businesses access money and conduct transactions. However, the implications of CBDCs for financial stability are complex and may include both stabilizing effects and disruptive risks, depending on their design and implementation. Two main hypotheses— the CBDC-stability hypothesis and the CBDC-disruption hypothesis—offer contrasting perspectives on the potential impacts of CBDCs on financial stability (BIS, 2021).

The CBDC-stability hypothesis posits that a well-designed CBDC issued by a central bank can support financial stability by bolstering central banks' core objectives, such as maintaining monetary and price stability. Proponents argue that central banks, as prudent custodians of the financial system, will design CBDCs to complement, rather than disrupt, the existing financial landscape. The Bank for International Settlements (BIS) (2021) suggests that central banks are unlikely to issue CBDCs if doing so would hinder their ability to meet core mandates, which include ensuring stable inflation, a reliable payment system, and overall financial stability. Therefore, the CBDC-stability hypothesis assumes that a CBDC, designed with these objectives in mind, will foster stability in the financial system rather than pose material risks (BIS, 2021).

One key aspect supporting this hypothesis is that CBDCs are generally intended to coexist with private forms of money, such as commercial bank deposits. Most CBDC models, particularly those targeting retail use, are designed to work harmoniously within the existing financial system, integrating seamlessly with existing payment infrastructures (Maniff, 2020). For instance, CBDCs are envisioned to complement rather than replace other forms of digital payments, providing an additional layer of security and trust by offering a central bank-backed option that could enhance public confidence in digital payments. Moreover, central banks are expected to allow sufficient time for financial institutions and individuals to adapt to CBDCs, ensuring that adoption occurs gradually and with minimal disruption to current systems (Bofinger & Haas, 2020). This measured approach to adoption is intended to mitigate any potential shocks that might otherwise destabilize the financial sector.

Additionally, a CBDC can contribute to financial stability by offering a safe asset that serves as a reliable store of value, especially during times of economic uncertainty. CBDCs, backed directly by central banks, could provide an alternative to bank deposits and cash, reducing reliance on less stable private sector financial products. This could enhance the public's trust in the financial system, as central banks provide a safety net for digital transactions. For instance, during periods of economic crisis or significant disruptions in the financial system, individuals might view CBDCs as a secure alternative, potentially reducing the likelihood of bank runs and other destabilizing events (Ward & Rochemont, 2019).

On the other hand, the CBDC-disruption hypothesis contends that CBDCs could introduce substantial risks to financial stability by fundamentally altering the financial ecosystem. According to this view, the adoption of CBDCs may disrupt traditional financial intermediation processes and challenge established business models of financial institutions (Allen et al., 2022). One primary concern is the risk of deposit substitution, where consumers might shift their deposits from commercial banks to CBDCs, leading to a reduction in bank deposits and posing liquidity risks. As bank deposits decrease, banks could face funding constraints, reducing their ability to extend credit, which might trigger a credit crunch. This shift could increase the vulnerability of banks to liquidity shocks and intensify the risks of a bank run, as depositors move funds from banks to CBDCs during periods of uncertainty (Bian et al., 2021).

The issue of bank disintermediation, or the weakening of banks' role as intermediaries in the financial system, is central to the CBDC-disruption hypothesis. Banks rely on deposits to fund lending activities; thus, a significant reduction in deposits could compromise their ability to lend, ultimately reducing credit availability in the economy (Kumhof & Noone, 2018). Without sufficient deposits, banks may struggle to maintain liquidity, and the resulting funding pressure could create a ripple effect, impacting not only the banks themselves but also businesses and households that depend on bank loans. In a worst-case scenario, this disintermediation could heighten systemic risk and precipitate broader financial instability (Ward & Rochemont, 2019).

The disruptive potential of CBDCs on financial stability largely depends on the scale of adoption and the specific design choices made by central banks. For instance, if CBDCs are widely adopted and designed in a way that closely resembles cash, they might substitute for a large volume of bank deposits. This could result in increased volatility within the banking sector, as banks might be forced to seek alternative sources of funding or reduce lending activities, negatively impacting credit availability in the economy (BIS, 2021). Conversely, if CBDCs are designed with constraints on holdings or limited interest rates, they may have a lesser impact on deposit substitution and financial disintermediation, thereby posing fewer risks to financial stability (Bofinger & Haas, 2020).

Another factor influencing the potential stability or disruption posed by CBDCs is the architecture and system underlying the currency. Some CBDCs are designed to operate within a two-tiered system, where the central bank issues the CBDC but commercial banks distribute it to end-users. This two-tier model allows banks to maintain their intermediation role and reduces the risk of direct competition between banks and the central bank. By maintaining a role for commercial banks in the distribution and management of CBDCs, the two-tier system helps to preserve financial stability while allowing for the benefits of digital currency (BIS, 2021).

Figure 1. Two-tier system helps distribution and management of CBDCs.

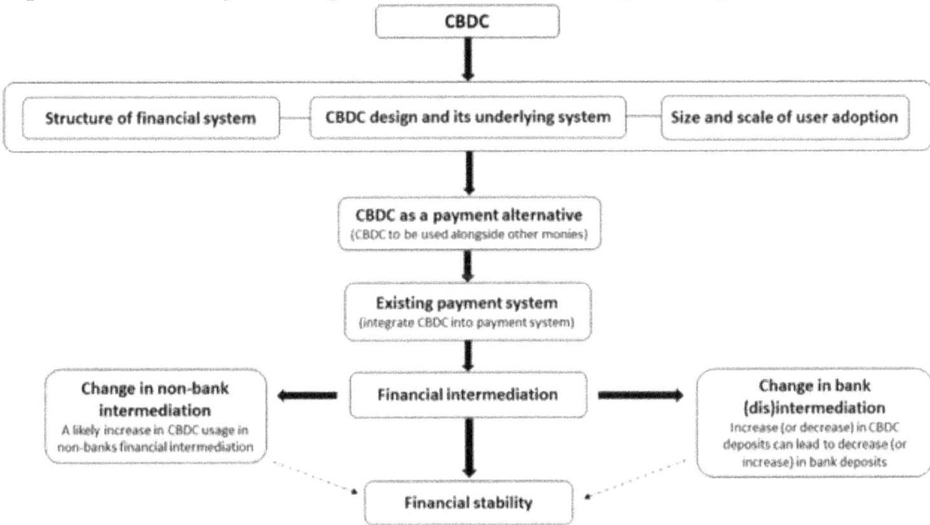

Table 1. Illustrates how CBDCs impact the financial system, focusing on their design, adoption and integration into payment systems. It highlights their effects on financial intermediation, including changes in bank and non-bank roles.

5. IMPACT OF CBDCs ON FINANCIAL INCLUSION IN ASIAN EMERGING ECONOMIES

Central Bank Digital Currencies (CBDCs) have emerged as a transformative financial innovation with the potential to reshape the landscape of financial inclusion, particularly in Asian emerging economies. Given the diverse socio-economic contexts of countries like India, China, Indonesia, and the Philippines, the implementation of CBDCs can play a pivotal role in enhancing access to financial services. This expanded analysis delves into the broader impacts of CBDCs, covering various aspects such as enhancing payment efficiency, supporting digital economies, reducing transaction costs, and fostering greater financial stability.

1. Enhancing Payment Efficiency and Reducing Transaction Costs

Table 1. illustrates the impact of CBDCs on Financial Inclusion Enhancing Payment Efficiency and Reducing Transaction Costs

Streamlining Domestic Payments	One of the most immediate impacts of CBDCs is the potential to streamline domestic payment systems. Traditional payment channels in many emerging economies are often slow, expensive, and unreliable, particularly for cross-border transactions. CBDCs can provide a more efficient alternative by enabling instant, low-cost digital payments directly between users. By eliminating intermediaries like payment processors and reducing the reliance on physical cash, CBDCs can lower transaction costs, making financial services more affordable for low-income populations
Facilitating Microtransactions	CBDCs can also facilitate microtransactions—small payments that are often impractical with traditional banking due to high fees. This capability is particularly beneficial for unbanked and underbanked individuals who rely on small-scale, daily transactions. With the availability of a digital currency that can be easily accessed and used without a bank account, individuals can engage in a wider range of economic activities, from paying for goods and services to saving small amounts regularly.
Promoting Digital Wallets and Mobile Payments	In countries with high mobile penetration but low banking penetration, CBDCs integrated with digital wallets and mobile payment platforms can significantly enhance financial access. For instance, in India, the Unified Payments Interface (UPI) system has already transformed the payment landscape. A CBDC integrated with such platforms could further increase the reach of digital payments, making it easier for people in remote areas to access financial services without needing a traditional bank account.

2. Supporting Digital Economies and E-commerce Growth

Table 2. illustrates the impact of CBDCs on Financial Inclusion in Supporting Digital Economies and E-commerce Growth

Boosting E-commerce and Digital Marketplaces	The rise of e-commerce in Asia has been exponential, driven by increasing internet penetration and mobile usage. However, many small businesses and consumers are still excluded from participating in the digital economy due to a lack of access to formal financial services. CBDCs can serve as a reliable and secure digital payment option, allowing unbanked individuals and micro-businesses to engage in online transactions. This can lead to a surge in e-commerce activities, enabling small businesses to expand their customer base beyond local markets and tap into regional and global markets.
Integration with Emerging Technologies	CBDCs can also be integrated with emerging technologies like blockchain, artificial intelligence (AI), and the Internet of Things (IoT), further enhancing their utility in the digital economy. For instance, smart contracts—automated, self-executing contracts—could use CBDCs for instant and conditional payments, reducing the need for manual intervention and minimizing the risk of fraud. This integration can enable innovative business models and services, such as pay-per-use schemes and microloans, which are particularly beneficial for small entrepreneurs and low-income consumers.

3. Promoting Greater Financial Stability

Table 3. illustrates the impact of CBDCs on Financial Inclusion in Promoting Greater Financial Stability

Reducing the Informal Economy	A significant challenge for many Asian emerging economies is the size of the informal economy, where transactions are predominantly conducted in cash, making it difficult for the government to track and regulate. By promoting the use of a digital currency, CBDCs can help reduce the reliance on cash, bringing more transactions into the formal economy. This increased transparency can enhance the government's ability to monitor economic activities, reduce tax evasion, and improve fiscal revenue.
Enhancing Monetary Policy Effectiveness	CBDCs offer central banks a new tool for implementing monetary policy. Unlike cash, which does not provide real-time data, CBDCs can offer valuable insights into spending patterns and economic activities. This data can enable central banks to make more informed decisions regarding interest rates, inflation control, and liquidity management. Additionally, CBDCs can facilitate more direct and efficient monetary interventions, such as distributing stimulus payments directly to individuals and businesses during economic downturns.
Mitigating the Risks of Stablecoins and Cryptocurrencies	The rapid rise of private cryptocurrencies and stablecoins poses challenges to the traditional financial system, particularly in terms of regulatory oversight and financial stability. In many emerging economies, the adoption of stablecoins as an alternative to local currencies could lead to a loss of monetary sovereignty. By introducing a CBDC, central banks can offer a safer and regulated digital alternative that mitigates the risks associated with private digital currencies while maintaining control over the monetary system.

Driving Financial Inclusion Through Technological Innovations

Table 4. illustrates the impact of CBDCs on Financial Inclusion in Driving Financial Inclusion Through Technological Innovations

Leveraging Offline Capabilities	One of the key features that can enhance the impact of CBDCs on financial inclusion is their ability to facilitate offline payments. In many rural and remote areas, internet connectivity is limited or non-existent, making digital financial services inaccessible. Offline-enabled CBDCs can allow individuals to conduct transactions without an active internet connection, significantly expanding the reach of digital financial services. This feature can be particularly impactful in countries like Indonesia and the Philippines, where a significant portion of the population lives in remote, underbanked regions.
Utilizing Digital Identification Systems	Many Asian countries have implemented or are in the process of developing digital identification systems, such as India's Aadhaar. Integrating CBDCs with these digital ID systems can simplify the onboarding process for individuals who do not have traditional identification documents, enabling them to access financial services easily. This integration can also enhance the security of transactions, reduce fraud, and ensure that financial services are delivered to the intended recipients, particularly in government welfare programs.
Encouraging Savings and Investment	CBDCs can also promote financial inclusion by encouraging savings and investment among low-income individuals. By providing a secure and easily accessible digital platform, CBDCs can help people save money and accumulate wealth over time. Central banks could also introduce features like interest-bearing CBDC accounts, offering incentives for individuals to save their digital currency. This could be a game-changer for populations that have limited access to formal savings products, helping them build financial resilience.

Potential Risks and Challenges

Table 5. illustrates the impact of CBDCs on Financial Inclusion showing Potential Risks and Challenges

Risk of Disintermediation	One of the main concerns surrounding the implementation of CBDCs is the potential disintermediation of commercial banks. If individuals prefer to hold CBDCs rather than deposit their money in bank accounts, it could lead to a reduction in bank deposits, limiting banks' ability to lend and impacting overall financial stability. To address this, central banks need to design CBDCs in a way that complements existing banking services rather than competes with them, possibly by setting limits on CBDC holdings for individuals or businesses.
Privacy and Data Security Concerns	The digital nature of CBDCs raises significant concerns about data privacy and security. Unlike cash transactions, digital transactions can be easily tracked, potentially compromising user privacy. Ensuring robust data protection measures and maintaining a balance between transparency and privacy will be critical to gaining public trust and encouraging widespread adoption of CBDCs.
Regulatory and Legal Frameworks	The successful deployment of CBDCs requires a comprehensive regulatory and legal framework that addresses issues such as cybersecurity, consumer protection, anti-money laundering (AML), and countering the financing of terrorism (CFT). Policymakers must develop clear guidelines that regulate the use of CBDCs, protect consumers, and ensure the stability of the financial system.

6. NAVIGATING THE RISKS AND CHALLENGES OF CBDC ADOPTION: POLICY RECOMMENDATION

The introduction of Central Bank Digital Currencies (CBDCs) offers significant potential benefits for enhancing financial inclusion, improving payment systems, and modernizing monetary policy. However, these benefits come with substantial risks and challenges, particularly concerning financial stability, the traditional banking system, monetary policy effectiveness, and issues surrounding cybersecurity and privacy. To ensure the successful adoption of CBDCs, it is essential to understand and address these risks through comprehensive policy measures.

1. Financial Stability and Bank Disintermediation

One of the critical concerns with CBDC implementation is the risk of bank disintermediation. If CBDCs become a preferred store of value, there is a possibility of significant shifts in deposits from commercial banks to CBDC accounts at central banks, especially during economic uncertainty. This phenomenon can lead to:

Reduced Bank Lending Capacity: The migration of deposits to CBDCs would limit the funding available for banks, reducing their ability to provide loans and finance economic activities, potentially stalling growth.

Increased Risk of Financial Instability: With fewer deposits, commercial banks may face liquidity challenges, increasing the likelihood of bank runs or failures. This scenario can exacerbate financial instability, shaking the confidence of investors and the public.

Centralization of Credit Allocation: As more funds move to CBDC accounts, central banks might play a more prominent role in credit allocation, leading to concerns about efficiency and the risk of political interference in credit decisions.

2. Monetary Policy Challenges

The widespread adoption of CBDCs could disrupt existing monetary policy mechanisms. A shift of a significant portion of the money supply into CBDCs could complicate the central bank's control over interest rates and liquidity, impacting the overall effectiveness of traditional monetary policies.

Interest Rate Distortions: Setting interest rates on CBDCs introduces a new tool in the monetary policy arsenal. However, if not carefully managed, this could distort market interest rates, influencing the broader financial market and potentially destabilizing the economy.

Liquidity Management Issues: The preference for CBDCs over cash and traditional bank deposits could reduce the predictability of the money supply, making it harder for central banks to manage liquidity through conventional tools like open market operations.

3. Cybersecurity, Privacy, and Regulatory Challenges

The digital nature of CBDCs makes them vulnerable to cybersecurity threats and raises concerns about user privacy. Ensuring robust security and a balanced approach to privacy is essential for gaining public trust and ensuring the smooth operation of CBDC systems.

Cybersecurity Risks: The centralization of digital currency systems creates a high-value target for cybercriminals. Successful attacks could disrupt financial systems, leading to significant economic and reputational damage.

Privacy Concerns: Striking a balance between user privacy and regulatory requirements is a key challenge. Full anonymity might facilitate illegal activities like money laundering, while extensive monitoring could deter adoption due to privacy concerns.

Regulatory Uncertainty: The lack of clear regulatory frameworks for CBDCs can create confusion about their issuance, use, and oversight, making it challenging to enforce compliance with existing financial regulations.

4. Additional Considerations for CBDC Adoption

While CBDCs have the potential to enhance financial inclusion, their impact heavily depends on how they are designed and implemented. Key considerations include:

Digital Divide: Unequal access to digital infrastructure and technology could limit the benefits of CBDCs, particularly in rural and underserved areas, where financial inclusion is most needed.

Cross-Border Complexity: Utilizing CBDCs for international transactions involves navigating issues related to exchange rates, capital flows, and regulatory differences, making coordination and standardization crucial.

Policy Recommendations

To navigate the risks and challenges associated with CBDC adoption effectively, the following policy measures should be considered:

Policies to Mitigate Financial Stability Risks:

Unattractive Interest Rates on CBDC Holdings: Set lower interest rates on CBDC accounts compared to traditional bank deposits to reduce the appeal of storing large sums in CBDC accounts, thus limiting potential deposit outflows from commercial banks.

Quantity Ceilings on CBDC Holdings: Impose caps on the amount of CBDC that individuals and businesses can hold. This would directly limit the extent of funds that could be transferred from commercial banks to CBDC accounts, helping to maintain bank liquidity.

Restrict Direct Convertibility: Implement limits on the direct conversion of bank deposits into CBDCs to slow down the potential outflow of funds from commercial banks. This approach can prevent sudden liquidity shocks but may affect the usability of CBDCs.

Two-Tiered Distribution Model: Utilize a two-tiered system where commercial banks act as intermediaries for CBDC distribution. This model helps maintain the traditional role of banks in the financial ecosystem and reduces the risk of disintermediation.

Policies to Address Monetary Policy Challenges:

Strategic Interest Rate Management: Carefully calibrate the interest rates on CBDCs to balance the need for attractiveness with the potential impact on bank deposits and overall financial stability. This ensures that CBDCs support monetary policy without disrupting the banking system.

Adaptation of Quantitative Tools: Enhance existing monetary policy tools, such as quantitative easing or tightening, to incorporate CBDCs into the central bank's liquidity management strategies, ensuring effective control over the money supply.

Policies for Cybersecurity and Privacy:

Invest in Robust Cybersecurity Infrastructure: Central banks should prioritize investments in advanced cybersecurity measures, including encryption, real-time monitoring, and multi-layered defense mechanisms to protect CBDC systems from cyber threats and ensure operational resilience.

Implement Privacy-Enhancing Technologies: Design CBDCs with features that support privacy while complying with regulatory requirements. For example, tiered anonymity can allow smaller transactions to be more private, while larger transactions undergo stricter verification processes.

Establish a Clear Regulatory Framework: Develop comprehensive regulations for CBDC issuance, usage, and oversight, aligned with international standards. This will provide clarity, ensure compliance, and facilitate cross-border CBDC transactions.

Policies for Enhancing Financial Inclusion:

Promote Digital Literacy and Infrastructure Development: Governments and central banks should work together to improve access to digital infrastructure and promote digital literacy, especially in rural and underserved areas, to maximize the financial inclusion benefits of CBDCs.

Facilitate International Coordination: Collaborate with other countries and international regulatory bodies to establish common standards and frameworks for cross-border CBDC transactions, addressing issues related to exchange rates and capital flows

7. BENEFITS AND CHALLENGES OF DIGITAL CURRENCY - FOCUSING ON CENTRAL BANK DIGITAL CURRENCIES

Over the past decade, rapid technological advancements, particularly the widespread use of the internet, have prompted a shift from cash and paper-based transactions to digital alternatives (Kraiwanit and Limsakul, 2022). Digital currencies have emerged as part of these disruptive innovations. Before the advent of Central Bank Digital Currencies (CBDCs), Bitcoin was the primary digital currency, operating without a centralized issuer (CPMI, 2015; Sankar, 2021). This decentralized nature allowed for swift, cost-effective, and efficient daily transactions (CPMI, 2015; Kraiwanit and Limsakul, 2022). However, the faceless nature of trading on Distributed Ledger Technology (DLT) platforms and the absence of sovereign oversight can lead to issues like invalid user agreements, money laundering, terrorism financing, and a lack of consumer trust (Latimer and Duffy, 2019). To address these flaws, many central banks are exploring the development of CBDCs, which would be under their regulation (Sankar, 2021; Boar et al., 2020).

CBDCs offer several advantages over other digital payment systems. They enable users to conduct both domestic and international transactions in real time and at lower costs, bypassing interbank settlements and minimizing payment delays (Sankar, 2021). This enhances the overall efficiency of the payment ecosystem (Ward and Rochemont, 2019). Additionally, being backed by fiat currencies makes CBDCs less susceptible to price volatility and operational disruptions (BIS, 2020; Sankar, 2021). CBDCs also allow central banks to monitor all transactions by individuals and businesses, both domestically and internationally (Cunha et al., 2021; Ojha, 2022). This capability helps reduce activities such as money laundering, terrorism financing, and tax evasion. Furthermore, offering interest-bearing CBDC accounts can help central banks mitigate the zero lower bound issue during economic downturns (Barontini and Holden, 2019; Riksbank, 2019). CBDCs have the potential to lower operational, regulatory, and political costs, thus promoting financial inclusion and contributing to GDP growth (Cunha et al., 2021).

While digital currencies operate on a global, internet-based system, their widespread use could potentially destabilize currency markets, presenting regulatory challenges for national authorities tasked with managing monetary and financial systems (Latimer and Duffy, 2019). The absence of regulatory frameworks for digital currencies like CBDCs may hinder the growth of currency markets (Bissessar, 2016). Therefore, increased regulation by technology-driven institutions is necessary to support the effective implementation of these digital assets (Bissessar, 2016).

A comparison of various CBDC projects across the globe reveals diverse approaches to their development, focusing on different ledger technologies and accessibility models. For instance, Uruguay's e-Peso uses a non-DLT retail token format in its pilot phase, while Saudi Arabia's Aber employs DLT for wholesale transactions using an account-based system. Other examples include Canada's Jasper, which utilizes DLT for both wholesale accounts and token-based transactions, and China's e-CNY, which operates with a non-DLT retail account system. Notable launched CBDCs include the Bahamas' Sand Dollar and Nigeria's e-Naira, both using DLT for retail purposes.

The shift to CBDCs could lead to liquidity issues and operational challenges for commercial banks, particularly if depositors move their funds to CBDC accounts during economic downturns (Ward and Rochemont, 2019; Mukherjee, 2022). To mitigate potential negative impacts on the economy, it is essential for public and private entities to collaborate in the design of CBDCs and to consider imposing restrictions on lending capabilities associated with CBDC accounts (BIS, 2021; Ward and Rochemont, 2019; Allen et al., 2020). These limitations may vary based on the specific structure, technology, and economic conditions of the countries implementing CBDCs (Foster et al., 2021).

Additional Benefits -

Combating Shadow Economies: CBDCs can reduce the prevalence of shadow economies by enabling governments to track all digital transactions, making it harder for illegal activities to go undetected.

Customized Economic Stimulus: Governments can use CBDCs to deploy direct, targeted economic relief or subsidies to specific demographic groups or regions, ensuring more equitable distribution of resources.

Enhanced Payment Ecosystems for Small Businesses: By reducing transaction fees and improving payment processing times, CBDCs can empower micro and small enterprises, especially in underserved areas.

Streamlining Public Sector Payments: CBDCs can facilitate faster disbursement of government benefits, pensions, and wages, eliminating inefficiencies associated with intermediaries.

Tourism-Friendly Currency: CBDCs can simplify currency exchange for international tourists by enabling them to use CBDCs directly in foreign countries, bypassing traditional currency exchange processes.

Integration with Emerging Technologies: CBDCs can leverage emerging technologies like IoT (Internet of Things) to enable micropayments in real time, such as toll payments or utility billing.

Support for Aging Populations: CBDCs can simplify financial management for aging populations by offering user-friendly platforms that integrate with public health and pension systems.

Rural and Remote Area Development: In areas with limited banking infrastructure, CBDCs can bridge the gap by providing digital financial services, promoting economic activity, and fostering growth.

Efficient Tax Collection: With all transactions recorded on a centralized system, CBDCs can help governments implement real-time tax collection, reducing tax evasion and improving public revenue streams.

Promoting Global Monetary Cooperation: CBDCs could pave the way for regional or global currency agreements, potentially reducing the dominance of major currencies like the US dollar.

Additional Challenges -

Privacy Concerns: CBDCs may lead to heightened fears of surveillance as governments gain the ability to monitor individual financial activities in real time, potentially infringing on citizens' privacy rights.

Technological Dependence and Vulnerability: Over-reliance on digital infrastructure could make economies vulnerable to systemic risks, such as cyberattacks, system outages, or data breaches.

Resistance from Financial Institutions: Commercial banks and financial intermediaries may resist CBDC adoption, perceiving it as a threat to their traditional business models.

Impact on Informal Economies: Many developing countries rely on informal economies, and the transition to CBDCs could marginalized communities dependent on cash transactions.

Legal and Jurisdictional Challenges: Different countries may face conflicts regarding the legal status, regulation, and cross-border application of CBDCs, complicating their global implementation.

Technological Exclusion Risks: In countries with low digital literacy or inadequate access to technology, the widespread use of CBDCs may exacerbate inequalities, leaving certain populations behind.

Economic Displacement Risks: The shift to CBDCs may disrupt traditional financial sector employment, requiring large-scale reskilling efforts for workers in obsolete roles.

Dependency on Central Banks: Widespread adoption of CBDCs may centralize financial power in central banks, increasing systemic risks if these institutions face governance or operational challenges.

Potential for Misuse: Governments could exploit CBDCs for political or economic purposes, such as freezing accounts of dissenters or using them as tools for financial repression.

Environmental Concerns: While CBDCs are often viewed as more energy-efficient than cryptocurrencies, large-scale operations may still have a significant carbon footprint if not designed with sustainability in mind.

8. AN OVERVIEW OF DIGITAL RUPEE - INDIA

The introduction of Central Bank Digital Currency (CBDC) in India, particularly the digital rupee, represents a significant step toward modernizing the financial system, with the Reserve Bank of India (RBI) leading its development to enhance financial inclusion, streamline transactions, and reduce reliance on physical cash.

Utilizing blockchain technology for transparency and immutability, the digital rupee operates under the RBI's oversight, ensuring each transaction is securely recorded and verified. Key benefits of the digital rupee include its potential to provide digital financial services to India's unbanked population, thereby improving financial inclusion. Additionally, it promises cost efficiency by reducing the expenses related to printing, handling, and transporting physical currency, while also lowering transaction fees. The digital currency can enhance the transmission of monetary policy, allowing for more precise economic control, and its use of blockchain technology increases security and transparency, reducing the risks of fraud and counterfeiting. However, challenges remain, particularly around cybersecurity and privacy concerns, given the increased risks associated with digital transactions. The **Digital Personal Data Protection (DPDP) Act, 2023** governs the handling of personal data, ensuring compliance with stringent data protection regulations to maintain user trust. Implementing a CBDC also requires a robust regulatory framework to meet anti-money laundering (AML) and know-your-customer (KYC) standards, with the RBI playing a critical role in issuing and regulating the digital rupee to maintain monetary stability and prevent illicit activities. Another major issue is the potential impact on commercial banks, as users might prefer transferring funds directly to digital wallets, which could reduce deposit retention and affect banks' liquidity and operational stability. Furthermore, the transition to a digital currency system faces obstacles related to digital literacy and infrastructure, particularly in rural areas where familiarity with digital payment methods and access to necessary technology may be limited. India's approach to CBDC development has been informed by global initiatives, drawing lessons from countries like China, which has advanced its digital Yuan through extensive trials, and from the European Union, where discussions around the digital euro focus on privacy and security. By examining these international experiences, India aims to craft a comprehensive CBDC policy tailored to its unique economic environment. The RBI has initiated pilot projects and feasibility studies to assess the digital rupee's deployment, focusing on addressing technical challenges, regulatory compliance, and cybersecurity issues. Ongoing research aims to align the digital rupee with India's financial inclusion goals, enhance payment system efficiency, and ensure financial stability. As development continues, the digital rupee is expected to revolutionize transaction methods and become a cornerstone of India's digital economy. Despite the promising benefits, the successful implementation of the digital rupee will require overcoming significant challenges, particularly in cybersecurity, regulation, and improving digital literacy, making the ongoing research and stakeholder consultations by the RBI crucial for shaping a secure and effective CBDC ecosystem in India.

Comparison with Global CBDC Initiatives: India's approach to CBDC has drawn from the experiences of countries like China, which has advanced its digital Yuan through extensive trials. Similarly, discussions around the digital euro in the European Union focus on privacy and security concerns. In contrast, Sweden's largely cashless society has shaped its strategy for adopting a digital currency. By studying the frameworks and regulatory practices of these nations, India aims to develop a comprehensive and adaptable CBDC policy tailored to its unique economic environment.

Current Status and Future Prospects: The RBI has initiated pilot projects and feasibility studies to assess the deployment of the digital rupee. The focus remains on addressing technical challenges, regulatory compliance, and cybersecurity issues to ensure a smooth rollout. The ongoing research aims to align the digital rupee with India's broader financial inclusion objectives, enhance payment system efficiency, and maintain financial stability. As the development progresses, the digital rupee is expected to revolutionize transaction methods, potentially becoming a cornerstone of India's digital economy.

In summary, while the digital rupee offers promising benefits such as increased financial inclusion, reduced transaction costs, and enhanced transparency, its successful implementation will depend on overcoming significant challenges related to cybersecurity, regulation, and digital literacy. The RBI's continued research and stakeholder consultations will play a pivotal role in shaping a secure and effective CBDC ecosystem in India.

9. COMPARATIVE STUDY OF CBDC POLICY AND STRUCTURE

Table 6. illustrates a comparative study on CBDCs in various economies in regards with its structure and policy

Country	Objective	Features	Challenges	Sources
India	Aims for financial inclusion and modernization	Utilizes a two-tier structure, user-friendly interface, supports offline transactions	Issues with technological infrastructure, privacy, security, and rural adoption	Alaeddin et al. (2018), Al-Laham et al. (2009), Kharpal (2022)
China	Speed up the transition to a cashless society and strengthen control	Extensive pilot testing, centralized setup, accessible through commercial banks	Concerns over privacy, surveillance, the impact on banks, and technological risks	Allen et al. (2020), Shahzad et al. (2018)
European Union	Focus on data protection, security, and system compatibility	Emphasizes data privacy, compatibility with existing systems, and universal accessibility	Challenges with regulatory compliance, balancing innovation with stability, and cross-border issues	BIS (2020), Barontini and Holden (2019), So ¨ilen and Benhayoun (2022)
Sweden	Reducing reliance on cash, enhancing payment efficiency	Rapid shift towards a cashless system, interest-bearing e-krona, improved payment systems, central role of Riksbank	Issues with monetary policy, impact on commercial banks, digital divide, and readiness in rural areas	BIS (2021), Riksbank (2019), Gim enez and Tamaj on (2019)
USA	Improving payment processes and increasing financial inclusion	Multi-tier framework, partnerships with existing financial institutions	Regulatory challenges, privacy issues, and integration with traditional banking	Boar et al. (2020), Kumar and Ayodeji (2022a, 2022b), Shareef et al. (2011)
Japan	Maintain financial stability and improve payment efficiency	Collaboration with the private sector, integration with current payment systems	Regulatory concerns, public trust issues, and technological risks	Kumar and Ayodeji (2022a, 2022b), Tsai et al. (2019) BIS (2021), Shareef et al. (2011)
Canada	Modernize the payment system and test new technologies	Partners with financial institutions, emphasis on blockchain and DLT (Distributed Ledger Technology)	Concerns about privacy, security, regulatory compliance, and system integration	Chong et al. (2010), Tsai et al. (2019)

continued on following page

Table 6. Continued

Country	Objective	Features	Challenges	Sources
Singapore	Boost financial inclusiveness and foster innovation	Cooperative approach with the private sector, integration with existing payment infrastructure	Regulatory hurdles, cybersecurity threats, and challenges in public awareness and acceptance	Chong et al. (2010), Tsai et al. (2019)
Australia	Encourage innovation and enhance cross-border payments	Stakeholder consultations, focus on real-time payment solutions	Issues related to privacy, technological risks, and meeting regulatory standards	Foster et al. (2021), Latimer and Duffy (2019)

Central Bank Digital Currencies (CBDCs) are being explored and implemented by various countries to address unique economic, social, and financial goals. In India, the primary objective is financial inclusion and modernization of payment systems. India's CBDC employs a two-tier structure with a user-friendly interface and offline transaction support, catering to areas with limited internet connectivity. However, challenges such as underdeveloped technological infrastructure, privacy concerns, security vulnerabilities, and slow rural adoption remain significant obstacles to its success (Alaeddin et al., 2018; Al-Laham et al., 2009; Kharpal, 2022).

China's CBDC, on the other hand, aims to accelerate the transition to a cashless society and strengthen state control over financial systems. With extensive pilot testing, a centralized framework, and accessibility through commercial banks, China's CBDC is poised for widespread adoption. Yet, privacy concerns, potential surveillance, risks to traditional banking, and technological vulnerabilities pose significant risks (Allen et al., 2020; Shahzad et al., 2018).

The European Union (EU) focuses on data protection, system security, and compatibility with existing financial systems. Its CBDC initiative emphasizes robust data privacy, universal accessibility, and seamless integration with current financial frameworks. Nevertheless, challenges such as regulatory compliance, balancing innovation with economic stability, and cross-border complexities must be addressed (BIS, 2020; Barontini and Holden, 2019; Söilen and Benhayoun, 2022).

In Sweden, the rapid shift towards a cashless society has driven the development of the e-krona. This CBDC supports interest-bearing mechanisms, improved payment systems, and relies on the Riksbank's central role. However, issues such as the potential impact on monetary policy, challenges to commercial banks, the digital divide, and readiness in rural areas require significant attention (BIS, 2021; Riksbank, 2019; Giménez and Tamajón, 2019).

The United States focuses on improving payment processes and enhancing financial inclusion. Its CBDC framework is multi-tiered, collaborating with existing financial institutions to ensure seamless integration. Despite its promise, the initiative faces regulatory barriers, privacy concerns, and challenges in integrating CBDC with traditional banking systems (Boar et al., 2020; Kumar and Ayodeji, 2022a, 2022b; Shareef et al., 2011).

Japan's CBDC aims to maintain financial stability while improving payment efficiency. It involves collaboration with the private sector and integration with existing payment infrastructures. However, regulatory concerns, public trust issues, and technological risks remain key challenges (Kumar and Ayodeji, 2022a, 2022b; Tsai et al., 2019; BIS, 2021; Shareef et al., 2011).

Canada seeks to modernize its payment systems and test innovative technologies through its CBDC efforts. By partnering with financial institutions and leveraging blockchain and Distributed Ledger Technology (DLT), Canada aims to enhance its financial systems. Nonetheless, concerns regarding privacy, security, regulatory compliance, and system integration need to be addressed for successful implementation (Chong et al., 2010; Tsai et al., 2019).

Singapore Boost financial inclusiveness and foster innovation Cooperative approach with the private sector, integration with existing payment infrastructure Regulatory hurdles, cybersecurity threats, and challenges in public awareness and acceptance Chong et al. (2010), Tsai et al. (2019) Australia Encourage innovation and enhance cross-border payments Stakeholder consultations, focus on real-time payment solutions Issues related to privacy, technological risks, and meeting regulatory standards Foster et al. (2021), Latimer and Duffy (2019) do the same for this as well

Singapore and Australia are exploring Central Bank Digital Currencies (CBDCs) with distinct objectives and strategies, yet face common and unique challenges in their implementation. Singapore's primary goal is to boost financial inclusiveness and foster innovation within its financial systems. The country adopts a cooperative approach with the private sector and integrates CBDCs into its existing payment infrastructure. However, significant hurdles include regulatory challenges, cybersecurity threats, and difficulties in raising public awareness and ensuring acceptance of the new digital currency (Chong et al., 2010; Tsai et al., 2019).

Australia, on the other hand, aims to encourage financial innovation and improve cross-border payment efficiency through its CBDC initiatives. The country focuses on real-time payment solutions and conducts extensive stakeholder consultations to design effective systems. Despite these efforts, issues such as privacy concerns, technological risks, and the need to meet stringent regulatory standards pose significant challenges to Australia's CBDC development (Foster et al., 2021; Latimer and Duffy, 2019).

In conclusion, while Singapore emphasizes financial inclusiveness and private-sector collaboration, and Australia prioritizes innovation and cross-border payment efficiency, both nations must address critical concerns such as regulatory compliance, cybersecurity, and public adoption. Their tailored approaches reflect their unique priorities and underline the importance of overcoming these challenges for successful CBDC implementation.

10. IMPACT OF CENTRAL BANK DIGITAL CURRENCIES ON MONETARY POLICY TRANSMISSION AND MACROECONOMIC STABILITY

The introduction of a CBDC can influence how traditional monetary policies impact the economy. By adjusting the nominal interest rate of a CBDC, central banks can alter the spread between the CBDC's interest rate and the domestic nominal interest rate. This adjustment affects households' asset portfolios, influencing their preferences between holding cash, CBDCs, domestic bonds, and foreign assets, ultimately impacting overall consumption, current accounts, and final economic output. This dynamic remains valid even when external shocks occur. Moreover, adjusting the CBDC's interest rate in response to exchange rate risks can enhance macroeconomic interlinkages between countries. The study suggests that traditional monetary policy and CBDC-driven monetary policy can complement each other effectively. For instance, during economic overheating, combining traditional price-based policies with CBDC-driven policies can help mitigate potential economic booms or busts better than using only traditional methods. The findings of Barrdear and Kumhof (2022) support this notion, proposing that a CBDC could act as an additional policy tool to smoothen business cycles, although this is conditional on the substitutability between bank deposits and CBDCs. Interestingly, the results of this study suggest that these dynamics hold even without the involvement of traditional banking intermediaries. Furthermore, the analysis reveals that households are inclined to hold more CBDC assets if these assets offer higher liquidity, despite potential storage costs associated with cash. This behavior is illustrated through a dynamic model showing how households adjust their holdings between cash and CBDC based on liquidity preferences. The conclusions drawn indicate that combining price-based and quantity-based monetary policies involving CBDCs can reduce macroeconomic volatility more effectively than traditional approaches alone. The central bank, by managing the issuance and interest rates of CBDCs, can influence household asset allocations and indirectly impact consumption patterns, current account balances, and real exchange rates. However, the study notes that if CBDCs were issued with variable interest rates, they could potentially help central banks bypass the constraints of the zero lower bound on nominal interest rates. Unlike cash, which typically has a zero interest rate, a CBDC with a negative interest rate could incentivize people to hold digital currencies over cash or other financial assets in scenarios where traditional monetary policies are ineffective due to zero nominal rates. The findings suggest a new avenue for central banks to enhance their policy effectiveness, particularly in the absence of cash in the monetary system. However, further research is needed to explore the full implications of this approach, especially in scenarios where traditional assets reach zero or near-zero interest rates.

11. CONCLUSION

The exploration of Central Bank Digital Currencies (CBDCs) as a transformative financial innovation underscores their potential to significantly influence financial inclusion and stability, particularly in emerging economies. This chapter has delved into the multifaceted role of CBDCs in the modern financial landscape, highlighting both their promise and the challenges that must be navigated for their successful implementation. As the global economy continues to digitize, central banks are increasingly considering the adoption of CBDCs as a means to modernize monetary systems, enhance financial accessibility, and address the structural inefficiencies present in traditional banking systems.

Promoting Financial Inclusion

Financial inclusion remains a critical challenge, especially in developing countries where a substantial portion of the population lacks access to formal banking services. Traditional banking infrastructure often fails to reach remote and underserved areas, leaving millions unbanked and limiting their economic participation. CBDCs offer a viable solution by providing a direct, government-backed digital platform that reduces reliance on physical bank branches and expensive financial intermediaries. By facilitating access to digital financial services through mobile wallets or digital identification systems, CBDCs can empower unbanked individuals to engage in the formal economy, make secure payments, save funds, and access credit. The integration of CBDCs with national digital ID systems, such as India's Aadhaar, exemplifies how streamlined digital identity verification can eliminate barriers to financial access, making it easier for individuals to open and manage digital wallets without extensive documentation requirements.

The potential of CBDCs to enhance financial inclusion is further amplified by their capacity to simplify transaction processes and lower associated costs. By bypassing traditional financial intermediaries, CBDCs can reduce transaction fees, making financial services more affordable for low-income users. Moreover, CBDCs can leverage existing digital infrastructure, such as mobile money platforms, to expand access to financial services. This approach is particularly effective in regions where mobile penetration is high, but banking services are scarce. By integrating with mobile networks, CBDCs can extend their reach to millions of unbanked individuals, enabling them to participate in the digital economy.

Enhancing Financial Stability

While the primary appeal of CBDCs lies in their potential to boost financial inclusion, their introduction also raises important questions about financial stability. One of the central concerns is the risk of disintermediation, where individuals and businesses may prefer holding CBDC accounts directly with central banks rather than traditional deposits with commercial banks. This shift could lead to a significant outflow of deposits from commercial banks, undermining their capacity to provide credit and manage liquidity, which are critical functions for economic stability. As the literature suggests, the large-scale adoption of CBDCs could alter the dynamics of the banking sector, potentially destabilizing the financial system if not carefully managed.

To mitigate these risks, central banks must design CBDCs with features that complement rather than compete with existing financial services. A tiered distribution model, where CBDCs are delivered through licensed financial institutions rather than directly by the central bank, could help maintain the traditional role of commercial banks in credit provision while still expanding access to digital financial services. Furthermore, implementing interest-bearing CBDCs could disincentivize users from hoarding digital currency and encourage spending or investment, thereby reducing the risk of destabilizing traditional deposit mechanisms.

Regulatory and Security Considerations

The successful implementation of CBDCs hinges on a robust regulatory framework that can balance innovation with financial stability. The experiences of early adopters like China and India underscore the need for comprehensive policies that address the potential risks associated with digital currencies. Regulatory oversight must ensure that CBDCs are designed with safeguards against financial crimes, such as money laundering and fraud, which could undermine trust in the new system. Effective regulation will also need to address privacy concerns, ensuring that while CBDCs provide enhanced financial oversight capabilities, they do not infringe on users' rights to privacy.

Cybersecurity remains another critical consideration. Given the digital nature of CBDCs, they are inherently vulnerable to cyber threats, including hacking, data breaches, and other forms of digital fraud. A secure CBDC system must incorporate advanced encryption, two-factor authentication, and continuous monitoring to detect and prevent unauthorized transactions. These measures are essential to build user confidence and ensure the widespread adoption of CBDCs, particularly among populations that may be wary of digital financial systems due to concerns about security and privacy.

Case Studies and Practical Insights

The chapter also examined case studies from India, two of the most prominent countries piloting CBDCs, to illustrate the practical implications of digital currency adoption. India's pilot of the Digital Rupee highlights the importance of integrating CBDCs with existing digital ID systems to streamline onboarding and enhance accessibility. These case studies provide valuable insights into the potential pathways for CBDC implementation in other emerging economies. They also underscore the importance of designing CBDCs with features tailored to local contexts, such as user-friendly interfaces, multilingual support, and integration with existing digital payment ecosystems.

Balancing Innovation with Prudence

The promise of CBDCs lies in their ability to modernize the financial system, make payments more efficient, and provide a secure digital alternative to physical cash. However, central banks must approach this innovation with caution, considering the profound implications it could have on the existing financial infrastructure. The transition to a CBDC-based system must be gradual and carefully managed, allowing central banks to address any unforeseen challenges that arise. Pilot programs, phased rollouts, and comprehensive stakeholder engagement will be essential strategies in ensuring a smooth and stable transition.

As central banks move forward with the exploration and potential implementation of CBDCs, the focus must remain on creating a system that enhances financial inclusion without compromising financial stability. This requires a delicate balance of designing CBDCs with user needs in mind, implementing strong regulatory and security measures, and ensuring that the new digital currency complements rather than disrupts existing financial services.

REFERENCES

Al-Laham, M., Al-Tarawneh, H., & Abdallat, N. (2009). Development of electronic money and its impact on the central bank role and monetary policy. *Issues in Informing Science and Information Technology, 6*, 339–349. DOI: 10.28945/1063

Alaeddin, O., Al-Debei, M. M., & Al-Lozi, E. M. (2018). Consumer adoption of cloud computing in Jordan. *International Journal of Business Information Systems, 29*(1), 1–20.

Allen, D. W., Berg, C., Markey-Towler, B., Novak, M., & Potts, J. (2020). Blockchain and the evolution of institutional technologies: Implications for innovation policy. *Research Policy, 49*(1), 103865. DOI: 10.1016/j.respol.2019.103865

Allen, F., Gu, X., & Jagtiani, J. (2022). A survey of FinTech research and policy discussion. *The Review of Corporate Finance Studies, 11*(1), 1–45.

Allen, F., Gu, X., & Jagtiani, J. (2022). A survey of fintech research and policy discussion. *The Review of Corporate Finance Studies, 11*(1), 1–45.

Bank for International Settlements (BIS). (2021). CBDCs: Financial stability implications. *BIS Annual Economic Report 2021*, Chapter III. https://www.bis.org/publ/arpdf/ar2021e3.htm

Barontini, C., & Holden, H. (2019). *Proceeding with caution – A survey on central bank digital currency. BIS Papers No. 101*. Bank for International Settlements.

Barrdear, J., & Kumhof, M. (2022). The macroeconomics of central bank digital currencies. *Journal of Economic Dynamics & Control, 104*, 34–55. DOI: 10.1016/j.jedc.2021.104148

Beck, T. (2020). Finance in the time of COVID-19: The role of digital financial services. *European Journal of Development Research, 32*(2), 486–502.

Beck, T. (2020). Fintech and financial inclusion: Opportunities and pitfalls. European Economy – Banks, Regulation, and the Real Sector, 2, 55–70.

Bian, X., Liang, Y., & Ma, L. (2021). Impact of CBDC on the credit channel of monetary policy: Evidence from China. *Finance Research Letters, 43*, 101954.

Bian, X., Liu, Y., & Song, Y. (2021). Central bank digital currency and financial system stability. *Journal of Digital Economy, 3*(1), 35–54.

BIS. (2020). *Central bank digital currencies: Foundational principles and core features*. Bank for International Settlements.

BIS. (2021). *CBDCs: Financial stability implications. BIS Quarterly Review, March 2021*. Bank for International Settlements.

Bissessar, N. (2016). Regulating virtual currencies. *Journal of Financial Regulation and Compliance, 24*(3), 292–303.

Boar, C., Holden, H., & Wadsworth, A. (2020). *Impending arrival – A sequel to the survey on central bank digital currency. BIS Papers No. 107*. Bank for International Settlements.

Bofinger, P., & Haas, T. (2020). CBDCs and financial stability: A critical assessment. *CEPR Discussion Paper No. DP15472*. https://cepr.org/publications/dp15472

Carbó-Valverde, S., & Sánchez, F. R. (2013). Financial innovation, digital security, and cybersecurity risk. *Journal of Financial Regulation and Compliance, 21*(4), 354–369.

Carbó-Valverde, S., & Sánchez, F. R. (2013). Financial exclusion and public policies: A European perspective. *Journal of Policy Modeling, 35*(5), 764–782.

Chong, A. Y. L., Ooi, K. B., Lin, B., & Tan, B. I. (2010). Online banking adoption: An empirical analysis. *International Journal of Bank Marketing, 28*(4), 267–287. DOI: 10.1108/02652321011054963

CPMI. (2015). *Digital currencies. Committee on Payments and Market Infrastructures*. Bank for International Settlements.

Cunha, I., Almeida, J., & Silveira, P. (2021). Digital currencies: Macroeconomic and regulatory implications. Central Bank of Brazil Working Paper Series.

Foster, R., Gorajek, A., & Tellez, D. (2021). *The RBA's approach to central bank digital currency*. Reserve Bank of Australia Bulletin.

Giménez, G., & Tamajón, L. G. (2019). Exploring the role of central banks in a digital monetary system: The Swedish e-krona. *Journal of Digital Economy, 1*(2), 18–34.

Kabir, M. H. (2022). Financial technology and financial inclusion: A critical review. *International Journal of Finance and Banking Studies, 11*(1), 1–12.

Kabir, M. N. (2022). Financial inclusion through central bank digital currency: Evidence from India. *Journal of Emerging Financial Markets, 14*(1), 92–108.

Kharpal, A. (2022). India's digital rupee: How it will work and what it means for crypto. CNBC Tech. Retrieved from https://www.cnbc.com/

Kim, Y., & Kwon, O. (2019). Central Bank Digital Currency and Financial Stability. *SSRN, 7*(1), 23–48. DOI: 10.2139/ssrn.3330914

Kim, Y., Kwon, O., & Lee, S. (2018). Digital currency and the future of banking: Disruptions and risks. *Banking and Finance Review*, *50*(3), 112–129.

Kraiwanit, T., & Limsakul, C. (2022). Central Bank Digital Currency and its role in financial transformation. *Asian Journal of Economics and Banking*, *6*(1), 45–67.

Kumar, R., & Ayodeji, J. (2022a). CBDC and future financial infrastructure: A comparative analysis. *Journal of Central Banking Theory and Practice*, *11*(2), 145–164.

Kumar, R., & Ayodeji, J. (2022b). Implications of CBDCs for emerging markets. *International Journal of Monetary Economics and Finance*, *15*(1), 56–73.

Kumhof, M., & Noone, C. (2018). Central bank digital currencies: Design principles and balance sheet implications. *Bank of England Staff Working Paper No. 725*. https://doi.org/DOI: 10.2139/ssrn.3180713

Kumhof, M., & Noone, C. (2018). Central bank digital currencies – Design principles and balance sheet implications. Bank of England Staff Working Paper No. 725.

Latimer, P., & Duffy, M. (2019). Digital currencies and monetary policy: Exploring risks and opportunities. *International Review of Financial Analysis*, *62*, 119–129.

Lumpkin, S. (2010). Regulatory issues related to financial innovation. *OECD Journal: Financial Market Trends*, *2010*(1), 1–21. DOI: 10.1787/fmt-2010-5km7k9tpcjhf

Lumpkin, S. (2010). Consumer protection and financial innovation: A few basic propositions. *OECD Journal: Financial Market Trends*, *1*, 1–23.

Maniff, J. M. (2020). *The role of central banks in supporting digital payment systems*. Federal Reserve Bank of Kansas City Economic Review.

Maniff, J. (2020). A framework for analyzing central bank digital currency architecture. *Federal Reserve Bank of Kansas City Research Working Paper RWP 20-01*. https://doi.org/DOI: 10.18651/RWP2020-01

Mukherjee, S. (2022). Digital rupee and the threat to commercial banking: Risks and safeguards. *Economic and Political Weekly*, *57*(48), 16–20.

Ojha, A. (2022). A roadmap for the implementation of digital currency in India. *Journal of Banking and Financial Technology*, *6*(1), 1–14.

Ozili, P. K. (2018). Impact of digital finance on financial inclusion and stability. *Borsa Istanbul Review*, *18*(4), 329–340. DOI: 10.1016/j.bir.2017.12.003

Ozili, P. K. (2021a). Financial innovation and financial inclusion in developing countries: Evidence from Nigeria. *International Journal of Financial Studies*, *9*(2), 18. DOI: 10.3390/ijfs9020018

Ozili, P. K. (2021a). Financial inclusion and fintech during the COVID-19 pandemic. *Cogent Economics & Finance*, *9*(1), 1869782.

Ozili, P. K. (2022b). Central bank digital currency and financial inclusion: A global perspective. *Journal of Economic and Administrative Sciences*, *38*(3), 467–482.

Ozili, P. K. (2022b). The role of central bank digital currencies in financial inclusion. *Journal of Economic Studies (Glasgow, Scotland)*, *49*(7), 1403–1420.

Ozili, P. K. (2022e). FinTech, RegTech and SupTech: Financial innovation and the future of regulation. *Banking and Finance Review*, *11*(3), 77–95.

Ozili, P. K. (2022e). Digital transformation and financial inclusion: Risks and rewards. *Journal of Financial Regulation and Compliance*, *30*(2), 254–267.

Philippon, T. (2016). The FinTech opportunity. *NBER Working Paper No. 22476*. National Bureau of Economic Research. https://doi.org/DOI: 10.3386/w22476

Riksbank. (2019). The Riksbank's e-krona project: Report 2. Sveriges Riksbank.

Salampasis, D., & Mention, A. L. (2018). FinTech: Harnessing innovation for financial inclusion. *Journal of Innovation Management*, *6*(1), 7–14.

Salampasis, D., & Mention, A.-L. (2018). Fintech: Harnessing innovation for financial inclusion. *Journal of Business Research*, *88*, 479–481.

Sankar, T. (2021). *Central bank digital currencies: Conceptual framework and implementation in India*. Reserve Bank of India Bulletin.

Schindler, J. W. (2017). FinTech and financial innovation: Drivers and barriers. *Finance and Economics Discussion Series 2017-081*. Board of Governors of the Federal Reserve System. https://doi.org/DOI: 10.17016/feds.2017.081

Schindler, J. W. (2017). FinTech and financial innovation: Drivers and depth. Office of Financial Research Working Paper No. 17-04.

Shahzad, F., Xiu, G., Wang, F., & Wang, J. (2018). China's digital currency electronic payment system and its impact. *China Finance Review International*, *8*(1), 22–40.

Shareef, M. A., Archer, N., & Dwivedi, Y. K. (2011). Examining adoption behavior of e-government services in India. *Information Systems Management*, *28*(3), 217–233.

Söilen, K. S., & Benhayoun, L. (2022). Exploring the EU's approach to CBDC and monetary sovereignty. *European Journal of Government and Economics*, *11*(1), 102–118.

Tronnier, F. (2020). Central Bank Digital Currencies: Opportunities for financial inclusion. *Journal of Financial Innovation, 12*(2), 45–59.

Tronnier, J. (2020). The effects of digital currencies on financial systems. *Financial Innovation, 6*(1), 1–21.

Tsai, M.-T., Lee, K. W., & Lin, W. L. (2019). Exploring digital currency innovation and challenges. *Journal of Economic Development, 44*(1), 1–26.

Ward, O., & Rochemont, S. (2019). Understanding central bank digital currencies (CBDC). *Global Risk Institute White Paper*. Retrieved from https://globalriskinstitute.org

Ward, O., & Rochemont, S. (2019). Understanding central bank digital currencies. Institute and Faculty of Actuaries Research Paper.

Chapter 5
Global Digital Economy and Initiatives of Government of India

Lakshya Yadav
https://orcid.org/0009-0007-0410-7816
SGTB Khalsa College, University of Delhi, India

S. Satyanarayanan
Ministry of Electronics and Information Technology, India

ABSTRACT

The digital economy is expanding quickly, particularly in emerging nations. This paper aims to explain the digital economy—its meaning, estimation, government initiatives, and challenges. After analyzing the various definitions proposed by credible organizations and researchers across different reports, the paper selects the most appropriate definition for the estimation. Also, it ranks different nations in terms of digital advancement in their economies. Further, the paper gives an insight into the government's steps to increase digital penetration in India and its future plans.

A. INTRODUCTION

The term "digital economy" refers generically to the amalgamation of aspects involving an economy based on digital technologies (UNED, 2020). The intensive use of digital technologies in economic activities has revolutionized various in-

DOI: 10.4018/979-8-3693-9765-7.ch005

dustries, including electronics and IT manufacturing by optimizing processes and opening up new opportunities.

Nowadays, as digital technology develops very quickly, more and more industries are based on electronic devices and the internet, and the economy relies more on this digital economy. According to Tap-Scott Digital economy is a modern form of economy that takes digital knowledge as the main factors of production, modern information network being the main carrier, and relies on the use of information and communication technology in optimized way to improve economic efficiency and optimize economic structure.

The digital economy covers two aspects: digital industrialization and industry digitization.

Industrial digitalization involves employing advanced information technology to carry out a comprehensive digital transformation of conventional industries by digitalizing, networking, and incorporating intelligence into every aspect. The industries of software and information, electronic information production, and information and communication are all included in the information technology sector.

The rise of the digital economy has transformed conventional industries, created new business models, and created fresh opportunities for development and growth across various sectors. This shift includes the proliferation of e-commerce, the digitalization of services, the use of very large amounts of data for analysis i.e., big data and analytics, and the advancement of the Internet of Things (IoT) and artificial intelligence (AI), The business world is rapidly transformed by technological advancements. It has allowed businesses to reach a global audience through these channels while also making changes to their business models, and how they communicate with and employ technology for the consumer. all contributing to a more interconnected and efficient global economy.

Digital platforms have become effective instruments for increasing business productivity and efficiency, mostly through lower transaction costs. There is plenty of research showing that platforms have the potential to raise overall efficiency, even though there isn't any systematic proof linking platform utilization to higher business productivity. Employers are using talent platforms like Kaggle, Hacker Rank, and others more frequently for hiring, using hackathons, contests, and challenges to evaluate applicants' technical proficiency. This method helps to reduce prejudice during the selection process, expedites the screening process, minimizes time lags, and makes it easier to create a qualifying shortlist of candidates. Using these platforms also lowers transaction costs for businesses. Emerging economies face the challenge of low capital and low labour productivity, digitisation helps in higher productivity for relatively lower cost.

B. THE COMPARISON OF DIGITAL ECONOMIES AROUND THE WORLD

B. 1 Digital Economy dependency on the condition of technology

According to Fang (2024), in a report based on Google's *Consumer Barometer* data, users in Asia prefer mobile phones over computers for internet access. Of the 10 countries studied by Nielsen, mobile phone usage was highest in South Korea (85%) and Singapore (80%), followed by China (66%), Australia (65%), Italy (62%), the United Kingdom (61%), the United States (53%), Russia (37%), Brazil (36%), Turkey (19%), and India (10%).

In earlier times factors of production were different, labour and natural resources were the most essential elements in the time period of agricultural economy, and capital and technology were the key components of manufacturing during the era of the industrial economy. Upon entering the digital economy era, data eventually emerges as a new element that fuels the development of society and the economy.

Computer hardware is an important component for human beings to process operations and store data. Initially, people used equipment like Rune1 to help in recording, such as the Phoenicians used clay to record the number of livestock or grain, and the Minoan civilization excavated artifacts are similar, and the users of that time were mostly traders, accountants, and government officials. The auxiliary counting tools gradually transformed both recording and calculating functions, tools such as Analog computers, slide rules, abacuses, and contemporary digital computers. (Fang, 2024)

B. 2 The Comparison

Evaluation of progress in the digital economy landscape is essential for identifying wrongdoings and planning the next steps to enhance global digitization. Evaluation helps rank digitization across different nations, comparison helps countries improve, and Strong performers can help weak performers by giving funds and guidance for advancement.

The TIMG index assesses the global digital economy's degree of development.

There are three levels of indicators. The first-level index comprises four aspects:

Digital technology, Digital Infrastructure, Digital marketplace, and digital governance each contribute 25%. The secondary indicators break down the first-level indicators further. Digital technology encompasses research and development output, labour capital, and the level of innovation. Infrastructure includes inclusion, convenience, and security. The digital marketplace covers the demand side, supply side, and international markets. Lastly, digital governance includes government, economic and social environment, and political and legal environment. Each secondary indicator represents one-third of its respective category There are two additional components for the third-level indexes. For R&D output, these include digital patent size and the number of published mathematical and computer science papers. For labour capital, higher education enrollment and national digital literacy are considered. For the level of innovation, innovation activity, and industry-university-research cooperation are necessary. The second part, inclusion, covers active fixed broadband users and mobile phone subscriptions. Convenience is derived from mobile tariffs and cell phone prices. The third part, the demand side, includes digital consumer size and mobile social media penetration. The supply side includes several digital businesses, and the amount of financing secured by digital businesses. International markets mean digital services export scale. The last part, the digital government presents the E-government index, and the economic and social environment stands for ease of doing, business index, and degree of intellectual property protection. The political and legal environment includes the construction of digital-related legal regulations. ICT regulation tracking index, degree of government support. Secondly, The TIMG index considers both the scope of sample coverage and the indicator's comprehensiveness. From 2013 to 2021, the statistic shows how the digital economy developed in 106 economies worldwide.

According to the research made by Google, the average goal of the TIMG index increased from 45.33 in 2013 to 57.01 in 2021, with a proportion of 26%. In the era that the digital economy developed quickly, the Indian government showed their attitude towards the prospect of a digital economy. In terms of the total index, the TIMG index in America, Singapore and the UK are the highest. India has advantages in the competitive market, but still has a certain gap compared with the countries like America in the aspects like digital technology, and the management of digital information.

Then the NRI index, the total ranking is the same as the TIMG index but the difference between the two countries is bigger and will be larger. Next is the IMD World digital competitiveness ranking, this also has the overall trend with the two indexes mentioned above, but with the range in the middle.

The NRI index (Network Readiness Index) is a standard that measures the level a country prepares for digital transformation. It considers many factors, including infrastructure, technology adoption, digitalization ability, and the policy pushed out by the government. During 2021, the score of the index of digital infrastructure in America rose from 79.79 in 2013 to 93.07, closely following Singapore and China, with figures of 90.53 and 89.33 respectively. The UK, Luxembourg, Japan, India, Germany, Russia and Italy rank the 4th to the 10th, and their scores are all between

85-89. Considering all the data, the overall trend shows a rising trajectory, with many newcomers significantly improving their performance in the digital economy field.

Three tiers make up the CHIPS framework: indicators, sub-pillars, and pillars. Connect, Harness, Innovate, Protect, and Sustain are the five pillars. The full spectrum of digital transformation is evaluated by these pillars.

According to the CHIP(S) framework, which measures digitalization generally, India is the third most digitally advanced country in the world, overtaking the UK, Germany, and Japan while trailing only the US and China. (Mishra et al., 2024)

Table 1. The CHIPS Framework source: ICRIER

C	Connect
H	Harness
I	Innovate
P	Protect
S	Sustain

The CHIPS framework -:

Table 2. Measuring digitalization using the CHIP(S) framework Source: ICREIR

Rank	Country	Score
1	USA	65.1
2	China	62.3
3	India	39.1
4	UK	28.8
5	Germany	23.8
6	S.Korea	21.9
7	Australia	20.7
8	Indonesia	20.6
9	Japan	20.4
10	France	19.9

Integration of Digital Economy And Real Economy

The amalgamation of the digital economy and the real economy (hereinafter referred to as "digital and real integration") began in the consumer sector, particularly in the consumer-interacting retail sector. It started with retail because of the simplicity of the individual transaction process, especially the decision-making process. This form of digital and real integration develops rapidly and has a great impact on the entire retail business organization.

The quick development of digital technology. Also, Prediction technology and blockchain technology are playing an increasingly important role in the integration of data and reality. Traditional machine learning techniques for time series prediction have now shifted to deep learning based on neural networks, which has tremendous potential for performance enhancement. realize the integration of digital and real, this paper should consider the problem of digital cost. Digital technology has developed rapidly in the application of e-commerce, logistics, advertising and other fields, and has achieved great results, and now the digital manufacturing industry is lagging.

Another way to boost the expansion of the digital economy is to direct its industrialization.

Artificial intelligence, blockchain, cloud computing, and data are examples of new digital technologies that are part of the industrialization of the digital economy. Producing digital products including pure digital products like APPs, the digital economy industrializes intelligent connected products through the transformation of achievements.

C. ESTIMATION OF THE DIGITAL ECONOMY

C. 1 Frameworks

OECD Framework

The OECD first defined the Digital Economy as "the digital economy enables and executes the trade of goods and services through electronic commerce on the internet."

The latest definition of the digital economy, proposed by the OECD in 2020, states: " All economic activity that is dependent upon or greatly enhanced by the usage of digital inputs, such as data, digital technologies, digital infrastructure, and digital services, is referred to as the "digital economy." All producers, consumers, and even the government that use these digital inputs in their economic endeavors are included. Compared to the initial definition put forth by the OECD, this one is far more complete. (Office for National Statistics, 2022)

It demonstrates how the scope of the digital economy has expanded over time, making it necessary to take consideration of every possible linkage. the indicators as proposed under "Toolkit for measuring the digital economy" – published in G20 2018, based on which the OECD 2020 definition has been framed. THE INDICATORS:

1. Infrastructure - This indicator assesses the digital and physical infrastructure, such as mobile connectivity and broadband access, required for a strong digital economy. Reliable internet access is supported by a well-built infrastructure, which also improves the whole digital experience for both consumers and companies.
2. Empowering Society - This focuses on the ways in which digital technology might improve societal capacities, like expanding access to healthcare and education. It highlights the value of digital literacy and the need to eliminate the digital divide in order to ensure equitable access to technology for all groups.
3. Innovation and technology adoption - This metric assesses how new technologies are being incorporated into corporate operations and society at large. It monitors R&D expenditures, startup activity, and the uptake of cutting-edge technologies—all of which are essential for promoting economic expansion and competitiveness in the digital era.
4. Jobs and Growth - This metric evaluates how the digital economy affects employment and economic expansion. Metrics on automation-related changes in labour demand, productivity gains from digital tools, and job growth in technological sectors are also included. Comprehending these dynamics aids policymakers in tackling workforce issues and optimizing employment prospects in a swiftly changing digital environment.

Based on these indicators (important components), the OECD 2020 report provides two new definitions of the digital economy, each relating to the specific indicators it covers.

'Bottom-up definition:

Digital Economy is defined in a traditional manner. "As the aggregate of a specific indicator for an ensemble of industries or sectors identified as actors in the Digital Economy".

This is a narrow definition that considers only the industries and activities directly contributing to the production of digital inputs or that rely on these inputs. It is an approach used to quantify economic work, as employed by the BEA to estimate their digital economy.

It captures the fundamental l digital related activities, while it fails to capture the influence of digitalization on wider industries and products.

The IMF uses an approach which is more inclusive in the sense that it also includes "online platforms and platform enabled services" in addition to "suppliers of ICT goods and services". This definition is also narrowing some senses but it uses the existing frameworks and definitions –most importantly that of System of National Accounts.

All industries that use digital inputs in their production process are included in the Digital Economy, as per second, more expansive subset of the bottom-up definition.

Top-down definition:

"Top-down definitions start from the identification of broad trends at play in the digital transformation and define the Digital Economy as the result of their combined impact, including trends enabled by the progress and adoption of digital technologies by societies. These trends include ideas such as "platformization" or the growing reliance on digital data and E-commerce or government services being increasingly provided online".

"Additional difficulty comes with the fact that any definition built around one or a few specific trends will be limited to only providing a partial, often non-monetary, perspective on the Digital Economy, while definitions combining too many trends or too universal a trend, such as Internet use, might become too vague. As observed by the IMF, if the Digital Economy encompasses all activities that simply use digitized data, the entire economy could soon be included in the concept, making it likely unclear". (OECD, 2020)

Flexible Definition:

Bukht and Heeks' paper titled -Defining, Conceptualizing and Measuring the Digital Economy (2017) serves as the foundation for the flexible definition. It provides a three-level, flexible, and tiered definition of the digital economy across three levels.

1. The economic activity of businesses that produce ICT information services and goods is the primary indicator of the digital economy.

Figure 1. Framework of the Digital Economy's Core and Related Sectors.

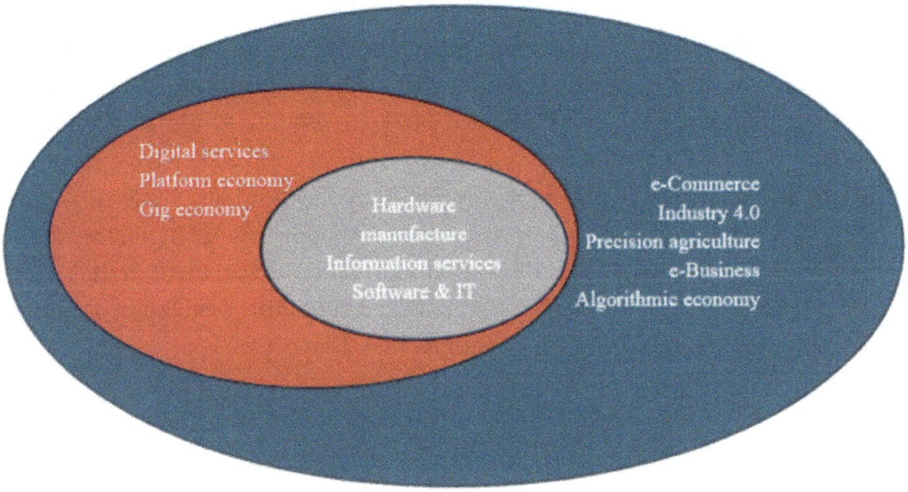

Note. Source (Bukht & Heeks, 2017)

2. Economic output from core sector economic activity generated by industries that depend on digital inputs is included in the limited definition of the digital economy.
3. The digital economy's broad measure is an expanded form of both as it consists of the first two measures in addition to the economic activity derived from sectors where the use of digital inputs has greatly improved their production. (Bukht & Heeks, 2017)

An alternate method of measuring the digital economy that runs parallel to the one mentioned above is:

A different way to gauge the digital economy that runs parallel to the one mentioned above is as follows- Digitally ordered and/or digitally delivered economic activity, which is based on the nature of the transaction rather than the goods or production methods of companies, is another measure of economic activity that can be viewed as an alternate perspective of the Digital Economy. As per IMF's 2023 digital trade report, digitally delivered trade is defined as "all international trade transactions that are delivered remotely over computer networks" and digitally ordered trade is defined as "the international sale or purchase of a good or service, conducted over computer networks by methods specifically designed for the purpose of receiving or placing orders".This measurement method focuses on the ordering or delivery process while ignoring the final product or manufacturing process.

Digital Society

The Digital Society concept extends beyond the Digital Economy. Digital society encompasses digital interactions and activities not included in GDP calculations, such as free digital platforms. These activities are essential for digital policy but are excluded from our estimation.

Additionally, the G20 Digital Economy Task Force acknowledges that, although not Directly related to a digital economy, various components of Digital interactions and activities that affect the economy and provide value are part of the digital society. . These activities are crucial for regional and economic development policies, among other things. (G20 Digital Economy Task Force, 2020)

Table 3. Typology of ICT sub-sectors Source: Heeks 2008

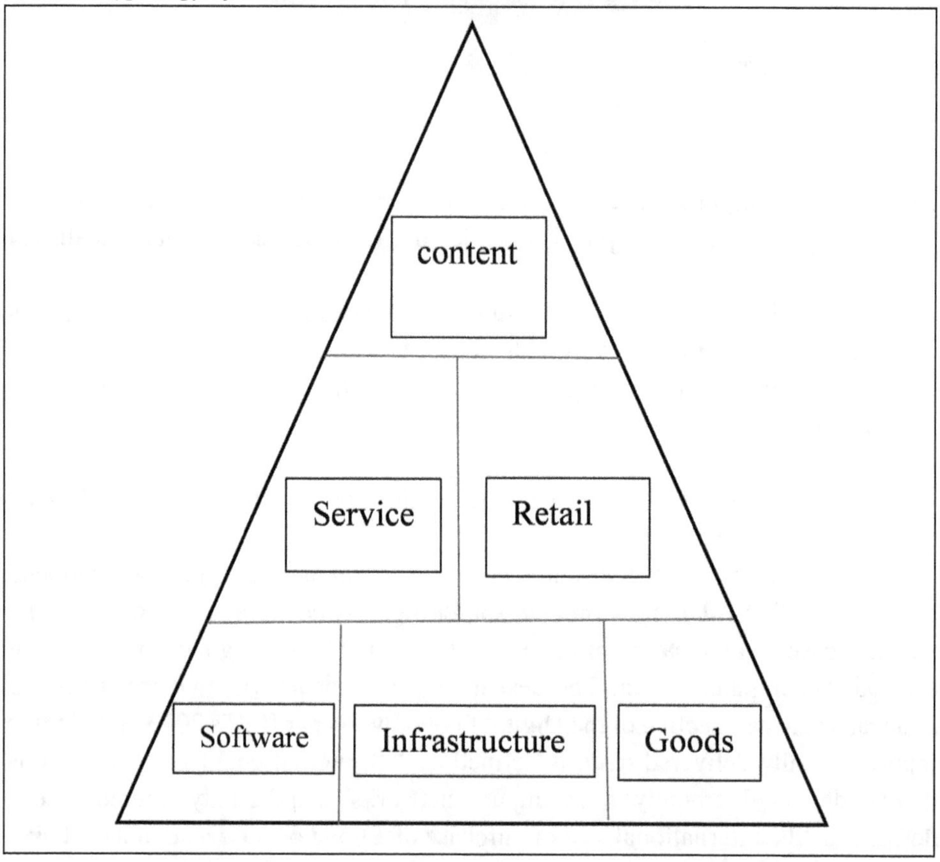

ADB Framework

The framework developed by the ADB in 2021 to measure the digital economy identifies forward and backward linkages concerning core digital economy.

The framework classifies fundamental digital products into five distinct categories namely:

(a) web publishing
(b) hardware
(c) specialized and support services
(d) software publishing
(e) telecommunications services

According to the ADB framework, the term "digital economy" describes how economic transactions involving digital industries and products affect GDP, or gross value added (GVA). (Srivastava et al., 2023)

In the proposed framework, digital products and industries are defined as "goods and services with the main function of generating, processing, and/or storing digitized data. The primary producers of such products (i.e., industries that supply these products) are considered the digital industries."

The core digital economy and digitally enabled goods are distinguished under the ADB framework. Digitally enabled products represent both forward and backward links within the core digital economy. Though they are not directly related to digital data, semiconductors are utilized for electrical conductivity, which is a necessary component of computer manufacturing.

Product manufacturing that incorporates digital elements into automobiles, such as self-driving capabilities, vehicle systems management, and in-car entertainment, is an example of a digitally enabled product.

As per the ADB definitions, three subsectors form digital basis –

(i) telecommunications;
(ii) computer and ICT service;
(iii) computer, electronics, and optical products (ADB, 2024)

C. 2 Estimation of digital economy of IT and Electronics Sector

According to the flexible definition -: The foundation of the digital economy is the development of key basic services and technology. This core can be referred to as the digital sector, which is more commonly known as the "IT sector" or the "ICT sector."

It is still common to define the ICT sector using the OECD's 1998 definition: "a combination of manufacturing and services industries that capture, transmit, and display data and information electronically". ISIC industrial codes (revision 4) 582 (software publication), 61 (telecommunications), 62 (computer programming, 63 (information service activities), consulting, and related activities, and 26 (manufacturing of computer, electronic, and optical devices) are now included in this classification.

Firms that produce ICT and information services as well as ICT products are included in the Core Measure of the Digital Economy.

Core Measure: Combination of ICT sectors defined under ISIC rev 4.0. and the content and media sector (OECD 2011 definition). By refining the definition further, trade flows can also include digitally ordered goods (as goods cannot be delivered digitally by nature), digitally delivered services, and ICT-enabled services.

ICT-enabled services are defined by UNCTAD as "all services that are remotely provided via ICT networks, or all activities that can be planned, carried out, delivered, assessed, and consumed electronically. (UNCTAD, 2015)

ADB classifies core digital products into five categories, which are as follows:

(a) web publishing
(b) hardware
(c) specialized and support services
(d) software publishing
(e) telecommunications services

We can summarize from all the above definitions that the IT and electronics sectors equate to the core industry for the estimation.

Methodological Requirements

The main sources of data for the digital economy framework are Input-Output Tables (IOTs) and National Supply and Use Tables (SUTs).

SUTs detail the production of goods and services domestically or imported for domestic use, while IOTs illustrate how these outputs are utilized within the economy, including exports, capital formation, intermediate consumption, and final consumption.

To implement this framework, matrices and vectors are directly derived from IOTs The SUTs can be transformed into IOTs by the prescribed transformation model of Eurostat from 2008. In that case, this ADB report used the "fixed product sales structure" assumption, which transforms a SUT by product and industry into an IOT by industry interactions.

Limitations of ADB Framework

First, very few data are available at the finest levels. Therefore, to be in a position where this high-level data could be disaggregated, questions need to be forwarded to the appropriate NSOs. Collection and maintaining uniformity and accuracy of all data is a challenge.

Secondly, It takes into account the most narrow definition of digital products. Non-digital product sales made online are not considered. Only the contribution of digital products, that means, products produced by the digital industries, are considered. For instance, a pen is sold through Zepto, an e-commerce platform. Only the contribution of the digital platform is accounted for in the framework, not of the non-digital product.

Thirdly, If one defines digital products in their narrowest sense, the digitally reliant economy is an added value from sectors that are digitally intensive businesses.

Fourth There are certain drawbacks to this methodology for calculating the digital economy's proportion of the national GDP. For example, since GDP counts do not include imports, neither do the digital economy estimates. This may, therefore, cause an understatement of the digital economy, especially in countries that make large imports of digital products. Therefore, such Estimates of the digital economy might be less in economies that import a lot of digital goods and in industries that heavily utilize core digital sectors than in others.

Table 4. Difference between ADB and OECD approach

ADB	OECD
Has a narrow definition of digital economy	Has a broader definition of digital economy
Uses IO (input output) table	Uses SUT (supply and use table)
Most recent data (IO Tables) available from MOSPI is for 2007-08	Most recent data (SUTs) available from MOSPI is for 2018-19
It does not account for the value additions of all digitally dependent sectors.	It considers all the digitally dependent sectors.

Calculation Methodology and Data Sourcing

We are using OCED framework in this report to calculate India's core digital Economy. We are using OCED framework in this report to calculate India's core digital Economy.

First, the primary benefit is the accessibility of data. The ADB framework utilizes national Input-Output tables provided by our national statistical office, MOSPI. Nevertheless, the latest available I-O tables from MOSPI are for the year 2007-08, and from NCAER for the year 2013-14, resulting in a lack of reliable data. This constraint made it necessary to adopt the OECD framework.

The second advantage addresses the ADB framework's inherent limitation, which results in underestimation. The ADB framework does not fully account for digitally dependent sectors, thereby underestimating the digital economy's actual contribution. On the other hand, the OECD framework adopts a more comprehensive approach, including all relevant industries and sectors contributing to the digital economy. This inclusive approach reduces the likelihood of underestimation and enhances the accuracy of the estimation.

The core industries identified in the Supply and Use table for the year 2018-19, based on the guidelines outlined in a report by the Organization for Economic Co-operation and Development (OECD, 2020), are as follows:

1. Manufacture of communication equipment
2. Manufacture of paper and paper products
3. Manufacture of machinery and equipment n.e.c.
4. Printing and reproduction of recorded media except publishing
5. Manufacture of computer and peripheral equipment
6. Manufacture of optical and electronic products n.e.c.
7. Manufacture of electrical equipment
8. Manufacture of electronic components, consumer electronics, magnetic and optical media
9. Communication
10. Other services

Table 5. Tiers of Digital Economy

1	Core Measure	Economic activity from producers of digital services and ICT goods
2	Narrow Measure	Economic activity from firms that depend on digital inputs plus the core measure
3	Broad Measure	Narrow measure + economic activity from firms that use digital inputs significantly to enhance production.
4	Digital Society	interactions and activities that have been digitalized, such as using digital platforms
5	Digitally ordered and/or delivered	Digital economy' ordering and delivery methods

Source: Report for the G20 Digital Task Force (OECD)

ICT Sector

Core Measure: According to the OECD (2011), a core measure involves the integration of the content and media sector with the ICT sectors, as defined by ISIC Revision 4.0. This concept can be further refined to include digitally ordered items (as physical goods cannot be provided digitally), digitally delivered services, and ICT-enabled services, especially when accounting for trade flows.

The United Nations Conference on Trade and Development (UNCTAD, 2021) defines ICT-enabled services as "all activities that can be specified, performed, delivered, evaluated, and consumed electronically," or more broadly as "all services that are delivered remotely through ICT networks". Digitally provided services are defined as "all services that are delivered remotely in an electronic format, using computer networks specifically designed for the purpose" in the Handbook on Measuring Digital Trade.

The primary distinction is that ICT-enabled services encompass services that are provided using means that do not necessitate computer networks, including phone conversations between people.

ICT Manufacturing Industries

2610 Manufacture of electronic components and boards
2620 Manufacture of computers and peripheral equipment
2630 Manufacture of communication equipment
2640 Manufacture of consumer electronics
2680Manufacture of magnetic and optical media

ICT Trade Industries

4651 Wholesale of computers, computer peripheral equipment and software
4652 Wholesale of electronic and telecommunications equipment and parts
ICT services industries
5820 Software publishing
61 Telecommunications
6110 Wired telecommunications activities
6120 Wireless telecommunications activities
6130 Satellite telecommunications activities
6190 Other telecommunications activities
62 Computer programming, consultancy activities and related
6201 Computer programming activities
6202 Computer consultancy and computer facilities management activities
6209 Other information technology and computer service activities
631 Data processing, hosting and related activities; web portals
6311 Data processing, hosting and related activities
6312 Web portals
8549 Other education
951 Repair of computers and communication equipment
9511 Repair of computers and peripheral equipment
9512 Repair of communication equipment

Content and Media Sector

581 Publishing of books, periodicals and other publishing activities
5811 Book publishing
5812 Publishing of directories and mailing lists
5813 Publishing of newspapers, journals and periodicals
5819 Other publishing activities
591 Motion picture, video and television programme activities
5911 Motion picture, video and television programme production activities
5912 Motion picture, video and television programme post-production activities
5913 Motion picture, video and television programme distribution activities
5914 Motion picture projection activities
592 Sound recording and music publishing activities
60 Programming and broadcasting activities

6010 Radio broadcasting
6020 Television programming and broadcasting activities
639 Other information service activities
6391 News agency activities
6399 Other information service activities n.e.c.

Narrow Measure

The narrow measure includes core + the industries which are totally reliant, and couldn't have existed in the absence of ICT inputs.

It consists of Digital services and platform economy.

The streams of income originating from electronic sources:

1. Revenue of a company from a digital order from their own website/app.
2. Revenue to a digital intermediary service provider for facilitating the service. This is the share that constitutes digital intermediary services like amazon, flipkart, uber etc.
3. Revenue to a seller/service provider whose services are facilitated via a digital intermediary service provider.
4. In case of free digital services like social media, YouTube etc., the advertisement stream of income is the income that is generated due to digitalisation.

Broad Measure

Includes the industries enhanced by the ICT puts, and the Narrow Measure.

To decide on such industries, we shall be using (Calvino et al.'s, 2018) taxonomy of sectors by digital intensity.

Table 6. Sectoral taxonomy of digital intensity: "global" indicator

Sector denomination	ISIC rev.4	Quartile of digital intensity: 2001-03	Quartile of digital intensity: 2013-15
Agriculture, forestry, fishing	01-03	Low	Low
Mining and quarrying	05-09	Low	Low
Food products, beverages and tobacco	10-12	Low	Low
Textiles, wearing apparel, leather	13-15	Medium-low	Medium-low

continued on following page

Table 6. Continued

Sector denomination	ISIC rev.4	Quartile of digital intensity: 2001-03	Quartile of digital intensity: 2013-15
Wood and paper products, and printing	16-18	Medium-high	Medium-high
Coke and refined petroleum products	19	Medium-low	Medium-low
Chemicals and chemical products	20	Medium-low	Medium-low
Pharmaceutical products	21	Medium-low	Medium-low
Rubber and plastics products	22-23	Medium-low	Medium-low
Basic metals and fabricated metal products	24-25	Medium-low	Medium-low
Computer, electronic and optical products	26	High	Medium-high
Electrical equipment	27	Medium-high	Medium-high
Machinery and equipment n.e.c.	28	High	Medium-high
Transport equipment	29-30	High	High
Furniture; other manufacturing; repairs of computers	31-33	Medium-high	Medium-high
Electricity, gas, steam and air cond.	35	Low	Low
Water supply; sewerage, waste management	36-39	Low	Low
Construction	41-43	Low	Low
Wholesale and retail trade, repair	45-47	Medium-high	Medium-high
Transportation and storage	49-53	Low	Low
Accommodation and food service	55-56	Low	Low
Publishing, audio and visual broadcasting	58-60	Medium-high	Medium-high
Telecommunications	61	High	High
IT and other information services	62-63	High	High
Finance and insurance	64-66	High	High
Real estate	68	Low	Low
Legal and accounting activities, etc	69-71	High	High
Scientific research and development	72	Medium-high	High
Advertising and market research; other business services	73-75	High	High

continued on following page

Table 6. Continued

Sector denomination	ISIC rev.4	Quartile of digital intensity: 2001-03	Quartile of digital intensity: 2013-15
Administrative and support service activities	77-82	High	High
Public administration and defence	84	Medium-high	Medium-high
Education	85	Medium-low	Medium-low
Human health activities	86	Medium-high	Medium-low
Residential care and social work activities	87-88	Medium-low	Medium-low
Arts, entertainment and recreation	90-93	Medium-low	Medium-high
Other service activities	94-96	Medium-high	High

Calculations for Core Measure Industries

To calculate the total output for the core measure industries while avoiding double counting, we will use the Gross Value Added (GVA) approach. This method ensures that outputs used as inputs by the same or other industries are not counted multiple times, which would artificially inflate the total value.

1. Obtain the total output data for each of the following industries for the year 2018-19:
    - Manufacture of paper and paper products
    - Manufacture of electrical equipment
    - Manufacture of communication equipment
    - Manufacture of optical and electronic products n.e.c.
    - Communication
    - Manufacture of electronic components, consumer electronics, magnetic and optical media
    - Manufacture of computer and peripheral equipment
    - Manufacture of machinery and equipment n.e.c.
    - Printing and reproduction of recorded media except publishing
    - Other services
2. Calculate the GVA:
    - For each industry, subtract the value of intermediate consumption (inputs used in production) from the total output. Since the industries under the core measure mostly use inputs supplied by industries outside

the digital economy, the intermediate consumption is zero as per the given definition.

GVA = Total Output – Intermediate Consumption
Given the assumption that intermediate consumption is zero:
GVA = TOTAL OUTPUT

3. Sum the GVA of All Core Industries:
   - Add the GVA of all ten core measure industries to get the total contribution of these industries to the digital economy.

Handling Taxes and Subsidies:

(Proportion of output of a product supplied by the core industries* Total taxes less subsidy of the product)

Addition by the core digital sector in the overall GDP:

Total output of core industries + Estimated net taxes = Portion of total GDP attributed to the core digital sector

Our calculations based on the SUT 2018-19 data yielded a result of approximately 20%.

Absolute values of the measure:

Core measure: 2104822 lakh cores (without net taxes)

D. ROLE OF R AND D

Research and Development (R&D plays part in the manufacturing and software industries through its being the propelling force behind innovation, technological progress, and, thus, general progress. This requirement is reflected by the substantial number of R&D claims in these segments. These is also a positive relation in R&D spending and G.D.P growth.

Net Zero Target: This only created challenges for the manufacturing and software industry when India committed to achieving a net zero target by 2070. Since these manufacturing industries are heavy users of energy, high emitters of gases, dependents on fossil fuel, and rich in production-related emissions, most of the R&D activities work on these lines to find new ways to decarbonize everyday processes and reduce dependency on fossil fuels.

Low Productivity—Low productivity is one of the major concerns of the manufacturing sector. This can be mainly due to outdated technology, inefficient processes, or an inadequate skill-set and quantity of workers.

Figure 2. Percentage of total R&D spending in computer, electronic and optical products manufacturing sector in selected countries in 2011 source: Statista

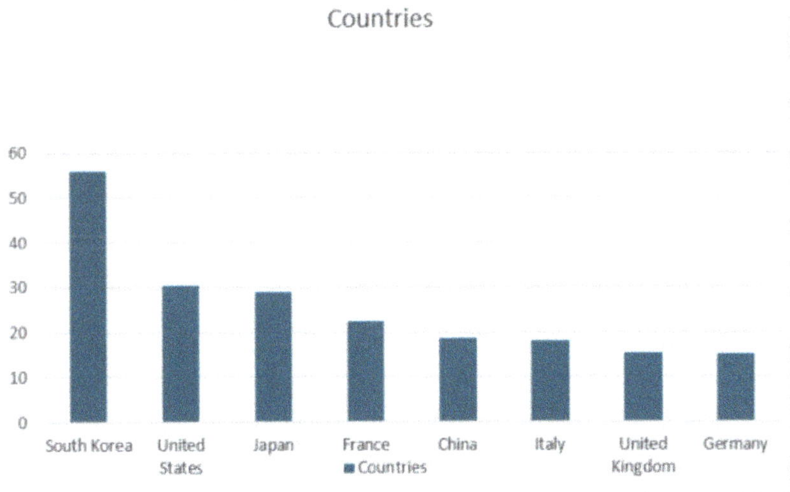

Percentage of total R&D spending in computer, electronic and optical products manufacturing sector in selected countries in 2011 source: Statista

D. 1 Measuring India's Digital Progress: The Comprehensive Effects of the Digital India Initiative

In India, the amount and value of digital payments have increased significantly in recent past, particularly during the COVID-19 pandemic that lasted from November 2019 to January 2023.

, as depicted in Chart 1. By January 2023, there were 1,052 crores of digital transactions, more than tripling from 300 crores in November 2019.

Figure 3. Measuring India's digital progress.

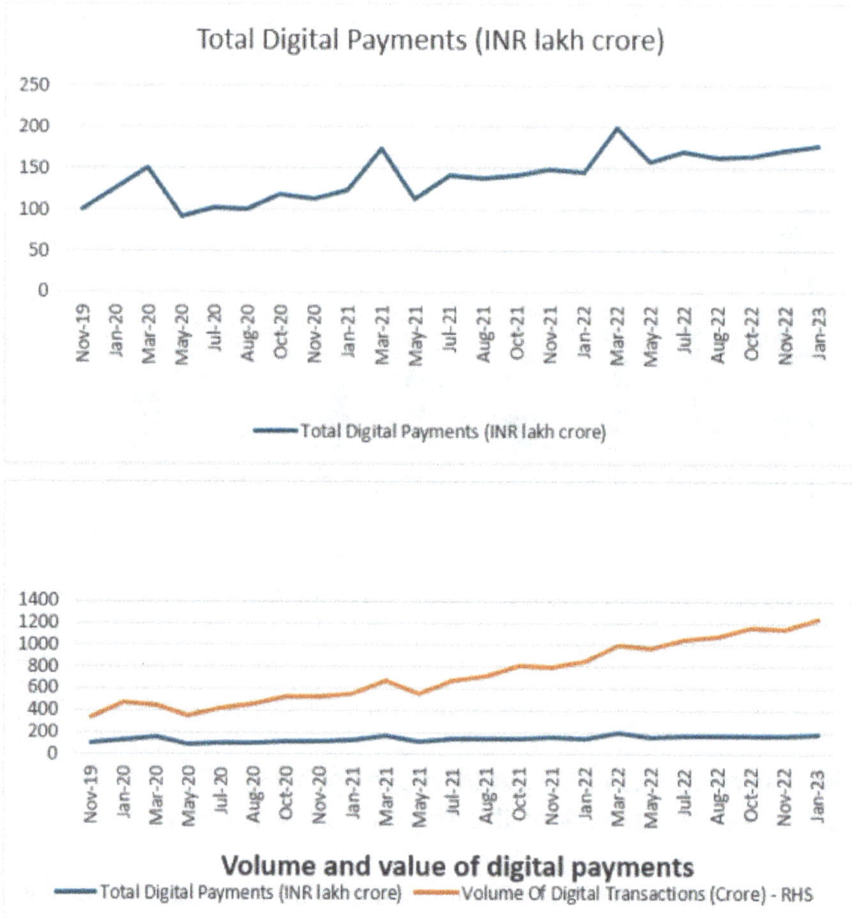

Source: RBI

Digital R&D Spending: The percentage of a nation's GDP that comes from the digital economy is correlated with its R&D spending as a percentage of GDP. With the largest percentage of its GDP going toward research and development, South Korea is a leader in this field. Its areas of interest include artificial intelligence (AI), AI semiconductors, 5G and 6G, quantum computing, the metaverse, and cybersecurity. To increase R&D and innovation investment, the Indian government launched Digital India futureLABS. Europe, on the other hand, lags behind in terms of digital investment; from 2024 to 2027, it is anticipated that yearly tech spending growth will reach €83 billion, far less than the €125 billion required to satisfy the European Commission's digital growth targets. Countries should focus on creating digital firms, improving public services, guaranteeing the availability of digital skills, raising R&D spending, and making tech investments that affect non-digital industries if they want to see a sustainable expansion in the digital economy. (Grady, 2024)

R&D in the Electronics Division

The electronics sector is a major contributor to the economy and one of the most globalized industries globally. In India, the demand for electronic hardware was projected to reach USD 400 billion by 2020. To gradually enhance the value addition in electronic product manufacturing, a continuous R&D program in the electronics sector is crucial. This will aid in developing indigenous technology, transferring it to industry for commercialization, and increasing the Intellectual Property (IP) content in product design and development. (MIETY, 2024)

The NASSCOM report on the adoption of Industry 4.0 in India says, "By 2025, with the advent of digital technologies, it is estimated that at least 40% of total expenditure on manufacturing will be on digital, against 20% of expenditure in 2021.". (Invest India, 2024)

Advantages of Digital India Programme

The Digital India programme is a major step towards achieving the digital revolution and digital empowerment of citizens. Few advantages of the programme are-

1. All government services are now accessible to the nation's citizens through standardized service delivery channels as a result of the digital India goal. By giving all of the nation's residents access to government services, healthcare, and education, this would be a significant step toward inclusive growth. Better health service advice is available to the public. Online education is an option for those who cannot afford to attend schools or universities.
2. Citizens will be able to digitally keep their passports, Pan cards, mark sheets, and other critical documents thanks to the digital locker facility.
3. The program would directly or indirectly create a significant number of employments in the IT, electronics, and telecommunications sectors.
4. This program will increasingly emphasize transparency because all of the data will be accessible to the nation's citizens online.
5. It will reduce long queues, as verification processes, and registrations can be done online. (Rani, 2021)

D. 2 Future Initiatives

The Government of India will support Digital India FutureLABS as a research and innovation framework under the future program to provide India's electronics and IT industry a boost by establishing leadership in standards, intellectual property, systems, and platforms.

The initiative shall thus promote domestic innovation along with collabouration for pushing sustainable growth and technological progressThe fields of automotive, mobility, computing, communication, strategic electronics, and industrial IoT will be the core focus of FutureLABS. In order to jointly build systems, standards, and intellectual property cores, it would make it easier for startups, multinational corporations, R&D institutions, and academia to collabourate.

Government labs, Indian start-ups, large corporations, and companies in the electronics sector will all work jointly on this project. These include automotive industrial platforms and tier 1 suppliers, where businesses are creating future technologies and system designs.

In the virtual presentation to the IESA Vision Summit 2024, Union Minister of State Shri Rajeev Chandrasekhar announced that the Government of India would shortly establish the India Semiconductor Research Centre. "We will soon establish the India Semiconductor Research Centre, which will function as a center for semiconductor innovation across all spectrums that will power future systems," the minister said. (PIB, 2024)

Additionally, the government is implementing programs such as:

The Modified Special Incentive Package (M-SIPS) has so far authorized 315 applications with a suggested investment of about Rs. 85,632 crores.

Electronic Manufacturing Clusters (EMC): In 15 states nationwide, 19 Greenfield EMCs and Common Facility Centers (CFCs) totaling 3,464 acres and costing Rs. 3,732 crore, including Rs. 1,529 crore in government grant-in-aid, have been sanctioned under the EMC scheme.

The government's Digital India plan aimed to transform India into a technologically empowered society and knowledge-based economy.

The aim of this initiative is to close the digital divide and provide digital access, empowerment, and inclusion. The three primary components of this initiative are ensuring that all residents have access to the Internet, enabling digital services, and establishing a secure digital infrastructure.

The gap between the government and its people has been greatly reduced by digital India, which makes it easier to provide beneficiaries with basic services in an open and corruption-free way. India is now a global leader in using technology to enhance the lives of its citizens because to this program. The drive for digitalization has also sped up the formalization of the economy.

The following are some of the major projects MeitY has carried out nationwide as part of the Digital India program:

Aadhar: A unique 12-digit biometric and demographic-based identification that is online, verifiable, and permanent is provided via Aadhaar. The Aadhaar Act of 2016, supporting its use for delivering subsidies, benefits, and services, was enacted on March 26, 2016 The number of enrolled residents exceeds 135.5 crore.

DigiLocker: Issuers can upload documents to digital archives through DigiLocker's ecosystem of repositories and gateways.

Unified Mobile Application for New-age Governance (UMANG) – for using mobile devices to deliver government services to residents. UMANG offers more than 20,197 bill payment services and more than 1668 e-services.

MyGov – MyGov a platform for citizen interaction was created to make participatory governance easier.

Unified Payment Interface (UPI), FutureSkills Prime, National Knowledge Network, Pradhan Mantri Gramin Digital Saksharta Abhiyaan (PMGDISHA), NCOG-GIS Applications, Jeevan Pramaan, CO-WIN, National Rollout of eDistrict MMP, eHospital/ Online Registration System (ORS), Open Government Data Platform. (PIB, 2022)

Overall, India's innovation and R&D have greatly increased, making it the best economy in Central and Southern Asia and placing it 40th in the world according to GII 2022.

As a result, the number of Intellectual Property Rights (IPRs) created by citizens of the nation has been steadily increasing.

The government's policies such as "National Education Policy 2020", "National Policy on Electronics 2019", "National Digital Communication Policy 2018", "Make in India, Digital India" startup India, etc. have quite contributed to the development of the R&D environment in the country. Besides, fresh approaches such as "Atmanirbhar Bharat", "Telecom Product-Linked Incentives (PLI) scheme", and 'Digital Communication Innovation Square' have been positive measures also in this respect.

Figure 4. Global Innovation Index

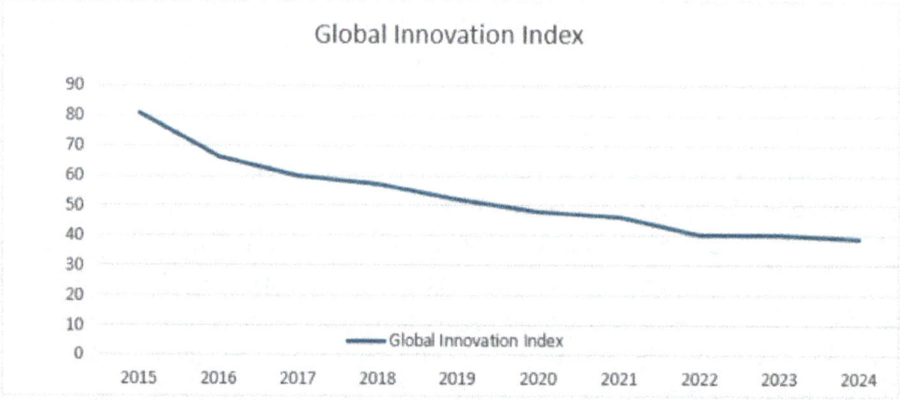

Source -: World Intellectual Property Organization (WIPO, 2024)

D.3 Case Study Why India Lags Behind China in Semiconductor R & D

A number of reasons, such as delayed policy action, poor infrastructure, restricted domestic manufacturing, and weakened industry-academia collabouration, contribute to India's lagging behind China in semiconductor R&D.

1) Poor Policy Support

Early and current government assistance for China's semiconductor sector was provided by programs such as the "National IC Industry Development Guidelines" (2014) and the "Made in China 2025" plan, which provided more than $150 billion in subsidies to create a completely "closed-loop" semiconductor industry in China. Unabashedly, the plan called for China to become the world's leading manufacturer of integrated circuits (ICs) and to eliminate its trade imbalance in ICs by 2030. 27 Some of these goals were clarified in 2015 when China unveiled its "Made in China 2025" strategy, which aimed to achieve 70% semiconductor self-sufficiency by 2025 and 40% by 2020. Also, China's part of the worldwide value added in the semiconductor sector increased from 8 to 31 percent between 2001 and 2016, whereas the US portion decreased from 28 to 22 percent and Japan's share dropped by more than two-thirds, from 30 to 8 percent. (Information Technology and Innovation Foundation, 2024) India's "Semiconductor Policy" (2007), on the other hand, was poorly funded and implemented, and the $10 billion "India Semiconductor Mission (ISM)" (2021) is still in its infancy (MeitY, 2021).

2) Weak Domestic Manufacturing System

Lack of Commercial Semiconductor Fabs

China's Dominance: More than 300 semiconductor factories may be found in China, including well-known companies like Yangtze Memory Technologies Corp. and Semiconductor Manufacturing International Corporation.

India's Struggle: As of 2024, India has no commercial factories in operation. Delays in finance and policy caused previous initiatives (such as HSMC and ISMC) to fail. The absence of a fab environment deters R&D expenditures.

3) Low Investment in R&D

India invests about 0.7% of GDP on research and development, whereas China spends over 3%, with a focus on semiconductors (NSF, 2023). While Indian companies depend on foreign technology, Chinese companies such as Huawei and SMIC make significant patent investments.

Delays in governmental action, low R&D funding, manufacturing flaws, and talent exodus are the main causes of India's semiconductor R&D gap. Even if recent projects like ISM and alliances with Micron, Tata, and Foxconn are promising, catching up to China will necessitate sustained investment, cooperation between academics and industry, and a more robust supply chain.

E. SIZE OF DIGITAL ECONOMIES AROUND THE GLOBE

E. 1 India

According to the Reserve Bank of India, the core digital economy's share of the nation's gross domestic product increased from 5.4% in 2014 to 8.5% in 2019. India's digital economy grew at a rate of 15.6% per year in US dollars between 2014 and 2019, which was 2.4 times faster than the nation's overall economic growth rate.

In addition, the digitally enabled sectors of the digitally reliant economy were estimated to have contributed 22.4% in 2019. According to analysis, the Reserve Bank of India calculated the output multipliers for the digital and non-digital sectors, which show how a unit change in final demand affects the economy's overall production. Between 2014 and 2019, the non-digital production multiplier decreased from 1.68 to 1.57. During this time, the digital output multiplier increased from 1.34 in 2014 to 1.50 in 2019.

India's digital economy was valued at US$200 billion in 2019, and under normal conditions, it was projected to grow to US$500 billion by 2025, according to a recent report by MIETY in 2019However, with targeted policy initiatives spanning 30 digital themes under nine national goals, the digital economy may reach USD 1 trillion. These objectives are:

1. Doubling Farmers Income
2. Quality Education for All
3. Make in Digital India, make for India, make for the world
4. Next-gen banking services
5. Jobs and Skills for the Future
6. Energy for All
7. E-governance of the future
8. 21st-century IT infrastructure and software capabilities
9. Health for All (PIB, 2019)

In 2019, the RBI reported that 6.1 percent of India's total forward linkages from the core digital economy were in the construction sector, followed by 4.2 percent for the rental of machinery and equipment, 3.8 percent for food and beverage and tobacco, 3.6 percent for textiles and textile products, and 3.5 percent for electrical and optical equipment.

E. 2 Global Digital Economy

Measuring the digital economy has become very essential given increasing proportion of digitally-driven economic activities and growing economic importance, though the process is not free from flaws. Challenges:

1. Definition/boundaries: As already remarked, definitions of the "digital economy" vary and differ. That inconsistency does not by itself make measurement difficult but does complicate comparisons. Additionally, the definitions that draw unclear boundaries between the rest of the economy, including the digital economy, does make measurement more challenging.
2. Issues with data quality: More precisely, there are fundamental issues with data in developing nations —either it does not exist or it is of low quality. This is further compounded by the fact that innovation is constant; hence, collection of data cannot keep pace with technological changes, ibid.
3. Invisibility of digital economy: Most economic activities made possible by digital technology are difficult to quantify as production. They might include services that act as a middleman between companies and/or customers for which valuation of inputs is problematic, let alone their value-added. Moreover, often

virtual these activities are challenging to trace, in particular in the context of inter-border digital trade and digital consumers-as-producers.

Size of Overall Global Economy

In a world where the digital landscape is going to set the future, there stand the twin giants: the United States of America and China. The two dominate nearly two-thirds of the global digital economy—a consideration that is amazing if not astonishing since these two nations together represent only 4.2% of the global population. Yet, figures tell a story of power—the US's 26 percent share of global GDP commands an astonishing 42 percent of all spending on technology. It's sewn e-commerce into the fabric of everyday life, where nearly 39 percent of the retail sales in 2024 flow through online channels—a figure primed to continue rising to 41 percent by 2028.

A Forrester forecast (2024) estimates that, as the digital economy charges forward, it will grow to $16.5 trillion by 2028 and account for 17% of global GDP across the 14 major economies that comprise North America, Europe, APAC, and Latin America.

From the vantage point of the World Economic Forum, in the next decade, close to half of all new value created will stem from digitally enabled platforms, and, by implication, will transform industries and societies alike in a similar vein With six key players leading the charge—the US, China, the UK, Japan, Germany, and South Korea—the global stage is set for action. By 2023-2028, the digital economy will sustain 6.9 percent growth year on year, strongly outperforming the pace of global GDP growth. It is being driven by a trio of e-commerce, technology spending, and exports, with the US and China anchoring nearly 40% of global value added in the information and communications technology sector. (World Economic Forum, 2022)

This is no fleeting digital revolution. The World Bank estimates that today, the digital economy represents more than 15% of global GDP and has grown 2.5 times faster in this past decade than the physical world's GDP. The digital economy is expected to provide 30 million jobs and contribute over 30% of the world's GDP by 2030, according to Deemah AlYahya, Secretary-General of the Digital Cooperation Organization, among others. (Devi, 2023)

Depending on the definition, the digital economy can account for anywhere between 4.5% and 15.5% of the world's gross domestic product.

In some countries, such as Taiwan, Ireland, and Malaysia, the ICT sector constitutes an appreciable share of their economies. Viewed in global terms, there is no denying the current boom in digital services in 2018, ICT and other digitally delivered services accounted for half of all services exported worldwide, with $2.9 trillion in exports.

An even more dramatic account of the digital economy's rise emerges from a study conducted by Huawei and Oxford Economics. In 2016, they estimated its size at $11 trillion; by 2025, that number was projected to grow to as much as $23 trillion, roughly the equivalent of almost a quarter of worldwide GDP. This is a story of a world transformed, where digital isn't just a part of the economy—it is the economy.

Table 7. Pace of digitalization: a cross country perspective (% CAGR in the ICT sector) Source (basic data): European Commission, PREDICT database (Srivastava, 2023)

Country	2001 to 2010	2010 to 2019	2001 to 2019
China	18.00	11.00	14.70
India	11.20	10.60	10.8
South Korea	6.10	2.50	4.70
Taiwan	5.70	3.30	4.40
Brazil	9.70	-2.10	4.30
Germany	2.00	4.10	3.10
EU	2.60	3.20	2.80
France	1.80	3.00	2.20
United states	-3.30	6.80	1.20
United Kingdom	-1.30	3.90	1.20

E.3 Labour Markets And Effect On Their Growth By Digitization

Employment is low in India's digital sectors. In calendar year 2022, out of a worker population ratio of 38.2%, There were almost 4.9 million people employed in the core digital economy.

Computer programming, consultancy, and related activities occupy 59.8% of this employment; it is followed by telecommunication services with 15.2%.

With these definitions, it would be probable that the percentage of digital workers will lie at around 1% in developing countries and almost 4% in developed ones, adding up to approximately 2.5% of the workforce worldwide. This might be interpreted as an implication that some 3% of the global workforce is working for the digital economy, as defined in Figure 3

, in the current scenario. There are, however, some large exceptions in the global South. Indeed, in the Philippines alone, there are already an estimated 2 million workers working online nearly 5% of the workforce many of them, at least half, being employed in call centers. In 2014, the number of people directly employed by the Indian IT sector was more than 3 million, with another 7-10 million working indirectly, Further, it is expected that a total of 6 million people work either directly or indirectly for the Indian Internet economy. It is said that the Internet has created 3.1 jobs for every job it replaces, with a more significant impact in aspiring economies, where 3.2 jobs are created than the developed ones where 1.6 jobs are created. Through digitization, 17 million jobs have been created in emerging economies from 2009-2011.

In the mid-2010s, the average labour productivity per worker in India was around $10,000, whereas in the software sector, it exceeded $37,000.

According to Deemah AlYahya, Secretary-General of the Digital Cooperation Organization, the digital economy can be expected to generate 30 million jobs by 2030.

On the global level, employment in ICT grew from 34 million in 2010 to 39 million in 2015; computer services accounted for the biggest share with 38%. The ICT sector's contribution to total employment rose from 1.8% to 2%. Computer services contributed 40% of the total value-added within the ICT sector.

F. CHALLENGES

F.1 Digital Inclusion and Equity

For a digital society to be equitable and accessible, digital inclusion and equality are essential elements. Existing socioeconomic inequalities are made worse by differences in access, opportunities, and skills as technology becomes more and more integrated into daily life.

The goal of digital inclusion is to guarantee that all people and communities have access to ICTs, such as digital devices, broadband internet, and the knowledge and abilities necessary to use them efficiently. Systemic inequalities in digital access, literacy, and involvement are addressed to further advance digital equity. Significant disparities still exist based on financial class, region, age, race, and disability, despite worldwide technological breakthroughs.

The Digital Divide: Barriers to Inclusion

The disparity in opportunities to access information and communication technologies (ICTs) and use the internet for a wide range of purposes between people, households, enterprises, and geographic locations at various socioeconomic levels is known as the "digital divide." The skills and abilities required to use digital technologies efficiently are also included in this difference, in addition to actual access to technology.

Infrastructure Gaps: Rural and low-income urban areas often lack affordable, high-speed internet (Van Dijk, 2020).

Device Affordability: Low-income households struggle to afford computers or smartphones.

Policy & Market Failures: Privatized telecom markets may neglect underserved regions.

Skills and Literacy Barriers

Digital literacy: Using digital technologies can be difficult for older folks and those with less education.

Language & Content: Accessibility concerns affect nonnative speakers and those with disabilities. (UNESCO,2021)

Socioeconomic and Cultural Barriers

Income Inequality: Cost remains a primary obstacle for disadvantaged groups (OECD, 2020).

Policy Intervention: Governments, NGOs, and private entities have implemented strategies to promote digital equity.

Broadband Expansion Programs

USA's Affordable Connectivity Program (ACP): Subsidizes internet costs for low-income families

EU's Digital Decade Initiative: Aims for 100% broadband coverage by 2030

Digital Literacy Programs

India's Digital Saksharta Abhiyan (DISHA): Trails rural populations in digital skills (MeitY, 2020).

Singapore's Seniors Go Digital: Helps elderly citizens adapt to technology (IMDA, 2021).

Public-Private Partnerships

Google's Project Loon: Provided internet via balloons in remote areas (before discontinuation).

Microsoft's Airband Initiative: Expands rural broadband in developing nations.

Digital inclusion and equity are essential for social and economic participation in the 21st century. While progress has been made, systemic barriers persist. Future efforts must prioritize affordability, accessibility, and education to ensure no one is left behind in the digital era.

Case Study : Digital Inclusion in Kerala, India – The "Kerala Fibre Optic Network (KFON)" Initiative

In 2021, the Indian state of Kerala announced the Kerala Fibre Optic Network (KFON) to give all residents access to reasonably priced broadband and free high-speed internet to two million low-income families. One of the most comprehensive public-sector digital inclusion initiatives in the world, this program treats internet access as a fundamental right in an effort to close the digital divide.

The following are KFON's main objectives.

- To close the connectivity gap, provide a core network infrastructure (information highway) that all service providers can access without discrimination.
- Establish a dependable, safe, and expandable network that links all government buildings, hospitals, schools, and other establishments.
- Collabourate with MSOs, TSPs, and ISPs to offer economically disadvantaged homes free internet, (up to 20 Mbps) to Below Poverty Line (BPL) families. (Kerala State IT Infrastructure Ltd., 2023)

Implementation

Infrastructure Development Laid 35,000 km of optical fibre across Kerala. Installed 30,000 Wi-Fi hotspots in public spaces. Partnered with BSNL (Bharat Sanchar Nigam Limited) for last-mile connectivity.

Impact and Outcome

- Digital Inclusion Successes
- 2 million+ households received free internet (KFON Report, 2023).
- Schools & colleges integrated with e-learning platforms.

Lessons for Global Digital Equity

- Public ownership of infrastructure can prevent corporate monopolies.
- Free internet for marginalized groups is feasible with government support.
- Digital literacy programs must accompany connectivity efforts.

Conclusion KFON demonstrates that government-led digital inclusion can significantly reduce inequality. However, long-term success depends on sustained funding, digital training, and private-sector collabouration. Similar models can be replicated in other developing regions.

F.2 Labour Right Vulnerabilities Caused By Gig Economy

Digital platforms have changed the nature of labour markets around the world by enabling "gig" or "platform-mediated" work, which is defined by flexible, task-based interactions that are controlled by algorithms rather than conventional employment procedures. Although this shift creates chances for people to enter the workforce, especially underprivileged groups, it also brings up serious issues with social justice, employment safeguards, and labour rights.

Misclassification: gig workers are frequently classified as independent contractors, they are not entitled to fundamental labour protections including the right to collective bargaining, paid leave, unemployment insurance, occupational health and safety, and minimum pay.

Economic Vulnerability and Income Instability: Earnings from platform-mediated employment are unstable because of shifting demand, algorithmic modifications, and consumer reviews. According to a World Bank research, there are 435 million gig workers worldwide. This number shows that the gig economy is growing quickly, but it also highlights the lack of social protections like savings accounts, pensions, and minimum salary guarantees. (Hussein, 2023)

India's Case

Depending on the type of job and the workers' status, several laws in India recognize digital labour platforms. For instance, labour regulations including the Industrial Disputes Act (MeitY, 2020), the Minimum Wages Act (MeitY, 2021), and the Employees' Provident Fund and Miscellaneous Provisions Act (MeitY, 2024) apply to workers who are categorized as employees. Nevertheless, these regulations do not apply to employees who are categorized as self-employed or independent contractors, and their legal safeguards are restricted (Mishra, 2024).

The Indian government has suggested the regulation on Social Security, a new labour regulation, to address this problem. Its goal is to give social security benefits to all workers, including those in the gig economy. Parliament is now considering the code. (Singh & Bhushan, 2023)

USA' Case

Platform employees are exempt from the majority of labour laws in the US since they are regarded by federal law as independent contractors. Nonetheless, several states have enacted legislation granting gig workers advantages including unemployment insurance and sick leave. (Singh & Bhushan, 2023)

While gig work made possible by digitalization has increased labour-market flexibility, it also carries significant concerns, especially in relation to worker classification, algorithmic governance, economic security, and systemic inequality. Even if new institutional developments and legal frameworks provide avenues for change, there are still many obstacles to overcome, especially with regard to enforcement, global inequality, and the conformity of digital labour regimes with accepted labour standards.

F.3 Potential Risks Of Modern Digital Economy

1. Platformization of the Economy: Risks and Challenges

Platformization is the term used to describe how digital platforms are becoming more and more dominant in economic activity, which can result in systemic vulnerabilities, data monopolies, and market concentration. While the economy has benefited greatly from the growing platformization of the industry due to the dominance of digital platforms like Amazon, Google, and Alibaba, there are also systemic problems.

Because the Platform Economy prevents low-skilled, less educated, and technologically illiterate persons from finding profitable employment, it may contribute to income and occupational health inequities in the traditional labour market. Conventional workers who are unable to adjust to the platform technologies will be forced into low-paying, unstable jobs with bad labour rights protections. This will intensify the race to the bottom between platform workers and traditional economy workers, sustaining the grey economy—the labour market's foundation of unreported work.(Samant, 2019)

Mitigation Policies: OECD and ILO

Both the OECD and the ILO have promoted global measures to address the platform economy's numerous issues. Both strategies view platform work as a component of a larger global movement toward digitalization in the labour and economic sectors, where international digital companies are becoming more and more prevalent. Both stress how important it is to provide all workers, regardless of employment position, proper social protection, labour and collective rights, and access to training. The OECD has a broader focus that includes economic and fiscal policy, whereas the ILO only analyzes working conditions and social protection. (Hauben et al., 2020).

OECD

- Address the primary issue of ambiguous employment status, guarantee accurate worker classification, and minimize the gray area between self-employment and dependent employment by implementing more standardized and transparent definitions of employment status and by stepping up law enforcement to combat abuse by employers or employees;
- Broaden specific labour rights and safeguards to encompass non-standard workers, particularly the self-employed, in the domains of equitable compensation, working time limits, occupational health and safety, anti-discrimination laws, and certain aspects of employment protection;
- • Improve legislation and enforcement to combat abuses of monopsony power in labour markets and circumstances where a small number of enterprises can set prices for labour and purchases of inputs.

ILO

- establishing a Universal Labour Guarantee that assures minimum workers' rights, a sufficient living wage, restrictions on maximum working hours, and protection of health and safety at work for all workers, irrespective of their contractual arrangement and employment status;
- adoption of an international governance framework for digital labour platforms that mandates that platforms (and clients) uphold a set of fundamental rights and safeguards for each and every one of their employees; the framework may include the means to enable cross-border social security payments and create a dispute resolution mechanism;

2. Financial Globalization: Spillover Effects & Currency Mismatches Financial globalization increases interconnectedness but also creates vulnerabilities, such as:

Spillover Effects in Financial Globalization

Cross-border capital flows are made easier by financial globalization, but it also makes nations more susceptible to spillover effects, in which financial or economic shocks in one nation spread to others. There are several ways in which these spillovers happen:

A. Capital Flow Volatility

Sudden Stops & Surges: Financial instability is frequently caused by rapid reversals of foreign capital inflows ("sudden stops") or excessive inflows ("surges") in emerging markets (EMs).

B. Financial Contagion

Herding Behavior: Even when only one nation is experiencing a crisis, investors frequently pull out of several emerging markets at once out of fear.

C. Spillovers from Monetary Policy

Policies of the US Federal Reserve: Capital frequently leaves EMs when the Fed raises interest rates, leading to currency devaluation and financial strain.

2. Currency Mismatches: A Serious risk in International Finance

Currency mismatches create vulnerabilities when assets or revenues are in local currency but liabilities are in foreign currencies (such as USD or EUR).

A. Balance Sheet Risks
B. Financial Instability & Crises

F.4 Cybersecurity Risk

With more of digital R&D, cyber threats are real. Protection on intellectual property and sensitive data is important to spearhead sustainable competitive advantage. A prediction by Cybersecurity Ventures has estimated that cybercrime could cost the world as much as US$10.5 trillion annually by the year 2025 (Cybersecurity Ventures, 2024); thus, this calls for the appropriate cybersecurity measures within digital R&D. The India Government has drafted various programs that tend to overcome part of the concerns related to data security and privacy through the very essence of implementation of the IT Act 2000, which embodies laws concerning data protection. India has marked great growth in terms of cyber safety, with a placement of tenth in the GCI 2020 as released by ITU on June 29th, 2021, hence moving up 37 places. (Jagran Josh, 2021)

Impact of Cybersecurity Dangers

A. Dangers to National Security

Critical infrastructure, such as energy, telecom, and banking networks, is disrupted by cyberattacks. They make private communications public and erode defenses.

B. Economic and Business Impact

Businesses lose money as a result of ransomware, fraud, and outages. Demands for compliance cause recovery costs to increase and customer trust to erode.

C. Personal consequences

Financial scams and identity theft are caused by breaches of personal data. Additionally, cyberthreats propagate false information and induce mental distress.

D. Innovation Challenges

Digital investments are discouraged by security concerns, and the adoption of new technologies is slowed by legislative changes.

Government Measures (Indonesia's Case)

- Infrastructure: National Security Operation Center (SOC) to detect/respond to threats.
- Legal: ITE Law (Law No. 19 of 2016), Presidential Regulation No. 53/2017.
- Training: Cybersecurity education and certification programs.
- Public-Private Collabouration: Industry partnerships to co-develop defenses.

F.5 More Challenges

Lack of Coordination Or Interoperability

The primary players in the digital economy in the majority of nations are not creating a unified or compatible digital environment. MNOs are new to digital financial services, whereas banks are centred around payment switches. There is a lack of coordination between legislation concerning mobile and finance, and regulators are slow to identify and respond to emerging mobile financial services and their potential effects on the larger financial industry. (Vital Wave et al., 2014)

Digital Illiteracy

The biggest barrier to the success of the Digital India program in terms of technology adaptation is a high degree of digital illiteracy. An estimated 950 million Indians do not yet have access to the internet, per the ASSOCHAM-Deloitte study on Digital India, published in November 2016. (ASSOCHAM & Deloitte, 2016)

The slow and delayed construction of infrastructure is one of the primary barriers to the growth of the digital economy. Digital infrastructure in developing and emerging nations is insufficient to handle the rapidly expanding digitalization of sectors such as digital payments.

The lengthy and complex regulatory procedures in emerging economies hinder the private sector's involvement in government initiatives.

G. CONCLUSION

The digital economy has reconstituted business methods by facilitating opportunities for growth, innovation, and efficiency. It allows firms to connect with distant customers easily, hastens processes, and accommodates business models that boost economic development. However, it also raises concerns such as cybersecurity vulnerabilities, uneven access to digital devices, and job displacement due to disruptions in conventional industries. While it is also forecasted to grow very fast, it needs to be judiciously managed to handle the digital divide in a manner that provides equitable access. The digital economy is undeniably vital to world prosperity, notwithstanding challenges along the way, due to developments in digital infrastructure, data analytics, and e-commerce. Policymakers, businesses, and society should work together to maximize benefits and reduce risks for fair digital transformation.

REFERENCES

G20 Digital Economy Task Force & International Telecommunication Union. (2020). *A roadmap toward a common framework for measuring the digital economy*. https://www.itu.int/en/ITUD/Statistics/Documents/publications/OECDRoadmapDigitalEconomy2020.pdf

Acquier, A., Daudigeos, T., & Pinkse, J. (2017). Promises and paradoxes of the sharing economy: An organizing framework. *Technological Forecasting and Social Change*, *125*, 1–10. DOI: 10.1016/j.techfore.2017.07.006

Asian Development Bank. (2024). *Capturing the digital economy: A proposed measurement framework and its applications*. https://www.adb.org/publications/capturing-digital-economy-measurement-framework

ASSOCHAM & Deloitte. (2016). *Digital India: Unlocking the trillion dollar opportunity*. https://www2.deloitte.com/content/dam/Deloitte/in/Documents/technology-media-telecommunications/in-tmt-digital-india-unlock-opportunity-noexp.pdf

Bukht, R., & Heeks, R. (2017). Defining, conceptualising and measuring the digital economy (Development Informatics Working Paper No. 68). *SSRN*. https://doi.org/ DOI: 10.2139/ssrn.3431732

Calvino, F., Criscuolo, C., Marcolin, L., & Squicciarini, M. (2018). A taxonomy of digital intensive sectors (OECD Science, Technology and Industry Working Papers, No. 2018/14). *OECD Publishing*. https://doi.org/DOI: 10.1787/18151965

Cybersecurity Ventures. (2024). *Cybercrime to cost the world $10.5 trillion annually by 2025*. https://cybersecurityventures.com/hackerpocalypse-cybercrime-report-2016/

Devi, A. (2023). DCO 2030: Digital economy to contribute 30% of global GDP and create 30 million jobs by 2030. *ITP.NET*. https://www.itp.net/industry/dco-2030-digital-economy-to-contribute-30-of-global-gdp-and-create-30-million-jobs-by-2030

Fang, Y. (2024). *The future development of the electronic technology industry under the trend of the digital economy*. ResearchGate. https://www.researchgate.net/publication/381304736

Forrester. (2024). *The global digital economy will reach $16.5 trillion and capture 17% of global GDP by 2028*. https://www.forrester.com/blogs/the-global-digital-economy-will-reach-16-5-trillion-and-capture-17-of-global-gdp-by-2028/

Grady, M. (2024). The global digital economy will reach $16.5 trillion and capture 17% of global GDP by 2028. *Forrester Blog*. https://www.forrester.com/blogs/the-global-digital-economy-will-reach-16-5-trillion-and-capture-17-of-global-gdp-by-2028/

Hauben, H., Lenaerts, K., & Kraatz, S. (2020). *Platform economy and precarious work: Mitigating risks*. European Parliament. https://www.europarl.europa.eu/RegData/etudes/BRIE/2020/652721/IPOL_BRI(2020)652721_EN.pdf

Hussein, F. (2023). Online gig work is growing rapidly, but workers lack job protections, a World Bank report says. *AP News*. https://apnews.com/article/online-gig-workers-labour-employment-world-bank-40b81a789fd5f0fb366e83f0223d832f

Jagran Josh. (2021). *ITU Global Cybersecurity Index 2020: India ranked among the top 10 nations*. https://www.jagranjosh.com/general-knowledge/itu-global-cybersecurity-index-1625207203-1

Kerala State IT Infrastructure Ltd. (KSITIL). (2023). *Kerala Fibre Optic Network (KFON)*. https://kfon.kerala.gov.in

Ministry of Electronics and Information Technology (MeitY). (2020). *Pradhan Mantri Gramin Digital Saksharta Abhiyan (PMGDISHA)*. https://www.pmgdisha.in

Ministry of Electronics and Information Technology (MeitY). (2021). *India Semiconductor Mission*. https://www.meity.gov.in

Ministry of Electronics and Information Technology (MeitY). (2024). *R & D in electronics division*. https://www.meity.gov.in/content/r-d-electronics

Mishra, D., Kedia, M., Reddy, A., & Ramnath, K. (2024). *State of India's Digital Economy (SIDE) Report, 2024*. ICRIER. https://icrier.org/pdf/State_of_India_Digital_Economy_Report_2024.pdf

National Science Foundation (NSF). (2023). *Science and Engineering Indicators 2023*. https://ncses.nsf.gov/pubs/nsb20231

Neos Networks. (2024). What is digital infrastructure. https://neosnetworks.com/resources/blog/what-is-digital-infrastructure/

Office for National Statistics. (2022). *UK digital economy research*. https://www.ons.gov.uk/economy/economicoutputandproductivity/output/methodologies/ukdigitaleconomyresearch2019

Organisation for Economic Co-operation and Development. (2020a). *Bridging the digital divide: Include, upskill, innovate*. https://www.oecd.org/digital/bridging-the-digital-divide.pdf

Organisation for Economic Co-operation and Development. (2020b). OECD Digital. *Economic Outlook, 2020*. Advance online publication. DOI: 10.1787/bb167041-en

Press Information Bureau. (2019). *Report on India's Trillion Dollar Digital Opportunity Released.* https://pib.gov.in/PressReleaseIframePage.aspx?PRID=1565669

Press Information Bureau. (2022). *Achievements made under Digital India programme.* https://pib.gov.in/PressReleaseIframePage.aspx?PRID=1885962

Press Information Bureau. (2024). *Indian government future plan on semiconductor and electronics manufacturing.* https://www.pib.gov.in/PressReleaseIframePage.aspx?PRID=2039638

Rani, A. (2021). Digital economy in India: Opportunities and challenges. *JETIR, 8*(2), 290–297. https://www.jetir.org/papers/JETIR2102290.pdf

Samant, Y. (2019). *The promises and perils of the platform economy: Occupational health and safety challenges, and the opportunities for labour inspection.* International Labour Organization. https://www.ilo.org/resource/statement/promises-and-perils-platform-economy-occupational-health-and-safety

Singh, R., & Bhushan, V. (2023). The global workforce revolution: Exploring digital labour platforms and the gig economy in the era of globalization. *International Journal of Civil Law and Legal Research, 3*(2), 421–435. https://www.civillawjournal.com/article/52/3-2-2-421.pdf. DOI: 10.22271/civillaw.2023.v3.i2a.52

Srivastava, D. K., Bharadwaj, M., Kapur, T., & Trehan, R. (2023). *Economy watch: Monitoring India's macro-fiscal performance.* EY. https://www.ey.com/content/dam/ey-unified-site/ey-com/en-in/insights/tax/documents/ey-economy-watch-april-2023-v1.pdf

UNCTAD. (2021). *Manual for the production of statistics on ICT-enabled services.* https://unctad.org/system/files/official-document/dtlstict2021d1_en.pdf

UNED. (2020). *Introduction to digital economy in the EU.* https://blogs.uned.es/digitaleconomy/wp-content/uploads/sites/253/2020/12/Introduction-to-Digital-Economy-in-the-EU.pdf

UNESCO. (2021). *The role of inclusive digital content for inclusive digital learning.* https://unesdoc.unesco.org/ark:/48223/pf0000375703

van Dijk, J. A. G. M. (2020). *The digital divide.* Polity Press. https://www.researchgate.net/publication/339751402

World Economic Forum. (2022). *Digital trust: How to unleash the trillion-dollar opportunity for our global economy.* https://www.weforum.org/stories/2022/08/digital-trust-how-to-unleash-the-trillion-dollar-opportunity-for-our-global-economy/

KEY TERMS AND DEFINITIONS

Core measure: The Core Measure of the Digital Economy includes only the economic activities of producers specializing in ICT goods and ICT-related information services. It includes industries that create digital products, software, telecommunications, and data services, focusing on firms that enable, process, or distribute digital information. This measure helps in calculating the sheer impact of the digital sector on other industries, as a bigger core sector makes digitalization faster thus making a positive impact on narrow and broad sector of the digital economy.

Narrow measure: Although this definition is still in line with the existing GDP production boundaries, it does not concentrate on the end product or the mode of transaction. Rather, the limited measure is defined by whether or not the production of the good or service depends on digitalization. Numerous new business models have emerged as a result of digitalization, but they do not produce ICT commodities or ICT and information services as defined by the core measure; instead, they are entirely dependent on digital inputs, such as digital services or data, to function. This differs with the other businesses included in the broad measure, where digital inputs simply serve to improve output rather than to enable it. For the production to occur, digital information and technologies are used intensively by intermediary platforms, such as public digital platforms, that enable transactions between producers and consumers. Although they are not regarded as manufacturers of ICT goods or ICT and information services, these companies heavily utilize ICT products and services to generate new kinds of value added.

Broad Measure: Industries that rely on digital technology to enhance their current economic activities in some manner are classified under the broad measure of the digital economy. Broad measures include firms that produce digital products, outputs that rely on digital inputs, and production of firms in which the use of digital inputs significantly improves production. Estimation for broad measure is a little tricky as the word significantly may be interpreted differently. The use of the word "significantly" also recognizes that there is no clear rigid boundary between digital and non-digital activities. It is essential for countries to differentiate between digital and non-digital activities, for example, in recent years sectors like agriculture and mining have been enhanced by digital inputs. If these sectors were included in the predetermined definition of the "digitally produced economy," it might be applied to nations where mining and agriculture account for sizable shares of the GDP but use digitalization very little, greatly overestimating the measure of the "digital economy".

The Digital Society: This definition of the digital society extends beyond the digital economy. Digital interactions and activities can not be included in GDP, for example, free digital platforms do not have a significant impact on value addition to the economy but these activities are essential for fostering equitable development and thus are essential for digital policy but are excluded from the estimation of the digital economy. Furthermore, the G20 Digital Economy Task Force recognizes that while not directly tied to a digital economy, many elements of a digital society include digital interactions and activities that have an effect on the economy and add value. Among other things, regional and economic development policies depend on these activities.

Digital Economy: Around 1996, American businessman Tapscott Don came up with the term "digital economy".The meaning of the term "digital economy" has been changing ever since. Early definitions and analysis focused mostly on Internet uptake and usage, as well as some of its effects on the economy. But as internet technology advanced, attention turned to analyzing the characteristics of the expanding digital economy. The dissemination of ideas, services, and products based on information and communication technologies (ICTs), as well as the skills required to operate the technologies, are currently the main focus in the shift to a digital economy. The term "digital economy" refers generically to the amalgamation of aspects involving "an economy based on digital technologies." (UNED,2020) Digital economy describes the wide range of economic activities that depend on digital technology, such as cloud computing, big data, artificial intelligence, the internet, and the Internet of Things (IoT). Digital services, financial technology, internet commerce, and platform-based companies that support global communication, transactions, and innovation are all included. The digital economy is revolutionizing established sectors by facilitating remote work, increasing productivity, and developing new business models like gig work and subscription services. In addition, technology promotes economic growth by automating processes and making decisions based on data, but it also raises issues with cybersecurity, privacy, and digital inequality. The digital economy has different definitions, each setting different boundaries. Two approaches, ADB and OECD, can be used to estimate the digital economy.

Platform Economy: Acquier et al. (2017) define the platform economy as "a set of initiatives that use digital platforms to mediate decentralized exchanges among peers." Digital platforms operate as intermediaries that help different user groups—like customers, service providers, and developers—interact and trade with one another. With the development of digital technologies and the internet, this new model has emerged, drastically changing conventional business processes in a wide range of industries.

Platform Types: There are other categories into which the platform economy can be divided, such as: Transaction platforms, such as Amazon and eBay, function as online markets for the purchase and sale of products and services. Platforms for innovation: These offer technical structures on which users can expand (e.g., Microsoft Azure). Integration platforms, like the Apple App Store, combine the features of transaction and innovation platforms. (Gunther,2022)

Digital Infrastructure: The real hardware and software-based technologies that make digital services possible are known as digital infrastructure. It comprises the networks and IT systems that let firms function and interact. It includes essential components such as: • Hardware includes computers, servers, networking equipment (such as switches and routers), and Internet of Things (IoT) devices that provide data processing and connectivity. • Software includes middleware, operating systems, and apps that help businesses run and make it easier for hardware to communicate with one another. • Data centers are establishments that contain networking hardware and computers, offering the ideal setting for storing, processing, and sharing massive amounts of data. • Networks: Both virtual and physical networks, such as the internet, wide area networks (WANs), and local area networks (LANs), are essential for data transfer. • Cloud computing: Internet-based services like Infrastructure as a Service (IaaS) and Software as a Service (SaaS) that enable scalable computing and storage resources. (Neos networks,2024).

Chapter 6
Security and Privacy in AI: IoT-Enabled Banking and Finance Services

R. Seranmadevi
https://orcid.org/0000-0002-4559-4100
Christ University, Bangalore, India

Santosh Reddy Addula
https://orcid.org/0009-0000-3286-8224
University of the Cumberlands, USA

Deepak Kumar
https://orcid.org/0009-0009-2137-0864
University of the Cumberlands, USA

Amit Kumar Tyagi
https://orcid.org/0000-0003-2657-8700
National Institute of Fashion Technology, New Delhi, India

ABSTRACT

The integration of Artificial Intelligence (AI) and the IoThas led to significant advancements in the banking and finance sector, providing personalized, efficient, and data-driven services. However, these AI-IoT enabled systems also introduce complex security and privacy challenges that need to be addressed to protect sensitive financial data and maintain customer trust. This paper surveys the key security and privacy issues in AI-IoT enabled banking, including data breaches, cyber-attacks, unauthorized access, and data misuse. We examine current methodologies for securing AI-IoT systems, such as encryption, blockchain, alongside AI-driven threat detection and response techniques.The survey explores regulatory considerations and compliance requirements that shape security protocols in financial services. By

DOI: 10.4018/979-8-3693-9765-7.ch006

identifying gaps in existing security measures and highlighting advanced privacy-preserving technologies, this study aims to provide a comprehensive understanding of the challenges and future directions in securing AI-IoT applications within banking and finance.

1. INTRODUCTION TO AI, IOT, BANKING AND FINANCE

The banking and finance sector is moving with a huge transformative shift which is driven by emerging technologies, particularly Artificial Intelligence (AI) and the Internet of Things (IoT) (Aji, A., & Nurhasanah, N. (2020), Alavi, A. S., & Jafari, A. (2021)). AI, with its ability to analyze large data sets, make predictions, and automate decision-making, provides banks and financial institutions powerful tools for personalizing services, reducing operational costs, and improving risk management. IoT, which enables devices to connect, collect, and exchange data in real-time, complements AI by providing a continuous flow of data from various sources. Together, AI and IoT make a connected ecosystem where customer behavior, market trends, and financial transactions can be analyzed and acted upon in real time. In banking and finance, these technologies provide promising applications. AI-powered chatbots and virtual assistants are transforming customer service, while predictive analytics support more accurate credit scoring, fraud detection, and investment strategies. IoT devices, such as wearables and smart home systems, are increasingly integrated with banking apps to provide users with personalized spending insights, location-based offers, and risk assessments. However, the use of AI and IoT also presents new security and privacy issues. Financial data is highly sensitive, and the extensive connectivity facilitated by IoT expands the potential attack surface for cyber threats. Hence, this work discusses how AI and IoT are redefining the banking and finance landscape, enabling unprecedented levels of personalization and operational efficiency. At the same time, it makes the importance of implementing robust security and privacy frameworks to protect customer data and maintain trust as the industry uses these cutting-edge technologies. The following sections will discuss several applications, benefits, challenges, and strategies for secure deployment of AI-IoT solutions within the financial sector.

1.1 Background of AI and IoT in Banking and finance

The integration of AI and IoT in banking and finance is part of a larger trend towards digital transformation in financial services. The evolution of AI has enabled machines to process complex financial data, identify patterns, and make data-driven decisions, reducing human intervention in various financial processes (Baig, M. Z.,

& Shah, F. (2020)). Here, few key advancements in AI, such as machine learning, natural language processing (NLP), and deep learning, have opened new avenues for automating customer service, predicting market trends, and enhancing fraud detection.

And IoT connects physical devices to the internet, allowing them to collect and share data autonomously. In banking, IoT has enabled "smart" applications that can monitor client behavior, facilitate seamless transactions, and even provide location-based offers. For example, IoT-integrated ATMs, biometric systems, and mobile wallets enhance convenience and accessibility, improving the overall customer experience. IoT also allows financial institutions to use data from connected devices to develop more accurate risk profiles, allowing for better-informed credit decisions and personalized offerings.

Historically, the banking sector has been cautious in adopting new technology due to strict regulatory requirements and the need to protect sensitive financial information. However, as consumer expectations for seamless, real-time services grow, financial institutions are increasingly adopting AI and IoT to remain competitive. AI-driven virtual assistants, automated credit scoring systems, and real-time transaction monitoring are now becoming industry standards, as they streamline operations and improve accuracy. IoT's contribution has been equally important, providing new data points and touchpoints for enhancing customer engagement and operational efficiency. Note that despite the advantages, the interconnected nature of AI and IoT provide new security risks. The reliance on IoT devices increases vulnerability to cyber-attacks, while the large amount of data required by AI systems introduces privacy issues. Thus, ensuring data security and regulatory compliance is important for successful AI-IoT adoption. The background of AI and IoT in banking and finance demonstrates a powerful shift toward data-driven decision-making, improved customer interaction, and innovative service models, yet have the need for a secure, privacy-conscious approach to safeguard customer data and trust.

1.2 Importance of Security and Privacy in Banking and finance

Security and privacy are foundational pillars in the banking and finance sector, where the trust of millions of customers relies on the safe handling of highly sensitive data. With the industry's rapid digitalization, fueled by advancements in AI and IoT ensuring robust security and privacy is more important than ever. Financial institutions handle large amount of personal and financial information, including transaction data, account details, and biometric identifiers, all of which, if exposed, could lead to serious consequences for both individuals and institutions.

The importance of security in banking and finance is underscored by the industry's exposure to cyber threats. Unauthorized access, data breaches, and fraudulent activities can lead to substantial financial losses, reputational damage, and regulatory penalties. Strong security protocols are essential to protect against these threats, safeguard the institution's integrity, and maintain operational stability. AI and IoT introduce additional complexities, as interconnected systems increase potential entry points for cyber-attacks, while the processing of large data volumes heightens vulnerability.

Privacy, too, is important, as financial data is particularly sensitive and highly regulated by privacy laws such as the GDPR in Europe and CCPA in the United States. Customers expect institutions to protect their personal information, and any violation of privacy can erode trust and lead to legal repercussions. AI's need for extensive data to make accurate predictions and improve customer experience must be balanced against the rights of individuals to control and protect their data. IoT-enabled financial services, which gather real-time user data, further amplify the need for privacy protections, as breaches can reveal behavioral patterns and personal information. In summary, security and privacy are essential for maintaining customer trust, regulatory compliance, and operational resilience in banking and finance.

2. UNDERSTANDING AI AND IOT IN BANKING AND FINANCE

2.1 Role of AI Technologies, IoT and their Applications in Banking and Finance

The convergence of AI and IoT has reshaped the banking and finance sector, enabling institutions to enhance operational efficiency, provide personalized customer experiences, and improve security measures (Bashir, M., & Kumar, M. (2021), Chen, Y., & Zhao, H. (2020)). These technologies work together to transform data into actionable insights, allowing for more informed decision-making and innovative financial solutions.

A. AI Technologies in Banking and Finance

AI technologies are used across various applications in banking and finance, particularly through machine learning (ML), NLP, and robotic process automation (RPA). AI's primary role is in data analysis and decision-making, allowing banks and financial firms to analyze customer data, understand behavioral patterns, and predict future trends. Few of the key applications include:

Customer Service: AI-powered chatbots and virtual assistants provide 24/7 support, helping customers with account queries, transaction histories, and routine tasks, leading to improved customer experience and cost savings.

Risk Management: Machine learning algorithms assess credit risk, detect fraudulent activities, and monitor transactions in real time to identify suspicious behavior. This enables proactive responses and minimizes financial losses.

Personalized Financial Planning: AI enables hyper-personalization by analyzing individual customer data to provide customized product recommendations, tailored investment advice, and budget planning.

Algorithmic Trading: AI analyzes large amount of financial data to make trading decisions faster than human traders, improving the accuracy of predictions and optimizing returns in financial markets.

B. IoT in Banking and Finance

IoT extends the data landscape by connecting physical devices, such as smartphones, ATMs, wearables, and connected cars, to the internet. By gathering real-time data from these devices, IoT enables banks to deliver contextualized, location-based services and gain deeper insights into customer needs (refer figure 1).

Connected ATMs and Branches: IoT-enabled ATMs monitor cash levels and send alerts for timely refills, reducing operational downtime. In branches, IoT sensors improve queue management and streamline the customer experience.

Figure 1. Benefits of IoT in Banking and Finance

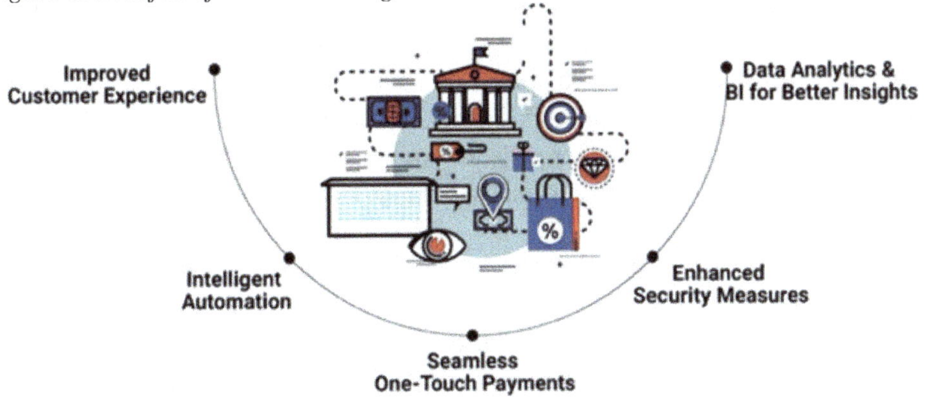

Wearables and Mobile Banking: IoT-powered wearables, like smartwatches, facilitate quick transactions, provides biometric authentication, and enable contactless payments, adding a layer of convenience for customers.

Fraud Prevention and Security Monitoring: IoT enhances security by enabling biometric authentication methods (fingerprint, facial recognition) and tracking device-based transactions to prevent unauthorized access.

Usage-Based Insurance (UBI): Banks and insurers use data from IoT devices, such as connected cars, to provide personalized insurance products based on customer behavior, creating fairer pricing models and improving risk assessment.

C. Integrated Applications of AI and IoT in Banking and Finance

The fusion of AI and IoT allows banks to maximize the value of IoT-generated data through advanced analytics and predictive insights. For example:

Smart Branches: AI analyzes data from IoT sensors in branches to optimize staffing, monitor customer flows, and improve service times.

Real-Time Credit Scoring: IoT-enabled devices provide contextual data about an individual's lifestyle or business activities. AI processes this data to generate a more accurate and dynamic credit score, allowing for real-time loan decisions.

Proactive Maintenance and Asset Monitoring: AI and IoT monitor ATMs and other banking equipment, identifying maintenance needs before issues arise, reducing downtime, and cutting repair costs.

Enhanced Fraud Detection: By analyzing data from connected devices, AI systems detect irregularities in transaction patterns, alerting financial institutions to potential fraud in real time.

AI and IoT are thus revolutionizing the banking and finance industry, providing new ways to deliver customer-centered services and increase efficiency (Dandash, B. H., & Aldabbas, H. (2021)). However, the interconnected nature of these technologies introduces complex challenges in data privacy and security, making the need for a robust security framework. Embracing these technologies responsibly can enable financial institutions to provide innovative, secure, and data-driven services that meet evolving customer demands in the digital era.

2.2 Benefits of Integrating AI and IoT in Banking and Finance

Integrating AI and IoT in the banking and finance sector has unlocked several advantages, allowing institutions to provide more responsive, personalized, and efficient services (Eze, U. C., & Ayo, C. K. (2020), Ghasemaghaei, M., & H. A. (2021), and Gupta, D., & Yadav, A. (2021).). Together, AI and IoT create a powerful ecosystem for real-time data processing, predictive insights, and enhanced operational capabilities. Here are some of the key benefits:

a. Enhanced Customer Experience: AI and IoT provides seamless, personalized experiences by enabling banks to anticipate and respond to customer needs in real-time. For example, AI-driven chatbots provide 24/7 support, while IoT-powered mobile and wearable devices allow instant, contactless transactions. This level of convenience makes customer loyalty and increases satisfaction.
b. Improved Fraud Detection and Security: The integration of AI and IoT strengthens security by providing advanced, multi-layered protections. IoT devices enable biometric authentication (like fingerprint and facial recognition) and transaction monitoring, while AI algorithms detect abnormal transaction patterns, alerting banks to potential fraud in real-time. This proactive approach reduces the risk of data breaches and unauthorized access.
c. Real-Time Data Analysis and Decision-Making: IoT continuously collects data from various devices, such as mobile phones, ATMs, and wearable devices. AI then analyzes this data, allowing banks to make real-time decisions. For example, dynamic credit scoring based on real-time data enables more accurate risk assessment, improving loan and credit decisions and expanding access to financial services.
d. Operational Efficiency and Cost Savings: Automation through AI, combined with IoT connectivity, reduces manual tasks, streamlines operations, and lowers costs. IoT-enabled devices can track inventory in ATMs, optimize branch staffing, and facilitate predictive maintenance for banking equipment, reducing downtime and operational expenses. AI-driven robotic process automation (RPA) further automates repetitive tasks like data entry, accelerating processes and improving efficiency.
e. Hyper-Personalization of Financial Services: AI can analyze IoT-generated data to provide highly customized financial products and recommendations based on individual behavior, spending patterns, and location. This enables banks to provides personalized loan terms, tailored investment advice, and customized financial planning, which aligns with each customer's unique financial needs and goals.
f. Enhanced Risk Management: IoT devices provide additional data points that help banks better assess risks, such as credit and insurance risks. By combining IoT data with AI analytics, banks can monitor customers' real-time financial behaviors, such as spending habits or driving patterns for usage-based insurance. This data-driven approach leads to more accurate risk profiles and more reliable financial products.

g. Predictive Maintenance and Reduced Downtime: IoT-connected ATMs and other banking infrastructure can alert banks to maintenance needs before issues escalate. AI algorithms can analyze this data to predict when equipment might fail, scheduling proactive maintenance and minimizing downtime. This reduces service interruptions and ensures consistent availability for customers (Hussain, A., & Raza, B. (2020), Khan, M. A., & Javed, M. Y. (2019)).
h. Streamlined Financial Operations and Supply Chains: AI and IoT integration can enhance supply chain and logistics management for financial institutions with physical assets or branches. For example, IoT sensors monitor asset locations, and AI systems optimize supply chain logistics, minimizing delays and ensuring better resource allocation.
i. Faster, Data-Driven Decision-Making: Real-time data from IoT devices combined with AI analytics enables banks to make faster, informed decisions. Whether approving a loan, adjusting credit limits, or identifying investment opportunities, banks can act promptly to meet market demands and customer expectations.

Hence, the integration of AI and IoT in banking and finance enables institutions to deliver innovative, customer-centric services while driving operational efficiencies and cost savings. Hence, by using these technologies, banks can respond to real-time needs, enhance security, improve customer satisfaction, and better manage risks, positioning themselves for sustainable growth in an increasingly digital financial landscape.

3. SECURITY CHALLENGES IN AI-IOT ENABLED BANKING AND FINANCE SYSTEMS

The integration of AI and IoT in banking and finance introduces advanced capabilities, but it also amplifies security vulnerabilities (Khan, M. N., & Ullah, A. (2021), Lin, Y., & Wang, Z. (2020), Murtaza, N., & Al-Hawari, M. (2020).). Financial institutions must address these unique security challenges to safeguard sensitive data and maintain customer trust. Note that here are some primary security challenges in AI-IoT enabled banking systems:

i. Increased Attack Surface: IoT devices, such as ATMs, mobile banking apps, and connected wearables, create multiple points of entry for cyber-attacks. Each IoT-enabled device added to a network increases the system's vulnerability, as these devices often lack robust security protocols, making them potential gateways for attackers to infiltrate broader financial networks.

ii. Data Privacy Risks: AI-IoT systems gather extensive amounts of personal and financial data in real time, which, if compromised, can lead to severe privacy violations. AI algorithms process sensitive data to deliver personalized services, but this data must be stored, managed, and protected under stringent privacy laws like GDPR and CCPA. Unauthorized access to this data could result in identity theft, financial fraud, and loss of customer trust.
iii. Vulnerability to Cyber-Attacks and Malware: Financial IoT devices are susceptible to various forms of cyber-attacks, including Distributed Denial of Service (DDoS), ransomware, and man-in-the-middle attacks. A breach in any connected device can allow attackers to gain access to the broader network. AI-driven systems, if compromised, could amplify these attacks by automating malicious activities and bypassing traditional security controls.
iv. AI Model Manipulation and Adversarial Attacks: AI models used in banking systems for risk assessment, fraud detection, and customer service can be manipulated by adversaries. Attackers may use adversarial inputs—maliciously crafted data designed to deceive AI algorithms—to manipulate AI decisions. For example, an adversary could manipulate credit scoring or loan approval algorithms to influence outcomes in their favor.
v. Insufficient Encryption and Authentication: IoT devices in banking often transmit data over unsecured networks, making encryption important. However, many IoT devices have limited processing power, which can result in weak or inconsistent encryption practices. Moreover, IoT devices and AI systems often lack multi-factor authentication, increasing the risk of unauthorized access and data breaches.
vi. Limited Security in Legacy Systems: Many financial institutions operate with legacy systems that were not designed to handle the security demands of AI and IoT. Integrating these modern technologies into outdated infrastructures can expose security gaps, making it easier for attackers to exploit vulnerabilities within the system.
vii. Real-Time Data Vulnerabilities: AI-IoT systems continuously process real-time data, which, if intercepted, can reveal valuable insights about customers, transactions, and operations. Hackers can exploit this data to disrupt operations or manipulate financial markets. Protecting real-time data in transit is important, as any breach can result in important financial and reputational losses.
viii. Device and Network Interoperability Issues: With several devices from different manufacturers connected to a single network, maintaining consistent security standards across all devices can be challenging. Differences in protocols, operating systems, and security configurations make it harder to manage vulnerabilities, leaving systems open to attacks.

ix. Regulatory Compliance Challenges: AI-IoT enabled banking systems must comply with strict regulatory standards for data protection, including GDPR, CCPA, and PCI-DSS. However, the fast-paced nature of technological advancements can make it difficult for banks to stay fully compliant. Failure to comply with these regulations not only exposes financial institutions to legal penalties but also makes them vulnerable to security breaches.
x. Insufficient Security in Device Firmware: IoT devices often operate on pre-installed firmware, which may contain vulnerabilities that are difficult to patch. Since firmware updates may not be consistent across all devices, unpatched devices can serve as entry points for attackers, exposing the entire system to security threats.
xi. Limited Transparency and Accountability in AI Algorithms: AI algorithms in banking may operate as "black boxes," making it challenging to understand how decisions are made. This lack of transparency can complicate detecting biases, errors, or manipulations in decision-making processes. Ensuring algorithmic accountability and establishing explainable AI practices are important to improving trust and security.
xii. Insider Threats: The highly interconnected nature of AI-IoT systems in banking also increases the risk of insider threats. Employees or third-party vendors with access to sensitive data may misuse their privileges, leading to data leaks or fraudulent activities. Establishing strict access controls, audit trails, and monitoring is essential to mitigate these risks.

In summary, AI-IoT enabled banking systems provides huge potential but are also highly susceptible to sophisticated security threats. Addressing these challenges requires a multi-layered security approach, including strong encryption, multi-factor authentication, regular firmware updates, and robust monitoring of AI algorithms.

4. POPULAR ISSUES AND PRIVACY CHALLENGES IN AI-IOT ENABLED BANKING AND FINANCE SYSTEMS

The convergence of AI and IoT in the banking and finance industry has introduced powerful capabilities but also several privacy issues (Rahman, M. A., & Hossain, M. S. (2021), Shamsi, J., & Bafghi, A. M. (2021), Tufekci, Z., & Korukoglu, S. (2020), Wang, H., & Zhou, Z. (2021), Zhang, Y., & Lu, Q. (2019)). The large amount of sensitive data collected, processed, and transmitted by these systems raise important privacy issues. Here are some of the most important privacy challenges (refer figure 2):

A. Data Collection and Surveillance issues: AI-IoT systems continuously collect data from users, including location, behavior patterns, transaction histories, and biometric data, often without full transparency to the users. While this data improves service personalization, it also raises issues about over-surveillance, as users may feel uncomfortable with the level of tracking and monitoring.

B. Lack of User Control Over Data: In many AI-IoT enabled systems, users have limited control over how their data is collected, processed, and shared. Once shared, it can be challenging for users to track where their information goes or to revoke permissions. This lack of control leads to privacy issues, as customers may not fully understand or agree to the extent of data sharing, increasing the potential for misuse.

C. Consent Management and Transparency Issues: AI and IoT rely on large amounts of personal data to provide insights and make decisions. Ensuring that customers are aware of and consent to data collection practices is important. However, many financial institutions face challenges in communicating complex data practices in a transparent manner, leading to inadequate consent and a lack of user understanding about how their data is used.

Figure 2. IoT Privacy and Security: Challenges and Solutions

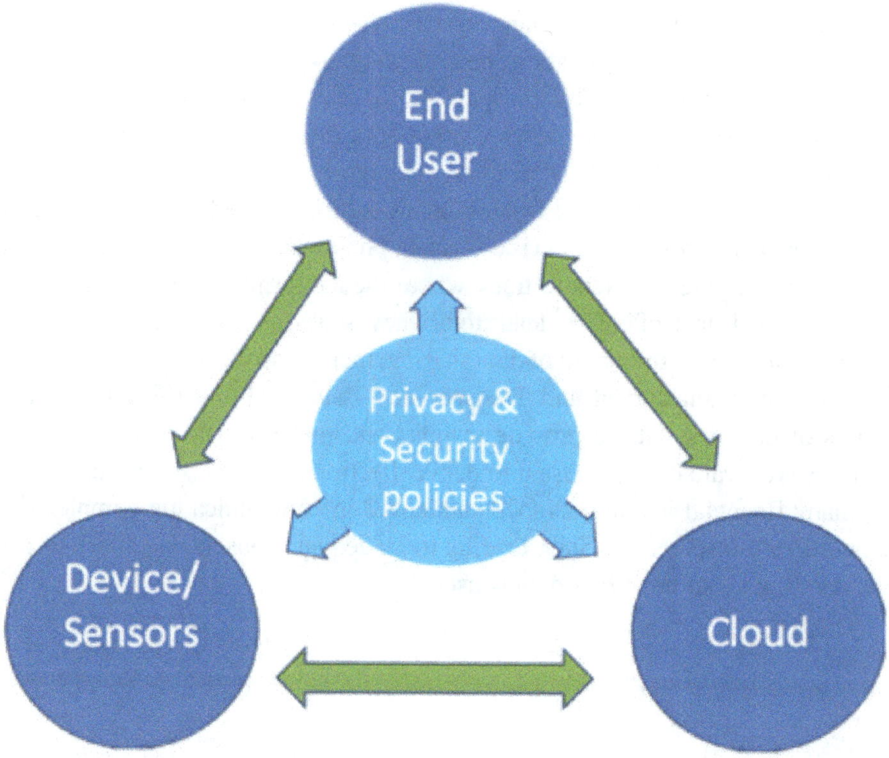

D. Unauthorized Data Sharing with Third Parties: AI-IoT enabled systems often involve multiple third-party service providers, from device manufacturers to data analytics firms. Financial institutions may share customer data with these third parties to improve services, but this also increases the risk of unauthorized data access or misuse. If third-party vendors lack robust privacy protocols, customer data is at risk of being exposed or mishandled.

E. Data Breaches and Unauthorized Access: The interconnectivity in AI-IoT enabled banking systems creates multiple entry points for unauthorized access. Sensitive data stored and transmitted between devices, such as financial records, personal information, and transaction data, is highly vulnerable to cyber-attacks. Data breaches can result in identity theft, financial fraud, and important reputational damage for financial institutions.

F. Privacy Risks from Location and Biometric Data: IoT devices often collect geolocation and biometric data for authentication and to provide contextualized services. However, this data is highly sensitive, and if compromised, it can expose users to privacy violations. Unauthorized access to location data can lead to tracking issues, while misuse of biometric data, like fingerprints or facial recognition, can have irreversible privacy consequences.

G Algorithmic Bias and Discrimination: AI algorithms, particularly in areas like credit scoring, loan approvals, and insurance underwriting, may inadvertently perpetuate biases. If an algorithm is trained on biased data, it can result in discriminatory decisions that unfairly impact certain groups. Such biases not only lead to privacy issues regarding the fairness of AI-driven decisions but can also expose financial institutions to legal and ethical liabilities.

H. Inadequate Data Anonymization Techniques: Financial data often requires de-identification to protect individual privacy. However, if anonymization techniques are weak, there is a risk that individuals can be re-identified by correlating anonymized data with other datasets. This creates a privacy challenge, as even supposedly "anonymous" data could lead to exposure of personal information.

I. Data Retention and Deletion Issues: AI-IoT systems store enormous amounts of data, and it can be challenging for financial institutions to implement effective data retention and deletion policies. Retaining data for extended periods increases the risk of exposure in the event of a breach. Additionally, compliance with data protection regulations, which often mandate data deletion upon request, can be difficult to enforce across interconnected AI-IoT systems.

J. Edge Computing Privacy Challenges: To reduce latency, many IoT devices process data at the edge (i.e., closer to where data is generated). While this reduces reliance on cloud storage, it presents privacy challenges, as edge devices may lack the robust security of centralized systems. Processing sensitive data on the edge makes it more vulnerable to local attacks, and ensuring data privacy across distributed devices becomes more complex.

K. Limited Privacy Protections in Device Firmware: IoT devices are often manufactured with fixed firmware that may not support advanced privacy features, making it difficult to implement necessary privacy controls. Unsecured firmware can leave devices open to vulnerabilities, and since firmware updates can be infrequent, these devices remain at risk of exposing personal data over time.

L. Lack of Transparency in AI Decision-Making: AI models used in banking are often complex and operate as "black boxes," making it difficult to understand how they arrive at certain decisions. This lack of transparency can lead to privacy issues, as customers have limited insights into how their data is used to make decisions that affect them, such as loan approvals or credit scoring.

M. Insider Threats and Internal Privacy Risks: Financial institutions must also account for internal privacy risks faced by employees or third-party contractors with access to sensitive data. Insider threats can lead to intentional or accidental data exposure, making the need for strict access controls, monitoring, and employee training on privacy protocols.

Note that Privacy challenges in AI-IoT enabled banking systems stem from the extensive data collection, transmission, and processing involved. Ensuring privacy requires robust data protection measures, transparency, and user control over data sharing. Financial institutions must adopt advanced data anonymization techniques, enforce strict data retention policies, and adhere to regulatory requirements to address these privacy issues effectively. Note that building customer trust will depend on the ability to provide secure, transparent, and privacy-respecting AI-IoT solutions in banking.

5. EFFECTIVE SECURITY FRAMEWORKS AND BEST PRACTICES FOR SAFE AND SECURE BANKING AND FINANCE SYSTEMS

To safeguard sensitive data and maintain customer trust, banking and finance institutions must implement robust security frameworks and focused to best practices tailored to address the unique challenges faced by AI and IoT technologies (Prakash M. et al., 2024, M Kiran Kumar, et al., 2024, Naveen Kumar C. M et al., 2024, K. R. Pundareeka Vittala, et al., 2024). Hence, here are some effective security frameworks and best practices to consider as:

A. Adopt a Layered Security Approach
    - Defense in Depth: Utilize multiple layers of security measures, including network security, endpoint security, application security, and physical security, to create a robust defense against cyber threats.
    - Segmentation: Segregate important systems and data into distinct zones to limit exposure and mitigate the impact of a potential breach.

B. Implement Strong Access Controls
    - Role-Based Access Control (RBAC): Enforce strict access controls based on user roles and responsibilities, ensuring employees only have access to the data necessary for their job functions.
    - Multi-Factor Authentication (MFA): Require MFA for all sensitive transactions and system access to add an extra layer of security against unauthorized access.

C. Data Encryption
    - At Rest and In Transit: Use strong encryption protocols to protect sensitive data both when stored and during transmission across networks.

Use established standards like AES (Advanced Encryption Standard) and TLS (Transport Layer Security).
- End-to-End Encryption: Implement end-to-end encryption for customer communications and transactions to ensure data privacy and integrity.

D. Regular Security Audits and Assessments
- Vulnerability Assessments: Conduct routine vulnerability assessments and penetration testing to identify and remediate security weaknesses in systems and applications.
- Compliance Audits: Regularly review compliance with industry regulations and standards, such as PCI DSS, GDPR, and others, to ensure adherence to legal requirements.

E. Endpoint and Device Security:
- Device Management: Secure IoT devices through robust device management practices, including regular updates, patch management, and configuration management.
- Antivirus and Anti-Malware Solutions: Deploy endpoint protection solutions to detect and mitigate malware and other malicious threats on devices used within the organization.

F. Data Minimization and Retention Policies:
- Limit Data Collection: Collect only the necessary data required for operations and minimize the storage of sensitive information.
- Data Retention Policies: Establish clear data retention and deletion policies to ensure that personal data is only retained for as long as necessary, reducing exposure to data breaches.

G. Secure Application Development Lifecycle (SDLC):
- Security by Design: Incorporate security into the software development lifecycle, ensuring that security assessments are performed at every stage of application development.
- Code Reviews and Testing: Conduct regular code reviews and security testing (static and dynamic) to identify vulnerabilities before applications are deployed.

H. Adopt Secure APIs:
- API Security Standards: Implement security protocols for Application Programming Interfaces (APIs) to protect data in transit. Use OAuth, API gateways, and rate limiting to control access and prevent abuse.
- API Monitoring: Monitor API activity to detect unusual access patterns and potential security threats.

I. Collaboration with Third Parties:

- Vendor Risk Management: Assess and manage the security posture of third-party vendors, ensuring they adhere to similar security standards and practices.
- Shared Responsibility Model: Clearly define security responsibilities between the organization and third-party vendors in contracts and service level agreements (SLAs).

J. Incident Reporting and Feedback Loops:
   - Establish Reporting Channels: Create clear channels for reporting security incidents or suspicious activities, encouraging employees to promptly report potential threats.
   - Continuous Improvement: Regularly review and update security practices based on lessons learned from security incidents and changes in the threat landscape.

Hence, implementing an effective security framework in banking and finance systems involves a holistic approach that integrates technology, processes, and people. By adopting layered security measures, strong access controls, and continuous monitoring, financial institutions can enhance their resilience against cyber threats and protect sensitive customer data.

6. TECHNOLOGICAL SOLUTIONS FOR ENHANCING SECURITY IN BANKING AND FINANCE SYSTEMS

6.1 Encryption Techniques for Data Protection in Banking and Finance systems

Encryption is an important component of data protection in banking and finance systems, ensuring the confidentiality, integrity, and authenticity of sensitive information. By converting plaintext into ciphertext, encryption protects data from unauthorized access and ensures secure transactions. Below is the primary encryption techniques used in the banking and finance sector:

A. Symmetric Key Encryption

In symmetric key encryption, the same key is used for both encryption and decryption. This method is efficient for encrypting large amounts of data. Its common Algorithms are:

- Advanced Encryption Standard (AES): A widely used symmetric encryption algorithm that supports key sizes of 128, 192, and 256 bits. AES is known for its security and speed, making it suitable for banking applications.
- Triple Data Encryption Standard (3DES): An enhancement of the original DES algorithm, applying the DES encryption process three times to each data block. While more secure than DES, it is slower than AES and is gradually being phased out in favor of AES.

B. Asymmetric Key Encryption

Asymmetric encryption uses a pair of keys—one public and one private. The public key encrypts the data, while the private key is used for decryption. This method is commonly used for secure key exchange and digital signatures. Few Common Algorithms are:

- Rivest-Shamir-Adleman (RSA): A widely used asymmetric encryption algorithm that relies on the mathematical difficulty of factoring large prime numbers. RSA is commonly used for secure communications and digital signatures in banking.
- Elliptic Curve Cryptography (ECC): A modern asymmetric encryption technique that provides similar security to RSA with smaller key sizes. This makes ECC efficient for resource-constrained environments, such as IoT devices in finance.

C. Hashing

Hashing is a one-way cryptographic function that converts data into a fixed-size hash value, making it impossible to reverse-engineer the original data. Hashing is primarily used for data integrity verification and password storage. Few Common Algorithms are:

- Secure Hash Algorithm (SHA-2): A family of cryptographic hash functions (including SHA-256 and SHA-512) widely used in security applications, including digital signatures and certificate generation.
- Message Digest Algorithm 5 (MD5): Although historically popular, MD5 is now considered weak and vulnerable to collisions. It is generally not recommended for new systems.

D. Transport Layer Security (TLS)

TLS is a cryptographic protocol designed to provide secure communication over computer networks. It ensures that data transmitted between clients and servers is encrypted and protected from eavesdropping and tampering. TLS is used to secure web transactions, mobile banking applications, and APIs by encrypting data in transit. Banks commonly implement TLS for secure online banking and e-commerce transactions.

E. Database Encryption

Database encryption protects sensitive data stored in databases, ensuring that data remains secure even if unauthorized access occurs. This includes encrypting both data at rest and data in use. Few Common Techniques are:

- Transparent Data Encryption (TDE): A method that encrypts database files at the storage level without requiring application changes. TDE is commonly used in relational database management systems (RDBMS).
- Column-Level Encryption: Allows specific columns in a database (e.g., credit card numbers, Social Security numbers) to be encrypted independently, providing granular control over data protection.

F. File and Disk Encryption

File and disk encryption protects sensitive data stored on devices, such as servers, laptops, and external drives. It ensures that data remains secure even if the physical device is lost or stolen. Few Common Tools are:

- File Containers: Software like VeraCrypt allows users to create encrypted volumes or containers to store sensitive files securely.

G. End-to-End Encryption (E2EE)

E2EE ensures that data is encrypted on the sender's device and only decrypted on the recipient's device, preventing intermediaries (including service providers) from accessing the data. Note that E2EE is often used in secure messaging applications for communication between clients and banks, ensuring that sensitive information remains private throughout the transmission.

H. Secure Sockets Layer (SSL)

SSL is an earlier version of TLS that was used to secure communications over networks. While largely replaced by TLS, some legacy systems may still use SSL. SSL was important for securing online transactions, but financial institutions are encouraged to transition to TLS for improved security.

I. Key Management

Effective key management is important for maintaining the security of encryption systems. This includes generating, storing, distributing, and retiring encryption keys securely. Few of best practices are:

- Use of Hardware Security Modules (HSM): HSMs provide a secure environment for key generation, storage, and management, reducing the risk of key compromise.
- Regular Key Rotation: Implementing a policy for regularly rotating encryption keys to minimize the impact of a compromised key.

Note that encryption is essential for protecting sensitive data in banking and finance systems. By utilizing a combination of symmetric and asymmetric encryption, hashing, TLS, and effective key management, financial institutions can enhance their data security, safeguard customer information, and comply with regulatory requirements.

6.2 Blockchain Technology for Transaction Security

Blockchain technology has emerged as a transformative solution for enhancing transaction security in banking and finance (Senthil Kumar Arumugam et al., 2024, Amit Kumar Tyagi et al., 2024, K. R.Pundareeka Vittala, et al., 2024, Archana Ambekar, et al., 2024, Manita D. Shah et al., 2024, Senthil Kumar Arumugam et al., 2024, B. N. Prathap et al., 2024,). Its decentralized, transparent, and immutable nature makes it particularly suitable for addressing the security challenges faced by traditional financial systems. Here's an overview of how blockchain technology enhances transaction security in this sector (refer figure 3):

a. Decentralization: Unlike traditional banking systems that rely on a central authority (like banks or payment processors), blockchain operates on a decentralized network of nodes. Each participant in the network maintains a copy of the entire blockchain, which mitigates the risk of a single point of failure. As benefit, Decentralization reduces the chances of fraud and corruption, as no single entity can manipulate the transaction data without consensus from the majority of network participants.

b. Immutability: Once a transaction is recorded on the blockchain, it cannot be altered or deleted without the consensus of the network. This immutability is achieved through cryptographic hashing and consensus mechanisms. As benefit, Immutability ensures that transaction records are secure and reliable, providing a permanent and tamper-proof audit trail. This feature is important for preventing fraud and enhancing trust among users.
c. Transparency: Blockchain technology provides transparency as all transactions are visible to participants in the network. Depending on the type of blockchain (public or private), users/ consumers can view transaction details, including timestamps and participants involved. As benefit, Transparency enhances accountability, as any discrepancies can be easily traced back to the source. This feature is particularly useful for regulatory compliance and auditing processes.
d. Cryptographic Security: Blockchain uses advanced cryptographic techniques to secure data and transactions. Each transaction is encrypted and linked to the previous one, forming a secure chain. As benefit, Cryptographic security prevents unauthorized access and ensures that only legitimate participants can initiate or verify transactions. It also protects sensitive information, such as financial data.
e. Consensus Mechanisms: Blockchain networks use consensus mechanisms to validate transactions and ensure agreement among participants. Common mechanisms include Proof of Work (PoW), Proof of Stake (PoS), and Practical Byzantine Fault Tolerance (PBFT). As benefit, these mechanisms prevent double-spending and ensure that only valid transactions are added to the blockchain. They enhance overall network security by requiring participants to agree on the state of the ledger.
f. Smart Contracts: Smart contracts are self-executing contracts with the terms of the agreement directly written into code on the blockchain. They automatically execute transactions when predefined conditions are met. As benefit, Smart contracts reduce the need for intermediaries, thereby streamlining processes and minimizing fraud risks. They also enhance transparency, as all parties can view and verify contract terms and execution.

Figure 3. Key benefits of Blockchain in banking

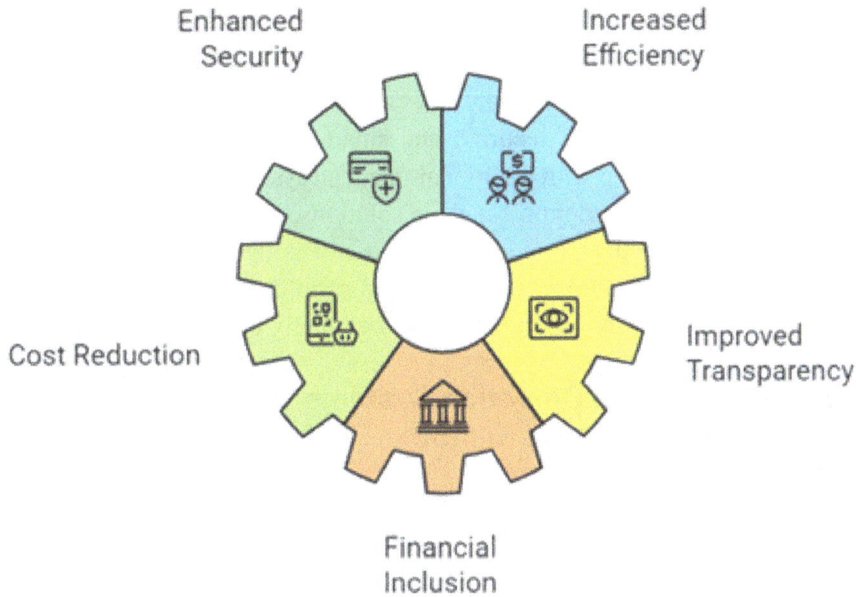

g. Tokenization of Assets: Blockchain enables the tokenization of real-world assets (e.g., real estate, commodities) by creating digital tokens that represent ownership. These tokens can be traded or transferred on the blockchain. As benefit, Tokenization increases liquidity, reduces transaction costs, and enhances security by providing a secure, immutable record of ownership and transaction history.
h. Enhanced Identity Verification: Blockchain can provide a secure and decentralized identity verification system. Users can control their digital identities through cryptographic keys, reducing reliance on centralized identity providers. As benefit, Enhanced identity verification helps prevent identity theft and fraud, as individuals can authenticate their identities without exposing sensitive information.
i. Reduction of Transaction Costs: By eliminating intermediaries (like banks and payment processors), blockchain can importantly reduce transaction costs associated with cross-border payments and remittances. As benefit, Lower costs enhance accessibility and encourage broader participation in financial systems, particularly for underserved populations.
j. Resilience to Attacks: The distributed nature of blockchain makes it highly resilient to cyber-attacks. A successful attack would require compromising a majority of nodes in the network, which is extremely difficult. As benefit, this

resilience enhances overall security, making blockchain a more reliable option for secure transactions compared to traditional centralized systems.

Hence, blockchain technology provides a robust framework for enhancing transaction security in banking and finance. Its features decentralization, immutability, transparency, cryptographic security, and smart contracts, address many of the vulnerabilities associated with traditional financial systems. As banks and financial institutions increasingly adopt blockchain solutions, they can importantly improve transaction security, reduce fraud, and make trust among customers and regulators. The ongoing evolution of blockchain technology holds the potential to reshape the future of banking and finance, making it more secure, efficient, and accessible.

6.3 AI-Driven Threat Detection Systems for Banking and Finance sector

In the banking and finance sector, safeguarding sensitive data and ensuring the security of transactions is paramount. With the rise of cyber threats, financial institutions are increasingly turning to AI-driven threat detection systems. These systems use advanced algorithms and machine learning techniques to enhance security measures, detect anomalies, and respond to potential threats in real-time. Here's an overview of how AI is transforming threat detection in this sector:

A. Anomaly Detection: AI algorithms analyze large amount of transactional data to identify patterns and behaviors that deviate from the norm. This helps in detecting unusual transactions that may indicate fraudulent activity. Few of its benefits are:
   - Early Detection: By flagging anomalies in real-time, banks can respond swiftly to potentially fraudulent transactions.
   - Reduced False Positives: Machine learning models can improve accuracy over time, minimizing the number of legitimate transactions incorrectly flagged as fraudulent.

B. Behavioral Analytics: AI systems utilize behavioral analytics to create profiles of typical user behavior. Any important deviations from these profiles can trigger alerts for further investigation. Here, few of its benefits are:
   - Personalized Security: By understanding individual customer behavior, banks can tailor security measures to specific user profiles.
   - Dynamic Threat Detection: Behavioral analytics adapts to changes in user behavior, enhancing the system's ability to detect evolving threats.

C. Real-Time Monitoring: AI-driven systems continuously monitor transactions, user activities, and network traffic in real time to identify and respond to suspicious activities. Here, few of its benefits are:
    - Immediate Response: Real-time alerts enable security teams to act quickly to mitigate risks and prevent financial losses.
    - Proactive Threat Mitigation: Continuous monitoring allows banks to detect and address potential vulnerabilities before they are exploited.

D. NLP: AI systems equipped with NLP capabilities can analyze unstructured data, such as emails, customer feedback, and news articles, to detect emerging threats and vulnerabilities. Here, few of its benefits are:
    - Threat Intelligence: NLP can identify potential threats from various sources, including social media and forums, enhancing overall security awareness.
    - Sentiment Analysis: By analyzing customer sentiments, banks can detect potential issues before they escalate.

E. Fraud Detection and Prevention: AI systems analyze historical transaction data to develop models that identify fraudulent activities, such as credit card fraud, money laundering, and account takeover. Here, few of its benefits are:
    - Adaptive Learning: AI models continuously learn from new data, improving their ability to detect sophisticated fraud schemes.
    - Risk Scoring: Transactions can be assigned risk scores based on various factors, allowing banks to prioritize investigations effectively.

F. Machine Learning for Threat Prediction: Machine learning algorithms can predict potential threats based on historical data and patterns, enabling proactive security measures. Few of its benefits are:
    - Anticipatory Defense: By identifying potential vulnerabilities and attack vectors, banks can strengthen their defenses ahead of time.
    - Resource Allocation: Predictive analytics helps security teams allocate resources effectively to high-risk areas.

G. Integration with SIEM Systems: AI-driven threat detection systems can be integrated with Security Information and Event Management (SIEM) systems to enhance overall security monitoring and incident response capabilities. Here, few of its benefits are:
    - Comprehensive Security View: Integration allows for the aggregation and analysis of security data from multiple sources, improving threat detection accuracy.
    - Streamlined Incident Response: AI-driven insights can facilitate faster and more efficient incident response processes.

H. Phishing Detection: AI systems can analyze email content, links, and attachments to identify potential phishing attempts targeting customers and employees. Here, few of its benefits are:
    - User Protection: By flagging suspicious emails before they reach users, banks can reduce the risk of successful phishing attacks.
    - Training and Awareness: AI can identify common phishing techniques, helping banks educate employees and customers on recognizing threats.

I. Automated Incident Response: AI systems can automate certain aspects of incident response, such as blocking suspicious accounts or transactions, to minimize human intervention. Here, few of its benefits are:
    - Rapid Response: Automation speeds up the response to threats, reducing potential damage.
    - Consistency: Automated responses ensure that security protocols are followed uniformly across the organization.

Hence, AI-driven threat detection systems represent an important advancement in the security capabilities of the banking and finance sector. By using machine learning, real-time monitoring, and behavioral analytics, these systems enhance the ability to detect, respond to, and prevent cyber threats. As the threat landscape continues to evolve, financial institutions that adopt and integrate AI technologies will be better positioned to protect sensitive data, maintain customer trust, and ensure regulatory compliance. Hence, the ongoing development of AI in threat detection will play an important role in shaping the future of cybersecurity in banking and finance.

7. FUTURE TRENDS IN AI-IOT BASED SECURITY AND PRIVACY FOR BANKING AND FINANCE SYSTEMS

As the banking and finance sectors increasingly use AI and IoT, the security and privacy of financial transactions and customer data become paramount. Emerging technologies and trends are set to redefine how these institutions approach security and privacy. Here are some future trends, c nabe discussed as:

A. Enhanced AI-Driven Security Analytics: Future systems will use advanced predictive analytics to foresee potential threats based on historical data patterns, enabling proactive security measures. Also, AI will continually analyze and learn from new threats, updating security protocols in real time without human intervention, enhancing the ability to respond swiftly to emerging risks.

B. Integration of Quantum Computing: With the rise of quantum computing, the banking sector will need to adopt quantum-resistant encryption algorithms to protect sensitive data against future decryption threats. Also, Quantum computing can importantly improve AI model training, enabling faster processing of large datasets for threat detection and risk assessment.
C. Decentralized Identity Management: Future banking systems may adopt Self-Sovereign Identity models that give users complete control over their identity and personal data, reducing reliance on centralized identity providers. Also, utilizing blockchain technology can enhance identity verification processes, providing secure and tamper-proof methods for customer identification.
D. Adaptive Security Frameworks: Future security systems will adopt adaptive frameworks that can change based on real-time assessments of risk and threat levels, enabling tailored security measures. Also, Systems will utilize contextual information (such as user behavior, location, and device type) to determine the appropriate security measures for each transaction or interaction.
E. IoT Security Enhancements: Future IoT systems will implement robust authentication protocols to ensure that only authorized devices can connect to financial networks. Also, Increased focus on end-to-end encryption will protect data transmitted between IoT devices and financial institutions, enhancing overall security.
F. AI-Powered Privacy Compliance: AI systems will increasingly monitor and analyze transactions to ensure compliance with regulations such as GDPR, CCPA, and others, reducing the risk of legal issues. Also, Techniques like federated learning will allow AI models to learn from decentralized data sources without exposing sensitive data, thereby maintaining privacy.
G. Behavioral Biometrics: Future banking systems will use behavioral biometrics, analyzing user behavior patterns (e.g., typing speed, mouse movement) to authenticate users without additional steps. Also, Systems will implement continuous authentication methods that evaluate user behavior throughout a session, providing an additional layer of security.
H. Collaborative Threat Intelligence Sharing: Financial institutions will collaborate to share threat intelligence, creating collective defense mechanisms that enhance overall security across the sector. Also, Shared intelligence will be analyzed using AI, enabling institutions to detect and respond to threats more effectively by learning from one another's experiences.
I. Edge Computing for Enhanced Security: Edge computing will allow data to be processed closer to its source, reducing latency and enhancing real-time threat detection capabilities. Also, by processing data locally on IoT devices, edge computing minimizes the risk of data breaches associated with transmitting sensitive information to centralized servers.

J. Regulatory Technology (RegTech) Integration: AI and IoT will be integrated into RegTech solutions that automate compliance processes, ensuring that financial institutions can swiftly adapt to changing regulations. Also, these systems will facilitate real-time monitoring and reporting to regulatory bodies, improving transparency and reducing compliance costs.
K. Ethical AI and Privacy-By-Design: Future developments will emphasize ethical AI use, ensuring that algorithms are transparent, fair, and unbiased in their decision-making processes. Also, Financial institutions will adopt privacy-by-design principles, integrating privacy issues into the design of systems and processes from the outset.
L. Increased Use of AI for Fraud Detection: Financial institutions will continue to develop and implement advanced machine learning models that can analyze larger datasets for more accurate fraud detection. Also, AI systems will provide immediate alerts to customers and financial institutions in case of suspicious activities, enhancing response times and reducing potential losses.

In summary, the future of security and privacy in banking and finance will be importantly influenced by advancements in AI and IoT technologies. As financial institutions adopt these technologies, they must remain vigilant about emerging threats while using innovative solutions to enhance their security posture (Khushboo et al., (2021), Somisetti, K. et al., 2020, S. Subasree, et al., 2022, Kushal Kumar, et al., 2023, I. Mapanga, et al., 2017, D. Agarwal et al., 2022, G. Vishnuram, et al., 2022, J. Jangir, et al., 2024, Sharma, S., et al., 2024, Agarwal, Deepshikha, et al., 2023, and P. Prasad et al., 2021). By focusing on adaptive security frameworks, robust identity management, and ethical AI practices, the banking and finance sector can protect sensitive information and maintain customer trust in an increasingly digital landscape. Hence, the integration of these technologies will play an important role in shaping a secure and efficient future for financial services.

8. NEXT DECADE TRENDS/ PREDICTIONS FOR THE FUTURE OF SECURITY IN BANKING

As the banking sector continues to evolve, the future of security will be shaped by technological advancements, changing regulatory landscapes, and the increasing sophistication of cyber threats. Here are several key trends and predictions for the next decade regarding security in banking:

A. AI and Machine Learning Integration: Banks will increasingly use AI and machine learning for predictive analytics to identify potential security threats before they materialize. These technologies will analyze historical data and current trends to forecast possible attack vectors. Also, AI systems will automate responses to detected threats, allowing for faster and more effective mitigation of risks, reducing the reliance on human intervention.
B. Zero Trust Security Model: The zero trust model, which operates on the principle of "never trust, always verify," will become a standard in banking security. This approach will involve continuous verification of users and devices, regardless of their location within or outside the network. Also, Banks will implement micro-segmentation strategies to create isolated environments within their networks, limiting the impact of potential breaches.
C. Enhanced Biometric Authentication: The use of biometric authentication will expand beyond fingerprints and facial recognition to include behavioral biometrics, voice recognition, and even gait analysis. Also, Banks will implement multi-factor authentication systems that combine several biometric methods, enhancing security while maintaining user convenience.
D. Quantum Computing and Cryptography: As quantum computing becomes more accessible, banks will need to adopt quantum-resistant cryptographic algorithms to protect sensitive data against future decryption threats. Also, Ongoing research will focus on developing and standardizing cryptographic methods that can withstand quantum attacks, ensuring long-term data security.
E. Integration of Blockchain Technology: Blockchain technology will be utilized to enhance security in transaction processing, identity verification, and fraud detection, providing tamper-proof records and increased transparency. Also, Smart contracts will automate security protocols, ensuring compliance and facilitating faster responses to security incidents.
F. Rise of Cyber Insurance: As cyber threats become more prevalent, banks will increasingly invest in cyber insurance to mitigate financial losses resulting from data breaches and cyber-attacks. Also, Cyber insurance policies will evolve to address emerging threats, including coverage for ransomware attacks and regulatory fines.
G. IoT Security Enhancements: As IoT devices become more prevalent in banking (e.g., smart ATMs), industry standards will emerge to ensure their security, including secure device authentication and data encryption. Also, Edge computing will allow for the processing of data closer to the source, reducing latency in threat detection and response.
H. Cybersecurity Awareness and Training: Banks will prioritize cybersecurity awareness and training for employees to reduce human error and enhance overall security posture. Also, Institutions will implement simulation training

REFERENCES

Agarwal, D., & Tripathi, K. (2022). A framework for structural damage detection system in automobiles for flexible insurance claim using IoT and machine learning. In *2022 International Mobile and Embedded Technology Conference (MECON)* (pp. 5–8). IEEE. DOI: 10.1109/MECON53876.2022.9751889

Agarwal, D., Tripathi, K., Krishen, K., & Kumar, [First name not provided]. (2023). Concepts of artificial intelligence and its application in modern healthcare systems. CRC Press. DOI: 10.1201/9781003333081

Aji, A., & Nurhasanah, N. (2020). The impact of IoT and AI on banking services: A comprehensive review. *Journal of Banking and Finance Technology*, *4*(1), 1–12. DOI: 10.1007/s42786-019-00009-2

Alavi, A. S., & Jafari, A. (2021). Cybersecurity risks in IoT: A review of recent literature. *Computers & Security*, *110*, 102423. DOI: 10.1016/j.cose.2021.102423

Ambekar, A., Anusha, K. M., Kumar, M. K., & Tyagi, A. K. (2024). Smart banking solutions for modern society: Opportunities and challenges. In *Convergence of technology and operations management in modern businesses*. IGI Global., DOI: 10.4018/979-8-3693-6200-6.ch011

Arumugam, S. K., Seranmadevi, R., Susendiran, S., & Tyagi, A. K. (2024). Blockchain-IoT-based solutions for smart banking and finance systems: Architecture, issues, challenges, and way ahead for the next generation. In *Convergence of technology and operations management in modern businesses*. IGI Global., DOI: 10.4018/979-8-3693-6200-6.ch008

Arumugam, S. K., Susendiran, S., Seranmadevi, R., & Tyagi, A. K. (2024). Artificial intelligence-enabled innovative and advanced solutions for banking and finance sector: Potential, benefits, opportunities, and challenges. In *Convergence of technology and operations management in modern businesses*. IGI Global., DOI: 10.4018/979-8-3693-6200-6.ch007

Arumugam, S. K., Tyagi, A. K., Tiwari, S., & Kumari, S. (2024). The role of futuristic technologies in building sustainable environment. In *Creating AI synergy through business technology transformation*. IGI Global., DOI: 10.4018/979-8-3693-4187-2.ch012

Baig, M. Z., & Shah, F. (2020). AI-based privacy-preserving methods in banking: A systematic review. *Journal of Financial Services Marketing*, *25*(2), 105–120. DOI: 10.1057/s41264-020-00060-2

Bashir, M., & Kumar, M. (2021). Securing IoT-enabled banking services through blockchain technology. *Journal of Information Security and Applications*, *57*, 102726. DOI: 10.1016/j.jisa.2020.102726

Chen, Y., & Zhao, H. (2020). Data security and privacy in IoT-based financial services: Challenges and solutions. *IEEE Access : Practical Innovations, Open Solutions*, *8*, 74622–74632. DOI: 10.1109/ACCESS.2020.2986683

Dandash, B. H., & Aldabbas, H. (2021). AI and IoT for secure financial services: The role of machine learning. *Future Generation Computer Systems*, *115*, 1–13. DOI: 10.1016/j.future.2020.10.035

Eze, U. C., & Ayo, C. K. (2020). Security and privacy in IoT banking: The case for a hybrid framework. *International Journal of Information Management*, *52*, 102065. DOI: 10.1016/j.ijinfomgt.2020.102065

Ghasemaghaei, M., & H. A. (. (2021). The role of AI in enhancing cybersecurity in the banking sector. *Journal of Business Research*, *124*, 360–368. DOI: 10.1016/j.jbusres.2020.11.048

Gupta, D., & Yadav, A. (2021). Security and privacy challenges in IoT-based financial services: A review. *Journal of Financial Services Marketing*, *26*(3), 137–150. DOI: 10.1057/s41264-021-00101-x

Hussain, A., & Raza, B. (2020). Blockchain technology for data security in IoT-based banking services. *Journal of Banking and Finance Technology*, *4*(2), 73–84. DOI: 10.1007/s42786-020-00016-7

Jangir, J., Tripathi, K., Punetha, N., & Srivastava, A. (2024). An efficient meta-heuristic dimensionality LSTM model for dimensionality reduction and clustering for attack classification. In *2024 International Conference on Intelligent Systems for Cybersecurity (ISCS)* (pp. 1–5). IEEE. DOI: 10.1109/ISCS61804.2024.10581351

Khan, M. A., & Javed, M. Y. (2019). AI and IoT: The backbone of financial security in banking. *Journal of Information Technology*, *34*(3), 215–228. DOI: 10.1177/0268396219831900

Khan, M. N., & Ullah, A. (2021). Risk assessment of IoT in banking services: A framework for security and privacy. *Computers & Security*, *109*, 102382. DOI: 10.1016/j.cose.2021.102382

Kumar, K., Tripathi, K., & Gupta, R. (2023). Plant disease detection from image using CNN. [IJIRCST]. *International Journal of Innovative Research in Computer Science and Technology*, *11*(4), 24–27. DOI: 10.55524/ijircst.2023.11.4.5

Kumar, M. K., Srinidhi, V., Shamanth, B. S., & Tyagi, A. K. (2024). Modern smart banking with cutting-edge technologies: A sustainable banking and financial world. In *Creating AI synergy through business technology transformation*. IGI Global., DOI: 10.4018/979-8-3693-4187-2.ch004

Kumar, N. C. M., Addula, S. R., Seranmadevi, R., & Tyagi, A. K. (2024). Advanced banking solutions for Industry 5.0: From industry's perspective. In *Creating AI synergy through business technology transformation*. IGI Global., DOI: 10.4018/979-8-3693-4187-2.ch001

Lin, Y., & Wang, Z. (2020). Privacy-preserving data mining for banking transactions in IoT environments. *IEEE Transactions on Dependable and Secure Computing*, *17*(1), 33–45. DOI: 10.1109/TDSC.2018.2865865

Mapanga, I., Kumar, V., Makondo, W., Kushboo, T., Kadebu, P., & Chanda, W. (2017). *Design and implementation of an intrusion detection system using MLP-NN for MANET. In 2017 IST-Africa Week Conference (IST-Africa)*. IEEE., DOI: 10.23919/ISTAFRICA.2017.8102374

Murtaza, N., & Al-Hawari, M. (2020). AI in banking: Balancing innovation and privacy. *Journal of Business Research*, *118*, 414–422. DOI: 10.1016/j.jbusres.2019.11.048

Prakash, M., Tyagi, A. K., Arumugam, S. K., & Rawat, A. (2024). Internet of Things for building a smart and sustainable environment: A survey. In *Achieving sustainability with AI technologies*. IGI Global., DOI: 10.4018/979-8-3693-5247-2.ch002

Prasad, P., & Tripathi, K. (2021). Natural scene text localization and removal: Deep learning and Navier-Stokes inpainting approach. In *2021 IEEE International Conference on Electronics, Computing and Communication Technologies (CONECCT)* (pp. 1–5). IEEE. DOI: 10.1109/CONECCT52877.2021.9622609

Prathap, B. N., Devaraju, N., Chidambaram, N., & Tyagi, A. K. (2024). Modern banking solutions in Industry 5.0: Evolution, impacts, and potential applications for the future. In *Convergence of technology and operations management in modern businesses*. IGI Global., DOI: 10.4018/979-8-3693-6200-6.ch013

Prathap, B. N., Kulkarni, P. G., Harish, N., & Tyagi, A. K. (2024). Modern banking and finance systems using artificial intelligence: A view from citizen's perspective. In *Convergence of technology and operations management in modern businesses*. IGI Global., DOI: 10.4018/979-8-3693-6200-6.ch004

Rahman, M. A., & Hossain, M. S. (2021). Data privacy and security issues in IoT: Implications for banking and finance. *Journal of Financial Regulation and Compliance*, *29*(3), 307–324. DOI: 10.1108/JFRC-06-2020-0070

Shah, M. D., Seranmadevi, R., Jose, S., & Tyagi, A. K. (2024). Blockchain for banking and finance: A survey. In *Convergence of technology and operations management in modern businesses*. IGI Global., DOI: 10.4018/979-8-3693-6200-6.ch009

Shamsi, J., & Bafghi, A. M. (2021). A comprehensive survey of security and privacy in IoT-enabled financial services. *Journal of Financial Services Marketing*, *26*(4), 223–237. DOI: 10.1057/s41264-021-00120-8

Sharma, S., Verma, P., Singh, R., & Tripathi, K. (2024). Advancements in facial expression recognition: A comprehensive analysis of techniques. In N. Chauhan, D. Yadav, G. K. Verma, B. Soni, & J. M. Lara (Eds.), Machine learning, image processing, network security and data sciences (Vol. 2128, pp. [page numbers not available]). Springer. DOI: 10.1007/978-3-031-62217-5_18

Somisetti, K., Tripathi, K., & Verma, J. K. (2020). Design, implementation, and controlling of a humanoid robot. In *2020 International Conference on Computational Performance Evaluation (ComPE)* (pp. 831–836). IEEE. DOI: 10.1109/ComPE49325.2020.9200020

Subasree, S., Sakthivel, N. K., Tripathi, K., Agarwal, D., & Tyagi, A. K. (2022). Combining the advantages of radiomic features based feature extraction and hyper-parameters tuned RERNN using LOA for breast cancer classification. Biomedical Signal Processing and Control, 72(Part A), 103354. DOI: 10.1016/j.bspc.2021.103354

Tufekci, Z., & Korukoglu, S. (2020). Cybersecurity in banking: The impact of IoT and AI on privacy. *Computers & Security*, *104*, 102109. DOI: 10.1016/j.cose.2020.102109

Tyagi, A. K., Kumari, S., Tiwari, S., & Subbiah, P. (2024). Industry 5.0 at the core of Society 5.0: A revolution in the modern era of the health care sector. In Sustainable innovation for Industry 6.0 (Chap. 17). IGI Global. DOI: 10.4018/979-8-3693-3140-8.ch017

Vishnuram, G., Tripathi, K., & Tyagi, A. K. (2022). Ethical hacking: Importance, controversies and scope in the future. In *2022 International Conference on Computer Communication and Informatics (ICCCI)* (pp. 1–6). IEEE. DOI: 10.1109/ICCCI54379.2022.9740860

Vittala, K. R. P., Ahmad, S. S., Seranmadevi, R., & Tyagi, A. K. (2024). Emerging technology adoption and applications for modern society towards providing smart banking solutions. In *Enhancing medical imaging with emerging technologies*. IGI Global., DOI: 10.4018/979-8-3693-5261-8.ch018

Vittala, K. R. P., Arumugam, S. K., Kumar, N. S., & Tyagi, A. K. (2024). Artificial intelligence: Blockchain integration for modern business. In *Advancing software engineering through AI, federated learning, and large language models*. IGI Global., DOI: 10.4018/979-8-3693-3502-4.ch006

Vittala, K. R. P., Hemamalini, V., Seranmadevi, R., & Tyagi, A. K. (2024). The road to smart banking: Opportunities and challenges for the next generation. In *Convergence of technology and operations management in modern businesses*. IGI Global., DOI: 10.4018/979-8-3693-6200-6.ch002

Vittala, K. R. P., Kumar, K., Seranmadevi, R., & Tyagi, A. K. (2024). Artificial intelligence-Internet of Things integration for smart marketing: Challenges and opportunities. In *Advancing software engineering through AI, federated learning, and large language models*. IGI Global., DOI: 10.4018/979-8-3693-3502-4.ch019

Vittala, K. R. P., Nagarathnamma, J., Chidambaram, N., & Tyagi, A. K. (2024). Smart financial services through smart banking in the era of Industry 5.0: Opportunities and challenges. In *Creating AI synergy through business technology transformation*. IGI Global., DOI: 10.4018/979-8-3693-4187-2.ch010

Wang, H., & Zhou, Z. (2021). AI-enhanced cybersecurity in banking: A systematic review. *Future Generation Computer Systems*, *115*, 287–299. DOI: 10.1016/j.future.2020.11.027

Zhang, Y., & Lu, Q. (2019). Managing privacy and security in IoT-enabled banking systems. *Journal of Financial Services Marketing*, *24*(4), 241–256. DOI: 10.1057/s41264-019-00064-1

Chapter 7
Exchange Rates and Trade Dynamics

Roop Raj
H.N.B. Garhwal University, India

Anagha Bhope
Indira School of Business Studies, India

Pratik Ajay Kodmalwar
https://orcid.org/0000-0003-1757-4441
Datta Meghe Institute of Management Studies, India

V. R. Sudindra
ICFAI Business School, ICFAI Foundation for Higher Education, India

Ashwarya Sharma
https://orcid.org/0009-0005-8510-3862
Chandigarh School of Business, Chandigarh Group of Colleges, India

P. Selvakumar
https://orcid.org/0000-0002-3650-4548
Department of Science and Humanities, Nehru Institute of Technology, Coimbatore, India

T. C. Manjunath
https://orcid.org/0000-0003-2545-9160
Rajarajeswari College of Engineering, India

ABSTRACT

The interplay between exchange rates, trade, and economic policies shapes the way nations engage with each other economically. Understanding exchange rates, their fluctuations, and how they influence trade flows is crucial for governments, businesses, and individuals involved in international trade. This overview will explore the concept of exchange rates, stability and growth. On the other hand, political instability or economic uncertainty can lead to depreciation, as investors seek safer assets in other countries.Government interventions, particularly in the form of monetary and fiscal policies, can also affect exchange rates. Conversely, a currency appreciation can worsen a trade deficit by making exports more expensive

DOI: 10.4018/979-8-3693-9765-7.ch007

and imports cheaper. moreover, exchange rate movements can affect the timing of trade flows. For instance, if a country expects its currency to appreciate in the future, it may delay its purchases of foreign goods to take advantage of lower prices later.

INTRODUCTION TO EXCHANGE RATES AND TRADE DYNAMICS

The interplay between exchange rates, trade, and economic policies shapes the way nations engage with each other economically. Understanding exchange rates, their fluctuations, and how they influence trade flows is crucial for governments, businesses, and individuals involved in international trade. This overview will explore the concept of exchange rates, stability and growth. On the other hand, political instability or economic uncertainty can lead to depreciation, as investors seek safer assets in other countries.Government interventions, particularly in the form of monetary and fiscal policies, can also affect exchange rates. Conversely, a currency appreciation can worsen a trade deficit by making exports more expensive and imports cheaper. moreover, exchange rate movements can affect the timing of trade flows. For instance, if a country expects its currency to appreciate in the future, it may delay its purchases of foreign goods to take advantage of lower prices later. Similarly, The Role of Speculation and Market Sentiment Traders and investors in the currency markets buy and sell currencies based on their expectations of future economic conditions, interest rates, and geopolitical events. they may sell its currency, leading to a depreciation. Conversely, positive economic news or political stability can lead to currency appreciation.. Understanding the factors that determine exchange rates, their impact on trade dynamics, and the broader economic implications is essential for businesses, policymakers, and investors engaged in international trade. While exchange rates are subject to fluctuations due to a variety of factors, their overall impact on the global economy remains profound. By shaping the competitiveness of nations in global markets, exchange rates play a pivotal role in driving economic growth and stability in an interconnected world.

The Foreign Exchange Market: Structure, Functions, and Participants

The market allows governments, businesses, investors, and individuals to convert one currency into another for a variety of purposes, including trade, investment, and speculation. The vast size and liquidity of the FX market, with daily turnover surpassing $6 trillion, make it a key driver of economic activity. This comprehensive overview will examine the structure of the foreign exchange market, its key functions, and the primary participants who engage in currency trading.

Structure of the London, Tokyo, and Sydney, allowing for continuous trading of currencies across different time zones.Unlike traditional stock markets that are centralized in specific locations, the FX through electronic platforms, telephone systems, or other communication channels. There is no physical exchange where currency trading is carried out through a global network of banks, brokers, and dealers, operating through various platforms.most liquid and active segment of the FX market, with traders often making short-term trades to profit from fluctuations in currency prices.standardized contracts traded on exchanges, such as the Chicago Mercantile Exchange (CME), allowing traders to buy or sell currencies at predetermined future dates. These contracts provide a hedge against future exchange rate movements and are commonly used by businesses and investors to manage currency risk.The Swap Market: The currency swap market allows institutions and corporations to exchange currency to manage foreign exchange risk and obtain better financing terms in different currencies.Investment Opportunities and Speculation:(Athanasiou G et al., 2008) The FX market also serves as a platform for investors and speculators seeking to profit from fluctuations in exchange rates. Forex trading provides opportunities for profit through both short-term speculation and long-term investment. Speculators, such as hedge funds and individual traders, attempt to predict future currency price movements and engage in buying or selling currencies to make profits. These participants contribute to market liquidity and help to ensure that exchange rates reflect the underlying economic fundamentals. exchange market, as they control national monetary policy and manage their country's currency reserves. They may intervene in the FX market to stabilize their domestic currency or achieve specific economic goals, such as diversify their foreign currency reserves.They also engage in proprietary trading, buying and selling currencies for their own profit. Banks often act as intermediaries, providing liquidity and ensuring that buyers and sellers can execute currency transactions.Corporations: Multinational corporations conduct business operations in foreign countries. They exchange currencies to pay for goods and services, manage foreign operations, and repatriate profits. foreign exchange market, seeking to profit from currency price movements. These investors engage in speculative trading, taking large positions in currencies based on their analysis of economic indicators, interest rates, and geopolitical events. Hedge funds may also use currency trading as part of a broader investment strategy to diversify their portfolios and enhance returns.due to the accessibility of online platforms and the ability to trade with relatively small amounts of capital. However, retail traders also face significant risks, as currency markets can be highly volatile and unpredictable.liquidity by buying and selling currencies on behalf of their clients or for their own accounts. They help ensure that the market operates smoothly and that there is a continuous flow of transactions. The market's decentralized nature and continuous 24-hour operation make it unique among financial markets(Bashir U et al., 2019), providing liquidity and price discovery for currencies globally. As the market continues to evolve, it remains a central component of the global financial system, influencing everything from the prices of goods and services to the broader macroeconomic stability of nations.

Theoretical Frameworks: Exchange Rates, Trade, and Economic Growth

Various theoretical frameworks have been developed to explain how exchange rates impact trade and economic growth, with different schools of thought offering diverse perspectives on the mechanisms at play. This comprehensive exploration will examine the major theoretical models that link exchange rates, trade, and economic growth, focusing on classical, Keynesian, and modern theories.Classical Theories: The Role of By focusing on these goods and engaging in trade, countries can achieve higher levels of economic welfare and growth than they could by producing everything domestically.In the classical framework, This mechanism highlights the central role of exchange rates in balancing trade between countries and in facilitating the efficient allocation of resources globally. However, while comparative advantage suggests that trade benefits all parties involved, it assumes that exchange rates are stable and does not fully account for the complexities of currency fluctuations or the role of speculative forces in the market.The (PPP) Theory According to PPP, an appreciation or depreciation of a currency should correct for differences in inflation rates and price levels between trading countries. Keynesian Theories: Exchange Rates, Trade, and Economic Fluctuations Keynesian economic theory, which emerged during exchange rates and trade flows, especially in the context of short-term economic fluctuations. According to Keynesian theory, exchange rates do not always adjust automatically to maintain balance in international trade. Instead, they can be influenced by government policies, investor sentiment, and speculative forces.In Keynesian economics, in aggregate demand. When a country experiences a trade deficit, for example, its currency may depreciate, making exports more attractive and imports more expensive. In the Keynesian framework, exchange rate movements thus act as a mechanism for adjusting trade balances and maintaining overall economic stability.Keynesians also emphasize interest rate changes, currency interventions, or capital controls. By adjusting monetary and fiscal policies, countries can influence their exchange rates and trade flows, helping to mitigate and exchange rate relationships.Monetarist theory, largely developed by economist Milton Friedman, places significant emphasis on the role of money supply in determining exchange rates and, by extension, trade and economic growth (Bender J C et al., 2013) As a result, the country's currency depreciates, making its exports cheaper and imports more expensive. Conversely, a country with lower inflation rates will see its currency appreciate relative to others. In this framework, exchange rates are seen as a reflection of a country's monetary policy and inflationary conditions. Monetarists emphasize the importance of maintaining a stable money supply to avoid excessive inflation and currency volatility, which could disrupt trade and economic growth boosts exports by making domestic goods cheaper, while an appreciating currency can make exports more expensive and reduce demand.

However, the monetarist approach tends to focus more on the role of money supply and inflation in driving exchange rates than on the broader factors affecting trade dynamics and economic growth.According to RBC theory, fluctuations in output and employment are largely the result of exogenous changes in technology and productivity,(Beine M et al., 2009) rather than demand-side factors like government intervention or money supply.Endogenous growth theory, which emerged in the 1980s and 1990s as a challenge to the neoclassical growth models, focuses on how investments in human capital, innovation, and knowledge drive long-term economic growth. Unlike exogenous models, which treat technological progress as an outside factor, Integrating Theories and Understanding the Complexity While classical theories like comparative advantage and PPP provide foundational insights into how exchange rates influence trade patterns, modern theories such as Keynesian, monetarist,(Bloomfield R et al., 2009) RBC, and endogenous growth models offer deeper understandings of how exchange rates interact with broader economic forces. Ultimately, exchange rates are not just a reflection of relative prices; they are also shaped by government policies, technological advancements, inflationary conditions, and investor sentiment. Understanding these theoretical frameworks is crucial for policymakers, businesses, and economists who seek to navigate the interconnected global economy and make informed decisions about trade and investment strategies.

Supply and Demand in the Foreign Exchange Market: Exchange Rate Determination

The balance of trade is a critical factor in exchange rate determination. Market speculation further drives exchange rate movements(Brianzoni S et al., 2020). Traders in the Forex market often act can lead to a sell-off, causing depreciation. Short-Term vs. Long-Term DeterminantsWhile supply and demand govern the immediate fluctuations in the Forex market, long-term exchange rate trends are often dictated by fundamental factors productivity, and fiscal policies. In the short term, however, market sentiment and speculative trading dominate. For example, political instability or unexpected central remain unchanged.In conclusion,(Calin O, 2012) the determination of and geopolitical events. Understanding these dynamics is crucial for policymakers, investors, and businesses as they navigate the global economy.

Exchange Rate Theories: Purchasing Power Parity, Interest Rate Parity, and Balance of Payments

While PPP provides a useful long-term perspective(Day R H et al., 2000), it is less effective in explaining short-term exchange rate fluctuations. Market imperfections, trade restrictions, and speculative capital flows often lead to deviations from PPP in the short term. equal when adjusted for forward exchange rates. Like PPP, IRP is more applicable in idealized markets. Real-world factors such as transaction costs, exchange rate volatility, and central bank interventions can cause deviations from the theory.The BOP is a comprehensive record of all economic transactions between a country and the rest of the world, including trade in goods and services, capital flows, and foreign investments(Choe G H, 2016). This theory posits that exchange rates adjust to ensure that the BOP remains in equilibrium.A country running a trade surplus, for instance, experiences increased demand for its currency, leading to appreciation. Conversely, a trade deficit increases the supply of the currency in the global market, causing depreciation. In addition to the trade balance, the financial and capital accounts also play a significant role. For example, inflows of foreign direct investment (FDI) or portfolio investments can strengthen a country's currency, while outflows exert downward pressure. but it may be less effective in explaining short-term volatility driven by speculative activities. For instance, PPP is particularly useful for analyzing long-term trends driven by inflation differentials, while IRP focuses on capital flows and interest rate differentials in the short to medium term. The BOP approach bridges the gap by incorporating trade and financial transactions into the analysis.In practice, deviations from these theories are common due to market imperfections, speculative activities, and government interventions. For example, speculative capital flows can cause short-term volatility that may not align with fundamentals such as inflation or interest rates. Similarly, central banks often implement monetary policies or currency interventions that distort natural market dynamics, leading to temporary deviations from theoretical predictions(Einstein A, 2005)., their combined application offers a robust framework for analyzing the interplay of economic forces in the global foreign exchange market. Understanding these theories is crucial for policymakers, investors, and businesses navigating the complexities of international finance.

Exchange Rate Systems: Fixed, Flexible, and Managed Float

Exchange rate systems define. Each system has its distinct characteristics, advantages, and limitations, shaping how governments and markets interact in the foreign exchange arena.One of the primary advantages of a fixed exchange rate system is the stability it provides. By eliminating significant fluctuations, it fosters predictable trade and investment conditions, which are especially beneficial for countries heavily reliant on international trade. Additionally, a fixed system can help control inflation, as the currency's value is tied to a more stable or stronger foreign currency. However, fixed systems have notable drawbacks.(Fama E F, 2010) or speculative attacks. Moreover, the rigidity of the system can prevent the natural adjustment of the exchange rate in response to economic imbalances, such as trade deficits or surpluses. Countries using fixed systems often face challenges in maintaining monetary policy independence, as domestic interest rates must align with the pegged currency's rate.Examples the currency board arrangements seen in countries like Hong Kong, where the Hong Kong dollar is pegged to the U.S. dollar.The primary advantage of a floating system is its ability to adjust automatically to economic conditions. For instance, if a country experiences a trade deficit, its currency depreciates, making exports cheaper and imports more expensive, which helps restore balance over time. Floating systems also provide greater autonomy for domestic monetary policy, as central banks are not required to maintain fixed currency levels.Despite these benefits(Feng G F et al., 2021), Sudden changes in currency values can impact the competitiveness of exports, the cost of imports, and the repayment of foreign debt. Developing economies with less stable financial systems are particularly vulnerable to the risks associated with a freely floating exchange rate. In this approach, exchange rates are primarily determined by market forces but are subject to periodic intervention by central banks to prevent excessive volatility or to achieve specific economic objectives.In a managed float system, governments may intervene currency appreciates excessively, the central bank may sell its currency in the market to stabilize its value. Conversely, if the currency depreciates sharply, the bank may purchase it to prevent further decline.This system offers flexibility while allowing governments to address short-term imbalances and maintain economic stability. China manages its currency, the yuan, within a narrow band around a reference rate, allowing limited fluctuations while maintaining control over broader economic conditions.Each exchange rate system has unique implications for economic policy and performance. Fixed systems promote stability but limit flexibility in responding to and policy objectives. For instance, small, open economies with significant trade exposure often prefer fixed systems to stabilize their trade environment, while larger, diversified economies tend to adopt floating systems to leverage monetary policy autonomy.In practice, no system is perfect. Fixed systems can collapse under sustained economic pressures, attacks and destabilizing capital flows(Franke R et al., 2016). Managed float systems attempt to mitigate these challenges but require effective policy frameworks and robust institutions to succeed.Conclusion Exchange rate systems—fixed, flexible, and managed float—are foundational to international finance and trade. Each system presents trade-offs between stability, flexibility, and monetary autonomy, influencing a nation's economic strategy and resilience. While fixed systems provide predictability, they demand significant reserves and policy discipline.

The Impact of Exchange Rates on Trade: Export-Led Growth and Import Competition

For example, nations pursuing export-led growth strategies, such as China and South Korea, have historically leveraged favorable exchange rates to make their products competitive in global markets. These countries often use policies(Hassler U et al., 2016), including managed exchange rate systems, to maintain currency values that support export-driven industrialization.However, a depreciated currency is not without challenges., eroding the initial competitive advantage. On the other hand, currency appreciation can have the opposite effect, making exports more expensive and potentially reducing global demand. This scenario is a concern for countries reliant on export revenue, as seen in Japan during periods of yen appreciation. as cheaper imports often lead to increased competition. Industries that are unable to compete with lower-priced foreign goods may experience declining revenues, layoffs, and, in severe cases, closures. particularly in sectors vulnerable to international competition. However, it may also lead to higher costs for consumers and businesses reliant on imported goods, potentially reducing overall purchasing power and investment.Exchange rates directly impact trade balances—the difference between a country's exports and imports. A depreciating currency often leads to improved trade balances by making exports more competitive and reducing the appeal of imports. This adjustment is known as the J-curve effect, where the initial impact of depreciation may worsen the trade balance before it improves as export volumes increase and import volumes decrease.Countries with trade surpluses, such as Germany or China, often benefit from weaker currencies that support their export-oriented economies. In contrast, nations with persistent trade deficits, like the United States, are more vulnerable to exchange rate fluctuations. Large deficits can lead to currency depreciation, increasing the cost of servicing foreign debt and creating potential macroeconomic instability.successful in East Asian economies, where governments have maintained competitive exchange rates to support export industries while investing in infrastructure and innovation.However, overreliance on export-led growth exposes countries to external shocks.

Global recessions, changes in foreign demand, or protectionist policies in trading partners can undermine export earnings, highlighting the importance of diversification in economic strategies. Additionally, competitive devaluations—where countries deliberately weaken their currencies to boost exports—can lead to trade tensions and retaliatory measures, disrupting global trade. A weaker currency makes imports more expensive, creating a price advantage for domestic producers. This can encourage investment in local industries and reduce reliance on volatile global markets. For example, central banks may use foreign reserves to stabilize the currency or implement monetary policies to influence exchange rates. Additionally, trade policies such as tariffs, subsidies, and export incentives are often used alongside exchange rate management to support trade objectives.Market forces also play a significant role in shaping the impact of exchange rates on trade. Speculative activities in the Forex market, changes in investor sentiment, and global economic conditions can lead to exchange rate volatility, creating uncertainty for businesses and governments(Hung J II, 2007). Companies involved in international trade often use hedging strategies, such as forward contracts and options, to manage exchange rate risks and stabilize earnings., such as manufacturing and agriculture, are highly sensitive to currency fluctuations. For example, a depreciating currency can significantly boost agricultural exports by making them more affordable in global markets. influencing export performance, import competition, and overall economic stability. Whether driving export-led growth or shaping domestic markets through import dynamics, exchange rate movements create both opportunities and challenges for economies. Policymakers and businesses must navigate these complexities, balancing exchange rate

Exchange Rates and Trade Balance: J-Curve Effect and Marshall-Lerner Condition

Two prominent concepts that explain how exchange rate movements influence These frameworks highlight the complexities of trade dynamics and the time-lagged responses to currency depreciation or appreciation. expensive. Conversely, currency appreciation makes exports more expensive and imports more affordable(Jawad M, 2019). These changes can alter trade volumes and the trade balance over time. However, the relationship is not immediate or linear, as it depends on factors such as price elasticity of demand, trade contracts, and market adjustment periods. This occurs because trade volumes are relatively inflexible in the short term due to existing contracts and limited immediate substitution between domestic and foreign goods.(Jackson J D, 2008)For example, when a currency depreciates, the value of imports increases in the short term as exporters capitalize on the price advantage and importers reduce demand for expensive foreign goods, trade volumes adjust, and the trade balance improves, forming the characteristic "J" shape.$|E_x + E_m| > 1$ the adjustment in trade volumes following depreciation offsets the initial increase in the cost of imports, leading to an overall improvement in the trade balance.For instance, in export-driven economies like Germany, where demand for exports is relatively elastic, currency depreciation can significantly enhance trade surpluses. In contrast, in economies reliant on essential imports, such as oil-dependent countries, depreciation may not always lead to trade balance improvement, as import demand is often inelastic.Interplay Between emphasizing the initial deterioration due to price and volume rigidities. The Marshall-Lerner Condition, on the other hand, explains the long-term equilibrium effects based on the responsiveness of export and import demand to price changes.For example, a country experiencing depreciation may initially face a worsening trade balance (J-Curve effect) but ultimately see improvement the trade balance may fail to recover, and depreciation could lead to persistent deficits. provide valuable insights, their practical application depends on several real-world factors. These include: Trade Elasticities: Many developing economies face challenges in meeting the Marshall-Lerner Condition due to inelastic demand for their exports, which are often raw materials or low-value-added goods.

Similarly, import dependence on essential goods like energy or food limits the responsiveness of import demand to price changes.strain foreign reserves and create short-term economic instability in countries reliant on external financing.(Jovanovic B, 2009) For instance, if global demand is weak, even a more competitive currency may fail to boost exports significantly.in some cases, exporters absorb currency depreciation costs to maintain market share, limiting the expected trade balance improvement., such as trade tariffs or subsidies, can distort the natural adjustment process predicted by the J-Curve and Marshall-Lerner Condition., typically benefit more from currency depreciation than service sectors. Similarly, countries with diversified export bases are better positioned to leverage exchange rate adjustments than those reliant on a few commodities.For instance, Asian economies like South Korea and Japan have successfully used currency depreciation to enhance export competitiveness and trade surpluses. In contrast, oil-exporting countries may struggle to improve trade balances through depreciation due to the inelastic nature of oil demand and limited export diversification. While the J-Curve highlights the initial deterioration and eventual recovery of trade balance, the Marshall-Lerner Condition underscores the importance of demand elasticities in achieving sustainable improvements. Policymakers must carefully assess these factors when implementing exchange rate policies, ensuring they align with broader economic objectives and global market conditions.

Exchange Rates and Foreign Direct Investment: Multinational Enterprises and Global Value Chains

Exchange rates significantly influence (FDI) by shaping the decisions of exchange rates affect the relative costs of investments, production, and trade, impacting how MNEs allocate resources across countries and integrate their activities globally. Currency depreciation in a host country reduces the relative cost of acquiring assets, land, and labor, making it more appealing for foreign investors. For example, a weaker currency allows MNEs to purchase more with their home currency, enhancing investment affordability. Conversely, currency appreciation in a host country can deter FDI by increasing the cost of investment. Depreciation can also enhance the competitiveness of export-oriented FDI, where MNEs establish operations in the host country to produce goods for export. Lower production costs, combined with favorable exchange rates, as it creates uncertainty about future returns, especially for long-term projects requiring stable economic conditions.For instance, developing countries often attract FDI during periods of currency weakness, as MNEs take advantage of lower entry costs. Yet, excessive depreciation or instability may signal economic vulnerabilities, discouraging investors. In contrast, stable and predictable exchange rate regimes tend to foster higher levels of FDI by reducing risk Investment Decisions: Exchange rates affect the relative cost of capital and expected returns on investments. For example, a U.S.-based company may choose to invest in a European country if the euro depreciates against the dollar, making European assets cheaper and potentially increasing the value of future returns when converted back to dollars. Cost Management: MNEs often seek to hedge against exchange rate risks by diversifying their investments across multiple countries or regions. By spreading operations, they can reduce exposure to currency-specific volatility and leverage exchange rate differentials for cost advantages(Kahneman D et al., 2019). For example, if a host country's currency depreciates, an MNE may experience lower revenues when converting local earnings to its home currency. To counter this, companies may adjust local pricing or seek to reduce costs in the host country.

Reinvestment of Earnings: Exchange rate movements also affect decisions on whether to repatriate profits or reinvest earnings in the host country. Favorable exchange rates may incentivize reinvestment to capitalize on local opportunities, while unfavorable rates may encourage MNEs to repatriate funds.. MNEs design GVCs to optimize efficiency, cost, and market access, and exchange rate changes can disrupt or enhance these arrangements.Cost of Inputs: Currency depreciation in a country supplying inputs to GVCs lowers the cost of materials and intermediate goods for MNEs. For export-oriented GVCs, depreciation in the currency of the production base enhances global competitiveness. However, for import-dependent chains, depreciation can increase costs, particularly for inputs sourced from countries with stronger currencies.Currency Risk Management:(Koch P D et al., 2001) MNEs involved in GVCs must actively manage currency risks to maintain profitability and stability. Techniques such as forward contracts, currency swaps, and natural hedging through local financing are commonly used to mitigate exchange rate exposure.Governments in host and home countries play a vital role in creating an environment conducive to FDI by addressing exchange rate concerns. Stable and predictable exchange rate regimes encourage investment by reducing uncertainty, while excessive volatility or misaligned currency policies can deter investors. Policymakers often pursue measures such as currency stabilization, trade agreements, and tax incentives to attract FDI and integrate their economies into GVCs.Attracting FDI: Host countries with undervalued or stable currencies are more likely to attract export-oriented FDI. Policies that complement exchange rate advantages, such as infrastructure development and labor market reforms, can enhance investment attractiveness.Promoting GVC Participation: Countries seeking to integrate into GVCs must address exchange rate-related barriers to trade and investment(LeBaron B, 2006). For example, improving currency convertibility and reducing transaction costs can facilitate smoother integration into global production networks. support investment. Managed float systems, for instance, allow for periodic intervention to stabilize exchange rates while preserving some market flexibility. Bilateral and Regional Agreements: Trade and investment agreements often include provisions addressing exchange rate stability to ensure fair competition and encourage cross-border investments. Examples include provisions in free trade agreements or regional initiatives like the European Union's single market. Exchange Rate Volatility: Sudden and unpredictable currency fluctuations increase risk, particularly for long-term investments in volatile markets.(Levy M et al., 2002)Non-Price Factors: Exchange rates are only one of many factors influencing FDI decisions.

Exchange Rate Volatility: Causes, Consequences, and Measurement

For instance, a surge in demand for a country's exports or investments can lead to appreciation, while reduced demand or capital Exchange rate volatility affects exporters and importers by creating uncertainty in pricing and profitability. For exporters, currency depreciation can boost competitiveness, while appreciation reduces it. Importers face higher costs when a domestic currency depreciates, potentially leading to inflation. High volatility can discourage trade agreements and long-term contracts. This reduces the effectiveness of monetary policy and can lead to hyperinflation in extreme cases., excessive intervention may deplete foreign reserves or create distortions in the currency market. measured using various statistical and econometric tools to quantify the degree of currency fluctuation over time.The simplest method is calculating the standard deviation or variance of exchange rate changes over a specific period. Higher values indicate greater volatility.Historical volatility measures the fluctuation in exchange rates(Lo A W, 2004) . It is widely used in forecasting and risk assessment.Technical indicators such as moving averages and Bollinger Bands assess volatility by analyzing trends and deviations in exchange rate movements over time.Businesses and investors use financial instruments such as futures, options, and swaps to hedge against exchange rate risks. These tools provide a fixed rate for future transactions, reducing uncertainty.. By spreading exposure, firms reduce reliance on a single currency. regional currency agreements or fixed exchange rate systems can reduce volatility.Firms can adjust pricing strategies in response to exchange rate changes, such as using local currencies for transactions or implementing dynamic pricing models.models enable businesses to anticipate currency movements and prepare contingency plans. Measures such as maintaining adequate foreign reserves, pursuing sound fiscal and monetary policies, and fostering transparent Forex markets can enhance stability.In addition, international cooperation, . Countries with high volatility may benefit from pegged exchange rates or managed float systems to reduce uncertainty. requiring careful management by businesses and policymakers alike. Accurate measurement tools and effective strategies are essential to mitigate risks and leverage opportunities in an increasingly interconnected world. Through a combination of financial innovation, risk management, and sound economic policies, the challenges of exchange rate volatility can be navigated successfully.

Exchange Rate Risk Management: Hedging, Speculation, and Arbitrage

Exchange investors, and financial institutions adopt Hedging is the process of reducing exposure to exchange rate fluctuations by using financial instruments or operational strategies. It is widely used by businesses, institutional investors, and multinational corporations to ensure predictable outcomes(Mourtas S D et al., 2022) They provide liquidity and transparency but lack customization compared to forwards. Companies often use operational strategies like matching revenue and expenses in the same currency to offset risks.For instance, sourcing materials locally in foreign markets or invoicing customers in the domestic currency reduces exposure.Hedging is a defensive strategy aimed at minimizing risk rather than maximizing profit. While it provides stability, it comes with costs, such as premiums for options or reduced flexibility.Unlike hedging, speculation involves taking deliberate risks in the foreign exchange market to profit from anticipated currency movements. Speculators include traders, hedge funds, and individual investors who seek to exploit market inefficiencies or price trends.(Mandelbrot B B, 2004)Speculators use leverage to amplify potential gains (and losses) from currency movements. For example, a trader might speculate on the U.S. dollar appreciating against the euro, using leverage to magnify profits.In carry trades, speculators borrow in a low-interest-rate currency and invest in a high-interest-rate currency, profiting from the interest rate differential. However, sudden exchange rate changes or shifts in monetary policy can result in significant losses.Speculators analyze trends and momentum indicators to predict short-term exchange rate movements. By buying undervalued currencies and selling overvalued ones, they aim to capture quick gains.While speculation adds liquidity to foreign exchange markets, it also introduces volatility. Excessive speculative activity can lead to destabilizing currency swings, prompting regulatory scrutiny. This strategy involves buying a currency in one market where it is undervalued and simultaneously selling it in another where it is overvalued.For example, if the USD/EUR rate differs between London and New York markets, arbitrageurs act quickly to profit from the discrepancy.Covered interest arbitrage involves using forward contracts to lock in profits from interest rate differentials between two currencies.

Uncovered interest arbitrage, on the other hand, involves higher risks as it assumes future exchange rates will align with interest rate differentials.Arbitrage helps align exchange rates across markets and ensures efficiency. However, technological advancements and algorithmic trading have made it increasingly competitive, reducing profit margins for manual traders.In practice, hedging, speculation, and arbitrage often overlap in the foreign exchange market. Institutional players, such as banks and hedge funds, may use all three strategies depending on market conditions and their objectives. For instance:Predicting exchange rate movements is inherently difficult due to the complex interplay of economic, political, and market factors.Hedging instruments come with fees, premiums, and administrative costs, which can erode profitability.Sudden and extreme events, such as financial crises or geopolitical shocks, can render even well-hedged positions vulnerable.Regulatory frameworks may limit speculative activities or impose restrictions on certain arbitrage strategies, affecting market flexibility.Over-the-counter (OTC) derivatives, such as forward contracts, expose participants to counterparty default risk.Governments and central banks play a crucial role in fostering stable foreign exchange markets to reduce the need for excessive risk management(Neely C J, 2000). Key measures include:nderstanding the principles and challenges of these approaches, businesses and investors can better navigate the complexities of the global currency markets. Policymakers, too, must ensure that financial systems support effective risk management while safeguarding market stability. Through a combination of proactive strategies and sound governance, exchange rate risks can be effectively managed to sustain global economic growth.

Derivatives and Currency Markets

These instruments provide flexibility and security for market participants while also enhancing liquidity and efficiency in foreign exchange (Forex) markets.Options help reduce potential losses while allowing participants to benefit from favorable rate changes.Standardization: Futures contracts are standardized in terms of contract size, maturity, and other terms, making them liquid and accessible(Nelson E, 2020). Margin Requirements: Participants must post an initial margin and maintain a margin balance, ensuring contract performance.Mark-to-Market: Futures positions are marked to market daily, reflecting changes in market value. an exporter expecting revenue in GBP can sell GBP futures to hedge against potential depreciation.traders use futures to take positions based on anticipated currency movements. Leverage amplifies potential profits but also increases risk.Futures enable arbitrage between spot and futures markets, aligning exchange rates across time frames.Transparency: Futures are traded on exchanges, providing clear pricing and high liquidity.Reduced Counterparty Risk: Clearinghouses act as intermediaries, ensuring contract performance.A currency swap is a financial agreement between two parties to exchange principal and interest payments in different currencies over a specified period. Fixed-for-Fixed: Both parties exchange fixed interest payments in their respective currencies. Fixed-for-Floating: One party pays a fixed rate while the other pays a floating rate, or vice versa.Customizability: Currency swaps can be tailored to meet specific needs, such as duration, payment frequency, and principal amounts.(Nuno A et al., 2018). Swaps are often used for managing long-term currency risks, such as foreign-denominated loans or investments.companies borrowing in foreign currencies can use swaps to convert liabilities into their domestic currency, avoiding exchange rate risk.For example, a U.S. company with a loan in euros may swap its euro-denominated obligations for dollar payments.Swaps allow firms to adjust their interest rate exposure, optimizing financing costs.

Financial institutions use swaps to profit from differences in interest rates and currency values across markets. Often more cost-effective than other hedging methods for long-term risk management.Derivatives reduce uncertainty, enabling businesses to focus on core operations without worrying about currency fluctuations. By allowing participants to hedge, speculate, or arbitrage, derivatives enhance liquidity and price discovery in currency markets.Instruments like swaps enable firms to manage financing costs effectively, particularly in volatile markets.Derivatives provide customized solutions for managing diverse risk profiles.The use of leverage can amplify losses, particularly in volatile currency markets.Advanced derivatives require sophisticated understanding and expertise, posing challenges for smaller firms. Regulatory changes, such as limits on derivative usage or reporting requirements, can affect market participants.Derivatives are indispensable tools in the currency markets, offering solutions for hedging, speculation, and arbitrage. Instruments such as options, futures, and swaps provide flexibility, liquidity, and efficiency, enabling market participants to manage risks and capitalize on opportunities.

Classical and Neoclassical Trade Theories: Comparative Advantage and Gains from Trade

Classical and neoclassical trade theories form the foundation of international trade economics, providing essential insights into why nations engage in trade and how they benefit. Rooted in principles like comparative advantage, opportunity cost, and the role of production factors, these theories illustrate how trade enhances global efficiency, promotes specialization, and fosters economic growth. This discussion delves into the core concepts of classical and neoclassical trade theories, focusing on comparative advantage and the gains from trade.Example: If England produces cloth more efficiently and Portugal excels at wine production, both nations can trade these goods for mutual benefit.Illustration: If Portugal is AdvantageBuilding on classical foundations, neoclassical trade theories introduced new imensions, such as the role of preferences, factor endowments, and production technologies(Zivot E et al., 2006). These refinements address limitations in Ricardo's model and provide a more comprehensive understanding of trade dynamics.The H-O model, developed by Eli Heckscher and Bertil Ohlin, explains trade patterns based on differences in factor endowments, such as labor, capital, and land.Example: Labor-abundant countries export labor-intensive goods, while capital-abundant nations export capital-intensive goods.This theorem explains how changes in factor endowments affect output in a two-good economy, illustrating the dynamic adjustments in trade patterns over time. Classical and neoclassWhile trade benefits nations overall, it can create winners and losers within economies, leading to income inequality and social discontent. The assumption of immobile factors across countries is unrealistic in a globalized world with multinational corporations and capital flows.Despite their limitations, classical and neoclassical trade theories remain highly relevant:Policy Formulation: They guide trade policies that promote specialization and liberalization.Global Trade Agreements: Concepts of comparative advantage underpin agreements(Zhang X et al., 2017) like WTO negotiations.

New Trade Theories: Increasing Returns, Imperfect Competition, and Strategic Trade Policy

New trade theories, emerging in the late 20th century, significantly expanded upon classical and neoclassical trade models. These theories account for real-world complexities, largely overlooked by traditional frameworks. By integrating elements from industrial organization, technology, and strategic decision-making, new trade theories provide a more nuanced understanding of how trade occurs in a globalized economy. This discussion explores the key concepts behind new trade theories, focusing on increasing returns to scale, imperfect competition, and strategic trade policy, and how these factors shape the global trading environment suggest that as the production of a good expands, the cost per unit of output decreases, leading to more efficient production at larger scales. This principle plays a central role in new trade theories, particularly in understanding why countries might specialize in certain industries, even when they do not have a comparative advantage based on traditional resource endowments.its production increases. This happens because, with larger production volumes, firms can utilize economies of scale—such as more specialized labor, advanced machinery, or better use of technology—leading to a lower average cost per unit produced.Example: A country that specializes in high-tech industries, like semiconductor manufacturing, may experience decreasing costs as production volume rises.(Yellen J L, 2015) specialization, and technological advancements. Implications for Trade, it may still dominate global trade in specific goods, like automobiles or electronics, by producing them more efficiently at a large scale. First-Mover Advantage: Firms or countries that are the first to enter a market and achieve high output may enjoy cost advantages. control over pricing. The concept of imperfect competition, including monopolistic competition, is central to new trade theories. that firms can differentiate their products through innovation, branding, and product features, which allows them to charge prices above marginal cost and still maintain market share.Example: The automobile industry, where firms such as Ford, Toyota, and Volkswagen produce differentiated cars that cater to different tastes, budgets, and geographic preferences, is a typical example of monopolistic competition. Despite being in the same industry, each firm has some level of market power due to differentiation., or branding. This leads to a more diverse range of traded goods, with each country specializing in particular varieties.Strategic trade policy, a concept derived from new trade theory, challenges the traditional free trade perspective by suggesting that governments can intervene in international trade to enhance the competitive position of domestic firms in global markets. Unlike classical trade theories, which argue for minimal government intervention, strategic trade theory proposes that governments can use policy tools—such as subsidies, tariffs, and investment in research and development (R&D)—to help domestic industries gain a competitive advantage imperfect competition, a government can shift the global market equilibrium to its advantage by supporting its domestic firms.(Yuan Y et al., 2019)

A tariff is a tax imposed on imported goods or services, designed to raise the price of foreign products and make them less competitive relative to domestic alternatives. Quotas are used to protect domestic industries by limiting foreign competition and ensuring that a specific percentage of the market is reserved for domestic producers. While quotas protect certain industries from foreign competition, they also lead to inefficiencies by distorting market forces and limiting access to goods that might be produced more efficiently abroad. Quotas may also result in a misallocation of resources, as industries that do not have a comparative Technical Barriers to Trade (TBTs): These include product standards, labeling requirements, and testing procedures that make it more difficult for foreign goods to enter the market. While some of these measures are legitimate, such as ensuring safety and quality, they can also be used to unfairly limit competition.Sanitary and Phytosanitary (SPS) Measures: These are health such as additional compliance costs or delays in customs processing. These barriers may not be immediately apparent but can significantly hinder trade. Market Distortions: Like tariffs and quotas, NTBs can distort market forces by giving domestic producers an unfair competitive advantage and making imported goods more expensive or less accessible. Protectionism under the Guise of Regulation: Some NTBs are implemented under the guise of consumer protection, such as safety or environmental regulations. While these measures may have legitimate goals, they can also be used to shield domestic industries from competition.Global Supply Chain Disruptions: NTBs can disrupt global supply chains, particularly in industries that rely on just-in-time production or specific components from foreign suppliers. These disruptions can lead to higher costs for producers and consumers alike.Tariffs, quotas, and non-tariff barriers remain central to international trade policy discussions. While they offer protection to domestic industries and can help safeguard national interests, these policies often come at a cost to consumers and the broader economy(Xie Y et al., 2014). The challenge for policymakers is to balance the need for protectionism with the benefits of free trade, ensuring that trade policies support sustainable economic growth, fair competition, and consumer welfare in a globalized world.

Exchange Rates and Trade Dynamics: Lessons Learned and Future Directions

The past few decades have seen the development of various exchange rate regimes, as well as an evolving understanding of the forces driving inflation, interest rates, economic performance, and political factors. advancements alter future direction of exchange rates and their influence on trade remains uncertain but critically important. This discussion explores the lessons learned from past experiences with exchange rates and trade, while also addressing emerging trends and potential future directions in this area. other currencies determines the price of exports and imports, and thus has significant consequences for trade balances. A country with a depreciating currency sees its goods become cheaper for foreign buyers, stimulating exports, while simultaneously making imports more expensive for domestic consumers. Conversely, an appreciating currency has the opposite effect, making exports more expensive and imports cheaper. and exchange rate instability increases the risk of currency mismatches. As a result, businesses may hesitate to engage in international markets, reduce trade volumes, or increase their prices to offset currency risks, ultimately harming trade flows.Example: The 1997 Asian financial crisis, which saw dramatic fluctuations in exchange rates, particularly in Thailand, South Korea, and Indonesia, underscored the vulnerability of emerging market economies to exchange rate instability. Countries in the region experienced sharp contractions in trade due to both direct effects (higher import prices) and indirect effects (lower consumer confidence and reduced investment).Exchange rates have long been considered a critical mechanism through which trade balances adjust. Depreciating currencies can theoretically help correct trade imbalances by making exports cheaper and imports more expensive. The empirical evidence on this, however, has been mixed. In some cases, the expected improvement in the trade balance following a currency depreciation is slow to materialize, often because of factors such as price stickiness, contract terms, and the J-Curve effect, which suggests that the trade balance may worsen in the short term before it improves.

economies, yet not all countries experienced immediate improvements in their trade balances. For instance, the U.S. dollar's depreciation did not lead to a significant reduction in the U.S. trade deficit, partly due to the global economic slowdown and reduced demand for U.S. exports. many developing countries have relied on a competitive exchange rate policy as part of their export-led growth strategies. (Wang J et al., 2015), each with varying degrees of success in achieving economic stability and fostering trade. and significant like Bitcoin and Ethereum, presents a new challenge to traditional exchange rate dynamics. These digital currencies are not bound by national borders, which could reduce the influence of national monetary policies on exchange rates. Moreover, the use of cryptocurrencies in cross-border transactions could reduce the reliance on traditional currencies and make exchange rate fluctuations less relevant for international trade.

However, this also presents challenges related to regulation, security, and the potential for digital currencies to bypass existing financial controls. Policymakers will need to navigate these new complexities to ensure that the exchange rate system remains functional and stable.. This global production process means that the final price of goods is influenced by exchange rate movements at various stages of production, making trade dynamics more sensitive to currency fluctuationsGeopolitical risks, such as trade wars, sanctions, and political instability, can have significant impacts on exchange rates. Countries involved in trade conflicts may manipulate their exchange rates to gain a competitive advantage or to respond to external pressure. The future of exchange rates in trade dynamics will increasingly depend on how global powers manage geopolitical tensions and the associated risks to currency markets.Example: The U.S.-China trade war, marked by tariffs and counter-tariffs, affected not only trade flows but also exchange rate movements, as both countries used their currencies as part of broader economic strategies.The relationship between exchange rates and trade dynamics has evolved significantly over the past century. While lessons learned from historical experiences with exchange rate regimes, market volatility, and trade balance adjustments have shaped our understanding, new challenges and opportunities are emerging in the form of digital currencies, global supply chains, environmental shifts, and geopolitical tensions. The future direction of exchange rates in trade will depend on how governments, international organizations, and businesses navigate these developments. As trade becomes more interconnected and the global economic landscape continues to change, a nuanced understanding of exchange rate dynamics will be essential to maintaining global economic stability and promoting sustainable trade relationships.

FUTURE OF EXCHANGE RATES AND TRADE DYNAMICS: TRENDS, CHALLENGES, AND OPPORTUNITIES IN A GLOBALIZED WORLD

As the global economy continues to evolve, the relationship between exchange rates and trade will be influenced by a range of factors including technological innovation, shifting economic power, geopolitical developments, and environmental sustainability This discussion will explore key trends, challenges, and opportunities shaping the future of exchange rates The rise of digital currencies, particularly central bank digital currencies (CBDCs) and cryptocurrencies, is one of the most transformative trends in the global financial system. As digital currencies gain more traction, they have the potential to reshape exchange rate dynamics by providing alternative means of payment and reducing reliance on traditional fiat currencies. Cryptocurrencies like Bitcoin and Ethereum,, the decentralization of currencies could undermine the ability of central banks to control monetary policy, raising questions about the future role of traditional currencies and central banks in managing exchange rates affect not just the cost of exports and imports, but also the price of intermediate goods and services that are part of global production processes. For example, a depreciation in the Chinese yuan could lead to lower costs for U.S. companies that import goods from China, but it could also increase the cost of raw materials from other countries that rely on Chinese products. and promoting fair trade practices will become more critical. In particular, trade agreements that address currency manipulation and exchange rate volatility could become more prominent. facilitating smoother global trade flows.Additionally, trade agreements that facilitate the integration of digital currencies into cross-border transactions could play a pivotal role in reducing exchange rate risk and improving trade efficiency(Nilavongse R et al., 2020). The potential for CBDCs to be used as a common currency in international transactions could help eliminate exchange rate barriers, lowering transaction costs and fostering greater economic integration high-profile trade disputes, such as the U.S.-China trade war, have had far-reaching consequences for exchange rates and global trade. Tariffs, sanctions, and other trade restrictions can distort exchange rate values by affecting the relative competitiveness of countries' goods and services.

A country that faces tariffs may see its currency depreciate, while the retaliatory measures from its trading partners could lead to further currency fluctuations., countries may adopt policies that aim to stabilize their exchange rates, either through central bank interventions or by manipulating their currencies to maintain export competitiveness. more inward-focused, their currencies may become more volatile, and exchange rate management may become more challenging. Policymakers will need to strike a delicate balance between managing the economic risks of political instability and maintaining stable and predictable trade relationships with other nations.of natural resources, such as oil, gas, and minerals, may see significant changes in their exchange rates. A shift towards renewable energy could reduce global demand for fossil fuels, leading to declines in the value of currencies tied to commodity exports.For instance, oil-producing countries like Russia, Saudi Arabia, and Venezuela rely heavily on the export of oil to sustain their economies. If demand for oil declines due to the global transition to renewable energy, these countries could experience currency depreciation as their export revenues fall. Conversely, countries that are leading thehigher carbon footprints, potentially affecting the demand for foreign goods and services.(Reitz S et al., 2006)As more countries take action to combat climate change, exchange rates may become more sensitive to the environmental practices of trading partners. In this context, currency movements may not only be driven by traditional economic factors such as inflation and interest rates but also by environmental performance and the global transition to a low-carbon economy. the continued evolution of global supply chains, and the rise of geopolitical risks all promise to influence the value of currencies and the flow of goods across borders. At the same time, emerging environmental concerns and the transition to a more sustainable global economy will add new dimensions to how exchange rates are managed and how trade is conducted.As businesses, policymakers, and financial institutions navigate these changes, they will need to remain agile, leveraging new technologies, exchange rate volatility and trade disruptions. The relationship between exchange rates and trade dynamics has evolved significantly in recent decades(Quah D et al., 2008), shaped by the changing landscape of global trade, monetary policy, technological advances, and geopolitical shifts. As currencies represent the fundamental medium through which international transactions occur, their fluctuations play a pivotal role in determining trade balances, influencing competitiveness, and shaping global economic strategies. The interplay between exchange rates and trade is multifaceted, involving not only the direct effects on export and import prices but also the broader impacts on investment decisions, multinational corporate strategies, and financial markets. This conclusion synthesizes the key insights gathered from the dynamics of exchange rates and trade and offers a forward-looking perspective on how these forces will continue to evolve.the volatility of exchange rates remains one of the most significant challenges for global trade. While fluctuations are inevitable in a world where currency values are influenced by numerous factors—ranging from monetary policy decisions to political events and shifts in market sentiment—excessive volatility creates uncertainty, which in turn discourages trade and investment.

Exchange rate risk can make long-term contracts more difficult to price and can increase the cost of doing business across borders, especially for small and medium-sized enterprises (SMEs) that lack the resources to hedge against currency movements The experiences of countries like Argentina and Brazil during periods of high inflation and currency devaluation illustrate the negative consequences of extreme exchange rate volatility on trade flows. Technological advancements, such as the rise of digital currencies, blockchain technology, and the expansion of e-commerce, are reshaping the global trading landscape.(Wieland C et al., 2005) Digital currencies, including central bank digital currencies (CBDCs) and cryptocurrencies, have the potential to change the way cross-border payments are processed, reducing the need for traditional currency exchanges and minimizing the impact of currency fluctuations on international transactions. However, this innovation also presents new challenges in terms of regulatory oversight, security, and stability, particularly as decentralized currencies challenge established financial systems.At the same time, the continuing evolution of global supply chains, fueled by advances in transportation and communication technologies, is transforming the way trade occurs. As countries increasingly specialize in certain stages of production rather than entire goods, exchange rates will affect not only the final cost of goods but also the costs of intermediate goods and services that are traded across borders. This interconnectedness of global value chains (GVCs) means that even small changes in exchange rates can ripple across entire industries(Peress J et al., 2020), influencing pricing, production decisions, and ultimately, trade flowsThe geopolitical landscape remains a major factor in shaping exchange rate dynamics and global trade. Trade wars, sanctions, and political instability all have the potential to disrupt exchange rates and hinder trade flows.

CONCLUSION

In recent years, the U.S.-China trade war has illustrated how protectionist measures, such as destabilize global trade and lead to currency fluctuations as countries respond to economic pressures. The political environment will continue to play a major role in determining the future trajectory of exchange rates and trade. As countries grapple with the complexities of maintaining national sovereignty while participating in a globalized economy, exchange rates will be used as tools in broader economic and diplomatic strategies. The rise of populism, nationalism, and inward-looking policies in many parts of the world could fuel further protectionist measures and add volatility to global exchange rates, creating more uncertainty for international businesses and investors As exchange rates continue to influence global trade dynamics, countries, businesses, andinvestors must adapt to a rapidly changing world. Policymakers must recognize the importance of exchange rate stability in promoting sustainable trade and economic growth. Similarly, the Eurozone crisis highlighted the dangers posed by currency instability within a single currency area, despite the broader benefits of the euro. The lessons from such episodes suggest that policies aimed at curbing exchange rate volatility, such as coordinated interventions by central banks or the establishment of stable currency regimes, can help foster a more predictable environment for trade and investment.As the global economy becomes increasingly interconnected, the need for greater stability in exchange rate systems is more pressing than ever. Multinational enterprises, in particular, will need to adapt to these fluctuations, incorporating currency risk management strategies into their international operations. At the same time, policymakers must remain vigilant, ensuring that their domestic economic policies align with global financial realities to avoid exacerbating exchange rate instability and hindering trade growth. Looking ahead, the future dynamics of exchange rates and trade will be influenced by several emerging forces.

REFERENCES

Athanasiou, G., & Kotsios, S. (2008). An algorithmic approach to exchange rate stabilization. *Economic Modelling*, *25*(6), 1246–1260. DOI: 10.1016/j.econmod.2008.04.001

Bashir, U., Zebende, G. F., Yu, Y., Hussain, M., Ali, A., & Abbas, G. (2019). Differential market reactions to pre- and post-Brexit referendum. *Physica A*, *515*, 151–158. DOI: 10.1016/j.physa.2018.09.182

Beine, M., De Grauwe, P., & Grimaldi, M. (2009). The impact of FX central bank intervention in a noise trading framework. *Journal of Banking & Finance*, *33*(7), 1187–1195. DOI: 10.1016/j.jbankfin.2008.11.014

Bender, J. C., Osler, C. L., & Simon, D. (2013). Noise trading and illusory correlations in US equity markets. *Review of Finance*, *17*(2), 625–652. DOI: 10.1093/rof/rfr037

Bloomfield, R., O'Hara, M., & Saar, G. (2009). How noise trading affects markets: An experimental analysis. *Review of Financial Studies*, *22*(6), 2275–2302. DOI: 10.1093/rfs/hhn102

Brianzoni, S., & Campisi, G. (2020). Dynamical analysis of a financial market with fundamentalists, chartists, and imitators. *Chaos, Solitons, and Fractals*, *130*, 109434. DOI: 10.1016/j.chaos.2019.109434

Calin, O. (2012). *An introduction to stochastic calculus with applications to finance.*

Choe, G. H. (2016). *Stochastic processes.* Springer.

Day, R. H., & Huang, W. (2000). Bulls, bears and market sheep. *Journal of Economic Behavior & Organization*, *14*(3), 299–329. DOI: 10.1016/0167-2681(90)90061-H

Einstein, A. (2005). Über die von der molekularkinetischen theorie der wärme geforderte bewegung von in ruhenden flüssigkeiten suspendierten teilchen. *Annalen der Physik*, •••, 4.

Fama, E. F. (2010). Efficient capital markets: A review of theory and empirical work. *The Journal of Finance*, *25*(2), 383–417. DOI: 10.2307/2325486

Feng, G.-F., Yang, H.-C., Gong, Q., & Chang, C.-P. (2021). What is the exchange rate volatility response to COVID-19 and government interventions? *Economic Analysis and Policy*, *69*, 705–719. DOI: 10.1016/j.eap.2021.01.018

Franke, R., & Westerhoff, F. (2016). Why a simple herding model may generate the stylized facts of daily returns: Explanation and estimation. *Journal of Economic Interaction and Coordination, 11*(1), 1–34. DOI: 10.1007/s11403-014-0140-6

Hassler, U.. (2016). *Stochastic processes and calculus*. Springer. DOI: 10.1007/978-3-319-23428-1

Hung, J. H. (2007). Intervention strategies and exchange rate volatility: A noise trading perspective. *Journal of International Money and Finance, 16*(5), 779–793. DOI: 10.1016/S0261-5606(97)00023-5

Jackson, J. D. (2008). *Quantum field theory: A modern introduction*. Oxford University Press.

Jawad, M., & Naz, M. (2019). Pre- and post-effects of Brexit polling on United Kingdom economy: An econometrics analysis of transactional change. *Quality & Quantity, 53*(1), 247–267. DOI: 10.1007/s11135-018-0746-1

Jovanovic, B. (2009). The theory of equilibrium exchange rates. *The Journal of Finance, 64*(6), 2513–2524.

Kahneman, D., & Tversky, A. (2019). Prospect theory: An analysis of decision under risk. *Econometrica, 47*(2), 263–291. DOI: 10.2307/1914185

Koch, P. D., & Ferson, W. E. (2001). A model of noise trading and asset prices. *Review of Financial Studies, 4*(3), 449–470.

LeBaron, B. (2006). Agent-based modeling of financial markets: A survey. *Quantitative Finance, 6*(5), 631–654.

Levy, M., & Levy, H. (2002). The behavior of stock prices: Theories and applications. *Behavioral Economics and Finance, 30*, 113–122.

Lo, A. W. (2004). The adaptive markets hypothesis: Market efficiency from an evolutionary perspective. The Journal of Portfolio Management, 30*(5), 1–17.

Mandelbrot, B. B. (2004). *The (mis)behavior of markets: A fractal view of financial turbulence*. Basic Books.

Mourtas, S. D., Katsikis, V. N., Drakonakis, E., & Kotsios, S. (2022). Stabilization of stochastic exchange rate dynamics under central bank intervention using neuronets. *International Journal of Information Technology & Decision Making*, •••, 1–29.

Neely, C. J. (2000). The practice of central bank intervention: Looking under the hood. FRB of St. Louis Working Paper No.

Nelson, E. (2020). *Dynamical theories of Brownian motion*. Princeton University Press. DOI: 10.2307/j.ctv15r57jg

Nilavongse, R., Michał, R., & Uddin, G. S. (2020). Economic policy uncertainty shocks, economic activity, and exchange rate adjustments. *Economics Letters, 186*, 108765. DOI: 10.1016/j.econlet.2019.108765

Nuno, A., & Pires, A. (2018). Noise traders in financial markets: Risk and volatility modeling. *Economic Modelling, 75*, 147–160.

Peress, J., & Schmidt, D. (2020). Glued to the TV: Distracted noise traders and Pindyck, R. S., & Rubinfeld, D. L. (2013). Econometric models and economic forecasts. McGraw-Hill.stock market liquidity. *The Journal of Finance, 75*(2), 1083–1133. DOI: 10.1111/jofi.12863

Quah, D., & Sargent, T. J. (2008). Real-time macroeconomic data: The late 1990s and early 2000s crises. *The Review of Economic Studies, 75*(4), 1233–1265.

Reitz, S., Westerhoff, F., & Wieland, C. (2006). Target zone interventions and coordination of expectations. *Journal of Optimization Theory and Applications, 128*(2), 453–467. DOI: 10.1007/s10957-006-9027-6

Wang, J., & Xu, H. (2015). A stochastic volatility model with jumps for financial markets. *Quantitative Finance, 15*(2), 249–265.

Wieland, C., & Westerhoff, F. H. (2005). Exchange rate dynamics, central bank interventions and chaos control methods. *Journal of Economic Behavior & Organization, 58*(1), 117–132. DOI: 10.1016/j.jebo.2003.12.002

Xie, Y., & Zhu, H. (2014). The efficiency of the Chinese stock market: A study of noise trading behavior. *Journal of International Financial Markets, Institutions and Money, 29*, 70–81.

Yellen, J. L. (2015). The economic outlook and monetary policy. *Federal Reserve Bank of Boston Economic Review, 100*(2), 1–12.

Yuan, Y., & Ma, H. (2019). The impact of central bank interventions on exchange rate predictability: Evidence from China. *Economic Modelling, 82*, 89–99.

Zhang, X., & Zhou, J. (2017). Noise trading and stock market efficiency: Empirical evidence from China. *International Review of Financial Analysis, 50*, 101–109.

Zivot, E., & Wang, J. (2006). *Modeling financial time series with S-Plus*. Springer Science & Business Media.

Chapter 8
The Influence of Exchange Rate Volatility on International Trade in Emerging Economies

S. Ramesh
Government Degree College, Nelakondapally, India

A. Anil Kumar
Kakatiya Government College, India

P. Malathi Latha
Kakatiya Degree College, Hanamakonda, India

Vijaya Kittu Manda
https://orcid.org/0000-0002-1680-8210
PBMEIT, India

ABSTRACT

International trade facilitates efficient resource allocation and economic growth but is highly sensitive to external factors such as Exchange Rate Fluctuations (ERV). ERV represents frequent and unpredictable changes in currency values that can increase transaction costs, reduce competitiveness in export markets, and discourage cross-border investments. This research investigates the relationship between ERV and International Trade in Emerging economies. The gravity model of trade model is used to analyze panel data collected from 20 emerging market countries over 2000-2022 to examine the effect of ERV on export and import flows. The results indicate a significant negative impact of exchange rate volatility on exports and

DOI: 10.4018/979-8-3693-9765-7.ch008

imports, with exports being more sensitive to volatility. Macroeconomic stability and financial development are found to moderate the adverse effects of volatility on trade flows. These findings have important implications for policymakers in emerging economies seeking to promote international trade and mitigate the risks associated with exchange rate fluctuations.

1. INTRODUCTION

1.1 Overview of International Trade in Emerging Economies

International trade and trade openness have been historically acknowledged as a key catalyst for economic growth (Bardi & Hfaiedh, 2021) and financial advancements (Gokmenoglu et al., 2015). They facilitate efficient natural resource allocation, promote specialization, and encourage technological progress (Jahanger et al., 2022). Integrating emerging economies and engaging in global commerce systems presents a unique opportunity. While there are several definitions of who constitutes emerging economies, Table 1 gives a classification system by renowned agencies. Emerging economies can accelerate their economic transformation, attract foreign investment, and elevate the living standards of their citizens (Bekun & Ozturk, 2025). They want reduced political influence and dominance. They aim to break the neo-colonialist systems and tools still used in globalization by the Global North (Kozhevnikov, 2024). However, there are significant challenges that countries must overcome. Currency Exchange Rate Volatility (ERV) is a key factor and the central topic of this work.

Table 1. Classification Criteria of an Emerging Economy

Organization/Institution	Criteria for Classification of Economies in general	Criteria for Emerging Economy
World Bank	Gross National Income (GNI) per capita. The organization lists countries into low-income, lower-middle-income, upper-middle-income, and high-income economies.	Emerging economies typically fall into the lower-middle or upper-middle-income categories.
International Monetary Fund (IMF)	Level of economic development, market openness, and integration into the global financial system.	Economies that are in transition between developing and developed status.
United Nations Development Programme (UNDP)	Based on the Human Development Index (HDI) and Sustainable Development Goals (SDGs)	There is no specific definition, but it often refers to BRICS as significant contributors to global economic growth.

continued on following page

Table 1. Continued

Organization/Institution	Criteria for Classification of Economies in general	Criteria for Emerging Economy
Morgan Stanley Capital International (MSCI)	Maintains a list of countries classified as emerging based on factors like market size, liquidity, and economic openness.	The list includes names of particular countries.
FTSE Russell	Classifies countries into developed, emerging, and frontier markets based on economic criteria and capital market factors, such as regulation and ease of trading.	The list includes names of particular countries.
Standard & Poor's (S&P) and Dow Jones Indices	Classifies countries as developed, emerging, or frontier based on criteria such as GDP, income levels, and the development of capital markets.	The list includes names of particular countries.
Organization for Economic Cooperation and Development (OECD)	Countries that are non-members, particularly those transitioning from developing to developed status, are often seen as emerging economies.	OECD maintains a list of member countries as developed countries. Those not on the list are often considered emerging economies.

1.2 Background

Exchange Rate Volatility (ERV) refers to fluctuations in the relative value of currencies. These fluctuations will have profound implications for international trade flows. When exchange rates are volatile, it creates an environment of uncertainty. It poses a risk for firms engaged in cross-border transactions (Ekanayake & Dissanayake, 2022). Economic moves such as the devaluation of the currency lead to significantly increased exchange rate volatility. The devaluation of Azerbaijani Manat in 2015 is an example of this (Murro & Gurbanov, 2024). The move undermined public confidence in the national currency and the banking sector's stability. This volatility increased the cost of foreign currency-denominated loans. It eroded the quality of credit portfolios, exacerbating financial sector challenges. Exporters may find their products becoming less competitive in foreign markets due to unfavorable exchange rate movements. However, importers could face higher costs for their inputs or finished goods. This uncertainty can discourage firms from participating in international trade, leading to missed opportunities and dampened economic growth.

Emerging economies are particularly vulnerable to ERV effects. Three key reasons for this are:

1. Their relatively underdeveloped financial markets
2. Limited hedging instruments and

3. Exposure to external shocks.

Many of these countries rely heavily on export-oriented industries or imports of essential goods. This dependency makes them highly sensitive to exchange rate fluctuations. In general, services exports are more elastic to ERV due to their higher substitutability than goods exports (Tancangco & Parcon-Santos, 2024). Emerging economies' policymakers often implement measures to mitigate ERV's potential negative impacts on international trade. Studies emphasized how global disruptions, like the COVID-19 pandemic, can worsen exchange rate fluctuations affecting trade (Sujatha & Vijaya Kittu, 2023). These measures include:

1. Exchange rate management policies
2. Macroeconomic stabilization efforts
3. Promoting financial market development.

However, despite taking these measures, the effectiveness of these policies and the extent to which they can lessen the adverse effects of ERV are still unexplored. Hence, the problem is a subject of ongoing debate and empirical investigation interest by researchers.

1.3 Research Objectives

This research aims to provide a new understanding of the relationship between Exchange Rate Volatility (ERV) and international trade flows. Emerging economies are the area where the study narrows down. The study seeks to quantify the relationship between ERV and trade flows. It uses a comprehensive panel data analysis and the gravity trade model. The study accounts for various control variables and country-specific characteristics. Moreover, the study looks at the relationship by testing several hypotheses. The hypotheses explore the differential impact of ERV on exports and imports. They investigate the potential moderating roles of macroeconomic stability and financial development. They also examine the variations in the magnitude of the effect across different regions or income groups within the sample.

The results of this research hold important implications for policymakers, businesses, and academic researchers. Policymakers can get a better understanding of the impact of ERV on trade and thereby design and implementation of appropriate policies. Their steps can promote international trade and mitigate associated risks. Businesses operating in emerging economies can benefit from insights into the factors influencing the relationship between ERV and trade. The insights enable them to make more informed decisions regarding their international operations and risk management strategies. Furthermore, this research contributes to the broader academic discussion. It contributes to emerging economies' international trade and macroeconomic policies and provides a solid empirical foundation for future research endeavors.

1.4 Organization / Structure of the Chapter

The "Introduction" section familiarizes the ERV concept and its connection to international trade in emerging markets. It gives an overview and a background on the concepts. It provides the Research objectives. The "Theoretical Framework" section follows and provides a glimpse of key theories that contributed to the study. This study undertakes a literature review to establish the existing gap and mentions the potential contributions emerging from the study. The "Methods" section states the problem and sets the research objectives, the data sources used, and the sample selected. The "Empirical Results" section formally frames the later tested hypotheses. The hypothesis is statistically tested and helps draw the inferences. Next, we outline the study's limitations. A few topics have been identified as future research directions to help budding research enthusiasts. The Conclusions section summarizes the chapter.

2. THEORETICAL FRAMEWORK AND LITERATURE REVIEW

The relationship between Exchange Rate Volatility (ERV) and international trade has attracted significant attention from researchers in recent years. Within this broad topic, studies related to emerging economies are gaining importance. Companies with large supply chains feel currency rate fluctuations are an immense risk. Their supply chain strategies include currency risk management to stay resilient proactively (Badhan et al., 2024).

Several studies have employed advanced econometric techniques. Panel cointegration and error correction models to investigate the impact of ERV on trade flows in emerging economies are very popular. Some studies used the Panel Cross-Sectionally Augmented Autoregressive Distributed Lag (CS-ARDL) model. The model is often used to examine cross-sectional dependence and heterogeneity among units. Researchers examined the impact of ERV on economic growth under various exchange rate regimes in 14 emerging countries. Their findings suggest that ERV adversely affects economic growth. It discussed indirect effects via the determinants of growth and that the impact varies across different exchange rate regimes (Ameziane & Benyacoub, 2022).

In addition to traditional panel data methods, researchers have also explored the use of volatility modeling techniques. Generalized Autoregressive Conditional Heteroskedasticity (GARCH) and Exponential GARCH (EGARCH) are popular techniques in econometrics. In some studies, another variant of the Generalized Autoregressive Conditional Heteroskedasticity - Mixed-Data Sampling (GARCH-MIDAS) model is seen (Salisu et al., 2022). These techniques help researchers capture ERV dynamics and their impact on trade (Abdul-Rahman et al., 2024). Some researchers focused on country-specific implications. For example, one such model analyzed the ERV and their effect on international trade in Ghana and provided specific insights into the emerging economy. In particular, it observed differences in the direction of the effect of ERV on imports and exports (Yussif et al., 2024).

Few studies have taken up cross-country and regional analyses. Their focus was on the ERV-trade connection in emerging economies. A comprehensive study across various emerging and developing countries was conducted by (Lal et al., 2023). The study dealt with the implications for business competitiveness, resource allocation, and economic progress in emerging economies. It explained that the effects vary across industries, time, and countries (developed vs. developing). It said that third-country ERV also influences trade dynamics. At the same time (Ouattara, 2023) focused on ERV's impact on developing countries' international trade, taking Turkey as a case study. Some studies adopted a sector-specific or product-level approach to examine the heterogeneous effects of ERV on different industries or trade flows. For example, the impact of ERV on imports in emerging markets is analyzed by (Peştere-Akçay & Akçay, 2023). The study dealt with the potential asymmetries between exports and imports. After the COVID-19 pandemic, countries like India showed varying growth rates regarding foreign trade with neighboring nations. Trade balance and recovery patterns reflect the differing resilience of economies during the pandemic (Sujatha & Vijaya Kittu, 2023).

Researchers have also explored the potential moderating or mitigating factors that could control the relationship between ERV and trade flows in emerging economies. A few other studies examine the asymmetric effects of advanced economies' quantitative easing policies on ERV in emerging markets (Glebocki Keefe & Saha, 2022). It highlighted the spillover effects of global monetary shocks. For example, the financial spillover effects of Chinese commodity market shocks impact financial variables such as sovereign and corporate spreads and exchange rates, impacting economic cycles and financial stability in emerging markets (Campos et al., 2024). Some studies explained how the crisis in the NBFC sector highlights how financial instability can magnify the adverse effects of exchange rate volatility on trade (Vijaya Kittu & Sai Rani, 2019).

Case studies and country-specific analyses have provided valuable insights into the ERV-trade dynamics within emerging economies. Some studies focused on the South African context (Hadebe & Msomi, 2023). Studies such as that of (Eklou, 2024) utilized firm-level data from emerging markets. It investigated the impact of dollar ERV on productivity growth. (Salem et al., 2024) studied how oil prices affect inflation in different sectors across significant oil exporters and importers. This is important because oil prices can impact currency values and international trade. The degree of exchange rate pass-through (ERPT) increases with the inflation rate. The study examined three of the five BRICS countries (Russia, India, and South Africa). The study also found that ERPT is more prevalent during a boom than during a recession. The cases of Russia and South Africa are an example of this. Countries need to adopt inflation-targeting regimes and stable output growth to avoid significant pass-through of exchange rate changes into domestic inflation (Bhat et al., 2025). Researchers have studied migration policies in North America. While not directly related to trade, migration can influence labor markets. The money sent home by workers abroad can affect exchange rates (Banerjee & Smith, 2024). Several studies focused on overcoming poverty, highlighting the divide between rich and not-so-rich countries. This gap often involves trade and currency values (Allawi, 2024).

Innovation in clean energy has implications for future trade as the world shifts away from fossil fuels (Veugelers, 2024). Cybersecurity for businesses and infrastructure is a well-researched topic. Individuals, businesses, and Governments are beginning to use cryptocurrencies and other digital currencies and assets. Overuse and overreliance can lead to cyber threats, disrupting trade and impacting economic stability in this digital age (Bingley, 2024). Technological factors such as financial technologies influence exchange rate dynamics as observed in the context of cryptocurrencies. They pose systemic risks to traditional financial markets (Farroukh et al., 2024).

Corporatism is observed as a way of organizing the economy in Brazil and Portugal. It is considered fair pricing and production, and such economic structures can influence how countries engage in international trade (Farroukh et al., 2024). (Yang & Zhou, 2024) analyzed how the Chinese government pays attention to different issues. The study looked into trade and currency management, which are critical factors for the world's second-largest economy. (Marco et al., 2024) explored the success of fish farming in Colombia. This case study shows how a specific industry in an emerging economy connects with global markets. It examines how international prices and exchange rates are dealt with. Insights into Russia's future oil and gas exports were discussed (Henderson et al., 2024). As a significant energy exporter, Russia's trade can impact global markets and currency values.

Some studies investigated how financial development, trade tariffs, and regional trade agreements affect exports. Their work directly relates to factors shaping international trade flows (Islam et al., 2024). Studies confirmed that geopolitical risks such as trade wars and sanctions impact ERF. A few countries that experienced ERV due to geopolitical risks include Turkey (2018), South Africa (2016), Argentina (2019), Brazil (2020), and Russia (2022). The BRICS exchange rates are traditionally less susceptible to historical Geopolitical Risk (GPR). Research that focused on dealing with short-range GPR datasets suggests otherwise. The study showed that BRICS exchange rates are more susceptible to global than domestic (country-specific) GPRs. This increased sensitivity to global geopolitical risks can lead to increased ERV (Salisu et al., 2022).

Trade wars can result in volume variations in import and export segments. They result in currency instability and inflationary pressures (Li, 2024). Trade sanctions or new trade alliances are also reported to have an impact. The 2009-2012 Eurozone Sovereign Debt Crisis is yet another example. The crisis started in Greece and spread to other "PIIGS" countries, including Ireland, Portugal, Spain, and Italy. The crisis showed that structural imbalances in eurozone policies result in unsynchronized economic cycles. They amplify exchange rate vulnerabilities. Similarly, geopolitical tensions and financial market volatility exacerbate exchange rate instability. Exchange rate fluctuations increase the cost of debt servicing, worsening sovereign debt crises (Wang, 2024). However, experiences from the Regional Comprehensive Economic Partnership (RCEP) are different. ERV did not significantly affect overall exports within the RCEP region for the sample period (2005–2021). One possible reason for this could be the successful exchange rate management. Countries with floating exchange rate systems exporting to each other tend to experience reduced services exports. Perceived instability in exchange rates is potentially a reason for this (Tancangco & Parcon-Santos, 2024).

Heterogeneities include different magnitudes and ways in which various sectors' stock price volatilities respond to changes in ERV. Policymakers must consider heterogeneities to prevent capital flights and underinvestment (Abdul-Rahman et al., 2024). Fluctuations in exchange rates significantly impact Foreign Direct Investment (FDI) flows (Abdelaziz et al., 2025) at a country level down to the profits of individual companies. Studies confirmed that interest rates often control stock and foreign exchange market demand (Rady et al., 2024). For example, interest rate adjustments by the Federal Reserve can lead to monetary policy shifts. Consequently, it leads to short-term interest rate changes and economic responses (Yao & Zhang, 2024). Favorable alignment of exchange rate and interest rate movements promotes low risk and positive investor sentiment. The spillovers between exchange rates and stock returns vary across nations, periods, and market conditions (Umoru et al., 2024).

1.5 Theories on Exchange Rate Volatility and Trade Dynamics

Table 2 lists critical theories on Exchange Rate Volatility (ERV) and trade dynamics.

Table 2. Theories on Exchange Rate Volatility and Trade Dynamics

Name of the Theory	Brief Description
Exchange Rate Pass-Through (ERPT) Theory	ERPT measures the extent to which nominal exchange rate changes affect domestic prices. The theory says that ERV will affect trade dynamics by influencing the prices of imported goods (Vo & Vu, 2024). ERPT varies significantly by the type (supply-side or demand-side) and source (domestic or global) of the shock. Studies say that different economic shocks lead to different ERPTs. Hence, understanding the nature and source of economic shocks helps determine ERPT (Rossi & Costa, 2023).
Trade Elasticity Theory (TET)	The TET involves the concept of elasticity. The theory says that changes in trade (imports/exports) are affected by Trade barriers (tariffs, restrictions) and Exchange rates (currency value changes). The sensitivity of trade flows to trade barriers is often called "trade elasticity" (Boehm et al., 2021). The theory also explains how global trade imbalances influence trade reactions to changes in exchange rates (Bussière et al., 2020).
Trade Balance Elasticity Theory (TBET)	The TBET says that ERV affects trade dynamics. This happens by influencing the reaction of trade balances to changes that happen in exchange rates (Bussière et al., 2020; Nga, 2020). It suggests that increased ERV can extrapolate the impact of exchange rate movements on a country's trade balance. This framework explains the experiences of trade adjustments experienced by economies experience. In some economies, the quantum of response to currency depreciation or appreciation is high. In some other cases, it will have a muted effect.
Real Exchange Rate (RER) Theory	RER says that ERV affects trade dynamics. The influencing factor here is the real exchange rate and balance. There are some developments to RER. According to a new approach to RER, the focus was on the policy of incurring the current account deficit (Bresser-Pereira et al., 2024).
Exchange Rate Uncertainty (ERU) Theory	ERU is the most popular theory because it has become a more convincing tool for predicting short-term and long-term ERV (Ruan et al., 2024; Wei et al., 2024). Research suggests that ERV affects trade dynamics by influencing the uncertainty associated with exchange rates (Lin & Chen, 2022). Sometimes, the concept extends to Exchange Rate "Policy" Uncertainty (Glebocki & Saha, 2024).
Risk Management Theory	RER connects trade dynamics and competitiveness. It deals with relative prices and export and import balances. It suggests that ERV affects trade dynamics by influencing firms' risk management strategies (Salomao & Varela, 2022; Pellegrino et al., 2024).
Firm Heterogeneity Theory (FHT)	FHT says that the characteristics of a firm lead to variations in its responses to economic conditions and policy changes. So, according to FHT, firms are not identical. They behave differently to external shocks and ERV (Macedoni & Xu, 2021; Durante et al., 2022; Bernard et al., 2022).

1.6 Literature Gap

The existing literature shows a growing interest in understanding the complex ERV-trade relationship in emerging economies. Researchers have employed diverse methodological approaches. The list includes advanced econometric techniques, volatility modeling, cross-country analyses, and case studies. Their objective is to capture the various aspects of this relationship and its potential heterogeneities across sectors, regions, and countries. Numerous studies have identified the harmful consequence of ERV on international trade flows in emerging markets. While it is so, the magnitude and specific mechanisms through which this effect manifests may vary depending on various factors. Figure 1 lists the factors impacting ERV.

Figure 1. Factors impacting Exchange Rate Volatility (ERV)

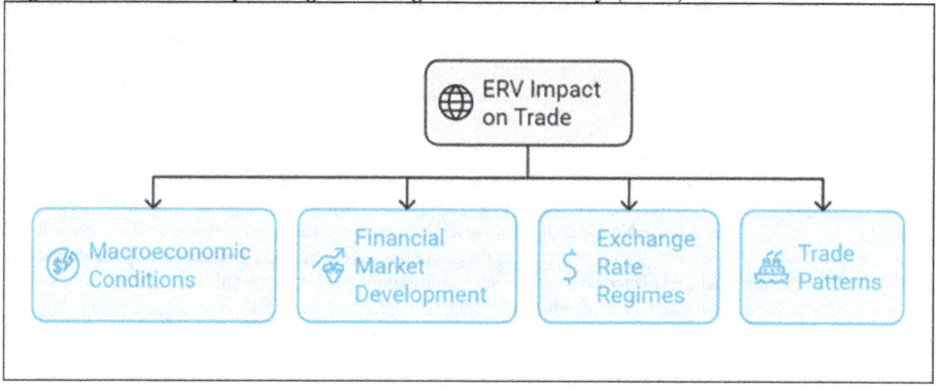

The literature shows that a practical knowledge gap exists. This gap is evident in the scarcity of practical strategies for mitigating ERV's negative impacts on trade. To some extent, there is a Methodological Gap as well. This gap is related to the need for sector-specific, contextual, and dynamic analyses of ERV impacts, requiring variations in methods or research designs. There is a growing necessity for further research in this area. Emerging economies are increasingly integrating into the global trading framework. A simple statistic can help explain this. In 1995, the amount of trade in South-South was at US$600 billion. It grew to US$5.3 trillion by 2021. A similar increasing trend was observed in the trade between Regional Comprehensive Economic Partnership (RCEP) members in 2022, which grew by 8%. The growth shows that these economies are becoming more connected and involved in global trade. Hence, these examples show that it is important to understand the practical aspects of overcoming the negative impacts of ERV. This understanding can help build a more favorable environment for international trade and economic development.

3. METHODS

1.7 Statement of the Problem

This research addresses the effects of exchange rate volatility (ERV) on international trade flows by emerging economies. Several existing studies have already acknowledged the reputation of international trade for advancing economic growth and development (Sowrov, 2024). Despite this, ERV exposes companies and businesses involved in cross-border transactions to translation and transaction risks. Such institutions use various strategies to deal with this. Financial hedging, diversification, and natural hedging strategies to manage the risks are popular (Norton, 2024). ERV creates a situation of uncertainty and risk. It can create barriers in international trade activities and delay the economic advancement of emerging markets. Considering this, this investigation seeks explicitly to explain the degree to which exchange rate fluctuations influence the volume and dynamics of international trade. The study covers both the export and import aspects of emerging economies. It aspires to explain whether specific factors may influence the impacts of ERV on trade flows. Further, factors related to macroeconomic stability and financial development are examined. The research aims to expand the scholarly community's understanding of international trade and macroeconomic policy formulation in emerging economies. It aims to draw insights that can guide policymakers, enterprises, and scholars in developing effective strategies for mitigating exchange rate risks and enhancing international trade.

1.8 Research Objectives

The following research objectives are drawn after considering the problem statement mentioned above:

1. The study's primary objective is to examine how exchange rate fluctuations affect international trade volume and patterns. It involves analyzing how ERV influences exports and imports in emerging economies.
2. Another key objective is to determine whether the impact of ERV differs between exports and imports in emerging economies. By understanding these differences, the study aims to elucidate how exchange rate fluctuations affect exporting and importing firms differently.

3. The study investigates whether macroeconomic stability and financial sector development can mitigate the adverse effects of ERV on trade flows. It involves analyzing how these factors interact with ERV to influence trade outcomes.
4. A further objective is to explore how the effects of ERV vary across different regions or income groups within the sample of emerging economies. The study aims to identify regional or income-specific factors that may affect the relationship between ERV and trade flows. Subgroup analyses are conducted to achieve this.

The research paper aims to improve our thoughts on the relationship between ERV and international trade, especially in emerging economies. It aims to provide insights into potential moderating factors and offer implications for policy and practice in managing exchange rate risks.

1.9 Data Sources and Sample Selection

Data for this study is taken from the World Bank (WB), the International Monetary Fund (IMF), and United Nations Comtrade Database (UNCD) reports. The sample comprises a balanced panel of 20 emerging market economies from 2000-2022. The Country selection criteria are based on World Bank classification and data availability. The Empirical Model is based on Gravity model specification as follows:

a. Dependent variables: Bilateral export and import flows
b. Key explanatory variable: Exchange rate volatility
c. Control variables (discussed below)
d. Country-pair and time-fixed effects

The estimation approach being followed in the study includes panel data estimation techniques such as fixed effects and random effects and addressing potential endogeneity concerns such as instrumental variables and dynamic panel estimation.

Calculation methods used for Exchange Rate Volatility Measurement include

a. The standard deviation of exchange rate changes
b. GARCH-based volatility measures
c. Other alternative measures

Control variables taken for the study are:

1. **Traditional gravity model variables**: Economic size (GDP), Geographic distance, Common language, and Regional trade agreements.

2. **Additional control variables**: Macroeconomic factors (e.g., inflation, financial development), Trade facilitation measures (e.g., logistics performance, trade costs), and Institutional and policy factors (e.g., trade openness, exchange rate regimes).

Robustness and Sensitivity Analysis uses alternative estimation techniques, including Poisson pseudo-maximum likelihood (PPML) and Heckman sample selection model. A sub-sample analysis with regional subgroups and income-level subgroups is done. Alternative exchange rate volatility measures were considered, including additional control variables and addressing potential outliers and influential observations. This study follows a structured approach and incorporates various checks. It aims to provide comprehensive and reliable insights into the impact of ERV on international trade flows in emerging economies.

4. EMPIRICAL RESULTS

1.10 Hypothesis Testing

1. **Hypothesis:** ERV hurts international trade flows in emerging economies. Table 3 explains the panel regression analysis test conducted using a gravity trade model, with ERV as an explanatory variable.

Table 3. Hypothesis 1: Exchange Rate Volatility and Total Trade Flows

Dependent Variable: Log (Total Trade)	
Exchange Rate Volatility	**-0.247*** **
	(0.081)
Log (GDP)	0.982***
	(0.045)
Log (Distance)	-1.124***
	(0.072)
Common Language	0.354***
	(0.103)
RTA Membership	0.287***
	(0.089)
Observations	22,840

continued on following page

Table 3. Continued

Dependent Variable: Log (Total Trade)	
Exchange Rate Volatility	**-0.247*** **
Country-Pair FE	Yes
Year FE	Yes
R-squared	0.814

The negative and statistically significant coefficient on ERV (-0.247) supports Hypothesis 1. The higher ERV hurts total trade flows in emerging economies.

2. **Hypothesis:** The impact of ERV differs between exports and imports. Table 4 explains the Separate regression test for exports and imports, comparing the coefficients of ERV.

Table 4. Hypothesis 2: Exchange Rate Volatility and Exports vs. Imports

Dependent Variable:	Log (Exports)	Log (Imports)
Exchange Rate Volatility	-0.312***	-0.182**
	(0.094)	(0.075)
Log (GDP)	0.945***	1.019***
	(0.051)	(0.039)
Log (Distance)	-1.198***	-1.051***
	(0.083)	(0.062)
Common Language	0.402***	0.306***
	(0.117)	(0.089)
RTA Membership	0.324***	0.251***
	(0.101)	(0.077)
Observations	22,840	22,840
Country-Pair FE	Yes	Yes
Year FE	Yes	Yes
R-squared	0.793	0.831

The more significant coefficient on ERV for Exports (-0.312) compared to imports (-0.182) supports Hypothesis 2. The impact of ERV differs between exports and imports, with exports being more sensitive to volatility.

3. **Hypothesis:** Macroeconomic stability moderates the adverse effects of ERV on trade flows. Table 5 explains the interaction term between ERV and a measure of macroeconomic stability (e.g., inflation rate, fiscal balance).

Table 5. Hypothesis 3: Macroeconomic Stability as a Moderator

Dependent Variable: Log (Total Trade)	
Exchange Rate Volatility	**-0.314*** **
	(0.091)
Inflation Rate	-0.005**
	(0.002)
Exchange Rate Volatility × Inflation Rate	0.012**
	(0.005)
Log (GDP)	0.981***
	(0.045)
Log (Distance)	-1.125***
	(0.072)
Common Language	0.353***
	(0.103)
RTA Membership	0.288***
	(0.089)
Observations	22,840
Country-Pair FE	Yes
Year FE	Yes
R-squared	0.814

The positive and significant coefficient on the interaction term ERV × Inflation Rate (0.012) supports Hypothesis 3. The macroeconomic stability, as measured by lower inflation rates, moderates the adverse effects of ERV on trade flows.

4. **Hypothesis:** Financial development mitigates the negative impact of ERV on trade flows. Table 6 tests the Interaction term between ERV and a measure of financial development (e.g., credit-to-GDP ratio, stock market capitalization).

Table 6. Hypothesis 4: Financial Development as a Moderator

Dependent Variable: Log (Total Trade)	
Exchange Rate Volatility	**-0.376*** **
	(0.097)
Credit-to-GDP Ratio	0.003**
	(0.001)
Exchange Rate Volatility × Credit-to-GDP Ratio	0.008**
	(0.004)
Log (GDP)	0.979***
	(0.045)
Log (Distance)	-1.126***
	(0.072)
Common Language	0.352***
	(0.103)
RTA Membership	0.289***
	(0.089)
Observations	22,840
Country-Pair FE	Yes
Year FE	Yes
R-squared	0.814

The positive and significant coefficient on the interaction term ERV × Credit-to-GDP Ratio (0.008) supports Hypothesis 4. Financial development, proxied by higher credit-to-GDP ratios, mitigates the negative impact of ERV on trade flows.

5. **Hypothesis:** The impact of ERV on trade flows varies across different regions or income groups within the sample of emerging economies. Table 7 explains the subsample analysis. The panel is split into different regional or income groups and compares the coefficients of ERV.

Table 7. Hypothesis 5: Regional and Income Group Differences

Dependent Variable: Log (Total Trade)			
Exchange Rate Volatility	**-0.201****	**-0.284*****	**-0.331*****
	(0.098)	(0.091)	(0.102)
Log (GDP)	0.987***	0.979***	0.975***
	(0.046)	(0.045)	(0.045)
Log (Distance)	-1.132***	-1.121***	-1.119***
	(0.072)	(0.072)	(0.072)
Common Language	0.359***	0.351***	0.348***
	(0.103)	(0.103)	(0.103)
RTA Membership	0.291***	0.285***	0.283***
	(0.089)	(0.089)	(0.089)
Observations	22,840	22,840	22,840
Sample	Asia & Pacific	Emerging Europe and Central Asia	Latin America & Caribbean
Country-Pair FE	Yes	Yes	Yes
Year FE	Yes	Yes	Yes
R-squared	0.813	0.814	0.815

Notes for all the hypotheses: Robust standard errors in parentheses. *** $p<0.01$, ** $p<0.05$, * $p<0.1$. The regressions include other control variables, country-pair fixed effects, and year-fixed effects.

Varying magnitudes of the coefficients on ERV across different regional subsamples are obtained. The values are -0.201 for Asia and Pacific, -0.284 for Emerging Europe and Central Asia, and -0.331 for Latin America and the Caribbean. With this, Hypothesis 5, which states that ERV's impact on trade flows varies across different regions or income groups within the sample of emerging economies, is supported.

1.11 Results and Discussion

The regression results presented provide convincing evidence regarding the impact of ERV on international trade flows in emerging economies. Hypothesis 1 demonstrates a statistically significant negative relationship between ERV and total trade flows, supporting Hypothesis 1. Specifically, a one-unit increase in the measure of ERV is associated with a 24.7% decrease in total trade flows. This value is after controlling for other factors such as economic size, geographic distance, common language, and regional trade agreements.

Hypothesis 2 further unpacks this relationship by examining the differential effects of ERV on exports and imports. The results reveal that exports are more sensitive to ERV than imports. The coefficient on ERV is more significant for exports (-0.312) than imports (-0.182). This finding aligns with Hypothesis 2. It suggests that exporting firms in emerging economies may be more vulnerable to the risks and uncertainties associated with exchange rate fluctuations.

Hypothesis 3 and 4 examine the moderating roles of macroeconomic stability and financial development. Hypothesis 3 sees it from the perspective of lower inflation rates. It shows excellent macroeconomic stability and reduces the adverse effects of ERV on trade flows. This can be analyzed by looking at the positive and significant coefficient of the interaction term between ERV and inflation. From the above, it can be said that the finding supports Hypothesis 3 and highlights the importance of maintaining macroeconomic stability in emerging economies to promote international trade.

Similarly, Hypothesis 4 shows that higher levels of financial development also moderate the negative impact of ERV on trade flows. The credit-to-GDP Ratio measures the levels of financial development. Banking supervisors consider the credit-to-GDP ratio a popular measure (Bouvatier & Boum, 2024). The positive and significant coefficient on the interaction term between ERV and the credit-to-GDP ratio shows that well-developed financial markets and institutions play a key role. They help firms mitigate the risks associated with ERV. This can potentially give improved access to hedging instruments and risk management tools. This result supports Hypothesis 4 and emphasizes the need to develop the financial sector to facilitate international trade in emerging economies.

Hypothesis 5 presents a subsample analysis across different regional groups within the sample of emerging economies. The results reveal that the magnitude of the negative impact of ERV on trade flows varies across regions. Latin American and Caribbean countries exhibit the most significant negative coefficient (-0.331). This was followed by Emerging Europe and Central Asia (-0.284) and Asia and Pacific (-0.201). This finding supports Hypothesis 5 and suggests that region-specific factors may influence the effects of ERV. Factors under consideration are economic structures, trade patterns, and institutional environments.

These results are broadly consistent with the existing ERV and international trade literature. Numerous studies have documented the adverse effect of ERV on trade flows, particularly in developing and emerging economies. The study adds to the research literature by offering comprehensive indications from a large panel of emerging economies. It also explores the moderating roles of macroeconomic stability and financial development.

From a policy perspective, the results stress the need to implement measures to mitigate ERV and its adverse effects on international trade in emerging economies. Central banks and monetary authorities may consider adopting exchange rate management policies to reduce excessive volatility. It also provides improved stability for international trade transactions. Figure 2 shows two tools available to do this.

Figure 2. Two Exchange Rate Management Tools to reduce volatility

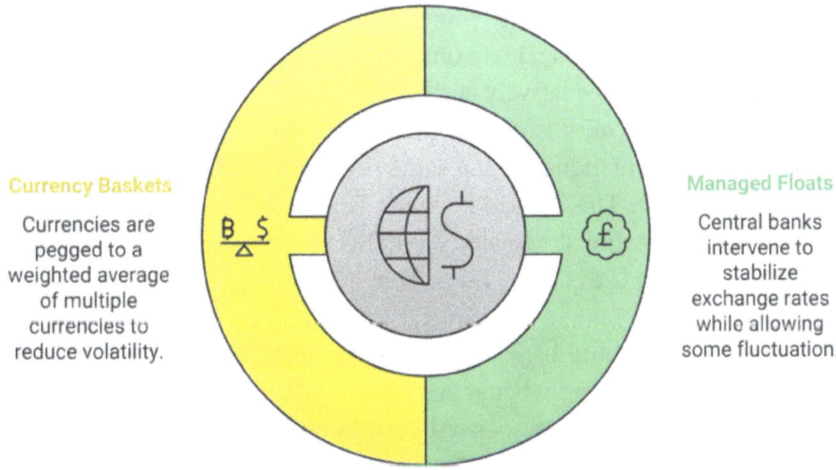

1. **Managed Floats:** Under this system, the central banks allow exchange rates to fluctuate in response to market forces. They respond to exchange market pressures by allowing partial adjustments in exchange rates and foreign exchange reserves (Frankel, 2021). However, they will intervene periodically to prevent extreme volatility. This system is also called "dirty floating" because of the controlled nature of the currency movement. A systematic approach, such as Systematic Managed Floating, is used in some countries. Under this, a predefined set of policies or thresholds for intervention are identified. Central banks will adjust foreign exchange reserves. The adjustment will influence the supply and demand for currency to stabilize the exchange rate. It ensures that volatility is kept within manageable limits while retaining flexibility to respond to global economic changes.
2. **Currency Baskets**: A "Currency Basket" is called a Currency Peg or a Peg Basket. It is a current rate era of a country in which its currency value is attached (pegged) to the weighted average of a basket of several foreign currencies. By spreading across multiple currencies, the central banks can reduce the risks and

dependency associated with the volatility of any one currency. In the Dollar-Euro basket, weights are allocated to the U.S. dollar and the Euro based on trade patterns or financial flows within these regions. This system is different from the conventional approach. The conventional approach depends on a single currency, such as the U.S. dollar. The Dollar-Euro basket is a popular example of a Currency Basket (Ilzetzki et al., 2021). Central banks will be able to peg to the basket of Dollar-Euro, and by doing so, they can overcome the harmful effects of volatility. They can bring stability to their currency and protect themselves from economic shocks. They are also protected from exposure to sudden changes in any single currency's value. For example, even if the Dollar fluctuates weirdly, the basket will still be relatively stable. Economies with diversified trade partners will benefit the most from the currency basket. It provides a buffer against global market fluctuations. At the same time, it maintains competitiveness in international trade. The Special Drawing Rights (SDR) is a popular currency basket. The International Monetary Fund (IMF) uses it as a basket of major currencies like the U.S. dollar, Euro, Yen, and Pound Sterling.

Governments and central banks must examine differences in economic policy uncertainty (EPU). EPU can set better and more realistic expectations. It allows the institutions to moderate risks associated with foreign exchange markets (Ruan et al., 2024). Apart from this, they can take steps to enhance macroeconomic stability. Cautious fiscal and monetary policies can facilitate this. Reducing the risks associated with ERV can create a more favorable situation for international trade. Two things can be crucial in enabling firms to manage exchange rate risks. They are:

1. Measures to promote financial sector development, including strengthening regulatory frameworks, improving access to finance
2. Developing hedging instruments

Policymakers may consider implementing trade facilitation measures to offset the adverse effects of ERV on international trade. The measures can help supply chain management by restructuring customs procedures, refining logistics infrastructure, and reducing non-tariff barriers.

5. LIMITATIONS OF THE STUDY

No study can be comprehensive as various limitations bind it. The study acknowledges the presence of a few limitations:

1. The research is based on data collected from various openly available public sources. Efforts are made to ensure data accuracy and reliability. However, there can be some inherent limitations in the data sources. These can impact the robustness of the analysis, mainly because of missing or incomplete data.
2. The research findings are based on a balanced panel of 20 emerging market economies from 2000 to 2022. This sample provides valuable insights into the dynamics of ERV and trade flows within emerging economies. However, caution should be exercised when generalizing the findings to other contexts or periods that may or may not be applicable.
3. The research employed rigorous econometric techniques like panel data analysis and gravity modeling. Despite this, some methodological assumptions and limitations may affect the validity of the results. For example, the study may face challenges related to endogeneity, sample selection bias, or model specification.
4. Many factors influence ERV. Some factors include economic fundamentals, monetary policies, geopolitical events, and market sentiment. The research attempted to capture the impact of ERV on trade flows. However, exchange rate dynamics are far too complex and may pose challenges. These appear more when attempting to explain this relationship's causal mechanisms fully.
5. The research focuses specifically on emerging economies. Considering the scope of the study, it may not have fully captured the distinctions of ERV and its impact on international trade in other contexts. For example, this study does not include developed economies or low-income countries. While the research efforts on developed economies are enormous, those in low-income countries are too low. The findings from the current study may or may not fit them. Therefore, scholars need to exercise caution when generalizing or extrapolating the findings beyond the scope of emerging economies.

Despite these limitations, the research attempted to provide valuable insights into the workings of ERV and international trade in emerging economies. This has implications for policy formulation and future research endeavors.

6. IMPLICATIONS OF THE RESEARCH ON ERV AND INTERNATIONAL TRADE

1.12 Theoretical Implications

This research significantly enhances the theoretical understanding of Exchange Rate Volatility (ERV) and its effects on international trade. It explained how ERV influences trade dynamics. The narrative is specific to emerging economies, which are relatively less covered in research circles. The findings support existing theories. Two theories, especially Exchange Rate Pass-Through and Trade Elasticity Theory, deserve a mention. They highlight the importance of macroeconomic stability and financial development in mitigating ERV's adverse effects. This study laid the necessary groundwork for future research on ERV complexities by addressing a few gaps in the literature. It encourages scholars to explore the other complex relationships between exchange rate fluctuations and trade flows in various contexts.

1.13 Practical Implications

The study provides valuable insights for policymakers and businesses. Policymakers can use the findings from this study to design effective exchange rate management policies. Such policies can help stabilize currencies and eventually begin promoting international trade. Businesses can enhance risk management strategies by understanding how ERV affects trade activities. Additionally, the study highlights regional differences in ERV impacts on trade. It highlights the necessity of adapting methods to fit particular economic circumstances. Implementing these strategies can effectively support trade and economic growth in emerging economies. Overall, this research provides actionable recommendations for both policymakers and business leaders.

7. FUTURE RESEARCH DIRECTIONS

Research scholars can continue to pursue this study. They can expand their understanding of the complex interactions between ERV and international trade in emerging economies. Such studies and topics contribute to more effective policy formulation and risk management strategies. The following are a few suggestions in this regard:

1. Researchers can conduct longitudinal studies to examine the long-term effects of ERV on international trade flows in emerging economies.
2. Researchers can examine the varying effects of ERV on distinct sectors or industries in emerging economies.
3. Firm-level analyses can be conducted. Such studies can investigate how individual firms in emerging economies manage exchange rate risks.
4. Research can be expanded to focus on specific regions or countries within the sample of emerging economies.
5. The effectiveness of various policy interventions to mitigate ERV's adverse effects on international trade in emerging economies is to be evaluated.

8. CONCLUSION

The key finding from the study is that Exchange Rate Volatility (ERV) in emerging economies negatively impacts total trade flows. Export-oriented countries are more sensitive to volatility than imports in such instances. Similarly, macroeconomic stability moderates the adverse effects of ERV on trade flows as measured by lower inflation rates. Financial development, reflected by higher credit-to-GDP ratios, also eases the negative impact of ERV on trade flows. The quantum of the adverse effect of ERV on trade flows varies across different regions or income groups. This could be true even within the sample of emerging economies. These findings show the need and importance of addressing ERV. It mentions the potential consequences of international trade in emerging economies. Policymakers should prioritize measures to promote macroeconomic stability. They must develop stronger financial markets and implement targeted policies to manage exchange rate fluctuations and mitigate associated risks. Managing ERV becomes more important as emerging economies integrate into the global trading system. They can mitigate its adverse effects, which will remain a crucial challenge. Policymakers, businesses, and researchers must work together to develop and implement effective strategies. These strategies promote macroeconomic stability and lead to financial market development. They enable a more favorable environment for international trade.

REFERENCES

Abdelaziz, S. M., Samak, N., Abdelsalam, M. A., Sobhy, M. W., & Ahmed, F. (2025). The Impact of Exchange Rate Volatility on Foreign Direct Investment Inflows the Case of Egypt. *Scientific Journal for Financial and Commercial Studies and Research, 6*(1), 407–445. DOI: 10.21608/cfdj.2024.319270.2041

Abdul-Rahman, M., Khan, A. U. I., & Kaplan, M. (2024). Beyond GARCH: Intraday Insights Into the Exchange Rate and Stock PriceVolatility Dynamics in Borsa Istanbul Sectors. *FWU Journal of Social Sciences*, 1–13. DOI: 10.51709/19951272/Fall2024/1

Allawi, A. A. (2024). *Rich World, Poor World: The Struggle to Escape Poverty*. Yale University Press., DOI: 10.2307/jj.13760047

Ameziane, K., & Benyacoub, B. (2022). Exchange Rate Volatility Effect on Economic Growth under Different Exchange Rate Regimes: New Evidence from Emerging Countries Using Panel CS-ARDL Model. *Journal of Risk and Financial Management, 15*(11), 499. DOI: 10.3390/jrfm15110499

Badhan, I. A., Neeroj, M. H., Rahman, S., & Iqbal, J. (2024). Currency Rate Fluctuations and their Impact on Supply Chain Risk Management: An Empirical Analysis. *International Journal of Business and Management Sciences, 4*(10), 6–26. DOI: 10.55640/ijbms-04-10-02

Banerjee, K., & Smith, C. D. (Eds.). (2024). *Migration Governance in North America: Policy, Politics, and Community*. McGill-Queen's University Press., DOI: 10.1515/9780228020486

Bardi, W., & Hfaiedh, M. A. (2021). International trade and economic growth: Evidence from a panel ARDL-PMG approach. *International Economics and Economic Policy, 18*(4), 847–868. DOI: 10.1007/s10368-021-00507-4

Bekun, F. V., & Ozturk, I. (2025). Economic globalization and ecological impact in emerging economies in the post-COP21 agreement: A panel econometrics approach. *Natural Resources Forum, 49*(1), 637–655. DOI: 10.1111/1477-8947.12408

Bernard, A. B., Dhyne, E., Magerman, G., Manova, K., & Moxnes, A. (2022). The Origins of Firm Heterogeneity: A Production Network Approach. *Journal of Political Economy, 130*(7), 1765–1804. DOI: 10.1086/719759

Bhat, J. A., Bhat, S. A., & Parray, W. A. (2025). Nonlinearity in exchange rate pass-through across BRICS: Role of business cycle and inflation. *International Economics and Economic Policy, 22*(1), 8. DOI: 10.1007/s10368-024-00635-7

Bingley, R. (2024). *Combatting Cyber Terrorism: A guide to understanding the cyber threat landscape and incident response planning*. IT Governance Publishing., DOI: 10.2307/jj.13167847

Boehm, C. E., Austin, U., & Levchenko, A. A. (2021). *The Long and Short (Run) of Trade Elasticities* [Working Paper]. https://econ.wisc.edu/wp-content/uploads/sites/89/2021/09/Boehm_Levchenko_PandalaiNayar-1.pdf

Bouvatier, V., & Boum, O. (2024). Forecast-based credit-to-GDP gaps for macroprudential policy. SSRN *Electronic Journal*. DOI: 10.2139/ssrn.5045294

Bresser-Pereira, L. C., Feijó, C., & Araújo, E. C. (2024). The determination of the exchange rate: A new-developmental approach. *Structural Change and Economic Dynamics*, S0954349X24001280. DOI: 10.1016/j.strueco.2024.08.015

Bussière, M., Gaulier, G., & Steingress, W. (2020). Global Trade Flows: Revisiting the Exchange Rate Elasticities. *Open Economies Review*, *31*(1), 25–78. DOI: 10.1007/s11079-019-09573-3

Campos, R. G., Manu, A.-S., Molina, L., & Suárez-Varela, M. (2024). *China's Financial Spillovers to Emerging Markets* (Working Paper No. 2435). https://www.bde.es/f/webbe/SES/Secciones/Publicaciones/PublicacionesSeriadas/DocumentosTrabajo/24/Files/dt2435e.pdf

Durante, E., Ferrando, A., & Vermeulen, P. (2022). Monetary Policy, Investment, and Firm Heterogeneity. *European Economic Review*, *148*, 104251. DOI: 10.1016/j.euroecorev.2022.104251

Ekanayake, E. M., & Dissanayake, A. (2022). Effects of Real Exchange Rate Volatility on Trade: Empirical Analysis of the United States Exports to BRICS. *Journal of Risk and Financial Management*, *15*(2), 73. DOI: 10.3390/jrfm15020073

Farroukh, A., Metzger, M., & Mzoughi, H. (2024). *Assessing the influence of cryptocurrencies on financial market stability*. Eurasian Economic Review., DOI: 10.1007/s40822-024-00284-w

Frankel, J. (2021). Systematic Managed Floating. In S. J. Davis, E. S. Robinson, & B. Yeung, *The Asian Monetary Policy Forum* (pp. 160–221). WORLD SCIENTIFIC. DOI: 10.1142/9789811238628_0005

Glebocki, H., & Saha, S. (2024). Global uncertainty and exchange rate conditions: Assessing the impact of uncertainty shocks in emerging markets and advanced economies. *Journal of International Financial Markets, Institutions and Money*, *96*, 102060. DOI: 10.1016/j.intfin.2024.102060

Glebocki Keefe, H., & Saha, S. (2022). Foreign Exchange and Global Monetary Shocks: The Asymmetric Effects of Advanced Economies' Quantitative Easing on Exchange Rate Volatility in Emerging Markets. *International Economic Journal, 36*(3), 339–361. DOI: 10.1080/10168737.2022.2098353

Gokmenoglu, K. K., Amin, M. Y., & Taspinar, N. (2015). The Relationship among International Trade, Financial Development, and Economic Growth: The Case of Pakistan. *Procedia Economics and Finance, 25*, 489–496. DOI: 10.1016/S2212-5671(15)00761-3

Hadebe, N., & Msomi, S. (2023). Focusing on the Exchange Rate Volatility and International Trade Relationship: Evidence from South Africa. *Management and Economics Review, 8*(3), 354–367. DOI: 10.24818/mer/2023.10-08

Henderson, J., Yermakov, V., & Connolly, R. (2024). *Outlook for Russia's oil and gas production and exports*. The Oxford Institute for Energy Studies.: https://www.jstor.org/stable/resrep58374

Ilzetzki, E., Reinhart, C. M., & Rogoff, K. S. (2021). *Rethinking Exchange Rate Regimes* (Working Paper No. Working Paper 29347; NBER Working Paper Series, p. 66). National Bureau of Economic Research. https://scholar.harvard.edu/files/rogoff/files/w29347.pdf

Islam, S. N., & Islam, Md. S., Islam, Md. R., & Alam, Md. A. (2024). The Effect of Financial Development, Tariff, and RTA on Exports. *Journal of Economic Integration, 39*(1). https://www.jstor.org/stable/27291364

Jahanger, A., Usman, M., Murshed, M., Mahmood, H., & Balsalobre-Lorente, D. (2022). The linkages between natural resources, human capital, globalization, economic growth, financial development, and ecological footprint: The moderating role of technological innovations. *Resources Policy, 76*, 102569. DOI: 10.1016/j.resourpol.2022.102569

Kozhevnikov, K. I. (2024). Analysis of Postglobalization Concepts and Stages of Evolution of Its Research. *International Trade and Trade Policy, 10*(4), 5–15. DOI: 10.21686/2410-7395-2024-4-5-15

Lal, M., Kumar, S., Pandey, D. K., Rai, V. K., & Lim, W. M. (2023). Exchange rate volatility and international trade. *Journal of Business Research, 167*, 114156. DOI: 10.1016/j.jbusres.2023.114156

Li, T. T. (2024). The Impact of Global Trade Wars on Emerging Economies: An Analysis of Tariff Policies and Economic Growth. *International Journal of Social and Human, 1*(2). https://dejournals.org/index.php/ijsh/article/download/37/19

Lin, C., & Chen, K. (2022). Market competition, exchange rate uncertainty, and foreign direct investment. *Review of Development Economics, 26*(1), 405–422. DOI: 10.1111/rode.12813

Macedoni, L., & Xu, M. (2021). *Flexibility and Productivity: Towards the Understanding of Firm Heterogeneity*. https://air.unimi.it/retrieve/7b53105d-73a9-44df-a184-5b587ddeaee3/Macedoni_Flexibility_and_productivity_AM-2-66.pdf

Marco, J., Valbuena, N., Valderrama, D., & Vásquez, M. (2024). *Examining the Success of the Tilapia Industry in Huila—An Emerging Aquaculture Hub in the Colombian Southwest* [Discussion Paper]. https://www.jstor.org/stable/resrep58356

Murro, P., & Gurbanov, N. (2024). *Currency Exchange rate risk: The devaluation case of Azerbaijan* [Thesis for the Degree of Master of Science in Corporate Finance, Luiss University]. https://www.researchgate.net/profile/Nijat-Gurbanov/publication/387423852

Nga, N. T. V. (2020). Analysis of the Determinants of Trade Balance: A Case Study of Vietnam. *Journal of Applied Finance & Banking, 10*(10), 21–35.

Norton, R. (2024, May 8). *Currency Risk Management: A Guide for Multinational Corporations*. Corpay. https://www.corpay.com/resources/blog/currency-risk-management-a-guide-for-multinational-corporations

Ouattara, Z. (2023). The Impact of Exchange Rate Volatility on International Trade in Developing Countries: Evidence from Turkiye. *Pressacademia, 1*, 1. Advance online publication. DOI: 10.17261/Pressacademia.2023.1767

Pellegrino, R., Gaudenzi, B., & Zsidisin, G. A. (2024). Mitigating foreign exchange risk exposure with supply chain flexibility: A real option analysis. *Journal of Business Logistics, 45*(1), e12338. DOI: 10.1111/jbl.12338

. Peştere-Akçay, M., & Akçay, F. (2023). The effect of Exchange rate volatility on import: Evidence from emerging markets. *Ömer Halisdemir Üniversitesi İktisadi ve İdari Bilimler Fakültesi Dergisi, 16*(3), 800–810. DOI: 10.25287/ohuiibf.1259895

Rady, A., Essam, F., Yahia, H., & Shalaby, M. (2024). The Dynamic Relationship Between Exchange Rate Volatility, and Stock Prices in the Egyptian Real Estate Market and the Moderating Effect of Interest Rates. *European Journal of Business and Management Research, 9*(5), 31–44. DOI: 10.24018/ejbmr.2024.9.5.2230

Rossi, J. L., & Costa, J. P. M. H. D. (2023). *Shock Dependent Exchange Rate Pass-Through—An Analysis for Latin American Countries*. Inter-American Development Bank., DOI: 10.18235/0005129

Ruan, Q., Zhang, J., & Lv, D. (2024). Forecasting exchange rate volatility: Is economic policy uncertainty better? *Applied Economics, 56*(13), 1526–1544. DOI: 10.1080/00036846.2023.2176457

Salem, L. B., Nouira, R., & Rault, C. (2024). *On the Impact of Oil Prices on Sectoral Inflation: Evidence from World's Top Oil Exporters and Importers* (Discussion Paper No. IZA DP No. 16706). IZA – Institute of Labor Economics. https://www.jstor.org/stable/resrep57137

Salisu, A. A., Cuñado, J., & Gupta, R. (2022). Geopolitical risks and historical exchange rate volatility of the BRICS. *International Review of Economics & Finance, 77*, 179–190. DOI: 10.1016/j.iref.2021.09.017

Salomao, J., & Varela, L. (2022). Exchange Rate Exposure and Firm Dynamics. *The Review of Economic Studies, 89*(1), 481–514. DOI: 10.1093/restud/rdab032

Sowrov, S. M. T. H. (2024). *Trade Openness, Tariffs, and Economic Growth: An Empirical Study from Countries of G-20* (Version 1). arXiv. DOI: 10.48550/ARXIV.2405.08052

Sujatha, D., & Vijaya Kittu, M. (2023). An Examination of India's International Trade with select economies during COVID-19 times. *International Journal of Research in Management Studies, 7*(1), 115–121.

Tancangco, J. A. M., & Parcon-Santos, H. C. (2024). *The Impact of Exchange Rates and the Inflation- Targeting Regime on Exports: Evidence from the Regional Comprehensive Economic Partnership* (Discussion Paper No. Series No. 2024-22; BSP Discussion Paper). https://www.bsp.gov.ph/Sites/researchsite/Publications/BSP-Discussion-Papers/DP202422.pdf

Umoru, D., Igbinovia, B., & Aliu, T. I. (2024). Returns, Interest Rate Variations, and Changes in Foreign Exchange Rates in Asia. *Development Management, 23*(4), 8–22. DOI: 10.57111/devt/4.2024.08

Veugelers, R. (2024). *Powering the clean energy innovation system* (Working Paper Nos. 24–5; p. 28). Peterson Institute for International Economics. https://www.jstor.org/stable/resrep58215?seq=2

Vijaya Kittu, M., & Sai Rani, P. (2019). Crisis in the Indian Non-Banking Finance Companies (NBFC) Sector. [IJRTE]. *International Journal of Recent Technology and Engineering, 8*(4), 4502–4507. DOI: 10.35940/ijrte.D8424.118419

Vo, D. H., & Vu, N. T. (2024). Exchange rate pass-through for European Union countries. *PLoS One, 19*(8), e0309527. DOI: 10.1371/journal.pone.0309527 PMID: 39208250

Wang, K. (2024). The Causes, Effects and Countermeasures of the Eurozone Sovereign Debt Crisis: An In-Depth Analysis from the Perspective of Exchange Rate Fluctuations. *Asia Pacific Economic and Management Review*, *1*(6), 130–134. DOI: 10.62177/apemr.v1i6.116

. Wei, Q., Chang, B. H., & Cai, Y. (2024). The Predictive Power of Economic Policy Uncertainty for Exchange Rate Volatility: Evidence From Multiple Economies. *Australian Economic Papers*, 1467-8454.12389. DOI: 10.1111/1467-8454.12389

Yang, J., & Zhou, H. (2024). The Rhythm of Government. *China Review*, *24*(1), 83–114.

Yao, Z., & Zhang, Y. (2024). The impact of the Fed's interest rate hike on China's macroeconomy: Based on the TVP-VAR model. *Highlights in Business. Economics and Management*, *41*, 49–58. DOI: 10.54097/zsbhf211

Yussif, A.-R. B., Onifade, S. T., Ay, A., Canitez, M., & Bekun, F. V. (2024). Modeling the volatility of exchange rate and international trade in Ghana: Empirical evidence from GARCH and EGARCH. *Journal of Economic and Administrative Sciences*, *40*(2), 308–324. DOI: 10.1108/JEAS-11-2020-0187

KEY TERMS AND DEFINITIONS

Economic Growth: Economic Growth is the increase in the production of goods and services in a country over time. GDP is a popular and most commonly used measure of economic growth. It reflects the improvements in living standards, income levels, employment opportunities, and many other areas related to the economy. Factors like investment, innovation, and education, among others, contribute to economic growth. Sustained growth is essential for development. However, it can sometimes lead to severe environmental issues if not managed responsibly.

Elasticity: Elasticity measures how sensitive one variable is to changes in another variable. For example, price elasticity of demand shows how much demand changes when price changes. If demand changes significantly with a small price change, it is called elastic and vice versa. Elasticity helps understand consumer behavior, set prices, and predict market outcomes.

Emerging Economies: These are countries with rapid economic growth and increasing industrialization. These countries have rising living standards and increasing integration into global trade and finance. They have high GDP growth rates and generally transition from agriculture-based to industrial. They are service-driven economies with a rising middle class. They seek to integrate with the global economy and witness infrastructure development. They often have a youthful workforce, take up political and economic reforms, and have institutional transformation.

Exchange Rate Volatility: Exchange Rate Volatility is the frequent and unpredictable change in currency values over time. Several reasons contribute to the volatility, including changes in interest rates, inflation, political stability, and economic performance. High volatility will make international trade and investments riskier as the value of payments or profits can fluctuate. For any business organization involved in international trade and governments across the globe, managing the risk of exchange rate volatility is a significant challenge.

Exchange Rate: The Exchange Rate refers to the price of one country's currency in terms of another. Exchange rates can be fixed, floating, or pegged, depending on how they are determined. They are of significant importance in international trade and investment.

Gross Domestic Product (GDP): Gross Domestic Product refers to the total value of all goods and services produced in a country in a specific time, usually a year. It indicates the robustness of a country's economy. Production, income, or expenditure data can help measure GDP.

Inflation: Inflation is the reason behind the general rise in the prices of goods and services over time. It decreases the purchasing power of money. Inflation times are those when people need more money to buy the same items. Several factors influence inflation. Increased demand or higher production costs can cause it. While moderate inflation is expected in a growing economy, high inflation may lead to significant economic trouble like erosion of savings and affect economic stability.

International Trade: International Trade or Foreign Trade refers to exchanging goods and services between or among countries. It enables countries to obtain goods they cannot efficiently produce themselves. International Trade leads to economic growth, creates jobs, and promotes global cooperation. It can also lead to dependency on other countries and trade imbalances. Free trade agreements and tariffs, among others, often influence international trade flows.

Macroeconomics: Macroeconomics refers to the study of the economy as a whole. It examines how governments, businesses, and households interact within an economy. Key macroeconomic goals include stable prices, low unemployment, and sustainable growth. It uses many tools, like monetary and fiscal policies, to influence economic outcomes.

Panel Data: Panel Data is the type of data that combines information across both time and individuals, such as countries, firms, or people. Panel data helps the researchers analyze changes over time while considering individual differences, which may persist. Panel data is widely used extensively in economics and social sciences for its ability to provide richer insights than cross-sectional or time-series data alone, among others.

Regional Comprehensive Economic Partnership (RCEP): RCEP is a regional economic agreement between ASEAN and Free Trade Agreement (FTA) member partners. This agreement unites 15 countries in a free-trade partnership, representing nearly a third of the global population and GDP.

Chapter 9
Unraveling Dynamic Shock Transmission Between Tunisian Economic Growth and Key Economic Indicators

Maroua Jerbi
https://orcid.org/0000-0002-0530-0630
Mediterranean School of Business, Tunisia

Nourhaine Nefzi
https://orcid.org/0000-0003-3524-928X
Mediterranean School of Business, Tunisia

Houda Boubaker
https://orcid.org/0009-0006-6016-7285
Mediterranean School of Business, Tunisia

ABSTRACT

In this paper, we analyze the connectedness between the Tunisian growth rate and its key macroeconomic drivers, namely Foreign Direct Investment, inflation, and exchange rate. The purpose is to evaluate how economic growth responds to shocks induced by a variety of economic indicators using the Time- Varying Parameter Vector autoregressive (TVP-VAR). The findings indicate that the 90s and 2000s reform policies were critical in restructuring the dynamics of Tunisia's macroeconomic network. In particular, the network visualization analysis shows that the behavior of the Tunisian growth rate in the past years has changed from being a net shock

DOI: 10.4018/979-8-3693-9765-7.ch009

receiver to net shock transmitter. Interestingly, there has been a declining shock transmission between the Tunisian growth rate and the Foreign Direct Investment, showing that over time the economy was diversified, while policy response mechanisms have strengthened. Such findings, therefore, provide insights from the perspective of an investor as well as policymakers who strive to understand the dynamics of the Tunisian economy.

INTRODUCTION

Tunisia's economy has weathered a storm of major setbacks in the past decade, starting with the 2011 revolution that fundamentally altered the socio-political landscape of the country but resulted in several years of lost economic growth. Adding to this period of instability, the global COVID-19 pandemic struck in 2020, disrupting supply chains and trade, while exerting enormous pressure on public health and social infrastructure. Moreover, the decision to suspend the Tunisian parliament on July 25, 2021, marked the beginning of an extended period of political transition contributing to the uncertainty surrounding the economy. The situation was worsened by the Ukrainian war along with Russia, which started its active phase in early 2022 and dramatically impacted the dynamics of several global markets, including Tunisia's economy (Duho et al., 2022). This conflict interrupted global energy and food supply lines, resulting in substantial increases in energy prices and higher expenses for vital items, worsening inflationary pressures in Tunisia.

Moreover, in 2022, the government met major difficulties in obtaining foreign financial help, as discussions with the Foreign Monetary Fund (IMF) for economic reform packages were postponed, heightening budgetary vulnerabilities. In 2023, Tunisia experienced further economic pressure as public sector strikes became increasingly frequent due to wage disputes and dissatisfaction with economic reforms. The country's agricultural sector continued to suffer from an extended drought, reducing local food output and increasing reliance on expensive imports, expanding the trade imbalance. Also, inflation remained a persistent problem, reducing household buying power and aggravating social unrest. The combined consequences of these crises slowed job creation, weakened labor market dynamics, worsened the rapid expansion of state debt, and most importantly, decreased the economic growth rate.

Considering frequent destabilizing events and their significant influence on the Tunisian economic growth, it becomes necessary to assess the extent to which the growth rate is sensitive to different economic shocks. In this regard, studies confirm that, for low-income countries, domestic shocks, such as those coming from FDI, inflation and real effective exchange rate (REER) have a greater impact on the country's growth rate than external shocks. (Ahmed, 2003; Can et al., 2020;

Olamide et al., 2021; Raddatz, 2007). This could be attributed to the immediate effects of these key economic indicators on the economic growth of the country, compared to external factors, such as geopolitical factors and global financial stress.

Many studies highlight that FDI is particularly important for countries especially those with developing economies like Tunisia, as it allows for the modernization of industries, competitiveness and integration into a global network of trade (Baliamoune-Lutz, 2004; Kurtishi-Kastrati, 2013; Zghidi et al.,2016). In addition, FDI provides capital and access to modern management techniques, which may facilitate sustainable economic growth over a long period of time.

In addition, identifying the appropriate exchange rate regime for Tunisia has been the purpose of many studies, including Ameziane and Benyacoub (2022) and Barguellil et al. (2018), as it allows managing international trades, external debt, and economic stability. In this regard, Bouoiyour and Selmi (2014) found that a fixed exchange rate regime positively affects the Tunisian economy by stabilizing prices, reducing inflationary pressures, and creating a predictable environment for trade and investment. This stability is an important element in establishing investor confidence and sustaining export competitiveness.

However, contrary to Bouoiyour and Selmi (2014) findings, other studies focusing on the adoption of the flexible exchange rate show a positive effect on boosting economic development and making the adaptation process to external shocks (i.e., fluctuations in commodity prices or movements in demand throughout the world) easier. According to Cerra et al. (2013), during fiscal crisis episodes, countries with flexible exchange rates suffer less production loss than those with fixed exchange rates because flexibility makes it easier for the economy to adjust to shocks, which helps to stabilize output and employment levels.

Another key economic indicator that plays an important role in shifting the growth rate pattern is the inflation rate of the country, evidenced by the rise of price level, which contributes to the decrease in consumer purchasing power over time. High inflation rates are usually associated with high economic uncertainty, which may lead enterprises to postpone or downsize capital investment. Inflation can also retard productivity by creating operational inefficiencies while reducing the competitiveness of Tunisian products in international markets. All these conditions reinforce the need for prudent monetary policy measures aimed at preserving price stability to safeguard long-term growth.

While previous literature has helped to shed light on the interconnections between Tunisian GDP and these macroeconomic variables, there has been relatively little exploration of the propagation of shocks into the Tunisian economy, particularly in the wake of the revolution. Those shocks mean unanticipated changes in key economic statistics which have visible effects on the economy of a nation concerning gross growth, stability, and development. This is very important, as shown by the number of studies that seek to assess the effect of macroeconomic shocks and uncertainty on GDP, across myriad countries and timeframes (Stockhammar and Österholm, 2016).

In Tunisia, the ongoing economic challenges are illustrative of shocks. The AFD (2024) Report shows how sectoral disruptions such as droughts affecting agriculture and inflationary pressures arising from surging commodity prices badly affected GDP growth and thus give testimony to the economy's vulnerability to domestic and external shocks. In addition, Diwan et al. (2024) engage in discussing how high subsidy expenditure and policy inertia combine with other shocks to further erode Tunisia's macroeconomic stability. With these findings, rather general considerations on uncertainty and disruptions to growth are confirmed.

By understanding transmission mechanisms and consequent effects of macroeconomic shocks on GDP, policymakers can make informed decisions on how to mitigate uncertainty and negative effects while promoting economic growth. For instance, stabilizing Tunisia's economy and boosting investor confidence depend heavily on tackling inflation and strengthening budgetary restraint. Given the unique circumstances surrounding the revolution and the ensuing changes to the country's economic environment, including changes in governance and structural inefficiencies, more study is necessary to clarify the reasons behind the instability of the economic growth in Tunisia.

By expanding on previous research on the relationship between macroeconomic determinants and Tunisian economic growth, with an emphasis on their dynamic interconnectedness, we build upon these discoveries in our study. Precisely, our analysis encompasses an examination of the sources of shock spillovers and the identification of the primary transmitter and absorber of shocks affecting the Tunisian growth rate.

To this end, we use the Time-Varying Parameter Vector Autoregressive Model (TVP-VAR) to assess the degree of interconnectedness between Tunisian GDP and its primary macroeconomic drivers, i.e., FDI, inflation, and exchange rates. We seek to offer a thorough study that helps identifying and crafting strategies to reach increased stability and sustained economic growth. This approach represents a considerable improvement compared to previous studies, which usually assumed the connectedness between macroeconomic variables to be static and the causality pattern between them to change seldom, if at all, over time. These studies have mainly relied on common interaction techniques such as VAR, cointegration, and GARCH-based models. In contrast, the TVP-VAR model allows us to move beyond a mere estimation of dependence towards a more realistic representation of the dynamics between economic variables.

The current research holds profound implications for both policymakers and investors. On the one hand, investors will better comprehend the fundamental forces behind Tunisia's economic growth by peering into the time-varying causal linkages between macroeconomic factors and GDP. Such insight enables assessing the sustainability of economic trends, possible risks and opportunities that might not be glaringly visible through the well-recognized lens of investment analysis. Investors can also rebalance their portfolios, refine their asset allocation decisions, and adopt the timing of their investments based on their superior knowledge of the changing economic environment in relation to individual macroeconomic factors influencing GDP growth, such as inflation, exchange rates, and fiscal policies.

Furthermore, the identification of the net shock transmitter and net shock receiver of macroeconomic variables connected with Tunisian GDP can deliver crucial information to policymakers concerning the origins and pathways of economic shocks. Thus, this information is necessary for the development of appropriate policy measures that could address the peculiar weaknesses in the economy.

In the same way, understanding the mechanics by which shocks are transmitted can increase the ability of policymakers to prioritize measures for stability in the worst-hit sectors or to foster resilience in sectors of key economic importance. Furthermore, the focus on dynamic shock transmissions might contribute to the broader policy debate concerning long-term growth strategies and macroeconomic stability. Having knowledge of the interrelationship amongst these macroeconomic variables with respect to their influence on GDP over time can better equip policymakers during the management of inflation, exchange rate variations, and fiscal policy. Such an examination can go a long way in directing regional economic integration schemes and global partnerships with a view to establishing a stronger and more diversified economic environment.

The remainder of this chapter is organized as follows: Section 1 describes the literature review on every macroeconomic variable interacting with the Tunisian GDP. Section 2 describes the econometric methodology followed by an empirical analysis in Section 4. Policy implications are given in Section 5, while Section 6 concludes the discussion.

LITERATURE REVIEW

This study aims to delve into the dynamic interaction and shock transmission between the Tunisian growth rate and key macroeconomic indicators. The literature behind this subject is extensive and can be split into two main strands, each of which will be covered in this section. On the one hand, we will begin with a review of prior studies on the nature and direction of relationships between economic growth and main economic indicators, namely exchange rate, inflation and Foreign Direct

Investment (FDI). On the other hand, our review will focus on previous research that outlines the dynamic connectedness and shock spillover within a specific region.

Macroeconomic Dynamics

To explain the rationale behind the choice of FDI, inflation and exchange rate as main variables and test their connectedness with economic growth, we provide, in this section, three subsections aiming to review studies that focus on the different findings explaining the relationship between economic growth and (1) Foreign direct investment, (2) inflation, and (3) exchange rate.

Economic Growth and FDI. The interaction of economic growth and FDI has been the subject of many research papers (Adams & Opoku, 2015; Alfaro et al., 2004; Borensztein et al.,1998; Maza & Hierro, 2024). This can be justified by the importance of FDI as a key economic driver for a nation's growth, as it constitutes a vital source of financing that promotes domestic investment, encourages firm integration into international markets, and contributes to job creation in many sectors.[1]

Although numerous research studies confirm a positive relationship between these two variables, the extent and factors driving such interaction continue to be under debate. In this regard, studies focusing on Tunisia provide mixed conclusions depending on the period of study and the factors considered. For example, few studies claim that FDI has a negative impact on Tunisian economic growth, which can be attributed to the type of investments and the high level of corruption. This was confirmed by Herzer (2012) who discusses how some forms of FDI, particularly those focused on resource extraction or low-value businesses, might crowd out local investments, impeding long-term growth. Similarly, Bouchoucha and Benammou (2020) underline the negative impact of institutional inadequacies and corruption, which not only discourage high-quality investments but also impair the potential advantages of current FDI inflows. On another side, the negative impact of FDI on GDP can be explained through the negative impact of FDI on environment which could lead to adverse effects on tourism, agriculture production and shortage in water resources. In this context, Hfaiedh and Bardi (2021) confirm that FDI inflows contribute to an increase in environmental degradation which supports the pollution heaven hypothesis.

However, a significant strand of the literature has demonstrated that, in Tunisia, FDI and GDP have a positive relationship, a trend that is commonly observed in other countries worldwide (De Mello, 1997; Ford et al., 2008; Sijabat, 2023). For instance, according to Zghidi et al. (2016), FDI can stimulate economic growth by raising production capacity, improving infrastructure, advancing innovative knowledge and technology, and increasing the operational competitiveness of domestic firms. In the same line, Baliamoune-Lutz (2004) focuses on Arab countries and highlight how the FDI contributes to the country's growth rate through exports. Another study conducted by Kurtishi-Kastrati (2013) provides an overview of economic theories that drive FDI, including Ricardo's comparative advantage, Heckscher-Ohlin model, and Hymer's firm specific advantages, among others. The author provides different categorizations of FDI highlighting its positive effect on economic growth through capital formation, technology transfer and human capital development.

However, the study shows that the FDI impact might change depending on the host country's conditions with a possible adverse effect in case of foreign firms' dominance. Kurtishi-Kastrati (2013) also covers some empirical research papers around the impact of FDI on economic growth. According to the review presented in the paper, a country should have strong institutions, policies and absorptive capacity to benefit from FDI advantages.

A second strand of studies has shown that FDI and economic growth are positively causally related in both directions, meaning that FDI stimulates economic growth, which in turn draws in more FDI. For instance, based on the work of M.K. Hossain and M.S. Hossain (2022), FDI boosts growth in emerging economies by transferring technology, creating job opportunities, and improving infrastructure. Similarly, a thriving economy attracts more international investors because of improved market conditions and financial stability.

In a similar vein, Omri and Sassi-Tmar (2015) use data of three different north African countries, namely, Tunisia, Morocco, and Egypt to assess the nature of interaction between FDI and economic growth in these economies. By employing the generalized method of moments, the authors confirm the existence of bi-directional interaction, where an increasing FDI inflows lead to an acceleration in economic growth, while a steady economic growth constitutes a favorable signal for foreign investors.

Economic Growth and Inflation. The study of the relationship between economic growth and inflation has long been the area of focus for many researchers (Bittencourt, 2012; Bruno & Easterly, 1998; Chu et al., 2017; Malec et al., 2024). Theoritically, the neoclassical economic model argues that inflation could increase economic growth through capital accumulation (Mundell,1963; Tobin,1965). In this case, higher inflation makes it less desirable to hold money and nominal assets, thereby attracting capital investments. This meant that individuals and firms would shift their preferences from holding money to investing in productive assets, propelling the economy forward by increasing capital accumulation, and hence output in the economy.

In the Tunisian context, the studies provide mixed conclusions relative to their goals, studied periods, and models. For instance, Ghandri et al. (2021) compare the pre- and post-revolution periods and illustrate two contrasting trends. The pre-revolution was characterized by rising growth with moderate inflation. The post- revolution period Tunisia witnessed economic turbulence, with a consequent upsurge in the inflationary rate of prices reflecting a negative relationship. The study questions whether adopting inflation targeting would be a good policy option for promoting economic growth in Tunisia. By considering the predictable linkage between the consumer price index and its determinants, including the economic growth, the authors confirm the positive relationship between inflation rate and growth rate in both short and long terms. They also conclude the possibility of Tunisia to adopt inflation-targeting regime, which would help stabilizing prices and promote the economy.

Other studies focus on different economic regions and indicate negative relationship between the inflation rate and a growth rate (Baharumshah et al.,2016; Balcilar et al., 2017; De Gregorio,1993; Malec et al., 2024). This could be explained by the monetary theory showing that an increase in inflation rate leads to a drop in stability which negatively impacts economic growth (Stockman's, 1985). Turning to the Tunisian context, Balkouti and Boujelbène (2019) corroborate previous studies by explaining that high inflation in Tunisia lowers economic growth as it distorts stability and economic well-being. A recent study conducted by Boukraine (2021) examines the linkage between inflation, exchange rate, and Tunisian external debt during the period 2011 – 2019. Using Smooth Transition Autoregressive (STAR) model, the author shows a high pass-through impact from exchange rate to inflation, which negatively affects the country's growth rate.

Bouyacoub (2022) analyzes the relationship between inflation targeting and economic growth in 20 MENA countries, including Tunisia over the period 2000 – 2020. The findings suggest the existence of a unidirectional causal negative relationship, from inflation to economic growth. The author explains that high inflation can lead to a decrease in overall product, and a worsening in employment, resulting in a slowdown of the economy. A more extensive body of literature emphasizes that the relationship between inflation and economic growth is non-linear and is related to thresholds (Baglan & Yoldas, 2014; Baharumshah et al., 2016; Omay & Öznur Kan, 2010; Thanh, 2015). The few studies that focus on Tunisian context confirm these findings. For example, Boujelbène and Helali (2017) find that the period from 1993 to 2012 shows evidence of a threshold effect with non-stationary and non-linear inflation rate. They conclude that inflation promotes economic growth when the threshold is below 3.48% and generates a negative and significant correlation between them above this threshold. In the same vein, Becha et al. (2023) identify an inflation threshold of 3.63% under which inflation has a positive significant impact on economic growth. However, if the threshold is above that value, the inflation is expected to have a negative impact on economic growth. Dammak and Helali (2017) confirm the non-linearity relationship between the inflation rate and Tunisian growth rate. The authors identify a threshold level of 3.48% for the period 1993 – 2012, above of which, the impact of inflation becomes negative. This has been clearly seen during the Gulf War (1994-1996), the global financial crisis (2008-2009), and the revolution era, when the high inflation coincided with economic slowdown in Tunisia. Similarly, Helali et al. (2021) highlight an indirect relationship between inflation and growth rate based on a threshold. They argue when inflation is below a threshold of 4.89%, financial depth stimulates economic growth. However, when this threshold exceeds the identified value, this positive impact weakens.

Overall, based on the literature review discussed above, it is evident that the interaction between the Tunisian growth rate and the inflation follows a non-linear pattern, suggesting the inconvenience of linear models, which reflect the need to employ more adaptive models that consider structure breaks and non-linear behaviors.

*Economic Growth and Exchange Rate***.** The adoption of financial liberalization has exposed different countries to significant fluctuations of the exchange rate which raised the interest of many researchers to study the controversial relation between exchange rates and economic growth.

Studies such as Edwards and Levy Yeyati (2005) and Mundell (1961) show that exchange rate flexibility can boost economic growth as it helps in the absorption of external shocks thanks to high adaptability. This can be explained by the smaller production losses found for countries with flexible rate regimes in the period of crisis, along with the greater monetary policy independence (Cerra et al, 2013; Mundell, 1963).

Other studies confirm, however, that exchange rate volatility has a negative impact on different macroeconomic aggregates, including investment, employment and trade, which would harm economic growth (Demir, 2010; Servén, 2003). In the same perspective, Dollar (1992) and Vieira et al. (2013) indicate that exchange rate volatility slows the economic growth. When examining the Tunisian context, different conclusions are provided by the literature. For instance, Sakli et al. (2022) found that there is no relationship between economic growth and exchange rate in the short run. While, in the long run, an appreciation in the real effective exchange rate (REER) plays a key role in reducing the competitiveness of domestic products compared to foreign ones, thus deteriorating the trade balance and reducing the economic growth. This can be also attributed to the negative impact of exchange rate volatility on exports driven by oil fluctuations, regime switching and leverage effects (Bouoiyour & Selmi, 2014).

Moreover, it is noteworthy to mention that the misalignment of REER has a significant impact on the nation's growth rate. Indeed, it has been proven that overvaluation can generate a negative signal to foreign investors, which may lead to a deficit in current account, an increase in external debts along with risks of speculative attacks and currency crisis (Kaminsky et al., 1998). Undervaluation, however, shows two different impacts. Precisely, small undervaluation of the currency might stimulate economic growth, especially for developing countries, as it helps to achieve competitiveness and boosting exports (Gala, 2008).

Large undervaluation, on the other hand, hurts growth in middle income countries and may cause an economic slowdown in these economies (Couharde et al. 2025). In this context, Amor et al. (2023) confirm that the undervaluation of the Tunisian REER promotes economic growth up to a threshold of 10.02% deviation from equilibrium, beyond which the undervaluation of the currency can inhibit the economic growth. The study also shows that overvaluation can boost growth, but only up to 9.02% threshold, after which the overvaluation becomes harmful for Tunisian growth rate. Recently, Elsharif (2024) studies the REER misalignment and its impact on economic growth in three Maghreb countries, i.e., Tunisia, Algeria and Morocco. The results show a negative relationship, implying that an undervalued currency leads to high long-term economic growth, while an overvalued currency harms economic growth in the long run.

For their part, Ameziane and Benyacoub (2022) focus on direct and indirect effects of exchange rate volatility on economic growth by considering the mitigating role of exchange rate regimes. Based on their results, fluctuations in exchange rates negatively impact economic growth in emerging countries, both directly and indirectly. Their study also emphasizes the importance of selecting an appropriate exchange rate regime to control exchange rate fluctuations and promote economic growth. Indeed, the authors conclude that countries with fixed or floating exchange rate regimes are most affected by exchange rate shocks, compared to intermediate regime, as the latter offers some flexibility to manage volatility while reducing at the same time economic vulnerability.

Barguellil et al. (2018) focus on a sample of developing countries including Tunisia and validate that both nominal and real exchange rate volatilities negatively impact the economic growth. A more pronounced effect is noticed in countries with flexible exchange rate regimes compared to countries adopting fixed exchange rate regime, due to limited uncertainty.

In this context, many studies provide different channels through which the exchange rate regime might impact economic growth. For instance, according to Dumas and Solnik (1995) and G. Ramey and V.A. Ramey (1995), flexible regimes create uncertainty and decrease investments, including FDI, as investors will be asking for a higher risk premium, leading to a negative impact on economic growth. Researchers also confirm that fixed regimes provide stability and confidence which promotes foreign investment, reduces transaction costs and fosters trade openness (Cushman and De Vita, 2017; Rose, 2000).

As a final point, it is important to highlight that exchange rate regimes can impact economic growth through their ability to act as shock absorbers and their role in the transmission of shocks (Flood & Marion, 1982). A deeper analysis of shock transmissions is developed in the next section.

Shock Spillover

Frequent and important economic recessions have given rise to significant literature bodies aiming to analyze the impact of dynamic shocks on macroeconomic and financial aggregates. While the literature on factors affecting the Tunisian GDP is very rich, little attention has been provided to shock spillovers in the Tunisian context, although it is of great importance not only for investors in tailoring their investment decisions, but also for policymakers, as it helps designing appropriate economic policies to promote sustainable economic growth in the country. In this section, we start by reviewing studies that focus on static and dynamic shock transmission between different economic aggregates, including the case of Tunisia. The second sub-section is addressed to examine studies that use the Time-Varying Vector Autoregression (TVP-VAR) model in the case of Tunisia. The purpose is to highlight the lack of works focusing on Tunisia and the extent to which its economy is affected by dynamic shock transmission from key economic indicators.

Static and Dynamic Shock Transmission. Studying the impact of shocks has been a focus area for extended international literature. While Caballero and Hammour (1994) state that shocks can eliminate inefficiencies and build long-term growth based on reforms, Cerra and Saxena (2008) argue that, for all types of countries (emerging, developing and transitioning), financial and political crises cause long-lasting economic growth downturn with possible economic recovery only for civil wars. The importance and the direction of these impacts depends on the type of shock, its origin, the resilience of the receptive economy, along with other factors (Edwards, 2010). Rand and Trap (2002) suggest that shocks starting in advanced economies represent a major growth driver of emerging markets while Dooley and Hutchinson (2009) find that emerging markets did not react to the US subprime crisis immediately. A similar conclusion is found in the work of Didier et al. (2012) which argues the significant resilience of emerging countries to the global financial crisis of 2008. The authors state that, despite the growth decline like developed countries, emerging economies were able to generate their pre-crisis growth rates more quickly. A possible explanation is the implementation of countercyclical policies, which was reflected in their stronger economic adaptability and quick absorption of external shocks, thus, permitting the quick recovery of economic growth.

Hoffmaister and Roldós (2001) use the Structural Vector Autoregression (SVAR) model to identify factors causing the macroeconomic variation in both Brazil and Korea. According to their results, domestic shocks are the primary drivers of GDP volatility in these countries, while external shocks play a minor role. Raddatz (2007) also supports the fact that, for low-income countries, external shocks explain a small portion of output variance as they are dominated by internal factors. Ahmed (2003) studies the extent to which internal and external shocks can impact the economic fluctuation in Latin American countries.

Based on a dynamic panel model, the authors conclude that an effective exchange rate regime capable of managing external shocks can positively influence the economic growth in these countries. In the same vein, Can et al. (2020) and Olamide et al. (2021) focus on Turkey and East African countries, and indicate that exchange rate movements are the primary drivers of shock transmission to GDP.

Drawing from the above literature review, it can be concluded that domestic shocks have greater impact on the growth rate in developing countries, than external shocks. This provides a compelling motivation to explore how shocks of the three economic indicators considered in this study, i.e., FDI, inflation and exchange rate, can influence the Tunisian economic growth rate.

Nevertheless, a review of prior research suggests limited existing papers assessing shock transmission between the Tunisian growth rate and its key economic variables. For example, Guenichi and Benamou (2010) investigate the relationship between world oil prices, economic growth and inflation in Tunisia for the period from 1970 to 2008, using univariate and multivariate tests for structural breaks along with cointegration analysis with multiple structural changes. According to their results, an increase in oil price negatively impacts real output through the price level increase, this means that inflation plays the role of oil shock transmitter to economic growth.

Makni (2019) uses a revised form of the New Keynesian model to analyze time-varying interaction and shock transmission between main macro-economic variables in Tunisia. The objective is to offer insights around the impact of various chocks on Tunisian economy.

Based on author's results, shock spillovers to Tunisian GDP are mainly driven by inflation, interest rate, demand and exchange rate shocks. The author explains that an inflationary shock increases inflation which pushes central banks to increase interest rate resulting in an exchange rate and output depreciation.

On the other hand, an increase in interest rates due to monetary shock would at the same time attract foreign investment but decrease spending and output, thus creating an economic imbalance. Conversely, positive shocks in the exchange rate help lowing inflation and interest rates, which stimulates capital inflows, investment and output in Tunisia. Finally, the author highlights the dependence of Tunisian GDP fluctuation on external shocks, namely global recession, foreign output changes and the Arab spring which weakens the growth. This was confirmed by Balcicar et al. (2022) and Nouira et al. (2018) who demonstrated that Tunisia acts as a financial shock receiver during periods of financial stress and that oil price decrease led to Tunisian exchange rate depreciation, which negatively impacts the economic growth.

Dynamic shock transmission using the TVP-VAR Model. As research interest on studying shock transmission between economic aggregates continues to rise, there has been a recent shift toward using time-varying models that are capable to capture not only dynamic interactions, but also the extent to which shocks can evolve over time, allowing a more realistic representation of the economic impacts. Time-Varying Parameter Vector Autoregression (TVP – VAR) constitutes one of these models that has been recently used by many studies. For instance, Asomaning et al. (2024) employ the TVP – VAR to measure the extent to geopolitical risk can affect economic aggregates in Ghana. The paper concludes that this variable constitutes the primary shock transmitter affecting the country's foreign exchange reserve, real exchange rate, consumer price index, and debt. Shu-ping and Xiao-meng (2017) use monthly data from China for the period 2001 – 2016 to assess to what extent the Chines economic growth is affected by the FDI and the REER. According to the authors, exchange rate presents a negative impact on China economic growth, while the connectedness between FDI and growth rate indicates different behaviors, varying before and after the global financial crisis of 2008.

Precisely, the study notices a delayed response of the growth rate to FDI shocks during the pre- crisis, while, after 2008, shock transmission from FDI become more immediate, highlighting the effectiveness of policy changes in China in terms of regulations and financial market development.

In the context of Tunisia, there has been a significant lack of studies that focus on the dynamic behavior between economic variables. In this regard, Dahem et al. (2017), highlight the necessity to consider structural and political changes that Tunisia has witnessed in the past decade. Based on the TVP – VAR, the authors show that the inflation response to exchange rate shocks is time evolving in Tunisia, especially after significant events (subprime crisis 2008, Arab Spring 2011 and the 2014 oil price crash). Using the same model, Samir and Tarek (2014), examine the dynamic impact of exchange rate on prices in Tunisia. According to the authors, the influence of exchange rates has been persistently increasing over the last years because of the country's exchange rate policy, lack of monetary policy and reduced subsidies on controlled products.

Research Gap and Hypothesis

Existing research studies, as highlighted in the literature review, reveal a lack of deep analysis on how the relationship between growth rate in Tunisia and domestic economic indicators evolve over time and whether internal shock transmission coming from these domestic indicators exert a significant impact on shaping Tunisian growth rate. This study attempts to describe the size and direction of the shock spillovers among the main macroeconomic factors. Precisely, our paper evaluates the response of Tunisian Economy, through the GDP changes, to any chock coming from the real exchange rate, the inflation, and the foreign direct investment, which is an unprecedented research topic.

To this end, we test the following hypotheses:

Hypothesis 0: There is significant connectedness and shock spillover effects between Tunisian GDP and exchange rate, FDI and inflation.
Hypothesis 1: No significant connectedness is observed between Tunisian GDP and exchange rate, FDI and inflation.

DATA AND RESEARCH METHODS

Data

In this research, we focus on four principal economic indicators to assess the dynamic of their interactions and the extent to which they contribute to the instability of the Tunisian economy. The variables under study cover the GDP per capita growth which measures the annual economic output in Tunisia per person, reflecting the overall economic growth of the country. The Consumer Price Index (CPI) (2010 = 100) is used as measure of inflation, as it embodies changes in price level of the consumption basket over the years. We also include The Foreign Direct Investment (FDI), net inflows as a percentage of the GDP. This variable measures the amount of the value of foreign investments in the Tunisian economy relative to its GDP. Finally, we consider the Real Effective Exchange Rate (REER) Index (2010 = 100) to assess the international competitiveness of Tunisia, based on its currency value in comparison to weighted average of foreign currencies. All data are extracted from the word bank and cover the period 1983 – 2023.

Methods of Analysis

This study uses the time-varying parameter vector autoregressions (TVP-VAR) model, a noteworthy empirical method put forth by Diebold and Ylmaz's (2009, 2012, 2014) and improved by Antonakakis et al. (2020).

This model proposes a variety of connectedness measures to track and evaluate dynamic spillovers in a preselected network. This method is based on the forecast error variance decomposition that was generated from the rolling-window VARs.

The key benefits of this approach are as follows: First, it overcomes the issues associated with rolling window analysis, which helps avoid the loss of important observations. Second, it helps measure dynamic connectedness for both low frequency and limited time-series data. Finally, the model uses Kalman filter technique with forgetting factors which allows variance to vary across time. The TVP-VAR model is defined as follows.

$$Z_t = \beta_t Z_{t-1} + \varepsilon_t \tag{1}$$

$$vec(\beta_t) = vec(\beta_{t-1}) + u_t \tag{2}$$

Where Z_t and Z_{t-1} dimensional endogenous variable vectors at time t and t – 1, respectively. ε_t and u_t are $N \times 1$ and $N^2 \times 1$ disturbance vectors at time t, respectively. Both $\varepsilon_t \sim (0, S_t)$ and $u_t \sim (0, R_t)$ are assumed to be normally distributed with $N \times N$ and $N^2 \times N^2$ dimensional matrices, respectively. β_t is a $N \times N$ time-varying coefficient matrix.

In order to calculate the H-step-ahead generalized forecast error variance decomposition GFEVD; (Koop et al., 1996; Pesaran & Shin, 1998), we transform the estimated TVP-VAR model into its Vector Moving Average (TVP-VMA), i.e., $Z_t - \sum_{i=1}^{p} \beta_{it} Z_{t-i} + \varepsilon_t = \sum_{j=0}^{\infty} A_{jt} \varepsilon_{t-j}$

The scaled GFEVD ($\widetilde{\theta^g_{ij,t}}(H)$) is then computed based on the $\theta^g_{ij,t}(H)$. To be precise,

$$\widetilde{\theta^g_{ij,t}}\left(H\right) = \frac{\theta^g_{ij,t}(H)}{\sum_{j=1}^{N} \theta^g_{ij,t}(H)} \tag{3}$$

Where; $\widetilde{\theta^g_{ij,t}}(H)$) represents the pairwise directional connectedness, i.e., the impact of variable j on variable i.

$$\theta^g_{ij,t}(H) = \frac{S^{-1}_{ii,t} \sum_{t=1}^{H-1} (f_i' A_t S_t f_j)^2}{\sum_{j=1}^{k} \sum_{t=1}^{H-1} (f_i A_t S_t A_t' f_i)} \tag{4}$$

Where, $\sum_{j=1}^{k} \theta^g_{ij,t}(H) = 1, \sum_{i,j=1}^{k} \widetilde{\theta}^g_{ij,t}(H) = k$, and f_i corresponds to a $N \times 1$ selection vector, which is equal to unity on the f_i^{th} position and zero otherwise.

within the framework of Diebold and Yılmaz (2014), the “to”, “from”, “net” and “total” connectedness measures can be computed, based on the GFEVD:

$$Total_t = \frac{\sum_{i,j=1,\, i\neq j}^{N} \widetilde{\theta^g_{ij,t}}(H)}{\sum_{i,j=1}^{N} \widetilde{\theta^g_{ij,t}}(H)} \times 100 \tag{5}$$

We can examine the scenario in which variable i transmits its shock to all other variables j. This situation is known as “*total directional connectedness to others*” and is described as:

$$TO_{jt} = \frac{\sum_{j=1,\, i\neq j}^{N} \widetilde{\theta_{ij,t}^{g}}(H)}{\sum_{j=1}^{N} \widetilde{\theta_{ij,t}^{g}}(H)} \times 100 \tag{6}$$

We can also examine the scenario in which variable *i* receives shocks from other variables *j*. This situation is known as "*total directional connectedness from others*" and can be defined as:

$$FROM_{jt} = \frac{\sum_{j=1,\, i\neq j}^{N} \widetilde{\theta_{ij,t}^{g}}(H)}{\sum_{i=1}^{N} \widetilde{\theta_{ij,t}^{g}}(H)} \times 100 \tag{7}$$

Finally, by substracting equation (7) from equation (6), we can have the "*net total directional connectedness*", which measures the net contribution of each variable to the whole network:

$$NET_{jt} = TO_{jt} - FROM_{jt} \tag{8}$$

Based on this equation, if the index is positive, it suggests that variable *i* is a net transmitter as it influences all other variables more than itself being influenced. If the index is negative, it indicates that all other variables are the one driving variable *i*, thus, this later is considered as a net receiver.

Finally, the bidirectional relationships between two variables can be measured by the "*net pairwise connectedness index*" ($NPDC_{ij}$) and has the following expression:

$$NPDC_{ij,t} = \widetilde{\theta_{ij,t}^{g}}(H) - \widetilde{\theta_{ji,t}^{g}}(H) \tag{9}$$

The equation above can be simply defined as the difference of the shocks transmitted from *i* to *j* and that transmitted from *j* to *i*. If $NPDC_{ij}$ is positive (negative), this means that variable *i* is impacting (impacted by) variable *j* more (less) that variable *j* impacts variable *i*.

EMPIRICAL RESULTS

Data Description

The descriptive statistics in Table 1 show that all macroeconomic variables have almost the same Mean value. The GPD exhibits the lowest volatility, positive skewness and a highest kurtosis, suggesting the presence of low fluctuations as well as greater likelihood of positive performance. Regarding other macroeconomic variables, the FDI stands out as the only variable with the highest standard deviation coupled with positive skewness and high kurtosis.

These high fluctuations accompanied with occasional spikes to high values may reflect the unexpected shocks or external events that could influence the FDI in Tunisia. Lastly, Jarque-Bera statistics reject the normal distribution hypothesis for GPD series.[2]

The initial examination of Table 1 reveals the heterogeneity of the different macroeconomic variables considered in this study.

Table 1. Summary statistics

	Main Variable	Other Macroeconomic variables		
	GPD	**CPI**	**FDI**	**EER**
Mean	2.924899	0.089631	0.208508	-0.02178
Std. Dev.	21.88305	1.538955	0.874662	0.048836
Skewness	5.791476	0.334624	2.197243	-1.45358
Kurtosis	34.96811	0.586716	4.822317	4.325217
Jarque-Bera	15.678 (0.000)	1.234 (0.539)	4.567 (0.102)	0.789 (0.674)

Note: mean values are expressed in percentage. Values between parentheses indicate the p-values for the Jarque-Bera Test.

Total Connectedness Analysis

Table 2 displays the results of the total dynamic connectedness between the studied variables. Three information matters in this table: total spillover value, Spillovers to and from others, and the net directional spillovers for individual variable. Starting with the analysis of the total spillover index, the table shows an average of 43.61 percent, indicating that nearly half of the network fluctuations are due to spillovers among the four macroeconomic variables considered in this study. The contributions of FDI and GDP to other variables are significantly stronger than those of EER and CPI. Precisely, FDI and GDP account for 49.5 percent and 45.9 percent of the total contribution to other variables, respectively, whereas EER and CPI contribute 40.2 percent and 39.66 percent, respectively. In addition, it can be observed from the table that the CPI receives the largest spillover from others, as 58.97 percent of its variability is explained by other variables. This highlights its sensitivity to external shocks. In contrast, FDI receives the least spillover from others (31.9 percent), corroborating that it is less affected by the network.

These observations are consistent with the net spillover analysis. Indeed, the FDI stands as the main net shock transmitter, with a positive value of 17.6 percent, followed by EER with a value of 5.3 percent. On the other hand, CPI and GPD function as net shock receivers, with net spillover values of -19.31 percent and -3.58 percent, respectively, which means that they receive more shocks than they transmit.

Table 2. Total Dynamic connectedness

	CPI	FDI	GPD	EER	Contrib. from others
CPI	41.03	18.14	25.52	15.31	58.97
FDI	6.81	68.1	10.69	14.41	31.9
GPD	23.61	14.58	51.33	10.48	48.67
EER	9.25	16.78	8.89	65.09	34.91
Direct. To others	39.66	49.5	45.09	40.2	174.45
Direct. including own	80.69	117.6	96.42	105.3	**Total Spillover Index**
NET	-19.31	17.6	-3.58	5.3	43.61

Note: The above table exhibits the results of the total dynamic connectedness between the different studied variables, using the TVP-VAR model of Chatziantoniou et al. (2021), with a lag length of order one and a 20-step ahead forecast error variance.

Figure 1 depicts the dynamic total connectedness in the macroeconomic network. The analysis shows that the level of connectedness reached its peak in 1984 and in late 1993, at roughly 74%, before embarking on a gradual decline starting from 2002. The sharp rise in connectedness in 1984 can be directly traced back to the policy changes initiated in the 1970s, a period marked by a determined push to stimulate private sector activity and encourage industrial development.

Precisely, laws enacted in 1972 and 1974 aimed to promote industrial development by offering incentives to exporting enterprises and encouraging investment in economically deprived areas (Baliamoune-Lutz, 2009).

This, together with ongoing tariff safeguards, created a favorable environment for company expansion within the Tunisian economy. The decrease in total connectedness after 1990 can be attributed to Tunisia's 1990s policies of liberalizing and diversifying its economy by expanding into new markets, encouraging privatization, and promoting exports, which helped to reduce the sensitivity of these variables to one another. (Ayadi, Mattoussi, 2016).

Figure 1. Total Dynamic Spillovers

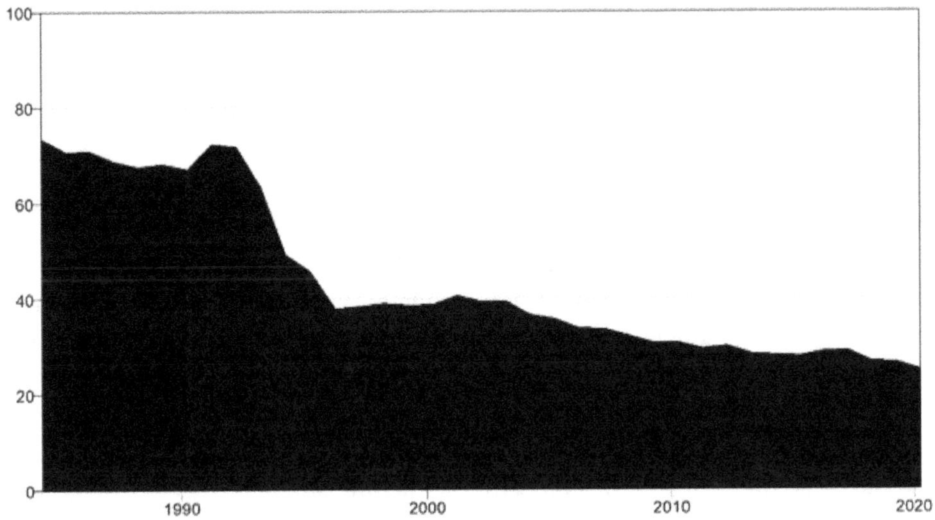

Net Total Connectedness Analysis

The purpose of this sub-section is to provide a comprehensive picture about how the dynamic of GDP prices contributes to or is affected by the dynamics of interconnected systems. Notably, the analysis of Figure 2 will help identifying moments during which the Tunisian GDP functions as a source of economic shocks and when it serves as a receiver of such shocks. A thorough examination of Figure 2 reveals several noteworthy findings. Firstly, between 1984 and approximately 1991, the Tunisian GPD consistently receives shocks from other macroeconomic factors, surpassing a threshold of 60 percent, on average.

However, starting from 1992, the Tunisian GPD transitions to become a net transmitter of shocks, influencing other macroeconomic variables in the system. This shift in the GPD function from receiver to contributor of shocks can be explained by the transformative measures aimed at supporting the country's growth, enhancing productivity, and integrating into the international market. An example of Tunisia undertaking structural adjustment program is its joining to the General Agreement on Tariffs and Trade (GATT) in 1990 and free-trade agreement signed with the European Union in 1995, to facilitate trade liberalization and demonstrate its commitment to international trade standards (Bechri and Naccache, 2005; International Monetary Fund,1999). Consequently, these reforms positively impacted the Tunisian GDP, by transforming its function from passively absorbing the different economic shocks to actively transmitting the effects of reforms and influencing other key macroeconomic indicators.

Secondly, Since the connectedness dropped off sharply and became more or less stable around 2002, the Tunisians claim that there were very deliberate interventions on the part of the administration to keep things stagnant through 2002. More specifically, with an aim to improve efficiency and competitiveness, a full-scale approach to economic liberalization was taken. It was a comprehensive initiative comprising a plethora of reforms aimed at diversifying the economy, improving fiscal management, and providing an economic climate conducive to doing business. Another important aspect consisted of reducing the economy's heavy dependence on a few sectors. Whereas Tunisia had traditionally been very much dependent on tourism and agriculture, the government has intervened with initiatives aimed at stimulating the growth of other sectors: information technology, renewable energy, and manufacturing (IMF, 2004).

Third, the Tunisian GPD acts mostly as a net transmitter of shocks in the period 1992-2020; yet there have also been times when its interconnection with the considered network is very low, especially in the period 2008-2011. The reason for this behavior was the increased sensitivity of the Tunisian economy during this period to international macroeconomic variables that have a far-reaching bearing on global stability.

In particular, extreme events like the financial crisis and the September terrorist attack further decreased the connectedness between the Tunisian GPD and other national macroeconomic factors. Starting in 2016, there has been a remarkable increase in shock transmission from the Tunisian GPD to other variables, and this behavior has remained stable since then, representing a significant switch in the role and power of the Tunisian GPD within the network.

To sum up, the overall net total connectedness suggests that the position of the Tunisian GPD in the network has been shaped over time by global events and specific local economic dynamics.

Figure 2. Net Total Connectedness (NTC)

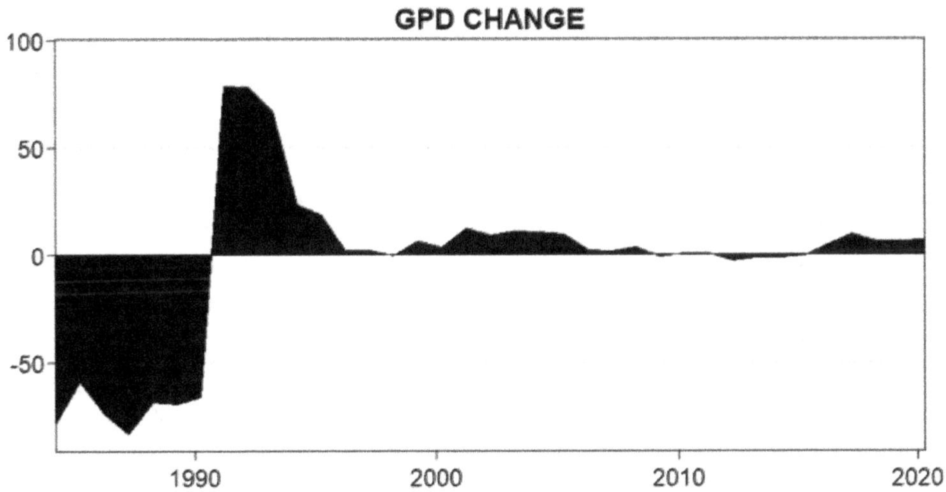

Net Pairwise Connectedness

Our focus in this part is on examining how the shock between the Tunisian growth rate and each macroeconomic indicators evolves over time, and whether there are specific economic factors acting as shock transmission channels to the GDP. To this end, we use the net pairwise connectedness measure.

Taking the case of the FDI vs. GDP nexus in Figure 3, we observe three distinct phases: an early phase of FDI dominance as shock contributor, a second phase of significant shift between 1991 and 2005, where the GDP becomes the primary shock transmitter, and a final phase of relative independence where the shock transmission from FDI to GDP didn't surpass the 10 percent, on average. As previously mentioned, the transition from FDI-driven to GDP-driven shocks around the 90's can be attributed to the sustained economic growth experienced during that period. This growth had a favorable impact on FDI inflows into Tunisia. Our findings corroborate the conclusion of Hamdi et al. (2013) confirming that the FDI did not have obvious impacts on Tunisia's economic growth during in that period. Looking at the third phase of the graph, it is evident that the dynamics changed significantly after the 2007 subprime crisis.

The increased turbulence and the frequent occurrence of global economic crises had a profound impact on the Tunisian growth, which was reflected in FDI behavior turning to main shock transmitter to the GDP. In other words, global economic disruptions have had repercussions, affecting the flow of foreign investment in

Tunisia and, consequently, the country's GDP. However, the FDI shock transmission remains very low, compared to the previous years, highlighting more stability in the Tunisian economy and less asymmetry in the shock transmission dynamics between FDI and GDP.

Regarding the connectedness between the CPI and GDP, an overall examination of Figure 4 confirms a low shock transmission dynamic between the two economic variables. Precisely, the first half of the studied period, i.e., 1984 and 2003, was characterized by a low contribution of shocks from CPI to GDP, consistently remaining below 10 percent. This could be attributed to various factors: (1) the adoption of the Structural Adjustment Plan (SAP) (1986-1994) which usually involves measures such as devaluation, subsidy reductions, and public sector wage constraints. These actions often trigger immediate inflationary pressures. As the CPI increased due to these measures, it impacted investments and overall economic activity, thus affecting the GDP, (2) 1992 Financial Sector Reforms which aimed at modernizing the banking sector and introducing capital market instruments.

As the financial sector became more responsive to market signals, it reacted more to inflationary tendencies (reflected in CPI) than before and, (3) The Tunisian economy, during this period, was heavily reliant on sectors like tourism and agriculture. Fluctuations in global prices or bad agricultural years could lead to a significant variation in the CPI, which would consequently impact GDP.

On the other hand, since 2003 the CPI has become the net receiver. A possible explanation can be traced to significant economic events, particularly, (1) Global Financial Crisis (2007-2008): While Tunisia was not directly hit by this crise, its GDP was affected due to its ties with European economies (trade partnerships and tourism). As the GDP declined, this led to lower spending and investments, reducing demand, and consequently impacting the CPI, (2) The political instability during the Jasmine Revolution (2010-2011) and its aftermath significantly impacted Tunisia's GDP.

The reduced economic activity and tourism fall resulted in a lower demand for goods and services, which then put a downward pressure on prices and the CPI, and (3) Economic Policies: Post the revolution, Tunisia underwent several policy changes aimed at stabilizing the economy. These changes often centered around boosting the GDP by focusing on investments, infrastructure, and diversifying the economy. As GDP started growing and stabilizing, it began influencing the CPI more directly.

Regarding the shock transmission between the Exchange rate and GDP, we note in figure 5 two main phases: a first phase reflecting a shock transmission from the EEF toward the Tunisian GPD, and a second phase where the economic growth indicator is primary shock transmitter. Exploring this further, we notice that the Tunisia's liberalization and economic diversification post-1986 played a significant impact in shifting the dynamic relationship between these two economic variables.

Precisely, it is evident that the period 1983 – 1990 was characterized by a significant instability in the national currency which negatively impacted the nation's economic growth. However, economic reconstruction and liberalization have led to a significant improvement in the GDP compared to the previous years. The current account deficit has decreased between 1986 and 1992 from 8 percent of GDP to 5.3 percent (International Monetary Fund., 1996). Such a change has been reflected in the behavior of exchange rate indicator, as it becomes more shock receiver starting from late 1990. This shift signals the extent to which monetary policy changes have impacted the GDP performance, which in turn has affected the international competitiveness of the country, reflected in EER responses. In other words, the Tunisian economic growth become more sensitive the international fluctuations, due to the country's economic integration with the global market.

However, it is worth mentioning that the impact of GDP on the exchange rate starts to decrease gradually, reaching its lowest level in 2005. The flattening of the dynamic connection around zero reflects the decreasing responsiveness of each variable to the other. This could be attributed to two main factors, (1) Stabilized monetary policies and (2) the country's global integration. On the one hand, the monetary policy in Tunisia has gone through several phases, the aim of which was to promote the country's economic growth. For instance, End et al (2020) highlight the efforts undertaken by the Tunisian monetary policy after Arab Spring to stabilize the financial system through targeting inflation and interest rate transmission. Given the stable economic climate, swings in key economic factors, including the country's economic growth and EER become less frequent, and thus, shock transmission between them become low, compared to previous years. On the other hand, the global integration of the Tunisian economy led to a varied economic exposure, enabling the country to rely more on international economic conditions rather than solely on domestic key factors. This diversification helps reduce the direct connectedness between a national economy and its currency.

Figure 3. Net Pairwise Connectedness between FDI and GPD

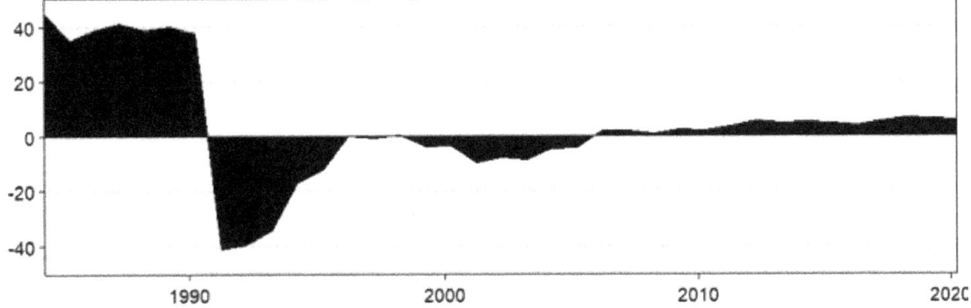

Figure 4. Net Pairwise Connectedness between CPI and GPD

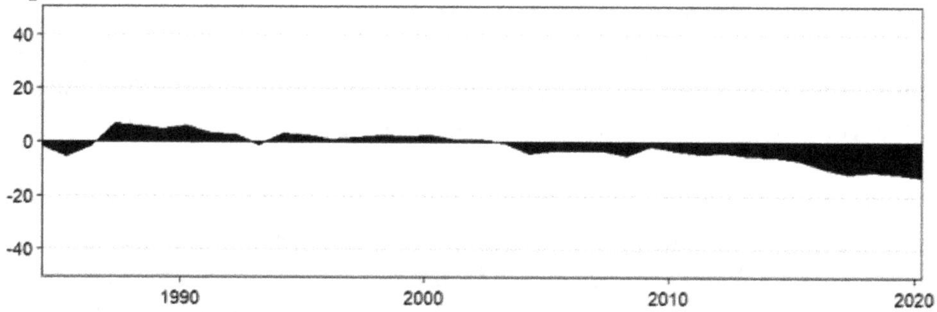

Figure 5. Net Pairwise Connectedness between GPD and EER

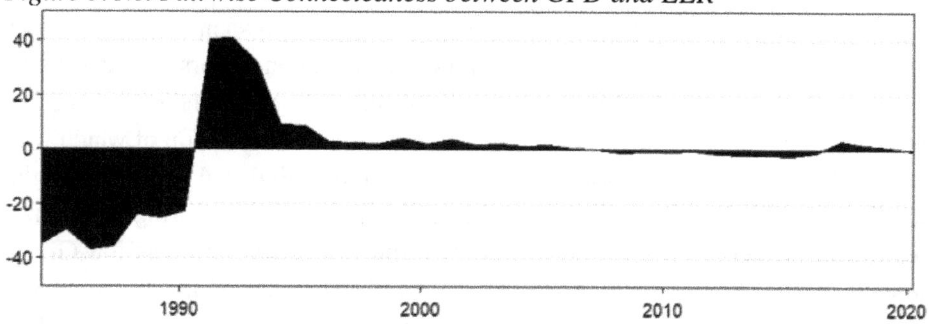

Based on the above analysis, our findings contribute to the existing literature, by providing, for the first time, insights into how the dynamic shock transmission between the Tunisian growth rate and key economic indicators evolve over time. Therefore, the null hypothesis implying that there is a significant connectedness and shock spillover effects between Tunisian GDP and exchange rate, FDI and inflation is confirmed while hypothesis 1 suggestion no significant connectedness is rejected.

POLICY IMPLICATIONS

Based on our empirical results, we make several important policy suggestions. First and foremost, governments ought to give priority to diversifying FDI sources by emphasizing investments from a greater number of countries and sectors. Growing industries like technology, healthcare, and renewable energy, for instance, may reduce dependency on traditional sectors while boosting economic resilience. Secondly, it is imperative to establish robust and uniform regulations. To increase investor trust and provide a stable environment conducive to long-term economic growth, these frameworks ought to include tax incentives, streamlined bureaucratic procedures, and investment protections. Furthermore, the central bank should take more initiative in curbing inflation. Inflation targeting, interest rate changes, and maintaining appropriate foreign reserves can all assist in keeping prices stable and reduce the impact of GDP variations on inflationary pressures. Policymakers should also look at exchange rate stability methods to protect the economy from external financial shocks. Finally, promoting public-private partnerships (PPPs) to co-finance infrastructure and innovation projects might enhance the domestic economy's base, making it more resilient to shocks coming from FDI and REER. Collectively, these policies would lower Tunisia's economic vulnerability to different shocks and encourage a more robust route to prosperity.

CONCLUSION

Studying macroeconomic trends in Tunisia over a long period since 1983 toward the year 2023 is a rare opportunity to examine how closely intertwined local and global economic phenomena turn out to be. The Tunisian economy over these four decades has exhibited an unusual degree of flexibility and adaptability and has shown pronounced ability to overcome severe policy changes, political upheavals, and gigantic occurrences in the world.

This stage captures not only the challenges faced by a nation but its response to the chronic domestic and international contexts, thereby further amplifying our understanding of the complex and resilient nature of the Tunisian economic setting.

In this paper, we have contributed to the literature on the Tunisian economy by analyzing for the first time the time-varying response of GDP to various unprecedented shocks through the TVP-VAR modeling environment. From thereon, the macroeconomic connectedness of Tunisia is forever changed by the increasing moves with respect to time for this GDP response. Indeed, according to the overall spillover index, interconnectedness among key economic variables reached a summit in 1984, then again during the early 1990s, and a slow decline from 2002 onwards. This transitional period coincides with Tunisia's undertakings at economic liberalization, especially with regard to diversification policies and structural reforms to shield domestic variables from external shocks. In addition, the network visualization demonstrates that the behavior of Tunisian GDP has evolved over time: from initially receiving shocks between 1984 and 1991, it transformed into a net shock transmitter since 1992.

After 1992, net shock transmission seems to have been caused by trade agreements-the GATT accession of Tunisia in 1990 and the free-trade agreement with the EU signed in 1995-from the perspective of economic integration but turning the entire map of economic shock transmission upside down. This is well supported by the notable structural change in GDP behavior vividly etched in the net pairwise-connectedness.

For example, a remarkable transition has been observed, around the 90’s, in FDI – GDP nexus, moving from FDI-driven to GDP-driven shocks. A third pattern of shock transmission has been observed after 2007, where the shock transmission from FDI to GDP was very low, highlighting a relative independence, which reflects more stability in the Tunisian economy.

Even in the CPI-GDP relationship, shocks were transmitted by CPI in the late 1980s and 1990s, mainly due to the SAP and subsequent financial-sector reforms. But after 2003, CPI became a net shock receiver, reflecting the impact of the global financial crisis of 2007-08 and political instability during the Jasmine Revolution in Tunisia during 2010-11. The association of the exchange rate and GDP was affected by the reforms of the 90's: the latter drifted from being a net receiver of shocks to a net transmitter. Over time, this connectedness waned, demonstrating some effectiveness of the monetary policy to stabilize the exchange rate and achieve equilibrium in the economy.

Overall, our findings suggest that, despite historical vulnerabilities, Tunisia's economy has become more resilient to external disturbances, benefiting from deeper economic diversification and stronger policy responses.

The current research has valuable insights to offer for scholars, investors, and policymakers, although its limitations must be acknowledged. One of the main limitations is regarded as having possible lapses in capturing all underlying factors and microeconomic subtleties that, despite well spanning over 40 years of data, would still be considered a bit limited. From a macroeconomic point of view, these phenomena could be said to have very complicated dynamics, which may not be fully captured in the scope of this study. The potential findings from the present merged methodology would be richly complemented with higher-frequency data that will allow for an even more fine-tuned investigation of dynamic connectedness patterns across macroeconomic variables. This would give insights into the complex interplay in detail in terms of the time scale, that is, how the relationship changes in the short run and responds to sudden economic shocks.

This, in turn, would allow for a better grasp of consciously making recommendations on the decision along with revealing some key nuances that go unnoticed in the present framework. There are numerous avenues for future research that stretch into other forms of industry for fine-grained assessments for hidden interplays and nuances to arise. Comparative studies on countries going through parallel transitions can further enrich our understanding of macroeconomics in dynamically evolving political and economic landscapes.

STATEMENT AND DECLARATIONS

- Availability of Data and Material: The datasets generated and/or analyzed during the current study are not publicly available but are available from the corresponding author upon request.
- Competing Interests: The authors declare no competing interests.
- Funding: This manuscript did not receive any external funding.
- Authors' Contributions: All authors of this research paper have actively contributed to the planning, execution, and analysis of this study.
- Acknowledgements: Not Applicable.

REFERENCES

Adams, S., & Opoku, E. E. O. (2015). Foreign direct investment, regulations and growth in sub-Saharan Africa. *Economic Analysis and Policy*, *47*, 48–56. DOI: 10.1016/j.eap.2015.07.001

AFD. (2024). African. *Economic Outlook, 2024*. https://www.afdb.org/en/documents/african-economic-outlook-2024

Ahmed, S. (2003). Sources of economic fluctuations in Latin America and implications for choice of exchange rate regimes. *Journal of Development Economics*, *72*(1), 181–202. DOI: 10.1016/S0304-3878(03)00073-7

Ameziane, K., & Benyacoub, B. (2022). Exchange Rate Volatility Effect on Economic Growth under Different Exchange Rate Regimes: New Evidence from Emerging Countries Using Panel CS-ARDL Model. *Journal of Risk and Financial Management*, *15*(11), 499. DOI: 10.3390/jrfm15110499

Amor, T. H., Nouira, R., Rault, C., & Sova, A. D. (2023). Real exchange rate misalignments and economic growth in Tunisia: New evidence from a threshold analysis of asymmetric adjustments. *The Quarterly Review of Economics and Finance*, *88*, 215–227. DOI: 10.1016/j.qref.2023.01.007

Antonakakis, N., Chatziantoniou, I., & Gabauer, D. (2020). Refined Measures of Dynamic Connectedness based on Time-Varying Parameter Vector Autoregressions. *Journal of Risk and Financial Management*, *13*(4), 84. DOI: 10.3390/jrfm13040084

Asomaning, K., Shah, H., & Emmanuel, U. (2024). A TVP-VAR assessment of the spillover effects of geopolitical risk shocks on macroeconomic variability: A study of the Ghanaian economy. Future Business Journal, 10(1), DOI: 10.1186/s43093-024-00341-5

Ayadi, M., & Mattoussi, W. (2016). Scoping of the Tunisian economy. In Working Paper Series. https://doi.org/DOI: 10.1007/978-3-030-91088-4_6

Baglan, D., & Yoldas, E. (2014). Non-linearity in the inflation–growth relationship in developing economies: Evidence from a semiparametric panel model. *Economics Letters*, *125*(1), 93–96. DOI: 10.1016/j.econlet.2014.08.015

Baharumshah, A. Z., Slesman, L., & Wohar, M. E. (2016). Inflation, inflation uncertainty, and economic growth in emerging and developing countries: Panel data evidence. *Economic Systems*, *40*(4), 638–657. DOI: 10.1016/j.ecosys.2016.02.009

Balcilar, M., Gupta, R., & Jooste, C. (2017). The growth-inflation nexus for the U.S. From 1801 to 2013: A semiparametric approach. *Journal of Applied Econometrics, 20*(1), 105–120. DOI: 10.1016/S1514-0326(17)30005-3

Baliamoune-Lutz, M. (2004). Does FDI Contribute to Economic Growth? *Business Economics (Cleveland, Ohio), 39*(2), 49–56. https://www.proquest.com/scholarly-journals/does-fdi-contribute-economic-growth/docview/199864100/se-2

Baliamoune-Lutz, M. (2009). Tunisia's development experience: A success story? (WIDER Research Paper No. 2009/32). The United Nations University World Institute for Development Economics Research (UNU-WIDER). https://www.econstor.eu/bitstream/10419/45097/1/601812603.pdf

Barguellil, A., Ben-Salha, O., & Zmami, M. (2018). Exchange Rate Volatility and Economic Growth. *Journal of Economic Integration, 33*(2), 1302–1336. DOI: 10.11130/jei.2018.33.2.1302

Becha, H., Kalai, M., & Helali, K. (2023). Smooth transition regression model relating inflation to economic growth in Tunisia. *Journal of Economic Structures, 12*(1), 1–26. DOI: 10.1186/s40008-023-00308-9

Bechri, M. Z., & Naccache, S. (2005). *The Political Economy of Development Policy in Tunisia* (Vol. 278). Contributions to Economic Analysis. DOI: 10.1016/S0573-8555(06)78010-5

Bittencourt, M. (2012). Inflation and economic growth in Latin America: Some panel time-series evidence. *Economic Modelling, 29*(2), 333–340. DOI: 10.1016/j.econmod.2011.10.018

Borensztein, E., De Gregorio, J., & Lee, J. (1998). How does foreign direct investment affect economic growth? *Journal of International Economics, 45*(1), 115–135. DOI: 10.1016/S0022-1996(97)00033-0

Bouchoucha, N., & Benammou, S. (2020). Does institutional quality matter for foreign direct investment? Evidence from African countries. *Journal of the Knowledge Economy, 11*(1), 390–404. DOI: 10.1007/s13132-018-0552-y

Boujelbène, T., & Helali, K. (2017). Threshold effects on the relationship between inflation rate and economic growth in Tunisia. *International Economic Journal, 31*(2), 310–325. DOI: 10.1080/10168737.2017.1289546

Boukraine, W. (2021). Asymmetric behavior of exchange rate in Tunisia: A nonlinear approach. FORCE: Focus on Research in Contemporary Economics, 2(1), 41-52. https://www.forcejournal.org/index.php/force/article/view/22

Bouoiyour, J., & Selmi, R. (2014). Exchange volatility and trade performance in Morocco and Tunisia: What have we learned so far? *Macroeconomics and Finance in Emerging Market Economies*, *8*(3), 244–274. DOI: 10.1080/17520843.2014.880150

Bouyacoub, B. (2022). Inflation targeting and economic growth in the Middle East and North Africa (MENA): Empirical modeling using ARDL approach. Financial Markets. *Institutions and Risks*, *6*(1), 5–12. DOI: 10.21272/fmir.6(1).5-12.2022

Bruno, M., & Easterly, W. (1998). Inflation crises and long-run growth. *Journal of Monetary Economics*, *41*(1), 3–26. DOI: 10.1016/S0304-3932(97)00063-9

Caballero, R. J., & Hammour, M. L. (1994). The Cleansing Effect of Recessions. *The American Economic Review*, *84*(5), 1350–1368. https://www.jstor.org/stable/2117776

Can, U., Bocuoglu, M. E., & Can, Z. G. (2020). How does the monetary transmission mechanism work? Evidence from Turkey. *Borsa Istanbul Review*, *20*(4), 375–382. DOI: 10.1016/j.bir.2020.05.004

Cerra, V., Panizza, U., & Saxena, S. C. (2013). International Evidence On Recovery From Recessions. *Contemporary Economic Policy*, *31*(2), 424–439. DOI: 10.1111/j.1465-7287.2012.00313.x

Cerra, V., & Saxena, S. C. (2008). Growth dynamics: The myth of economic recovery. *The American Economic Review*, *98*(1), 439–457. DOI: 10.1257/aer.98.1.439

Chu, A. C., Cozzi, G., Furukawa, Y., & Liao, C. (2017). Inflation and economic growth in a Schumpeterian model with endogenous entry of heterogeneous firms. *European Economic Review*, *98*, 392–409. DOI: 10.1016/j.euroecorev.2017.07.006

Couharde, C., Grekou, C., Mignon, V., & Morvillier, F. (2025). Reconciling contrasting views on the growth effect of currency misalignments. *Journal of International Money and Finance*, *151*, 103237. DOI: 10.1016/j.jimonfin.2024.103237

Cushman, D. O., & De Vita, G. (2017). Exchange rate regimes and FDI in developing countries: A propensity score matching approach. *Journal of International Money and Finance*, *77*, 143–163. DOI: 10.1016/j.jimonfin.2017.07.018

Dahem, A., Skander, S., & Siala Guermazi, F. (2017). Time-varying VAR analysis for disaggregated exchange rate pass-through in Tunisia (MPRA Paper No. 79759). Munich Personal RePEc Archive. https://mpra.ub.uni-muenchen.de/79759/

Dammak, T. B., & Helali, K. (2017). Threshold Effects on the Relationship Between Inflation Rate and Economic Growth in Tunisia. *International Economic Journal*, *31*(2), 310–325. DOI: 10.1080/10168737.2017.1289546

De Gregorio, J. (1993). Inflation, taxation, and long-run growth. *Journal of Monetary Economics, 31*(3), 271–298. DOI: 10.1016/0304-3932(93)90049-L

De Mello, L. R.Jr. (1997). Foreign direct investment in developing countries and growth: A selective survey. *The Journal of Development Studies, 34*(1), 1–34. DOI: 10.1080/00220389708422501

Demir, F. (2010). Exchange Rate Volatility and Employment Growth in Developing Countries: Evidence from Turkey. *World Development, 38*(8), 1127–1140. DOI: 10.1016/j.worlddev.2009.12.019

Didier, T., Hevia, C., & Schmukler, S. L. (2012). How resilient and countercyclical were emerging economies during the global financial crisis? *Journal of International Money and Finance, 31*(8), 2052–2077. DOI: 10.1016/j.jimonfin.2012.05.007

Diebold, F. X., & Yilmaz, K. (2009). Measuring Financial Asset Return and Volatility Spillovers, with Application to Global Equity Markets. *Economic Journal (London), 119*(534), 158–171. DOI: 10.1111/j.1468-0297.2008.02208.x

Diebold, F. X., & Yilmaz, K. (2012). Better to give than to receive: Predictive directional measurement of volatility spillovers. *International Journal of Forecasting, 28*(1), 57–66. DOI: 10.1016/j.ijforecast.2011.02.006

Diebold, F. X., & Yılmaz, K. (2014). On the network topology of variance decompositions: Measuring the connectedness of financial firms. *Journal of Econometrics, 182*(1), 119–134. DOI: 10.1016/j.jeconom.2014.04.012

Diwan, I., Alaya, H., & Meddeb, H. (2024). Tunisia's Economy in the Eye of the Storm. Retrieved from: https://carnegie-production-assets.s3.amazonaws.com/static/files/Diwan_Tunisia%20Economy_draft.pdf

Dollar, D. (1992). Outward-Oriented Developing Economies Really Do Grow More Rapidly: Evidence from 95 LDCs, 1976-1985. *Economic Development and Cultural Change, 40*(3), 523–544. Advance online publication. DOI: 10.1086/451959

Dooley, M., & Hutchison, M. (2009). Transmission of the U.S. Subprime crisis to emerging markets: Evidence on the decoupling–recoupling hypothesis. *Journal of International Money and Finance, 28*(8), 1331–1349. DOI: 10.1016/j.jimonfin.2009.08.004

Duho, K. C. T., Abankwah, S. A., Agbozo, D. A., Yonmearu, G., Aryee, B. N. A., & Akomanin, O. (2022). Exploring the Russo-Ukrainian crisis and its impact on African countries: A cross-regional analysis. Dataking Policy Brief 005, Accra, Dataking Consulting 2022, Available at *SSRN*: https://ssrn.com/abstract=4085903DOI: 10.2139/ssrn.4085903

Dumas, B., & Solnik, B. (1995). The World Price of Foreign Exchange Risk. *The Journal of Finance, 50*(2), 445–479. DOI: 10.1111/j.1540-6261.1995.tb04791.x

Edwards, S. (2010). The international transmission of interest rate shocks: The Federal Reserve and emerging markets in Latin America and Asia. *Journal of International Money and Finance, 29*(4), 685–703. DOI: 10.1016/j.jimonfin.2010.01.003

Edwards, S., & Levy Yeyati, E. (2005). Flexible exchange rates as shock absorbers. *European Economic Review, 49*(8), 2079–2105. DOI: 10.1016/j.euroecorev.2004.07.002

End, N., El Hamiani Khatat, M., & Kolsi, R. (2020). Tunisia monetary policy since the Arab Spring: The fall of the exchange rate anchor and rise of inflation targeting (IMF Working Paper, Volume 2020, Issue 167). International Monetary Fund. DOI: 10.5089/9781513555027.001

Flood, R. P., & Marion, N. P. (1982). The transmission of disturbances under alternative exchange-rate regimes with optimal indexing. *The Quarterly Journal of Economics, 97*(1), 43–66. DOI: 10.2307/1882626

Ford, T. C., Rork, J. C., & Elmslie, B. T. (2008). Foreign direct investment, economic growth, and the human capital threshold: Evidence from US states. *Review of International Economics, 16*(1), 96–113. DOI: 10.1111/j.1467-9396.2007.00726.x

Gala, P. (2008). Real Exchange Rate Levels and Economic Development: Theoretical Analysis and Econometric Evidence. *Cambridge Journal of Economics, 32*(2), 273–288. DOI: 10.1093/cje/bem042

Ghandri, M., Soltani, H., & Maktouf, S. (2021). Inflation targeting as a future framework for Tunisian monetary policy: Between perception and reality in an inflationary context. *Journal of International Students, 14*(4), 174–186. DOI: 10.14254/2071-8330.2021/14-4/12

Guenichi, H., & Benamou, S. (2010). World oil price, economic growth, inflation & interest rate relationships in Tunisia. *Energy Studies Review, 17*(2), 25–42. DOI: 10.15173/esr.v17i2.523

Hamdi, H., Sbia, R., Hakimi, A., & Hakimi, W. K. (2013). Multivariate Granger causality between foreign direct investment and economic growth in Tunisia. *Economic Bulletin, 33*(2), 1193–1203. http://www.accessecon.com/Pubs/EB/2013/Volume33/EB-13-V33-I2-P113.pdf

Helali, K., Ben Jedidia, K., & Boujelbène, T. (2021). Threshold effects of inflation on the financial development-economic growth nexus in Tunisia. *International Journal of Monetary Economics and Finance, 14*(5), 438–459. DOI: 10.1504/IJMEF.2021.118282

Herzer, D. (2012). How Does Foreign Direct Investment Really Affect Developing Countries' Growth? *Review of International Economics, 20*(2), 396–414. DOI: 10.1111/j.1467-9396.2012.01029.x

Hfaiedh, M. A., & Bardi, W. (2021). Does FDI and Corruption affect Environmental Quality in Tunisia? *International Journal of Energy Economics and Policy, 11*(4), 267–275. DOI: 10.32479/ijeep.11089

Hoffmaister, A. W., & Roldôs, J. E. (2001). The sources of macroeconomic fluctuations in developing countries: Brazil and Korea. *Journal of Macroeconomics, 23*(2), 213–239. DOI: 10.1016/S0164-0704(01)00162-8

Hossain, M. K., & Hossain, M. S. (2022). Causal Interaction between Foreign Direct Investment Inflows and China's Economic Growth. *Sustainability (Basel), 15*(10), 7994. DOI: 10.3390/su15107994

International Monetary Fund. (1996). Currency convertibility in Tunisia. IMF eLibrary. https://www.elibrary.imf.org/display/book/9781557755643/C06.xml

International Monetary Fund. (1999). Tunisia: Staff report for the Article IV consultation (Vol. 1999, Issue 104). International Monetary Fund. https://doi.org/DOI: 10.5089/9781451837766.002

International Monetary Fund. (2004). *Tunisia: 2004 Article IV consultation—Staff report; Public information notice on the Executive Board discussion; and statement by the Executive Director for Tunisia.* International Monetary Fund. https://www.imf.org/en/Publications/CR/Issues/2016/12/30/Tunisia-2004-Article-IV-Consultation-Staff-Report-Public-Information-Notice-on-the-18006

Kaminsky, G., Lizondo, S., & Reinhart, C. (1998). *Leading Indicators of Currency Crises. International Monetary Fund., 45.* Advance online publication. DOI: 10.1596/1813-9450-1852

Koop, G., Pesaran, M., & Potter, S. M. (1996). Impulse response analysis in nonlinear multivariate models. *Journal of Econometrics, 74*(1), 119–147. DOI: 10.1016/0304-4076(95)01753-4

Kurtishi-Kastrati, S. (2013). Impact of FDI on economic growth: An overview of the main theories of FDI and empirical research. *European Scientific Journal, 9*(7), 56–77. https://eujournal.org/index.php/esj/article/view/855/898

Makni, A. (2019). A macro-model to monetary transmission analysis in Tunisia. IHEID Working Papers 13-2019, Economics Section, The Graduate Institute of International Studies. https://repec.graduateinstitute.ch/pdfs/Working_papers/HEIDWP13-2019.pdf

Malec, K., Maitah, M., Rojik, S., Aragaw, A., & Fulnečková, P. R. (2024). Inflation, exchange rate, and economic growth in Ethiopia: A time series analysis. *International Review of Economics & Finance, 96*, 103561. DOI: 10.1016/j.iref.2024.103561
Malec, K., Maitah, M., Rojik, S., Aragaw, A., & Fulnečková, P. R. (2024). Inflation, exchange rate, and economic growth in Ethiopia: A time series analysis. *International Review of Economics & Finance, 96*, 103561. DOI: 10.1016/j.iref.2024.103561
Maza, A., & Hierro, M. (2024). Delving into the FDI-economic growth relationship at the regional level: Headquarters effect in FDI data. *International Review of Economics & Finance*, *97*, 103829. DOI: 10.1016/j.iref.2024.103829

Mundell, R. A. (1961). A Theory of Optimum Currency Areas. *The American Economic Review*, *51*, 657–665. https://www.jstor.org/stable/1812792

Mundell, R. A. (1963). Inflation and Real Interest. *Journal of Political Economy*, *71*(3), 280–283. DOI: 10.1086/258771

Nouira, R., Amor, T. H., & Rault, C. (2018). Oil price fluctuations and exchange rate dynamics in the MENA region: Evidence from Non-Causality-in-Variance and Asymmetric Non-Causality Tests. *The Quarterly Review of Economics and Finance*. Advance online publication. DOI: 10.1016/j.qref.2018.07.011

Olamide, E., Maredza, A., & Ogujiuba, K. (2021). Monetary Policy, External Shocks and Economic Growth Dynamics in East Africa: An S-VAR Model. *Sustainability (Basel)*, *14*(6), 3490. DOI: 10.3390/su14063490

Omay, T., & Öznur Kan, E. (2010). Re-examining the threshold effects in the inflation–growth nexus with cross-sectionally dependent non-linear panel: Evidence from six industrialized economies. *Economic Modelling*, *27*(5), 996–1005. DOI: 10.1016/j.econmod.2010.04.011

Omri, A., & Sassi-Tmar, A. (2015). Linking FDI inflows to economic growth in North African countries. *Journal of the Knowledge Economy*, *6*(1), 90–104. DOI: 10.1007/s13132-013-0172-5

Pesaran, H., & Shin, Y. (1998). Generalized impulse response analysis in linear multivariate models. *Economics Letters*, *58*(1), 17–29. DOI: 10.1016/S0165-1765(97)00214-0

Raddatz, C. (2007). Are external shocks responsible for the instability of output in low-income countries? *Journal of Development Economics*, *84*(1), 155–187. DOI: 10.1016/j.jdeveco.2006.11.001

Ramey, G., & Ramey, V. A. (1995). Cross-Country Evidence on the Link Between Volatility and Growth. *The American Economic Review*, *85*(5), 1138–1151. https://www.jstor.org/stable/2950979

Rand, J., & Tarp, F. (2002). Business Cycles in Developing Countries: Are They Different? *World Development*, *30*(12), 2071–2088. DOI: 10.1016/S0305-750X(02)00124-9

Rose, A. K. (2000). One money, one market: The effect of common currencies on trade. Economic Policy, 15(30), 8-45. DOI: 10.1111/1468-0327.00056

Sakli, H., Hniya, L., Lassoued, T., & Telmoudi, F. (2022). The effect of real exchange rate on economic growth: Evidence from Tunisia and Morocco. *Revue d'Economie Financiere*, *2022*(20), 971–977. DOI: 10.55365/1923.x2022.20.109

Samir, B. A., & Tarek, J. (2014). Exchange Rate Pass-Through in Tunisia: Evidence from a Time Varying Parameter Model. *Journal of Developing Areas*, *48*(1), 145–164. DOI: 10.1353/jda.2014.0007

Servén, L. (2003). Real Exchange-Rate Uncertainty and Private Investment in LDCS. *The Review of Economics and Statistics*, *85*(1), 212–218. DOI: 10.1162/rest.2003.85.1.212

Shu-ping, W., & Xiao-meng, W. (2017). Relationships between exchange rates, economic growth and FDI in China: An empirical study based on the TVP-VAR model. Littera Scripta, 10(1), 166-179. https://littera-scripta.com/wp-content/uploads/2019/05/Wang-1.pdf

Sijabat, R. (2023). The Association between Foreign Investment and Gross Domestic Product in Ten ASEAN Countries. *Economies*, *11*(7), 188. DOI: 10.3390/economies11070188

Stockhammar, P., & Österholm, P. (2016). The impact of US uncertainty shocks on small open economies. *Open Economies Review*, *28*(2), 347–368. DOI: 10.1007/s11079-016-9424-x

Stockman, A. C. (1985). Effects of Inflation on the Pattern of International Trade. *The Canadian Journal of Economics. Revue Canadienne d'Economique*, *18*(3), 587–601. DOI: 10.2307/135021

Thanh, S. D. (2015). Threshold effects of inflation on growth in the ASEAN-5 countries: A Panel Smooth Transition Regression approach. *Journal of Economics, Finance and Administrative Science*, *20*(38), 41–48. DOI: 10.1016/j.jefas.2015.01.003

Tobin, J. (1965). Money and Economic Growth. *Econometrica, 33*(4), 671–684. DOI: 10.2307/1910352

Vieira, F. V., Holland, M., Gomes da Silva, C., & Bottecchia, L. C. (2013). Growth and exchange rate volatility: A panel data analysis. *Applied Economics, 45*(26), 3733–3741. DOI: 10.1080/00036846.2012.730135

Zghidi, N., Sghaier, I. M., & Abida, Z. (2016). Does economic freedom enhance the impact of foreign direct investment on economic growth in North African countries? A panel data analysis. *African Development Review, 28*(1), 64–74. DOI: 10.1111/1467-8268.12167

KEY TERMS AND DEFINITIONS

Exchange Rate: The value of one currency expressed in terms of another currency, determining how much of one currency is needed to purchase a unit of another.

FDI (Foreign Direct Investment): Investments made by individuals, companies, or governments in a foreign country, typically to establish business operations, acquire assets, or gain management control in another country.

GDP (Gross Domestic Product): The total monetary value of all goods and services produced within a country's borders in a specific time period. It serves as a primary indicator of a country's economic performance.

Inflation: The rate at which the general level of prices for goods and services in an economy rises over a period of time, reducing the purchasing power of money.

Monetary Policy: The process by which central banks regulate the money supply, interest rates, and credit availability to achieve macroeconomic objectives such as controlling inflation, stabilizing the currency, and fostering economic growth.

Shock Transmission: The process by which economic disturbances or shocks (e.g., changes in monetary policy, external trade disruptions, financial shocks, sectoral shocks) in one sector, country, or variable are propagated in the economy or to other economies through different channels such as interest rates, exchange rates, credit rates and expectation channels.

TVP-VAR (Time-Varying Parameter Vector Autoregression): A statistical model that analyzes the dynamic relationships between multiple economic variables over time, allowing for changes in their interactions and coefficients due to structural shifts or economic conditions.

ENDNOTES

1. Detailed analyses of FDI contribution are discussed in the subsequent paragraphs.

2. To ensure stationarity in the studied data, we applied the first difference to all the studied variables. However, we use the third differencing for the EER variable. According to Augmented Dickey–Fuller (Said & Dickey, 1984) test, we reject the presence of unit roots in the series, confirming that all the variables are stationary.

Chapter 10
Economic Impact Assessment Through Input–Output Modeling:
The Case of Canada

Nesibe Varoglu
https://orcid.org/0000-0001-7473-3248
Istanbul University, Turkey

Aysel Varoglu
https://orcid.org/0000-0003-4629-4326
Independent Researcher, Canada

ABSTRACT

This study examines how economic impact analysis is conducted through the Input-Output Model. The paper discusses the structure of Input-Output tables in detail, examines the mathematical dimension of the model based on matrices, and discusses how multipliers are determined. Unlike other studies, after examining how all these variables are calculated, how the economic impact analysis is conducted is explained with examples from the Canadian economy. In other words, the mathematical and economic dimensions of the model are examined together, the Input-Output analysis is compared with other analyses, and a detailed contribution to the literature is made.

INTRODUCTION

The capitalist system, which is based on consumption, has triggered even more consumption with globalization and technological developments. The increase in demand not only increases the production of new products but also leads to the

DOI: 10.4018/979-8-3693-9765-7.ch010

emergence of new industries. Therefore, economic calculations have had to keep pace with the development. However, economic calculations such as Gross domestic product (GDP) only take into account the value of final goods and services and therefore do not allow for detailed economic analysis. Hence, Input-Output (I-O) Analysis, Computable General Equilibrium modeling (GCE), and Dynamic Stochastic General Equilibrium (DSGE) methods are preferred for economic impact assessment. Among these, I-O tables, which are very suitable for cross-sectoral analysis, continue to be used and developed, especially by developed economies. It is widely used in economies divided into provinces, such as the US and Canada, as it is suitable for macroeconomic analysis as well as detailed intra- and inter-provincial economic analysis. The analysis is frequently preferred not only in economic impact assessments but also in project evaluations.

Simon Kuznets, a Russian-American economist trying to make sense of the 1929 Great Depression and its impact on the economy, developed the GDP formula to recover the US economy after the crisis (Vanham, 2021). GDP is the total monetary or market value of all final goods and services produced within a country's borders within a specified period. (Bondarenko, 2024). Since the product produced in one sector can be an input to another sector, goods, and services are only included in the economy at the final stage in GDP. This is to avoid double counting. Since none of the GDP calculations provide information on inter-sectoral flows, but only calculate the value of final goods and services, inter-sectoral flows can only be seen through economic tables. The first economic table was the "Tableau Economique" created by the Quesnay in 1758. In the table, Quesnay showed the relationship between different economic sectors and the payment flow between them (Leontief, W. (1936). Leon Walras, influenced by Quesnay's economic picture, developed General Equilibrium analysis through Inter-industrial flows. Leontief, on the other hand, was inspired by Walras' analysis of maintaining general equilibrium through inter-industry flows in the I-O model (Horowitz & Planting, 2006-2009). I-O analysis, also known as the Leontief Model, was developed by Russian-American Professor Wassily Leontief in the late 1930s. Thanks to this analysis, Leontief was awarded the Nobel Prize in Economic Science in 1973 (Leontief, 1986).

I-O analysis is a macroeconomic analysis method that explains the interdependencies between different economic sectors and industries through the multiplier mechanism. In addition to industries and sectors, the model also includes macroeconomic indicators such as government spending, investment, imports, exports, and household consumption expenditures. The inclusion of all these variables allows the model to estimate the effects of economic shocks (positive or negative) and to analyze the fluctuation effects across the economy. The I-O model is therefore a highly efficient method for economic impact assessment to understand the aggregate change in an economy. On the other hand, the model has been criticized for some of its basic assumptions. One of the criticisms is the assumption that the relationship between industrial inputs and outputs is linear and constant. This assumption implies that the change in demand is also linear and constant. Within the structural design of the model, prices are assumed to remain fixed and the model outputs industry averages and average input costs for technology use (Christ, 1955). In contrast, CGE models include the supply side in the analysis, ensuring that prices are variable rather than fixed. Hence, it is possible to adjust both quantities and prices after a policy shock in CGE models (Scottish Government, 2016).

The I-O model does not include economies of scale and structural changes in production technologies and the model is static, which does not take into account the time needed for changes to take place (Christ, 1955). Despite all these criticisms, the model is still widely used in advanced economies such as the US, Canada and Australia, as well as in New Zealand and some European and Asian countries because, unlike other economic calculations, it allows for a detailed economic assessment that takes into account inter-sectoral flows. This is why this study was conducted.

This paper is organized as follows. The first section provides an overview of related literature on I-O modeling with a focus on economic impact assessment. The second section describes the data and methods used in this paper and explains the methodological approach of the I-O Model. It discusses the Structure of I-O Tables, Type I and Type II Multipliers, direct effects, indirect effects, induced effects. The third section provides the techno-economic background for I-O analysis by calculating multipliers and their effects through matrices. In this section, technical coefficients are derived for the sectors in the table, the Leontief Inverse Matrix (I-A)-1, simple multipliers, and total multipliers are calculated. In the wake of this, output multipliers, income multipliers, employment multipliers, and value-added multipliers are found to calculate the total effects on the economy. Apart from that, it is presented as well how to calculate cumulative effects. In the fourth section, an economic impact assessment is made using multipliers from Statistic Canada and the Government of Alberta. Finally, the fifth section delves into the core findings of the study and actionable recommendations are provided based on these insights.

LITERATURE REVIEW

The study "Research on the Development of Textile Industry in Shandong Province Based on I-O Model" written by Qi Xiaonan and Cai Jun (2022)" examined the relationship between the textile industry sector in Shandong Province and other industrial sectors in the province using the I-O analysis table of Shandong Province in 2017 and they concluded that the textile industry has a great radiation effect on other industries in Shandong province. The textile industry in the province belongs to the type II intermediate product type industry sector, which has a strong driving force on the upstream industry, and the downstream industry is also more dependent on it. That's why authors have concluded that it should increase government support to the textile industry, and prioritize the development of the textile industry to stimulate the growth of total social demand (Xiaonan & Jun, 2022).

The study “Identifying the Role of Knowledge-Intensive Business Services in the Korean Economy as a Sustainable Innovation Tool Using the I–O Analysis (2024)” written by Yong Jae Shin investigated the impact of knowledge-intensive business services (KIBSs) on the Korean economy and which industries are more significantly impacted by KIBS sectors. According to the study, KIBS is a growing sector, in the Korean economy. The total output has grown at an average annual rate of 9.6% over the past 10 years indicating that the demand for KIBSs in other industries is increasing. The study claimed indicators have emerged that clearly demonstrate distinct roles within the South Korean economic system based on the type of KIBS, all KIBSs were classified as medium-demand manufacturing, with forward linkage effects higher than the standard value of one and backward linkage effects lower than one. Furthermore, the author found that The KIBS sector was found to have a high production inducement effect on other industries and affected secondary and tertiary industries evenly (Jae Shin, 2024).

The paper “French Economy and Clean Energy Transition: A Macroeconomic Multi-Objective Extended I-O Analysis (2024)” has used I-O analysis to focus on the influence of several current macroeconomic parameters such as value add, GDP, employment, energy consumption, and CO2 emissions on each other and on the French economy and examined various scenarios for clean energy transition, with the aim of reducing pollution intensity within the electricity grid of the French economy. Using dynamic analysis, the study finds that “Air Transport” is the first sector where a cut in final demand would optimize the sustainability of the economy. The 75% substitution of fossil fuels with clean energy sources in the French economy provides evidence that the 'Air Transport' sector continues to hold the position of the first-largest contributor.

However, the electricity sector ranked 5th before the 75% substitution of fossil fuels by clean energies and 7th afterward. This indicates that the regulation of this sector will indeed lead to a reduction in CO2 emissions along with a higher GDP (Lochot, Khalilpour, Sánchez, & F.A. Hoadley, 2024).

METHODOLOGY

In this study, the economic impact assessment was made with I-O analysis. The mathematical structure of the I-O table is presented in Figure 1, which offers a brief overview of its components. The basic I-O relationship is mathematically represented as X = L.Y, where X is total output, L is the Leontief Inverse Matrix ($(I - A)^{-1}$) and Y is final demand. (Leontief Inverse Matrix derived from Z).

Figure 1. Basic Framework of the I-O Table

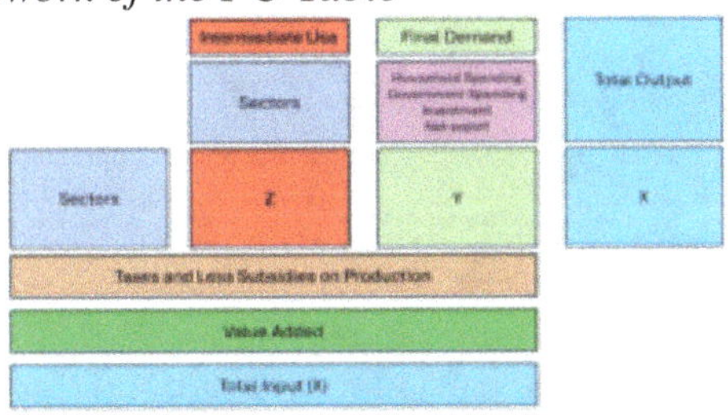

Source. Created by the authors.

I-O tables reflect the I-O characteristics of a specific economy, or selected countries, regions, or provinces over a defined period. In the paper, the I-O table represents an economy. The table data is obtained from Statistics Canada's 2020 utilization table at basic prices and consists of industries, final demand, value-added, total output, and total input.

STRUCTURE OF I-O TABLE

Inter-industry relations in the model are reflected in the economy through multipliers. The concept of multiplier is a macroeconomic term that can be defined as an economic factor that, when changed in an economy, causes changes in many other related economic variables. The concept was first introduced into economic theory in the paper 'The Relation of Household Investment to Unemployment' written by R.F. Kahn. Multiplier effects measure the impact of a change in economic activity, such as investment or spending, on total economic output. This means that, in an I-O model, it is necessary to estimate economic multipliers for specific industries to understand the flow of products and resources within a given economy and between that economy and the outside world (Hughes, 2018). The model uses I-O tables, which are a combination of several matrices with data covering the supply chain for all sectors. In economic terms, the data in each column corresponds to the inputs used in the production function of that sector. From a mathematical point of view, the main matrix in the table illustrates the input components used in the production of a sector. In other words, in this model, the output of one industrial sector becomes the input of another industrial sector (Leontief 1986). Figure 2 outlines the general structure of the model.

Figure 2. I-O Table Structure

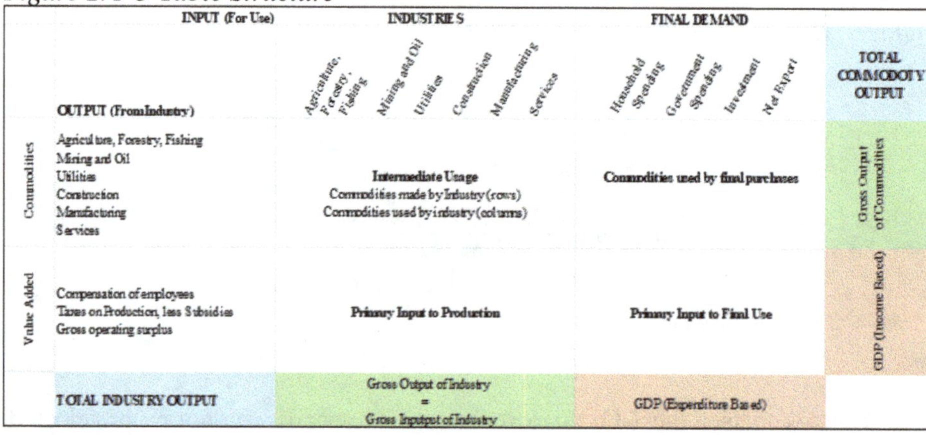

Source. Horowitz & Planting, 2009.

The mathematical structure of the model is explained by the formula $X = (I - A)^{-1} .Y$. The components of the formula are; gross output (X), the identity matrix (I), the technical coefficient Matrix (A) which describes the units of intermediate goods required to produce one unit of gross output, the Leontief inverse matrix (L) refers to the total output required to produce one unit of goods for final demand, and another component is final demand (Y) (Nugroho, 2022).

According to model assumptions, in the I-O table, gross industrial output must be equal to gross industrial input. The output of goods is the sum of the goods used as inputs and those used by the final buyers. The sum of the total industry use of primary factors and the total final demand use of primary factors should equal income-based GDP. The sum of the total final demand for all commodities, including primary factors across all sectors, should equal expenditure-based GDP. Furthermore, income-based GDP must equal expenditure-based GDP (NWT Bureau of Statistics, 2006). The general structure of the table is as seen in Figure 2. However, countries and provinces develop the sectors part of the table according to their industrial structures and the final consumption part according to their economic structures. For example, the Australian Government has used the table, as presented in Figure 3, in line with its particular needs.

Figure 3. Structure of Australian I-O Tables

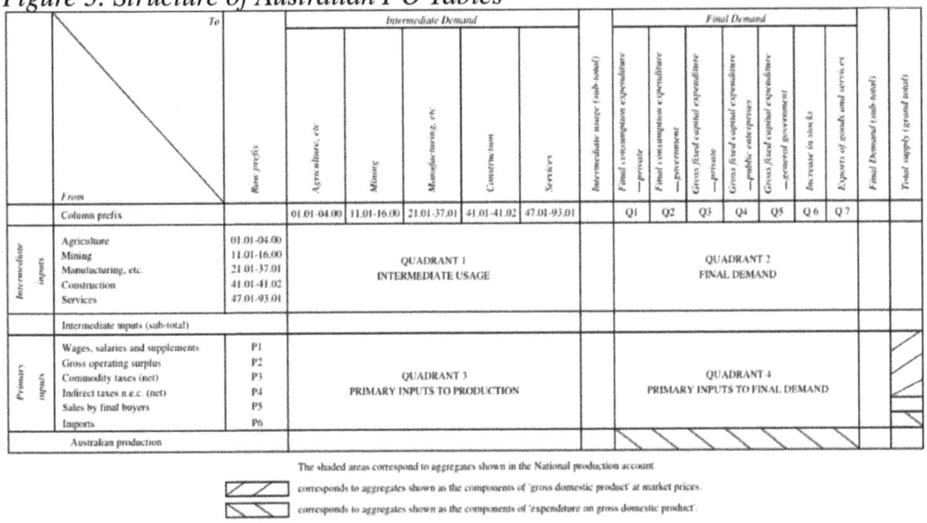

Source. McLennan, 1996-1997.

Multipliers and The Types of Effects

The I-O model accounts for three effects. The first of these is the direct effect, which illustrates the impact of the initial change in spending following an economic shock. The second is the indirect effect or the secondary effect, that is any effect resulting from employment. The third is the induced effect, which occurs as a result of the consumption of goods and services by workers who create employment in production (Hughes, 2018). The I-O model contains two types of multipliers, Type I and Type II. Direct and indirect effects are calculated through these multipliers. In some sources, Type I multipliers are called simple multipliers, and Type II multipliers are called total multipliers.

In the direct effect

If there is an increase in final demand, producers will increase the production of that good to meet the increased demand.

In the indirect effect

As the demand for intermediate goods will increase as a result of the increased production within the scope of the direct effect, the increase in demand will continue throughout the supply chain. The sum of direct and indirect effects is also calculated via the Type I inverse matrix (NISRA, 2024).

Type I Multipliers

These multipliers indicate how much of each industry's output is needed to produce one unit of output of a given industry. In the Type I Multiplier, the effects of household consumption expenditures are not included. This means there is no induced effect. The indirect and purely industry-based multiplier effect is divided by the direct effect (Hughes, 2018).

The calculation is; Type I Multiplier = (Direct + Indirect) / Direct

Type II Multipliers

These multipliers are the type of multiplier that includes the effects of household consumption expenditures. In this multiplier, the sum of the direct effect, indirect effect, and induced effect is divided by the direct effect (Hughes, 2018).

The calculation is; Type II Multiplier = (Direct + Indirect + Induced) / Direct

CALCULATION OF MULTIPLIERS AND THEIR EFFECTS THROUGH MATRICES

How the multipliers are determined using the data in Table 1 is examined.

Table 1. Basic Transaction Table

	INDUSTRIES						FINAL DEMAND					
	Agriculture Fishing Forestry	Mining, Quarrying, and Oil and Gas Extraction	Utilities	Construction	Manufacturing	Services	Household Consumption Expenditure	Governments Consumption Expenditure	Gross Fixed Capital Formation	Changes in Inventories	Export	Total use ((Gross Output at basic Prices))
Agriculture fishing forestry	18,674.1	122.3	30.4	1,067.3	49,542.0	2,439.0	6,533.7	7,187.5	3,811.2	13,627.1	19,104.9	122,139.6
Mining quarrying and oil and gas extraction	2,676.3	14,202.2	2,608.0	9,796.5	70,470.3	3,345.6	2,130.5	2,143.5	945.4	1,168.7	294.3	109,681.3
Utilities	2,333.4	3,439.4	506.8	329.3	21,233.1	4,577.6	1,016.0	1,756.0	2,243.6	596.0	1,266.6	39,297.7
Construction	4,421.1	2,586.8	2,860.2	142.6	2,028.9	41,927.6	29,046.1	21,443.2	23,694.8	659.9	23,575.6	182,626.9
Manufacturing	36,154.9	23,046.8	3,571.2	80,577.4	286,439.2	86,765.7	12,049.1	14,049.1	13,237.0	106,059.7	12,626.5	674,576.4
Service	11,123.3	31,004.2	27,985.0	59,846.0	77,712.8	710,602.1	1,342.0	1,342.0	466.1	244.3	799.7	922,466.5
Import	1,516.9	205.3	403.8	512.4	745.2	150.1	-4,614.9	-4,412.4	-4,449.7	-4,562.0	-1,130.0	
Net taxes on Products	1,465.3	2,055.4	203.6	68.2	8,043.5	15,133.3	-4,858.5	-3,365.3	-1,687.0	-1,453.2		
Total Intermediate Use	78,395.4	76,662.4	38,169.0	152,338.7	516,214.8	864,941.0						
Compensation of Employees	11,742.5	24,081.5	332.0	115.0	125,165.0	57,007.1						
Gross Operating Surplus	29,978.4	7,124.0	644.4	25.7	33,082.1	424.2						
Net taxes on Production	2,023.2	863.4	152.3	147.5	164.5	94.2						
Gross Value-added at basic prices	43,744.1	33,018.8	1,128.7	288.2	158,361.6	57,525.5						
TOTAL (Gross Output at basic Prices)	122,139.6	109,681.3	39,297.7	182,626.9	674,576.4	922,466.5	42,644.0	40,143.6	38,401.4	116,340.4	56,537.6	

Source. The table is derived from Statistics Canada's 2020 usage table at basic prices, with changes made to some figures and inputs. Matrix A is derived from the red-framed area.

Each value in the column is divided by the total expenditure value under that column to find the multipliers, which is the first step in making an economic impact assessment using the I-O model. For instance, in Table 1, the agricultural, fishing, and forestry multiplier is 18,674.1 / 122,039.05 = 0.15. The multipliers derived from the table are called "technical coefficients". The technical coefficients calculate the input requirement of any increase in output. In our example, we will obtain Matrix A for six sectors from the technical coefficients. Mathematically, Matrix A (6*6) is as follows.

Figure 4. Matrix A

$$A = \begin{bmatrix} a11 & a12 & a13 & a14 & a15 & a16 \\ a21 & a22 & a23 & a24 & a25 & a26 \\ \cdots & \cdots & \cdots & \cdots & \cdots & \cdots \\ \cdots & \cdots & \cdots & \cdots & \cdots & \cdots \\ \cdots & \cdots & \cdots & \cdots & \cdots & \cdots \\ a61 & a62 & a63 & a64 & a65 & a66 \end{bmatrix}$$

Table 2 presents the technical coefficients obtained from Table 1.

Table 2. Technical Coefficients Table

	Agriculture, Fishing Forestry	Mining, Quarrying, Oil and Gas Extraction	Utilities	Construction	Manufacturing	Services	Household Consumption Expenditure
Agriculture Fishing Forestry	0.153	0.001	0.001	0.007	0.073	0.003	0.153
Mining, Quarrying, Oil and Gas Extraction	0.022	0.129	0.066	0.064	0.104	0.004	0.050
Utilities	0.019	0.031	0.013	0.002	0.031	0.005	0.024
Construction	0.036	0.024	0.073	0.001	0.003	0.045	0.681
Manufacturing	0.296	0.210	0.091	0.528	0.425	0.094	0.283
Services	0.091	0.283	0.712	0.392	0.115	0.770	0.031
Compensation of Employees	0.096	0.227	0.008	0.001	0.186	0.062	-

Source. Data processed by the authors.

In order to produce an extra dollar's worth of output from the utilities industries, the mining, quarrying, and oil and gas extraction industries must have produced an extra $0.066 worth of output, and the construction industry must have produced an extra $0.073 worth of output. In short, as seen in the table, extra output from one industry will cause extra output in all industries of the economy. With the aim of calculating the simple multipliers, we select six rows and columns of the Technical Coefficient Table and create A Matrix (6*6) in Table 3. In some sources, Matrix A can be referred to as an intermediate-use matrix.

Table 3. Matrix A

	1	2	3	4	5	6
(1) Agriculture Fishing Forestry	0.15	0.00	0.00	0.01	0.07	0.00
(2) Mining, Quarrying, and Oil and Gas Extraction	0.02	0.13	0.07	0.06	0.10	0.00
(3) Utilities	0.02	0.03	0.01	0.00	0.03	0.00
(4) Construction	0.04	0.02	0.07	0.00	0.00	0.05
(5) Manufacturing	0.30	0.21	0.09	0.53	0.42	0.09
(6) Services	0.09	0.28	0.71	0.39	0.12	0.77

Source. Data processed by the authors.

In Table 4, we set up a Matrix I (6*6) with all its diagonal elements equal to 1 and all its other elements equal to zero in order to calculate a Matrix (I – A).

Table 4. The Identity Matrix (Matrix I)

1	0	0	0	0	0
0	1	0	0	0	0
0	0	1	0	0	0
0	0	0	1	0	0
0	0	0	0	1	0
0	0	0	0	0	1

Source. Data processed by the authors.

Table 5 presents a Matrix (I-A).

Table 5. Matrix (I-A)

	1	2	3	4	5	6
(1) Agriculture Fishing Forestry	0.85	- 0.00	- 0.00	- 0.01	- 0.07	- 0.00
(2) Mining, Quarrying, and Oil and Gas Extraction	- 0.02	0.87	- 0.07	- 0.06	- 0.10	- 0.00
(3) Utilities	- 0.02	- 0.03	0.99	- 0.00	- 0.03	- 0.00
(4) Construction	- 0.04	- 0.02	- 0.07	1.00	- 0.00	- 0.05
(5) Manufacturing	- 0.30	- 0.21	- 0.09	- 0.53	0.58	- 0.09
(6) Services	- 0.09	- 0.28	- 0.71	- 0.39	- 0.12	0.23

Source. Data processed by the authors.

In Table 6, Leontief's inverse matrix is computed using the matrix inversion function, followed by the calculation of the column sums. These are simple multipliers. The Leontief inverse matrix represents the ratio of total output change to final demand change for Type I and its calculation is as follows;

Table 6. Leontief Inverse Matrix $(I-A)^{-1}$ for Type I

	1	2	3	4	5	6
(1) Agriculture Fishing Forestry	1.29	0.12	0.15	0.20	0.23	0.15
(2) Mining, Quarrying, and Oil and Gas Extraction	0.20	1.33	0.32	0.36	0.33	0.24
(3) Utilities	0.08	0.10	1.10	0.10	0.11	0.09
(4) Construction	0.14	0.18	0.33	1.21	0.14	0.31
(5) Manufacturing	1.18	1.19	1.53	1.99	2.50	1.48
(6) Services	1.84	2.88	5.20	3.89	2.31	6.25

Source. Data processed by the authors.

In calculating simple multipliers (Type I) household consumption expenditures are excluded from the model. This means that there is no interaction between the household sector and other sectors. That's why it's called the open model. On the other hand, since the household sector and wages are also included in the model in calculating the total multipliers (Type II), household consumption expenditures are linked to other sectors in the economy. Therefore, the model is called a closed model. Consumption-induced effects are obtained by subtracting simple multipliers from the total multipliers (McLennan, 1996-1997). In other words, Type II contains the induced effect as well as the Type I components. The induced effect is the demand created by the household to meet its consumption and provides a monetary return to the economy. Hence, when determining the technical coefficients matrix in Type II, it is necessary to include the compensation of employees row and the household consumption expenditures column in addition to the Type I components. Since the Type II technical coefficient matrix has 7 rows and 7 columns, the identity matrix should taken as 7*7. All other steps are performed in the same way as in Type I. The total factors are obtained from this 7*7 matrix. For convenience, this matrix can be called the B matrix. After Type I and Type II multipliers are found, output, income, employment, and GDP multipliers must also be found to calculate the total effects on the economy.

Output Multipliers

Type I output multiplier is the sum of all outputs from each domestic industry to produce an additional unit of output in an industry. This sum is obtained from the column sums of the Type I Leontief inverse matrix. Similarly, Type II output multipliers are obtained from the column sums of the Type II Leontief inverse matrix (Scottish Government, 2023). Table 7 displays the output multipliers by sector, respectively (The following output multipliers are simple output multipliers from Type I. The output multipliers obtained from Type II are called total output multipliers).

Table 7. Output Multipliers for Type I

Agriculture, Fishing, Forestry	4.73
Mining, Quarrying, and Oil and Gas Extraction	5.80
Utilities	8.64
Construction	7.73
Manufacturing	5.61
Services	8.52

Source. Data processed by the authors.

Industrial support effects are obtained by subtracting the initial effects and first-round effects from the simple multiplier. Production-induced effects also are found by adding the first-round effects to industrial support effects (McLennan, 1996-1997).

Income Multipliers

The income multiplier calculates the total value of income from workers' wages required to meet the demand for one dollar of final output. This impact on employees' employment or compensation is designated as the income impact (McLennan, 1996-1997). In this paper; compensation of employees' coefficients (w), and total input (X). Income Multipliers are obtained from w/ X . L (Cassar, 2015).

Table 8 displays the income multipliers by sector, respectively (The following income multipliers are simple income multipliers from Type I. The income multipliers obtained from Type II are called total income multipliers). Total income multipliers are obtained by multiplying the technical coefficients of compensation of employees by Matrix B. The first round of income effects is obtained by multiplying the technical coefficients of employees' by Matrix A (McLennan, 1996-1997).

Table 8. Income Multipliers

Agriculture, Fishing, Forestry	0.50
Mining, Quarrying, and Oil and Gas Extraction	0.71
Utilities	0.70
Construction	0.71
Manufacturing	0.70
Services	0.73

Source. Data processed by the authors.

Employment Multipliers

To find employment multipliers, employment coefficients must first be found. Employment coefficients are found by dividing the number of people employed in a particular industry by the level of output. After that, employment multipliers are obtained by using the formula of Lb/X . L (Sukma et al., 2018). In this paper, Lb represents labour.

Value-Added Multipliers

Value-added multipliers are calculated just like income multipliers. The multipliers in question are obtained from Gross Value Added/X.L for each sector (Cassar, 2015). Table 9 presents the value-added multipliers for each sector, respectively.

Table 9. Value-Added Multipliers

Agriculture, Fishing, Forestry	0.92
Mining, Quarrying, and Oil and Gas Extraction	0.90
Utilities	0.87
Construction	0.89
Manufacturing	0.91
Services	0.87

Source. Data processed by the authors.

Calculating Cumulative Effects

As per the assumption of the model, the total sector output change (ΔX) must be equal to the final demand change (ΔY). For this reason, after an external shock in order to calculate cumulative effects, the first round effect is found by multiplying the change in output by Matrix A. The second round effect is obtained by multiplying the first round effect by Matrix A. The third round effect is obtained by multiplying the second round effect by Matrix A. In this way, the total effect is reached with increasing summation. The total impact consists of the sum of direct impacts and indirect impacts (Elhan-Kayalar and Oum, 2022).

ECONOMIC IMPACT ASSESSMENT

Assuming that the Government of Canada increases residential building construction by $5 million due to the escalating housing crisis, the economic impact assessment would be as follows. Multipliers are from Statistic Canada and the type of multipliers is total. In multipliers that measure impacts on the Canadian economy, impacts on output, GDP, and labour income are expressed per dollar of output change, while employment impacts are expressed as the number of jobs per

$1,000,000 of output. The calculation in our example was made accordingly as well (Statcan, 2024).

The impact on Output: 2.095* $5,000,000 = $ 10,475,000

The impact on Labour Income: 0.592 * $5,000,000 = $ 2,960,000

The impact on GDP at Basic Prices: 0.983 * $5,000,000 = $ 4,915,000

Employment Required: 8.527 * ($5,000,000 /$1,000,000) = 43 Jobs

In another example, assuming that a factory will be established in Alberta in 2024 in the non-residential building construction industry at $4 million (at basic prices). While the cost of industrial machines is 2 million dollars, the economic effects of the project in 2024 will be as follows.

The impact on GDP at Basic Prices: 0.716 * $4,000,000 = $ 2,864,000

The impact on Labour Income: 0.505 * $4,000,000 = $ 2,020,000

Employment Required: 5.4 * ($4,000,000 /$1,000,000) = 22 Jobs

The effects of commercial and service sector machinery purchases in 2024 are as follows;

Total value of Alberta machinery: 0.112 * $2,000,000 = $224,000

The impact on GDP at basic prices: 0.466* $224,000 = $104,384

The impact on labour income: 0.329 * $224,000 = $73,696

Employment required: 2.7 * ($224,000 /1,000,000) = less than 1 Job.

The multipliers in our example are from the Government of Alberta and the type of multipliers is total. In multipliers that measure impacts on the Alberta economy, impacts on output, GDP, and labour income are expressed per dollar of output change, while employment impacts are expressed as the number of jobs per $1,000,000 of output. The calculation in our example was made accordingly as well (Alberta Government, 2024). When the results are interpreted, it is seen that the Government of Alberta gained economic benefit from Project 1 and the purchase of industrial machinery within the scope of the project.

CONCLUSION AND RECOMMENDATIONS

This study discusses in detail how economic impact analysis is carried out through the I-O model. The structural details of the I-O tables are provided, the mathematical dimension of the model is examined through matrices, and how the multipliers are determined is explained. In addition to all these, the economic impact analysis is elucidated by means of examples. The I-O model is frequently preferred in predicting and analyzing the effects of positive or negative economic shocks and economic fluctuations. Changes in the output of sectors with strong forward and backward linkages have the greatest impact on the economy and are affected to a greater extent by changes in the general level of economic activity. Since I-O tables are a powerful analytical tool, they are used to determine production, demand structure, employment, prices, and costs, as well as export, import, and investment rates. I-O economics, when applied at high sectoral and spatial resolution, successfully analyzes trade relations between countries and sectors and predicts changes in production technologies and consumption patterns that may be caused by policies. The model is also commonly utilized in sensitivity analysis. Apart from that, I-O analysis is highly efficient in structural domain analysis such as energy and environment. The I-O analysis enables the calculation of the energy content of products in intermediate and final demand and to calculate energy demand through energy matrices. With I-O analysis, it is possible to identify direct and indirect pollution sources using data on emissions in I-O tables, and to conduct environmental analysis by calculating the pollution content in final demand.

It is advised to employ that the I-O model together with Cost-Benefit Analysis to determine which project is more efficient when comparing alternative investments. Along with this one, in calculating major changes that have a significant impact on the economy by changing the flow of goods, services, and labour, CGE modeling must preferred because it takes into account resource constraints in the economy and can effectively deal with large investments and structural policy changes. Moreover, CGE models are stronger than macro-econometric forecasting models incorporating time series data and economic theory in that they deal with detailed industrial data. However, for the most comprehensive calculations, DSGE should be preferred. Because, in addition to having many common features with CGE models, the model focuses on shorter-term effects. That's why, it is a more dynamic model.

REFERENCES

Alberta Government. (2024). Open Government Program, https://open.alberta.ca/dataset?tags=GDP&dataset_type=publications&dataset_type=publications

Bondarenko, P. (2024). Gross Domestic Product. *Encyclopedia Britannica*. https://www.britannica.com/money/gross-domestic-product

Cassar, I. P. (2015). Estimates Of Output, Income, Value Added And Employment Multipliers For The Maltese Economy, Central Bank of Malta, 2015.

Christ, C. F. (1955). A review of I-O analysis. *I-O analysis: An appraisal*, (p.137-182). Princeton University Press: the National Bureau of Economic Research. https://www.nber.org/system/files/chapters/c2866/c2866.pdf

Elhan-Kayalar, Y. And Oum, S. (2022). Estimating the Job Creation Impact of Development Assistance. Manila: Asian Development Bank. https://www.adb.org/sites/default/files/publication/850336/job-creation-impact-development-assistance.pdf

Horowitz, K. J., & Planting, M. A. (2009). *Concepts and Methods of the U.S. I-O Accounts. The U.S. Bureau of Economic Analysis of the U.S.* Department of Commerce., https://www.bea.gov/sites/default/files/methodologies/IOmanual_092906.pdf

Hughes, D. (2018). *A Primer in Economic Multipliers and Impact Analysis Using I-O Models*. University of Tennessee, Department of Agricultural & Resource Economics., https://utia.tennessee.edu/publications/wp-content/uploads/sites/269/2023/10/W644.pdf

Jae Shin, Y. (2024). Identifying the Role of Knowledge-Intensive Business Services in the Korean Economy as a Sustainable Innovation Tool Using Input–Output Analysis. *Sustainability (Basel)*, *16*(5), 1823. Advance online publication. DOI: 10.3390/su16051823

Leontief, W. (1936). Quantitative Input and Output Relations in the Economic Systems of the United States. *The Review of Economics and Statistics*, *18*(3), 105–125. DOI: 10.2307/1927837

Leontief, W. (1986). *I-O Economics* (2nd ed.). Oxford University Press.

Lochot, V., Khalilpour, K., Sánchez, D., & Hoadley, F. A. (2024). French economy and clean energy transition: A macroeconomic multi-objective extended I-O analysis. *Sustainable Futures : An Applied Journal of Technology, Environment and Society*, *8*, 100285. Advance online publication. DOI: 10.1016/j.sftr.2024.100285

McLennan, W. (1996-97). Information Paper: Australian National Accounts Introduction to I-O Multipliers, Catalog No.5246.0. Australian Bureau of Statistics

Nugroho, Y. D. (2022). Analysis of I-O Table: Identifying Leading Sectors in Indonesia (Case Study in 2010, 2016 and 2020). *Proceedings of The International Conference on Data Science and Official Statistics*, 2021(1), 985–997. doi:DOI: 10.34123/icdsos.v2021i1.251

NISRA (North Ireland Statistic and Research Agency). (2024). The Analytical I-O tables. https://www.nisra.gov.uk/statistics/economic-accounts-project/analytical-I -O -tables

NWT Bureau of Statistics (2006). NWT I-O Model – An Overview –, NWT Bureau of Statistics Government of the Northwest Territories, June 2006.

Scottish Government. (2016). *Computable General Equilibrium (CGE) Modelling and SG's CGE Model.* Scottish Government.

Scottish Government. (2023). Supply, Use and I-O Tables. https://www.gov.scot/ publications/about-supply-use-I-O -tables/pages/user-guide-multipliers

Statcan (2024). I-O multipliers, detail level. *Statistics Canada.* https://www150.statcan .gc.ca/t1/tbl1/en/tv.action?pid=3610059401&pickMembers%5B0%5D=2.5& pickMembers%5B1%5D=4.25&cubeTimeFrame.startYear=2020&cubeTimeFrame .endYear=2020&referencePeriods=20200101%2C20200101

Sukma, M., Hartono, D., & Prihawantoro, S. (2018). The Impacts Analysis of Creative-Products Export on the Economy. *JEJAK, 11*(1), 92–107. DOI: 10.15294/ jejak.v11i1.11337

Vanham, P. (2021). A brief history of GDP-and what could come next, The World Economic Forum, 2022. https://www.weforum.org/agenda/2021/12/stakeholder -capitalism-episode-1-a-brief-history-of-gdp/

Xiaonan, Q., & Jun, C. (2022). Research on the Development of Textile Industry in Shandong Province Based on I-O Model. *Information Systems and Economics (2022) Clausius Scientific Press*, ISSN 2523-6407 Vol. 3 Num. 4, DOI: DOI: 10.23977/ infse.2022.030402

Chapter 11
RBI's Decision of Moratorium and Trust of Middleclass Depositors in India:
An Analytical Study

Nitin Bansal
https://orcid.org/0000-0001-5514-2194
Banasthali Vidyapeeth, India

ABSTRACT

Reserve Bank of India sometimes takes the decision to impose moratorium on specific bank for short term after identification of any unfair practices in the banking system. RBI has to take the permission from the Government of India to impose a moratorium on a specific banking institution for a specific time frame to minimize the effect of irregularities and safeguard the interest of the depositors. This research paper focused on to examine the impact of RBI's decision to impose moratorium on specific bank on the trust of middle-class depositors in the Indian context. A self-structured questionnaire has been used to collect the data from the bank's customers from the Delhi region. 474 useful schedules were considered and analyzed through statistical tools. The study revealed that moratorium is having a significant negative impact on the trust level of the middle-class depositors and customers avoid maintaining their accounts in such banks in the future.

DOI: 10.4018/979-8-3693-9765-7.ch011

INTRODUCTION

The moratorium is derived from the Latin word moratorius which means tending to delay or authorizing delay of payment. Moratorium word usually refers to the legal postponement of payment. Initially, RBI imposed a moratorium for six months on Punjab and Maharashtra Co-operative Bank Limited (PMC) on 23rd September 2019 (Arekar, 2019). RBI restricted the bank customers to withdraw up to Rs. 1,000 only during the moratorium period. PMC Bank was also not allowed to sanction any loan, renewal of loans and advances, incur any liability, borrowal of funds, investments, and disburse any payment. RBI put all these restrictions under section 35A of the Banking Regulation Act.

Mathew and Verma (2020) stated that RBI imposed a moratorium on Lakhsmi Vilas Bank on 17th November 2020 for 30 days period. RBI restricted the bank to pay more than Rs. 25,000 to any customer without permission during the moratorium period. RBI has assured the bank's customers that their money is safe and their interests will be protected. Bank's capital had been eroded during the last three years because of continuous losses. Bank tried to raise the funds from external sources, but could not raise the funds and continuous withdrawal of funds by depositors raised liquidity concerns. RBI had to merge Lakhsmi Vilas Bank with DBS India to safeguard the interest of the depositors. This merger vanished the infusion of more capital as the balance sheet of the merged entity has a healthy balance sheet, adequate capital adequacy ratio, and common entity Tier 1 capital.

Kumar (2020) stated that regulator of banks in India i.e., RBI has the power to be permitted by the government of India to impose a moratorium for a specific period. During the moratorium period, depositors of the bank cannot withdraw the funds at will as the ceiling restricts the bank's customers to withdraw the amount beyond a specified amount. Basu (2003) stated that disbursement of the loan and advance without precise knowledge of the borrower and projects emerges the probabilities of non-payment and loans convert into non-performing assets. During the last two years, RBI had to impose restrictions (moratorium) on three private banks back-to-back in India.

Dayal (2020) stated that Banking Regulation Act 1949 allowed the RBI to impose the moratorium on Yes Bank under section 45. Sood (2020) mentioned that RBI had superseded the management of Yes Bank Limited on 5th March 2020 and imposed a moratorium of one month. RBI restricted the bank to pay more than Rs. 50,000 per customer without its permission. Yes Bank's financial position was declined during the last two years. Bank was trying to raise the funds to address the liquidity crisis and loan losses, but the bank failed to infuse any capital as investors were having high-risk probabilities in investment with Yes Bank Ltd. RBI had to impose the moratorium to safeguard the interest of the depositors. Then RBI bailed out Yes bank where major investment was done by the SBI and some other major banks collectively. Banking customers need a comprehensive training program to adopt the digital banking services, so, RBI and the Government of India should provide the training to bank's customers to enhance adoption rate (Bansal, 2020a; Bansal et al., 2022).

The moratorium is a short-term solution and meanwhile, RBI needs to safeguard the interest of the depositors. RBI intervenes in the business activities of banks when RBI finds irregularities in the banking operations, liquidity concerns, and any other major concern in front of banks.

Research Gap

Many researchers have researched banking aspects like profitability of banks, impacts of non-performing assets, liquidity management of banks, and many more, but no study has been conducted in past in the context of moratorium's effect on middle-class customers. This study has focused on this missing aspect as the last two years have evidenced a major financial crisis to middle-class customers in India because of the moratorium imposed by RBI. RBI imposed a moratorium on 3 banking institutions and restricted the customers to withdraw their funds beyond a certain amount during the last two years.

Objectives

1. To identify the numerous factors of moratorium having an impact on the trust level of middle-class depositors in India.
2. To study the effect of the restriction on funds withdrawal due to moratorium on the trust level of middle-class depositors in India.
3. To study the effect of the period of moratorium on the trust level of middle-class depositors in India.
4. To study the effect of irregularities in banking services on the trust level of middle-class depositors in India.
5. To study the effect of the failure of corporate governance on the trust level of middle-class depositors in India.
6. To study the effect of the role of bank staff on the trust level of middle-class depositors in India.
7. To study the effect of the negative image of banks due to moratorium on the trust level of middle-class depositors in India.

LITERATURE REVIEW

Mathew and Verma (2020) stated that RBI decided to restrict the Lakshmi Vilas Bank (LVB) customers to avail the banking services for 30 days as RBI imposed moratorium after the failures of Punjab and Maharashtra Co-Operative Bank Limited, IL&FS, DHFL, and Yes Bank Limited on 17th November 2020. They mentioned that LVB has booked its one-fourth of advances as bad debts. LVB's gross non-performing assets were 25.4 percent of the bank's total advances. Depositors are withdrawing their funds continuously which has raised the liquidity crisis. Bank tried to raise the funds but could not raise adequate funds to meet out its liquidity crisis. RBI has merged LVB with DBS India to safeguard the interest of the depositors, but equity share capital has been written off. So, all the investors who invested in the shares of LVB, have lost their money. Nair (2020) stated that RBI has merged Lakshmi Vilas Bank with DBS Bank India (DBIL). This merger is effective from 27th November 2020 as earlier the moratorium was for 30days, but RBI has merged the bank and lifted the moratorium before the expiry of the period. Password management strategies are highly crucial to hance the trust level of the bank's customers. Most of the people are now using digital services, and to access the digital accounts, passwords are the first check point (Bansal and Pandey, 2023; Bansal, 2020b).

Nair (2020) stated that the central government of India made an order of moratorium after getting an application by RBI under sub-section 1. The Ministry of Finance decided the moratorium on Yes Bank after considering the application of RBI. Yes Bank was the first large private bank where the Government of India imposed a moratorium. State Bank of India had given in-principle approval to invest funds in Yes Bank Limited, but the depositors of the bank have to bear the burden of limited withdrawals.

RBI had permitted to withdraw up to Rs. 50,000 but in some special circumstances withdrawal up to Rs. 5,00,000 was possible. These circumstances include:

1. If depositor / dependent on the depositor needs any medical treatment.
2. If dependent / dependent on the depositor needs funds for higher education in India or outside India.
3. If dependent / dependent on the depositor need funds for the marriage function.
4. If there is any other unavoidable emergency.

Karthikeyan (2020) stated that RBI provided no reprieve to the bank's customers who are in extreme financial crisis due to the moratorium imposed on Punjab and Maharashtra Co-operative Bank Limited on 23rd September 2019. RBI has extended the moratorium period for another six months till 22nd December 2020, and only relief to the customers allowed to withdraw up to Rs. 1,00,000. Customers are having restricted withdrawal permission even they have huge amounts deposited in their bank accounts. Six depositors have passed away due to the insufficient cash withdrawal since the incident took place. Sen (2020) stated that RBI has further extended the moratorium period for the next three months ending 31st March 2021. RBI has not given any relief to the bank's depositors as of now. Bank's depositors were stressed to get their life's savings and asking the relief from RBI and the Ministry of Finance. Punjab and Maharashtra Co-operative Bank Limited have invited the investors to take the management of the bank and run regular banking activities of the bank. Investors can buy any financial institution, trust, society, individual, or company. Four investors have shown their interest in investment in PMC Bank.

Sood (2020) mentioned the reason for the moratorium on Yes Bank limited. She said that during the last two years Yes Bank's financial position declined significantly. This decline is due to the the inability of the bank to raise adequate funds to meet out bank's loan losses, continuous withdrawal of funds by depositors, shrinkage of deposit books, and triggering invocation of bond covenants by investors. Bank has also faced many governance issues in the last few years which leads to the bank's steady decline. RBI has imposed restricted cash withdrawal up to Rs. 50,000 only irrespective of any amount in the customer's savings account, current account, and investment accounts.

Motiani (2020) stated that RBI has assured the bank's depositors regarding the safety of their funds deposited in the bank. RBI restricted the bank's customers to withdraw money beyond Rs. 25,000, but in special circumstances up to Rs. 5,00,000 is allowed. All the auto credit into Lakshmi Vilas Bank was stopped such as salary, dividends, and interest. The auto debit was also restricted up to Rs. 25,000 during the moratorium period in case any EMIs, SIPs, insurance premiums, or any other instructions are given by the account holder. So, this is advised to all the account holders to either change their bank account details with the debtor, investment company, and employer.

RESEARCH METHODOLOGY

Data collection: A questionnaire on 5 points Likert scale has been used. Questionnaires were distributed through a stratified random sampling method to 525 participants in the Delhi region which is having multi variant customer base from different parts of the country.

Sample size: Questionnaires were distributed among 525 customers to obtain the useful 384 responses. Out of 525, 474 useful responses have been received.

Reliability: To check the reliability, Cronbach's Alpha was used, and found the value above 0.7, which is acceptable.

Normality: To check the normality of data, Skewness and Kurtosis values were checked and the values are between -2 to +2 i.e. the acceptable range.

Tools for analysis: This study has applied the Factor analysis and multiple linear regression.

Hypothesis: Following hypotheses have been formed:

H_{01}: There is no impact of the restriction on funds withdrawal due to the moratorium on the trust level of middle-class depositors in India.
H_{02}: There is no impact of the period of moratorium on the trust level of middle-class depositors in India.
H_{03}: There is no impact of irregularities in banking services on the trust level of middle-class depositors in India.
H_{04}: There is no impact of the failure of corporate governance on the trust level of middle-class depositors in India.
H_{05}: There is no impact of the role of bank staff on the trust level of middle-class depositors in India.
H_{06}: There is no impact of the negative image of the bank due to the moratorium on the trust level of middle-class depositors in India.

Data Analysis:

Data has been analyzed using exploratory factor analysis and multiple linear regression.

Table 1. Demographic profile

Variable Details	Frequency	Percentage
Gender		
Male	272	57.38
Female	202	42.62
Age		
Less than 25	104	21.94
25-35	175	36.92
35-45	149	31.43
45 & above	46	9.71
Qualification		
Up to higher secondary	89	18.78
Graduate	139	29.32
Post Graduate	166	35.02

continued on following page

Table 1. Continued

Variable Details	Frequency	Percentage
Ph.D	80	16.88
Monthly Income		
Upto Rs. 20,000	115	24.26
Rs. 20,001-35,000	134	28.27
Rs. 35,001-50,000	189	39.87
Rs. 50,001 & above	36	7.60

For the data collection, 474 respondents of various demographic profiles were considered (Table 1). Out of 474 respondents, 272 respondents were male (57.38%), and 202 respondents were female (42.62%).

104 respondents have less than 25 years of age (21.94%), 175 respondents were in the age group of 26-35 years (36.92%), 149 respondents were in the age group of 36-45 years (31.43%) and 46 respondents were in the age group of 45 years & above (9.71%).

89 respondents were having qualifications up to higher secondary level (18.78%), 139 respondents were graduates (29.32%), 166 respondents were postgraduates (35.02%) and 80 respondents were having Ph. D degree (16.88%).

115 respondents have their monthly income upto Rs. 20,000 (24.26%), 134 respondents have their monthly income between Rs. 20,001-35,000 (28.27%), 189 respondents have their monthly income between Rs. 35,001-50,000 (39.87%) and 36 respondents have their monthly income from Rs. 50,001 & above (7.60%).

Table 2. Variables coding

Variable Details	Variable Name	Nature
Trust level of middle-class depositors	D_1	Dependent
Restriction on funds withdrawal	ID_1	Independent
Period of moratorium	ID_2	Independent
Irregularities in banking services	ID_3	Independent
Failure of corporate governance	ID_4	Independent
Role of bank staff	ID_5	Independent
Deterioration of bank's image due to moratorium	ID_6	Independent

Variables: The study has been conducted in consideration of 6 main independent variables (Table 2) i.e., Restriction on funds withdrawal is ID_1, Period of the moratorium is ID_2, Irregularities in banking services is ID_3, Failure of corporate governance is ID_4, Role of bank staff is ID_5 and Deterioration of bank's image due to moratorium is ID_6 along with other overarching variables. Here is one dependent variable i.e., the Trust level of middle-class depositors in India (D_1).

Table 3. Normality Analysis

Descriptive Statistics				
	N Statistic	Mean Statistic	Skewness Statistic	Kurtosis Statistic
D1	474	3.51	-.638	-.333
ID11	474	3.73	-.486	-.543
ID12	474	3.61	-.414	-.336
ID13	474	3.75	-.498	-.546
ID21	474	3.40	.389	-1.047
ID22	474	3.15	-.110	-1.238
ID23	474	3.48	.369	-1.215
ID31	474	3.50	-.378	.123
ID32	474	3.61	-.498	-.253
ID33	474	3.69	-.535	-.326
ID41	474	3.17	-.123	-1.014
ID42	474	3.11	-.065	-1.072
ID43	474	3.11	-.076	-1.137
ID51	474	3.41	-.261	-.809
ID52	474	3.35	-.192	-.848
ID53	474	3.29	-.315	-.619
ID61	474	3.43	-.296	-.174
ID62	474	3.26	-.401	-.209
ID63	474	3.29	-.458	-.511
Valid N (listwise)	474			

Normality Analysis: The skewness and kurtosis values of all the 19 variables (1 dependent and 18 independent) have been checked (Table 3), and accepted (George & Mallery, 2010).

Table 4. KMO and Bartlett's Test

	KMO and Bartlett's Test	
Kaiser-Meyer-Olkin Measure of Sampling Adequacy.		0.811
Bartlett's Test of Sphericity	Approx. Chi-Square	4592.868
	df	136
	Sig.	0.000

KMO and Bartlett's Test: Acceptable range of KMO value is between 0.5 to 1.0 (Malhotra, 2008) as this range represents the appropriateness of factor analysis. Table 4 represents that the KMO value is 0.811 which is within the acceptable range.

Table 5. Communalities

Communalities		
	Initial	**Extraction**
ID11	1.000	.785
ID12	1.000	.787
ID13	1.000	.691
ID21	1.000	.657
ID22	1.000	.606
ID23	1.000	.591
ID32	1.000	.371
ID33	1.000	.507
ID41	1.000	.713
ID42	1.000	.834
ID43	1.000	.819
ID51	1.000	.864
ID52	1.000	.865
ID53	1.000	.781
ID61	1.000	.775
ID62	1.000	.828
ID63	1.000	.803

Extraction Method: Principal Component Analysis.

Communalities: All the 18 variables have communalities values above 0.5 (Table 5). Malhotra, 2008 stated that communalities value should be above 0.5 to accept the variables. So, all 18 variables have been considered for the study.

Table 6. Total Variance Explained

Total Variance Explained									
Component	Initial Eigenvalues			Extraction Sums of Squared Loadings			Rotation Sums of Squared Loadings		
	Total	% of Variance	Cumulative %	Total	% of Variance	Cumulative %	Total	% of Variance	Cumulative %
1	5.249	30.875	30.875	5.249	30.875	30.875	2.867	16.866	16.866
2	2.426	14.269	45.144	2.426	14.269	45.144	2.812	16.542	33.407
3	1.795	10.559	55.703	1.795	10.559	55.703	2.388	14.045	47.452
4	1.566	9.209	64.912	1.566	9.209	64.912	2.382	14.013	61.466
5	1.243	7.312	72.224	1.243	7.312	72.224	1.829	10.759	72.224
6	.759	4.464	76.688						
7	.649	3.815	80.504						
8	.598	3.518	84.021						
9	.536	3.155	87.176						
10	.410	2.411	89.587						
11	.357	2.102	91.689						
12	.325	1.912	93.602						
13	.293	1.721	95.323						
14	.253	1.491	96.814						
15	.223	1.311	98.125						
16	.182	1.073	99.198						
17	.136	.802	100.000						

Extraction Method: Principal Component Analysis.

Total Variance Explained: According to Hair et al., 2009, factor contribution should be above 60 percent to accept the variance by each factor. Table 6 represents the Eigenvalues. Here Eigenvalues represent the total variance explained by each factor i.e., 72.224 percent of the total variance. 72.224 percent is above the minimum acceptable value. So, the variance is acceptable.

Table 7. Rotated Component Matrix[a]

	1	2	3	4	5
ID11		.868			
ID12		.843			
ID13		.777			
ID21					.802
ID22					.768
ID23					.761

continued on following page

Table 7. Continued

ID32		.519			
ID33		.441			
ID41				.841	
ID42				.913	
ID43				.903	
ID51	.906				
ID52	.889				
ID53	.843				
ID61			.822		
ID62			.858		
ID63			.837		

Extraction Method: Principal Component Analysis.
Rotation Method: Varimax with Kaiser Normalization.
a. Rotation converged in 5 iterations.

Rotated Component Matrix: Table 7 represents the exploratory factor analysis to identify the prominent factors for the study (Churchill et al., 2010). Factors have been identified which revealed 5 components and covered 72.224% of the variability. Factor loadings of all 17 variables are above 0.4, which are above the minimum acceptable value (Nunnally's, 1967).

Out of 17 variables, ID_{51}, $ID_{52,}$ and ID_{53} have factor loadings on 1st component; ID_{11}, $ID_{12,}$ ID_{13}, $ID_{32,}$ and ID_{33} have factor loadings on 2nd component; ID_{61}, $ID_{62,}$ and ID_{63} have factor loadings on 3rd component; ID_{41}, ID_{42}, and ID_{43} have factor loadings on 4th component and ID_{21}, ID_{22} and ID_{23} have factor loadings on 5th component.

Table 8. Scale reliability

Variables/combined items	Anchor	Cronbach's α
1	3	0.913
2	5	0.816
3	3	0.876
4	3	0.865
5	3	0.663

Scale Reliability: Out of 5 combined items, 4 combined items i.e., 1, 2, 3, and 4 have Cronbach's α value above 0.70, and the remaining 1 combined item i.e., 5 has Cronbach's α value above 0.50 but less than 0.70. So, all the combined variables have been considered for the study as the scale is reliable enough (Cavana et al., 2001; George & Mallery, 2003).

MULTIPLE LINEAR REGRESSION

Table 9. Model Summary[f]

Model	*R*	*R Square*	*Adjusted R Square*	*Std. Error of the estimate*
1	.752[a]	0.566	0.564	0.719
2	.597[b]	0.483	0.480	1.084
3	.751[c]	0.564	0.559	0.929
4	.614[d]	0.499	0.495	1.035
5	.484[e]	0.234	0.230	0.955

a. Predictors: (Constant), ID11, ID13, ID33
b. Predictors: (Constant), ID21
c. Predictors: (Constant), ID41, ID43, ID42
d. Predictors: (Constant), ID52, ID51
e. Predictors: (Constant), ID62, ID61, ID63
f. Dependent Variable: D1

Table 10. ANOVA[a]

Model	*Sum of Squares*	*df*	*Mean Square*	*F*	*Sig.*
1 Regression	350.339	3	116.78	226.088	.000b
Residual	268.592	520	0.517		
Total	618.931	523			
2 Regression	205.823	1	205.823	96.498	.000c
Residual	413.108	522	1.175		
Total	618.931	523			
3 Regression	438.521	3	249.63	126.929	.000d
Residual	180.41	520	0.864		
Total	618.931	523			
4 Regression	61.066	2	30.533	28.515	.000e
Residual	557.865	521	1.071		
Total	618.931	523			

continued on following page

Table 10. Continued

Model	Sum of Squares	df	Mean Square	F	Sig.
5 Regression	145.035	3	48.345	53.048	.000f
Residual	473.896	520	0.911		
Total	618.931	523			

a. Predictors: (Constant), ID11, ID13, ID33
b. Predictors: (Constant), ID21
c. Predictors: (Constant), ID41, ID43, ID42
d. Predictors: (Constant), ID52, ID51
e. Predictors: (Constant), ID62, ID61, ID63
f. Dependent Variable: D1

Table 11. Coefficients[a]

Model		Unstandardized Coefficients		Standardized Coefficients	t	Sig.
		B	Std. Error	Beta		
1	(Constant)	0.091	.144		0.636	.525
	ID11	.519	.039	.490	13.316	.000
	ID13	.317	.041	.300	7.674	.000
	ID33	0.081	34.000	0.078	2.354	.019
2	(Constant)	3.856	.162		23.819	.000
	ID21	-.101	.046	-.097	-2.227	.026
3	(Constant)	-.103	.210		-0.490	.625
	ID41	.764	.041	.657	18.604	.000
	ID43	0.260	.062	0.191	4.222	.000
	ID42	-.201	.062	-.152	-3.265	.001
4	(Constant)	2.738	.147		18.663	.000
	ID52	0.453	.072	0.48	6.261	.000
	ID51	-0.218	.073	-0.228	-2.972	.003
5	(Constant)	1.717	.162		10.602	.000
	ID62	.470	.067	.437	7.019	.000
	ID61	.243	.065	.212	3.717	.000
	ID63	-.173	.060	-.174	-2.903	.004

a. Dependent Variable: D1

Data analysis and interpretation: Initially the impact of variables considered in the model 1, 2, 3, 4, and 5 have been analyzed by using multiple linear regression to test the hypotheses. Tables 9, 10, and 11 have shown the consolidated results.

Model 1: Here hypotheses H_{01a}, H_{01b}, H_{01c}, H_{03b}, and H_{03c} have been analyzed. Here trust level of middle-class depositors for banking institutions in India is D_1 and restriction on funds withdrawal from a bank account is the main independent variable ID_1 and irregularities observed in banking services is ID_3 along with 5 overarching variables i.e., ID_{11}, ID_{12}, ID_{13}, ID_{32}, and ID_{33}.

Model 1 (Table 9) represents 56.6 percent of the total variation of the dependent variable (D_1).

Table 10 of ANOVA indicates the implication of model 1. Here significance value is less than 0.001.

Table 11 of coefficients revealed that variables ID_{11}, ID_{13}, and ID_{33} have significance values below 0.05. So, null hypotheses have been rejected i.e., $H_{01a,}$ H_{01c}, and H_{03c}, and alternate hypotheses have been accepted i.e., H_{a1a}, $H_{a1c,}$ and H_{a3c}. Here variable ID_{12} and ID_{32} have significance values above 0.05, so accept the null hypothesis i.e., H_{01b} and H_{03b}.

The regression equation for model 1:

$$D_1 = 0.091 + 0.490*ID_{11} + 0.300*ID_{13} + 0.078*ID_{33} \tag{1}$$

Equation 1 reveals that one unit change in ID_{11} will impact of 0.490 unit change on the trust level of middle-class depositors for banking institutions in India, one unit change in ID_{13} will impact of 0.300 unit change on the trust level of middle-class depositors for banking institutions in India, one unit change in ID_{33} will impact of 0.078 unit change on the trust level of middle-class depositors for banking institutions in India.

It means that restriction on funds withdrawal from the bank account and irregularities observed in banking institutions have a significant impact on the trust level of middle-class depositors for banking institutions in India.

Model 2: Here hypotheses H_{02a}, H_{02b}, and H_{02c} have been analyzed. Here trust level of middle-class depositors for banking institutions in India is D_1 and the period of moratorium on banking services is the main independent variable ID_2 along with 3 overarching variables i.e., ID_{21}, ID_{22}, and ID_{23}.

Model 2 (Table 9) represents 48.3 percent of the total variation of the dependent variable (D_1).

Table 10 of ANOVA indicates the implication of model 2. Here significance value is less than 0.001.

Table 11 of coefficients revealed that variable ID_{21} has a significance value below 0.05. So, null hypotheses have been rejected i.e., H_{02a}, and alternate hypotheses have been accepted i.e., H_{a2a}.

Here variable ID_{22} and ID_{23} have significance values above 0.05, so accept the null hypothesis i.e., H_{02b} and H_{02}c.

The regression equation for model 2:

$$D_1 = 3.856 - 0.097*ID_{21} \quad (2)$$

Equation 2 reveals that one unit change in ID_{21} will impact of 0.097 unit change on the trust level of middle-class depositors for banking institutions in India.

It means that period of moratorium on banking services has a minor impact on the trust level of middle-class depositors for banking institutions in India.

Model 3: Here hypotheses H_{04a}, H_{04b}, and H_{04c} have been analyzed. Here trust level of middle-class depositors for banking institutions in India is D_1 and failure of corporate governance in banking institutions is the main independent variable ID_4 along with 3 overarching variables i.e., ID_{41}, ID_{42}, and ID_{43}.

Model 3 (Table 9) represents 56.4 percent of the total variation of the dependent variable (D_1).

Table 10 of ANOVA indicates the implication of model 3. Here significance value is less than 0.001.

Table 11 of coefficients revealed that variables ID_{41}, ID_{42}, and ID_{43} have significance values below 0.05. So, null hypotheses have been rejected i.e., H_{04a}, H_{04b}, and H_{04c}, and alternate hypotheses have been accepted i.e., H_{a4a}, H_{a4b}, and H_{a4c}.

The regression equation for model 3:

$$D_1 = -0.103 + 0.657*ID_{41} + 0.191*ID_{43} - 0.152*ID_{42} \quad (3)$$

Equation 3 reveals that one unit change in ID_{41} will impact of 0.657 unit change on the trust level of middle-class depositors for banking institutions in India, one unit change in ID_{43} will impact of 0.191 unit change on the trust level of middle-class depositors for banking institutions in India, one unit change in ID_{42} will impact of 0.152 unit change on the trust level of middle-class depositors for banking institutions in India.

It means that the failure of corporate governance has a significant impact on the trust level of middle-class depositors for banking institutions in India.

Model 4: Here hypotheses H_{05a}, H_{05b}, and H_{05c} have been analyzed. Here trust level of middle-class depositors for banking institutions in India is D_1 and the role of bank staff for the a moratorium is the main independent variable ID_5 along with 3 overarching variables i.e., ID_{51}, ID_{52}, and ID_{53}.

Model 4 (Table 9) represents 49.9 percent of the total variation of the dependent variable (D_1).

Table 10 of ANOVA indicates the implication of model 4. Here significance value is less than 0.001.

Table 11 of coefficients revealed that variables ID_{51} and ID_{52} have significance values below 0.05. So, null hypotheses have been rejected i.e., H_{05}a and H_{05b}, and alternate hypotheses have been accepted i.e., H_{a5a} and H_{a5b}.

The regression equation for model 4:

$$D_1 = 2.738 + 0.480*ID_{52} - 0.228*ID_{51} \quad (4)$$

Equation 4 reveals that one unit change in ID_{52} will impact 0.480 unit change on the trust level of middle-class depositors for banking institutions in India and one unit change in ID51 will impact 0.228 unit change on the trust level of middle-class depositors for banking institutions in India.

It means that role of bank staff in the moratorium has a significant impact on the trust level of middle-class depositors for banking institutions in India.

Model 5: Here hypotheses H_{06a}, H_{06b}, and H_{06c} have been analyzed. Here trust level of middle-class depositors for banking institutions in India is D_1 and deterioration of the bank's image due to moratorium is the main independent variable ID_6 along with 3 overarching variables i.e., ID_{61}, ID_{62}, and ID_{63}.

Model 5 (Table 9) represents 23.4 percent of the total variation of the dependent variable (D_1).

Table 10 of ANOVA indicates the implication of model 5. Here significance value is less than 0.001.

Table 11 of coefficients revealed that variables ID_{61}, ID_{62}, and ID_{63} have significance values below 0.05. So, null hypotheses have been rejected i.e., H_{06a}, H_{06b}, and H_{06c} and alternate hypotheses have been accepted i.e., H_{a6a}, H_{a6b}, and H_{a6c}.

The regression equation for model 5:

$$D_1 = 1.717 + 0.437*ID_{62} + 0.212*ID_{61} - 0.174*ID_{63} \quad (5)$$

Equation 5 reveals that one unit change in ID_{62} will impact of 0.437 unit change on the trust level of middle-class depositors for banking institutions in India, one unit change in ID_{61} will impact of 0.212 unit change on the trust level of middle-class depositors for banking institutions in India and one unit change in ID_{63} will impact of 0.174 unit change on the trust level of middle-class depositors for banking institutions in India.

It means that the deterioration of the bank's image due to the moratorium has a significant impact on the trust level of middle-class depositors for banking institutions in India.

Table 12. Excluded Variables[a]

Excluded Variables[a]						
Model		Beta In	t	Sig.	Partial Correlation	Tolerance
1	ID12	.067[b]	1.457	.146	.064	.392
	ID32	-.014[b]	-0.424	.672	-.019	.767
2	ID22	-.017[c]	-0.354	.724	-.015	.799
	ID23	-.009[c]	-0.185	.853	-.008	.823
3	ID53	0.053[d]	0.808	.419	.035	.395

a. Dependent Variable: D1
b. Predictors: (Constant), ID11, ID13, ID33
c. Predictors: (Constant), ID21
d. Predictors: (Constant), ID52, ID51

Excluded Variables: Table 12 represents the information of excluded variables. ID_{12}, ID_{32}, ID_{22}, ID_{23}, and ID_{53} have been excluded based on their significance value as the significance value of all these variables is more than 0.05. So null hypotheses i.e., H_{01b}, H_{03b}, $H_{02}b$, H_{02c}, and H_{05c} are accepted.

CONCLUSION

After an in-depth analysis of the collected primary data, the study concluded that the moratorium on banking services imposement by RBI has a highly significant negative impact on the trust level of middle-class depositors in India. Middle-class customers have limited sources of income and these customers deposit their hard-earned money in the bank for safety purposes and interest income. But restrictions imposed by RBI on funds withdrawal from their accounts demoralize the customers and these restrictions restrict the customers to avail banking facilities for a specific period. During the period of the moratorium, customers lose their trust level in banks. After the imposement of the moratorium, customers lose their trust in the bank's top management as well as the bank's staff as the moratorium was imposed due to the mismanagement of banking operations by the concerned staff members which hamper the image of the bank. Overall the study concluded that due to many prominent factors which have a significant impact on the trust level of middle-class depositors, customers lose their trust in banking institutions.

Recommendations

These are the recommendations proposed based on the study:

1. RBI, a regulatory body should be highly vigilant and monitor high-value transactions.
2. Top management of the bank should be more concerned about banking operations to minimize the effect of irregularities.
3. Bank staff should also be highly vigilant while assessing the creditworthiness of the customers to minimize the effect of non-performing assets and anti-money laundering activities.
4. Banks should identify the high-risk intensive customers on regular basis and monitor the transactions in their bank accounts.

Future Implications

The outcomes of this paper can be considered for further research in related studies:

1. This study can be significant for the study of banking irregularities.
2. This study can be significant for the study of the moratorium.
3. This study can be significant for the study of corporate governance failure in banks.
4. This study can be significant for the study of the deterioration of a bank's image.

REFERENCES

Bansal, N. (2020a). The impact of training programme of digital banking services to employees of unorganised sector and their acceptability in India. *International Journal of Electronic Customer Relationship Management, 12*(3), 246–272. DOI: 10.1504/IJECRM.2020.110042

Bansal, N. (2020b). Awareness of password management and adoption of digital banking services in rural India. *Finance India, 34*(2).

Bansal, N., & Pandey, K. N. (2023). Impact of password management strategies on the trust enhancement in the digital era. *International Journal of Business Performance Management, 24*(3-4), 484–503. DOI: 10.1504/IJBPM.2023.132333

Bansal, N., Pareek, N., & Nigam, A. (2022). The impact of customer's training of digital banking services on its acceptability by customers' in India. *International Journal of Business and Globalisation, 30*(2), 207–231. DOI: 10.1504/IJBG.2022.122665

Basu, S. (2003). Why do banks fail? *International Review of Applied Economics, 17*(3), 231–248. DOI: 10.1080/0269217032000090469

Cavana, R. Y., Delahaye, B. L., & Sekaran, U. (2001). *Applied business research: Qualitative and quantitative methods.* John Wiley & Sons Australia.

Churchill, G. A., Iacobucci, D., & Israel, D. (2010). *Marketing research: A south Asian perspective.* Cengage Learning.

Dayal, Y. (2020). Yes Bank Ltd. was placed under Moratorium. Retrieved from Moratorium on yes bank. PDF., Retrieved May 10th, 2021, from.

George, D., & Mallery, P. (2003). *SPSS for Windows step by step: A simple guide and reference 11.0 update* (4th ed.). Allyn & Bacon.

George, D., & Mallery, P. (2010) *SPSS for Windows Step by Step: A Simple Guide and Reference 17.0* Update. 10th Edition, Pearson, Boston.

Hair, J. F., William, B. C., Barry, B. J., Anderson, R. E., & Tatham, R. L. (2009). *Multivariate Data Analysis* (6th ed.). Pearson Education.

Karthikeyan, S. (2020). RBI Extends Moratorium on PMC Bank Till December 22; Withdrawal Limit Capped At Rs. 1 Lakh. Retrieved from https://www.republicworld.com/business-news/india- business/rbi-extends-moratorium-on-pmc-bank-till-december-22-2020.html. (Accessed on 10th April 2021)

Kumar, K. B. (2020). What is a Bank Moratorium, and when does it come into play? Retrieved from https://www.thehindu.com/business/Economy/the-hindu-explains-what-is-a-bank-moratorium-and- when-does-it-come-into-play/article33151740.ece. (Accessed on 5th June 2021).

Malhotra, N. (2008). *Marketing Research – An Applied Orientation* (5th ed.). Pearson Education.

Mathew, G., & Verma, S. (2020). Moratorium on Lakshmi Vilas Bank: What does it mean for depositors, financial sector? Retrieved from https://indianexpress.com/article/explained/lakshmi-vilas-what-a- failed-bank-means-7056518/. (Accessed on 26th March 2021)

Motiani, P. (2020). What Lakshmi Vilas Bank account customers should do post imposition of moratorium? Retrieved from https://economictimes.indiatimes.com/wealth/save/what-lakshmi- vilas-bank-account-customers-should-do-post-imposition-of- moratorium/articleshow/79299602.cms?from=mdr. (Accessed on 19th April 2021)

Nair, V. (2020). Government Puts Yes Bank Under Moratorium, RBI Supersedes Board, Withdrawal Capped At Rs 50,000. Retrieved from https://www.bloombergquint.com/business/government-puts- yes-bank-under-moratorium-rbi-supersedes-board-withdrawals-capped-at-rs-50000. (Accessed on 9th March 2021)

Nair, V. (2020). Lakshmi Vilas Bank Under RBI Moratorium, To be merged With DBS India. Retrieved from https://www.bloombergquint.com/business/rbi-places-lakshmi-vilas-bank-under-moratorium. (Accessed on 30th March 2021)

Nunnally, J. (1967). *Psychometric Methods*. McGraw-Hill.

Sen, S. (2020). RBI extends restrictions on scam-hit PMC bank till March 31; receives four proposals for investment. Retrieved from https://www.dnaindia.com/business/news-rbi-extends-restrictions- on-scam-hit-pmc-bank-till-march-31-receives-four-proposals-for-investment-2862877. (Accessed on 10th February 2021).

Sood, J. (2020). RBI Imposes Moratorium on Yes Bank: All You Need to know. Retrieved from https://www.outlookindia.com/website/story/business-news-rbi-places-moratorium-on-yes-bank- withdrawal-all-you-need-to-know/348340. (Accessed on 10th March 2021).

Chapter 12
Navigating the Housing Crisis in Turkey:
Monetary Policy, Fiscal Tools, and Structural Challenges

Ozge Filiz Yildirim
https://orcid.org/0000-0001-7285-7255
Izmir Katip Celebi University, Turkey & King's College London, UK

ABSTRACT

Housing lies at the intersection of social necessity and economic significance, serving as both a fundamental human need for shelter and a major driver of economic activity and wealth accumulation across the world. However, the continuous rise in housing prices over recent years, coupled with uncertainties in monetary policy, supply-side limitations, and escalating demand, has transformed housing into a significant source of instability in Turkey. This study analyses the main trends of the housing market in Turkey and examines the effects of monetary policy on this market at a descriptive level. Structural factors such as housing supply, fiscal policies, demographic pressures, external capital flows and social effects are also examined. The findings reveal that house prices are sensitive to monetary policy actions and that the multidimensional nature of the housing crisis requires comprehensive solutions that include not only economic but also social and spatial policies. Accordingly, the study proposes holistic and sustainable policy recommendations to stabilise the housing market.

DOI: 10.4018/979-8-3693-9765-7.ch012

1. INTRODUCTION

The housing market plays a dual role both as a social element that fulfils a basic need for shelter and as a key component of household wealth and macroeconomic growth. Especially in emerging economies, housing is at the centre of financial stability and socio-economic development. In this context, the case of Turkey presents a unique case with its rapidly transforming structure, persistent accessibility problems and increasing macroeconomic vulnerabilities.

The impact of monetary policy on the housing market is one of the most debated and complex transmission mechanisms in modern macroeconomics. The 2008 global financial crisis, which was predominantly attributed to imbalances in the housing market, highlighted the significance of housing in maintaining financial stability and fostering economic resilience.

Due to its high sensitivity to interest rates, its close linkages with credit markets and its large share in household wealth, housing stands out as a channel through which the effects of monetary policy are strongly transmitted. Changes in housing prices determine not only consumption and investment decisions but also wealth inequalities, thus generating spillover effects across the economy.

The housing market in Turkey is shaped within a multi-layered dynamic where macroeconomic fluctuations, institutional structures and government policies intersect. In recent years, factors such as rapid urbanisation, migration, demographic transformation and changing household structures have significantly increased the demand for housing. However, structural factors such as limitations in land supply, zoning regulations, and high construction costs restrict housing supply. At the same time, high inflation, volatile monetary policies and expansionary credit conditions have caused housing prices to rise much faster than household incomes, making Turkey one of the leading emerging economies in terms of housing inflation. The increasing transformation of housing into an investment instrument deepens asset-based inequalities and increases intergenerational injustice.

In this context, the housing crisis in Turkey has moved beyond a cyclical problem and turned into a permanent and multidimensional socio-economic issue. Access to housing is becoming increasingly difficult, especially for young people and low-income groups, while ownership rates are declining and precarious tenancy is becoming widespread. Increasing financialisation of the housing market, external investor demand, fiscal incentives and macroprudential policy gaps further complicate the nature of the crisis.

This chapter analyses the channels through which monetary policy affects the housing market in Turkey, focusing on the main transmission mechanisms such as interest rates, credit expansion and expectations. It also analyses how structural dynamics such as housing supply, fiscal policy, demographic pressures and foreign capital inflows interact with these macroeconomic influences. This study, which is accompanied by descriptive data, aims to identify the main trends in the Turkish housing market, analyse policy implications and shed light on the multidimensional nature of the housing crisis. In this framework, the second section presents the literature review, the third section discusses the theoretical framework and transmission mechanisms, and the fourth section presents data on the Turkish housing market. The concluding section develops comprehensive recommendations to address the housing crisis.

2. RELATED LITERATURE

This section aims to present the main research themes and important studies on the relationship between the housing market and monetary policy at two levels. Firstly, the main transmission mechanisms and key controversies on the effects of monetary policy on the housing market in the international literature will be summarised. Then, the structural characteristics of the housing market in the Turkish economy, research themes related to this market and empirical studies on the role of monetary policy will be analysed in more detail.

2.1. Monetary Policy and the Housing Market: International Evidence

In the international literature, the impact of monetary policy on the housing market is analysed within the framework of multiple transmission mechanisms. Research in this field has witnessed a growing depth and sophistication over time. The impact of monetary policy on housing demand and prices is explored through both direct and indirect channels. Among the main transmission channels, changes in the user cost of capital through interest rates, expectations about house prices, construction financing, wealth and credit channels and the recently prominent deposit and securitisation channels (Drechsler et al., 2022; Bernanke and Gertler, 1995; Mishkin, 2007) stand out.

The role of monetary policy in the formation of asset price bubbles is also a contentious issue in the literature. While Taylor (2007) argues that keeping interest rates "too low for too long" fuelled the housing bubble in the US in the 2000s, Bernanke (2010) and Luciani (2015) argue that the impact of monetary policy in this process is limited and the main determinants are financial innovations and inadequate regulatory framework. In this context, another important debate in the literature is whether monetary policy or macroprudential policies are more effective in preventing asset bubbles (Mishkin, 2007; Drechsler et al., 2022). The question of whether central banks should proactively target bubbles or focus on managing the possible effects of bubbles after the crisis is among the main issues that have been emphasised in international research.

2.2. Research on the Turkish Housing Market

Academic studies on the Turkish housing market are centred around five main themes to understand the multidimensional structure of the market. These themes include: the determinants of housing supply and demand, macroeconomic and financial factors affecting housing prices, the financialization process (the gradual transformation of housing into an investment instrument), the establishment of the legal framework for the mortgage system, the relationship between monetary policy and housing market, and the debates on affordability and inequality.

2.2.1. Determinants of Housing Demand and Supply

Studies on housing demand in Turkey have revealed that many factors, particularly household income, interest rates, demographic changes and house prices play a determining role (Halıcıoğlu, 2005; Lebe and Aktaş, 2014). In particular, low interest rates, migration and shrinking household structure are among the factors that support housing demand. Bekmez and Özpolat (2014) comparatively analysed the determinants of housing demand in the case of Turkey, Hungary and the United Kingdom and found that economic-financial variables have different effects across countries. On the supply side, construction costs, land prices, interest rates, bureaucratic processes and government policies come to the fore (Varlı and Erdem, 2014). Çiftçi (2020) emphasises that the qualitative transformation in housing production in the last decade and the orientation towards luxury housing have made it more difficult for low-income groups to access housing.

2.2.2. Relationship between House Prices and Macroeconomic Indicators

Empirical studies on house prices in Turkey show that many macroeconomic variables such as GDP, inflation, exchange rate, housing loans and foreign demand have an impact on prices (Badurlar, 2008; Akkay, 2021). Particularly in metropolitan cities like Istanbul, Ankara, and Izmir, empirical evidence suggests that price deviations from fundamentals occur occasionally, and speculative trading strategies can be effective in such markets (Zeren and Ergüzel, 2015). Nevertheless, it is also noted that such valuations do not disseminate throughout the entire market (Coşkun et al., 2020). Varlık (2020) showed that economic growth has asymmetric effects on house prices and that the upward effect of an increase in industrial production on house prices is greater than the downward effect of a decrease. In addition, it is also revealed that house purchases by foreigners have an impact on regional house prices (Ceritoğlu et al., 2019; Erol, 2019; Ergüven, 2020).

2.2.3. Financialization and Mortgage System

Various academic studies emphasise that the housing market in Turkey has been significantly financialised since the 2000s and that housing has gradually turned into an investment instrument rather than a means of shelter (Ergüven, 2020; Erol, 2019; Aslan and Dinçer, 2018). This transformation was further accelerated by the widespread use of housing loans, the active role of public institutions such as TOKİ in housing production, and state intervention in the mortgage market (Aslan and Dinçer, 2018; Çelik, 2023).

The development of the mortgage market in Turkey has expanded housing finance opportunities but has also brought new risks and controversies. The 2007 Housing Finance Law was an important step in establishing the legal infrastructure of the market. Özsan and Karakaş (2005) emphasise the importance of the regulatory framework for the development of the secondary market. Coşkun and Yalçıner (2014) examined the functional conditions of the mortgage finance system in Turkey and the relationship between housing loan volume and macroeconomic variables. Tunç (2019) analysed the effect of housing and general-purpose loans on house prices and found that loans have a significant effect on prices. Akgündüz et al. (2023) show that the reduction in housing loan interest rates by public banks in the summer of 2020 increased house prices by 2.1%, and this effect occurred through a 6.6% increase in retail housing loans.

2.2.4. Monetary Policy and Housing Market

The extent and channels through which monetary policy affects house prices, especially the effectiveness of non-interest rate instruments and macroprudential policies, remain controversial. While some studies find that monetary policy has significant effects on house prices, there is no consensus on the size and transmission mechanisms of this effect. Studies reveal that monetary policy instruments such as interest rates and money supply have a direct impact on housing prices, credit volume and construction activities (Ergeç and Taşdemir, 2008; Darıcı, 2018; Bayır, 2019). In particular, it is stated that low interest rates temporarily increase housing demand and prices, while high interest rates suppress this demand. The literature also emphasises that expansionary monetary policy has a stronger impact on prices in markets with limited housing supply while tightening policies affect the market by narrowing long-term financing channels such as mortgage loans (Aastveit and Anundsen, 2022; Drechsler et al., 2022).

In Turkey, there is an inverse relationship between CBRT policy rates and house prices (Duca et al., 2021). Expansions in the money supply, another important component of monetary policy, can also push house prices upwards; studies in this context show that liquidity abundance has an impact on prices, especially through asset loans (Cihangir, 2020). Although the effects of macroprudential policies on the housing market have been increasingly analysed in the international literature (Svensson, 2018; Shi et al., 2014; Carro, 2023; Kannan et al., 2012; Bruneau et al., 2016) empirical studies on the effectiveness of these policies in Turkey are still limited. Although the CBRT and related institutions implement various measures and regularly announce them to the public, the impact of these measures on the Turkish housing market has not been sufficiently researched at the academic level.

2.2.5. Housing Bubbles

Another controversial area is the existence of housing price bubbles. The rapid price increases in Turkey, particularly in certain periods, have raised the question of whether there exists overvaluation in the housing market. Studies analysing this issue in the literature reveal that speculative tendencies can be observed in certain periods and regions (Zeren and Ergüzel, 2015; Afşar and Doğan, 2018). However, there is no conclusive evidence of a continuous and widespread bubble formation at the overall market level (Coşkun et al., 2020; Ceritoğlu et al., 2019). These findings suggest that price movements in the housing market may be shaped not only by economic fundamentals but also by market expectations and behavioural dynamics.

2.2.6. Affordability and Income Distribution

Studies on housing affordability and income inequalities also constitute an important area of research on the housing market. The disconnect between the increase in housing prices and household income growth has led to serious access problems, particularly for low- and middle-income groups. Studies reveal that homeownership rates in Turkey have declined gradually, rental rates have increased, and this process has further deepened income inequality (Ceritoğlu, 2020; Coşkun, 2021). These developments suggest that the evolving dynamics of the housing market may have broader economic and social implications, particularly for lower-income groups.

Even though there is increasing interest in the nexus between housing markets and monetary policy in Turkey, the literature remains limited in offering comprehensive, data-driven insights into this relationship. This study aims to contribute to the literature by providing a structured, data-driven assessment of Turkey's housing market, with a special focus on monetary transmission channels, policy interactions, and social implications.

3. THEORETICAL FRAMEWORK: TRANSMISSION MECHANISMS BETWEEN MONETARY POLICY AND THE HOUSING MARKET

This section analyses the channels through which monetary policy affects the housing market, the theoretical foundations of these channels and their reflections on the macro-financial system. To comprehend the mechanism by which monetary policy influences the housing market, the framework of monetary transmission mechanisms will be employed. This framework posits that the impact of monetary policy on the housing market is manifested through five main channels: interest rate channel, credit channel, wealth effect channel, expectations channel and exchange rate channel.

3.1. Interest Rate Channel

Among these channels, the most direct and prevalent mechanism is the conventional interest rate channel. A change in the policy rate by the central bank directly affects market interest rates and mortgage interest rates. This channel plays a decisive role in both housing demand and housing supply. From the demand side, a fall in the policy rate reduces the cost of borrowing by lowering mortgage rates. This makes house purchases more attractive for households and increases demand (DiMaggio, 2017; Koeniger et al., 2022). On the other hand, an increase in interest rates raises borrowing costs and suppresses housing demand. Empirical studies on Turkey reveal that tight monetary policy particularly interest rate hikes harm real house prices. From the supply side, interest rates are a critical factor affecting construction investments. Since construction firms usually finance their projects with loans, an increase in interest rates increases financing costs and weakens the tendency to start new housing projects (Mishkin, 2007; Topel and Rosen, 1988).

3.2. Credit Channel

While the interest rate channel manifests the effects of monetary policy on housing demand and supply directly through borrowing costs, the credit channel complements this effect indirectly through credit conditions and balance sheets. From this perspective, monetary policy affects not only the cost of credit but also the lending capacity of banks and borrowers' access to credit. In this respect, the credit channel can be considered as a mechanism that deepens and reinforces the impact of the interest rate channel. The credit channel is analysed under two sub-headings: bank lending channel and balance sheet channel.

3.2.1. Bank Lending Channel

The Bank Lending Channel argues that a tightening in monetary policy reduces banks' reserves and limits their lending capacity. Banks with a deposit-based funding structure may be forced to withdraw long-term loans, especially mortgages, due to increased funding costs. Drechsler et al. (2022) show that in the US case, such contractions lead to a reduction in bank portfolio lending, which in turn leads to a shift towards the securitised loan market.

3.2.2. Balance Sheet Channel

The Balance Sheet Channel, on the other hand, focuses on how the financial position of borrowers is affected by monetary policy. An expansionary monetary policy strengthens balance sheets by raising asset prices (including housing) and improving firms' cash flows. Borrowers with increased net wealth and higher collateral values become less risky for banks and can obtain easier and cheaper credit. This stimulates investment and consumption, further boosting economic activity and asset prices.

3.2.3. Wealth Effect Channel

Housing is the most important component of household wealth. The impact of monetary policy on house prices also affects consumption expenditures through the wealth channel. An increase in house prices leads homeowners to experience a sense of wealth, which subsequently boosts their consumption levels (Mian and Sufi, 2011; Mishkin, 2007). This effect is more pronounced in advanced financial systems where households can borrow additional funds by pledging their houses as collateral (home equity-based borrowing).

3.2.4. Expectations Channel

Monetary policy decisions and central bank communication shape economic agents' expectations about future house price changes, affecting current user cost and demand (Mishkin, 2007). A sustained expansionary monetary policy stance may create an expectation among households and investors that house prices will continue to rise. This could result in a speculative spiral and potentially lead to price deviations from their fundamental values, as demand may be driven by the desire to purchase before prices increase further.

3.2.5. Exchange Rate Channel

Finally, in open and capital flow-sensitive economies like Turkey, the effects of monetary policy on the exchange rate also affect the housing market indirectly. A tight monetary policy usually appreciates the local currency, while a loose monetary policy may lead to depreciation. Changes in the exchange rate can affect the housing market in two ways. Firstly, a depreciating local currency can potentially boost external demand by reducing the cost of housing for foreign residents. In Turkey, legal regulations facilitating the sale of housing to foreigners have made this channel more important. Secondly, as some inputs used in the construction sector are import-based, an increase in the exchange rate may raise construction costs, adversely affect housing supply and put upward pressure on prices.

The impact of monetary policy on the housing market does not stem from a single channel but from the complex and simultaneous interaction of the interest rate, credit, wealth, expectations and exchange rate channels described above. For example, low interest rates both increase demand by lowering borrowing costs (interest rate channel) and encourage banks to expand credit supply (credit channel). Increased credit utilisation and demand push up house prices, which in turn increases household wealth, supports consumption (wealth effect) and strengthens balance sheets, making additional borrowing possible (balance sheet channel). This process can create a self-feeding cycle by fuelling expectations of further price increases (expectations channel).

The strength and efficiency of transmission mechanisms also vary depending on structural conditions such as the country's mortgage system (Mishkin, 2007), the elasticity of housing supply, financial depth and home ownership ratio (Koeniger et al., 2022), household indebtedness and the macroprudential policy framework. These factors shape both the sensitivity of housing demand to interest rates and the transmission of policy shocks through the credit and price channels within and across countries (Fratantoni, 2003). For example, in Switzerland, despite the prevalence of fixed-rate mortgages, interest rate pass-through is strong because rental contracts are directly indexed to mortgage rates and the proportion of public rental housing is low. In contrast, in Germany and Italy, the high proportion of public housing and the less elasticity of rents limit the impact of monetary policy shocks on rents. Similarly, mortgage utilisation and interest rate pass-through are stronger in more financially developed regions (Koeniger et al., 2022). Especially in markets with inelastic housing supply, demand shocks have a faster and stronger impact on prices. Therefore, stabilising the housing market requires a holistic policy approach that includes not only monetary policy but also macroprudential instruments such as loan-to-value ratio restrictions, tax regulations and structural reforms to increase housing supply.

In the case of Turkey, the loose monetary policy implemented in the post-2018 period has effectively activated both the interest rate and credit channels. In addition, high inflation expectations supported housing demand, while the sharp depreciation of the Turkish lira both suppressed supply by increasing FX-linked construction costs and stimulated foreign demand due to rising geopolitical risks and relative price advantage. As a result of these multiple effects, Turkey has become one of the countries where house prices have risen the fastest worldwide.

To operationalise the theoretical framework presented above, the following section provides a comprehensive descriptive analysis of the Turkish housing market. By examining the interaction of housing supply, demand, macroeconomic conditions and monetary policy indicators, it aims to uncover the stylised facts that characterise Turkey's housing dynamics and trace the channels through which policy shocks are transmitted.

4. DESCRIPTIVE ANALYSIS

Based on the theoretical framework of housing market dynamics, this section presents a descriptive data analysis of the Turkish housing market. The general characteristics of the housing market in Turkey and the changes it has undergone in recent years will be analysed using data. We aim to take a bird's eye view of Turkey's housing market and derive stylised facts specific to this market. Statistics on home ownership and tenants use annual data for the period 2006-2024, while all other indicators are compiled using monthly data covering 2010-2024. All data were obtained from TURKSTAT and Central Bank Electronic Data Delivery System (EDDS). The section first examines the development of housing supply through indicators such as production volume, construction costs and housing stock, and then evaluates the demographic and economic factors determining housing demand. Thirdly, the effects of monetary policy on the housing market will be analysed; this analysis will include developments related to mortgage loan dynamics and interest rates. Finally, the evolution of house prices over time will be analysed in the context of price indices and regional differences, and the section will conclude by discussing the social consequences of rising housing costs.

4.1. Housing Supply

Housing supply has a complex structure shaped not only by economic and financial factors but also by demographic and political factors. One of the most important factors directly affecting housing supply is construction costs.

Figure 1 shows the evolution of the Construction Cost Index (CCI) in Turkey between 2015 and 2024. There is a sharp increase in construction costs with a significant acceleration, especially after 2021. Three factors are very important in this increase. The first is the sharp depreciation in late 2018. The construction industry in Turkey mainly uses imported materials such as iron and steel. The depreciation of the Turkish lira has significantly increased the costs of these commodities. Another factor is rising inflation, which pushed up material and labour costs. Lastly, the rise in energy prices, both locally and globally, is another cost-pushing factor.

Figure 1. Trends in Construction Costs in Turkey (2015-2024)

Source: Compiled by the author with data from TURKSTAT.

On the economic and financial side, the most important variables affecting housing supply are interest rates, inflation and exchange rates. Interest rates affect both opportunity costs and financing for contractors. Rising interest rates increase financing costs and reduce expected profits, discouraging investments in new housing projects. Macroeconomic stability also has an indirect effect on supply. As discussed above, the exchange rate may reduce housing supply by increasing construction costs. Moreover, uncertainty in indicators such as inflation or the exchange rate can increase the risk of long-term investments such as housing, forcing developers to reduce their activities.

Another important factor is land supply and land zoning/construction regulations. Urban regeneration policies[1], changes in land use, large infrastructure investments, social housing projects (undertaken by the Housing Development Administration), and legal and bureaucratic changes in housing construction can be considered within this framework. Although there have been some short-term implementations in this field in the last 15 years, no structural change has been observed.

Natural disasters are one of the contributing actors in shaping housing supply, particularly in countries with high disaster risk, such as Turkey. Turkey is situated at the intersection of three major tectonic plates and a highly seismically active region. Many of its fault lines have the potential to generate violent earthquakes. In the last 50 years, there have been seven earthquakes of magnitude seven and above. Hence, it is a high-risk region in terms of disasters. Earthquakes in particular pose a significant threat. According to CSSB (2023), a total of 35,355 buildings were demolished in the affected provinces. In addition, emergency demolition orders were taken for 17,491 buildings and 179,786 buildings were identified as heavily damaged. The number of buildings with medium damage was 40,228 and the number of buildings with minor damage was 431,421.

Finally, government policies and incentives play a critical role in supporting the housing supply. Subsidies for affordable housing projects or tax incentives to developers can mitigate the effects of rising costs and ease regulatory barriers. The most recent and major development is the large-scale Housing Development Administration of Turkey (TOKİ) housing projects initiated for earthquake victims after the 2023 Kahramanmaraş earthquake.

Figure 2. Change in Annual Housing Supply (2010-2024).

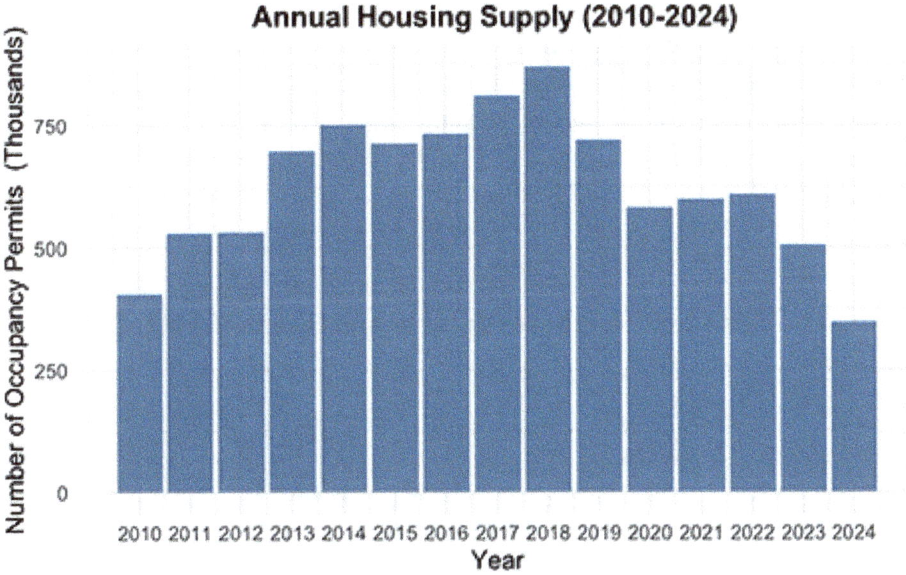

Source: Compiled by the author with data from Central Bank EDDS.

A building permit is an official document showing that the building has been completed per the zoning plan, project and legal regulations and must be obtained after the construction is completed to carry out purchase and sale transactions. It is one of the most frequently used variables in the literature to proxy housing supply. Figure 2 shows the annual number of building permits issued between 2010 and 2024. Since data is available until September, the 2024 annual value reflects the first 9 months. Between 2010 and 2024, the housing supply averaged 626,000 units annually, peaking before 2017 and sharply declining thereafter.

The 2010-2017 period was a period of rapid growth in the housing market due to low interest rates, social housing projects and increasing domestic demand. A significant decline is observed in the graph after 2018. Factors such as the impact of the rise in construction costs due to the currency crisis in 2018, tightening monetary policy and the pandemic played a role in this decline. During the pandemic (2020-2022), there was a short-term increase in housing demand due to the decrease in borrowing costs led by public banks and the elevated demand for larger houses (such as detached houses with gardens) due to pandemic dynamics (Akgündüz et al., 2023). However, towards the end of 2023, housing supply started to decline again due to difficulties in access to credit and unsustainable cost and borrowing pressures.

4.2. Housing Demand

As housing supply, housing demand is determined by the interaction of economic, financial and demographic factors. As with all goods and services, income level is one of the main determinants of housing demand. Important macro-financial components include mortgage rates (especially for mortgages), inflation and macroeconomic stability which will be discussed in the next section.

Figure 3. Housing Sales to Foreigners: Volume and Share of Total Sales

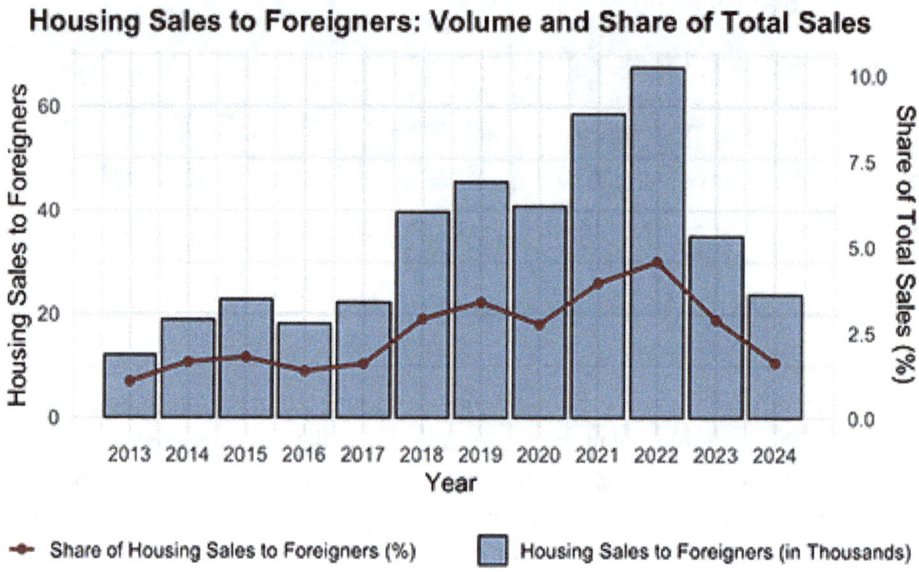

Source: Compiled by the author with data from TURKSTAT.

Demographic conditions directly influence housing demand. Population growth, marriage and divorce rates, separate household formation rates, and internal and external migration movements have a significant impact on both total demand and geographical distribution. The average household size of 4,5 persons in 2001 decreased over time to 3.5 persons in 2015 and 3.1 persons in 2023. According to TURKSTAT data, the number of one-person households exceeded 5 million 192 thousand, while the number of households consisting of two-person families reached 5 million 311 thousand. The shift in the demographic structure from the traditional patriarchal family model to smaller-scale, single or two-person nuclear families, as well as the increase in divorce rates and the spread of individual life preferences, have led to significant changes like the housing need and the typological structure of the supply (Gökçe, 2024). This transformation has led to an increase in housing demand beyond the population growth rate.

Over the past 15 years, Turkey has emerged as a key destination for individuals seeking refuge from political instability and conflicts in neighbouring countries. The implications of this situation on the housing market have also become a highly debated topic. The sharp increases in rents, especially in big cities and border regions, have increased not only economic but also social tensions. Housing sales to foreigners, both in terms of level and ratio to total sales, increased steadily until 2022, after which they dropped dramatically (Salami et al., 2023). However, even in 2022, when it reached its peak, it did not exceed 5% of total sales, which can be interpreted as the limited role of foreign housing demand in determining total housing demand.

4.3. Role of Monetary Policy

The most critical monetary policy variable that directly affects housing demand is the mortgage rate. Mortgage rate is the interest rate faced by individuals who become homeowners by taking out a mortgage loan. Therefore, the mortgage rate represents the cost of borrowing for the housing market. Ceteris paribus, an increase in the mortgage rate reduces the demand for housing by increasing the cost of borrowing. As can be seen in Figure 4, in most cases, the mortgage rate closely follows the central bank policy interest rate (weighted average cost of funding, WAFC).

Figure 4. Weighted Average Funding Cost (WAFC) and Mortgage Rates (2011-2024)

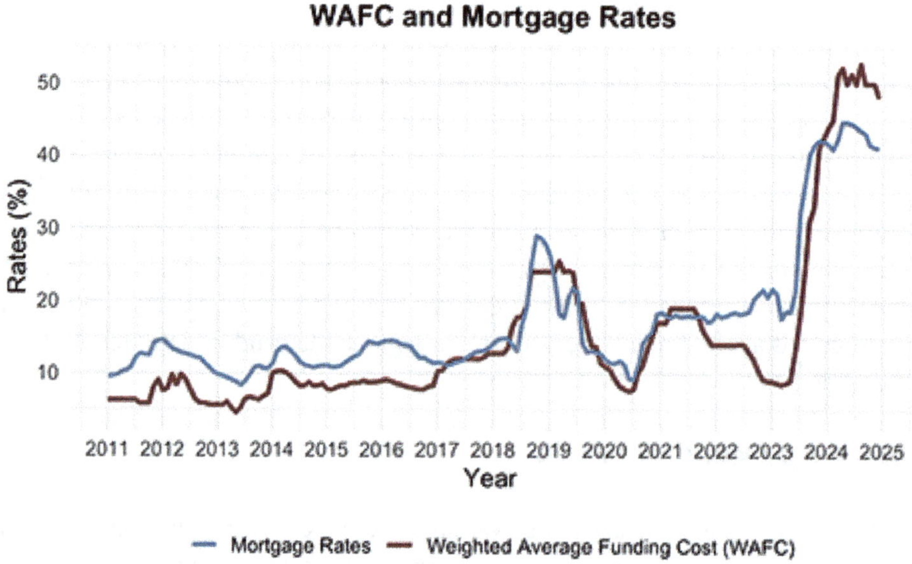

Source: Compiled by the author with data from Central Bank EDDS.

Post-2010 monetary policy in Turkey has taken both domestic and external factors into account. In particular, the effects of inflation and exchange rates have a significant impact on these trends. In an environment of global liquidity abundance created by the loose policies implemented by advanced economies in the aftermath of the global financial crisis, the CBRT supported its traditional interest rate policy with a complex set of instruments. In this period, relatively low interest rates stimulated economic growth and led to a rapid expansion in the housing market.

In August and September 2018, exchange rate shocks, a sharp rise in the CDS risk premium and inflationary pressures forced the CBRT to raise interest rates to 24 per cent. The increase in the mortgage rate following the policy rate severely suppressed housing demand. The tight stance against inflation, which was maintained until July 2019, started to ease afterwards. This process continued until the policy rate fell to 8.25% in May 2020. In September 2020, as the inflationary effects of the pandemic were felt more strongly, the interest rate hike period started again and continued for a year.

In September 2021, although inflationary pressure continued, the tight monetary policy stance could not be maintained and gradual interest rate cuts resumed. While mortgage and policy rates were quite close to each other until this period, they started to diverge after this period. In contrast to the artificially low policy rate, the mortgage rate remained relatively high. The spread between the two reached

15% by mid-2023. In late 2023, following the appointment of a new Central Bank Governor, a return to orthodox monetary policies was initiated. To combat inflation, which had reached 65%, the policy rate was raised to 50%. Mortgage interest rates followed suit and rose above 40%, reaching a historical record high.

Figure 5. Housing Loans and Consumer Loans in Turkey (2010–2024)

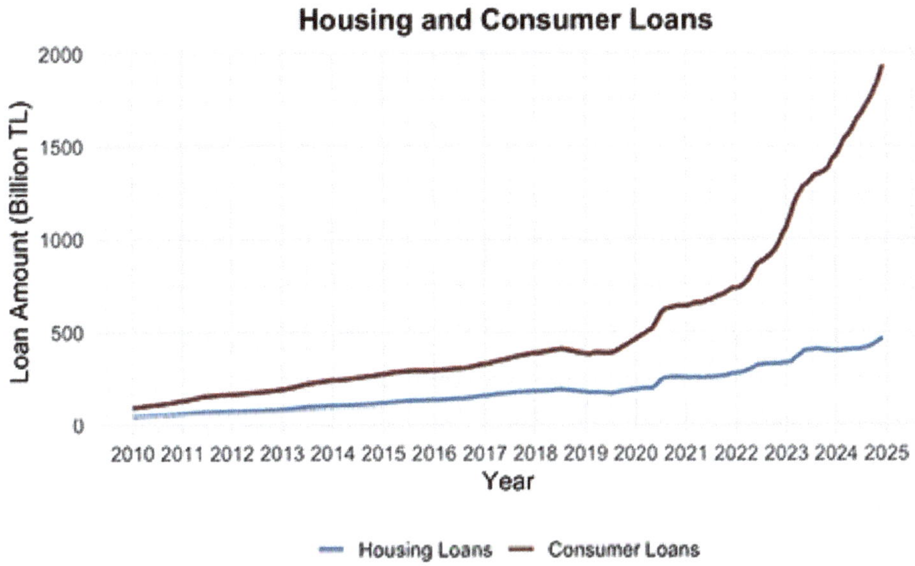

Source: Compiled by the author with data from Central Bank EDDS.

The next step is to analyse how mortgage interest rates affect mortgage lending. Figure 5 shows the volume of housing loans and consumer loans in Turkey between 2010 and 2025. After the 2001 financial crisis, structural programs facilitated households' access to credit through the banking sector. Thus, housing loans started to play an important role in housing demand (Tunc, 2020). Consumer loans have been increasing steadily since 2010. The acceleration of the increase, especially after 2021, is also noteworthy. Although the trend in housing loans is upward, the increase is milder compared to consumer loans. Considering the rising mortgage interest rates, the tight anti-inflationary monetary policy has driven housing demand downwards by increasing borrowing costs through the traditional channel of the monetary transmission mechanism.

Figure 6. Share of Housing Credits in Total Credit Volume in Turkey (2010–2024)

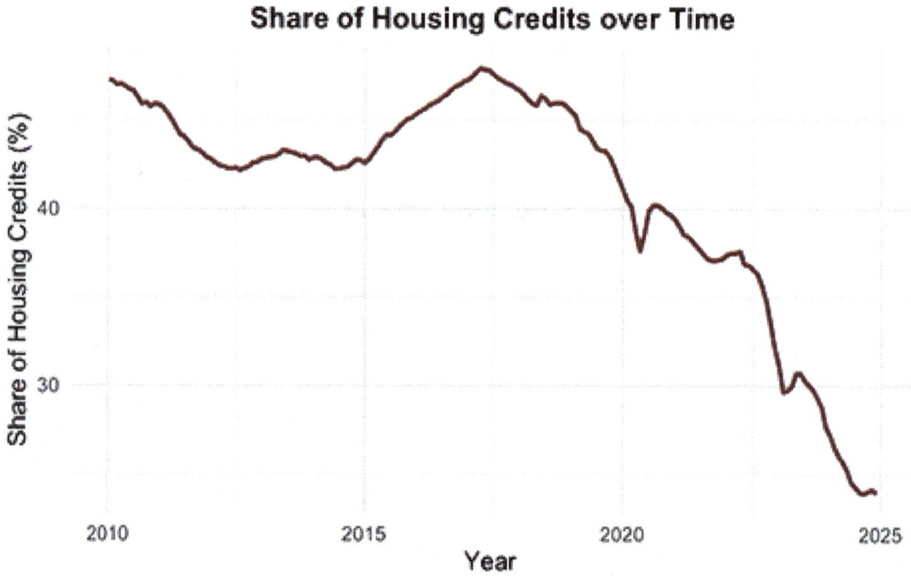

Source: Compiled by the author with data from Central Bank EDDS.

Monetary policy in Turkey has alternated between periods of encouraging credit expansion (e.g. low interest rate policies during the 2020 pandemic) and tightening monetary policies. The rapid increase after 2021 may reflect the government's efforts to keep credit channels open to support consumption. However, rising housing costs and prices, as well as households' tendency to use short-term loans to maintain their existing consumption levels, have limited the availability of housing loans.

Figure 6 shows the share of housing loans in total loans over time. The dramatic decrease in the whole sample is quite remarkable. The volume of housing loans has increased as a combination of economic growth, demographic changes, inflation, the construction sector and government policies. However, the diversification of consumer loans and growth in total volume led to a decline in the overall share of housing loans. The change in the period until 2020 is characterised by relatively milder fluctuations. This period is a period in which credit-driven growth in the housing market is also supported by the state. This period ended with the 2018 currency crisis and the subsequent high interest rate period. After 2020, the decline in this rate continued at an accelerated pace. This can be explained by the increase in housing loan costs, the rise in housing prices and the high inflationary environment. From a macroeconomic perspective, households prioritised more urgent consumption loans, while policymakers prioritised production and export-oriented loans, which led to a considerable decline in the share of retail housing loans in total loans.

Figure 7 shows mortgage rates and the ratio of mortgage sales to Total Housing Sales over time in Turkey. The net negative relationship between the share of mortgaged sales in total sales and mortgage rates is noteworthy. Between 2013 and 2018, mortgage rates followed a course close to inflation. During the tight monetary policy period in 2018, mortgage rates followed suit. This increase caused the share of mortgaged sales in housing sales to fall to a historically low level.

With a looser monetary policy, the share of mortgaged sales started to increase again. In the aftermath of the COVID-19 pandemic, there has been a significant increase in individuals' demand for mortgaged housing purchases due to the low-interest loans. The mortgage rate fell below 1 percentage point, mainly through public banks, which shows that the share of mortgaged sales reached a record high of 57%. In this period, individuals' shift towards housing loans with low interest rates provided a kind of resource transfer to those who could access their loans in an inflationary environment (Kurtbaş and Timur, 2024). It is important to emphasise that this situation makes it more difficult for low-income households to access housing finance and further increases inequality within society. On the contrary, in the period after 2022, when interest rates increased, there was a significant decline in the share of mortgaged sales. High interest rates limited households' access to mortgaged purchases and reduced the share of mortgaged sales in total sales. After June 2023, the gap between the two series widened and the inverse correlation was further emphasised. The mortgage rate approached and settled around 45%. The rising cost of financing has dramatically reduced the share of mortgaged sales in total sales. In December 2023, the mortgage rate reached 42%, while the share of mortgaged sales dropped to 4.36%.

Figure 7. Mortgage Rates and Ratio of Mortgaged Sales to Total Housing Sales (2013–2024)

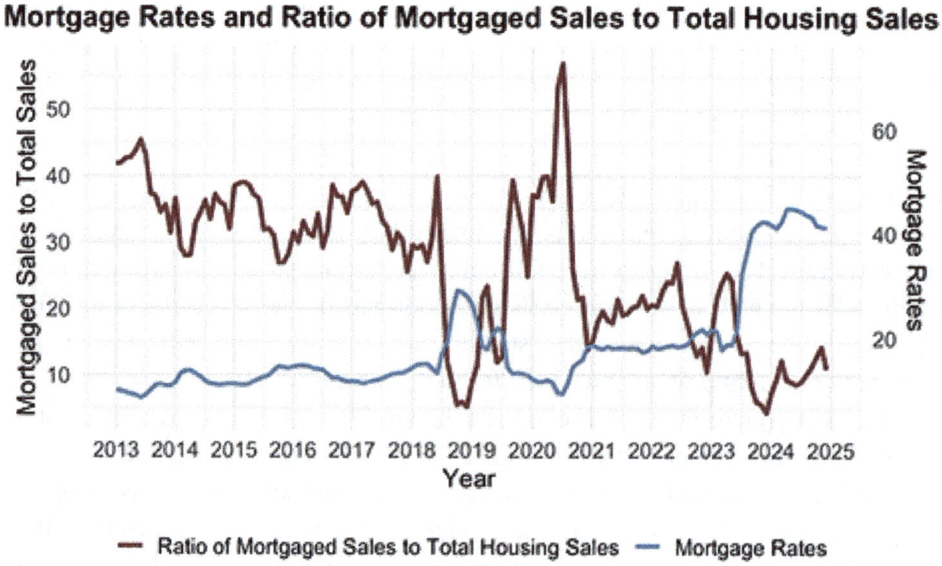

Source: Compiled by the author with data from Central Bank EDDS.

Figure 8 demonstrates the relationship between Consumer Price Index (CPI) inflation and rent inflation in Turkey. Until 2021, CPI inflation and rent inflation followed a generally similar course. This shows that rents, as an important component of household expenditures, are heavily affected by general inflation dynamics. After 2021, rent inflation significantly exceeded CPI inflation. The reasons for this divergence can be attributed to 3 factors: supply constraints due to increased construction costs, demand pressures as a consequence of demographic changes and migration and economic uncertainties.

Figure 8. Consumer Price Index (CPI) inflation and Rent Inflation

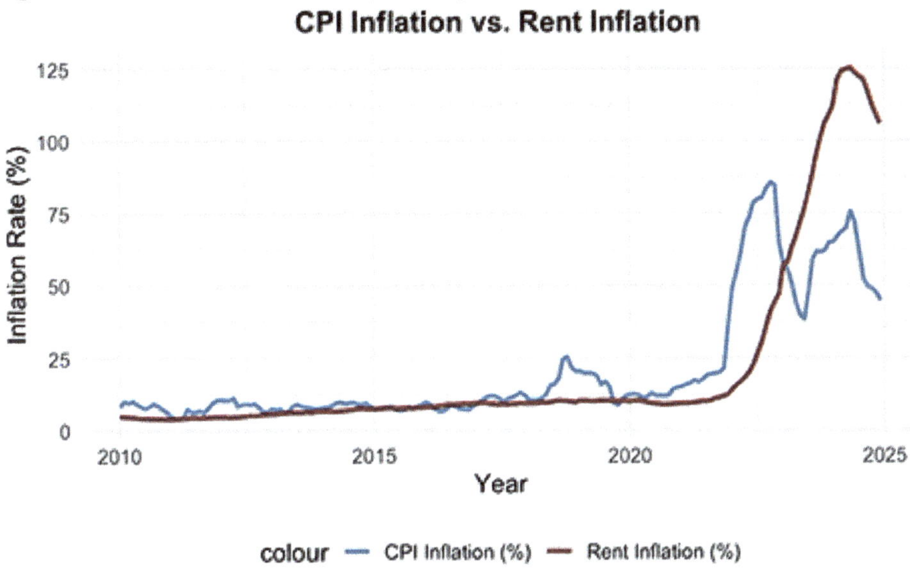

Source: Compiled by the author with data from Central Bank EDDS.

The high CPI inflation in the post-2021 period also had significant repercussions on the housing market. Increasing construction material, labour and financing costs pushed up rental prices. Moreover, the indexation of rent increases to the CPI further accelerated the increase in rent inflation.

4.4. Development of House Prices

Housing prices are determined by the interaction of housing demand and supply. Consequently, any factor influencing either housing demand or supply plays a crucial role in shaping housing prices. This interconnection underscores the importance of examining both sides of the market to understand fluctuations in housing prices effectively. However, it should be noted that, in general, supply-side factors have a longer-term effect, while demand-side factors have a shorter-term effect.

Figure 9. Nominal and Real House Prices in Turkey (2010-2024)

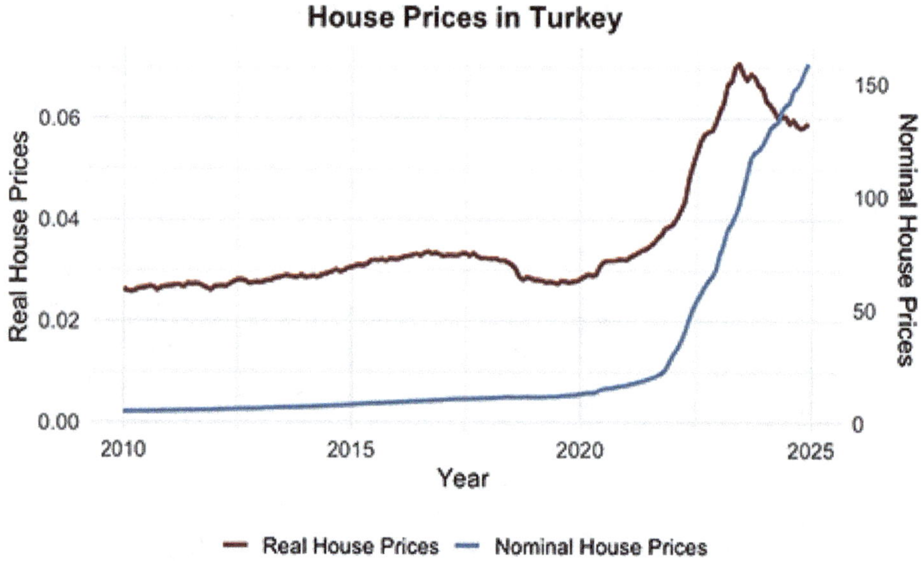

Source: Compiled by the author with data from Central Bank EDDS.

Figure 9 shows the behaviour of nominal and real house prices in Turkey between 2010 and 2025. Here, the right axis shows the nominal house price index, while the left axis shows the development of the realised house price index with the CPI over time. According to Figure 9, there has been a relentless rise in nominal house prices in Turkey since 2010. The moderate increase in the 2010-2020 period accelerated especially after 2020 and reached its peak towards 2024. Real house prices remained relatively stable in the 2010-2020 period, while a substantial rise was observed from 2020 onwards. Whether this sharp rise in prices is a bubble has also been much debated (Akkaya 2024; Doruk, 2024). However, this increase is more limited compared to nominal prices. This indicates that high inflation pushes up nominal prices but suppresses real prices.

Figure 10 shows the rate of growth in nominal and real house prices. The right axis shows the increase in the nominal house price index while the left axis shows the change in the real house price index. Since real prices are adjusted for inflation, the real rate of increase is lower than the nominal rate of increase. However, this difference may vary depending on the severity of inflation. Figure 10 can be analysed in 3 phases. In the first phase, 2010-2016, the house price index followed a relatively stable course with a moderate increase. The second phase, 2017-2021, can be characterised with serious fluctuations.

Figure 10. Growth Rate of Nominal and Real House Prices in Turkey (2010-2024)

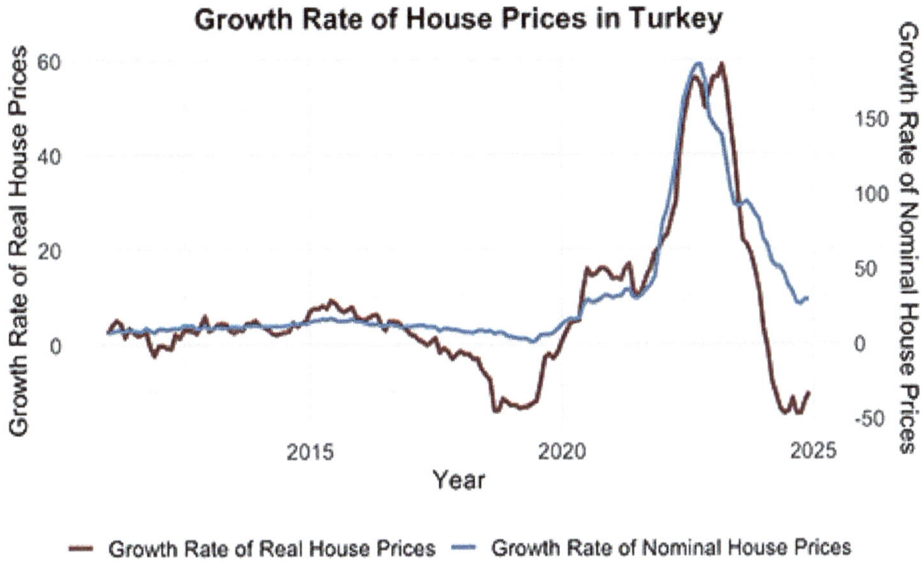

Source: Compiled by the author with data from Central Bank EDDS.

In this period, we see a fall in the real house price index due to the shrinking housing demand caused by exchange rate fluctuations and tight monetary policy. Subsequently, we see a dramatic rise in both nominal and reel house price index growth rates. It can be argued that both the demand and supply sides were effective in this increase. On the supply side, rising inflation increased construction costs, while the reasons for the increase on the demand side can be attributed to both the loosening monetary policy, rising inflationary pressure and the search for a safe haven for savings caused by this, and the impact of the pandemic(Akçay and Akyüz, 2024).

The period after the end of 2021, shaped by high inflation, can be considered as phase 3. High inflation drastically reduced the rate of increase in real house prices. In mid-2022, the fruits of the Central Bank's tight monetary policy implementation to combat inflation at 90% levels began to be reaped, and the rate of increase in the nominal house price index began to decline. In late 2023, real house prices started to decline.

Figure 11. Mortgage Rates and Real House Price Growth in Turkey (2010-2024)

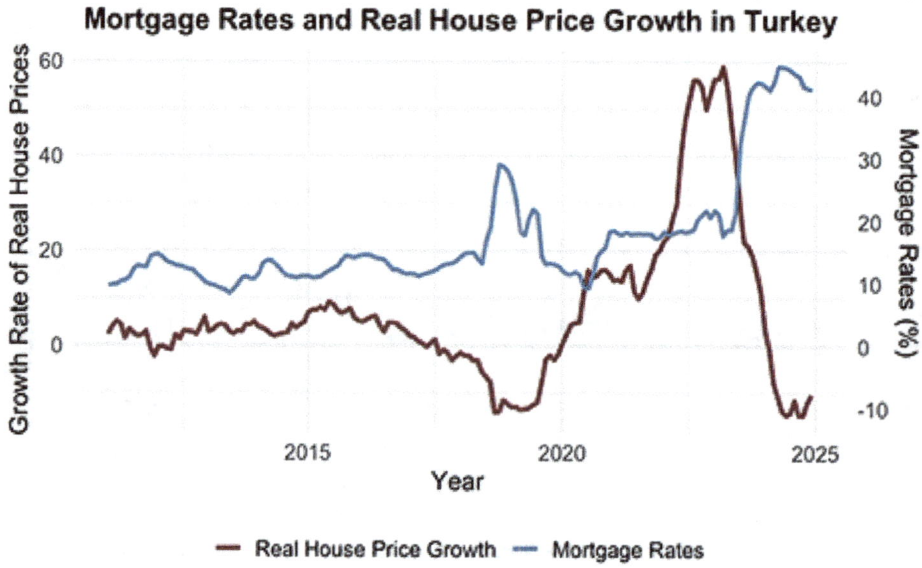

Source: Compiled by the author with data from Central Bank EDDS.

Figure 11 shows the relationship between the real house price growth rate in Turkey and mortgage interest rates over time. Mortgage interest rates are one of the most critical determinants of the housing market. In Turkey, during periods of rising interest rates, housing demand decreases due to the increase in mortgage loan costs, which slows down the rate of real house price growth. The impact of mortgage rates and interest rates in general on house prices is not limited to the demand side through mortgage costs. High interest rates also limit the financing capacity of the construction sector from the supply side.

Until 2018, the moderate mortgage rate was accompanied by a moderate and soft house price growth rate. Following the exchange rate shock, the real house price growth rate saw negative levels after the rapid rise in mortgage rates. The effects of the second shock, the anti-inflationary tight monetary policy shock after COVID-19, were more persistent. In the period following 2020, there is a sharp increase in real house prices. This is also associated with the increase in demand for real estate due to the credit incentive packages implemented during the pandemic, low interest rates and the depreciation of the Turkish lira. Especially in this period, when the government organised low-interest rate loan campaigns to support the housing market, the increase in housing demand was rapidly reflected in prices.

4.5. The Broader Landscape: Non-Monetary Forces Shaping the Turkish Housing Market

Although monetary policy is one of the key determinants of the housing crisis in Turkey, there are many other structural, institutional and social factors shaping this process. This section analyses such complementary factors and highlights the multidimensional nature of the housing crisis.

4.5.1. Fiscal Policy and Government Regulations

Fiscal policy influences the housing market through various tax incentives, subsidies and public expenditures (Wolswijk, 2009; Holmans et al., 2002). Policies implemented in many countries aim to incentivise home ownership. Tax deductibility of mortgage interest, non-taxation of deemed rental income and exemptions to capital gains tax for primary residences are prominent instruments in this framework (Wolswijk, 2009; McDonald and Stokes, 2015). For example, in Spain, the 1998 tax reform provided a tax credit on mortgage principal, which led to a significant increase in the homeownership rate (Raya Vilchez and Kucel, 2023). In addition, reduced VAT rates on new housing and direct subsidies for purchases also shape housing demand (Wolswijk, 2009; Kirwan, 1987).

Within the broader fiscal policy framework, the impact of public spending and budget deficits on growth is also reflected in the housing market through income and employment (Stockhammer and Otero, 2023; Afonso and Sousa, 2012). However, in cases where housing expenditures are not sufficiently prioritised or social housing budgets are cut, it can be difficult for low-income groups to access housing. For example, the contraction of affordable rental housing programmes during periods of austerity is a factor that exacerbates market imbalances (Goering and Whitehead, 2017).

Fiscal policies towards the housing market in Turkey were characterised by public housing production, tax exemptions, rent controls and credit support provided through state banks (e.g. Emlak ve Eytam Bank, 1926) in the Early Republican period, while in the post-1980 period, with the neo-liberal transformation, the state withdrew from direct housing production and prioritised market mechanisms (Ulusoy, 2020). In the post-2002 period, TOKİ's powers were expanded and public-private partnership projects were made widespread with privileges such as free transfer of treasury lands, and tax and fee exemptions (Ayan, 2011). TOKİ produced over 1.27 million housing units in the 2003-2023 period and although it is claimed that most of these units were "social housing", in practice, a significant portion of these units were targeted at groups with incomes three times the minimum wage, leading to criticisms of deviation from social targets (Gökçe, 2024).

On the demand side, Turkey aimed to increase homeownership through low-interest housing loan campaigns (e.g. 10-year loans with 0.99% interest rates) and tax incentives (T.C. Hazine ve Maliye Bakanlığı., 2022). In addition, instruments such as low VAT rates on new housing, property tax exemptions and income tax deductions for renovation expenditures have supported both new production and housing demand. However, due to the inelasticity of housing supply, these policies were largely reflected in prices, pushing up prices rather than facilitating access to housing. This situation shows that policies aimed solely at stimulating demand cannot provide a solution to the developing housing crisis and that more holistic, supply-based and socially just fiscal policies are needed.

State interventions have not only been aimed at stimulating housing demand or increasing housing supply but also at regulating the rental market. In June 2022, a 25 per cent cap on annual rent increases was introduced in response to the acceleration of rent increases and the deepening housing crisis, especially in metropolitan areas. This regulation, which initially entered into force for one year, was later extended and remained in force until July 2024. The main purpose of this practice was to protect especially low- and middle-income tenants against rent increases that far exceeded income increases and to ensure housing security. In the post-2021 period, annual rent increases exceeded 100% in some cities, creating serious housing insecurity for low-income households.

However, although this regulation provided relief in the short term, it brought along various problems in practice. While the 25 per cent limit applied to existing tenants, new leases were made under free market conditions, which led some landlords to try to evict tenants and resort to informal methods such as payment by hand. On the other hand, the expectation of a decline in real rental incomes pushed some property owners to keep their properties vacant and the supply of rental housing contracted. The weak legal infrastructure of the regulation and slow judicial processes created uncertainty for both tenants and landlords and led to the spread of informal rental relations.

4.5.2. Informal Housing Sector and Squatter Settlements

An important element of the housing crisis is the existence of informal housing markets and squatter settlements. These structures often arise from a combination of factors such as rapid urbanisation, inadequate planning, income inequality and a lack of affordable formal housing supply (UN-Habitat, 2016). Although they provide temporary shelter for low-income households, they create structural problems in the long term. Insufficient supply of formal housing can increase demand in these areas, creating a price gap between formal and informal markets. The proliferation of slums hinders sustainable urbanisation due to problems such as irregular construction, lack of infrastructure and poor access to public services (UN-Habitat, 2016). This situation both reduces the quality of life in the cities and increases land costs for official housing projects, making planned urban development difficult. Households living in these areas are both vulnerable to disaster risks and disadvantaged in terms of social justice.

In Turkey, squatter settlements have spread rapidly around metropolises, especially with the wave of rural-urban migration that accelerated since the 1950s and has become a chronic problem in many cities, particularly in Istanbul, Ankara and Izmir (Öztürk and Doğan, 2010). Unplanned settlements, infrastructure inadequacies and property problems have created structural problems in these areas that have been waiting for solutions for many years. In recent years, increasing migrant flows due to regional instabilities, particularly the Syrian civil war, have increased the housing pressure in metropolises again and created a second wave of concentration in existing shantytown areas. These developments have led to a re-expansion of the informal housing market and a deepening of spatial inequalities.

4.5.3. Capital Flows and Foreign Direct Investment

Foreign direct investments (FDI) and portfolio flows have both direct and indirect effects on the housing market. FDI can increase housing demand and prices through foreign direct purchases and real estate development projects, particularly in touristic or high-quality-of-life areas, which can contribute to the formation of housing bubbles (Rodríguez and Bustillo, 2010). Portfolio flows, on the other hand, affect the housing market through more indirect mechanisms. They create a rebalancing in households' portfolio preferences, increasing the preference for riskier assets (e.g. housing) (Boddin et al., 2025), expanding credit supply by providing liquidity to the financial system (Favilukis et al., 2013) and thereby pushing up house prices. Moreover, in some developing countries, capital inflows have been observed to increase house prices both through the money supply channel and through investor behaviour (Ahmed et al., 2021; Feng, Lin and Wang, 2017).

4.5.4. Housing Financialisation and Investment-Oriented Ownership

In recent years, the concept of housing financialisation, the shift from housing as a basic need to a financial asset, has gained prominence in international research. This transformation is marked by the growing perception of housing as a vehicle for wealth accumulation rather than shelter (Hochstenbach and Aalbers, 2024). Although the OECD (2021) highlights that housing is more widely held and accessible than many other financial assets, the fact that house prices have outpaced income growth in many countries has eroded this stabilising effect. The rise of buy-to-let investments, reinvestment of housing wealth by older generations, and increased intergenerational property transfers all point to a deeper structural change. These developments have led to new forms of inequality along generational, spatial, and socio-economic lines (Long and Zhuang, 2025; Matha et al., 2025; Lux et al., 2021).

Turkey reflects this global trend with its distinct dynamics. Housing has increasingly become a store of value in the face of chronic inflation and currency depreciation. As noted by Ergüven (2020), this process has been reinforced by state-led growth strategies that positioned the housing sector as a central policy tool. Market-oriented public housing production by TOKİ, the monetisation of public land, and policy incentives promoting housing as a capital asset have reoriented the sector away from social objectives and toward wealthier segments of society (Solak, 2024). This shift has widened the divide between income groups, particularly in terms of access to ownership.

A widely used metric to capture the financialisation of housing markets is the price-to-rent ratio, which compares median house prices to median annual rents. Elevated ratios signal that housing prices have become detached from rental values, often a symptom of speculative demand and constrained affordability. Figure 12 shows a sharp increase in the price/rent ratio in Turkey, especially in the post-2020 period, and a decline in recent years. The loose monetary policies implemented by central banks after the COVID-19 pandemic led to low interest rates. In Turkey, falling mortgage interest rates have encouraged house purchases and pushed up house prices. During this period, high inflation in Turkey and the depreciation of the Turkish Lira fuelled demand for housing. People turned to real estate to protect the value of their money. The supply of new housing was limited due to rising construction costs and problems in the supply chain. This situation has pushed prices even higher.

Figure 12. Price-to-Rent Ratio Trends in Turkey (2010–2024)

Source: Compiled by the author with data from OECD.

After 2022, this process was reversed, and the rise in mortgage interest rates reduced the demand for housing and slowed the price increase. Persistent high inflation and economic uncertainties reduced the purchasing power of households and had a negative impact on the housing market. In this period, the slowdown in the rate of increase in house prices and the relatively faster increase in rents led to a decline in the price/rent ratio.

This increase in the price/rent ratio in Turkey highlights the difficulties households face in accessing housing and the affordability problems in the housing market. The rise in the ratio reduces the chances of home ownership, especially for low- and middle-income groups, and deepens income and wealth inequality.

4.6. Social Consequences

The housing crisis has had a disproportionate effect on low-income households. Rising housing costs have deepened income inequality and placed immense pressure on vulnerable groups. Analysing home ownership is particularly important to understand the contribution of housing market problems arising from housing supply and the rapid increase in house prices to the solution of the housing affordability problem. Figure 13 and Figure 14 analyse the ownership status of housing in Turkey in terms of homeowners and renters in the period 2006-2024. While Figure 13 provides a breakdown of total households according to TUIK (2024), Figure 14 provides an analysis of households with less than 60 per cent of median income.

In Figure 13, the homeownership rate decreases from 60.9 per cent in 2006 to 56.1 per cent in 2024. In contrast, the proportion of total households that are renters increases from 23.5 per cent in 2006 to 28 per cent in 2024, an increase of about 5 percentage points.

Figure 13. Total Homeowners and Renters

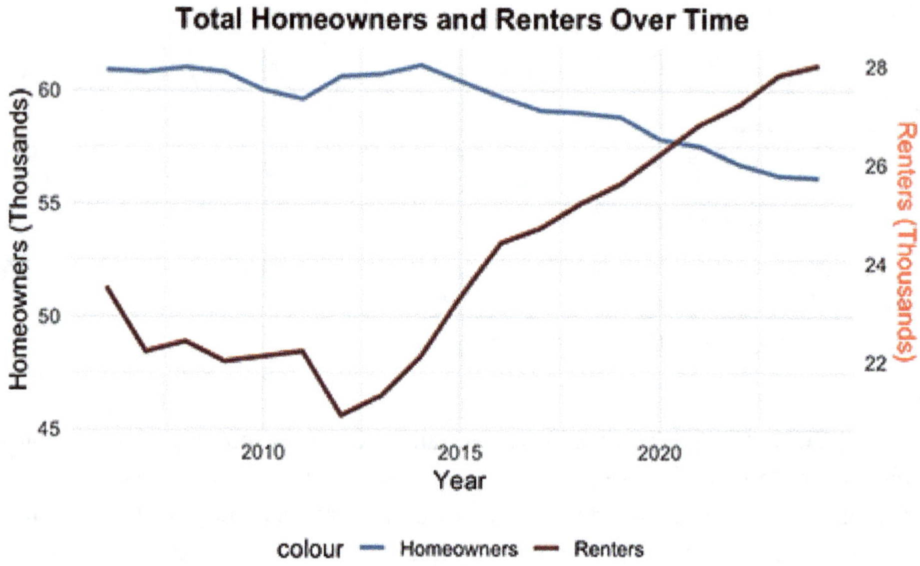

Figure 14. Homeowners and Renters Below %60 of Median Income

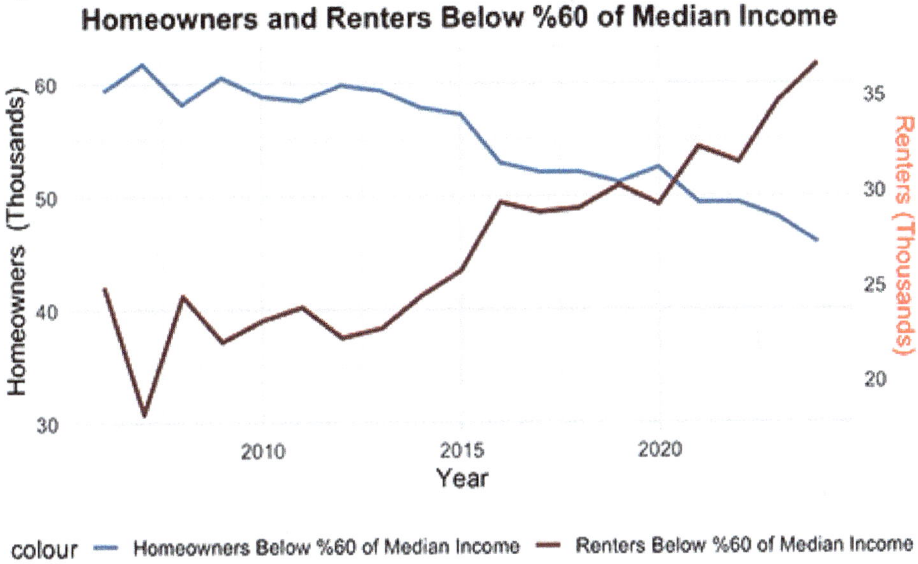

Source: Compiled by the author with data from TURKSTAT.

When this analysis is conducted for those below 60% of the median income, the homeownership rate drops rapidly from 59.3% in 2006 to 45.8% in 2024. On the other hand, the renter rate rose from 25 per cent in 2006 to 29.3 per cent in the year of the COVID-19 pandemic and to 36.7 per cent in 2024, continuing its rapid rise in the following years. As a sign of the affordability crisis, this implies that Turkey's purely market-based housing finance structure has led to a shift in home ownership, with a gradually increasing intensive process of renting for low-income households (Yıldırım, 2023).

For instance, the fact that these rates have fallen despite housing production may imply that housing production/supply could mean that only households with a house are becoming homeowners again. Alternatively, it may also indicate that households are purchasing housing as an alternative investment instrument. Therefore, the ever-increasing housing supply has not helped to solve the housing affordability problem for low-income households.

This trend is not only limited to the decline in homeownership rates but is also deepened by the increasing reliance on rental housing and the increasingly serious problem of access to housing. As the purchasing power of housing decreases, the demand for rental properties increases, leading to a rapid rise in rental rates, especially in big cities. As of 2024, while the net minimum wage is around 22,000 TL, average rents in metropolises such as Istanbul, Ankara and Izmir have reached 20,000-25,000

TL. This high rent burden makes it difficult for young individuals and newly formed families to establish independent housing; many young people continue to live in their parents' houses for economic reasons. This trend reduces the living space per capita in households in Turkey and worsens the problem of overcrowding. 51 per cent of young people aged 15-29 live in overcrowded households, which is almost double the European Union average (26 per cent) (Duvar English, 2023).

In addition to financial burdens, legal insecurity for tenants has also become a serious social problem. Due to increasing rent pressure and legal loopholes, many tenants in Turkey cannot rent a house without signing an eviction undertaking. These documents are widely used by landlords to evict tenants, especially after rent increase limits. In addition, in recent years, informal eviction practices such as verbal pressure, non-renewal of contracts and forced eviction have also become widespread (Sağlam, 2022). This situation seriously weakens both tenants' security of tenure and their bargaining power.

Overall, the descriptive analysis reveals that the housing market in Turkey is highly sensitive to monetary policy and that this relationship operates through multiple transmission channels. The determinant effects of changes in mortgage interest rates on both housing demand and prices suggest that the interest rate channel functions strongly. Likewise, fluctuations in credit volume and the decline in the share of housing loans in total loans reveal that the credit channel has weakened, especially in recent years. The effects of rising house prices on consumption patterns and wealth distribution emphasise the social dimension of the wealth effect channel. The price increases caused by periodic low-interest loan campaigns and the role of expectations in price formation point to the functioning of the expectations channel. Finally, the impact of exchange rate fluctuations on construction costs and foreign demand reveals that the exchange rate channel is also a factor that cannot be ignored. These multiple transmission mechanisms suggest that monetary policy in Turkey shapes the housing market not only at the economic level but also at the social and regional levels.

5. CONCLUSION

The Turkish housing market is characterised by a complex interplay of economic fluctuations, financial developments, demographic transformations and policy preferences. This study indicates that high inflation, volatile monetary policies and structural supply constraints have severely limited housing affordability and disproportionately affected low-income groups. The increasing transformation of housing into an investment instrument exacerbates wealth-based inequalities and makes it more difficult for young and low-income groups to access housing.

The findings suggest that the housing crisis should be addressed with a holistic approach, with not only economic but also social and spatial dimensions. In this framework, it is important for policymakers to enhance mortgage market stability by ensuring predictability in monetary policy and managing credit expansion in a balanced manner through macroprudential tools. For instance, countries like South Korea and New Zealand have adopted effective loan-to-value (LTV) and debt-to-income (DTI) regulations to curb speculative demand and stabilise credit conditions.

At the same time, structural interventions to boost housing supply, such as zoning reforms, public-private partnerships and the transformation of vacant buildings, are vital. On the demand side, financial support mechanisms for first-home buyers, social assistance for tenants and diversification of affordable rental housing are needed. Australia and Canada have implemented first-time homebuyer assistance programmes, while France and Austria provide direct rent subsidies and strong public rental housing alternatives to support vulnerable populations.

Regulation of the rental market, strengthening tenants' rights, quotas for the production of affordable housing and incentives based on energy efficiency should also be considered in solving the housing crisis. For instance, the Netherlands has introduced rental caps and strict regulations to ensure affordability, while Sweden and Denmark apply mandatory affordability quotas in new housing developments. Germany and the UK have supported retrofitting policies with fiscal incentives to promote energy-efficient housing stock.

The effectiveness of these proposals depends to a large extent on structural factors such as the country's financial system structure, the elasticity of housing supply, regional inequalities and governance capacity. Therefore, an effective housing policy requires a data-driven and long-term strategic approach that is compatible with monetary and fiscal policies, integrated with social policies, and data-driven. Such a policy framework will not only alleviate the housing problem but will also be one of the building blocks of social justice and economic stability.

REFERENCES

Aastveit, K. A., & Anundsen, A. K. (2022). Asymmetric effects of monetary policy in regional housing markets. *American Economic Journal. Macroeconomics, 14*(4), 499–529. DOI: 10.1257/mac.20190011

Afonso, A., & Sousa, R. M. (2012). The macroeconomic effects of fiscal policy. *Applied Economics, 44*(34), 4439–4454. DOI: 10.1080/00036846.2011.591732

Afsar, A., & Dogan, E. (2018). Analyzing asset of bubbles in the housing market with right-tailed unit root tests: The case of Turkey. *Journal of Business Economics and Finance, 7*(2), 139–147. DOI: 10.17261/Pressacademia.2018.836

Ahmed, R., Jawaid, S. T., & Khalil, S. (2021). Foreign capital inflows and housing market in Pakistan. *International Journal of Housing Markets and Analysis, 14*(5), 936–952. DOI: 10.1108/IJHMA-07-2020-0089

Akçay, S. B., & Akyüz, M. (2024). Why Did House Prices Go Up During COVID-19 Pandemic? Policy-Driven or Market-Driven? *International Real Estate Review, 27*(2), 303–328. DOI: 10.53383/100384

Akgündüz, Y. E., Dursun-de Neef, H. Ö., Hacihasanoğlu, Y. S., & Yılmaz, F. (2023). Cost of credit, mortgage demand and house prices. *Journal of Banking & Finance, 154*, 106953. DOI: 10.1016/j.jbankfin.2023.106953

Akkay, R. C. (2021). The macroeconomic determinants of the housing prices in Turkey. *Erciyes Üniversitesi İktisadi ve İdari Bilimler Fakültesi Dergisi*, (58), 241–264. DOI: 10.18070/erciyesiibd.801319

Akkaya, M. (2024). Konut fiyat balonu ve konut fiyatını etkileyen faktörlerin analizi: Türkiye uygulaması. *Gazi İktisat ve İşletme Dergisi, 10*(1), 33–45.

Aslan, A., and Dinçer, İ. (2018). The impact of mortgage loans on the financialization process in Turkey. *Planlama*, 28(2).

Ayan, E. (2011). Konut Finansmanı Sistemi ve Türkiye'de TOKİ Uygulamalarının Analizi. *Muhasebe ve Finansman Dergisi*, (51), 139–156.

Bayır, M. (2019). Türkiye'de Para Politikasının Konut Fiyatlarına Etkisi. *Eskişehir Osmangazi Üniversitesi İktisadi ve İdari Bilimler Dergisi, 14*(3), 657–674. DOI: 10.17153/oguiibf.486955

Bekmez, S., & Özpolat, A. (2014). A dynamic analysis on determining of housing demand: A comparison for Turkey, Hungary, and UK. *Management Studies, 2*(3), 179–190.

Bernanke, B. S. (2010) "Monetary policy and the housing bubble: a speech at the Annual Meeting of the American Economic Association, Atlanta, Georgia, January 3, 2010," Speech 499, Board of Governors of the Federal Reserve System (U.S.).

Bernanke, B. S., & Gertler, M. (1995). Inside the black box: The credit channel of monetary policy transmission. *The Journal of Economic Perspectives*, *9*(4), 27–48. DOI: 10.1257/jep.9.4.27

Boddin, D., te Kaat, D. M., Ma, C., & Rebucci, A. (2025). Portfolio flows and household portfolios. *European Economic Review*, *172*, 104904. DOI: 10.1016/j.euroecorev.2024.104904

Bruneau, G., Christensen, I., & Meh, C. A. (2016). Housing market dynamics and macroprudential policy (No. 2016-31). *Bank of Canada Staff Working Paper.*

Carro, A. (2023). Taming the housing roller coaster: The impact of macroprudential policy on the house price cycle. *Journal of Economic Dynamics & Control*, *156*, 104753. DOI: 10.1016/j.jedc.2023.104753

Çelik, Ö. (2023). The roles of the state in the financialisation of housing in Turkey. *Housing Studies*, *38*(6), 1006–1026. DOI: 10.1080/02673037.2021.1928003

Ceritoğlu, E. (2020). Homeownership, housing demand, and household wealth distribution in Turkey. *Emerging Markets Finance & Trade*, *56*(5), 1146–1165. DOI: 10.1080/1540496X.2018.1555461

Ceritoğlu, E., Cılasun, S. M., Demiroğlu, U., & Ganioğlu, A. (2019). An analysis to detect exuberance and implosion in regional house prices in Turkey. *Central Bank Review*, *19*(2), 67–82. DOI: 10.1016/j.cbrev.2019.06.002

Çiftçi, M. (2020). Türkiye'de konut üretim özelliklerinin 1964-2019 arasında uzun dönemli dönüşümü. *Kırklareli Üniversitesi Sosyal Bilimler Dergisi*, *4*(1), 83–98.

Cihangir, Ç. K. (2020). Para, Ayriştirilmiş Krediler, Konut Fiyatlari ve Gsyh Arasindaki Nedensellik İlişkisi. *Bolu Abant İzzet Baysal Üniversitesi Sosyal Bilimler Enstitüsü Dergisi*, *20*(2), 469–488.

Coskun, Y. (2021). Measuring homeownership affordability in an emergent market context: An exploratory analysis for Turkey. *International Journal of Housing Markets and Analysis*, *14*(3), 446–480. DOI: 10.1108/IJHMA-04-2020-0033

Coskun, Y., Seven, U., Ertugrul, H. M., & Alp, A. (2020). Housing price dynamics and bubble risk: The case of Turkey. *Housing Studies*, *35*(1), 50–86. DOI: 10.1080/02673037.2017.1363378

Coşkun, Y., and Yalçıner, K. (2014). İpotekli konut finansmanı sisteminin gelişme koşulları: Türkiye için ampirik bir analiz. *İktisat İşletme ve Finans*, 29(339), 59-94.

Darıcı, B. (2018). Para politikası ve konut fiyatları ilişkisi: Türkiye ekonomisi için ampirik bir analiz. *Anemon Muş Alparslan Üniversitesi Sosyal Bilimler Dergisi*, 6(ICEESS'18), 221-228.

Di Maggio, M., Kermani, A., Keys, B. J., Piskorski, T., Ramcharan, R., Seru, A., & Yao, V. (2017). Interest rate pass-through: Mortgage rates, household consumption, and voluntary deleveraging. *The American Economic Review*, *107*(11), 3550–3588. DOI: 10.1257/aer.20141313

Doruk, Ö. T. (2024). Exploring the determinants of housing price bubbles in the Turkish economy: a COVID-related framework. *International Journal of Housing Markets and Analysis*. https://doi.org/DOI: 10.1108/IJHMA-05-2024-0073/FULL/XML

Drechsler, I., Savov, A., & Schnabl, P. (2022). How monetary policy shaped the housing boom. *Journal of Financial Economics*, *144*(3), 992–1021. DOI: 10.1016/j.jfineco.2021.06.039

Duca, J. V., Muellbauer, J., & Murphy, A. (2021). What drives house price cycles? International experience and policy issues. *Journal of Economic Literature*, *59*(3), 773–864. DOI: 10.1257/jel.20201325

English, D. (2023, June 27). Overcrowded homes plague half of Turkey's young population. https://www.duvarenglish.com/overcrowded-homes-plague-half-of-turkeys-young-population-news-62331

Ergeç, E. H., & Taşdemir, M. (2008). Türkiye'de İnşaat Sektörü Ve Para Politikalari Arasindaki Nedensellik İlişkileri. *Eskişehir Osmangazi Üniversitesi Sosyal Bilimler Dergisi*, *9*(1), 115–132.

Erguven, E. (2020). The political economy of housing financialization in Turkey: Links with and contradictions to the accumulation model. *Housing Policy Debate*, *30*(4), 559–584. DOI: 10.1080/10511482.2019.1681017

Erol, I. (2019). New geographies of residential capitalism: Financialization of the Turkish housing market since the early 2000s. *International Journal of Urban and Regional Research*, *43*(4), 724–740. DOI: 10.1111/1468-2427.12794

Favilukis, J., Kohn, D., Ludvigson, S. C., and Van Nieuwerburgh, S. (2013). International Capital Flows and House Prices. Housing and the financial crisis, 235-300.

Feng, L., Lin, C. Y., & Wang, C. (2017). Do capital flows matter to stock and house prices? Evidence from China. *Emerging Markets Finance & Trade*, *53*(10), 2215–2232. DOI: 10.1080/1540496X.2016.1180283

Fratantoni, M., & Schuh, S. (2003). Monetary policy, housing, and heterogeneous regional markets. *Journal of Money, Credit and Banking*, *35*(4), 557–589. DOI: 10.1353/mcb.2003.0029

Goering, J., & Whitehead, C. M. E. (2017). Fiscal austerity and rental housing policy in the United States and United Kingdom, 2010-2016. *Housing Policy Debate*, *27*(6), 875–896. DOI: 10.1080/10511482.2017.1321568

Gökce, B. (2024). Türkiye'de 2000 Yılı Sonrası Uygulanan Konut Politikaları ve Yaşanan Konut Sorununun Değişen Arz-Talep Dengeleri Üzerinden Değerlendirmesi. *Van Yüzüncü Yıl Üniversitesi Sosyal Bilimler Enstitüsü Dergisi*, (65), 135–152.

Halıcıoğlu, F. (2005). The demand for new housing in Turkey: An application of ARDL model. *Business and Economics Society International Conference*, AZ, ABD.

Hochstenbach, C., & Aalbers, M. B. (2024). The uncoupling of house prices and mortgage debt: Towards wealth-driven housing market dynamics. *International Journal of Housing Policy*, *24*(4), 642–670. DOI: 10.1080/19491247.2023.2170542

Holmans, A., Whitehead, C., & Scanlon, K. (2002). *Fiscal policy instruments to promote affordable housing*. Cambridge Centre for Housing and Planning Research.

Kannan, P., Rabanal, P., & Scott, A. M. (2012). Monetary and macroprudential policy rules in a model with house price booms. *The B.E. Journal of Macroeconomics*, *12*(1). Advance online publication. DOI: 10.1515/1935-1690.2268

Kirwan, R. M. (1987). Fiscal Policy and the Price of Land and Housing in Japan. *Urban Studies (Edinburgh, Scotland)*, *24*(5), 345–360. DOI: 10.1080/00420988720080581

Koeniger, W., Lennartz, B., & Ramelet, M. A. (2022). On the transmission of monetary policy to the housing market. *European Economic Review*, *145*, 104107. DOI: 10.1016/j.euroecorev.2022.104107

Lebe, F., & Akbaş, Y. E. (2014). Türkiye'nin konut talebinin analizi: 1970-2011. *Atatürk Üniversitesi İktisadi ve İdari Bilimler Dergisi*, *28*(1), 57–82.

Long, J., & Zhuang, L. (2025). Housing finance and inequality: Mortgage debt in urban China. *Habitat International*, *161*, 103411. DOI: 10.1016/j.habitatint.2025.103411

Luciani, M. (2015). Monetary policy and the housing market: A structural factor analysis. *Journal of Applied Econometrics*, *30*(2), 199–218. DOI: 10.1002/jae.2318

Lux, M., Sunega, P., & Kážmér, L. (2021). Intergenerational financial transfers and indirect reciprocity: Determinants of the reproduction of homeownership in the post-socialist Czech Republic. *Housing Studies*, *36*(8), 1294–1317. DOI: 10.1080/02673037.2018.1541441

Mathä, T. Y., Pulina, G., & Ziegelmeyer, M. (2025). Private wealth transfers and homeownership: Evidence from Luxembourg. *Applied Economics*, •••, 1–12. DOI: 10.1080/00036846.2025.2471589

McDonald, J. F., & Stokes, H. H. (2015). Monetary Policy, Fiscal Policy, and the Housing Bubble. *Modern Economy*, *6*(2), 165–178. DOI: 10.4236/me.2015.62014

Mian, A., & Sufi, A. (2011). House Prices, Home Equity-Based Borrowing, and the US Household Leverage Crisis. *The American Economic Review*, *101*(5), 2132–2156. DOI: 10.1257/aer.101.5.2132

Mishkin, F. S. (2007). Housing and the monetary transmission mechanism. NBER Working Paper.

Badurlar, Ö. (2008). Türkiye'de konut fiyatları ile makro ekonomik değişkenler arasındaki ilişkinin araştırılması. *Anadolu üniversitesi sosyal bilimler dergisi*, 8(1), 223-238.

Organisation for Economic Co-operation and Development (OECD). (2021). *Brick by Brick: Building Better Housing Policies*. OECD Publishing., DOI: 10.1787/b453b043-

Özsan, O., Konut, O., & Karakas, C. (2005). Housing finance practices and development of a secondary mortgage market in Turkey. *Housing Finance International*, *19*(3), 19.

Öztürk, N. ve Doğan, A. (2010). Konut Sektörünün Sorunları ve Çözüm Önerileri. *Bütçe Dünyası Dergisi*, *33*(1), 139–154.

Raya Vilchez, J. M., & Kucel, A. (2023). How fiscal policy affects housing market dynamics: Evidence from Spain. *Bulletin of Economic Research*, *75*(2), 323–347. DOI: 10.1111/boer.12358

Rodríguez, C., & Bustillo, R. (2010). Modelling foreign real estate investment: The Spanish case. *The Journal of Real Estate Finance and Economics*, *41*(3), 354–367. DOI: 10.1007/s11146-008-9164-9

Sağlam, İ. (2022). Tahliye taahhütnamesinin hukuki niteliği ve geçerlilik şartları. *Sakarya Üniversitesi Hukuk Fakültesi Dergisi*, *24*(2), 345–368. DOI: 10.35307/sauhf.2022.24.2.14

Salami, M. A., & Tanrivermis, H., and Aliefendioğlu (Tanrivermis), Y. (2023). Interdependence between foreign housing acquisitions and housing price increase in Turkey during the COVID-19 pandemic era. *International Journal of Housing Markets and Analysis, 16*(3), 575–597. DOI: 10.1108/IJHMA-08-2022-0109

Shi, S., Jou, J. B., & Tripe, D. (2014). Can interest rates really control house prices? Effectiveness and implications for macroprudential policy. *Journal of Banking & Finance, 47*, 15–28. DOI: 10.1016/j.jbankfin.2014.06.012

Solak, A. O. (2024). Housing policies in Turkey post-2002. *International Journal of Housing Policy, 24*(2), 372–387. DOI: 10.1080/19491247.2022.2154905

Stockhammer, E., & Otero, A. N. (2023). A tale of housing cycles and fiscal policy, not competitiveness. Growth drivers in Southern Europe. *New Political Economy, 28*(3), 483–505. DOI: 10.1080/13563467.2022.2141702

Svensson, L. E. (2018). Housing prices, household debt, and macroeconomic risk: Problems of macroprudential policy I. Unpublished. https://www. larseosvensson. se/files/papers/housing-priceshousehold-debt-and-macroeconomic-risk.pdf

Taylor, J. B. (2007). *Housing and monetary policy (No. w13682)*. National Bureau of Economic Research. DOI: 10.3386/w13682

T.C. Hazine ve Maliye Bakanlığı. (2022, Mayıs 20). Hazine ve Maliye Bakanlığı Konut Finansmanına İlişkin Detayları Paylaştı. Anadolu Ajansı.

Topel, R., & Rosen, S. (1988). Housing investment in the United States. *Journal of Political Economy, 96*(4), 718–740. DOI: 10.1086/261560

Tunç, C. (2019). Konut kredilerinin konut fiyatları üzerindeki etkisi: Türkiye örneği. *23. Finans Sempozyumu Conference Proceeding*, Kayseri, Türkiye.

Tunc, C. (2020). The Effect of Credit Supply on House Prices: Evidence From Turkey. *Housing Policy Debate, 30*(2), 228–242. DOI: 10.1080/10511482.2019.1661266

Ulusoy, A. E. (2020). Türkiye'de Konut Politikaları: Tarihsel Süreç Ve Aktörlerin Rolü. *Kamu Yönetimi Ve Politikaları Dergisi, 1*(3), 87–123.

UN-Habitat. (2016). *World Cities Report 2016: Urbanization and Development – Emerging Futures*. UN-Habitat.

Varlı, Y., & Erdem, O. (2014). The Demand and Supply Model of Housing: Evidence from the Turkish Housing Market Available at *SSRN*: https://ssrn.com/abstract= 2479794 or http://dx.doi.org/DOI: 10.2139/ssrn.2479794

Varlık, N. (2020). Ekonomik büyümenin konut fiyatları üzerindeki asimetrik etkisi: NARDL uygulaması. *Hitit Üniversitesi Sosyal Bilimler Enstitüsü Dergisi, 13*(2), 352–367. DOI: 10.17218/hititsosbil.800641

Wolswijk, G. (2009). Fiscal aspects of housing in Europe. In *Housing market challenges in Europe and the United States* (pp. 158–177). Palgrave Macmillan UK. DOI: 10.1057/9780230246980_8

Yıldırım, M. O. (2023). Housing affordability in Turkey: How big is it and who are the most vulnerable? In *Citizen-centered public policy making in Turkey* (pp. 331–347). Springer International Publishing. DOI: 10.1007/978-3-031-35364-2_18

Zeren, F., and Ergüzel, O. S. (2015). Testing For Bubbles in The Housing Market: Further Evidence From Turkey. *Financial Studies*, 19(1).

ENDNOTE

1 The practice of decontaminating buildings in areas of high potential disaster risk through transformation, renovation or transfer to ensure the creation of healthier and safer areas.

Chapter 13
An Empirical Analysis of Borsa Istanbul:
Some Answers to the Questions on Investors' Minds

Mercan Hatipoglu
https://orcid.org/0000-0003-3307-5458
Cankırı Karatekin University, Turkey

ABSTRACT

Investors often confronts challenges about which financial product outperforms the others. Sharp ratio tests demonstrated that BIST-100 index is a second superior investment after gold for risk-averse investors in Türkiye. However, the probability of yielding above the risk-free rate, Borsa Istanbul-100 index is the highest among alternative investment instruments. In terms of international portfolio diversification, the evidence suggests that correlations between Türkiye and other markets have generally declined towards the 2020s. In our analysis of the US dollar and stock market returns, we found that the depreciation of the TL was the cause of the fall in the stock market price. Emprically, Borsa Istanbul's contribution to the Turkish economy is less straightforward but still positive: the Turkish stock market promotes long-term growth.The results show that stock returns and inflation tend to move together, but this relationship is not one-to-one in Turkish case. Therefore, Borsa Istanbul compensates the investor for below the inflation.

INTRODUCTION

Emerging markets have come of age and provided remarkable opportunities to investors along worldwide over the decades (Errunza, 1983). In most cases,

DOI: 10.4018/979-8-3693-9765-7.ch013

developing countries have liberalized their capital markets since the 1980s in an effort to lower the cost of capital and encourage foreign investment (Henry, 2000). From the perspective of international investors, the effort to integrate into world capital markets has broken prejudices towards emerging markets. For precisely this reason, portfolio flows in the form American depositary receipt (ADR) accelerated towards emerging markets (Mullin, 1993). Thus, the emergence of borrowing opportunities by issuing equities to overseas financial markets has made developing countries shin (Tesar & Werner, 1995). As argued in literature, formerly emerging markets was characterized by low liquidity and higher volatility. Only after that, thanks to the financial reforms (cutting withholding tax, easing the listing process, reducing bureaucratic restrictions, gradually easing transaction cost, modifying the accounting system, reinforcing the underwriting regulation and computerizing the equity transaction) that have been successfully maintained to date, emerging markets have gained a privileged place in the global market (Cornelius, 1994). Consistent with preceding reforms, many of the emerging multinationals have become capital intensive and largely technology driven (Agtmael, 2009). Evidently, on the policy front, the growth-oriented strategy pursued through the privatization of state-owned companies and stabilized exchange rates have led to a decline in risk premiums in many developing countries (Papaioannou & Duke, 1993). More to the point, relatively low interest rate policy in the early 1990s due to the Stock Market Crash of 1987 in the United States (October 19, 1987, the day known as "Black Monday") induced significant capital inflows towards emerging markets (Feldman & Kumar, 1995). In this direction, it can be said that in light of market performance, underlying economic conditions, declining fiscal deficits, realistic exchange rates cause the equity markets has begun to flourish. In large part, ongoing financial flows spurred by domestic pension and mutual funds contributed the equity capitalization across the emerging markets (Bailey, 2010). In essence, developing countries left no doubt about the policies to be implemented in the capital markets. As a matter of fact, as developing countries become more integrated into world markets, more sound financial reforms (prudential and adequate regulation) will be implemented (Obstfeld, 1998). For example, if we need to refer to current developments that will help developing countries to stand out, the US elections may be discussed. With the expectation that the Trump administration will impose tariffs on China, much Chine multinational company may begin to provide products from outside of US. In the event that China tends to emerging markets, corporate earnings of emerging markets firms potentially can be stimulated. In this respect, global portfolio managers seek to add to emerging markets equities. On the negative side, developing countries still have a room to go in terms of stock market size relative to their share in world national income (Barry et al., 1998). The progress of emerging markets can be illustrated through data on international statistics.

Table 1. Overview of selected emerging stock markets 2010-2022

Country Name	Market Capitalization (current US$ billion)		Turnover ratio (%)	
	2010	2022	2010	2022
Africa				
Egypt, Arab Rep.	84.28	38.85	44.16	28.89
Morocco	69.15	53.71	8.82	5.71
Tunisia	10.65	7.75	17.23	7.35
Asia				
Indonesia	360.39	610.29	28.98	31.93
Malaysia	408.69	381.21	28.09	28.98
Europe				
Greece	67.59	59.04	60.13	31.60
Poland	190.71	147.66	36.41	44.44
Türkiye	302.44	330.01	133.33	270.99
Latin America				
Argentina	63.91	52.95	3.98	15.03
Brazil	1545.57	794.42	58.76	162.65
Middle East				
Jordan	302.44	330.01	27.86	9.98

Source: data.worldbank.org

Table 1 shows data on 11 developing countries in different regions. At first glance, emerging markets in questions seems to be lagged in terms of capitalization. But, we should not forget that, while the market size of these countries was expressed in million dollars in the 1990s, the same figures mentioned in billion dollars in the 2010s. On this basis, the fact that developing countries have a highly concentrated bank-based financial system may have put market-based finance on standstill (Loser, 2008). Some, but not all, of emerging markets have sustained the growth trend. For instance, Türkiye has raised market capitalization approximately from US$ 300 billion in 2010 to US$ 330 billion in 2022. Unfortunately, in many developing countries, capitalization values are seen to decrease. Specifically, a fall in the market capitalization of Africa and Asia regions are noteworthy. In practice, the World Bank prefer turnover ratio as proxy to measure the liquidity of the stock market. Similarly, a commonly held view of portfolio managers posits that investors prefer to trade in liquid markets. In addition, the decrease in market liquidity also widens the difference between bids and ask price. The most active trade markets are Türkiye and Brazil, with rates exceeding 250 percent and 150 percent, respectively. In one respect, low transaction costs manifested by higher turnover ratio enabled the aforementioned countries provides the cost advantage. Admittedly, as macroeconomic outlook of emerging markets improve, this facilitate the firms operate at lower transaction cost (Claessens et al., 2002).

Figure 1. Price Performance of Borsa İstanbul and MSCI Emerging Markets Index (2002-2024)

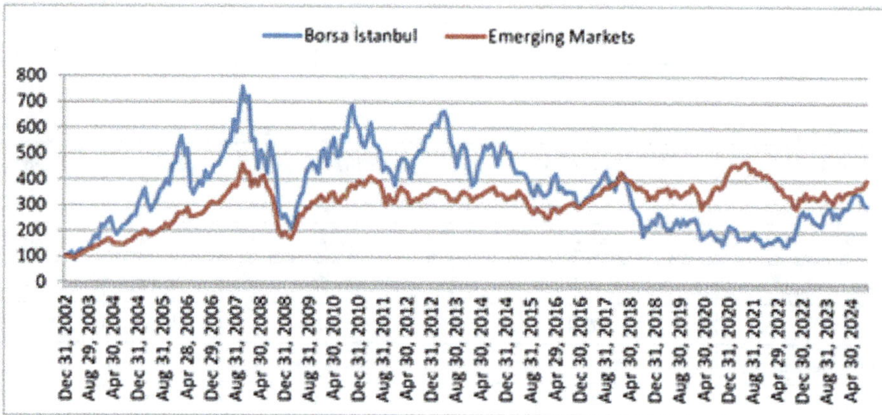

Source: https://www.msci.com/end-of-day-data-country

Figure 1 compares the performance of Borsa Istanbul with MSCI Emerging Markets Index. It shows that Borsa Istanbul equities roughly outperform the MSCI-Emerging market index during the period 2002-2017. Following market decline in 2017, the outperformance of the Borsa Istanbul disappeared and the stock market's weak performance due to political volatility becomes more apparent. For much of 2019, unconventional monetary policies elevated the fears of early interest rate cuts and BIST-100 index saw no gains over the peer markets.Inflation over this period reached roughly 20 per cent in 2020 and was still at 80 percent in 2022. According to figure 1, Borsa Istanbul appears to be at a discount.

Figure 2. Real return of BIST, %, (1998-2023)

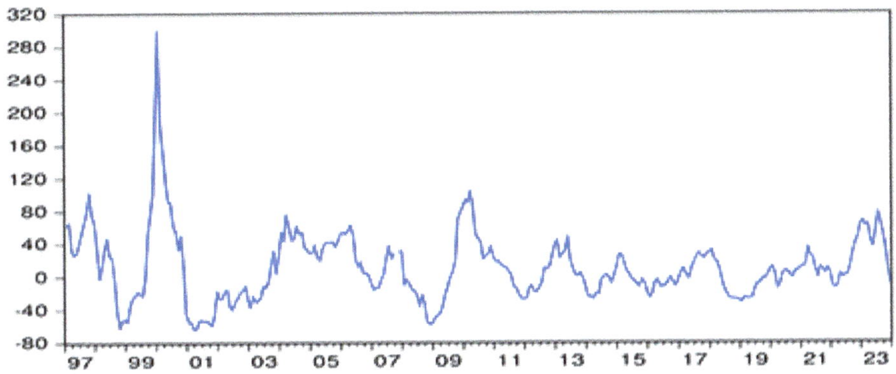

Source: https://data.tuik.gov.tr/Bulten/Index?p=Finansal-Yatirim-Araclarinin-Reel-Getiri-Oranlari

We observe steepest decline in equity returns following 2001 economic crisis from figure 2. The BIST-100 index had lost more than threefold its value. The second largest annual decline in returns of around 70 percent occurred in 2007. Besides, we see an extreme return that BIST-100 index went up nearly 300% on January 2001 but index approximately went down %70 on March 2001. After 2002, there was a downtrend in volatility of returns. The index also has been under pressure because of the Mortgage crisis throughout 2008 and European debt crisis from 2011 to 2013. The stock returns rose almost continuously, often gradually, but exhibited less large cycles. Notwithstanding, generously large gains throughout cycles were offered to investors.

Türkiye started a decisive shift in financial markets by liberalizing its economy in the early 1980's. Perhaps the liberalization effort would be to achieve the sound financial system, protection of property rights by independent law, elimination of corruption and facilitating the entry of foreign investments into the country and to benefit from their knowledge and experience that Mishkin (2009) emphasizes as the benefits of globalization. Apart from the mentioned benefits, Feldman & Kumar (1995) listed the underlying determinants of emerging stock markets as follows: domestic demand, export, declining budget deficits, stable inflation, realistic exchange rates, reducing taxes and fees on transactions, institutional settings and privatizations. Moreover, they strongly emphasized that equity issuance reduces firms' vulnerability to interest rate fluctuations. In addition according to them, the continuous valuation of share prices, takeovers and mergers make the market more disciplined. Cecchetti & Kharroubi (2012) stated that, as the financial system develops, it can stimulate investment by reducing transaction costs. Levine (2002) pointed out that if the firms have not enough bargaining power, there exists the possibility that banking sector retains future profits much more. In such cases, it becomes easier for companies to choose capital markets for their funding needs. Baier et al., (2004) presented findings that economies grew faster after the stock market was established. Bekaert & Harvey, (2002) listed the obstacles to emerging market investment as a legal barriers, indirect barriers that due to asymmetric information, accounting standards and investor protection rights and risks about liquidity, political, economic policy and exchange rate. This chapter addresses several questions about Borsa Istanbul Stock Exchange and financial markets in Türkiye. The chapter is structured as follows. First, the position of Borsa Istanbul among its peers is explained. Then, for those who use mathematical models to make investment decisions, the return distribution of the stock market and its advantages over alternative investment instruments in Türkiye are discussed. Subsequent sections focus on diversification, which is essential to reduce portfolio risk. We also show which countries have a low correlation with Türkiye. Investors often use a wide range of macroeconomic factors to predict the future value of stock market indices. In the following chapters, the effects of exchange rate and inflation on Borsa Istanbul are investigated separately with simple regression models. The final chapter is devoted to the relationship between capital markets and economic growth. This is because the existence of financial markets in each country is assessed according to their contribution to the real economy.

Characteristics of Borsa Istanbul as an Emerging Market

Emerging stock markets expected to provide higher return due to higher economic growth. What could cause emerging capital markets were portfolio selections. Roughly speaking, emerging markets make portfolio more diversified because of low correlation with the developed markets. Erb et al., (1997) pointed out these features and stated that market classification based only on national income does not reflect reality. On the other hand, exchange rates shocks, new regulatory settings and political instability induces emerging market return than imagined. Bekaert et al., (2023) affirmed that emerging markets roughly featured by low GDP per capita, financial integration and weak valuations ratio. However, first and foremost many developing country markets in the early 1990s transformed from segmented market to integrated market. This drastic changes one hand caused the price hikes other hand led to skewness and kurtosis to decrease in developing countries. Because, while former market returns was affected by only by local economy but later lead to more companies to be listed (Bekaert et al., 1998). Furthermore, Erb et al., (1996a) work underlined that beta coefficient does not work in segmented capital markets as a risk measure. Erb et al., (1998) argued that it makes risk management difficult because returns are not normally distributed in many emerging markets. Therefore, when developed markets are in a bear market, developing countries are not the right option. Erb et al., (1996b) defined political risk as willingness to pay debt and they argued that financial and economic risks are related to debt payment capacity and ability. The author documented empirically the variation of emerging market returns can be explain nearly %29 by political risks. Harvey (2000) put forward the idea that coskewness has ability to explain emerging markets returns. Bekaert & Harvey (2002) implied that developing country stock markets are more insensitive to company-specific news, and the underlying reason is insider trading. Another variable that explains the difference in returns in developing countries is commercial legal system. Most of countries legal foundation derived from relatively English common law or French, German and Scandinavian civil law. Buchanan & English (2007) conservative results indicated that returns of emerging markets with French law systems are higher than operated with English common law. Finally, there was the coronavirus pandemic that hit the world in March 2020. It disrupted all financial markets for a long time. The COVID-19 pandemic, which has affected the whole world from labour markets to supply chains, has also deeply affected developing countries. Topcu & Gulal (2020) proved that emerging Asian stock markets were the worst affected by the pandemic. Harjoto & Rossi (2023) pointed out that the negative impact of the pandemic was mostly in the energy and financial sectors, but developing countries recovered in a shorter time compared to the 2008 crisis. Feyen et al. (2021) concluded that emerging countries implementing the Basel III standards were less affected by the global pandemic. Beck et al., (2020) in their firm-level survey studies in developing countries, found that firms reduced investment spending but were also cautious about laying off workers. Ahmed et al. (2020) stated that increases in CDS premiums caused financial fragility in countries such as Brazil, Chile, Colombia, Indonesia, India, Malaysia, Mexico, the Philippines, South Africa, Thailand and Turkiye during the pandemic period.

The Istanbul Stock Exchange, which commenced its operations on January 3, 1986 with 19 stocks, was undoubtedly established to contribute the economy (Gülay & Aydoğmuş, 2024). Because well-functioning stock market pools domestic savings, attracts foreign capital inflows and prevent the mispricing of equity by providing information. In addition, by reducing discount rates, capital markets enable investment projects to be realized more cheaply, thus the economy grows and employment would be increased. It is also worth noting that an effective financial system offers small companies new and less costly funds, saving them from being dependent on bank loans (Bekaert & Harvey 1998). Considering that there are approximately 3.7 million SMEs[1] operating in Türkiye, it is clear why the expansion of capital markets is desired. This article explores the features of Borsa Istanbul stock exchange. How BIST evolved from its foundation in terms of return distribution and relation with economic aggregates.

In the first stage, Capital Market Law came into force in 1981 and then Capital Markets Boards was established in 1982 with the regulatory authority for Borsa Istanbul. The primary revenue sources of BIST come from fees charged on transactions and listing procedures. Besides, these profits are retained in order to meet costs and are not distributed to other persons or institutions. To be listed on the BIST, also depends on some regulations such as at least 15 per cent of firm's shares floating and last two years of firms income statement have to document profit (Altunbas vd., 2008,152, 153).

Figure 3. Nominal level of the BIST and total trade value, (1986-2023)

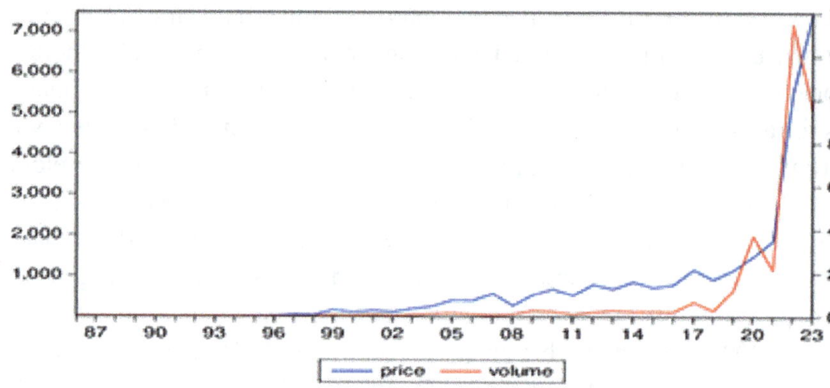

*Source: https://evds2.tcmb.gov.tr/ * Price Indices BIST-100 (XU100), According to Closing Price (January, 1986=0.01), ** Total Traded Value (TRY, Billion)*

Figure 3 plots the yearly nominal level of the BIST from its inception in 1986 and trade value. Based on 0.02 points in 1986, Borsa Istanbul index stood at 7470 by the end of 2023. Furthermore, Borsa Istanbul transaction volume was 95 billion TL as of the closing of 2023. While the period from 1986 to 2002 indicated stagnation in nominal terms, after 2002 Borsa Istanbul index had passed to accelerating pace of appreciation. In a similar vein, by 2022, stocks entered bull market territory and continued upward. Investors saw stock prices appreciate by more than imagined. BIST broke 5500 in 2022 and then surpassed 7,000 in a following year. Obviously, there appears to be a strong positive trend in prices through in the midst of 2021 until end of 2022. Perhaps, the reason behind trend was stock market response to anticipated expansionary monetary policy of CBRT[2]. Considering the disasters and financial crises BIST fell more than 50 points (152 to 94) after 1999 Marmara Earthquake and 250 (558 to 267) points during 2008 global financial crisis. Nevertheless, on the following year stock prices soared and BIST jumped 263 points from 267 to 530 in 2010. In the light of remarkable performance of 2021-2023, It would not be surprising to expect an abrupt correction.

Empirical Distributions Properties of Borsa Istanbul Retuns in Different Frequency

The annual rates of return on the BIST-100 calculated with compounded return formula, Log $(Price_t/Price_{t-1})$, span the years 1986-2023, for a 37 observations. Quarterly return series covers the period between 1986-Q1 and 2024-Q3 for a 154 observations. The data at monthly frequency covers the period between February 1986 and September 2024 and totally 463 observations lie in the period.

Table 2. BIST-100 return summary statistics

Return series	Art.Mean*	Geo.Mean	Median	Std.dev	Skewness	Kurtosis	JB***
BIST-100 (annual)	%35.10	%20.71	%29.40	%62.11	0.737	3.179	0.18
BIST-100 (quarterly)	%8.86	%6.12	%7.36	%24.22	0.414	3.940	0.00
BIST-100 (monthly)	%2.94	%2.10	%2.30	%16.40	0.891	7.326	0.00

*Arithmetic mean, ** Geometric mean,*** Jarque-Bera

As is seen in table, BIST-100 rewarded investors on average, annually %35.10, quarterly %8.86 and monthly %2.94. The geometric mean highlights how much the value of the investment in the last observation has increased compared to the initial value in the first observation. Accordingly, the BIST index provided investors with a return of 20.74% annually, 6.12% quarterly and 2.10% monthly. Standard deviation coefficients show that the highest variability is in annual frequency returns. The lower standard deviations of shorter frequency data implies that the fluctuations in quarterly and monthly returns around the average return are relatively smaller.

The Rates of Nominal Profits Provide by Means of Financial Investments in Türkiye

Table 3 illustrates the mean and standard deviations for several financial instruments in monthly frequency, obtained from TURKSTAT[3] (Turkish Statistical Institute) database. Data cover the period January 2005 and August 2024. Returns are calculated based on the same month of the previous year. In this way, the performance of the Borsa Istanbul index compared to alternative asset class is revealed.

Table 3. Arithmetic mean and standard deviation of real return of asset class in Türkiye

	Arithmetic mean	standard deviation	CV*	Sharpe Ratio
Deposit interest	13.32%	4.29%	0.32	0.17
BIST 100	27.70%	43.31%	1.56	0.37
US Dollar	19.38%	25.05%	1.29	0.27
Euro	18.11%	22.12%	1.22	0.24
Gold (ingot)	29.82%	26.88%	0.90	0.64
Government Domestic Debt[4]	12,59%	13.38%	1.06	-

According to CV, the most risky asset is BIST-100 index, while the least risky ones are deposits and gold. As measured by standard deviation, return variability of BIST is far above other instruments but its average return is well above others except gold. However, Sharp ratio tells us that, BIST-100 index is a second superior investment with the second highest positive value for risk-averse investors. Again, from the table, we can easily calculate that the risk premium of Turkish stocks is approximately 15.11% by subtracting the return of government bonds from the return of the BIST index. In terms of Sharpe ratio, BIST investors' compensated with additional return above government bonds for bearing extra risks. Therefore investors who center on only return, BIST is a favorable destination.

Table 4. The probability of returns of different asset class below and above risk free

	P ≤ %12.59*	P ≥ 12.59*
Deposit interest	43,24%	56,76%
BIST 100	26,08%	73,92%
US Dollar	40,18%	59,82%
Euro	39,32%	60,68%
Gold (ingot)	36,36%	63,64%

* Government Domestic Debt mean rate is assumed risk free rate

According to table 4, the probability of BIST 100 index underperform risk free rate is 26%. The probability of a return above the risk-free interest rate is roughly 74%. These probability values appear more attractive than competing instruments such as exchange rates and gold. In addition, the possibility of deposit returns yielding almost 50% below the risk-free interest rate is due to high inflation in Türkiye. Table 5 presents the test results for decades.

Table 5. Returns and variances of the BIST 100: A Test of Equality across the decades

	1990s	2000s
Number of Months (n)	120	297
Monthly Return (%)	5.44%	1.40%
Variance of Returns	0.0276	0.009
Standard Deviation (%)	16.63	9.90
T test of mean differences	1,975	
The P value of mean differences test	0,013	
F test of variance differences	2,819	
The P value of variance differences test	0.000	

The average monthly return of BIST in the 1990s appears to substantially more than in the 2000s. According to the t-test findings, the difference between returns is meaningful at the level of significance of 0.05. But the P value of calculated t statistic is not significant at the 0.01 level; therefore, investors may not reject the null hypothesis that monthly returns for both periods are same. When we investigate whether the variance of the BIST Index has changed after the 2000s, result of F-test is significant at the 0.01 confidence level. For, the null hypothesis that the variances of returns are the same in the 1990s and 2000s is rejected. It seems that the Turkish equity market was more volatile before the 2000s although many financial crises happened during 2000s such as 2000-2001 crises (led by IMF), 2007-2008 global finance crisis, 15 July 2016 coup attempt and COVID-19 pandemic. However, in the 1990s, only April 1994 devaluation took place and the dollar exchange rate, which was 14,500 TL on April 5, climbed to 39,933 TL on April 7.

Table 6. Correlations of monthly returns to selected investment classes Jan 2005 –Aug 2024

	BIST	INT	GOLD	EURO	USD	GOV
BIST	1,00					
INT	0,31	1,00				
GOLD	0,30	0,26	1,00			
EURO	0,27	-0,01	0,78	1,00		
USD	0,24	-0,02	0,77	0,91	1,00	
GOV	0,23	0,51	-0,17	-0,39	-0,28	1,00

Table 6 shows positive linear relationships between BIST and other investment instruments. Therefore, if the correlation coefficient is positive, when the BIST return increases (decreases), it is expected that others tend to increases (decreases). The fact that the stock market index has a positive correlation with the returns of other investment instruments means that the possibility of domestic diversification is limited. On the other hand, the correlation coefficient of Gov captures the negative associations to Gold, Euro and USD. One plausible outcome is that, holding the currency, gold and government bonds is beneficial for asset allocation in domestic capital market.

International Diversification facilities of Borsa Istanbul

Portfolio managers are sometimes skeptical about investing in emerging markets due to high debt ratios. Nevertheless, given the long-term performance of emerging markets, capital is expected to flow to developing countries (Errunza & Padmanabhan, 1988). On the positive side, deregulation policies implemented in developing countries, the publication of reliable information about the markets, harmonization of trading systems and the cheaper transaction costs invite portfolio investments to developing countries (Odier & Solnik, 1993). The essential of holding diversified portfolios is to reduce the risks. Indeed, domestic firms also are useful in reducing risks but the ability to reduce risk is very limited. Hence, prudent investors seek the way of deals with risk by focusing overseas market. Because any development that may be considered negative for another country means gain for the other one. For example, while oil shocks multiply costs for the US economy, the same shocks mean additional income for oil-exporting countries (Shapiro & Hanouna, 2019). By building an internationally diversified portfolio with the help of emerging markets, portfolio managers have been tried to achieving efficient portfolios. From a practical point of view, as a prerequisite for diversification, firms traded on the stock exchange must have a high publicy rate (Solnik, 1995). In the study of Markowitz (1952), instead of including many stocks in the portfolio, Markowitz has proven that diversification can be only achieved with negative covariance and correlation coefficients. Dwyer & Hafer (1988) identified the developments that increase the correlation between stock markets as the expansion of international trade volume and the areas of activity of multinational companies. In addition, the authors listed the factors that reduce the correlation as having different expected returns of companies traded in different industries and changing country risks. In Conover's work (2002), specifically, the volatility of stock returns and economic contractions have been shown as components that strengthen the correlation between stock markets. Moreover, the authors argued that the correlations between developing country stock markets decrease during periods when the United States implements tight monetary policy. More empirical evidences documented that increasing volatility limits diversification opportunities (Solnik et al., 1996). Another reason for the low correlation across stock markets is the different fiscal and monetary policies implemented by countries due to being in different economic conjunctures (Erb et al., 1994; Kumar, 2011). However, the liberalization process of emerging capital market, the removal of barriers to trade and the financial crises caused the markets to move in the same direction (Gilmore et al., 2005). One of the studies investigating the co-movements of financial markets, Karolyi & Stulz (1996) contended that higher correlation of stock markets leads to volatility of portfolios, increase in risk premiums of world markets, and raises of capital costs of local firms.

Table 7. Correlation coefficients with the BIST Index[5]

EMERGING MARKETS	2000-2010 (Monthly)	2010-2020 (Monthly)	2020-2024* (Daily)
Brazil	0,51	0,59	0,26
Egypt	0,44	0,27	0,13
Greece	0,50	0,42	0,31
Malaysia	0,43	0,48	0,16
South Africa	0,54	0,59	0,31
DEVELOPED MARKETS			
Germany	0,61	0,51	0,36
Hong Kong	0,57	0,43	0,20
Japan	0,45	0,41	0,17
UK	0,61	0,52	0,37
USA	0,64	0,40	0,25

* data spanning the January, 2020 to January 2024

Table 7 reports return correlations between equity markets and Borsa Istanbul in terms of US dollars. To provide the relative performance of different indexes comparable, starting dates of the each index are set to base value of 100. These settings are valid for all three time periods in both monthly and daily frequencies. At first inspection, the coefficients appear in table 7, affirm that movements in stock return in different markets are almost unrelated between each other. Therefore, changes in Borsa Istanbul returns are roughly independent from other emerging or developed markets since the correlations are smaller than 1. Further, evidence implies that Türkiye and other markets correlations have generally declined towards the 2020's. This result can be interpreted as the cash flows of companies traded on different stock exchanges are no longer affected by similar economic factors. When we analyze by sample periods, for 2000-2010, Borsa Istanbul is most correlated with the US, UK and Germany stock market, ranging the coefficients from 0.61 to 0.64. These findings reveal that BIST tracks the developed market's ups and downs.

But, in the same period, the correlation between Türkiye and other emerging equities ranged from 0.44 to 0.53. Compared with the all markets, Malaysia has the lowest correlation with Türkiye during 2010s. The period from January 2020 to January 2024 witnessed the decline in the correlation coefficients of Türkiye and other countries' stock markets. The coefficients calculated with daily data did not remain steady and has dropped significantly. Correlations vary somewhat across countries; the coefficients are around 0.25 for emerging markets and less than 0.30 for developed markets. Several conclusions may be drawn from findings. First, the correlation coefficients are not invariant over a monthly or a daily holding period, though they do not follow the same pattern. Largely, Borsa Istanbul tends to less correlated with the rest of world stock exchange. The evidence supports the argument that portfolio risk can be substantially reduced by including firms traded in Borsa Istanbul stock exchange in both emerging and developed markets portfolios. Note that again, in the eye of financial market participants, the Borsa Istanbul linkages with other markets have fluctuated over decades. Accordingly, within the scope of asset allocations, the most favorable country for the 2000s was Malaysia, whereas the 2010s was Egypt. The outline of results indicate that Borsa Istanbul stock exchange will serves as attractive allocation input for investors in developed and developing countries. However, in-depth look to correlation coefficients, findings imply that practicality of diversification is quite limited. Because no any market has a negative correlation with the Borsa Istanbul Index, investment managers may conclude that diversifications will failure or erode in the upcoming years. As a final note on this subject, we can discuss the correlations and contagion nexus. The high degree of correlation between two markets can be assessed as a road to financial contagion. Given our results, correlations are downturn trend which supports the lack of contagion. Simply put, financial shocks are unlikely to be transmitted across markets. Lastly, the correlations between the Türkiye and the rest of the world stock markets are generally lower today than they were during the last two decades.

Table 8. Stock market comparisons, number of companies listed, market capitalization and Value of share trading, end of 2023 Source: The World Federation of Exchanges, https://www.world-exchanges.org/our-work/articles/2023-annual-statistics-guide

	Domestic	Foreign	Capitalization*	Value Of Share Trading**
Athens Stock Exchange	152	6	81.317	27.266
B3 - Brasil Bolsa Balcão	345	8	991.198	5.818.810
Borsa Istanbul	517	1	337.585	32.148.543
Bursa Malaysia	987	6	378.055	484.858
Deutsche Boerse AG	388	45	2.178.053	1.030.572

continued on following page

Table 8. Continued

	Domestic	Foreign	Capitalization*	Value Of Share Trading**
Hong Kong Exchanges	2428	181	3.974.783	17.799.722
Japan Exchange Group	3929	6	6.149.200	898.624.750
Johannesburg Stock Exchange	224	60	1.025.827	4.853.827
Nasdaq - US	2606	826	23.414.747	20.666.688
NYSE	1709	563	25.564.650	NA
The Egyptian Exchange	241	0	55.654	619.506

Note:*USD millions, **in millions of local currencies, Athens Stock Exchange and Deutsche Boerse AG are denominated in EURO

Looking at table 8, the domestic equity market capitalization stood at approximately 337 billion USD for Borsa Istanbul by the end of 2023. This value closely mirrors the Türkiye's financial market relative performance. While the number of companies traded on the Brazilian stock exchange is close to that of Borsa Istanbul, market value is nearly more than 3 times that of Borsa Istanbul. The number of foreign companies traded within Borsa Istanbul is one. Therefore, compared to peer stock exchanges, Türkiye has a hard time attracting foreign companies. Many studies in the literature link the listing shares abroad and its financial benefits. Let's make a brief summary, foreign companies listed in the USA are successful in increasing their visibility and reducing their cost of capital by increasing their liquidity (Doidge et., 2004). Additionally, trading on US stock exchanges is an activity that increases the transaction volume even on the company's own stock exchange (Karolyi, 1998).

Borsa Istanbul and Exchange Rate Behavior

Although many companies' assets are located in domestic, over half of the sales have been abroad. On that account, the problem of exchange rate fluctuations emerges. Because volatile currencies will have impacts on pricing overseas selling, buying and cash flow of foreign subsidiaries. Here, a less obvious point is the extent to which firms will be affected by the exchange rate. Countries follow different exchange rate policies due to their unique economic conditions. If a country pursues an overvalued currency, it makes domestic firms products more expensive and imports cheaper. These policies ultimately lessen the competitiveness of domestic companies in foreign markets. Conversely, monetary policy that depreciates the local currency will enhance the competitiveness. Further, the revenues of exporting companies may go up somewhat with the help of devaluations implemented by governments (Shapiro & Hanouna, 2019). Accordingly, the stock price of Turkish firm cannot be treated as an only Turkish asset. In essence, share prices must not expected continually going up or down when the Lira depreciates or appreciates (Diermeier & Solnik, 2001). In this part, semiannual data covers 1996 and 2024 period was analyzed to uncover the impact of exchange rates on stock market. The return of Borsa İstanbul-100 index as dependent variable and the growth rate of US Dollar / Turkish Lira (depreciation of TL) as independent variable are used. The data relating to variables are collected from the database of CBRT.

Table 9. Exchange rate exposure on equity return

Variable	Coefficient	Std. Error	t-Statistic	Prob.
USD	0.635	0.254	2.493	0.015
C	0.061	0.036	1.687	0.097
Diagnostics				
Observation	56			
R square	0.082			
Correlation LM Test[Prob]*:	0.504			
Heteroskedasticity Test[Prob]**:	0.422			

Note: *, **, respectively denotes, Breusch-Godfrey Serial Correlation LM Test for one lag and Heteroskedasticity Test:Breusch-Pagan-Godfrey

The finding[6] in Table 9 shows that coefficient of the US dollar is significant and the R-square is not large. So that, in this regression, US dollar appreciations against Turkish Lira explain approximately 8 percent of the variation of the Borsa Istanbul return between 1996 and 2024. For the Turkish stock market, the coefficient of the exchange rate is 0.63, implying for a 10% increase in the exchange rate (TL depreciation), stock prices are expected to decrease by 6%, holding all other variables constant. The regression equation also favor the US dollar changes have predictive power for future BIST returns in the longer horizons. What is more, the exchange rate depreciations cause domestic investors shifts from Borsa Istanbul firms to foreign currency (US dollar). Apart from, the weaker exchange rates (conducting low interest rates policy) do not provide foreign investors to buy domestic stocks at lower prices. In terms of economic policy, findings are compatible with the widely accepted idea of strong dollar is bad news for the Turkish economy. As a general rule, US dollar appreciation soar the energy prices, raises the cost of imports and disrupts the balance of payment of Türkiye. Solnik (1984) suggested that countries where exchange rates negatively affect stock prices should not adopt a "laissez-faire" attitude towards exchange rates.

Does Borsa Istanbul Protect Investors From Inflation?

Empirically, much has been written about examining the impact of inflation on stock prices. While early work of Erb et al., (1995) findings indicate that over longer horizon stock markets fail to protect investors against inflation, the study of Ang et al., (2012) defend the idea that the overall stock market may be adequate destination to avoid the inflation threaten. More specifically, authors documented the stocks covaried positively with inflation rates provide higher return that others. Predominantly, investors refer to inflation in decision making process. Because inflation means decrease in the value of the money, it retards the capital markets return. In this context, Barnes et al. (1999) argued that inflation causes volatility in the short term, reducing the depth of financial markets and shrinking the credit supply. Neville et al., (2021) focused more on the economic mechanisms of high inflationary regime experiences and stated that firms give up investing because inflation prevents long-term contracts. Therefore, the authors argued that rising inflation reduces expected future cash flows, making stocks more sensitive to inflation rates. Statistically, they claim that stock prices are negatively correlated with consumer price index. To the extent that inflation is accepted, investors will expect higher return rates from stocks (Homer, 1969). To make our task easy, an inflation hedge financial instrument is assumed to generate return, at least equal or above the prices increase (Reilly et al., 1970). Since stocks have rights over the cash flows of companies, they are considered real assets in a sense. Since the intrinsic value of asset is subject to the price of the goods or services, when input or output prices rise, the value of assets will also increase, therefore equities considered as hedges against inflation. Consequently, investors predict that stock prices move with inflation and must compensate for the devastating effects of inflation (Boudoukh & Richardsoni 1993). However, companies should not be fooled by the fact that, costs are historical but selling prices are instantaneously occurred in inflationary periods. Thus, inflation causes the profit margins to expand in an inflationary environment. But these profits do not mean “real earning” of the firm (Siegel, 2021). The sample begins in June 2012 and ends in October 2024. Again, the monthly closing price of BIST-100 index and headline inflation rates obtained from CBRT were used. As a common view, regression models that investigating the relationship between returns and inflation, if the coefficient of expected or unexpected inflation rates in the equation is equal to or greater than 1, it can be said that stock is a perfect inflation hedging security.

Table 10. Returns and Inflation

Variable	Coefficient	Std. Error	t-Statistic	Prob.
Inflation(-1)	0.609	0.296	2.056	0.041
C	0.007	0.007	0.930	0.353
Diagnostics				
Observation	147			
R square	0.028			
Correlation LM Test[Prob]*:	0.454			
Heteroskedasticity Test[Prob]**:	0.324			

Note: *, **, respectively denotes, Breusch-Godfrey Serial Correlation LM Test for one lag and Heteroskedasticity Test:Breusch-Pagan-Godfrey

As apparent from the table 10, stock return increases by 6 percentages when one lagged inflation increases by 10 percentages. The regression coefficient of stock returns on the one month lagged inflation rate is 0.609 and significantly positive. We can interpret the coefficient, nominal stock returns and inflation tend to move together over the sample but the relationship is not one-for-one. In an inflationary environment, there will be a positive correlation between stock return and inflation rates on the grounds that companies' sales or profits increase. Otherwise, companies' cash flows will decrease as rising inflation is a sign of future economic contraction. Findings[7] demonstrated that firms listed in BIST-100 index are not complete hedge but partial inflation hedging assets during the 2012-2024.

Contribution of Borsa Istanbul on Turkish Economic Growth

The benefits of capital markets to the economy are countless. Firstly, stock markets allow investors to invest in even small amounts; by portfolio diversification the way to reduce risks is paved. Thus, the rate of resources invested in companies increases and stabilizes the economic growth rates (Levine, 1991). Occasional changing and fluctuating stock prices provide investors with information about which companies are good and which are not. Clearly, companies that perform well are more likely to raise financing through IPOs (Guell, 2007). When share prices are high, if the company chooses to go public again for its new investments, new issues can be made at a high price. Therefore, the capital cost of new projects decreases (Howells & Bain, 2007). Additionally, if transaction costs are reduced thanks to stock exchanges, financial markets will be more liquid, thus more investment projects will be realized. As a matter of fact, Hermes & Lensink (2000) declared that, stock exchanges are one step ahead in providing liquidity to the financial system, because there are no factors such as asymmetric information or moral hazard, unlike banks. Besides, companies listed on stock exchanges are more closely subject to corporate governance principles, better managed companies have higher investment potential (Levine, 1997). CFO's base their investment decisions upon stock price performance. In this case, of firm's capitalization exceeds the replacement cost of capital, it becomes easier for managers to make new investment decisions (Mauro, 2003). Most notably, stock markets are also favorable destinations for investors who are reluctant to evaluate their investments in the long term because of uncertainty. But, in the stock market, when necessary, stocks can be bought and sold quickly, easily and with relatively affordable commission fees at any time, causing savings to flow into the capital markets (Demirgüç-Kunt, & Levine 1996). According to Errunza (2001), capital markets are a prerequisite for a country to attract both foreign direct investment and portfolio flows. Demirgüç-Kunt et al., (2008) emphasized that securing investor rights will undoubtedly accelerate the contribution of stock markets to economic growth. The affiliations between stock market and economy builds on long term intrinsic value of firms formulated as discount cash flow. In line with the model, when the investors make a downward revision in firm's dividends on the ground of economic slowdown, intrinsic value of firms will be fall. Therefore, the current value of stocks provides insight into the future performance of the economy. It is not for nothing that stock market indices are used as leading indicators by many economic institutions (Harvey, 1989). Also equity returns influences the rest of the real output. Because falling stock prices will reduce consumption through the wealth effect, there will be a decrease in demand in the overall economy (Friend, 1972). Despite literature disagree about the financial sector and economy nexus, works of Levine (2003), Mauro (2003), Madsen et al., (2013) and Zumba (2024) noted that countries with well-functioning financial markets tend to grow faster. This section uses market capitalization of listed domestic companies and GDP in terms of current US$ to find out whether stock market could help output growth. It analyzes the association between economic performance and one lagged market capitalization.

Table 11. Turkish economic growth and market capitalization

Variable	Coefficient	Std. Error	t-Statistic	Prob.
Market Cap(-1)	0.116	0.039	2.989	0.006
C	0.063	0.028	2.254	0.032
Diagnostics				
Observation	29			
R square	0.158			
F-statistic	4.885			
Prob(F-statistic)	0.036			

continued on following page

Table 11. Continued

Variable	Coefficient	Std. Error	t-Statistic	Prob.
Correlation LM Test[Prob]*:	0.408			
Heteroskedasticity Test[Prob]**:	0.339			

Note: *, **, respectively denotes, Breusch-Godfrey Serial Correlation LM Test for one lag and Heteroskedasticity Test:Breusch-Pagan-Godfrey

Table 11 presents the effects of the market capitalization of listed domestic companies on future GDP. For every 10 percentage increase in the lagged market capitalization of listed domestic companies for a Türkiye, the future growth rate is predicted to increase by 100 pps or 0.01 percentage point. In brief, an increase in market capitalization by 10 percentage point forecasts an 1 percentage point increase in GDP in the following year. Based on the coefficients in model, if the market capitalization growth is zero for Türkiye, the long-term rate of economic growth is predicted to be 6 percent. When stock exchanges were newly established, most of the investors trading strategy are passive. But as the market develops, it gains the ability to attract more professional investors whose decisions are more based on economic fundamentals and the latest information. Thus, the flow of news about publicly traded companies accelerates and more information about real production begins to arrive (Wilcox, 1992). Therefore, another factor that strengthens the association between Borsa Istanbul and the real economy is the corporate companies that trust the stock exchange. Demirgüç-Kunt & Levine (2001) showed that as the national income level rises, companies prefer capital markets as a financing method, but this does not exclude the banking sector. One plausible reason is that firms, not only issue new equity, but they borrow more from banks simultaneously. As equity financing develops, the amount of loans companies receive from banks also increases. More recently data about debt to equity ratio for some OECD members clearly demonstrate the issue. As seen from graph, outstanding debt is much larger than the market value of outstanding equity for Türkiye. So, Türkiye is one of highly leveraged country among OECD members. As a final step, we would like to emphasize that the Turkish economy benefits from capital markets as it grows.

Figure 4. Debt to equity ratio of financial corporations as year of 2022[8]

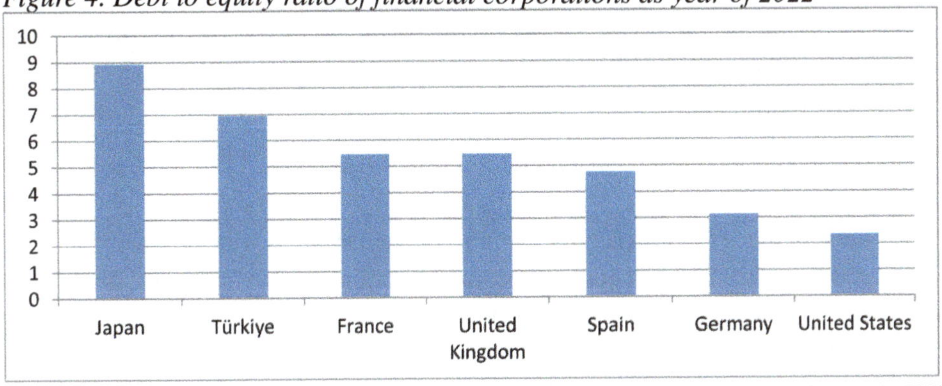

Source: OECD (2024), "Financial corporations debt to equity ratio" (indicator), https://doi.org/10.1787/a3108a99-en (accessed on 16 November 2024).

Data on companies distributing dividends and amounts for the selected Europe - Middle East – Africa countries are reported in Table 12. Let's take a closer look; Türkiye has the highest number of companies distributing dividends in 2022 and 2033. To a large extent, she ranks forefront in dividend payments denominated in US dollar. Apparently, investor must bear in mind that Türkiye's investment climate is supportive in terms of dividend payout.

Table 12. Number of companies distributing dividends and amounts of net dividends paid, 2022-2023 Source: https://www.world-exchanges.org/our-work/articles/2023-annual-statistics-guide

	Number of companies		Dividends paid (USD)	
Europe - Middle East - Africa	**2023**	**2022**	**2023**	**2022**
Athens Stock Exchange	71	71	3.861,5	2.019,9
Bahrain Bourse	0	0	0,0	0,0
BME Spanish Exchanges	136	142	33.207,9	26.533,4
Borsa Istanbul	183	163	4.797,7	4.406,7
Botswana Stock Exchange	17	16	232,5	190,8
Cyprus Stock Exchange	0	13	0,0	0,0
Namibian Stock Exchange	12	10	0,0	0,0
Palestine Exchange	0	30	0,0	221,0
Stock Exchange of Mauritius	38	35	277,8	353,4
Tel-Aviv Stock Exchange	0	233	0,0	8.128,8
The Egyptian Exchange	79	83	1.652,4	1.467,0

continued on following page

Table 12. Continued

	Number of companies		Dividends paid (USD)	
Europe - Middle East - Africa	**2023**	**2022**	**2023**	**2022**
Warsaw Stock Exchange	157	154	5.350,8	3.511,6
Zagreb Stock Exchange	16	NA	1.036,9	NA

Türkiye is one of the fastest growing emerging economies with an average annual GDP growth rate of 5% over the last decade. According to IMF statistics, Türkiye is the 17th largest economy and is also a member of OECD and G20 countries. However, there are many weak spots[9] particularly in the resilience of economy, Türkiye has pursued stimulate economic policies, and for the first time in its history, her national income has exceeded the one billion dollar as of 2023. Today, the psychology of the Turkish investors is ebullient and their confidence has been reassured. But it should not be forgotten that, fiscal policies constitute a minor source of risk in equity markets. Because like other developing countries, Türkiye spends a significantly share of their revenues to meet interest payments (Duttagupta & Pazarbasioglu, 2017).

CONCLUSION

Emerging markets have left behind the weak exchange rates and political instability of the 1960s. As the developing country's GDP increases, emerging stock markets become more integrated with the rest of the world. Thus access to emerging markets has become easier for international investors. Thanks to institutionalization, all kinds of information about the markets became available for investors, buying and selling of shares became easier, liquidity increased and audited financial statements of companies listed on the stock exchanges of developing countries began to be published regularly. For above mentioned reasons: today's emerging markets are an investment opportunities not to be missed (Mobius, 2012). Generally, portfolio manager and individual investors have been searching the way of coping with equity selection. From Turkish investor angle, relatively speaking, Borsa Istanbul has not lost its allure in terms of portfolio diversification. This is because Borsa Istanbul is less correlated with the rest of the world's capital markets. The companies listed in capital markets are also sensitive to exchange rate movements because of import and export operations. Empirical evidence has documented that a strong US dollar drags down the Borsa Istanbul market. For this reason, the US dollar appears as an alternative investment instrument to Borsa Istanbul. Based on empirical relationship between Borsa Istanbul and economic growth, it can be said that, stock market stimulates the long-term economic growth. Inflation has been a fearful economic problem in Türkiye for decades. In the face of inflation risk, the findings affirm that BIST-100 index provide some degree of hedging ability. The results can be interpreted as Borsa Istanbul will partially maintain its purchasing power during inflationary periods. This paper came to conclusion that Borsa Istanbul is a gain to the Turkish economy and there is still room for further developments. Needless to say, Türkiye's business-friendly policymakers will work to narrow the gap with developed markets and to build solid capital markets in the upcoming years. The first step in achieving this is to gradually reduce inflation to single-digit levels.

Finally, this chapter provides recommendations for all stakeholders in capital markets. As the equity financing model has no specific maturity, it is a permanent source of funding for listed companies. Companies can ensure their credibility by going public at any time and by raising capital through issuing stocks. Firms whose debt/equity ratio falls by issuing new shares also reduce the cost of raising additional funds. In addition, going public makes it easier to meet the need for additional resources by making companies more visible, requiring them to make accurate disclosures to the public and requiring independent external audit. In this way, the institutionalization of companies is ensured, while at the same time corporate governance skills are enhanced (Fabozzi & Peterson, 2003). By the same token, it is much easier to calculate the market capitalization of listed companies than of unlisted ones. Since the shares of companies traded at instrict price will be liquid, the cost of funding decreases. However, companies should not deprive themselves of resources by underpricing new equity issues, nor should they postpone investment projects by paying out excessive cash dividends. Companies need to approach the capital markets with different instruments to reach new investors. For example, companies can issue dividend rights certificates for savers who have religious objections to interest. For example, the dividend rights certificates differs from a share in that it is only a shareholder in the profits and does not have the right to participate in the management of the company (Akgüç, 2010). In most cases, capital markets are the only source of low-cost financing. In fact, companies in Türkiye can benefit from certain incentives in return for financing new investments mainly with equity. Another advantage of equity-financing is that, in times of economic recession, companies with low fixed liabilities can continue to operate without going bankrupt. In other words, since the availability of bank credit is limited for start-ups, equity capital is once again the only option. Moreover, from a socio-economic point of view, offering investment opportunities to small savers by issuing shares on the stock exchange will contribute to the income distribution in the long run (Akgüç, 2010). Therefore, given the benefits of capital markets mentioned above, regulators are expected to introduce new rules to encourage companies to issue shares. In this context, the easing of the conditions for capital increases in the commercial code and the shortening of the public offering process would be the shortest way. In addition, the multinational companies that are active in Türkiye should be encouraged to be listed on the Borsa Istanbul. Reductions in the costs of offering new shares, such as announcement costs, intermediary transaction costs and stamp duty, should be fair to all market participants. The reduction of listing costs by the management of Borsa Istanbul will also encourage companies to go public. Finally, the role of listed companies is to increase the market value of the company by investing in projects with an internal rate of return above the cost of equity. In terms of economic policies, budget deficits should be reduced and tax rates that deter investors should be avoided as much as possible.

REFERENCES

Agtmael, A. (2009). The emerging markets century revisited. *Indian Journal of Industrial Relations, 45*(1), 127–136.

Ahmed, S., Hoek, J., Kamin, S. B., Smith, B., & Yoldas, E. (2020). The Impact of COVID-19 on Emerging Market Economies' Financial Conditions (No. 2020-10-07-1). B*oard of Governors of the Federal Reserve System* (US).

Akgüç, Ö. (2010). *Finansal Yönetim*. Avcıol Basım Yayın.

Altunbas, Y., Kara, A., & Olgu, Ö. (2008). *Turkish Banking: Banking Under Political Instability and Chronic High Inflation*. Springer.

Ang, A., Brière, M., & Signori, O. (2012). Inflation and Individual Equities. *Financial Analysts Journal, 68*(4), 36–55. DOI: 10.2469/faj.v68.n4.3

Baier, S. L., Dwyer, G. P.Jr, & Tamura, R. (2004). Does Opening a Stock Exchange Increase Economic Growth? *Journal of International Money and Finance, 23*(3), 311–331. DOI: 10.1016/j.jimonfin.2004.01.001

Bailey, O. (2010). *Developments in Emerging Equity Markets, Bulletin, December-Quarter*. Reserve Bank of Australia.

Barnes, M., Boyd, J. H., & Smith, B. D. (1999). Inflation and Asset returns. *European Economic Review*, 43(4-6), 737-754. doi:.1016/S0014-2921(98)00090-7

Barry, C. B., Peavy, J. W.Jr, & Rodriguez, M. (1998). Performance Characteristics of Emerging Capital Markets. *Financial Analysts Journal, 54*(1), 72–80. DOI: 10.2469/faj.v54.n1.2147

Beck, T., Flynn, B., & Homanen, M. (2020). COVID-19 in emerging markets: Firm-survey evidence. *Covid Economics, 38*, 37–67.

Bekaert, G., Erb, C. B., Harvey, C. R., & Viskanta, T. E. (1998). Distributional Characteristics Of Emerging Market Returns and Asset Allocation. *Journal of Portfolio Management, 24*(2), 102–116. DOI: 10.3905/jpm.24.2.102

Bekaert, G., & Harvey, C. R. (1998). Capital markets: An engine for Economic Growth. *The Brown Journal of World Affairs, 5*(1), 33–53.

Bekaert, G., & Harvey, C. R. (2002). Research in Emerging Markets Finance: Looking To The Future. *Emerging Markets Review, 3*(4), 429–448. DOI: 10.1016/S1566-0141(02)00045-6

Bekaert, G., Harvey, C. R., & Mondino, T. (2023). Emerging Equity Markets in a Globalized World. *Emerging Markets Review, 101034*, 101034. Advance online publication. DOI: 10.1016/j.ememar.2023.101034

Boudoukh, J., & Richardson, M. (1993). Stock Returns and Inflation: A Long-horizon Perspective. *The American Economic Review, 83*(5), 1346–1355.

Buchanan, B., & English, P. C.II. (2007). Law, Finance, and Emerging Market Returns. *Emerging Markets Review, 8*(3), 181–193. DOI: 10.1016/j.ememar.2007.05.001

Cecchetti, S., & Kharroubi, E. (2012). *Reassessing the Impact of Finance on Growth (No. 381).* Bank for International Settlements.

Claessens, S., Klingebiel, D., & Schmukler, S. L. (2002). The Future of Stock Exchanges in Emerging Economies: Evolution and Prospects. *Brookings-Wharton Papers on Financial Services*, 2002(1), 167-212.

Conover, C. M., Jensen, G. R., & Johnson, R. R. (2002). Emerging Markets: When Are They Worth It? *Financial Analysts Journal, 58*(2), 86–95. DOI: 10.2469/faj.v58.n2.2525

Cornelius, P. K. (1994). The Internationalization of Emerging Stock Markets. *Inter Economics, 29*(3), 131–138. DOI: 10.1007/BF02926350

Demirgüç-Kunt, A., Beck, T. H. L., & Honohan, P. (2008). *Finance for All?: Policies and Pitfalls in Expanding Access.* World Bank.

Demirgüç-Kunt, A., & Levine, R. (1996). Stock Markets, Corporate Finance, and Economic Growth: An Overview. *The World Bank Economic Review, 10*(2), 223–239. DOI: 10.1093/wber/10.2.223

Demirgüç-Kunt, A., & Levine, R. (2001). *Financial Structure and Economic Growth: A Cross-Country Comparison of Banks, Markets, and Development.* MIT Press. DOI: 10.7551/mitpress/3001.001.0001

Diermeier, J., & Solnik, B. (2001). Global Pricing of Equity. *Financial Analysts Journal, 57*(4), 37–47. DOI: 10.2469/faj.v57.n4.2464

Doidge, C., Karolyi, G. A., & Stulz, R. M. (2004). Why Are Foreign Firms Listed in the US Worth More? *Journal of Financial Economics, 71*(2), 205–238. DOI: 10.1016/S0304-405X(03)00183-1

Duttagupta, R., & Pazarbasioglu, C. (2017). Miles to Go: The Future of Emerging Markets—IMF F&D. International Monetary Fund. Available online: https://www.imf. org/external/pubs/ft/fandd/2021/06/the-future-of-emerging-markets-duttagupta-andpazarbasioglu. htm (accessed on 5 Dec 2023).

Dwyer, G., & Hafer, R. (1988). Are National Stock Markets Linked? *Review - Federal Reserve Bank of St. Louis*, (Nov), 3–14.

Erb, C., Harvey, C., & Viskanta, T. (1998). Risk in Emerging Markets. *The Financial Survey*, *1998*, 42–46.

Erb, C. B., Harvey, C. R., & Viskanta, T. E. (1994). Forecasting International Equity Correlations. *Financial Analysts Journal*, *50*(6), 32–45. DOI: 10.2469/faj.v50.n6.32

Erb, C. B., Harvey, C. R., & Viskanta, T. E. (1995). Inflation and World Equity Selection. *Financial Analysts Journal*, *51*(6), 28–42. DOI: 10.2469/faj.v51.n6.1947

Erb, C. B., Harvey, C. R., & Viskanta, T. E. (1996a). Expected Returns and Volatility in 135 Countries. *Journal of Portfolio Management*, *22*(3), 46–58. DOI: 10.3905/jpm.1996.409554

Erb, C. B., Harvey, C. R., & Viskanta, T. E. (1996b). Political Risk, Economic Risk, and Financial Risk. *Financial Analysts Journal*, *52*(6), 29–46. DOI: 10.2469/faj.v52.n6.2038

Erb, C. B., Harvey, C. R., & Viskanta, T. E. (1997). The Making of an Emerging Market. *Emerging Markets Quarterly*, *1*, 14–19.

Errunza, V. (2001). Foreign Portfolio Equity Investments, Financial Liberalization, and Economic Development. *Review of International Economics*, *9*(4), 703–726. DOI: 10.1111/1467-9396.00308

Errunza, V. R. (1983). Emerging Markets: A New Opportunity for Improving Global Portfolio Performance. *Financial Analysts Journal*, *39*(5), 51–58. DOI: 10.2469/faj.v39.n5.51

Errunza, V. R., & Padmanabhan, P. (1988). Further Evidence on the Benefits of Portfolio Investments in Emerging Markets. *Financial Analysts Journal*, *44*(4), 76–78. DOI: 10.2469/faj.v44.n4.76

Fabozzi, F. J., & Peterson, P. P. (2003). *Financial management and analysis*. John Wiley & Sons.

Feldman, R. A., & Kumar, M. S. (1995). Emerging Equity Markets: Growth, Benefits, and Policy Concerns. *The World Bank Research Observer*, *10*(2), 181–200. DOI: 10.1093/wbro/10.2.181

Feyen, E., Gispert, T. A., Kliatskova, T., & Mare, D. S. (2021). Financial sector policy response to COVID-19 in emerging markets and developing economies. *Journal of Banking & Finance*, *133*, 106184. DOI: 10.1016/j.jbankfin.2021.106184 PMID: 34898821

Friend, I. (1972). The Economic Consequences of the Stock Market. *The American Economic Review*, *62*(1/2), 212–219.

Gilmore, C. G., McManus, G. M., & Tezel, A. (2005). Portfolio allocations and the Emerging Equity Markets of Central Europe. *Journal of Multinational Financial Management*, *15*(3), 287–300. DOI: 10.1016/j.mulfin.2004.12.001

Guell, R. C. (2007). *Issues in Economics Today*. McGraw-Hill/Irwin.

Gülay, G., & Aydoğmuş, M. (2024). Guest Editors' introduction: Borsa Istanbul history (1836–2023) and an overview of selected papers on the 150th anniversary of the founding of Borsa Istanbul. *Borsa Istanbul Review*.

Hachicha, F. (2024). Sentiment investor, exchange rates, geopolitical risk and developing stock market: Evidence of co-movements in the time-frequency domain during RussiaUkraine war. *Review of Behavioral Finance*, *16*(3), 486–509. DOI: 10.1108/RBF-04-2023-0119

Harjoto, M. A., & Rossi, F. (2023). Market reaction to the COVID-19 pandemic: Evidence from emerging markets. *International Journal of Emerging Markets*, *18*(1), 173–199. DOI: 10.1108/IJOEM-05-2020-0545

Harvey, C. R. (1989). Forecasts of Economic Growth from the Bond and Stock Markets. *Financial Analysts Journal*, *45*(5), 38–45. DOI: 10.2469/faj.v45.n5.38

Harvey, C. R. (2000). Drivers of Expected Returns in Emerging Markets. *Emerging Market Quarterly*, 32 – 49. DOI: 10.2139/ssrn.795385

Henry, P. B. (2000). Stock Market Liberalization, Economic Reform, and Emerging Market Equity Prices. *The Journal of Finance*, *55*(2), 529–564. DOI: 10.1111/0022-1082.00219

Hermes, N., & Lensink, R. (2000). Financial System Development in Transition Economies. *Journal of Banking & Finance*, *24*(4), 507–524. DOI: 10.1016/S0378-4266(99)00078-3

Homer, S. (1969). Inflation and the Capital Markets. *Financial Analysts Journal*, *25*(4), 143–145. DOI: 10.2469/faj.v25.n4.143

Howells, P., & Bain, K. (2007). *Financial Markets and Institutions*. Pearson Education.

Karahan, C. C., & Özsöylev, H. N. (2023). Inflation and the Stock Market: Money Illusion in Borsa Istanbul. In Managing Inflation and Supply Chain Disruptions in the Global Economy (pp. 24-40). IGI Global.

Karolyi, G. A. (1998). Why Do Companies List Shares Abroad?: A Survey of the Evidence and its Managerial Implications. *Financial Markets, Institutions and Instruments*, *7*(1), 1–60. DOI: 10.1111/1468-0416.00018

Karolyi, G. A., & Stulz, R. M. (1996). Why Do Markets Move Together? An Investigation of US-Japan Stock Return Comovements. *The Journal of Finance*, *51*(3), 951–986. DOI: 10.1111/j.1540-6261.1996.tb02713.x

Köse, N., & Ünal, E. (2024). The Effects of the Volatilities in Global Determinants on the Istanbul Stock Exchange. *Panoeconomicus*, •••(00), 1–38. DOI: 10.2298/PAN230213020K

Kumar, S. S. S. (2011). Are Emerging Markets Relevant for Portfolio Diversification? *Review of Market Integration*, *3*(2), 103–119. DOI: 10.1177/097492921100300201

Levine, R. (1991). Stock Markets, Growth, and Tax Policy. *The Journal of Finance*, *46*(4), 1445–1465. DOI: 10.1111/j.1540-6261.1991.tb04625.x

Levine, R. (1997). Financial Development and Economic Growth: Views and Agenda. *Journal of Economic Literature*, *35*(2), 688–726.

Levine, R. (2002). Bank-Based or Market-Based Financial Systems: Which is Better? *Journal of Financial Intermediation*, *11*(4), 398–428. DOI: 10.1006/jfin.2002.0341

Levine, R. (2003). More on Finance and Growth: More Finance, More Growth? *Review - Federal Reserve Bank of St. Louis*, *85*(4), 31–46. DOI: 10.20955/r.85.31-46

Loser, C. M. (2008). *Financial Markets in Latin America. Growth and Development in Emerging Market Economies: International Private Capital Flows, Financial Markets and Globalization*. Sage Publishing.

Madsen, J. B., Dzhumashev, R., & Yao, H. (2013). Stock Returns and Economic Growth. *Applied Economics*, *45*(10), 1257–1271. DOI: 10.1080/00036846.2011.613802

Markowitz, H. (1952). Modern Portfolio Theory. *The Journal of Finance*, *7*(11), 77–91.

Mauro, P. (2003). Stock Returns and Output Growth in Emerging and Advanced Economies. *Journal of Development Economics*, *71*(1), 129–153. DOI: 10.1016/S0304-3878(02)00136-0

Mishkin, F. S. (2009). Globalization and financial development. *Journal of Development Economics*, *89*(2), 164–169. DOI: 10.1016/j.jdeveco.2007.11.004

Mobius, M. (2012). *The Little Book of Emerging Markets: How to Make Money in the World's Fastest Growing Markets*. John Wiley & Sons.

Moussa, F., & Delhoumi, E. (2022). The asymmetric impact of interest and exchange rate on the stock market index: Evidence from MENA region. *International Journal of Emerging Markets*, *17*(10), 2510–2528. DOI: 10.1108/IJOEM-01-2020-0089

Mullin, J. (1993). Emerging Equity Markets in The Global Economy. *Quarterly Review-Federal Reserve Bank of New York*, *18*, 54–54.

Neville, H., Draaisma, T., Funnell, B., Harvey, C. R., & Van Hemert, O. (2021). The Best Strategies for Inflationary Times. *Journal of Portfolio Management*, *47*(8), 8–37. DOI: 10.3905/jpm.2021.1.274

Obstfeld, M. (1998). The Global Capital Market: Benefactor or Menace? *The Journal of Economic Perspectives*, *12*(4), 9–30. DOI: 10.1257/jep.12.4.9

Odier, P., & Solnik, B. (1993). Lessons for International Asset Allocation. *Financial Analysts Journal*, *49*(2), 63–77. DOI: 10.2469/faj.v49.n2.63

Özbay, F., & Tosun, N. (2022). The Fear Impact of COVID-19 on Stock Markets and Exchange Rates: An Empirical Application on Turkey. In Handbook of Research on Global Networking Post COVID-19 (pp. 1-22). IGI Global.

Papaioannou, M., & Duke, L. (1993). The Internationalization of Emerging Equity Markets. *Finance & Development*, *30*, 36–36.

Reilly, F. K., Johnson, G. L., & Smith, R. E. (1970). Inflation, Inflation Hedges, and Common Stocks. *Financial Analysts Journal*, *26*(1), 104–110. DOI: 10.2469/faj.v26.n1.104

Shapiro, A. C., & Hanouna, P. (2019). *Multinational Financial Management*. John Wiley & Sons.

Siegel, J. J. (2021). *Stocks for the Long Run: The Definitive Guide to Financial Market Returns & Long-Term Investment Strategies*. McGraw-Hill Education.

Solnik, B. (1984). Stock Prices and Monetary Variables: The International Evidence. *Financial Analysts Journal*, *40*(2), 69–73. DOI: 10.2469/faj.v40.n2.69

Solnik, B., Boucrelle, C., & Le Fur, Y. (1996). International Market Correlation and Volatility. *Financial Analysts Journal*, *52*(5), 17–34. DOI: 10.2469/faj.v52.n5.2021

Solnik, B. H. (1995). Why Not Diversify Internationally Rather than Domestically?. *Financial Analysts Journal*, 51(1), 89-94. doi:/DOI: 10.2469/faj.v30.n4.48

Spyrou, S. I. (2004). Are stocks a good hedge against inflation? Evidence from emerging markets. *Applied Economics*, *36*(1), 41–48. DOI: 10.1080/0003684042000177189

Tesar, L. L., & Werner, M. (1995). US Equity Investment in Emerging Stock Markets. *The World Bank Economic Review*, *9*(1), 109–129. DOI: 10.1093/wber/9.1.109

Topcu, M., & Gulal, O. S. (2020). The impact of COVID-19 on emerging stock markets. *Finance Research Letters*, *36*, 101691. DOI: 10.1016/j.frl.2020.101691 PMID: 32837378

Wilcox, J. W. (1992). Global Investing in Emerging Markets. *Financial Analysts Journal*, 15–19.

Zumba, Y. (2024). Stock Prices and Economic Activities in Nigeria: Sector Level Evidence. *Macroeconomics and Finance in Emerging Market Economies*, *17*(1), 5–24. DOI: 10.1080/17520843.2022.2027619

ENDNOTES

1 TurkStat, Small and Medium Sized Enterprises Statistics Bulletin, 2022, https://data.tuik.gov.tr/Bulten/Index?p=49438&dil=2

2 CBRT lowered the lending rate from %19 to 8.5% for the period from 19.03.2021 to 24.02.2023. https://www.tcmb.gov.tr/wps/wcm/connect/TR/TCMB+TR/Main+Menu/Temel+Faaliyetler/Para+Politikasi/Merkez+Bankasi+Faiz+Oranlari/1+Hafta+Repo

3 https://www.tuik.gov.tr/, *Coefficiant of variation is a ratio the standart deviation to mean.

4 Government Domestic Debt Instruments are calculated by using BIST-KYD GDS ALL Index under BIST-KYD GDS Indices, which is published by Borsa İstanbul. This index reflects the yield of zero coupon and fixed-rate coupon Turkish Government Debt Securities (GDS), which are traded in Debt Securities Market, by covering all maturity bands. See in details https://data.tuik.gov.tr/Bulten/Index?p=Finansal-Yatirim-Araclarinin-Reel-Getiri-Oranlari-Agustos-2024-53733.

5 All data collected from Morgan Stanley Capital International (MSCI) .The web link is https://www.msci.com/end-of-day-data-country

6 See: Özbay & Tosun (2022), Moussa & Delhoumi (2022) and Hachicha (2024) where time –varying methods and different crisis period analyzed.

7 See: Köse & Ünal (2024); Karahan,& Özsöylev (2023) and Spyrou (2004).

8 See time seriesi detail in OECD (2024), "National Accounts at a Glance (Edition 2023)", OECD National Accounts Statistics (database), https://doi.org/10.1787/c1524558-en (accessed on 16 November 2024).

9 To take an example, in the earthquake of Hatay that Türkiye experienced more than 50,000 casualties, injured 107,000 people, damaged 1.9 million house, displaced 3.3 million people, It is estimated that $81.5 billion is needed for the region's recovery (https://www.worldbank.org/en/country/turkey/overview#1)

Compilation of References

Aastveit, K. A., & Anundsen, A. K. (2022). Asymmetric effects of monetary policy in regional housing markets. *American Economic Journal. Macroeconomics*, *14*(4), 499–529. DOI: 10.1257/mac.20190011

Abdelaziz, S. M., Samak, N., Abdelsalam, M. A., Sobhy, M. W., & Ahmed, F. (2025). The Impact of Exchange Rate Volatility on Foreign Direct Investment Inflows the Case of Egypt. *Scientific Journal for Financial and Commercial Studies and Research*, *6*(1), 407–445. DOI: 10.21608/cfdj.2024.319270.2041

Abdul-Rahman, M., Khan, A. U. I., & Kaplan, M. (2024). Beyond GARCH: Intraday Insights Into the Exchange Rate and Stock PriceVolatility Dynamics in Borsa Istanbul Sectors. *FWU Journal of Social Sciences*, 1–13. DOI: 10.51709/19951272/Fall2024/1

Acquier, A., Daudigeos, T., & Pinkse, J. (2017). Promises and paradoxes of the sharing economy: An organizing framework. *Technological Forecasting and Social Change*, *125*, 1–10. DOI: 10.1016/j.techfore.2017.07.006

Adams, S., & Opoku, E. E. O. (2015). Foreign direct investment, regulations and growth in sub-Saharan Africa. *Economic Analysis and Policy*, *47*, 48–56. DOI: 10.1016/j.eap.2015.07.001

AFD. (2024). African. *Economic Outlook, 2024*. https://www.afdb.org/en/documents/african-economic-outlook-2024

Afonso, A., & Sousa, R. M. (2012). The macroeconomic effects of fiscal policy. *Applied Economics*, *44*(34), 4439–4454. DOI: 10.1080/00036846.2011.591732

Afsar, A., & Dogan, E. (2018). Analyzing asset of bubbles in the housing market with right-tailed unit root tests: The case of Turkey. *Journal of Business Economics and Finance*, *7*(2), 139–147. DOI: 10.17261/Pressacademia.2018.836

Agarwal, D., Tripathi, K., Krishen, K., & Kumar, [First name not provided]. (2023). Concepts of artificial intelligence and its application in modern healthcare systems. CRC Press. DOI: 10.1201/9781003333081

Agarwal, D., & Tripathi, K. (2022). A framework for structural damage detection system in automobiles for flexible insurance claim using IoT and machine learning. In *2022 International Mobile and Embedded Technology Conference (MECON)* (pp. 5–8). IEEE. DOI: 10.1109/MECON53876.2022.9751889

Agtmael, A. (2009). The emerging markets century revisited. *Indian Journal of Industrial Relations*, *45*(1), 127–136.

Ahmed, S., Hoek, J., Kamin, S. B., Smith, B., & Yoldas, E. (2020). The Impact of COVID-19 on Emerging Market Economies' Financial Conditions (No. 2020-10-07-1). B*oard of Governors of the Federal Reserve System* (US).

Ahmed, R., Jawaid, S. T., & Khalil, S. (2021). Foreign capital inflows and housing market in Pakistan. *International Journal of Housing Markets and Analysis*, *14*(5), 936–952. DOI: 10.1108/IJHMA-07-2020-0089

Ahmed, S. (2003). Sources of economic fluctuations in Latin America and implications for choice of exchange rate regimes. *Journal of Development Economics*, *72*(1), 181–202. DOI: 10.1016/S0304-3878(03)00073-7

Aji, A., & Nurhasanah, N. (2020). The impact of IoT and AI on banking services: A comprehensive review. *Journal of Banking and Finance Technology*, *4*(1), 1–12. DOI: 10.1007/s42786-019-00009-2

Akan, T. (2024). The impact of monetary policy on climate change through the mediation of sectoral renewable energy consumption. *Energy Policy*, *192*, 114244. DOI: 10.1016/j.enpol.2024.114244

Akat, A.S. (2004). Dalgalı Kur ve Para Politikası: Bir Parasal Kural Önerisi. iç. *Gülten Kazgan'a Armağan: Türkiye Ekonomisi*. İstanbul: İstanbul Bilgi Üniversitesi Yayınları, ss.57-80.

Akçay, S. B., & Akyüz, M. (2024). Why Did House Prices Go Up During COVID-19 Pandemic? Policy-Driven or Market-Driven? *International Real Estate Review*, *27*(2), 303–328. DOI: 10.53383/100384

Akgüç, Ö. (2010). *Finansal Yönetim*. Avcıol Basım Yayın.

Akgündüz, Y. E., Dursun-de Neef, H. Ö., Hacihasanoğlu, Y. S., & Yılmaz, F. (2023). Cost of credit, mortgage demand and house prices. *Journal of Banking & Finance*, *154*, 106953. DOI: 10.1016/j.jbankfin.2023.106953

Akkaya, M. (2024). Konut fiyat balonu ve konut fiyatını etkileyen faktörlerin analizi: Türkiye uygulaması. *Gazi İktisat ve İşletme Dergisi, 10*(1), 33–45.

Akkay, R. C. (2021). The macroeconomic determinants of the housing prices in Turkey. *Erciyes Üniversitesi İktisadi ve İdari Bilimler Fakültesi Dergisi*, (58), 241–264. DOI: 10.18070/erciyesiibd.801319

Alaeddin, O., Al-Debei, M. M., & Al-Lozi, E. M. (2018). Consumer adoption of cloud computing in Jordan. *International Journal of Business Information Systems, 29*(1), 1–20.

Alagöz, R. (2012). The Impacts Of Neo-Lıberal Polıcıes On Turkey In 2000-2001. City University of New York (CUNY) *CUNY Academic Works*. https://academicworks.cuny.edu/cc_etds_theses/133

Alavi, A. S., & Jafari, A. (2021). Cybersecurity risks in IoT: A review of recent literature. *Computers & Security, 110*, 102423. DOI: 10.1016/j.cose.2021.102423

Alberta Government. (2024). Open Government Program, https://open.alberta.ca/dataset?tags=GDP&dataset_type=publications&dataset_type=publications

Albertazzi, U., Fringuellotti, F., & Ongena, S. (2020). Monetary policy and bank stability: The analytical toolbox reviewed. *ECB Working Paper Series No. 2377*. European Central Bank. https://doi.org/DOI: 10.2866/13576

Aleem, A., & Lahiani, A. (2014). Monetary policy credibility and exchange rate pass-through: Some evidence from emerging countries. *Economic Modelling, 43*, 21–29. DOI: 10.1016/j.econmod.2014.06.020

Al-Jasser, M., & Banafe, A. (2008). Monetary policy transmission mechanism in Saudi Arabia. In *BIS Papers No. 35*. Bank for International Settlements.

Al-Laham, M., Al-Tarawneh, H., & Abdallat, N. (2009). Development of electronic money and its impact on the central bank role and monetary policy. *Issues in Informing Science and Information Technology, 6*, 339–349. DOI: 10.28945/1063

Allawi, A. A. (2024). *Rich World, Poor World: The Struggle to Escape Poverty*. Yale University Press., DOI: 10.2307/jj.13760047

Allegret, J. P., & Benkhodja, M. T. (2015). External shocks and monetary policy in an oil exporting economy (Algeria). *Journal of Policy Modeling, 37*(4), 652–667. DOI: 10.1016/j.jpolmod.2015.03.017

Allen, D. W., Berg, C., Markey-Towler, B., Novak, M., & Potts, J. (2020). Blockchain and the evolution of institutional technologies: Implications for innovation policy. *Research Policy, 49*(1), 103865. DOI: 10.1016/j.respol.2019.103865

Allen, F., Gu, X., & Jagtiani, J. (2022). A survey of fintech research and policy discussion. *The Review of Corporate Finance Studies, 11*(1), 1–45.

Allen, F., Gu, X., & Jagtiani, J. (2022). A survey of FinTech research and policy discussion. *The Review of Corporate Finance Studies, 11*(1), 1–45.

Altunbas, Y., Kara, A., & Olgu, Ö. (2008). *Turkish Banking: Banking Under Political Instability and Chronic High Inflation*. Springer.

Ambekar, A., Anusha, K. M., Kumar, M. K., & Tyagi, A. K. (2024). Smart banking solutions for modern society: Opportunities and challenges. In *Convergence of technology and operations management in modern businesses*. IGI Global., DOI: 10.4018/979-8-3693-6200-6.ch011

Ameziane, K., & Benyacoub, B. (2022). Exchange Rate Volatility Effect on Economic Growth under Different Exchange Rate Regimes: New Evidence from Emerging Countries Using Panel CS-ARDL Model. *Journal of Risk and Financial Management, 15*(11), 499. DOI: 10.3390/jrfm15110499

Amor, T. H., Nouira, R., Rault, C., & Sova, A. D. (2023). Real exchange rate misalignments and economic growth in Tunisia: New evidence from a threshold analysis of asymmetric adjustments. *The Quarterly Review of Economics and Finance, 88*, 215–227. DOI: 10.1016/j.qref.2023.01.007

Ang, A., Brière, M., & Signori, O. (2012). Inflation and Individual Equities. *Financial Analysts Journal, 68*(4), 36–55. DOI: 10.2469/faj.v68.n4.3

Antonakakis, N., Chatziantoniou, I., & Gabauer, D. (2020). Refined Measures of Dynamic Connectedness based on Time-Varying Parameter Vector Autoregressions. *Journal of Risk and Financial Management, 13*(4), 84. DOI: 10.3390/jrfm13040084

Arat, K. (2003). Türkiye'de Optimum Döviz Kuru Rejimi Seçimi ve Döviz Kurlarından Fiyatlara Geçiş Etkisinin İncelenmesi. Uzmanlık Yeterlilik Tezi. Ankara: TCMB Dış İlişkiler Genel Müdürlüğü.

Aren, S. (1991). *100 Soruda Para ve Para Politikası*. 4.b., İstanbul: Gerçek Yayınevi.

Arumugam, S. K., Tyagi, A. K., Tiwari, S., & Kumari, S. (2024). The role of futuristic technologies in building sustainable environment. In *Creating AI synergy through business technology transformation*. IGI Global., DOI: 10.4018/979-8-3693-4187-2.ch012

Ashcraft, A. B. (2006). New evidence on the lending channel. *Journal of Money, Credit and Banking, 38*(3), 751–775. DOI: 10.1353/mcb.2006.0037

Asian Development Bank. (2024). *Capturing the digital economy: A proposed measurement framework and its applications.* https://www.adb.org/publications/capturing-digital-economy-measurement-framework

Aslan, A., and Dinçer, İ. (2018). The impact of mortgage loans on the financialization process in Turkey. *Planlama*, 28(2).

Asomaning, K., Shah, H., & Emmanuel, U. (2024). A TVP-VAR assessment of the spillover effects of geopolitical risk shocks on macroeconomic variability: A study of the Ghanaian economy. Future Business Journal, 10(1), DOI: 10.1186/s43093-024-00341-5

ASSOCHAM & Deloitte. (2016). *Digital India: Unlocking the trillion dollar opportunity.* https://www2.deloitte.com/content/dam/Deloitte/in/Documents/technology-media-telecommunications/in-tmt-digital-india-unlock-opportunity-noexp.pdf

Athanasiou, G., & Kotsios, S. (2008). An algorithmic approach to exchange rate stabilization. *Economic Modelling*, *25*(6), 1246–1260. DOI: 10.1016/j.econmod.2008.04.001

Ayadi, M., & Mattoussi, W. (2016). Scoping of the Tunisian economy. In Working Paper Series. https://doi.org/DOI: 10.1007/978-3-030-91088-4_6

Ayan, E. (2011). Konut Finansmanı Sistemi ve Türkiye'de TOKİ Uygulamalarının Analizi. *Muhasebe ve Finansman Dergisi*, (51), 139–156.

Badhan, I. A., Neeroj, M. H., Rahman, S., & Iqbal, J. (2024). Currency Rate Fluctuations and their Impact on Supply Chain Risk Management: An Empirical Analysis. *International Journal of Business and Management Sciences*, *4*(10), 6–26. DOI: 10.55640/ijbms-04-10-02

Badurlar, Ö. (2008). Türkiye'de konut fiyatları ile makro ekonomik değişkenler arasındaki ilişkinin araştırılması. *Anadolu üniversitesi sosyal bilimler dergisi*, 8(1), 223-238.

Baglan, D., & Yoldas, E. (2014). Non-linearity in the inflation–growth relationship in developing economies: Evidence from a semiparametric panel model. *Economics Letters*, *125*(1), 93–96. DOI: 10.1016/j.econlet.2014.08.015

Baharumshah, A. Z., Slesman, L., & Wohar, M. E. (2016). Inflation, inflation uncertainty, and economic growth in emerging and developing countries: Panel data evidence. *Economic Systems*, *40*(4), 638–657. DOI: 10.1016/j.ecosys.2016.02.009

Baier, S. L., Dwyer, G. P.Jr, & Tamura, R. (2004). Does Opening a Stock Exchange Increase Economic Growth? *Journal of International Money and Finance, 23*(3), 311–331. DOI: 10.1016/j.jimonfin.2004.01.001

Baig, M. Z., & Shah, F. (2020). AI-based privacy-preserving methods in banking: A systematic review. *Journal of Financial Services Marketing, 25*(2), 105–120. DOI: 10.1057/s41264-020-00060-2

Bailey, O. (2010). *Developments in Emerging Equity Markets, Bulletin, December-Quarter*. Reserve Bank of Australia.

Balcilar, M., Demirer, R., Gupta, R., & van Eyden, R. (2017). The impact of US policy uncertainty on the monetary effectiveness in the Euro area. *Journal of Policy Modeling, 39*(6), 1052–1064. DOI: 10.1016/j.jpolmod.2017.09.002

Balcilar, M., Gupta, R., & Jooste, C. (2017). The growth-inflation nexus for the U.S. From 1801 to 2013: A semiparametric approach. *Journal of Applied Econometrics, 20*(1), 105–120. DOI: 10.1016/S1514-0326(17)30005-3

Baliamoune-Lutz, M. (2009). Tunisia's development experience: A success story? (WIDER Research Paper No. 2009/32). The United Nations University World Institute for Development Economics Research (UNU-WIDER). https://www.econstor.eu/bitstream/10419/45097/1/601812603.pdf

Baliamoune-Lutz, M. (2004). Does FDI Contribute to Economic Growth? *Business Economics (Cleveland, Ohio), 39*(2), 49–56. https://www.proquest.com/scholarly-journals/does-fdi-contribute-economic-growth/docview/199864100/se-2

Banerjee, K., & Smith, C. D. (Eds.). (2024). *Migration Governance in North America: Policy, Politics, and Community*. McGill-Queen's University Press., DOI: 10.1515/9780228020486

Bank for International Settlements (BIS). (2021). CBDCs: Financial stability implications. *BIS Annual Economic Report 2021*, Chapter III. https://www.bis.org/publ/arpdf/ar2021e3.htm

Bansal, N. (2020b). Awareness of password management and adoption of digital banking services in rural India. *Finance India, 34*(2).

Bansal, N. (2020a). The impact of training programme of digital banking services to employees of unorganised sector and their acceptability in India. *International Journal of Electronic Customer Relationship Management, 12*(3), 246–272. DOI: 10.1504/IJECRM.2020.110042

Bansal, N., & Pandey, K. N. (2023). Impact of password management strategies on the trust enhancement in the digital era. *International Journal of Business Performance Management, 24*(3-4), 484–503. DOI: 10.1504/IJBPM.2023.132333

Bansal, N., Pareek, N., & Nigam, A. (2022). The impact of customer's training of digital banking services on its acceptability by customers' in India. *International Journal of Business and Globalisation, 30*(2), 207–231. DOI: 10.1504/IJBG.2022.122665

Bardi, W., & Hfaiedh, M. A. (2021). International trade and economic growth: Evidence from a panel ARDL-PMG approach. *International Economics and Economic Policy, 18*(4), 847–868. DOI: 10.1007/s10368-021-00507-4

Barguellil, A., Ben-Salha, O., & Zmami, M. (2018). Exchange Rate Volatility and Economic Growth. *Journal of Economic Integration, 33*(2), 1302–1336. DOI: 10.11130/jei.2018.33.2.1302

Barnes, M., Boyd, J. H., & Smith, B. D. (1999). Inflation and Asset returns. *European Economic Review*, 43(4-6), 737-754. doi:.1016/S0014-2921(98)00090-7

Barontini, C., & Holden, H. (2019). *Proceeding with caution – A survey on central bank digital currency. BIS Papers No. 101*. Bank for International Settlements.

Barrdear, J., & Kumhof, M. (2022). The macroeconomics of central bank digital currencies. *Journal of Economic Dynamics & Control, 104*, 34–55. DOI: 10.1016/j.jedc.2021.104148

Barry, C. B., Peavy, J. W.Jr, & Rodriguez, M. (1998). Performance Characteristics of Emerging Capital Markets. *Financial Analysts Journal, 54*(1), 72–80. DOI: 10.2469/faj.v54.n1.2147

Bashir, M., & Kumar, M. (2021). Securing IoT-enabled banking services through blockchain technology. *Journal of Information Security and Applications, 57*, 102726. DOI: 10.1016/j.jisa.2020.102726

Bashir, U., Zebende, G. F., Yu, Y., Hussain, M., Ali, A., & Abbas, G. (2019). Differential market reactions to pre- and post-Brexit referendum. *Physica A, 515*, 151–158. DOI: 10.1016/j.physa.2018.09.182

Basu, S. (2003). Why do banks fail? *International Review of Applied Economics, 17*(3), 231–248. DOI: 10.1080/0269217032000090469

Batool, Z., & Bhatti, A. A. (2020). Macroeconomic policies and social inclusion in the developing world. [LASSIJ]. *Liberal Arts and Social Sciences International Journal, 4*(2), 114–129. DOI: 10.47264/idea.lassij/4.2.10

Bayır, M. (2019). Türkiye'de Para Politikasının Konut Fiyatlarına Etkisi. *Eskişehir Osmangazi Üniversitesi İktisadi ve İdari Bilimler Dergisi, 14*(3), 657–674. DOI: 10.17153/oguiibf.486955

Becha, H., Kalai, M., & Helali, K. (2023). Smooth transition regression model relating inflation to economic growth in Tunisia. *Journal of Economic Structures, 12*(1), 1–26. DOI: 10.1186/s40008-023-00308-9

Bechri, M. Z., & Naccache, S. (2005). *The Political Economy of Development Policy in Tunisia* (Vol. 278). Contributions to Economic Analysis. DOI: 10.1016/S0573-8555(06)78010-5

Beck, T. (2020). Fintech and financial inclusion: Opportunities and pitfalls. European Economy – Banks, Regulation, and the Real Sector, 2, 55–70.

Beck, T. (2020). Finance in the time of COVID-19: The role of digital financial services. *European Journal of Development Research, 32*(2), 486–502.

Beck, T., Flynn, B., & Homanen, M. (2020). COVID-19 in emerging markets: Firm-survey evidence. *Covid Economics, 38*, 37–67.

Beine, M., De Grauwe, P., & Grimaldi, M. (2009). The impact of FX central bank intervention in a noise trading framework. *Journal of Banking & Finance, 33*(7), 1187–1195. DOI: 10.1016/j.jbankfin.2008.11.014

Bekaert, G., Erb, C. B., Harvey, C. R., & Viskanta, T. E. (1998). Distributional Characteristics Of Emerging Market Returns and Asset Allocation. *Journal of Portfolio Management, 24*(2), 102–116. DOI: 10.3905/jpm.24.2.102

Bekaert, G., & Harvey, C. R. (1998). Capital markets: An engine for Economic Growth. *The Brown Journal of World Affairs, 5*(1), 33–53.

Bekaert, G., & Harvey, C. R. (2002). Research in Emerging Markets Finance: Looking To The Future. *Emerging Markets Review, 3*(4), 429–448. DOI: 10.1016/S1566-0141(02)00045-6

Bekaert, G., Harvey, C. R., & Mondino, T. (2023). Emerging Equity Markets in a Globalized World. *Emerging Markets Review, 101034*, 101034. Advance online publication. DOI: 10.1016/j.ememar.2023.101034

Bekmez, S., & Özpolat, A. (2014). A dynamic analysis on determining of housing demand: A comparison for Turkey, Hungary, and UK. *Management Studies, 2*(3), 179–190.

Bekun, F. V., & Ozturk, I. (2025). Economic globalization and ecological impact in emerging economies in the post-COP21 agreement: A panel econometrics approach. *Natural Resources Forum*, *49*(1), 637–655. DOI: 10.1111/1477-8947.12408

Bender, J. C., Osler, C. L., & Simon, D. (2013). Noise trading and illusory correlations in US equity markets. *Review of Finance*, *17*(2), 625–652. DOI: 10.1093/rof/rfr037

Bernanke, B. S. (2010) "Monetary policy and the housing bubble: a speech at the Annual Meeting of the American Economic Association, Atlanta, Georgia, January 3, 2010," Speech 499, Board of Governors of the Federal Reserve System (U.S.).

Bernanke, B. S. (2019). Monetary policy in a new era.

Bernanke, B. S. (2020). The new tools of monetary policy. *The American Economic Review*, *110*(4), 943–983. DOI: 10.1257/aer.110.4.943

Bernanke, B. S., & Gertler, M. (1995). Inside the black box: The credit channel of monetary policy transmission. *The Journal of Economic Perspectives*, *9*(4), 27–48. DOI: 10.1257/jep.9.4.27

Bernard, A. B., Dhyne, E., Magerman, G., Manova, K., & Moxnes, A. (2022). The Origins of Firm Heterogeneity: A Production Network Approach. *Journal of Political Economy*, *130*(7), 1765–1804. DOI: 10.1086/719759

Bevilacqua, E. (2022). European cooperative banks and sustainability. In *Contemporary Trends in European Cooperative Banking: Sustainability, Governance, Digital Transformation, and Health Crisis Response* (pp. 165–192). Springer International Publishing. DOI: 10.1007/978-3-030-98194-5_8

Bhat, J. A., Bhat, S. A., & Parray, W. A. (2025). Nonlinearity in exchange rate pass-through across BRICS: Role of business cycle and inflation. *International Economics and Economic Policy*, *22*(1), 8. DOI: 10.1007/s10368-024-00635-7

Bianchi, J., & Bigio, S. (2022). Banks, liquidity management, and monetary policy. *Econometrica*, *90*(1), 391–454. DOI: 10.3982/ECTA16599

Bian, X., Liang, Y., & Ma, L. (2021). Impact of CBDC on the credit channel of monetary policy: Evidence from China. *Finance Research Letters*, *43*, 101954.

Bian, X., Liu, Y., & Song, Y. (2021). Central bank digital currency and financial system stability. *Journal of Digital Economy*, *3*(1), 35–54.

Bingley, R. (2024). *Combatting Cyber Terrorism: A guide to understanding the cyber threat landscape and incident response planning*. IT Governance Publishing., DOI: 10.2307/jj.13167847

BIS. (2020). *Central bank digital currencies: Foundational principles and core features*. Bank for International Settlements.

BIS. (2021). *CBDCs: Financial stability implications. BIS Quarterly Review, March 2021*. Bank for International Settlements.

Bissessar, N. (2016). Regulating virtual currencies. *Journal of Financial Regulation and Compliance, 24*(3), 292–303.

Bittencourt, M. (2012). Inflation and economic growth in Latin America: Some panel time-series evidence. *Economic Modelling, 29*(2), 333–340. DOI: 10.1016/j.econmod.2011.10.018

Blanchard, O., & Brancaccio, E. (2019). Crisis and revolution in economic theory and policy: A debate. *Review of Political Economy, 31*(2), 271–287. DOI: 10.1080/09538259.2019.1644730

Bloomfield, R., O'Hara, M., & Saar, G. (2009). How noise trading affects markets: An experimental analysis. *Review of Financial Studies, 22*(6), 2275–2302. DOI: 10.1093/rfs/hhn102

Boar, C., Holden, H., & Wadsworth, A. (2020). *Impending arrival – A sequel to the survey on central bank digital currency. BIS Papers No. 107*. Bank for International Settlements.

Bocken, N. M., & Short, S. W. (2021). Unsustainable business models–Recognising and resolving institutionalized social and environmental harm. *Journal of Cleaner Production, 312*, 127828. DOI: 10.1016/j.jclepro.2021.127828

Boddin, D., te Kaat, D. M., Ma, C., & Rebucci, A. (2025). Portfolio flows and household portfolios. *European Economic Review, 172*, 104904. DOI: 10.1016/j.euroecorev.2024.104904

Boehm, C. E., Austin, U., & Levchenko, A. A. (2021). *The Long and Short (Run) of Trade Elasticities* [Working Paper]. https://econ.wisc.edu/wp-content/uploads/sites/89/2021/09/Boehm_Levchenko_PandalaiNayar-1.pdf

Bofinger, P., & Haas, T. (2020). CBDCs and financial stability: A critical assessment. *CEPR Discussion Paper No. DP15472*. https://cepr.org/publications/dp15472

Bondarenko, P. (2024). Gross Domestic Product. *Encyclopedia Britannica*. https://www.britannica.com/money/gross-domestic-product

Boneva, L., Ferrucci, G., & Mongelli, F. P. (2022). Climate change and central banks: What role for monetary policy? *Climate Policy, 22*(6), 770–787. DOI: 10.1080/14693062.2022.2070119

Borensztein, E., De Gregorio, J., & Lee, J. (1998). How does foreign direct investment affect economic growth? *Journal of International Economics, 45*(1), 115–135. DOI: 10.1016/S0022-1996(97)00033-0

Bouchoucha, N., & Benammou, S. (2020). Does institutional quality matter for foreign direct investment? Evidence from African countries. *Journal of the Knowledge Economy, 11*(1), 390–404. DOI: 10.1007/s13132-018-0552-y

Boudoukh, J., & Richardson, M. (1993). Stock Returns and Inflation: A Long-horizon Perspective. *The American Economic Review, 83*(5), 1346–1355.

Boujelbène, T., & Helali, K. (2017). Threshold effects on the relationship between inflation rate and economic growth in Tunisia. *International Economic Journal, 31*(2), 310–325. DOI: 10.1080/10168737.2017.1289546

Boukraine, W. (2021). Asymmetric behavior of exchange rate in Tunisia: A nonlinear approach. FORCE: Focus on Research in Contemporary Economics, 2(1), 41-52. https://www.forcejournal.org/index.php/force/article/view/22

Bouoiyour, J., & Selmi, R. (2014). Exchange volatility and trade performance in Morocco and Tunisia: What have we learned so far? *Macroeconomics and Finance in Emerging Market Economies, 8*(3), 244–274. DOI: 10.1080/17520843.2014.880150

Bouvatier, V., & Boum, O. (2024). Forecast-based credit-to-GDP gaps for macroprudential policy. SSRN *Electronic Journal.* DOI: 10.2139/ssrn.5045294

Bouyacoub, B. (2022). Inflation targeting and economic growth in the Middle East and North Africa (MENA): Empirical modeling using ARDL approach. Financial Markets. *Institutions and Risks, 6*(1), 5–12. DOI: 10.21272/fmir.6(1).5-12.2022

Bresser-Pereira, L. C., Feijó, C., & Araújo, E. C. (2024). The determination of the exchange rate: A new-developmental approach. *Structural Change and Economic Dynamics*, S0954349X24001280. DOI: 10.1016/j.strueco.2024.08.015

Brianzoni, S., & Campisi, G. (2020). Dynamical analysis of a financial market with fundamentalists, chartists, and imitators. *Chaos, Solitons, and Fractals, 130*, 109434. DOI: 10.1016/j.chaos.2019.109434

Bruneau, G., Christensen, I., & Meh, C. A. (2016). Housing market dynamics and macroprudential policy (No. 2016-31). *Bank of Canada Staff Working Paper.*

Bruno, M., & Easterly, W. (1998). Inflation crises and long-run growth. *Journal of Monetary Economics, 41*(1), 3–26. DOI: 10.1016/S0304-3932(97)00063-9

Buchanan, B., & English, P. C.II. (2007). Law, Finance, and Emerging Market Returns. *Emerging Markets Review, 8*(3), 181–193. DOI: 10.1016/j.ememar.2007.05.001

Bukht, R., & Heeks, R. (2017). Defining, conceptualising and measuring the digital economy (Development Informatics Working Paper No. 68). *SSRN*. https://doi.org/ DOI: 10.2139/ssrn.3431732

Bussière, M., Cao, J., de Haan, J., Hills, R., Lloyd, S., Meunier, B., Pedrono, J., Reinhardt, D., Sinha, S., Sowerbutts, R., & Styrin, K. (2021). The interaction between macroprudential policy and monetary policy: Overview. *Review of International Economics*, *29*(1), 1–19. DOI: 10.1111/roie.12505

Bussière, M., Gaulier, G., & Steingress, W. (2020). Global Trade Flows: Revisiting the Exchange Rate Elasticities. *Open Economies Review*, *31*(1), 25–78. DOI: 10.1007/s11079-019-09573-3

Caballero, R. J., & Hammour, M. L. (1994). The Cleansing Effect of Recessions. *The American Economic Review*, *84*(5), 1350–1368. https://www.jstor.org/stable/2117776

Calin, O. (2012). *An introduction to stochastic calculus with applications to finance*.

Calvino, F., Criscuolo, C., Marcolin, L., & Squicciarini, M. (2018). A taxonomy of digital intensive sectors (OECD Science, Technology and Industry Working Papers, No. 2018/14). *OECD Publishing*. https://doi.org/DOI: 10.1787/18151965

Campiglio, E. (2016). Beyond carbon pricing: The role of banking and monetary policy in financing the transition to a low-carbon economy. *Ecological Economics*, *121*, 220–230. DOI: 10.1016/j.ecolecon.2015.03.020

Campiglio, E., Dafermos, Y., Monnin, P., Ryan-Collins, J., Schotten, G., & Tanaka, M. (2018). Climate change challenges for central banks and financial regulators. *Nature Climate Change*, *8*(6), 462–468. DOI: 10.1038/s41558-018-0175-0

Campos, R. G., Manu, A.-S., Molina, L., & Suárez-Varela, M. (2024). *China's Financial Spillovers to Emerging Markets* (Working Paper No. 2435). https://www.bde.es/f/webbe/SES/Secciones/Publicaciones/PublicacionesSeriadas/DocumentosTrabajo/24/Files/dt2435e.pdf

Can, U., Bocuoglu, M. E., & Can, Z. G. (2020). How does the monetary transmission mechanism work? Evidence from Turkey. *Borsa Istanbul Review*, *20*(4), 375–382. DOI: 10.1016/j.bir.2020.05.004

Capelle-Blancard, G., Desroziers, A., & Zerbib, O. D. (2021). Socially responsible investing strategies under pressure: Evidence from Covid-19. *Journal of Portfolio Management*, *47*(9), 178–197. DOI: 10.3905/jpm.2021.1.288

Caporin, M., Pelizzon, L., & Plazzi, A. (2017). Does monetary policy impact market integration? Evidence from developed and emerging markets. *Journal of International Money and Finance, 70*, 147–168. DOI: 10.1016/j.jimonfin.2016.08.004

Carbó-Valverde, S., & Sánchez, F. R. (2013). Financial exclusion and public policies: A European perspective. *Journal of Policy Modeling, 35*(5), 764–782.

Carbó-Valverde, S., & Sánchez, F. R. (2013). Financial innovation, digital security, and cybersecurity risk. *Journal of Financial Regulation and Compliance, 21*(4), 354–369.

Carney, M. (2015). Breaking the tragedy of the horizon–climate change and financial stability. *Speech given at Lloyd's of London, 29*, 220-230.

Carro, A. (2023). Taming the housing roller coaster: The impact of macroprudential policy on the house price cycle. *Journal of Economic Dynamics & Control, 156*, 104753. DOI: 10.1016/j.jedc.2023.104753

Cassar, I. P. (2015). Estimates Of Output, Income, Value Added And Employment Multipliers For The Maltese Economy, Central Bank of Malta, 2015.

Cavana, R. Y., Delahaye, B. L., & Sekaran, U. (2001). *Applied business research: Qualitative and quantitative methods.* John Wiley & Sons Australia.

Cecchetti, S., & Kharroubi, E. (2012). *Reassessing the Impact of Finance on Growth (No. 381).* Bank for International Settlements.

Çelik, Ö. (2023). The roles of the state in the financialisation of housing in Turkey. *Housing Studies, 38*(6), 1006–1026. DOI: 10.1080/02673037.2021.1928003

Ceritoğlu, E. (2020). Homeownership, housing demand, and household wealth distribution in Turkey. *Emerging Markets Finance & Trade, 56*(5), 1146–1165. DOI: 10.1080/1540496X.2018.1555461

Ceritoğlu, E., Cılasun, S. M., Demiroğlu, U., & Ganioğlu, A. (2019). An analysis to detect exuberance and implosion in regional house prices in Turkey. *Central Bank Review, 19*(2), 67–82. DOI: 10.1016/j.cbrev.2019.06.002

Cerra, V., Panizza, U., & Saxena, S. C. (2013). International Evidence On Recovery From Recessions. *Contemporary Economic Policy, 31*(2), 424–439. DOI: 10.1111/j.1465-7287.2012.00313.x

Cerra, V., & Saxena, S. C. (2008). Growth dynamics: The myth of economic recovery. *The American Economic Review, 98*(1), 439–457. DOI: 10.1257/aer.98.1.439

Cham, T. (2016). Does monetary integration lead to an increase in FDI flows? An empirical investigation from the West African Monetary Zone (WAMZ). *Borsa Istanbul Review*, *16*(1), 9–20. DOI: 10.1016/j.bir.2016.01.002

Chebbi, T., & Derbali, A. (2019). US monetary policy surprises transmission to European stock markets. *International Journal of Monetary Economics and Finance*, *12*(1), 3–14. DOI: 10.1504/IJMEF.2019.098633

Chen, Y., & Zhao, H. (2020). Data security and privacy in IoT-based financial services: Challenges and solutions. *IEEE Access : Practical Innovations, Open Solutions*, *8*, 74622–74632. DOI: 10.1109/ACCESS.2020.2986683

Choe, G. H. (2016). *Stochastic processes*. Springer.

Chong, A. Y. L., Ooi, K. B., Lin, B., & Tan, B. I. (2010). Online banking adoption: An empirical analysis. *International Journal of Bank Marketing*, *28*(4), 267–287. DOI: 10.1108/02652321011054963

Christ, C. F. (1955). A review of I-O analysis. *I-O analysis: An appraisal*, (p.137-182). Princeton University Press: the National Bureau of Economic Research. https://www.nber.org/system/files/chapters/c2866/c2866.pdf

Chu, A. C., Cozzi, G., Furukawa, Y., & Liao, C. (2017). Inflation and economic growth in a Schumpeterian model with endogenous entry of heterogeneous firms. *European Economic Review*, *98*, 392–409. DOI: 10.1016/j.euroecorev.2017.07.006

Churchill, G. A., Iacobucci, D., & Israel, D. (2010). *Marketing research: A south Asian perspective*. Cengage Learning.

Çiftçi, M. (2020). Türkiye'de konut üretim özelliklerinin 1964-2019 arasında uzun dönemli dönüşümü. *Kırklareli Üniversitesi Sosyal Bilimler Dergisi*, *4*(1), 83–98.

Cihangir, Ç. K. (2020). Para, Ayriştirilmiş Krediler, Konut Fiyatlari ve Gsyh Arasindaki Nedensellik İlişkisi. *Bolu Abant İzzet Baysal Üniversitesi Sosyal Bilimler Enstitüsü Dergisi*, *20*(2), 469–488.

Claessens, S., Klingebiel, D., & Schmukler, S. L. (2002). The Future of Stock Exchanges in Emerging Economies: Evolution and Prospects. *Brookings-Wharton Papers on Financial Services*, 2002(1), 167-212.

Conover, C. M., Jensen, G. R., & Johnson, R. R. (2002). Emerging Markets: When Are They Worth It? *Financial Analysts Journal*, *58*(2), 86–95. DOI: 10.2469/faj.v58.n2.2525

Cornelius, P. K. (1994). The Internationalization of Emerging Stock Markets. *Inter Economics*, *29*(3), 131–138. DOI: 10.1007/BF02926350

Cortés, G. S., Gao, G. P., Silva, F. B., & Song, Z. (2022). Unconventional monetary policy and disaster risk: Evidence from the subprime and COVID–19 crises. *Journal of International Money and Finance*, *122*, 102543. DOI: 10.1016/j.jimonfin.2021.102543 PMID: 34949899

Coşkun, Y., and Yalçıner, K. (2014). İpotekli konut finansmanı sisteminin gelişme koşulları: Türkiye için ampirik bir analiz. *İktisat İşletme ve Finans*, 29(339), 59-94.

Coskun, Y. (2021). Measuring homeownership affordability in an emergent market context: An exploratory analysis for Turkey. *International Journal of Housing Markets and Analysis*, *14*(3), 446–480. DOI: 10.1108/IJHMA-04-2020-0033

Coskun, Y., Seven, U., Ertugrul, H. M., & Alp, A. (2020). Housing price dynamics and bubble risk: The case of Turkey. *Housing Studies*, *35*(1), 50–86. DOI: 10.1080/02673037.2017.1363378

Couharde, C., Grekou, C., Mignon, V., & Morvillier, F. (2025). Reconciling contrasting views on the growth effect of currency misalignments. *Journal of International Money and Finance*, *151*, 103237. DOI: 10.1016/j.jimonfin.2024.103237

CPMI. (2015). *Digital currencies. Committee on Payments and Market Infrastructures*. Bank for International Settlements.

Cuaresma, J. C., & Gnan, E. (2008). Four monetary policy strategies in comparison: How to deal with financial instability? *Monetary Policy & The Economy*, (Q1/08), 65–102. https://ideas.repec.org/p/onb/oenbfs/y2008iq1b3.html

Cunha, I., Almeida, J., & Silveira, P. (2021). Digital currencies: Macroeconomic and regulatory implications. Central Bank of Brazil Working Paper Series.

Cushman, D. O., & De Vita, G. (2017). Exchange rate regimes and FDI in developing countries: A propensity score matching approach. *Journal of International Money and Finance*, *77*, 143–163. DOI: 10.1016/j.jimonfin.2017.07.018

Cybersecurity Ventures. (2024). *Cybercrime to cost the world $10.5 trillion annually by 2025*. https://cybersecurityventures.com/hackerpocalypse-cybercrime-report-2016/

D'Orazio, P., & Popoyan, L. (2023). Do monetary policy mandates and financial stability governance structures matter for the adoption of climate-related financial policies? *Inter Economics*, *173*, 284–295. DOI: 10.1016/j.inteco.2023.01.004

Dahem, A., Skander, S., & Siala Guermazi, F. (2017). Time-varying VAR analysis for disaggregated exchange rate pass-through in Tunisia (MPRA Paper No. 79759). Munich Personal RePEc Archive. https://mpra.ub.uni-muenchen.de/79759/

Dandash, B. H., & Aldabbas, H. (2021). AI and IoT for secure financial services: The role of machine learning. *Future Generation Computer Systems, 115*, 1–13. DOI: 10.1016/j.future.2020.10.035

Darıcı, B. (2018). Para politikası ve konut fiyatları ilişkisi: Türkiye ekonomisi için ampirik bir analiz. *Anemon Muş Alparslan Üniversitesi Sosyal Bilimler Dergisi*, 6(ICEESS'18), 221-228.

David, R. J., & Han, S. K. (2004). A systematic assessment of the empirical support for transaction cost economics. *Strategic Management Journal, 25*(1), 39–58. DOI: 10.1002/smj.359

Dayal, Y. (2020). Yes Bank Ltd. was placed under Moratorium. Retrieved from Moratorium on yes bank. PDF., Retrieved May 10th, 2021, from.

Day, R. H., & Huang, W. (2000). Bulls, bears and market sheep. *Journal of Economic Behavior & Organization, 14*(3), 299–329. DOI: 10.1016/0167-2681(90)90061-H

De Gregorio, J. (1993). Inflation, taxation, and long-run growth. *Journal of Monetary Economics, 31*(3), 271–298. DOI: 10.1016/0304-3932(93)90049-L

De Mello, L. R.Jr. (1997). Foreign direct investment in developing countries and growth: A selective survey. *The Journal of Development Studies, 34*(1), 1–34. DOI: 10.1080/00220389708422501

Demir, F. (2010). Exchange Rate Volatility and Employment Growth in Developing Countries: Evidence from Turkey. *World Development, 38*(8), 1127–1140. DOI: 10.1016/j.worlddev.2009.12.019

Demirgüç-Kunt, A., Beck, T. H. L., & Honohan, P. (2008). *Finance for All?: Policies and Pitfalls in Expanding Access*. World Bank.

Demirgüç-Kunt, A., & Levine, R. (1996). Stock Markets, Corporate Finance, and Economic Growth: An Overview. *The World Bank Economic Review, 10*(2), 223–239. DOI: 10.1093/wber/10.2.223

Demirgüç-Kunt, A., & Levine, R. (2001). *Financial Structure and Economic Growth: A Cross-Country Comparison of Banks, Markets, and Development*. MIT Press. DOI: 10.7551/mitpress/3001.001.0001

Devi, A. (2023). DCO 2030: Digital economy to contribute 30% of global GDP and create 30 million jobs by 2030. *ITP.NET*. https://www.itp.net/industry/dco-2030-digital-economy-to-contribute-30-of-global-gdp-and-create-30-million-jobs-by-2030

Di Maggio, M., Kermani, A., Keys, B. J., Piskorski, T., Ramcharan, R., Seru, A., & Yao, V. (2017). Interest rate pass-through: Mortgage rates, household consumption, and voluntary deleveraging. *The American Economic Review*, *107*(11), 3550–3588. DOI: 10.1257/aer.20141313

Didier, T., Hevia, C., & Schmukler, S. L. (2012). How resilient and countercyclical were emerging economies during the global financial crisis? *Journal of International Money and Finance*, *31*(8), 2052–2077. DOI: 10.1016/j.jimonfin.2012.05.007

Diebold, F. X., & Yilmaz, K. (2009). Measuring Financial Asset Return and Volatility Spillovers, with Application to Global Equity Markets. *Economic Journal (London)*, *119*(534), 158–171. DOI: 10.1111/j.1468-0297.2008.02208.x

Diebold, F. X., & Yilmaz, K. (2012). Better to give than to receive: Predictive directional measurement of volatility spillovers. *International Journal of Forecasting*, *28*(1), 57–66. DOI: 10.1016/j.ijforecast.2011.02.006

Diebold, F. X., & Yılmaz, K. (2014). On the network topology of variance decompositions: Measuring the connectedness of financial firms. *Journal of Econometrics*, *182*(1), 119–134. DOI: 10.1016/j.jeconom.2014.04.012

Diermeier, J., & Solnik, B. (2001). Global Pricing of Equity. *Financial Analysts Journal*, *57*(4), 37–47. DOI: 10.2469/faj.v57.n4.2464

Dikau, S., & Volz, U. (2021). Central bank mandates, sustainability objectives and the promotion of green finance. *Ecological Economics*, *184*, 107022. DOI: 10.1016/j.ecolecon.2021.107022

Dinh, L. Q., Oanh, T. T. K., & Ha, N. T. H. (2024). Financial stability and sustainable development: Perspectives from fiscal and monetary policy. *International Journal of Finance & Economics*.

Diwan, I., Alaya, H., & Meddeb, H. (2024). Tunisia's Economy in the Eye of the Storm. Retrieved from: https://carnegie-production-assets.s3.amazonaws.com/static/files/Diwan_Tunisia%20Economy_draft.pdf

Doğan, Y. (1986). *IMF Kıskacında Türkiye 1946-1980. 2.b.* Tekin Yayınevi.

Doidge, C., Karolyi, G. A., & Stulz, R. M. (2004). Why Are Foreign Firms Listed in the US Worth More? *Journal of Financial Economics*, *71*(2), 205–238. DOI: 10.1016/S0304-405X(03)00183-1

Dolan, P., Shaw, R., Tsuchiya, A., & Williams, A. (2005). QALY maximization and people's preferences: A methodological review of the literature. *Health Economics*, *14*(2), 197–208. DOI: 10.1002/hec.924 PMID: 15386656

Dollar, D. (1992). Outward-Oriented Developing Economies Really Do Grow More Rapidly: Evidence from 95 LDCs, 1976-1985. *Economic Development and Cultural Change*, *40*(3), 523–544. Advance online publication. DOI: 10.1086/451959

Dooley, M., & Hutchison, M. (2009). Transmission of the U.S. Subprime crisis to emerging markets: Evidence on the decoupling–recoupling hypothesis. *Journal of International Money and Finance*, *28*(8), 1331–1349. DOI: 10.1016/j.jimonfin.2009.08.004

Doruk, Ö. T. (2024). Exploring the determinants of housing price bubbles in the Turkish economy: a COVID-related framework. *International Journal of Housing Markets and Analysis*. https://doi.org/DOI: 10.1108/IJHMA-05-2024-0073/FULL/XML

DPT. (1968). *İkinci Beş Yıllık Kalkınma Planı 1968 – 1972.* Ankara. http://www.sbb.gov.tr/ Lists/Kalknma%20Planlar/Attachments/8/plan2.pdf

DPT. (1973). *Üçüncü Beş Yıllık Kalkınma Planı 1973 – 1977.* Ankara. http://www.sbb.gov.tr/ Lists/Kalknma%20Planlar/Attachments/7/plan3.pdf

DPT. (1979). *Dördüncü Beş Yıllık Kalkınma Planı 1979 – 1983.* Ankara. http://www.sbb.gov.tr/ Lists/Kalknma%20Planlar/Attachments/6/plan4.pdf

DPT-SPO (Devlet Planlama Teşkilatı). (1963). *Birinci Beş Yıllık Kalkınma Planı 1963 – 1967.* Ankara. http://www.sbb.gov.tr/ Lists/Kalknma%20Planlar/Attachments/9/plan1.pdf

Drechsler, I., Savov, A., & Schnabl, P. (2022). How monetary policy shaped the housing boom. *Journal of Financial Economics*, *144*(3), 992–1021. DOI: 10.1016/j.jfineco.2021.06.039

Duca, J. V., Muellbauer, J., & Murphy, A. (2021). What drives house price cycles? International experience and policy issues. *Journal of Economic Literature*, *59*(3), 773–864. DOI: 10.1257/jel.20201325

Duho, K. C. T., Abankwah, S. A., Agbozo, D. A., Yonmearu, G., Aryee, B. N. A., & Akomanin, O. (2022). Exploring the Russo-Ukrainian crisis and its impact on African countries: A cross-regional analysis. Dataking Policy Brief 005, Accra, Dataking Consulting 2022, Available at *SSRN*: https://ssrn.com/abstract=4085903DOI: 10.2139/ssrn.4085903

Dumas, B., & Solnik, B. (1995). The World Price of Foreign Exchange Risk. *The Journal of Finance*, *50*(2), 445–479. DOI: 10.1111/j.1540-6261.1995.tb04791.x

Duncombe, R., & Boateng, R. (2009). Mobile phones and financial services in developing countries: A review of concepts, methods, issues, evidence and future research directions. *Development Informatics Working Paper No. 37*. Centre for Development Informatics, University of Manchester. https://diodeweb.files.wordpress .com/2010/09/di_wp37.pdf

Dünya Gazetesi (2016). Negatif faiz nedir, neden uygulanır? https://www.dunya .com/ finans/haberler/negatif-faiz-nedir-neden-uygulanir-haberi-307723

Durante, E., Ferrando, A., & Vermeulen, P. (2022). Monetary Policy, Investment, and Firm Heterogeneity. *European Economic Review*, *148*, 104251. DOI: 10.1016/j. euroecorev.2022.104251

Duttagupta, R., & Pazarbasioglu, C. (2017). Miles to Go: The Future of Emerging Markets—IMF F&D. International Monetary Fund. Available online: https://www. imf. org/external/pubs/ft/fandd/2021/06/the-future-of-emerging-markets-duttagupta-andpazarbasioglu. htm (accessed on 5 Dec 2023).

Dwyer, G., & Hafer, R. (1988). Are National Stock Markets Linked? *Review - Federal Reserve Bank of St. Louis*, (Nov), 3–14.

Edwards, S. (2010). The international transmission of interest rate shocks: The Federal Reserve and emerging markets in Latin America and Asia. *Journal of International Money and Finance*, *29*(4), 685–703. DOI: 10.1016/j.jimonfin.2010.01.003

Edwards, S., & Levy Yeyati, E. (2005). Flexible exchange rates as shock absorbers. *European Economic Review*, *49*(8), 2079–2105. DOI: 10.1016/j.euroecorev.2004.07.002

Eğilmez, M., & Kumcu, E. (2004).Ekonomi Politikası: Teori ve Türkiye Uygulaması. 22.b., İstanbul: Remzi Kitabevi.

Eichengreen, B., & Bordo, M. D. (2002). Crises now and then: What lessons from the last era of financial globalization.

Einstein, A. (2005). Über die von der molekularkinetischen theorie der wärme geforderte bewegung von in ruhenden flüssigkeiten suspendierten teilchen. *Annalen der Physik*, •••, 4.

Ekanayake, E. M., & Dissanayake, A. (2022). Effects of Real Exchange Rate Volatility on Trade: Empirical Analysis of the United States Exports to BRICS. *Journal of Risk and Financial Management*, *15*(2), 73. DOI: 10.3390/jrfm15020073

Elhan-Kayalar, Y. And Oum, S. (2022). Estimating the Job Creation Impact of Development Assistance. Manila: Asian Development Bank. https://www.adb.org/sites/ default/files/publication/850336/job-creation-impact-development-assistance.pdf

End, N., El Hamiani Khatat, M., & Kolsi, R. (2020). Tunisia monetary policy since the Arab Spring: The fall of the exchange rate anchor and rise of inflation targeting (IMF Working Paper, Volume 2020, Issue 167). International Monetary Fund. DOI: 10.5089/9781513555027.001

English, D. (2023, June 27). Overcrowded homes plague half of Turkey's young population. https://www.duvarenglish.com/overcrowded-homes-plague-half-of-turkeys-young-population-news-62331

Erb, C. B., Harvey, C. R., & Viskanta, T. E. (1994). Forecasting International Equity Correlations. *Financial Analysts Journal, 50*(6), 32–45. DOI: 10.2469/faj.v50.n6.32

Erb, C. B., Harvey, C. R., & Viskanta, T. E. (1995). Inflation and World Equity Selection. *Financial Analysts Journal, 51*(6), 28–42. DOI: 10.2469/faj.v51.n6.1947

Erb, C. B., Harvey, C. R., & Viskanta, T. E. (1996a). Expected Returns and Volatility in 135 Countries. *Journal of Portfolio Management, 22*(3), 46–58. DOI: 10.3905/jpm.1996.409554

Erb, C. B., Harvey, C. R., & Viskanta, T. E. (1996b). Political Risk, Economic Risk, and Financial Risk. *Financial Analysts Journal, 52*(6), 29–46. DOI: 10.2469/faj.v52.n6.2038

Erb, C. B., Harvey, C. R., & Viskanta, T. E. (1997). The Making of an Emerging Market. *Emerging Markets Quarterly, 1*, 14–19.

Erb, C., Harvey, C., & Viskanta, T. (1998). Risk in Emerging Markets. *The Financial Survey, 1998*, 42–46.

Ergeç, E. H., & Taşdemir, M. (2008). Türkiye'de İnşaat Sektörü Ve Para Politikalari Arasindaki Nedensellik İlişkileri. *Eskişehir Osmangazi Üniversitesi Sosyal Bilimler Dergisi, 9*(1), 115–132.

Ergin Ünal, A. & Yetiz, F. (2017). Parasal Genişlemeye Alternatif Arayışları: Negatif Faiz. *PEK-Politik Ekonomik Kuram,* c.1, S.2, ss.66-78.

Erguven, E. (2020). The political economy of housing financialization in Turkey: Links with and contradictions to the accumulation model. *Housing Policy Debate, 30*(4), 559–584. DOI: 10.1080/10511482.2019.1681017

Eroğlu, İ. & Erdoğmuş, M. (2017). Merkez Bankalarının Krizle Mücadele Çabaları: Negatif Faiz Politikası Tercihi ve İktisadi Yansımaları. *Namık Kemal Üniversitesi Sosyal Bilimler Metinleri Dergisi,* İCOMEP'17 Özel sayı, ss.82-97.

Erol, I. (2019). New geographies of residential capitalism: Financialization of the Turkish housing market since the early 2000s. *International Journal of Urban and Regional Research, 43*(4), 724–740. DOI: 10.1111/1468-2427.12794

Errunza, V. (2001). Foreign Portfolio Equity Investments, Financial Liberalization, and Economic Development. *Review of International Economics, 9*(4), 703–726. DOI: 10.1111/1467-9396.00308

Errunza, V. R. (1983). Emerging Markets: A New Opportunity for Improving Global Portfolio Performance. *Financial Analysts Journal, 39*(5), 51–58. DOI: 10.2469/faj.v39.n5.51

Errunza, V. R., & Padmanabhan, P. (1988). Further Evidence on the Benefits of Portfolio Investments in Emerging Markets. *Financial Analysts Journal, 44*(4), 76–78. DOI: 10.2469/faj.v44.n4.76

Evemy, J., Berry, C., & Yates, E. (2024). Low interest rates, low productivity, low growth? A multi-sector case study of UK-based firms' funding and investment strategies in the context of loose monetary policy. *New Political Economy, 29*(2), 240–259. DOI: 10.1080/13563467.2023.2240237

Eze, U. C., & Ayo, C. K. (2020). Security and privacy in IoT banking: The case for a hybrid framework. *International Journal of Information Management, 52*, 102065. DOI: 10.1016/j.ijinfomgt.2020.102065

Fabozzi, F. J., & Peterson, P. P. (2003). *Financial management and analysis.* John Wiley & Sons.

Fama, E. F. (2010). Efficient capital markets: A review of theory and empirical work. *The Journal of Finance, 25*(2), 383–417. DOI: 10.2307/2325486

Fang, Y. (2024). *The future development of the electronic technology industry under the trend of the digital economy.* ResearchGate. https://www.researchgate.net/publication/381304736

Farroukh, A., Metzger, M., & Mzoughi, H. (2024). *Assessing the influence of cryptocurrencies on financial market stability.* Eurasian Economic Review., DOI: 10.1007/s40822-024-00284-w

Faruq, A. T. M., & Huq, M. T. (2024). The Role of Central Banks in Advancing Sustainable Finance. arXiv preprint arXiv:2411.13576.

Favilukis, J., Kohn, D., Ludvigson, S. C., and Van Nieuwerburgh, S. (2013). International Capital Flows and House Prices. Housing and the financial crisis, 235-300.

Feldman, R. A., & Kumar, M. S. (1995). Emerging Equity Markets: Growth, Benefits, and Policy Concerns. *The World Bank Research Observer*, *10*(2), 181–200. DOI: 10.1093/wbro/10.2.181

Feng, G.-F., Yang, H.-C., Gong, Q., & Chang, C.-P. (2021). What is the exchange rate volatility response to COVID-19 and government interventions? *Economic Analysis and Policy*, *69*, 705–719. DOI: 10.1016/j.eap.2021.01.018

Feng, L., Lin, C. Y., & Wang, C. (2017). Do capital flows matter to stock and house prices? Evidence from China. *Emerging Markets Finance & Trade*, *53*(10), 2215–2232. DOI: 10.1080/1540496X.2016.1180283

Feyen, E., Gispert, T. A., Kliatskova, T., & Mare, D. S. (2021). Financial sector policy response to COVID-19 in emerging markets and developing economies. *Journal of Banking & Finance*, *133*, 106184. DOI: 10.1016/j.jbankfin.2021.106184 PMID: 34898821

Filho, W. L., Balogun, A. L., Ayal, D. Y., Bethurem, E. M., Murambadoro, M., Mambo, J., Taddese, H., Tefera, G. W., Nagy, G. J., Fudjumdjum, H., & Mugabe, P. (2018). Strengthening climate change adaptation capacity in Africa: Case studies from six major African cities and policy implications. *Environmental Science & Policy*, *86*, 29–37. DOI: 10.1016/j.envsci.2018.05.004

Flood, R. P., & Marion, N. P. (1982). The transmission of disturbances under alternative exchange-rate regimes with optimal indexing. *The Quarterly Journal of Economics*, *97*(1), 43–66. DOI: 10.2307/1882626

Ford, T. C., Rork, J. C., & Elmslie, B. T. (2008). Foreign direct investment, economic growth, and the human capital threshold: Evidence from US states. *Review of International Economics*, *16*(1), 96–113. DOI: 10.1111/j.1467-9396.2007.00726.x

Forrester. (2024). *The global digital economy will reach $16.5 trillion and capture 17% of global GDP by 2028.* https://www.forrester.com/blogs/the-global-digital-economy-will-reach-16-5-trillion-and-capture-17-of-global-gdp-by-2028/

Foster, R., Gorajek, A., & Tellez, D. (2021). *The RBA's approach to central bank digital currency.* Reserve Bank of Australia Bulletin.

Frankel, J. (2021). Systematic Managed Floating. In S. J. Davis, E. S. Robinson, & B. Yeung, *The Asian Monetary Policy Forum* (pp. 160–221). WORLD SCIENTIFIC. DOI: 10.1142/9789811238628_0005

Franke, R., & Westerhoff, F. (2016). Why a simple herding model may generate the stylized facts of daily returns: Explanation and estimation. *Journal of Economic Interaction and Coordination*, *11*(1), 1–34. DOI: 10.1007/s11403-014-0140-6

Fratantoni, M., & Schuh, S. (2003). Monetary policy, housing, and heterogeneous regional markets. *Journal of Money, Credit and Banking*, *35*(4), 557–589. DOI: 10.1353/mcb.2003.0029

Friend, I. (1972). The Economic Consequences of the Stock Market. *The American Economic Review*, *62*(1/2), 212–219.

G20 Digital Economy Task Force & International Telecommunication Union. (2020). *A roadmap toward a common framework for measuring the digital economy*. https://www.itu.int/en/ITUD/Statistics/Documents/publications/OECDRoadmapDigitalEconomy2020.pdf

Gala, P. (2008). Real Exchange Rate Levels and Economic Development: Theoretical Analysis and Econometric Evidence. *Cambridge Journal of Economics*, *32*(2), 273–288. DOI: 10.1093/cje/bem042

Gali, J., & Monacelli, T. (2005). Monetary policy and exchange rate volatility in a small open economy. *The Review of Economic Studies*, *72*(3), 707–734. DOI: 10.1111/j.1467-937X.2005.00349.x

Garber, P. M. Garber (1991). The Collapse of the Bretton Woods Fixed Exchange Rate System. NBER Chapters, in: *A Retrospective on the Bretton Woods System: Lessons for International Monetary Reform*, pp. 461-494, National Bureau of Economic Research, Inc. https://www.nber.org/system/files/chapters/c6876/c6876.pdf

George, D., & Mallery, P. (2010) *SPSS for Windows Step by Step: A Simple Guide and Reference 17.0* Update. 10th Edition, Pearson, Boston.

George, D., & Mallery, P. (2003). *SPSS for Windows step by step: A simple guide and reference 11.0 update* (4th ed.). Allyn & Bacon.

Ghandri, M., Soltani, H., & Maktouf, S. (2021). Inflation targeting as a future framework for Tunisian monetary policy: Between perception and reality in an inflationary context. *Journal of International Students*, *14*(4), 174–186. DOI: 10.14254/2071-8330.2021/14-4/12

Ghasemaghaei, M., & H. A. (. (2021). The role of AI in enhancing cybersecurity in the banking sector. *Journal of Business Research*, *124*, 360–368. DOI: 10.1016/j.jbusres.2020.11.048

Gilmore, C. G., McManus, G. M., & Tezel, A. (2005). Portfolio allocations and the Emerging Equity Markets of Central Europe. *Journal of Multinational Financial Management*, *15*(3), 287–300. DOI: 10.1016/j.mulfin.2004.12.001

Giménez, G., & Tamajón, L. G. (2019). Exploring the role of central banks in a digital monetary system: The Swedish e-krona. *Journal of Digital Economy*, *1*(2), 18–34.

Glebocki Keefe, H., & Saha, S. (2022). Foreign Exchange and Global Monetary Shocks: The Asymmetric Effects of Advanced Economies' Quantitative Easing on Exchange Rate Volatility in Emerging Markets. *International Economic Journal*, *36*(3), 339–361. DOI: 10.1080/10168737.2022.2098353

Glebocki, H., & Saha, S. (2024). Global uncertainty and exchange rate conditions: Assessing the impact of uncertainty shocks in emerging markets and advanced economies. *Journal of International Financial Markets, Institutions and Money*, *96*, 102060. DOI: 10.1016/j.intfin.2024.102060

Goering, J., & Whitehead, C. M. E. (2017). Fiscal austerity and rental housing policy in the United States and United Kingdom, 2010-2016. *Housing Policy Debate*, *27*(6), 875–896. DOI: 10.1080/10511482.2017.1321568

Gökce, B. (2024). Türkiye'de 2000 Yılı Sonrası Uygulanan Konut Politikaları ve Yaşanan Konut Sorununun Değişen Arz-Talep Dengeleri Üzerinden Değerlendirmesi. *Van Yüzüncü Yıl Üniversitesi Sosyal Bilimler Enstitüsü Dergisi*, (65), 135–152.

Gokmenoglu, K. K., Amin, M. Y., & Taspinar, N. (2015). The Relationship among International Trade, Financial Development, and Economic Growth: The Case of Pakistan. *Procedia Economics and Finance*, *25*, 489–496. DOI: 10.1016/S2212-5671(15)00761-3

Grady, M. (2024). The global digital economy will reach $16.5 trillion and capture 17% of global GDP by 2028. *Forrester Blog*. https://www.forrester.com/blogs/the-global-digital-economy-will-reach-16-5-trillion-and-capture-17-of-global-gdp-by-2028/

Ground, M., & Ludi, K. L. (2006). Investigating the bank-lending channel in South Africa: A VAR approach. *Working Paper 2006-4*, Department of Economics, University of Pretoria. https://ideas.repec.org/p/pre/wpaper/200604.html

Guell, R. C. (2007). *Issues in Economics Today*. McGraw-Hill/Irwin.

Guenichi, H., & Benamou, S. (2010). World oil price, economic growth, inflation & interest rate relationships in Tunisia. *Energy Studies Review*, *17*(2), 25–42. DOI: 10.15173/esr.v17i2.523

Gülay, G., & Aydoğmuş, M. (2024). Guest Editors' introduction: Borsa Istanbul history (1836–2023) and an overview of selected papers on the 150th anniversary of the founding of Borsa Istanbul. *Borsa Istanbul Review*.

Güneş, H. (1998). Dünden Bugüne Para Politikaları. iç. *75 Yılda Paranın Serüveni.* M. Sönmez (Ed.), İstanbul: Tarih Vakfı Yayınları, ss.187-194.

Gunji, H., Miura, K., & Yuan, Y. (2009). Bank competition and monetary policy. *Japan and the World Economy, 21*(2), 105–115. DOI: 10.1016/j.japwor.2007.11.001

Gunji, H., & Yuan, Y. (2018). Bank diversification and monetary policy. *Applied Economics Letters, 25*(15), 1087–1090. DOI: 10.1080/13504851.2017.1397845

Gupta, D., & Yadav, A. (2021). Security and privacy challenges in IoT-based financial services: A review. *Journal of Financial Services Marketing, 26*(3), 137–150. DOI: 10.1057/s41264-021-00101-x

Gupta, J., & Vegelin, C. (2016). Sustainable development goals and inclusive development. *International Environmental Agreement: Politics, Law and Economics, 16*(3), 433–448. DOI: 10.1007/s10784-016-9323-z

Hachicha, F. (2024). Sentiment investor, exchange rates, geopolitical risk and developing stock market: Evidence of co-movements in the time-frequency domain during RussiaUkraine war. *Review of Behavioral Finance, 16*(3), 486–509. DOI: 10.1108/RBF-04-2023-0119

Hadebe, N., & Msomi, S. (2023). Focusing on the Exchange Rate Volatility and International Trade Relationship: Evidence from South Africa. *Management and Economics Review, 8*(3), 354–367. DOI: 10.24818/mer/2023.10-08

Hair, J. F., William, B. C., Barry, B. J., Anderson, R. E., & Tatham, R. L. (2009). *Multivariate Data Analysis* (6th ed.). Pearson Education.

Halıcıoğlu, F. (2005). The demand for new housing in Turkey: An application of ARDL model. *Business and Economics Society International Conference*, AZ, ABD.

Hamdi, H., Sbia, R., Hakimi, A., & Hakimi, W. K. (2013). Multivariate Granger causality between foreign direct investment and economic growth in Tunisia. *Economic Bulletin, 33*(2), 1193–1203. http://www.accessecon.com/Pubs/EB/2013/Volume33/EB-13-V33-I2-P113.pdf

Hammoudeh, S., Nguyen, D. K., & Sousa, R. M. (2015). US monetary policy and sectoral commodity prices. *Journal of International Money and Finance, 57*, 61–85. DOI: 10.1016/j.jimonfin.2015.06.003

Hanim, T. F., Abdul Rahman, R., & Omar, N. (2011). Empirical evidence on the risk management tools practised in Islamic and conventional banks. *Qualitative Research in Financial Markets, 3*(2), 86–104. DOI: 10.1108/17554171111155339

Harjoto, M. A., & Rossi, F. (2023). Market reaction to the COVID-19 pandemic: Evidence from emerging markets. *International Journal of Emerging Markets, 18*(1), 173–199. DOI: 10.1108/IJOEM-05-2020-0545

Harvey, C. R. (1989). Forecasts of Economic Growth from the Bond and Stock Markets. *Financial Analysts Journal, 45*(5), 38–45. DOI: 10.2469/faj.v45.n5.38

Harvey, C. R. (2000). Drivers of Expected Returns in Emerging Markets. *Emerging Market Quarterly*, 32 – 49. DOI: 10.2139/ssrn.795385

Harvey, S. K., & Cushing, M. J. (2015). Is West African Monetary Zone (WAMZ) a common currency area? *Review of Development Finance, 5*(1), 53–63. DOI: 10.1016/j.rdf.2015.05.001

Hassen, G., & Hamdi, K. (2020). The impact of monetary policy on overall and sectoral economic growth: Evidence from Tunisian Central Bank in crisis periods. *International Journal of Monetary Economics and Finance, 13*(5), 471–484. DOI: 10.1504/IJMEF.2020.110558

Hassler, U.. (2016). *Stochastic processes and calculus*. Springer. DOI: 10.1007/978-3-319-23428-1

Hauben, H., Lenaerts, K., & Kraatz, S. (2020). *Platform economy and precarious work: Mitigating risks*. European Parliament. https://www.europarl.europa.eu/RegData/etudes/BRIE/2020/652721/IPOL_BRI(2020)652721_EN.pdf

Hazra, D. (2017). Monetary policy and alternative means of payment. *The Quarterly Review of Economics and Finance, 65*, 378–387. DOI: 10.1016/j.qref.2016.11.002

Helali, K., Ben Jedidia, K., & Boujelbène, T. (2021). Threshold effects of inflation on the financial development-economic growth nexus in Tunisia. *International Journal of Monetary Economics and Finance, 14*(5), 438–459. DOI: 10.1504/IJMEF.2021.118282

Henderson, J., Yermakov, V., & Connolly, R. (2024). *Outlook for Russia's oil and gas production and exports*. The Oxford Institute for Energy Studies.: https://www.jstor.org/stable/resrep58374

Henry, P. B. (2000). Stock Market Liberalization, Economic Reform, and Emerging Market Equity Prices. *The Journal of Finance, 55*(2), 529–564. DOI: 10.1111/0022-1082.00219

Hepaktan, E., Çınar, S. & Dündar, Ö. (2011). Türkiye'de Uygulanan Döviz Kuru Sistemlerinin Dış Ticaret İle İlişkisi. *Akademik Araştırmalar ve Çalışmalar Dergisi,* c.3, S.5, Kasım, ss.62-82.

Hermes, N., & Lensink, R. (2000). Financial System Development in Transition Economies. *Journal of Banking & Finance*, *24*(4), 507–524. DOI: 10.1016/S0378-4266(99)00078-3

Herzer, D. (2012). How Does Foreign Direct Investment Really Affect Developing Countries' Growth? *Review of International Economics*, *20*(2), 396–414. DOI: 10.1111/j.1467-9396.2012.01029.x

Hfaiedh, M. A., & Bardi, W. (2021). Does FDI and Corruption affect Environmental Quality in Tunisia? *International Journal of Energy Economics and Policy*, *11*(4), 267–275. DOI: 10.32479/ijeep.11089

Hochstenbach, C., & Aalbers, M. B. (2024). The uncoupling of house prices and mortgage debt: Towards wealth-driven housing market dynamics. *International Journal of Housing Policy*, *24*(4), 642–670. DOI: 10.1080/19491247.2023.2170542

Hoffmaister, A. W., & Roldôs, J. E. (2001). The sources of macroeconomic fluctuations in developing countries: Brazil and Korea. *Journal of Macroeconomics*, *23*(2), 213–239. DOI: 10.1016/S0164-0704(01)00162-8

Holmans, A., Whitehead, C., & Scanlon, K. (2002). *Fiscal policy instruments to promote affordable housing*. Cambridge Centre for Housing and Planning Research.

Homer, S. (1969). Inflation and the Capital Markets. *Financial Analysts Journal*, *25*(4), 143–145. DOI: 10.2469/faj.v25.n4.143

Horowitz, K. J., & Planting, M. A. (2009). *Concepts and Methods of the U.S. I-O Accounts. The U.S. Bureau of Economic Analysis of the U.S.* Department of Commerce., https://www.bea.gov/sites/default/files/methodologies/IOmanual_092906.pdf

Hossain, M. K., & Hossain, M. S. (2022). Causal Interaction between Foreign Direct Investment Inflows and China's Economic Growth. *Sustainability (Basel)*, *15*(10), 7994. DOI: 10.3390/su15107994

Ho, T., & Yeh, K. (2010). Measuring monetary policy in a small open economy with managed exchange rates: The case of Taiwan. *Southern Economic Journal*, *76*(3), 811–826. DOI: 10.4284/sej.2010.76.3.811

Hove, S., Mama, A. T., & Tchana, F. T. (2015). Monetary policy and commodity terms of trade shocks in emerging market economies. *Economic Modelling*, *49*, 53–71. DOI: 10.1016/j.econmod.2015.03.012

Howells, P., & Bain, K. (2007). *Financial Markets and Institutions*. Pearson Education.

Hughes, D. (2018). *A Primer in Economic Multipliers and Impact Analysis Using I-O Models*. University of Tennessee, Department of Agricultural & Resource Economics., https://utia.tennessee.edu/publications/wp-content/uploads/sites/269/2023/10/W644.pdf

Hung, J. H. (2007). Intervention strategies and exchange rate volatility: A noise trading perspective. *Journal of International Money and Finance*, *16*(5), 779–793. DOI: 10.1016/S0261-5606(97)00023-5

Hussain, A., & Raza, B. (2020). Blockchain technology for data security in IoT-based banking services. *Journal of Banking and Finance Technology*, *4*(2), 73–84. DOI: 10.1007/s42786-020-00016-7

Hussein, F. (2023). Online gig work is growing rapidly, but workers lack job protections, a World Bank report says. *AP News*. https://apnews.com/article/online-gig-workers-labour-employment-world-bank-40b81a789fd5f0fb366e83f0223d832f

Igan, D., Kabundi, A., De Simone, F. N., & Tamirisa, N. (2017). Monetary policy and balance sheets. *Journal of Policy Modeling*, *39*(1), 169–184. DOI: 10.1016/j.jpolmod.2016.09.003

Ikhide, S., & Uanguta, E. (2010). Impact of South Africa's monetary policy on the LNS economies. *Journal of Economic Integration*, *25*(2), 324–352. DOI: 10.11130/jei.2010.25.2.324

Ilzetzki, E., Reinhart, C. M., & Rogoff, K. S. (2021). *Rethinking Exchange Rate Regimes* (Working Paper No. Working Paper 29347; NBER Working Paper Series, p. 66). National Bureau of Economic Research. https://scholar.harvard.edu/files/rogoff/files/w29347.pdf

İnan, E. A. (2002). *Kur Rejimi Tercihi ve Türkiye*. TBB-Türkiye Bankalar Birliği.

International Monetary Fund (IMF). (2015). Monetary policy and financial stability. *IMF Policy Paper*. https://www.imf.org/en/Publications/Policy-Papers/Issues/2016/12/31/Monetary-Policy-and-Financial-Stability-PP5059

International Monetary Fund. (1996). Currency convertibility in Tunisia. IMF eLibrary. https://www.elibrary.imf.org/display/book/9781557755643/C06.xml

International Monetary Fund. (1999). Tunisia: Staff report for the Article IV consultation (Vol. 1999, Issue 104). International Monetary Fund. https://doi.org/DOI: 10.5089/9781451837766.002

International Monetary Fund. (2004). *Tunisia: 2004 Article IV consultation—Staff report; Public information notice on the Executive Board discussion; and statement by the Executive Director for Tunisia.* International Monetary Fund. https://www.imf.org/en/Publications/CR/Issues/2016/12/30/Tunisia-2004-Article-IV-Consultation-Staff-Report-Public-Information-Notice-on-the-18006

Isibor, A., Omankhanlen, A., Ehikioya, B., Osuma, G., Oladipo, A., Bunmi-Alo, A., & Ajalaadebowale, K. (2023). Achieving Sustainable Economic Growth in Sub-Saharan African Countries Using the Tool of Monetary Policy Effectiveness. *Journal of Central Banking Theory and Practice*, *12*(3), 111–132. DOI: 10.2478/jcbtp-2023-0027

Islam, S. N., & Islam, Md. S., Islam, Md. R., & Alam, Md. A. (2024). The Effect of Financial Development, Tariff, and RTA on Exports. *Journal of Economic Integration, 39*(1). https://www.jstor.org/stable/27291364

Issahaku, H., Harvey, S. K., & Abor, J. Y. (2016). Does development finance pose an additional risk to monetary policy? *Review of Development Finance*, *6*(2), 91–104. DOI: 10.1016/j.rdf.2016.06.001

Issing, O., & Wieland, V. (2012). Monetary theory and monetary policy: Reflections on the development over the last 150 years. *Institute for Monetary and Financial Stability, Goethe University Frankfurt.* Working Paper No. 67. https://www.imfs-frankfurt.de/de/forschung/imfs-working-papers.html

Jackson, J. D. (2008). *Quantum field theory: A modern introduction.* Oxford University Press.

Jae Shin, Y. (2024). Identifying the Role of Knowledge-Intensive Business Services in the Korean Economy as a Sustainable Innovation Tool Using Input–Output Analysis. *Sustainability (Basel)*, *16*(5), 1823. Advance online publication. DOI: 10.3390/su16051823

Jagran Josh. (2021). *ITU Global Cybersecurity Index 2020: India ranked among the top 10 nations.* https://www.jagranjosh.com/general-knowledge/itu-global-cybersecurity-index-1625207203-1

Jahanger, A., Usman, M., Murshed, M., Mahmood, H., & Balsalobre-Lorente, D. (2022). The linkages between natural resources, human capital, globalization, economic growth, financial development, and ecological footprint: The moderating role of technological innovations. *Resources Policy*, *76*, 102569. DOI: 10.1016/j.resourpol.2022.102569

Jangir, J., Tripathi, K., Punetha, N., & Srivastava, A. (2024). An efficient meta-heuristic dimensionality LSTM model for dimensionality reduction and clustering for attack classification. In *2024 International Conference on Intelligent Systems for Cybersecurity (ISCS)* (pp. 1–5). IEEE. DOI: 10.1109/ISCS61804.2024.10581351

Jawadi, F., Mallick, S. K., & Sousa, R. M. (2017). US monetary policy and global financial stability. *Research in International Business and Finance, 39*, 466–485. DOI: 10.1016/j.ribaf.2016.09.001

Jawad, M., & Naz, M. (2019). Pre- and post-effects of Brexit polling on United Kingdom economy: An econometrics analysis of transactional change. *Quality & Quantity, 53*(1), 247–267. DOI: 10.1007/s11135-018-0746-1

Jeon, B. N., & Wu, J. (2014). The role of foreign banks in monetary policy transmission: Evidence from Asia during the crisis of 2008–2009. *Pacific-Basin Finance Journal, 29*, 96–120. DOI: 10.1016/j.pacfin.2014.03.005

Jin, Y., Liu, D., & Li, Y. (2018). Factors That Have Led to the Collapse of the Bretton Woods System. *American Journal of Industrial and Business Management, 8*(10), 2133–2142. DOI: 10.4236/ajibm.2018.810141

Jovanovic, B. (2009). The theory of equilibrium exchange rates. *The Journal of Finance, 64*(6), 2513–2524.

Kabir, M. H. (2022). Financial technology and financial inclusion: A critical review. *International Journal of Finance and Banking Studies, 11*(1), 1–12.

Kabir, M. N. (2022). Financial inclusion through central bank digital currency: Evidence from India. *Journal of Emerging Financial Markets, 14*(1), 92–108.

Kabundi, A., Schaling, E., & Some, M. (2015). Monetary policy and heterogeneous inflation expectations in South Africa. *Economic Modelling, 45*, 109–117. DOI: 10.1016/j.econmod.2014.11.002

Kahneman, D., & Tversky, A. (2019). Prospect theory: An analysis of decision under risk. *Econometrica, 47*(2), 263–291. DOI: 10.2307/1914185

Kallianiotis, J. N. (2017). Central Banks, Monetary Policy, and their Efficiency. *Chapter in Monetary Policy: Perspectives, Strategies and Challenges, Harriet Ward (editor), New York: Nova Science Publishers.*

Kaminsky, G., Lizondo, S., & Reinhart, C. (1998). *Leading Indicators of Currency Crises. International Monetary Fund., 45.* Advance online publication. DOI: 10.1596/1813-9450-1852

Kang, K. H., & Do, K. (2024). Korea's neutral interest rate: Estimates, determinants, and monetary policy stance. *Journal of Asian Economics*, *92*, 101732. DOI: 10.1016/j.asieco.2024.101732

Kannan, P., Rabanal, P., & Scott, A. M. (2012). Monetary and macroprudential policy rules in a model with house price booms. *The B.E. Journal of Macroeconomics*, *12*(1). Advance online publication. DOI: 10.1515/1935-1690.2268

Karahan, C. C., & Özsöylev, H. N. (2023). Inflation and the Stock Market: Money Illusion in Borsa Istanbul. In Managing Inflation and Supply Chain Disruptions in the Global Economy (pp. 24-40). IGI Global.

Karolyi, G. A. (1998). Why Do Companies List Shares Abroad?: A Survey of the Evidence and its Managerial Implications. *Financial Markets, Institutions and Instruments*, *7*(1), 1–60. DOI: 10.1111/1468-0416.00018

Karolyi, G. A., & Stulz, R. M. (1996). Why Do Markets Move Together? An Investigation of US-Japan Stock Return Comovements. *The Journal of Finance*, *51*(3), 951–986. DOI: 10.1111/j.1540-6261.1996.tb02713.x

Karthikeyan, S. (2020). RBI Extends Moratorium on PMC Bank Till December 22; Withdrawal Limit Capped At Rs. 1 Lakh. Retrieved from https://www.republicworld.com/business-news/india- business/rbi-extends-moratorium-on-pmc-bank-till-december-22-2020.html. (Accessed on 10th April 2021).

Kashyap, A. K., & Stein, J. C. (2000). What do a million observations on banks say about the transmission of monetary policy? *The American Economic Review*, *90*(3), 407–428. DOI: 10.1257/aer.90.3.407

Kazgan, H., & Ateş, T. vd. (1999). *Osmanlı'dan Günümüze Türk Finans Tarihi*. c.2, İstanbul: Creative Yayıncılık.

Kepenek, Y. (2014). Türkiye Ekonomisi. 28.b., İstanbul: Remzi Kitabevi.

Kerala State IT Infrastructure Ltd. (KSITIL). (2023). *Kerala Fibre Optic Network (KFON)*. https://kfon.kerala.gov.in

Keränen, J., Piirainen, K. A., & Salmanen, R. T. (2012). Systematic review on B2B branding: Research issues and avenues for future research. *Journal of Product and Brand Management*, *21*(6), 404–417. DOI: 10.1108/10610421211264892

Khan, M. A., & Javed, M. Y. (2019). AI and IoT: The backbone of financial security in banking. *Journal of Information Technology*, *34*(3), 215–228. DOI: 10.1177/0268396219831900

Khan, M. N., & Ullah, A. (2021). Risk assessment of IoT in banking services: A framework for security and privacy. *Computers & Security, 109*, 102382. DOI: 10.1016/j.cose.2021.102382

Kharpal, A. (2022). India's digital rupee: How it will work and what it means for crypto. CNBC Tech. Retrieved from https://www.cnbc.com/

Kılıçbay, A. (1990). *İktisadi Planlama*. İ.Ü. İktisat Fakültesi Yayını.

Kim, J. (2000). Constructing and estimating a realistic optimizing model of monetary policy. *Journal of Monetary Economics, 45*(2), 329–359. DOI: 10.1016/S0304-3932(99)00054-9

Kim, Y., & Kwon, O. (2019). Central Bank Digital Currency and Financial Stability. *SSRN, 7*(1), 23–48. DOI: 10.2139/ssrn.3330914

Kim, Y., Kwon, O., & Lee, S. (2018). Digital currency and the future of banking: Disruptions and risks. *Banking and Finance Review, 50*(3), 112–129.

Kirwan, R. M. (1987). Fiscal Policy and the Price of Land and Housing in Japan. *Urban Studies (Edinburgh, Scotland), 24*(5), 345–360. DOI: 10.1080/00420988720080581

Koch, P. D., & Ferson, W. E. (2001). A model of noise trading and asset prices. *Review of Financial Studies, 4*(3), 449–470.

Koeniger, W., Lennartz, B., & Ramelet, M. A. (2022). On the transmission of monetary policy to the housing market. *European Economic Review, 145*, 104107. DOI: 10.1016/j.euroecorev.2022.104107

Kohler, P. (2015). Redistributive policies for sustainable development: looking at the role of assets and equity.

Koop, G., Pesaran, M., & Potter, S. M. (1996). Impulse response analysis in nonlinear multivariate models. *Journal of Econometrics, 74*(1), 119–147. DOI: 10.1016/0304-4076(95)01753-4

Köse, Y., Atik, M. & Yılmaz, B. (2015). Türkiye İçin Negatif Faiz Oranının Uygulanabilirliği ve Analitik Olarak İncelenmesi. *Finansal Araştırmalar ve Çalışmalar Dergisi*, c.7, S.13, Temmuz, ss.321-339.

Köse, N., & Ünal, E. (2024). The Effects of the Volatilities in Global Determinants on the Istanbul Stock Exchange. *Panoeconomicus*, •••(00), 1–38. DOI: 10.2298/PAN230213020K

Kozhevnikov, K. I. (2024). Analysis of Postglobalization Concepts and Stages of Evolution of Its Research. *International Trade and Trade Policy*, *10*(4), 5–15. DOI: 10.21686/2410-7395-2024-4-5-15

Kraiwanit, T., & Limsakul, C. (2022). Central Bank Digital Currency and its role in financial transformation. *Asian Journal of Economics and Banking*, *6*(1), 45–67.

Krause, S., & Rioja, F. (2006). Financial development and monetary policy efficiency. *Working Paper*, Department of Economics, Georgia State University.

Küçük, Y. (1985), Planlı Kalkınma ve Türkiye, 4.b., İstanbul: Tekin Yayınevi.

Kumar, K. B. (2020). What is a Bank Moratorium, and when does it come into play? Retrieved from https://www.thehindu.com/business/Economy/the-hindu-explains -what-is-a-bank-moratorium-and- when-does-it-come-into-play/article33151740. ece. (Accessed on 5th June 2021).

Kumar, K., Tripathi, K., & Gupta, R. (2023). Plant disease detection from image using CNN. [IJIRCST]. *International Journal of Innovative Research in Computer Science and Technology*, *11*(4), 24–27. DOI: 10.55524/ijircst.2023.11.4.5

Kumar, R., & Ayodeji, J. (2022a). CBDC and future financial infrastructure: A comparative analysis. *Journal of Central Banking Theory and Practice*, *11*(2), 145–164.

Kumar, R., & Ayodeji, J. (2022b). Implications of CBDCs for emerging markets. *International Journal of Monetary Economics and Finance*, *15*(1), 56–73.

Kumar, S. S. S. (2011). Are Emerging Markets Relevant for Portfolio Diversification? *Review of Market Integration*, *3*(2), 103–119. DOI: 10.1177/097492921100300201

Kumhof, M., & Noone, C. (2018). Central bank digital currencies – Design principles and balance sheet implications. Bank of England Staff Working Paper No. 725.

Kumhof, M., & Noone, C. (2018). Central bank digital currencies: Design principles and balance sheet implications. *Bank of England Staff Working Paper No. 725*. https://doi.org/DOI: 10.2139/ssrn.3180713

Kurtishi-Kastrati, S. (2013). Impact of FDI on economic growth: An overview of the main theories of FDI and empirical research. *European Scientific Journal*, *9*(7), 56–77. https://eujournal.org/index.php/esj/article/view/855/898

Kutu, A. A., & Ngalawa, H. (2016). Monetary policy shocks and industrial sector performance in South Africa. *Journal of Economics and Behavioral Studies*, *8*(3), 26–40. DOI: 10.22610/jebs.v8i3(J).1286

Lal, M., Kumar, S., Pandey, D. K., Rai, V. K., & Lim, W. M. (2023). Exchange rate volatility and international trade. *Journal of Business Research*, *167*, 114156. DOI: 10.1016/j.jbusres.2023.114156

Latimer, P., & Duffy, M. (2019). Digital currencies and monetary policy: Exploring risks and opportunities. *International Review of Financial Analysis*, *62*, 119–129.

Lavy, V., & Rapoport, H. (1992). External Debt and Structural Adjustment: Recent Experience in Turkey. *Middle Eastern Studies*, *28*(2), 313–332. https://www.jstor.org/stable/4283495. DOI: 10.1080/00263209208700903

Lawal, A. I., Somoye, R. O., Babajide, A. A., & Nwanjia, T. I. (2018). The effect of fiscal and monetary policies interaction on stock market performance: Evidence from Nigeria. *Future Business Journal*, *4*(1), 16–33. DOI: 10.1016/j.fbj.2017.11.004

LeBaron, B. (2006). Agent-based modeling of financial markets: A survey. *Quantitative Finance*, *6*(5), 631–654.

Lebe, F., & Akbaş, Y. E. (2014). Türkiye'nin konut talebinin analizi: 1970-2011. *Atatürk Üniversitesi İktisadi ve İdari Bilimler Dergisi*, *28*(1), 57–82.

Leontief, W. (1936). Quantitative Input and Output Relations in the Economic Systems of the United States. *The Review of Economics and Statistics*, *18*(3), 105–125. DOI: 10.2307/1927837

Leontief, W. (1986). *I-O Economics* (2nd ed.). Oxford University Press.

Levine, R. (1991). Stock Markets, Growth, and Tax Policy. *The Journal of Finance*, *46*(4), 1445–1465. DOI: 10.1111/j.1540-6261.1991.tb04625.x

Levine, R. (1997). Financial Development and Economic Growth: Views and Agenda. *Journal of Economic Literature*, *35*(2), 688–726.

Levine, R. (2002). Bank-Based or Market-Based Financial Systems: Which is Better? *Journal of Financial Intermediation*, *11*(4), 398–428. DOI: 10.1006/jfin.2002.0341

Levine, R. (2003). More on Finance and Growth: More Finance, More Growth? *Review - Federal Reserve Bank of St. Louis*, *85*(4), 31–46. DOI: 10.20955/r.85.31-46

Levy, M., & Levy, H. (2002). The behavior of stock prices: Theories and applications. *Behavioral Economics and Finance*, *30*, 113–122.

Lin, C., & Chen, K. (2022). Market competition, exchange rate uncertainty, and foreign direct investment. *Review of Development Economics*, *26*(1), 405–422. DOI: 10.1111/rode.12813

Lin, Y., & Wang, Z. (2020). Privacy-preserving data mining for banking transactions in IoT environments. *IEEE Transactions on Dependable and Secure Computing, 17*(1), 33–45. DOI: 10.1109/TDSC.2018.2865865

Li, T. T. (2024). The Impact of Global Trade Wars on Emerging Economies: An Analysis of Tariff Policies and Economic Growth. *International Journal of Social and Human, 1*(2). https://dejournals.org/index.php/ijsh/article/download/37/19

Lo, A. W. (2004). The adaptive markets hypothesis: Market efficiency from an evolutionary perspective. The Journal of Portfolio Management, 30*(5), 1–17.

Lochot, V., Khalilpour, K., Sánchez, D., & Hoadley, F. A. (2024). French economy and clean energy transition: A macroeconomic multi-objective extended I-O analysis. *Sustainable Futures : An Applied Journal of Technology, Environment and Society, 8*, 100285. Advance online publication. DOI: 10.1016/j.sftr.2024.100285

Long, J., & Zhuang, L. (2025). Housing finance and inequality: Mortgage debt in urban China. *Habitat International, 161*, 103411. DOI: 10.1016/j.habitatint.2025.103411

López-Villavicencio, A., & Mignon, V. (2017). Exchange rate pass-through in emerging countries: Do the inflation environment, monetary policy regime, and central bank behavior matter? *Journal of International Money and Finance, 79*, 20–38. DOI: 10.1016/j.jimonfin.2017.09.004

Loser, C. M. (2008). *Financial Markets in Latin America. Growth and Development in Emerging Market Economies: International Private Capital Flows, Financial Markets and Globalization*. Sage Publishing.

Luciani, M. (2015). Monetary policy and the housing market: A structural factor analysis. *Journal of Applied Econometrics, 30*(2), 199–218. DOI: 10.1002/jae.2318

Lumpkin, S. (2010). Consumer protection and financial innovation: A few basic propositions. *OECD Journal: Financial Market Trends, 1*, 1–23.

Lumpkin, S. (2010). Regulatory issues related to financial innovation. *OECD Journal: Financial Market Trends, 2010*(1), 1–21. DOI: 10.1787/fmt-2010-5km7k9tpcjhf

Lux, M., Sunega, P., & Kážmér, L. (2021). Intergenerational financial transfers and indirect reciprocity: Determinants of the reproduction of homeownership in the post-socialist Czech Republic. *Housing Studies, 36*(8), 1294–1317. DOI: 10.1080/02673037.2018.1541441

Macedoni, L., & Xu, M. (2021). *Flexibility and Productivity: Towards the Understanding of Firm Heterogeneity*. https://air.unimi.it/retrieve/7b53105d-73a9-44df-a184-5b587ddeaee3/Macedoni_Flexibility_and_productivity_AM-2-66.pdf

Madsen, J. B., Dzhumashev, R., & Yao, H. (2013). Stock Returns and Economic Growth. *Applied Economics, 45*(10), 1257–1271. DOI: 10.1080/00036846.2011.613802

Makni, A. (2019). A macro-model to monetary transmission analysis in Tunisia. IHEID Working Papers 13-2019, Economics Section, The Graduate Institute of International Studies. https://repec.graduateinstitute.ch/pdfs/Working_papers/HEIDWP13-2019.pdf

Malec, K., Maitah, M., Rojik, S., Aragaw, A., & Fulnečková, P. R. (2024). Inflation, exchange rate, and economic growth in Ethiopia: A time series analysis. *International Review of Economics & Finance, 96*, 103561. DOI: 10.1016/j.iref.2024.103561

Malhotra, N. (2008). *Marketing Research – An Applied Orientation* (5th ed.). Pearson Education.

Mandelbrot, B. B. (2004). *The (mis)behavior of markets: A fractal view of financial turbulence*. Basic Books.

Maniff, J. (2020). A framework for analyzing central bank digital currency architecture. *Federal Reserve Bank of Kansas City Research Working Paper RWP 20-01*. https://doi.org/DOI: 10.18651/RWP2020-01

Maniff, J. M. (2020). *The role of central banks in supporting digital payment systems*. Federal Reserve Bank of Kansas City Economic Review.

Mapanga, I., Kumar, V., Makondo, W., Kushboo, T., Kadebu, P., & Chanda, W. (2017). *Design and implementation of an intrusion detection system using MLP-NN for MANET. In 2017 IST-Africa Week Conference (IST-Africa)*. IEEE., DOI: 10.23919/ISTAFRICA.2017.8102374

Marco, J., Valbuena, N., Valderrama, D., & Vásquez, M. (2024). *Examining the Success of the Tilapia Industry in Huila—An Emerging Aquaculture Hub in the Colombian Southwest* [Discussion Paper]. https://www.jstor.org/stable/resrep58356

Markowitz, H. (1952). Modern Portfolio Theory. *The Journal of Finance, 7*(11), 77–91.

Masood, O., & Ashraf, M. (2012). Bank-specific and macroeconomic profitability determinants of Islamic banks: The case of different countries. *Qualitative Research in Financial Markets, 4*(2/3), 255–268. DOI: 10.1108/17554171211252565

Matemilola, B. T., Bany-Ariffin, A. N., & Muhtar, F. E. (2015). The impact of monetary policy on bank lending rate in South Africa. *Borsa Istanbul Review, 15*(1), 53–59. DOI: 10.1016/j.bir.2014.09.003

Mathä, T. Y., Pulina, G., & Ziegelmeyer, M. (2025). Private wealth transfers and homeownership: Evidence from Luxembourg. *Applied Economics*, •••, 1–12. DOI: 10.1080/00036846.2025.2471589

Mathew, G., & Verma, S. (2020). Moratorium on Lakshmi Vilas Bank: What does it mean for depositors, financial sector? Retrieved from https://indianexpress.com/article/explained/lakshmi-vilas-what-a- failed-bank-means-7056518/. (Accessed on 26th March 2021).

Mauro, P. (2003). Stock Returns and Output Growth in Emerging and Advanced Economies. *Journal of Development Economics*, *71*(1), 129–153. DOI: 10.1016/S0304-3878(02)00136-0

Ma, Y. (2016). Nonlinear monetary policy and macroeconomic stabilization in emerging market economies: Evidence from China. *Economic Systems*, *40*(4), 461–480. DOI: 10.1016/j.ecosys.2015.12.003

Ma, Y., & Lin, X. (2016). Financial development and the effectiveness of monetary policy. *Journal of Banking & Finance*, *68*, 1–11. DOI: 10.1016/j.jbankfin.2016.03.002

Maza, A., & Hierro, M. (2024). Delving into the FDI-economic growth relationship at the regional level: Headquarters effect in FDI data. *International Review of Economics & Finance*, *97*, 103829. DOI: 10.1016/j.iref.2024.103829

McDonald, J. F., & Stokes, H. H. (2015). Monetary Policy, Fiscal Policy, and the Housing Bubble. *Modern Economy*, *6*(2), 165–178. DOI: 10.4236/me.2015.62014

McLennan, W. (1996-97). Information Paper: Australian National Accounts Introduction to I-O Multipliers, Catalog No.5246.0. Australian Bureau of Statistics

Meurs, M., Seidelmann, L., & Koutsoumpa, M. (2019). How healthy is a 'healthy economy'? Incompatibility between current pathways towards SDG3 and SDG8. *Globalization and Health*, *15*(1), 83. DOI: 10.1186/s12992-019-0532-4 PMID: 31791366

Mian, A., & Sufi, A. (2011). House Prices, Home Equity-Based Borrowing, and the US Household Leverage Crisis. *The American Economic Review*, *101*(5), 2132–2156. DOI: 10.1257/aer.101.5.2132

Ministry of Electronics and Information Technology (MeitY). (2020). *Pradhan Mantri Gramin Digital Saksharta Abhiyan (PMGDISHA)*. https://www.pmgdisha.in

Ministry of Electronics and Information Technology (MeitY). (2021). *India Semiconductor Mission*. https://www.meity.gov.in

Ministry of Electronics and Information Technology (MeitY). (2024). *R & D in electronics division.* https://www.meity.gov.in/content/r-d-electronics

Mishkin, F. S. (2007). Housing and the monetary transmission mechanism. NBER Working Paper.

Mishkin, F. S. (2009). Globalization and financial development. *Journal of Development Economics, 89*(2), 164–169. DOI: 10.1016/j.jdeveco.2007.11.004

Mishra, D., Kedia, M., Reddy, A., & Ramnath, K. (2024). *State of India's Digital Economy (SIDE) Report, 2024.* ICRIER. https://icrier.org/pdf/State_of_India_Digital_Economy_Report_2024.pdf

Mishra, P., Montiel, P., Pedroni, P., & Spilimbergo, A. (2014). Monetary policy and bank lending rates in low-income countries: Heterogeneous panel estimates. *Journal of Development Economics, 111*, 117–131. DOI: 10.1016/j.jdeveco.2014.08.005

Mobius, M. (2012). *The Little Book of Emerging Markets: How to Make Money in the World's Fastest Growing Markets.* John Wiley & Sons.

Mohanty, M. S., & Turner, P. (2006). Monetary policy transmission in emerging market economies: What is new? *BIS Papers No. 35.* Bank for International Settlements. https://www.bis.org/publ/bppdf/bispap35.htm

Morgan, S. (2011). *Dynamic differentiated RRR adjustment to become the primary monetary policy tool.* Morgan Stanley Research Asia/Pacific.

Motiani, P. (2020). What Lakshmi Vilas Bank account customers should do post imposition of moratorium? Retrieved from https://economictimes.indiatimes.com/wealth/save/what-lakshmi- vilas-bank-account-customers-should-do-post-imposition-of- moratorium/articleshow/79299602.cms?from=mdr. (Accessed on 19th April 2021).

Mourtas, S. D., Katsikis, V. N., Drakonakis, E., & Kotsios, S. (2022). Stabilization of stochastic exchange rate dynamics under central bank intervention using neuronets. *International Journal of Information Technology & Decision Making*, •••, 1–29.

Moussa, F., & Delhoumi, E. (2022). The asymmetric impact of interest and exchange rate on the stock market index: Evidence from MENA region. *International Journal of Emerging Markets, 17*(10), 2510–2528. DOI: 10.1108/IJOEM-01-2020-0089

Muhammad, A. A. (2023). Examining the Relationship among Unemployment, Inflation, and Economic Growth. *Journal of Business and Economic Options, 6*(2), 23–31.

Mukherjee, S. (2022). Digital rupee and the threat to commercial banking: Risks and safeguards. *Economic and Political Weekly, 57*(48), 16–20.

Mullineux, A. W., & Murinde, V. (2014). Financial sector policies for enterprise development in Africa. *Review of Development Finance, 4*(2), 66–72. DOI: 10.1016/j.rdf.2014.05.001

Mullin, J. (1993). Emerging Equity Markets in The Global Economy. *Quarterly Review-Federal Reserve Bank of New York, 18*, 54–54.

Mundell, R. A. (1961). A Theory of Optimum Currency Areas. *The American Economic Review, 51*, 657–665. https://www.jstor.org/stable/1812792

Mundell, R. A. (1963). Inflation and Real Interest. *Journal of Political Economy, 71*(3), 280–283. DOI: 10.1086/258771

Murro, P., & Gurbanov, N. (2024). *Currency Exchange rate risk: The devaluation case of Azerbaijan* [Thesis for the Degree of Master of Science in Corporate Finance, Luiss University]. https://www.researchgate.net/profile/Nijat-Gurbanov/publication/387423852

Murtaza, N., & Al-Hawari, M. (2020). AI in banking: Balancing innovation and privacy. *Journal of Business Research, 118*, 414–422. DOI: 10.1016/j.jbusres.2019.11.048

Muzayyanah, M., Triyana, E., & Aura, K. A. N. (2023). Evaluating the impact of fiscal and monetary policies on Indonesia's macroeconomic stability and growth (2015-2019). [JIEMB]. *Journal of Islamic Economics Management and Business, 5*(2), 203–226. DOI: 10.21580/jiemb.2023.5.2.21672

Nair, V. (2020). Government Puts Yes Bank Under Moratorium, RBI Supersedes Board, Withdrawal Capped At Rs 50,000. Retrieved from https://www.bloombergquint.com/business/government-puts-yes-bank-under-moratorium-rbi-supersedes-board-withdrawals-capped-at-rs-50000. (Accessed on 9th March 2021).

Nair, V. (2020). Lakshmi Vilas Bank Under RBI Moratorium, To be merged With DBS India. Retrieved from https://www.bloombergquint.com/business/rbi-places-lakshmi-vilas-bank-under-moratorium. (Accessed on 30th March 2021).

Naraidoo, R., & Paya, I. (2012). Forecasting monetary policy rules in South Africa. *International Journal of Forecasting, 28*(2), 446–455. DOI: 10.1016/j.ijforecast.2011.04.006

National Science Foundation (NSF). (2023). *Science and Engineering Indicators 2023*. https://ncses.nsf.gov/pubs/nsb20231

Ncube, M. (1999). Financial systems and monetary policy in Africa (*Working Paper No.* 20, Graduate School of Business Administration, University of the Witwatersrand). https://wiredspace.wits.ac.za/handle/10539/19804

Ndikumana, L. (2016). Implications of monetary policy for credit and investment in Sub-Saharan African countries. *Journal of African Development, 18*(2), 1–18. DOI: 10.5325/jafrideve.18.2.0001

Neely, C. J. (2000). The practice of central bank intervention: Looking under the hood. FRB of St. Louis Working Paper No.

Nelson, E. (2020). *Dynamical theories of Brownian motion.* Princeton University Press. DOI: 10.2307/j.ctv15r57jg

Neos Networks. (2024). What is digital infrastructure. https://neosnetworks.com/resources/blog/what-is-digital-infrastructure/

Neville, H., Draaisma, T., Funnell, B., Harvey, C. R., & Van Hemert, O. (2021). The Best Strategies for Inflationary Times. *Journal of Portfolio Management, 47*(8), 8–37. DOI: 10.3905/jpm.2021.1.274

Nga, N. T. V. (2020). Analysis of the Determinants of Trade Balance: A Case Study of Vietnam. *Journal of Applied Finance & Banking, 10*(10), 21–35.

Nguyen, A. D. M., Dridi, J., Unsal, F. D., & Williams, O. H. (2015). On the drivers of inflation in Sub-Saharan Africa (*IMF Working Paper No.* WP/15/189). International Monetary Fund, African Department. https://doi.org/DOI: 10.5089/9781513519240.001

Nguyen, H. H., Nguyen, T. P., & Tran, A. N. T. (2022). Impacts of monetary policy transmission on bank performance and risk in the Vietnamese market: Does the COVID-19 pandemic matter? *Cogent Business & Management, 9*(1), 2094591. Advance online publication. DOI: 10.1080/23311975.2022.2094591

Nilavongse, R., Michał, R., & Uddin, G. S. (2020). Economic policy uncertainty shocks, economic activity, and exchange rate adjustments. *Economics Letters, 186*, 108765. DOI: 10.1016/j.econlet.2019.108765

NISRA (North Ireland Statistic and Research Agency). (2024). The Analytical I-O tables. https://www.nisra.gov.uk/statistics/economic-accounts-project/analytical-I-O -tables

Norton, R. (2024, May 8). *Currency Risk Management: A Guide for Multinational Corporations.* Corpay. https://www.corpay.com/resources/blog/currency-risk-management-a-guide-for-multinational-corporations

Nouira, R., Amor, T. H., & Rault, C. (2018). Oil price fluctuations and exchange rate dynamics in the MENA region: Evidence from Non-Causality-in-Variance and Asymmetric Non-Causality Tests. *The Quarterly Review of Economics and Finance*. Advance online publication. DOI: 10.1016/j.qref.2018.07.011

Nugroho, Y. D. (2022). Analysis of I-O Table: Identifying Leading Sectors in Indonesia (Case Study in 2010, 2016 and 2020). *Proceedings of The International Conference on Data Science and Official Statistics*, 2021(1), 985–997. doi:DOI: 10.34123/icdsos.v2021i1.251

Nunes, A. R., Lee, K., & O'Riordan, T. (2016). The importance of an integrating framework for achieving the Sustainable Development Goals: The example of health and well-being. *BMJ Global Health, 1*(3), e000068. DOI: 10.1136/bmjgh-2016-000068 PMID: 28588955

Nunnally, J. (1967). *Psychometric Methods*. McGraw-Hill.

Nuno, A., & Pires, A. (2018). Noise traders in financial markets: Risk and volatility modeling. *Economic Modelling, 75*, 147–160.

NWT Bureau of Statistics (2006). NWT I-O Model – An Overview –, NWT Bureau of Statistics Government of the Northwest Territories, June 2006.

Obstfeld, M. (1998). The Global Capital Market: Benefactor or Menace? *The Journal of Economic Perspectives, 12*(4), 9–30. DOI: 10.1257/jep.12.4.9

Odier, P., & Solnik, B. (1993). Lessons for International Asset Allocation. *Financial Analysts Journal, 49*(2), 63–77. DOI: 10.2469/faj.v49.n2.63

Office for National Statistics. (2022). *UK digital economy research*. https://www.ons.gov.uk/economy/economicoutputandproductivity/output/methodologies/ukdigitaleconomyresearch2019

Ojha, A. (2022). A roadmap for the implementation of digital currency in India. *Journal of Banking and Financial Technology, 6*(1), 1–14.

Oksay, S. (2001). *Döviz Kuru ve Ödemeler Bilançosu Politikaları: Türkiye (1923-2000)*. Beta Yayınevi.

Olamide, E., Maredza, A., & Ogujiuba, K. (2021). Monetary Policy, External Shocks and Economic Growth Dynamics in East Africa: An S-VAR Model. *Sustainability (Basel), 14*(6), 3490. DOI: 10.3390/su14063490

Omay, T., & Öznur Kan, E. (2010). Re-examining the threshold effects in the inflation–growth nexus with cross-sectionally dependent non-linear panel: Evidence from six industrialized economies. *Economic Modelling*, *27*(5), 996–1005. DOI: 10.1016/j.econmod.2010.04.011

Omri, A., & Sassi-Tmar, A. (2015). Linking FDI inflows to economic growth in North African countries. *Journal of the Knowledge Economy*, *6*(1), 90–104. DOI: 10.1007/s13132-013-0172-5

Organisation for Economic Co-operation and Development (OECD). (2021). *Brick by Brick: Building Better Housing Policies*. OECD Publishing., DOI: 10.1787/b453b043-

Organisation for Economic Co-operation and Development. (2020a). *Bridging the digital divide: Include, upskill, innovate*. https://www.oecd.org/digital/bridging-the-digital-divide.pdf

Organisation for Economic Co-operation and Development. (2020b). OECD Digital. *Economic Outlook, 2020*. Advance online publication. DOI: 10.1787/bb167041-en

Otker-Robe, I., & Podpiera, A. M. (2013). The social impact of financial crises: Evidence from the global financial crisis. *World Bank Policy Research Working Paper*, , 6703. DOI: 10.1596/1813-9450-6703

Ouattara, Z. (2023). The Impact of Exchange Rate Volatility on International Trade in Developing Countries: Evidence from Turkiye. *Pressacademia*, *1*, 1. Advance online publication. DOI: 10.17261/Pressacademia.2023.1767

Ouedraogo, R., & Sourouema, W. S. (2018). Fiscal policy pro-cyclicality in Sub-Saharan African countries: The role of export concentration. *Economic Modelling*, *71*, 1–11. DOI: 10.1016/j.econmod.2018.05.017

Owusu-Sekyere, E. (2017). The impact of monetary policy on household consumption in South Africa: Evidence from vector autoregressive techniques. *Suid-Afrikaanse Tydskrif vir Ekonomiese en Bestuurswetenskappe*, *20*(1), 1–12. DOI: 10.4102/sajems.v20i1.1660

Özbay, F., & Tosun, N. (2022). The Fear Impact of COVID-19 on Stock Markets and Exchange Rates: An Empirical Application on Turkey. In Handbook of Research on Global Networking Post COVID-19 (pp. 1-22). IGI Global.

Ozili, P. K. (2018). Impact of digital finance on financial inclusion and stability. *Borsa Istanbul Review*, *18*(4), 329–340. DOI: 10.1016/j.bir.2017.12.003

Ozili, P. K. (2021a). Financial inclusion and fintech during the COVID-19 pandemic. *Cogent Economics & Finance*, *9*(1), 1869782.

Ozili, P. K. (2021a). Financial innovation and financial inclusion in developing countries: Evidence from Nigeria. *International Journal of Financial Studies*, *9*(2), 18. DOI: 10.3390/ijfs9020018

Ozili, P. K. (2022b). Central bank digital currency and financial inclusion: A global perspective. *Journal of Economic and Administrative Sciences*, *38*(3), 467–482.

Ozili, P. K. (2022b). The role of central bank digital currencies in financial inclusion. *Journal of Economic Studies (Glasgow, Scotland)*, *49*(7), 1403–1420.

Ozili, P. K. (2022e). Digital transformation and financial inclusion: Risks and rewards. *Journal of Financial Regulation and Compliance*, *30*(2), 254–267.

Ozili, P. K. (2022e). FinTech, RegTech and SupTech: Financial innovation and the future of regulation. *Banking and Finance Review*, *11*(3), 77–95.

Özsan, O., Konut, O., & Karakas, C. (2005). Housing finance practices and development of a secondary mortgage market in Turkey. *Housing Finance International*, *19*(3), 19.

Öztürk, S. & Saygın, S. (2017). 1973 Petrol Krizinin Ekonomiye Etkileri ve Stagflasyon Olgusu. *BJSS-Balkan Sosyal Bilimler Dergisi,* c. 6, S. 12, ss. 1-12.

Öztürk, A., & Aslanoğlu, M. (1998). *Ekonomik Planlama*. Ekin Kitabevi.

Öztürk, N. ve Doğan, A. (2010). Konut Sektörünün Sorunları ve Çözüm Önerileri. *Bütçe Dünyası Dergisi*, *33*(1), 139–154.

Padoa-Schioppa, T. (2003). Central banks and financial stability: exploring the land in between. The transformation of the European financial system, 25, 269-310.

Pakdemirli, E. (1991). *Ekonomimizin 1923'ten 1990'a Sayısal Görünümü.* Milliyet Yayınları.

Papaioannou, M., & Duke, L. (1993). The Internationalization of Emerging Equity Markets. *Finance & Development*, *30*, 36–36.

Parasız, İ., Ekren, N., & Eroğlu, İ. (2016). Para Politikası ve Türkiye Uygulaması. 7.b., Bursa: Ezgi Kitabevi.

Parasız, İ. (2003). *Türkiye Ekonomisi*. Ezgi Kitabevi.

Parasız, İ. (2011). *Türkiye'de ve Dünyada Bankacılık*. Ezgi Kitabevi.

Patra, M. D., & Kapur, M. (2012). A monetary policy model for India. *Macroeconomics and Finance in Emerging Market Economies*, *5*(1), 16–39. DOI: 10.1080/17520843.2011.576453

Pellegrino, R., Gaudenzi, B., & Zsidisin, G. A. (2024). Mitigating foreign exchange risk exposure with supply chain flexibility: A real option analysis. *Journal of Business Logistics*, *45*(1), e12338. DOI: 10.1111/jbl.12338

Peress, J., & Schmidt, D. (2020). Glued to the TV: Distracted noise traders and Pindyck, R. S., & Rubinfeld, D. L. (2013). Econometric models and economic forecasts. McGraw-Hill.stock market liquidity. *The Journal of Finance*, *75*(2), 1083–1133. DOI: 10.1111/jofi.12863

Pesaran, H., & Shin, Y. (1998). Generalized impulse response analysis in linear multivariate models. *Economics Letters*, *58*(1), 17–29. DOI: 10.1016/S0165-1765(97)00214-0

Petticrew, M., & Roberts, H. (2006). *Systematic reviews in the social sciences.* Blackwell. DOI: 10.1002/9780470754887

Philippon, T. (2016). The FinTech opportunity. *NBER Working Paper No. 22476.* National Bureau of Economic Research. https://doi.org/DOI: 10.3386/w22476

Picault, M., Pinter, J., & Renault, T. (2022). Media sentiment on monetary policy: Determinants and relevance for inflation expectations. *Journal of International Money and Finance*, *124*, 102626. Advance online publication. DOI: 10.1016/j.jimonfin.2022.102626

Pinder, R. (2023). Was the Bretton Woods system bound to fail? *Knowles Review of Economic History*, *2*(1), 36–45.

Powel, J. H. (2014, June). Monetary policy accommodation, risk-taking, and spillovers. *Global Research Forum on International Macroeconomics and Finance*, Federal Reserve Bank of New York.

Prakash, M., Tyagi, A. K., Arumugam, S. K., & Rawat, A. (2024). Internet of Things for building a smart and sustainable environment: A survey. In *Achieving sustainability with AI technologies*. IGI Global., DOI: 10.4018/979-8-3693-5247-2.ch002

Prasad, P., & Tripathi, K. (2021). Natural scene text localization and removal: Deep learning and Navier-Stokes inpainting approach. In *2021 IEEE International Conference on Electronics, Computing and Communication Technologies (CONECCT)* (pp. 1–5). IEEE. DOI: 10.1109/CONECCT52877.2021.9622609

Press Information Bureau. (2019). *Report on India's Trillion Dollar Digital Opportunity Released.* https://pib.gov.in/PressReleaseIframePage.aspx?PRID=1565669

Press Information Bureau. (2022). *Achievements made under Digital India programme.* https://pib.gov.in/PressReleaseIframePage.aspx?PRID=1885962

Press Information Bureau. (2024). *Indian government future plan on semiconductor and electronics manufacturing.* https://www.pib.gov.in/PressReleaseIframePage.aspx?PRID=2039638

Primus, K. (2018). The effectiveness of monetary policy in small open economies. *Journal of Policy Modeling, 31*(1), 1–31. DOI: 10.1016/j.jpolmod.2018.03.001

Qin, J., Ge, J., & Lu, X. (2018). The effectiveness of monetary policy in China: New evidence from long-range cross-correlation analysis and the components of multifractality. *Physica A, 506*, 1026–1037. DOI: 10.1016/j.physa.2018.04.068

Quah, D., & Sargent, T. J. (2008). Real-time macroeconomic data: The late 1990s and early 2000s crises. *The Review of Economic Studies, 75*(4), 1233–1265.

Quartey, P., & Afful-Mensah, G. (2014). Financial and monetary policies in Ghana: A review of recent trends. *Review of Development Finance, 4*(2), 115–125. DOI: 10.1016/j.rdf.2014.07.001

Raddatz, C. (2007). Are external shocks responsible for the instability of output in low-income countries? *Journal of Development Economics, 84*(1), 155–187. DOI: 10.1016/j.jdeveco.2006.11.001

Rady, A., Essam, F., Yahia, H., & Shalaby, M. (2024). The Dynamic Relationship Between Exchange Rate Volatility, and Stock Prices in the Egyptian Real Estate Market and the Moderating Effect of Interest Rates. *European Journal of Business and Management Research, 9*(5), 31–44. DOI: 10.24018/ejbmr.2024.9.5.2230

Rafiq, M. S., & Mallick, S. K. (2008). The effects of monetary policy on output in EMU-3: A sign restriction approach. *Journal of Macroeconomics, 30*(4), 1756–1791. DOI: 10.1016/j.jmacro.2007.12.003

Rahman, M. A., & Hossain, M. S. (2021). Data privacy and security issues in IoT: Implications for banking and finance. *Journal of Financial Regulation and Compliance, 29*(3), 307–324. DOI: 10.1108/JFRC-06-2020-0070

Ramer, S. L. (2005). Site action pearl-growing methods and librarianship history and theory. *Journal of the Medical Library Association: JMLA, 93*(3), 397–403. DOI: 10.3163/1536-5050.93.3.397 PMID: 16059431

Ramey, G., & Ramey, V. A. (1995). Cross-Country Evidence on the Link Between Volatility and Growth. *The American Economic Review, 85*(5), 1138–1151. https://www.jstor.org/stable/2950979

Rand, J., & Tarp, F. (2002). Business Cycles in Developing Countries: Are They Different? *World Development, 30*(12), 2071–2088. DOI: 10.1016/S0305-750X(02)00124-9

Rani, A. (2021). Digital economy in India: Opportunities and challenges. *JETIR, 8*(2), 290–297. https://www.jetir.org/papers/JETIR2102290.pdf

Raya Vilchez, J. M., & Kucel, A. (2023). How fiscal policy affects housing market dynamics: Evidence from Spain. *Bulletin of Economic Research, 75*(2), 323–347. DOI: 10.1111/boer.12358

Reilly, F. K., Johnson, G. L., & Smith, R. E. (1970). Inflation, Inflation Hedges, and Common Stocks. *Financial Analysts Journal, 26*(1), 104–110. DOI: 10.2469/faj.v26.n1.104

Reitz, S., Westerhoff, F., & Wieland, C. (2006). Target zone interventions and coordination of expectations. *Journal of Optimization Theory and Applications, 128*(2), 453–467. DOI: 10.1007/s10957-006-9027-6

Rey, H. (2013, August). Dilemma not trilemma: The global financial cycle and monetary policy independence. *Symposium on "Reassessing the Fed's Roles"*, Jackson Hole. Federal Reserve Bank of Kansas City.

Riksbank. (2019). The Riksbank's e-krona project: Report 2. Sveriges Riksbank.

Rodríguez, C., & Bustillo, R. (2010). Modelling foreign real estate investment: The Spanish case. *The Journal of Real Estate Finance and Economics, 41*(3), 354–367. DOI: 10.1007/s11146-008-9164-9

Rose, A. K. (2000). One money, one market: The effect of common currencies on trade. Economic Policy, 15(30), 8-45. DOI: 10.1111/1468-0327.00056

Rossi, J. L., & Costa, J. P. M. H. D. (2023). *Shock Dependent Exchange Rate Pass-Through—An Analysis for Latin American Countries*. Inter-American Development Bank., DOI: 10.18235/0005129

Ruan, Q., Zhang, J., & Lv, D. (2024). Forecasting exchange rate volatility: Is economic policy uncertainty better? *Applied Economics, 56*(13), 1526–1544. DOI: 10.1080/00036846.2023.2176457

Rubio, M., & Schuh, S. (2017). Monetary policy and the role of inventory investment. *Applied Economics Letters*, *24*(21), 1605–1612. DOI: 10.1080/13504851.2017.1363855

Sağlam, İ. (2022). Tahliye taahhütnamesinin hukuki niteliği ve geçerlilik şartları. *Sakarya Üniversitesi Hukuk Fakültesi Dergisi*, *24*(2), 345–368. DOI: 10.35307/sauhf.2022.24.2.14

Saiti, B. Y. B. (2016). The effects of monetary policy on the Islamic financial services industry. *Qualitative Research in Financial Markets*, *8*(3), 218–228. DOI: 10.1108/QRFM-02-2016-0006

Sakli, H., Hniya, L., Lassoued, T., & Telmoudi, F. (2022). The effect of real exchange rate on economic growth: Evidence from Tunisia and Morocco. *Revue d'Economie Financiere*, *2022*(20), 971–977. DOI: 10.55365/1923.x2022.20.109

Salami, M. A., & Tanrivermis, H., and Aliefendioğlu (Tanrivermis), Y. (2023). Interdependence between foreign housing acquisitions and housing price increase in Turkey during the COVID-19 pandemic era. *International Journal of Housing Markets and Analysis*, *16*(3), 575–597. DOI: 10.1108/IJHMA-08-2022-0109

Salampasis, D., & Mention, A. L. (2018). FinTech: Harnessing innovation for financial inclusion. *Journal of Innovation Management*, *6*(1), 7–14.

Salampasis, D., & Mention, A.-L. (2018). Fintech: Harnessing innovation for financial inclusion. *Journal of Business Research*, *88*, 479–481.

Salem, L. B., Nouira, R., & Rault, C. (2024). *On the Impact of Oil Prices on Sectoral Inflation: Evidence from World's Top Oil Exporters and Importers* (Discussion Paper No. IZA DP No. 16706). IZA – Institute of Labor Economics. https://www.jstor.org/stable/resrep57137

Salisu, A. A., Cuñado, J., & Gupta, R. (2022). Geopolitical risks and historical exchange rate volatility of the BRICS. *International Review of Economics & Finance*, *77*, 179–190. DOI: 10.1016/j.iref.2021.09.017

Salomao, J., & Varela, L. (2022). Exchange Rate Exposure and Firm Dynamics. *The Review of Economic Studies*, *89*(1), 481–514. DOI: 10.1093/restud/rdab032

Samant, Y. (2019). *The promises and perils of the platform economy: Occupational health and safety challenges, and the opportunities for labour inspection*. International Labour Organization. https://www.ilo.org/resource/statement/promises-and-perils-platform-economy-occupational-health-and-safety

Samir, B. A., & Tarek, J. (2014). Exchange Rate Pass-Through in Tunisia: Evidence from a Time Varying Parameter Model. *Journal of Developing Areas*, *48*(1), 145–164. DOI: 10.1353/jda.2014.0007

Sankar, T. (2021). *Central bank digital currencies: Conceptual framework and implementation in India*. Reserve Bank of India Bulletin.

Schindler, J. W. (2017). FinTech and financial innovation: Drivers and barriers. *Finance and Economics Discussion Series 2017-081*. Board of Governors of the Federal Reserve System. https://doi.org/DOI: 10.17016/feds.2017.081

Schindler, J. W. (2017). FinTech and financial innovation: Drivers and depth. Office of Financial Research Working Paper No. 17-04.

Schmeling, M., Schrimpf, A., & Steffensen, S. A. (2022). Monetary policy expectation errors. *Journal of Financial Economics*, *146*(3), 841–858. DOI: 10.1016/j.jfineco.2022.09.005

Schwartz, A. J. (2003). Asset price inflation and monetary policy. *Atlantic Economic Journal*, *31*(1), 1–14. DOI: 10.1007/BF02298459

Scottish Government. (2016). *Computable General Equilibrium (CGE) Modelling and SG's CGE Model*. Scottish Government.

Scottish Government. (2023). Supply, Use and I-O Tables. https://www.gov.scot/publications/about-supply-use-I-O -tables/pages/user-guide-multipliers

Sen, S. (2020). RBI extends restrictions on scam-hit PMC bank till March 31; receives four proposals for investment. Retrieved from https://www.dnaindia.com/business/news-rbi-extends-restrictions-on-scam-hit-pmc-bank-till-march-31-receives-four-proposals-for-investment-2862877. (Accessed on 10th February 2021).

Şenses, F. (1991). Turkey's Stabilizatıon and Structural Adjustment Program in Retrospect and Prospect. *The Developing Economies*, *29*(3), 210–234. DOI: 10.1111/j.1746-1049.1991.tb00208.x

Servén, L. (2003). Real-Exchange-Rate Uncertainty and Private Investment in LDCS. *The Review of Economics and Statistics*, *85*(1), 212–218. DOI: 10.1162/rest.2003.85.1.212

Sezen, S. (1999). Devletçilikten Özelleştirmeye Türkiye'de Planlama. Ankara: TODAİE Yayını (No 293).

Shahzad, F., Xiu, G., Wang, F., & Wang, J. (2018). China's digital currency electronic payment system and its impact. *China Finance Review International*, *8*(1), 22–40.

Shamsi, J., & Bafghi, A. M. (2021). A comprehensive survey of security and privacy in IoT-enabled financial services. *Journal of Financial Services Marketing, 26*(4), 223–237. DOI: 10.1057/s41264-021-00120-8

Shapiro, A. C., & Hanouna, P. (2019). *Multinational Financial Management*. John Wiley & Sons.

Shareef, M. A., Archer, N., & Dwivedi, Y. K. (2011). Examining adoption behavior of e-government services in India. *Information Systems Management, 28*(3), 217–233.

Sharma, S., Verma, P., Singh, R., & Tripathi, K. (2024). Advancements in facial expression recognition: A comprehensive analysis of techniques. In N. Chauhan, D. Yadav, G. K. Verma, B. Soni, & J. M. Lara (Eds.), Machine learning, image processing, network security and data sciences (Vol. 2128, pp. [page numbers not available]). Springer. DOI: 10.1007/978-3-031-62217-5_18

Shi, S., Jou, J. B., & Tripe, D. (2014). Can interest rates really control house prices? Effectiveness and implications for macroprudential policy. *Journal of Banking & Finance, 47*, 15–28. DOI: 10.1016/j.jbankfin.2014.06.012

Shu-ping, W., & Xiao-meng, W. (2017). Relationships between exchange rates, economic growth and FDI in China: An empirical study based on the TVP-VAR model. Littera Scripta, 10(1), 166-179. https://littera-scripta.com/wp-content/uploads/2019/05/Wang-1.pdf

Siegel, J. J. (2021). *Stocks for the Long Run: The Definitive Guide to Financial Market Returns & Long-Term Investment Strategies*. McGraw-Hill Education.

Sijabat, R. (2023). The Association between Foreign Investment and Gross Domestic Product in Ten ASEAN Countries. *Economies, 11*(7), 188. DOI: 10.3390/economies11070188

Simo-Kengne, B. D., Balcilar, M., Gupta, R., Reid, M., & Aye, G. C. (2013). Is the relationship between monetary policy and house prices asymmetric across bull and bear markets in South Africa? Evidence from a Markov-switching vector autoregressive model. *Economic Modelling, 32*, 161–171. DOI: 10.1016/j.econmod.2013.02.006

Singh, R., & Bhushan, V. (2023). The global workforce revolution: Exploring digital labour platforms and the gig economy in the era of globalization. *International Journal of Civil Law and Legal Research, 3*(2), 421–435. https://www.civillawjournal.com/article/52/3-2-2-421.pdf. DOI: 10.22271/civillaw.2023.v3.i2a.52

Söilen, K. S., & Benhayoun, L. (2022). Exploring the EU's approach to CBDC and monetary sovereignty. *European Journal of Government and Economics, 11*(1), 102–118.

Solak, A. O. (2024). Housing policies in Turkey post-2002. *International Journal of Housing Policy*, *24*(2), 372–387. DOI: 10.1080/19491247.2022.2154905

Solnik, B. H. (1995). Why Not Diversify Internationally Rather than Domestically?. *Financial Analysts Journal*, 51(1), 89-94. doi:/DOI: 10.2469/faj.v30.n4.48

Solnik, B. (1984). Stock Prices and Monetary Variables: The International Evidence. *Financial Analysts Journal*, *40*(2), 69–73. DOI: 10.2469/faj.v40.n2.69

Solnik, B., Boucrelle, C., & Le Fur, Y. (1996). International Market Correlation and Volatility. *Financial Analysts Journal*, *52*(5), 17–34. DOI: 10.2469/faj.v52.n5.2021

Somisetti, K., Tripathi, K., & Verma, J. K. (2020). Design, implementation, and controlling of a humanoid robot. In *2020 International Conference on Computational Performance Evaluation (ComPE)* (pp. 831–836). IEEE. DOI: 10.1109/ComPE49325.2020.9200020

Sood, J. (2020). RBI Imposes Moratorium on Yes Bank: All You Need to know. Retrieved from https://www.outlookindia.com/website/story/business-news-rbi-places-moratorium-on-yes-bank- withdrawal-all-you-need-to-know/348340. (Accessed on 10th March 2021).

Sowrov, S. M. T. H. (2024). *Trade Openness, Tariffs, and Economic Growth: An Empirical Study from Countries of G-20* (Version 1). arXiv. DOI: 10.48550/ARXIV.2405.08052

Spyrou, S. I. (2004). Are stocks a good hedge against inflation? Evidence from emerging markets. *Applied Economics*, *36*(1), 41–48. DOI: 10.1080/0003684042000177189

Srithilat, K., & Sun, G. (2017). The impact of monetary policy on economic development: Evidence from Lao PDR. *[Conference paper]*.

Srivastava, D. K., Bharadwaj, M., Kapur, T., & Trehan, R. (2023). *Economy watch: Monitoring India's macro-fiscal performance*. EY. https://www.ey.com/content/dam/ey-unified-site/ey-com/en-in/insights/tax/documents/ey-economy-watch-april-2023-v1.pdf

Statcan (2024). I-O multipliers, detail level. *Statistics Canada*. https://www150.statcan.gc.ca/t1/tbl1/en/tv.action?pid=3610059401&pickMembers%5B0%5D=2.5&pickMembers%5B1%5D=4.25&cubeTimeFrame.startYear=2020&cubeTimeFrame.endYear=2020&referencePeriods=20200101%2C20200101

Stern, N. (2006). Stern Review: The economics of climate change.

Stockhammar, P., & Österholm, P. (2016). The impact of US uncertainty shocks on small open economies. *Open Economies Review*, *28*(2), 347–368. DOI: 10.1007/s11079-016-9424-x

Stockhammer, E., & Otero, A. N. (2023). A tale of housing cycles and fiscal policy, not competitiveness. Growth drivers in Southern Europe. *New Political Economy*, *28*(3), 483–505. DOI: 10.1080/13563467.2022.2141702

Stockman, A. C. (1985). Effects of Inflation on the Pattern of International Trade. *The Canadian Journal of Economics. Revue Canadienne d'Economique*, *18*(3), 587–601. DOI: 10.2307/135021

Stone, M. R., & Bhundia, A. J. (2004). A new taxonomy of monetary regimes (*IMF Working Paper No. 04/191*). International Monetary Fund. https://doi.org/DOI: 10.5089/9781451866390.001

Subasree, S., Sakthivel, N. K., Tripathi, K., Agarwal, D., & Tyagi, A. K. (2022). Combining the advantages of radiomic features based feature extraction and hyper-parameters tuned RERNN using LOA for breast cancer classification. Biomedical Signal Processing and Control, 72(Part A), 103354. DOI: 10.1016/j.bspc.2021.103354

Suhaibu, I., Harvey, S. K., & Amidu, M. (2017). The impact of monetary policy on stock market performance: Evidence from twelve African countries. *Research in International Business and Finance*, *42*, 1372–1382. DOI: 10.1016/j.ribaf.2017.07.075

Sujatha, D., & Vijaya Kittu, M. (2023). An Examination of India's International Trade with select economies during COVID-19 times. *International Journal of Research in Management Studies*, *7*(1), 115–121.

Sukma, M., Hartono, D., & Prihawantoro, S. (2018). The Impacts Analysis of Creative-Products Export on the Economy. *JEJAK*, *11*(1), 92–107. DOI: 10.15294/jejak.v11i1.11337

Svensson, L. E. (2018). Housing prices, household debt, and macroeconomic risk: Problems of macroprudential policy I. Unpublished. https://www. larseosvensson.se/files/papers/housing-priceshousehold-debt-and-macroeconomic-risk.pdf

T.C. Hazine ve Maliye Bakanlığı. (2022, Mayıs 20). Hazine ve Maliye Bakanlığı Konut Finansmanına İlişkin Detayları Paylaştı. Anadolu Ajansı.

Takım, A. & İslamoğlu, M. (2012). Serbest Piyasa Ekonomisine Geçiş Sürecinde Türkiye'de Uygulanan Para Politikaları İle İlgili Tartışmalar. *Afyon Kocatepe Üniversitesi İİBF Dergisi,* c.XIV, S.1, ss.179-189.

Tancangco, J. A. M., & Parcon-Santos, H. C. (2024). *The Impact of Exchange Rates and the Inflation- Targeting Regime on Exports: Evidence from the Regional Comprehensive Economic Partnership* (Discussion Paper No. Series No. 2024-22; BSP Discussion Paper). https://www.bsp.gov.ph/Sites/researchsite/Publications/BSP-Discussion-Papers/DP202422.pdf

Tarullo, D. K. (2017, February 10). Monetary policy without a working theory of inflation [Speech]. Federal Reserve Board. https://www.federalreserve.gov/newsevents/speech/tarullo20170210a.htm

Taylor, J. B. (1999). The robustness and efficiency of monetary policy rules as guidelines for interest rate set by the European Central Bank. *Journal of Monetary Economics*, *43*(3), 655–679. DOI: 10.1016/S0304-3932(99)00008-2

Taylor, J. B. (2007). *Housing and monetary policy (No. w13682)*. National Bureau of Economic Research. DOI: 10.3386/w13682

Tesar, L. L., & Werner, M. (1995). US Equity Investment in Emerging Stock Markets. *The World Bank Economic Review*, *9*(1), 109–129. DOI: 10.1093/wber/9.1.109

Thanh, S. D. (2015). Threshold effects of inflation on growth in the ASEAN-5 countries: A Panel Smooth Transition Regression approach. *Journal of Economics, Finance and Administrative Science*, *20*(38), 41–48. DOI: 10.1016/j.jefas.2015.01.003

Tobin, J. (1965). Money and Economic Growth. *Econometrica*, *33*(4), 671–684. DOI: 10.2307/1910352

Topcu, M., & Gulal, O. S. (2020). The impact of COVID-19 on emerging stock markets. *Finance Research Letters*, *36*, 101691. DOI: 10.1016/j.frl.2020.101691 PMID: 32837378

Topel, R., & Rosen, S. (1988). Housing investment in the United States. *Journal of Political Economy*, *96*(4), 718–740. DOI: 10.1086/261560

Tranfield, D., Denyer, D., & Smart, P. (2003). Towards a methodology for developing evidence-informed management knowledge by means of systematic analysis. *British Journal of Management*, *14*(3), 207–222. DOI: 10.1111/1467-8551.00375

Tronnier, F. (2020). Central Bank Digital Currencies: Opportunities for financial inclusion. *Journal of Financial Innovation*, *12*(2), 45–59.

Tronnier, J. (2020). The effects of digital currencies on financial systems. *Financial Innovation*, *6*(1), 1–21.

Tsai, M.-T., Lee, K. W., & Lin, W. L. (2019). Exploring digital currency innovation and challenges. *Journal of Economic Development*, *44*(1), 1–26.

Tufekci, Z., & Korukoglu, S. (2020). Cybersecurity in banking: The impact of IoT and AI on privacy. *Computers & Security, 104*, 102109. DOI: 10.1016/j.cose.2020.102109

Tunç, C. (2019). Konut kredilerinin konut fiyatları üzerindeki etkisi: Türkiye örneği. *23. Finans Sempozyumu Conference Proceeding*, Kayseri, Türkiye.

Tunc, C. (2020). The Effect of Credit Supply on House Prices: Evidence From Turkey. *Housing Policy Debate, 30*(2), 228–242. DOI: 10.1080/10511482.2019.1661266

Tyagi, A. K., Kumari, S., Tiwari, S., & Subbiah, P. (2024). Industry 5.0 at the core of Society 5.0: A revolution in the modern era of the health care sector. In Sustainable innovation for Industry 6.0 (Chap. 17). IGI Global. DOI: 10.4018/979-8-3693-3140-8.ch017

Ufoeze, L. O., Odimgbe, S. O., Ezeabalisi, V. N., & Alajekwu, U. B. (2018). Effect of monetary policy on economic growth in Nigeria: An empirical investigation. *Annals of Spiru Haret University. Economic Series, 9*(1), 123–140.

Ulusoy, A. E. (2020). Türkiye'de Konut Politikaları: Tarihsel Süreç Ve Aktörlerin Rolü. *Kamu Yönetimi Ve Politikaları Dergisi, 1*(3), 87–123.

Umoru, D., Igbinovia, B., & Aliu, T. I. (2024). Returns, Interest Rate Variations, and Changes in Foreign Exchange Rates in Asia. *Development Management, 23*(4), 8–22. DOI: 10.57111/devt/4.2024.08

UNCTAD. (2021). *Manual for the production of statistics on ICT-enabled services*. https://unctad.org/system/files/official-document/dtlstict2021d1_en.pdf

UNED. (2020). *Introduction to digital economy in the EU*. https://blogs.uned.es/digitaleconomy/wp-content/uploads/sites/253/2020/12/Introduction-to-Digital-Economy-in-the-EU.pdf

UNESCO. (2021). *The role of inclusive digital content for inclusive digital learning*. https://unesdoc.unesco.org/ark:/48223/pf0000375703

UN-Habitat. (2016). *World Cities Report 2016: Urbanization and Development – Emerging Futures*. UN-Habitat.

van Dijk, J. A. G. M. (2020). *The digital divide*. Polity Press. https://www.researchgate.net/publication/339751402

Vanham, P. (2021). A brief history of GDP-and what could come next, The World Economic Forum, 2022. https://www.weforum.org/agenda/2021/12/stakeholder-capitalism-episode-1-a-brief-history-of-gdp/

Varlık, N. (2020). Ekonomik büyümenin konut fiyatları üzerindeki asimetrik etkisi: NARDL uygulaması. *Hitit Üniversitesi Sosyal Bilimler Enstitüsü Dergisi*, *13*(2), 352–367. DOI: 10.17218/hititsosbil.800641

Varlı, Y., & Erdem, O. (2014). The Demand and Supply Model of Housing: Evidence from the Turkish Housing Market Available at *SSRN*: https://ssrn.com/abstract=2479794 or http://dx.doi.org/DOI: 10.2139/ssrn.2479794

Veugelers, R. (2024). *Powering the clean energy innovation system* (Working Paper Nos. 24–5; p. 28). Peterson Institute for International Economics. https://www.jstor.org/stable/resrep58215?seq=2

Vieira, F. V., Holland, M., Gomes da Silva, C., & Bottecchia, L. C. (2013). Growth and exchange rate volatility: A panel data analysis. *Applied Economics*, *45*(26), 3733–3741. DOI: 10.1080/00036846.2012.730135

Vijaya Kittu, M., & Sai Rani, P. (2019). Crisis in the Indian Non-Banking Finance Companies (NBFC) Sector. [IJRTE]. *International Journal of Recent Technology and Engineering*, *8*(4), 4502–4507. DOI: 10.35940/ijrte.D8424.118419

Vishnuram, G., Tripathi, K., & Tyagi, A. K. (2022). Ethical hacking: Importance, controversies and scope in the future. In *2022 International Conference on Computer Communication and Informatics (ICCCI)* (pp. 1–6). IEEE. DOI: 10.1109/ICCCI54379.2022.9740860

Vishwakarma, D., Sonkar, S., Keshari, S. K., & Jaiswal, A. K. (2024). Achieving Sustainable Development Goals Through Microfinance: An Incremental Steps Towards Growth. [EEL]. *European Economic Letters*, *14*(1), 2022–2031.

Vittala, K. R. P., Ahmad, S. S., Seranmadevi, R., & Tyagi, A. K. (2024). Emerging technology adoption and applications for modern society towards providing smart banking solutions. In *Enhancing medical imaging with emerging technologies*. IGI Global., DOI: 10.4018/979-8-3693-5261-8.ch018

Vittala, K. R. P., Arumugam, S. K., Kumar, N. S., & Tyagi, A. K. (2024). Artificial intelligence: Blockchain integration for modern business. In *Advancing software engineering through AI, federated learning, and large language models*. IGI Global., DOI: 10.4018/979-8-3693-3502-4.ch006

Vo, D. H., & Vu, N. T. (2024). Exchange rate pass-through for European Union countries. *PLoS One*, *19*(8), e0309527. DOI: 10.1371/journal.pone.0309527 PMID: 39208250

Waal, A., & van Eyden, R. (2012, October). Monetary policy and inflation in South Africa: A VECM augmented with foreign variables (*ERSA Working Paper No. 316*). Economic Research Southern Africa.

Waknis, P. (2014). A Leviathan central bank: Modeling seignorage in a money search model. *Economics Letters*, *125*(3), 386–391. DOI: 10.1016/j.econlet.2014.10.027

Waknis, P. (2016). Competitive supply of money in a new monetarist model. *Economics Letters*, •••, 1–25. DOI: 10.1016/j.econlet.2016.02.008

Walsh, C. E. (2004). Implications of a changing economic structure for the strategy of monetary policy (*Working Paper 03/18*). University of California, Santa Cruz, Center for International Economics.

Wang, H., & Zhou, Z. (2021). AI-enhanced cybersecurity in banking: A systematic review. *Future Generation Computer Systems*, *115*, 287–299. DOI: 10.1016/j.future.2020.11.027

Wang, J., & Xu, H. (2015). A stochastic volatility model with jumps for financial markets. *Quantitative Finance*, *15*(2), 249–265.

Wang, K. (2024). The Causes, Effects and Countermeasures of the Eurozone Sovereign Debt Crisis: An In-Depth Analysis from the Perspective of Exchange Rate Fluctuations. *Asia Pacific Economic and Management Review*, *1*(6), 130–134. DOI: 10.62177/apemr.v1i6.116

Wang, Y., Whited, T. M., Wu, Y., & Xiao, K. (2022). Bank market power and monetary policy transmission: Evidence from a structural estimation. *The Journal of Finance*, *77*(4), 2093–2141. DOI: 10.1111/jofi.13159

Ward, O., & Rochemont, S. (2019). Understanding central bank digital currencies (CBDC). *Global Risk Institute White Paper*. Retrieved from https://globalriskinstitute.org

Ward, O., & Rochemont, S. (2019). Understanding central bank digital currencies. Institute and Faculty of Actuaries Research Paper.

WB. (1976). *Turkey - Country economic memorandum.* Washington, D.C.: World Bank Group. http://documents.worldbank.org/curated/en/509561468172148573

WB. (1980). *Turkey - Postscript special economic report.* Washington, D.C.: World Bank Group. http://documents.worldbank.org/curated/en/621131468121489159

Were, M., Nyamongo, W., Kamau, A. W., Sichei, A. W., & Wambua, J. (2014). Assessing the effectiveness of monetary policy in Kenya: Evidence from a macroeconomic model. *Economic Modelling*, *37*, 193–201. DOI: 10.1016/j.econmod.2013.11.004

Wieland, C., & Westerhoff, F. H. (2005). Exchange rate dynamics, central bank interventions and chaos control methods. *Journal of Economic Behavior & Organization, 58*(1), 117–132. DOI: 10.1016/j.jebo.2003.12.002

Wilcox, J. W. (1992). Global Investing in Emerging Markets. *Financial Analysts Journal*, 15–19.

Wolswijk, G. (2009). Fiscal aspects of housing in Europe. In *Housing market challenges in Europe and the United States* (pp. 158–177). Palgrave Macmillan UK. DOI: 10.1057/9780230246980_8

Wong, K. M., & Chong, T. T. L. (2016). Does monetary policy matter for trade? *Department of Economics, The Chinese University of Hong Kong*. (Unpublished manuscript).

World Economic Forum. (2022). *Digital trust: How to unleash the trillion-dollar opportunity for our global economy*. https://www.weforum.org/stories/2022/08/digital-trust-how-to-unleash-the-trillion-dollar-opportunity-for-our-global-economy/

Xiaonan, Q., & Jun, C. (2022). Research on the Development of Textile Industry in Shandong Province Based on I-O Model. *Information Systems and Economics (2022) Clausius Scientific Press*, ISSN 2523-6407 Vol. 3 Num. 4, DOI: DOI: 10.23977/infse.2022.030402

Xie, Y., & Zhu, H. (2014). The efficiency of the Chinese stock market: A study of noise trading behavior. *Journal of International Financial Markets, Institutions and Money*, *29*, 70–81.

Yalçıner, K. & Çetinkaya, M. – Çevik, Y. E. (2017). Türkiye'nin 'De Facto' Döviz Kuru Rejiminin Belirlenmesi. *Selçuk Üniversitesi Sosyal Bilimler Enstitüsü Dergisi*, S.37, ss.265-272.

Yang, J., & Zhou, H. (2024). The Rhythm of Government. *China Review*, *24*(1), 83–114.

Yao, Z., & Zhang, Y. (2024). The impact of the Fed's interest rate hike on China's macroeconomy: Based on the TVP-VAR model. *Highlights in Business. Economics and Management*, *41*, 49–58. DOI: 10.54097/zsbhf211

Yaşar, S. (2005). *Global Ekonomide Makro Ekonomi Yönetimi*. Beta Yayınevi.

Yellen, J. L. (2015). The economic outlook and monetary policy. *Federal Reserve Bank of Boston Economic Review*, *100*(2), 1–12.

Yergin, D. (2023). The 1973 Oil Crisis: Three Crises in One—and the Lessons for Today. Testimonies & Speeches by Daniel Yergin, Columbia-SIPA, October 16. https://www.energypolicy.columbia.edu/ publications/the-1973-oil-crisis-three-crises-in-one-and-the-lessons-for-today/

Yıldırım, M. O. (2023). Housing affordability in Turkey: How big is it and who are the most vulnerable? In *Citizen-centered public policy making in Turkey* (pp. 331–347). Springer International Publishing. DOI: 10.1007/978-3-031-35364-2_18

Yılmaz, S. & Kalkan, D. K. (2017). Enerji Güvenliği Kavramı: 1973 Petrol Krizi Işığında Bir Tartışma. *ANKASAM Uluslararası Kriz ve Siyaset Araştırmaları Dergisi,* 1 (3), ss.169-199.

Yinusa, D. O., & Akinlo, A. E. (2008). *Exchange rate volatility and the extent of currency substitution in Nigeria (MPRA Paper No. 16257).* University Library of Munich.

Yuan, Y., & Ma, H. (2019). The impact of central bank interventions on exchange rate predictability: Evidence from China. *Economic Modelling, 82*, 89–99.

Yussif, A.-R. B., Onifade, S. T., Ay, A., Canitez, M., & Bekun, F. V. (2024). Modeling the volatility of exchange rate and international trade in Ghana: Empirical evidence from GARCH and EGARCH. *Journal of Economic and Administrative Sciences*, *40*(2), 308–324. DOI: 10.1108/JEAS-11-2020-0187

Zehri, C., El Amin, B. M., Inaam, Z., & Sekrafi, H. (2024). Exploring the nexus of decent work, financial inclusion, and economic growth: A study aligned with SDG 8. *Sustainable Futures : An Applied Journal of Technology, Environment and Society*, *7*, 100213. DOI: 10.1016/j.sftr.2024.100213

Zehri, C., Madjd-Sadjadi, Z., & Ammar, L. S. I. (2024). Asymmetric impacts of US monetary policy on emerging markets: Contagion and macroeconomic determinants. *Journal of Economic Asymmetries*, *29*, e00354. Advance online publication. DOI: 10.1016/j.jeca.2024.e00354

Zeren, F., and Ergüzel, O. S. (2015). Testing For Bubbles in The Housing Market: Further Evidence From Turkey. *Financial Studies*, 19(1).

Zghidi, N., Sghaier, I. M., & Abida, Z. (2016). Does economic freedom enhance the impact of foreign direct investment on economic growth in North African countries? A panel data analysis. *African Development Review*, *28*(1), 64–74. DOI: 10.1111/1467-8268.12167

Zhang, X., & Zhou, J. (2017). Noise trading and stock market efficiency: Empirical evidence from China. *International Review of Financial Analysis*, *50*, 101–109.

Zhang, Y., & Lu, Q. (2019). Managing privacy and security in IoT-enabled banking systems. *Journal of Financial Services Marketing*, *24*(4), 241–256. DOI: 10.1057/s41264-019-00064-1

Zivot, E., & Wang, J. (2006). *Modeling financial time series with S-Plus*. Springer Science & Business Media.

Zumba, Y. (2024). Stock Prices and Economic Activities in Nigeria: Sector Level Evidence. *Macroeconomics and Finance in Emerging Market Economies*, *17*(1), 5–24. DOI: 10.1080/17520843.2022.2027619

About The Contributors

Cláudio Félix Canguende Valentim is President at the Instituto Superior Politécnico Jean Piaget de Benguela, Angola. Cláudio received a Master's degree in Finance from Universidade Portucalense, Portugal. He holds a PhD in Business and Economic from the University of Aveiro, Portugal. He has published in high-impact journals such as: Journal of Risk and Financial Management; Journal of Global Marketing; Open Journal of Business and Management; IGI Global and Elsevier.

Mara Teresa da Silva Madaleno has a Ph.D. in Economics from the University of Aveiro (UA) since 2011, under the subject "Essays on Energy Derivatives Pricing and Financial Risk Management". Currently Coordinator of the Research Unit on Governance, Competitiveness and Public Policies (GOVCOPP), and effective member. Currently lectures Finance and Economics at the undergraduate, graduate MSc and Ph.D. levels as an Associate Professor at the UA Department of Economics, Management, Industrial Engineering and Tourism (DEGEIT). Mara Teresa da Silva Madaleno is a prolific researcher, actively contributing to the academic community. She co-authors scientific articles in peer-reviewed reference journals, books and book chapters in the fields of energy economics, finance, and economics. Her research interests span Financial Economics, Energy and Environmental Economics, Energy Financial Markets and Behavior in Finance and Financial Markets. She has also been a valuable cooperator in various research projects. Presently, she is the director of the Master of Economics (branches of Finance, Business and Organizations, Innovation and Internationalization, Energy and Sustainability) at the DEGEIT in UA, and vice-director of the Master in Data Science for Social Sciences. She is also a member of the Portuguese Economists Order (OE) and university and Aveiro district representative of OE, founding partner, member and vowel of the Fiscal Council of APEEN (Associação Portuguesa de Economia da Energia; Portuguese Association of Energy Economics).

Samuel Carlos Victorino is a Full Professor and Rector of the Universidade Jean Piaget de Angola, Angola. He has a PhD in agricultural sciences from the University of Christian-Albrechts-Universität zu Kiel-Germany, was a member of the Jury of several Public Tests for the category of Full Professor in Angola, supervised several Master's Dissertations in Science Teaching, is a lecturer in the Master's courses in International Economics and Finance, at ACITE - Academy of Social Sciences; at the Faculty of Sciences in partnership with the University of the Algarve - Portugal and; at the University of Belas. He has participated in several international congresses and has published several articles and books on statistics applied to biological, social and human sciences.

João Jungo is a PhD in Economic and Business Sciences, Finance branch, from the University of Aveiro. PhD thesis: "Financial inclusion and financial stability: an analysis of African countries". Master's Degree in Economics, Finance branch, from the University of Aveiro. Master's thesis: "Determinants of savings and financial inclusion: the case of Angolan families". Degree in Economics from the Agostinho Neto University, Faculty of Economics. Monograph: "Elements of regional and agrarian economics: a case study of Bengo province". Member of the Governance, Competitiveness and Public Policy Research Unit (GOVCOPP), research group Decision Support Systems (SAD). Professor of Macroeconomics and Economic and Financial Analysis at the Instituto Superior de Administração e Finanças; Visiting Assistant Professor, University of Aveiro-Department of Economics Management Industrial Engineering and Tourism and Instituto Superior de Contabilidada e Administração-Portugal, Curricular Units (UCs): Macroeconomics and Economics I; Collaborating Professor at the Metropolitan Polytechnic Institute of Angola. Courses taught: Microeconomics; Financial Mathematics; Angolan Financial System; Public Finance. Lecturer at the Kangonjo Institute of Angola: Macroeconomics, Monetary and Financial Economics. Author of books, book chapters and scientific articles in peer-reviewed journals and reviewer for various journals

***

Sakshi is a Research Scholar in the department of Mittal School of Business of Lovely Professional University. She earned her master's degree in management from Maharshi Dayanand University, Rohtak, Haryana. She is pursuing her PhD in the field of human resource management.

Anil Kumar Anumasu is an accomplished Assistant Professor of Commerce with a rich academic career. He began his journey as a Junior Lecturer in Commerce in 2008 under Intermediate Education. After clearing the National Eligibility Test

(NET), he was promoted to Assistant Professor in 2013. Specializing in Finance and Accounting, Dr. Anil Kumar was awarded a Ph.D. in November 2023 by Kakatiya University. He has presented research papers at various national seminars and published 12 scholarly articles in esteemed national and international journals. Currently, he serves at Kakatiya Government College (Autonomous), Hanumakonda, advancing teaching and research in commerce education.

Joshua Yindenaba Abor is a Financial Economist and Professor of Finance with expertise in monetary economics.

Santosh Reddy Addula, a Senior Member of IEEE, is a research scholar at the University of the Cumberlands. His educational qualifications include a Ph.D. and a Master of Science in Information Technology. With extensive experience in the IT industry, he has demonstrated expertise across multiple domains. Santosh is an innovator who has made significant contributions to academic research through his articles as an author and co-author. Additionally, he serves as a reviewer for esteemed journals, demonstrating his commitment to advancing knowledge and upholding high standards in scholarly publications within his field.

Elikplimi Komla Agbloyor is a Professor of Financial Risk and an expert in finance and monetary policy

Christopher Awinia is a senior lecturer in the department of economics and community economic development at the Open University of Tanzania (OUT). He lectures in evaluation studies and the impact of globalisation on international development. Dr. Awinia consults widely government as well as international development and non-profit organisations. He is the coordinator of the Professorial Chair on Industrialisation and Development at the OUT.

Anagha Bhope is an Associate Professor at Indira University, Pune. With a strong academic background and extensive experience in management education. Dr. Bhope is known for her student-centric teaching approach and commitment to academic excellence. She has contributed to several research initiatives and actively engages in mentoring future business leaders.

Houda Boubaker, Ph.D in Economics from the Aix-Marseille University and member of the "Economic and Statistic Modeling and Analysis (MASE)" research laboratory at the Higher School of Statistics and Information Analysis. More than 10 years teaching experience in public and private universities. She was a data analyst at MADAR consulting. Actually, she is assistant professor at the South Mediterranean University- Mediterranean School of Business (SMU-MSB). Her researcher is related to Monetary policy and business cycles using the Dynamic Stochastic General Equilibrium (DSGE) models.

Shivani Dhand is an Associate Professor (14+ years of experience),a Certified SHRM (Society for Human Resource Management)faculty in the department of Mittal School of Business of Lovely Professional University.She is NLP(Neuro Linguistics Programming) Practioner She is also a member of the Indian Society for Training and Development (ISTD) and the Indian Society of Labour Economics. She is also a core committee member and Mentor of an NGO(Shalini Fellowship) Shivani Dhand has worked in an IT company as an HR. She has published 15 research papers in various journals which include Scopus-indexed, UGC care and peer-reviewed journals. She is a certified POSH trainer. She has worked with CPSC (Columbo Plan Staff College) Manila Philippines, and trained the faculty and Principals of various Institutions in Bhutan (2015). In 2016, She worked on one of the projects," Austria as an Innovation leader in EU in Austria and was awarded as best presentation and Excellent paper. Her research is situated in the field of Startups, HR Practices Human Resource Management, Entrepreneurship, and social entrepreneurship with a special focus on academic entrepreneurship.

Mercan Hatipoglu is currently an Assoicate Professor of Finance at Çankırı Karatekin University in Çankırı, Türkiye. Prior to joining Çankırı Karatekin University, he was research assistant at Eskisehir Osmangazi University between 2011 and 2015. His research area focus on the risk management, financial markets and volatility in emerging markets. Dr. Hatipoglu received B.A. in Management from Dokuz Eylul University in 2008 and Ph.D. in Finance in 2015, with the thesis on " Nonlinear Time Series Models and an Application on Emerging Markets " at the University of Eskisehir Osmangazi. He teaches International Financial Management, Investment, Capital Markets and Econometrics courses at undergraduate and graduate level.

Marwa Jerbi is an Assistant Professor of Finance at Mediterranean School of Business (MSB), South Mediterranean University of Tunis. In 2017, she received her Ph.D. in Finance from the Institute of Higher commercial studies (IHEC Carthage, Tunisia). She has been a Senior Market Research Analyst for 6 years within FIS Tunisia. She has been teaching International Finance and derivatives, Econometrics, Finance 1 and Finance 2 courses for UPM students along with, fixed income and Alternative investment courses for master's degree students. Her research interests include International Finance, portfolio management, financial risk and economic studies. Her research activities are currently focusing on Green and sustainable investments, portfolio management, along with economic growth.

İrfan Kalaycı is a professor of Political Economy at İnönü University (Malatya / Turkey).

Pratik Kodmalwar is associated with the Department of Management Studies at Datta Meghe Institute of Management Studies, located in Nagpur, Maharashtra. As a part of the MBA program, he contributes to academic excellence through his knowledge, dedication, and commitment to shaping future business leaders.

Vijaya Kittu Manda has nearly 13+ years of experience in Business Management and Technology. He is a Researcher at PBMEIT, India and works in capital markets, financial planning, and investing. He is an Advocate, a technocrat, an academician, a book writer, and a stock market enthusiast. He has 11 University Postgraduate Degrees in various disciplines. He is a Ph.D. in Management (Finance). His thesis was on Mutual Funds and their Market Competition. His thesis won the prestigious NSE-IEA Best Thesis Award in 2023. He is currently pursuing his second Ph.D. in Computer Science with focus on Blockchain. He contributed over 780 articles to various magazines. He is the Chief Editor for a Management Book Series, is a Peer Review, is a Certified Peer Review Supervisor, is a Session Chair and an Advisor for various academic and industrial conferences. He has over 116+ Google Scholar publications and 785+ magazine article publications so far. He is the Chief Editor for a Management Book Series and the Editor of several Scopus-indexed books. He is a Peer Reviewer and is a Certified Peer Review Supervisor. He frequently reviews for leading publishers including IEEE, Springer, Emerald, Sage, amongst others. He sits as a Session Chair and an Advisor for various academic and industrial conferences. He is a guest speaker for colleges and universities. He serves as the host for a research talk show called PBMEIT Expert Insights. Information about his current research activities is available at www.vijaykittu.com.

T.C. Manjunath was born on 6th February 1967. He did his BE from RV College of Engg. in 1989, ME in Robotics & Automation from LD College of Engg. in 1992 with First Rank and PhD in Systems & Control Engg. from IIT Bombay in the year 2007. He is currently working as the Dean Research R D and as Professor in the Dept. of Computer Science & Engineering with specialization in IoT, Cyber Security & Blockchain Technology in Rajarajeswari College of Engineering, Bengaluru, Karnataka. He has completed B.E. Degree from R.V. College of Engg., M.E. Govt.'s LD College of Engg., Gujarat Univ., Ahmedabad in First Rank and Ph.D. in Systems and Control Engineering from the Indian Institute of Technology Bombay IIT Bombay He has got a teaching academic, research and administrative experience of more than 35+ years 10 years as Principal, 8 years as HoD rest as faculty and has published more than 1200+ research papers in various national &

international journals and conferences, with 175+ patents, 25 book-chapters, 25 awards and also published 25 text books in various field of science, engineering and technology, completed projects worth Rs. 9 Crores till date apart from guiding 10 PhD scholars. He is a member of 30 Professional Society Chapters and is a fellow of IE, IETE, AMIEE and a chartered engineer. He got the best research scholar award in 2006 in IIT Bombay amongst all the research scholars of the institute. He has got 10 awards in academics and research activities.

Nourhaine Nefzi is an Assistant Professor of Finance at the Mediterranean School of Business (MSB), South Mediterranean University of Tunis. In 2018, she received her Ph.D. in Finance from the Higher Institute of Management of Tunis (ISG), University of Tunis. Her research interest is in the field of Finance, with a special focus on Portfolio Management, Financial Risks, and International Finance. She participated as a peer-reviewed for the Journal of International Financial Markets, Institutions & Money and Finance Research Letters. She published three articles with two appearing in Q1 journals and has participated in several international conferences.

Daniel Ofori-Sasu is a financial economist and an expert in monetary economics and economic policies.

Prathikantam Malathi Latha is a distinguished academician and researcher with 25 years of teaching experience and 15 years of research expertise. She holds four postgraduate degrees in various disciplines, along with two postgraduate diplomas. Additionally, she has earned an M.Phil., Ph.D., and is SET qualified, showcasing her strong academic foundation. A prolific writer and researcher, Dr. Malathi Latha has authored 20 publications, including 15 articles in reputed magazines and numerous research papers. Her contributions extend to editorial boards, reflecting her leadership and expertise in academic publishing. Dr. Malathi Latha has actively contributed to academic and social programs, having served as an IQAC coordinator and NSS program officer. She has also been a member of several Boards of Studies (BOS), influencing curriculum design and academic policies. Beyond academics, she is a voluntary counselor and provides coaching for competitive exams, empowering students to achieve their career goals. Her multifaceted experience and dedication make her an inspiring figure in education and research.

P. Selvakumar is currently an Associate Professor in the Department of Science and Humanities at Nehru Institute of Technology, Coimbatore, Tamil Nadu, India. Prior to joining Nehru Institute of Technology, he held positions as an Assistant Professor in the Department of Science and Humanities various engineering colleges in Coimbatore, Tamil Nadu, India, spanning from 2011 to 2023. Dr.P. Selvakumar's academic and research interests lie primarily in the field of phytochemistry. He has made significant contributions to his field, with an impressive record that includes 30 journal publications, 12 patents, and 20 conference papers. Additionally, he has organized 5 seminars and conferences, further demonstrating his commitment to academic and scientific exchange. Throughout his career, Dr. P.Selvakumar has been recognized for his dedication and excellence in teaching, having been honored with several awards, including the Best Teacher Awards. He holds a prominent position in the academic community, contributing actively to research.

Seranmadevi R. has a Doctorate in Management and 24 years of rich experience in both industry and Academia, presently working for Christ University, Bangalore, qualified with MBA., M.Com., MCA., M.Phil., Ph.D., and UGC-NET for Management and UGC-NET/JRF – Commerce, recognized with 3 remarkable patents, having the citation index of 176, H index of 7, and publication track of 21 Scopus Indexed journals, 2 WoS journals, 21 UGC Care listed, 7 edited volume Research Books and 10 international and 11 peer-reviewed national journals, and granted the NPTEL Discipline Star Award, 2020, NPTEL Believer Award, 2021, NPTEL Enthusiast Award, 2021, and NPTEL Marketing Domain Star Award, 2022 as a recognition of a continuous learning and upskilling the recent trends like Business Modelling, Business Analytics and AI, ML, BCT and IoT in Business. She has presented papers in 46 international and 35 national level seminars and booked many Best Paper awards, and is trusted as a promising Resource person in different disciplines like exploring knowledge in Research framework, Statistical tools applications in Social Science Research, Digital Marketing, Emerging Technology Trends, etc attended 30 FDP to enrich knowledge and adjudicated four Ph.D. thesis for Bharathiyar University, Coimbatore. Currently working on the internal project work entitled “Civics view on Synergy and Trade-off effect of Sustainable Development Goals in Bangalore”.

Roop Raj is working as Associate Professor in Economics. Raj has done his 10th and 12th education from Jawahar Navodaya Vidyalaya Jhajjar, Haryana, after which he has obtained BA Economics Hons, MA Economics, UGC-NET-JRF Economics, M.Phil Economics and PhD Economics degree. Raj has published more than 70 research papers in international journals, most of which have been published by foreign publishers like Springer, Elsevier, Wiley, Emerald etc. Most of the research papers are Scopus, web of Science, SCI indexed and UGC-Care listed. Raj has also registered 17 patents till now, out of which 6 are design patents and 11 are utility patents. Dr. Raj has authored six books in his subject. He has also completed many research oriented training/FDP/orientation/ refresher programmes related to his subject. Dr. Raj has presented his research work in more than 67 national/ international seminars/ Conferences also.

S. Ramesh is currently serving as an Assistant Professor of Commerce at Government Degree College, Nelakondapalli, Khammam District, Telangana, India. With an impressive academic background, holding an M.Com., M.Ed., and Ph.D., Dr. Ramesh has accumulated vast experience in academia. He previously held the role of Principal (FAC) at Government Degree College, Manthani, and has also served as a Junior Lecturer in Mulakalapalli and Peddapalli (Boys). Additionally, he contributed his expertise as a faculty member at SR & BGNR Government Arts & Science College (A), Khammam. A distinguished scholar, Dr. Ramesh has actively participated in over 35 seminars, presenting papers across various forums. He has published more than 180 research articles in prestigious national and international journals and authored 18 books. He serves as a distinguished course writer for the Board of Intermediate Education, Telangana and the School of Distance Learning and Continuing Education, Kakatiya University, Warangal. His dedication to research has been recognized with an award from the Government of Andhra Pradesh for his significant contributions to the field.

S. Satyanarayanan is a scientist in Ministry of Electronics and Information Technology, Government of India. He is handling various activities in area of Digital Economy, Human Recourse Development and Cyber Laws.

Ashwarya Sharma is an accomplished academic and researcher in the field of commerce, currently serving as an Assistant Professor at Chandigarh Group of Colleges, Jhanjeri, Mohali since 2016. She holds an M.Com (Hons) in Finance, Banking, and Insurance from Panjab University and a B.Ed from Punjabi University, Patiala. She is also pursuing a Ph.D. from Punjabi University with a focus on corporate governance and social responsibility. With a strong background in research, Ashwarya has presented and published papers at national conferences and in international journals. Her academic contributions are complemented by certifications from the National Stock Exchange of India and multiple NCFM modules. Recognized for her dedication, she has received accolades such as "Employee of the Month," "Women Employee of the Year," and a "Certificate of Best Performance." Beyond academics, she actively volunteers for street animal welfare and has participated in environmental initiative

Amit Kumar Tyagi is working as Assistant Professor, at National Institute of Fashion Technology, 110016, New Delhi, India. Previously he has worked as Assistant Professor (Senior Grade 2), and Senior Researcher at Vellore Institute of Technology (VIT), Chennai Campus, 600127, Chennai, Tamilandu, India for the period of 2019-2022. He received his Ph.D. Degree (Full-Time) in 2018 from Pondicherry Central University, 605014, Puducherry, India. About his academic experience, he joined the Lord Krishna College of Engineering, Ghaziabad (LKCE) for the periods of 2009-2010, and 2012-2013. He was an Assistant Professor and Head- Research, Lingaya's Vidyapeeth (formerly known as Lingaya's University), Faridabad, Haryana, India for the period of 2018-2019. His supervision experience includes more than 10 Masters' dissertations and one PhD thesis. He has contributed to several projects such as "AARIN" and "P3- Block" to address some of the open issues related to the privacy breaches in Vehicular Applications (such as Parking) and Medical Cyber Physical Systems (MCPS). He has published over 350 papers in refereed high impact journals, conferences and books.

Sudindra V R is a seasoned finance professional with over 20 years of experience in the fields of Finance, Fintech, Training, and Education. He is currently associated with the Department of Finance at ICFAI Foundation for Higher Education, ICFAI Business School, Bangalore, Karnataka. Prof. Sudindra brings a wealth of industry and academic expertise, contributing significantly to the development of future finance professionals.

Aysel Varoglu She holds a BS degree in Economics from Gazi University (2013) and an MA degree in Energy Economics and Management from Social Sciences University of Ankara (2022). She works on energy economics and analysis at the Ministry of Trade. She has published research articles and book chapters on the strategic and economic importance of energy and climate change. Her research interests are mainly in the macroeconomic impacts of energy and climate change.

Özge Filiz Yıldırım is an Assistant Professor of Economics at İzmir Katip Çelebi University and currently a Visiting Research Associate at the Department of Banking and Finance, King's College London. She holds a Ph.D. in Economics from Ege University, where her research focused on DSGE modelling and macroeconomic shocks, along with an M.S. in Economics from Bilkent University and a B.S. in Economics from Dokuz Eylül University. Her research interests lie in open economy macroeconomics, monetary policy, housing markets, and macro-financial risks, including those related to climate change. Dr. Yıldırım has published in peer-reviewed international journals and contributed to several edited volumes on topics such as macroeconomic policy, financial crises, and housing market dynamics. Her work has been recognized with the TÜBİTAK International Postdoctoral Research Fellowship and the Turkish Economic Association's Doctoral Dissertation Award.

Index

Symbols

A

B

C

D

E

F

G

H

I

L

M

www.ingramcontent.com/pod-product-compliance
Lightning Source LLC
LaVergne TN
LVHW062333300926
849161LV00007B/1677

* 9 7 9 8 3 6 9 3 9 7 6 5 7 *